PERSONAL BRANDING EXPERT   LINKEDIN BRANDING EXPERT

JANE ANDERSON & KYLIE CHOWN

CONNECT

LEVERAGE *your* LINKEDIN PROFILE *for* BUSINESS GROWTH *and* LEAD GENERATION

... IN LESS THAN

7 *MINUTES PER DAY*

"Over the past 100 years, we have moved from the Industrial Age, through the Information Age to the Digital Age. To thrive today, you need to be online and your expertise needs to be on show. Jane Anderson and Kylie Chown have shone a light on the path to having a digital presence on LinkedIn that really connects with your target audience and makes your expertise stand out. Clear, practical and simple, *CONNECT* is a must-read for anyone using LinkedIn to do business."
– *Dermot Crowley, Productivity Expert and author of "Smart Work", Wiley, 2015*

"The rules of connection have changed. We can connect and influence at the touch of a button and, as a result, our ability to manage our personal brand across multiple channels is critical. In this book, Jane and Kylie share how LinkedIn can build and leverage your brand to drive commercial and personal success. A must read packed with learnings, tools and tips for anyone wanting to take leadership of self."
– *Janine Garner, Collaboration Expert and author of "From Me to We", Wiley, 2015*

"*CONNECT* offers insights and practical tips on how to use LinkedIn to leverage your profile and business. Helping the reader work through at a strategic level what they want to be known for and then providing valuable guidance to achieve this. Put simply, if you have a LinkedIn profile and you are serious about your professional brand, then you must read this book."
– *Gabrielle Dolan, author of "Ignite: Real Leadership, Real Talk, Real Results", Wiley, 2015*

Acknowledgements

Thank you first and foremost to my parents, who are tireless supporters of me and my sisters. I am eternally grateful.

To Matt Church, Gabrielle Dolan, Janine Garner, Dermot Crowley, Patrick Hollingworth, Simon Waller, Rachel Bourke, Tracey Ezard, Dan Gregory and the rest of the Thought Leaders Global Community: thank you for your guidance, support and inspiration.

A special thank you to Keith Abraham. I am so grateful for your insights, care and interest. I feel very lucky to have you as a mentor.

Thank you to Lauren Shay, our editor. Your patience and guidance has made this work happen.

– Jane Anderson

Thank you to my parents and family. Your support and encouragement allow me to do what I do.

Thank you to the clients I work with. I appreciate that you are so open to sharing, and allow me to be part of your journey.

Thank you to Lauren Shay, our editor. Your work is amazing and we couldn't have done this without you.

– Kylie Chown

About the Authors

Jane Anderson

Jane Anderson is a LinkedIn and Personal Branding Expert. She has worked with more than 13,000 clients on marketing and to position them in their industries. Her clients include Rio Tinto, Virgin Australia, the Australian Medical Association, Origin Energy and various Thought Leaders, speakers and authors.

She has been featured in *Business Insider*, *The Age*, *Sydney Morning Herald*, *Marie Claire* and *Today Tonight*. She is also the author of *IMPACT: How to Build Your Personal Brand for the Connection Economy*.

When Jane's not travelling, speaking and running workshops, she lives in Brisbane, Queensland. She enjoys running, the beach and playing with her nieces and nephew.

- https://au.linkedin.com/in/janeandersonpersonalimpact
- www.jane-anderson.com

Kylie Chown

Kylie Chown is a LinkedIn and Digital Branding Expert. For more than 10 years, she has worked with start-ups, consultants and businesses to successfully leverage their LinkedIn profiles to their full capabilities.

Kylie has been featured as an expert in the *Australian Institute of Management (AIM)*, *Franchise Business*, *HRM America* and *Leaders in Heels*. She is also a regular guest on the *Reach Personal Branding* blog.

She is currently one of eight Certified Master Writers in Australia, and one of three Reach Certified Branding Analysts.

Kylie lives in Brisbane, Queensland, and when she's not working, she enjoys all that the Queensland lifestyle has to offer with her family and friends.

- https://au.linkedin.com/in/kyliechown
- www.kyliechown.com

Contents

Chapter 1

Why is LinkedIn So Important For You?

Reid Hoffman, the co-founder of LinkedIn, recently said: "If you can get better at your job, you should be an active member of LinkedIn, because LinkedIn should be connecting you to the information, insights and people to be more effective."

In 2009, Jane began working with people on LinkedIn. It wasn't that LinkedIn was new; it was that it had been reserved for executives. She was helping people get jobs after the global financial crisis, and every so often she would meet someone who needed to be on LinkedIn. They were so reluctant to get online. She tried to find someone who could write their profiles. There wasn't anyone, so she began to write them herself.

Fast forward to 2011. Jane was on a plane next to a gentleman. She was flying between Brisbane and Canberra. She talked to the gentleman, and discovered he owned a technology company specialising in network security. He was also a professor of IT security at a university. He did a lot of consulting work in Canberra for the Australian Federal Government. Jane asked him: "Are all your team on LinkedIn? How do you use LinkedIn as part of your business?"

He said: "Actually, I've removed our sales team. I just have one sales manager now. I allow them to spend one day a week in forums on LinkedIn and other sites. Our technical experts answer questions and are connected to our customers. This is just how our customers want to communicate now, and our business has changed quite dramatically as a result."

Since then, we've noticed that traditional sales approaches and the new ways of selling and creating leads are quite different.

Most people will ask: "Isn't LinkedIn just like an online version of your resume?" Or: "Isn't it like Facebook, but for business?"

A LinkedIn profile is like your own personal website for your business and for you as someone in charge of sales or business growth. We're in the connection economy. When we're online, we want to be able to connect.

People do their research long before they get in touch with you. A CEB study found that about 60% of a buying decision is made before the person buys from you. It's a bit like TripAdvisor, where people do their research online before they decide to connect.

You can access people, information and misinformation more readily. If you need a financial planner and you're in Sydney, Australia, and you want to talk to someone in New York because you have been told they're the best, then that's what you can do. You're no longer restricted by location.

You can also access experts. Nowadays, if there is an expert in flamenco dancing and they are in Spain, you can go online and learn from a flamenco dancing teacher in Spain.

This is because of sites such as Elance, oDesk and Popexpert.

You might be thinking, "What does that have to do with LinkedIn?" What it means is that if you focus locally, you must have a strong presence, and LinkedIn is an effective way of achieving that.

It's getting more difficult to access decision makers because they're so busy. According to a study by the Radicati Group, business users sent and received on average 121 emails a day in 2014, and this is expected to grow to 140 emails a day by 2018. The amount of information landing in inboxes is extraordinary.

To cut through this noise is quite difficult, so we have to go to spaces where people hang out. Considering the average person spends two hours per day using social media, this is where we need to go to connect with them. We are in the connection economy.

The truth is we don't even know about missed opportunities because we don't get feedback.

Challenges with the Current Sales Process

Pigeonholing, Stereotypes and Unconscious Bias

You would have heard the saying: "first impressions last". In fact, Margaret Thatcher once said: "I usually make a decision about a person in the first 10 seconds and I usually find that I'm right."

There is a lot of information and misinformation out there. People want to understand who you are and where you're coming from. Otherwise, they will stereotype you very quickly. Their perception could be based on what you have done in the past, rather than what you can offer for the future.

You need to determine what you want their interpretation of you to be, and convey yourself in that light when you connect. They may not need your help right now, but they may know someone who does.

Something to remember is that your mistakes are not as obvious online as they are in the real world and you don't know the opportunities you're missing. People can look at your profile and move on, and you don't even know. There is a world of opportunity sitting at your fingertips. It's now time to take the opportunity to help those clients who are looking for you and need your help!

Some other challenges in the current selling climate include:

- **Access to decision makers:** This is more difficult as gatekeepers are becoming more challenging to manage.
- **"Digital First":** Increasingly customers are undertaking research online before making buying decisions. As mentioned, 60% of a buying decision is made before a customer makes contact. This means the use of Google searches are increasing. Sites such as Trip Advisor to choose hotels and Urban Spoon to choose a restaurant are examples of that.
- **The high cost of doing business:** Organisations are finding it increasingly challenging to meet skyrocketing overheads and wages. Businesses don't have money to waste any more.
- **Flexibility:** Businesses need to be able to move fast. Customers' needs change quickly and businesses need to be agile, yet stay on track.
- **The struggle to find more ideal customers:** It's difficult for businesses to position themselves for new clients and markets.
- **Time and money:** A business's growth isn't restricted to a local area anymore. We have access to markets nationally an internationally, but it takes time and money to build those markets and have a presence in those locations.
- **Unqualified leads:** We don't have time to waste on people who don't meet your sales criteria.
- **People do their research:** Customers research online to find the cheapest option.
- **The increasing cost of search engine optimisation and Google AdWords:** It's becoming extraordinarily expensive to get results from online advertising.
- **A feeling of paralysis:** With the sea of information available, combined with a lack of time and money, many businesses choose to do nothing. It can all seem too hard.

The Connection Economy

The old ways of selling have changed. It used to be about calling. It used to be about samples and then trying to get meetings with people. Now it's quite different. Now it's about leveraging people's social networks. It's about engagement, which means connecting with people, and it's about education. We need to be able to educate people about how we can help them. This is, essentially, the social sales model.

Past	Present	Future
Employees	Role Models	Ambassadors
Cold Calls	Tribes	Engagement
Sales Demonstrations	Education	Thought Leadership
Salesperson	Trusted Adviser	Expert
Transaction	Solution Selling	Lifetime Partnership

According to Ipsos Open Thinking Exchange, the average person spends two hours a day on the internet. IBM's Global CEO Study found that CEOs believe social media utilisation for customer engagement will increase by 256% over five years to become the second-most popular way to engage customers after face-to-face communication.

How You're Found in the Marketplace

Customers find you via various means when they work with you. The following quadrants are the most common.

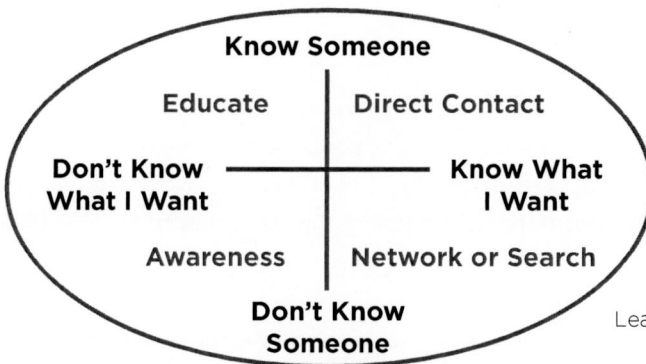

Lead Generation Matrix
© Jane Anderson

So, How Do People Find You?

"If I know someone and I don't know what I want."
If this is the case with a customer, they're going to ask the people they know. If they're more extroverted, they will probably go to their networks. If they're more introverted, then they will jump online and do a Google search.

The benefit of being referred in your networks means you have a good reputation. If you've got a good reputation, then you've got good positioning.

The problem with someone doing a Google search is that they don't know you, so you will be competing against others who have experience with search engine optimisation or Google AdWords. What it also means is that you will be like toothpaste on a supermarket shelf, looking the same as everybody else. You will compete on price, and that's a very difficult space in which to sell.

If you are well networked, then your referrals will come to the fore and that can be more effective.

"If I know someone and I know what I want, then what I'm going to do is direct contact."
If this is the case, the customer is going to pick up the phone and call you or email you because they already know who you are. The challenge for direct contact is that you have to be front of mind.

"For someone I don't know and I don't know what I want."
In that case, your job is to educate. You have to make sure you're putting content out there so people understand what you do and realise that they do have a particular problem. If someone has a problem, they're not going to know unless you keep educating them. You want them read your content and think, "There, that's exactly what I'm after."

"I don't know that I have a problem and I don't know someone."
In that case, your job is awareness. Your job is to make sure your profile is clear about how you help people, but you also must write blog posts and articles to help people become aware of the type of work you do. They might not need your help right now, but down the track they may realise there's a problem they need solving.

So the challenge is that we need to work on all quadrants of the Lead Generation Matrix. Yes, those who already know you make your job easy, but remember that someone out there is trying to find you, even if they don't know it yet.

What Type of LinkedIn Lead Generator Are You?

BLACK-BELT LINKEDIN LEAD GENERATOR

	TYPE	FOCUS	% LEAD GENERATION
ATTRACT	Ninja	Sales Maker	100
	Influencer	Thought Leader	85
	Active	Curator	70
	Positioned	Expert	50
REPEL	Resume	Commodity	10
	Account	Lost	5
	No Account	Judged	-10

© Jane Anderson 2015

Repel

Level 1 – No account. At this level, you'll be judged; judged that you're not up with the times or stereotyped in a way that may not be true. If you have no social media account, especially if you have no LinkedIn profile, you won't be seen as managing your presence. If you don't manage your brand, someone else will.

Level 2 – Account. This may be where a LinkedIn account came about unexpectedly for you. You didn't ask for an account but someone invited you, so you set one up. You haven't entered any information. It's an empty profile, with just your name and current position, and possibly a previous role. At least you're on LinkedIn, but it's not helping you or your organisation.

Level 3 – Resume. Your profile contains your career history and the tasks you did in your previous roles. Your summary is more about you and less about how you help your customer. With a profile that seems more like an obituary, you come across as a commodity in the market of talent instead of an expert in your field. You appear vanilla and boring, the same as everyone else, which is untrue.

Attract

Level 4 – Positioned. Your profile is written for your future and designed to attract the right people. When people land on your profile, it's clear who you help and you are positioned as an expert in your industry. There is nothing untrue in how your profile is written; it matches the human being and ensures the reader categorises you correctly without making assumptions.

Level 5 – Active. You're positioned and starting to become more active with your profile. You feel confident about liking, sharing and commenting on posts that are linked to what you're trying to achieve. You don't like or share anything that doesn't relate to your purpose.

Level 6 – Influencer. You are now creating original content and posts that link to your strategy. People are starting to follow you and like what you're saying. A tribe might even be forming and you're seeing the same people like and comment on your posts. Your profile may get 50-150 views per week. You're seeing more clients coming to you, wanting to do business.

Level 7 – Ninja. You're now leveraging your profile to create connections and open doors. You have specific scripts that you use to gain meetings with potential clients. You're starting to have more clout to ask for what you want as you've been contributing to your audience. You know how to move potential clients through your sales funnel.

Why LinkedIn?

With more than 365 million users, LinkedIn is a great opportunity to grow a business in front of a highly targeted audience. It was originally created for executives only, but it has grown to connect professionals at all levels – even graduates, who are the fastest-growing LinkedIn demographic. The most under-represented group is women, and this presents one of the greatest opportunities online.

LinkedIn was developed in 2003 by Reid Hoffman. He organised a team from PayPal and SocialNet to work on the idea. Growth was slow to begin with, some days only attracting 20 people at a time. Fast-forward to 2009 when Jeff Weiner, previously an executive at Yahoo!, took the reins as CEO while Hoffman managed product development. By the end of 2010, LinkedIn had 90 million members and 1000 employees around the world. By 2013, it had reached 225 million members, acquiring two members per second. Today, it has more than 7600 employees and is listed on the stock exchange. The site is available in 24 languages and has members listed in more than 200 countries. In 2015, LinkedIn acquired Lynda.com for $1.5 billion.

LinkedIn doesn't seem to be going anywhere any time soon. It has had a dramatic impact on the way business is done in the digital world and has been a game changer for professionals and businesses.

Fears of Using LinkedIn for Business Growth, Lead Generation and Networking

Time and Return on Investment

One fear people have about LinkedIn is how much time it will take out of their day. "Are you going to say that I have to sit on LinkedIn for half an hour a day or 20 minutes a day? I just don't have that kind of time." Definitely not. That's not a good use of time for a lot of. In some areas, such as business development and sales teams, it is a good use of time, but for most other roles it's about getting the profile written correctly and leveraging it to support other business activities.

Loss of Talent

One of the other fears leaders have about LinkedIn is that well-written profiles will lead to recruiters poaching their organisation's talent. If that happens, it means the profile has been written incorrectly. The LinkedIn profile-writing strategy for a team member versus a job seeker is very different. It is a different process, with a different result. If the profile is written based on what the organisation wants to achieve, then it won't appear in talent pools and it will be clear to a recruiter that the team member is not looking for a job.

Looking Stupid

Many clients we work with have a fear of looking stupid or failing to manage their profile successfully. They may also be concerned about not knowing how to handle the situation if they post something online that people disagree with.

Competitors

Some people are concerned that their competition will use LinkedIn to see what they're doing. "What if they try to steal my clients? How do I protect my connections, my clients and myself?"

So What's This Really About?

Connection

As humans, we have an innate need to belong. Our sense of community and tribe dictates our self-esteem. In today's digital world, it supports our need for connection through sites such as Facebook, Twitter, Instagram and LinkedIn.

People Buy From People

People buy from people, and they buy from people they know, like and trust. This marketing speak has been going around for years, but it is amplified in the connected and social-network economy.

Accessibility

If you have built a website, you may find it takes a few weeks to index correctly with Google. This has a high impact on your business if you're sitting and waiting for enquiries via your website. LinkedIn's indexing generally takes two days, so you can be found in a Google search much faster.

Experts

If you aren't positioning yourself effectively to your market, someone else is. Your expertise needs to be accessible to your market via blogs, videos, books and podcasts. LinkedIn is the perfect place to leverage your thought leadership.

24/7

Waiting to get in contact with people or doing your research by making phone calls doesn't work anymore. With websites, Facebook and LinkedIn, businesses are now open to the public 24/7 and marketing needs to be able to reach customers in the hours that suit them. Clients respond to emails at 2am and on Sundays. We no longer work 9-5 and no longer have a work-life balance. It's just life.

Low Cost

We live in a global – not just a local – marketplace. The internet has opened access to experts across the world on oDesk, Elance, Popexpert, Facebook and LinkedIn. Accessing experts in other countries used to be expensive, but we can now work with experts around the world at a competitive price.

Rely on Search

By purely relying on a Google search to get clients, you risk minimising your positioning. You become like toothpaste on the supermarket shelf, where people are trying to decide which one to buy but they're not sure, so they just buy the one on special. You need to stand out to maximise your positioning in the market and show what makes you different.

Connection

This is about being found for what you want to be found for, and creating networks and leads. It's about being positioned correctly in your client's mind so that leads convert to sales more easily. As Seth Godin in *Tribes* says, your network becomes your greatest asset for business growth.

Reflections and Actions

- How much does your marketing currently cost?
- How are you measuring the success of those activities?
- How do you manage your face-to-face relationships online?
- How do you educate your tribe?

Chapter 2

Where Are You Now?

Bill Owens, the 40th Governor of Colorado, once said: "We know that, when it comes to technology and the economy, if you're not constantly moving forward, then – without a doubt – you're moving backwards."

LinkedIn can seem like a huge beast and knowing where to start can be bewildering. This leads to procrastination and putting it into the too-hard basket. You may feel frustrated because you know there is an opportunity there, but you don't know how to make the most of it.

Furthermore, perhaps you don't want to use LinkedIn for selling but as a positioning tool when networking. People can view your profile for validation after face-to-face activity, such as attending events. You may also want to use your profile as a way of validating yourself as a leader if you're advertising a job for a new team member.

You

Is LinkedIn right for you?

Just having a profile for the sake of it is no reason to have one. At the moment, it might be a validator for you more than a business development tool.

Bridget Loudon, the CEO of Expert 360, an online brokerage site matching management consultants with clients across the world, tells a story about her parents, who live in South Africa, and her grandmother, who lives in Newcastle. Her parents were trying to find the right surgeon to help her grandmother who had a shoulder injury. They conducted their research for a surgeon in Newcastle from their home in South Africa.

In terms of your profile, you need to think outside your immediate surroundings and immediate location. Someone, somewhere in the world is trying to find you. We are not in a local marketplace any more. We're in a global marketplace and you need to be easily validated by people who can't physically see you or who aren't familiar with you.

LinkedIn is right for you if you:

- Have your own business
- Clients ask for you
- Are the leader of an organisation or school
- Are in business development or sales
- Are a consultant, trainer, coach, facilitator or an expert in your field
- Have the type of business that is reactive
- Rely on Google searches for clients

For example, if you have a pest control business, you could pay Google AdWords $10 – $10.50 for a click-through from a Google page. Your profile could still be well validated if you have a good relationship with real estate agents or property managers. It can still complement your business, even if you're not necessarily using it for aggressive business and sales growth. People buy from people and they buy from people they know, like and trust. In the LinkedIn field, this will mostly be business to business, but it can also be used for business to consumer, especially for referrals. For example, if I'm a personal trainer, my clients may be on LinkedIn, so it can be easier for them to refer me to their friends. They can get a feel for who I am far more quickly on LinkedIn than Facebook, especially if I'm not connected to my friends at work on Facebook.

When a potential client needs help, they will either ask their networks or undertake a search. You need to make sure your business turns up in both those cases easily. For example, if I hurt myself and I need to see a chiropractor, I will more than likely Google "Chiropractor Brisbane" and rely on the website that comes up. You can also use your LinkedIn profile to come up in the same search.

Metrics for Measuring Where You Are Now

All-Star Status

You may notice you have an area on your profile that shows if you have an "All-Star" status. This means that your profile has been fully completed. If it doesn't say "All-Star", then you need to fill your profile with more content. Bear in mind, though, that having an "All-Star" status doesn't mean you have an effective profile. It just means the fields have been completed.

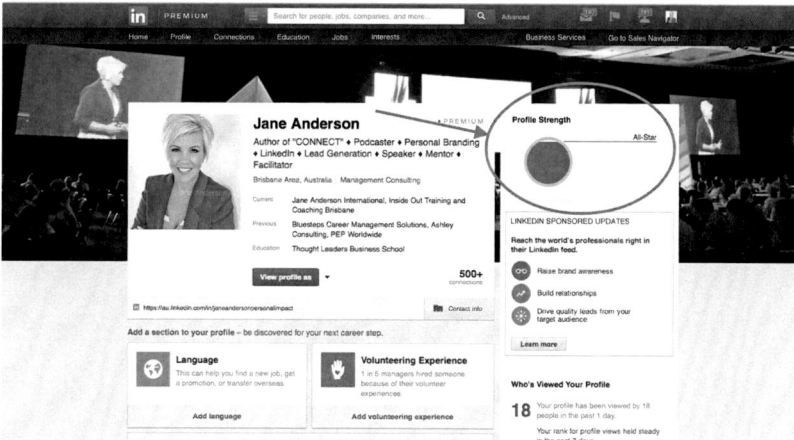

Visibility and Who Viewed Your Profile

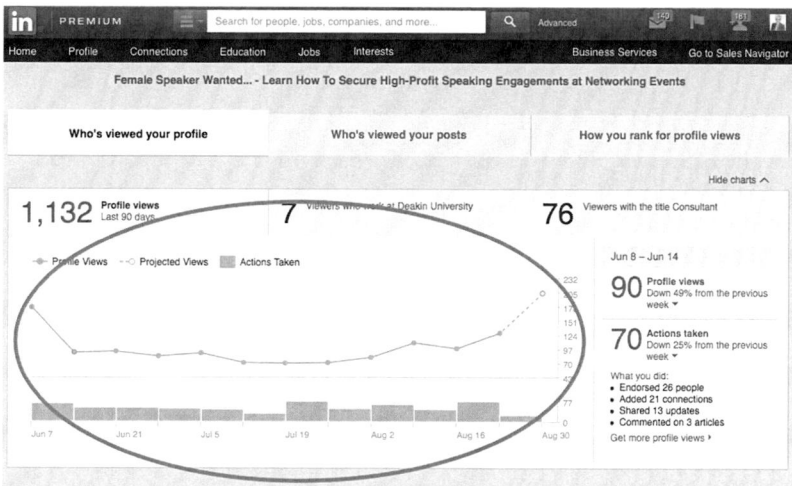

If you have a Premium Account, you may notice a graph in the "Who Viewed Your Profile" area that shows a line of how many people viewed your profile and, in the bar graph underneath, the action that was taken. If your line graph is going up but your bar graph is consistently going down, this may mean that your content is not relevant to your audience. If the line is going down but the bar graph is going up, this means the right person is looking at your profile. So a line going down isn't always a bad sign.

How You Rank for Profile Views

You'll also notice this option that shows you how you rank in your connections. Many people place a lot of importance on this. However, it depends on who you're connected to. If you're an IT salesperson and you're connected with lots of other IT sales people, you will rank low. If you're the only IT salesperson in your connections, you will rank highly. There are too many factors to take into consideration to lose a lot of time managing this metric.

How to Manage an Out-of-Control Account

"It is just bringing me more work, work I don't have time for."

We recently worked with a client who was a human resources manager. During the consultation, we talked about LinkedIn and he revealed that he didn't even log in to his LinkedIn account as "it is just bringing me more work, work I don't have time for."

He talked about how his inbox was being flooded with requests to connect and suppliers wanting his company's business. He saw LinkedIn as a medium that brought him more work and people wanting things from him. He didn't know how to control his account so he could use it to his benefit.

This client is not alone. A recent article on infoworld.com quoted professional developer Peter Wayner as saying this about LinkedIn: "It's sure cool and it's fun to look at hierarchies, but I've never had much luck with using it for more than idle curiosity."

David Linthicum, consultant and chief technology officer at Blue Mountain Labs, has a much more positive spin. He uses LinkedIn several times a day. He says: "I use LinkedIn to get the information on people I may want to work with, may want to hire, may want to network with. Most people in IT have LinkedIn profiles, and you can understand a lot about them from their profile." He has a problem with the site, though: "I get many people asking me to join their network who turn out to be spammers. You have to be careful who you accept."

Some ways to take control of your LinkedIn account and have it work for you include:

1. **Control your settings.** By controlling your settings, you can take control of incoming communication notifications and emails. To do this: Under the **Privacy and Settings** option, you will see you have five main areas you can manage. These include: Profile; Communications; Group, Companies and Applications; and Account.

2. **Manage your current connections.** You can keep your connections private. The default LinkedIn setting is that your first-degree connections can see who your other first-degree connections are. By making your connections private, you protect yourself and your connections. You can also block a connection's status updates if you still want to be connected, but don't want to see all their updates.

3. **Curb your connection requests.** Carefully review any requests to connect. Inadvertently connecting with a spammer can compromise your account. You can also control who can connect with you by stipulating that they need to have your email address to submit a connection request. When someone requests a connection, you will receive an email as well as a notification in your profile. If you click on the tick, the request will be accepted. If you would like to find out more about the person, click on their name.

Google Search

If you do a search for your profile in LinkedIn using keywords, you will turn up in the search result as the top-ranked profile, as LinkedIn search results are based on first, second and third-level connections. To get a real indication of where you're turning up in search results, you need to undertake a "clean search". You do need to be mindful of whether you're reviewing a public or individual profile.

LinkedIn public profiles come in two different formats: they start with www.linkedin.com/in/ or they start with www.linkedin.com/pub/

If there is an "in" in the URL this means the user has a premium subscription profile. "Pub" is for everyone else.

For example, if you were looking for a **LinkedIn Profile Writer** in Brisbane you would undertake the following search:

"site:linkedin.com/in | site:linkedin.com/pub -dir "LinkedIn Profile Writer" Brisbane"

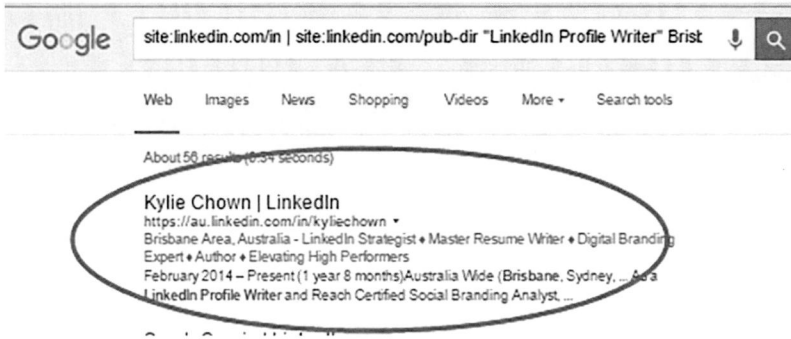

By doing this search you get all profiles returned regardless of whether they have paid for a premium account or not.

How People Find You

When assessing how people find you, you need to consider the purpose and patterns that lead to how you're found. Some of the patterns come from your contacts and who you're connected to. You may notice certain people keep looking at your profile and coming back to you that way. They may have also found you more easily if you've been undertaking aggressive search engine optimisation with your profile.

The amount of content you post will also affect how you're found and will give evidence of your visibility. The best way to review this is by looking through your newsfeed.

So the overall message is that you don't need to place high in search results for everything. It depends on your purpose and who your connections are.

Self-Assessment

Here is a checklist with some questions to help you determine if your LinkedIn profile is working for you and where you need to focus your efforts.

	Current score /10	Final score /10
Establish Your Profile		
1. Does your profile address the problems and fears of your ideal client?		
2. Do you have a professional headshot?		
3. Do you control updates clogging your inbox?		
4. Is your profile fully search engine optimised in the title, summary, current role, skills and expertise, and does it include a vanity URL and contact details?		
5. Are you well validated with recommendations and endorsements?		
Total score /50		
Engage Your Audience		
6. Do you like and comment professionally?		
7. Do you create personalised scripts to connect professionally?		
8. Do you leverage LinkedIn to support your face-to-face networks?		
9. Do you curate content in a time-efficient and relevant manner?		
10. Do you contribute to groups professionally?		
Total score /50		
Elevate Your Positioning		
11. Do you undertake advanced searches to find ideal connections?		
12. Are you positioned effectively when being introduced to a potential client or contact?		
13. Can you write a thought-leading post with a call to action to attract ideal clients?		
14. Do you know how to write a compelling script to connect with ideal stakeholders via Connect or InMail, knowing the difference between the two?		
Total score /40		
Empower Your Team		
15. Can you maintain and troubleshoot your profile?		
16. Do you know how to run your business page?		
Total score /20		
TOTAL SCORE /160		

Reflections and Actions

- Your score from the above activity will determine the actions you need to take in this book. Focus your efforts on where you have gaps and go to the chapter that relates to that area, so you can find out what you need to do to get a score of 10.
- Consider your Google search. Google yourself and see where you turn up in that search. If a current or potential client found it, would it be a favourable result?
- How many views per week do you currently get on your LinkedIn profile? Take a screen grab and record it.
- Give yourself a pat on the back for those areas where you have already scored 10 out of 10!

Chapter 3

How to Leverage Your Profile

Hollywood actress Hilary Duff once said: "I'm pretty good at thinking about everything – all of my consequences – before I make a decision, and I think about everything that's going to happen because of that decision. I'm a Libra, and I'm very strategic."

We recently worked with a client, Peter, in financial services, who said he was spending a lot of time trying to grow his business through LinkedIn but found he was wasting so much time that he gave up and decided to just focus on his old sales methods. He couldn't understand what he was doing wrong on LinkedIn, so he dismissed it. Maybe you have been in the same boat, where you have tried to use LinkedIn but received minimal results. The goal of this book is to help you have greater impact in as short amount of time as possible. A good place to start is to think about the type of user you are before beginning.

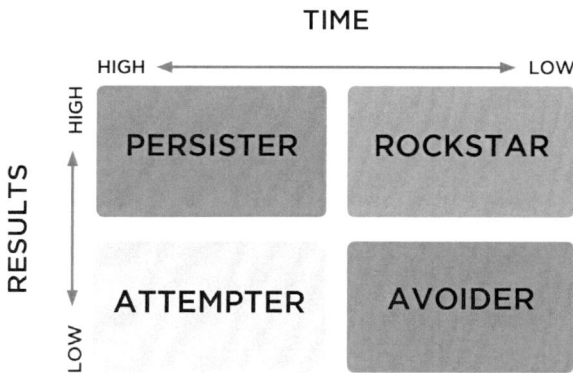

TIME

HIGH ⟷ LOW

RESULTS	
HIGH	
PERSISTER	**ROCKSTAR**
ATTEMPTER	**AVOIDER**
LOW	

© Jane Anderson 2015

Q1: Persister. You're getting results but it's taking a lot of time. You're posting content but unsure if it's the right content. You feel as though there must be a better way but you're not sure what that is. You'd like to know some more efficient ways to make your profile work and be less time consuming. If you're at this level, you need to focus on efficiency, effectiveness and getting your profile to work for you a lot more. You may also need to look at the sequence of what you're doing with your profile. The order of your activity may also be out of sequence and need to be adjusted.

Q3: Attempter. You've tried putting some time into your LinkedIn profile but you're not getting any results. You're about to give up if something doesn't change. You feel overwhelmed and it all seems too hard. At this level, you need to focus on creating the strategy for your profile that will create the results you're looking for. You also need to shift from the mindset of taking from others to giving to generate leads.

Q4: Avoider. You think LinkedIn is more a recruitment tool. You may think that if profiles are created for your team, they will leave and not attract clients. You have a private profile because you don't want attention and you don't see yourself as an integral part of the sales funnel. Alternatively, you don't have time to spend on social media and don't even see the value of it. If you're at this level, you need to look at the purpose of your role in the organisation and where LinkedIn's purpose intersects. From here, your strategy can be designed to leverage the time you spend on it and keep you focused on business-critical activity.

Q2: Rockstar. You're confident and killing it. You know how to design your profile to attract your ideal client. You're leveraging your content, approaching your clients with ease and generating leads. You know the process, have the system in place and it's a strategic part of your sales process. You know there is no replacement for face-to-face communication, but you know how to leverage LinkedIn to support other lead-generating activities. At this level, you can focus on helping others in your business or elevating the business through your profile and other thought-leadership activities.

There are three elements to get help you move to Rockstar Status:

- Search Engine Optimisation
- Positioning
- Connection

REACTIVE

SEO   Positioning

Pull

Perspire   Push

Connection

PROACTIVE

Search Engine Optimisation

LinkedIn, first and foremost, is a search engine. In other words, it's similar to Google in that it's designed for people to use to search for what they're looking for. Not only does this mean that you can turn up in a search result in LinkedIn; you can also turn up in a Google search if you have the right words in your profile. The advantage of this is that you can beat your competitors, even if they're large organisations, in a Google as well as a LinkedIn search.

So, one of the first things you need to have in your profile is search engine optimisation, or SEO. SEO is about having the correct words in your profile so that you turn up in search results and are found. There are three main elements to keep in mind when search engine optimising your profile:

1. **Relevance:** Ensure you use words that a customer uses when searching for you. For example, if you're a facilitator in leadership, a customer could type in "Leadership Facilitator Sydney", but there are also people who might type in "Leadership Trainer Sydney" or "Leadership Training Sydney". Ensuring you have enough of the words in your profile means that people can find you for what you want to be found for. By doing this, your profile will have a lot of pull. This means your profile will bring the right people to you like a magnet.

2. **Competitiveness:** Some keywords will be more competitive than others. This means that to get a strong, targeted result, you may need to be more specific. For example, the keyword "coach" would be a competitive keyword. It is also not very specific to what you do. By making the keyword "junior AFL coach" or "executive coach", you will get a more targeted response that aligns with your goals and ideal client.

3. **Location:** The third element of SEO is the location of keywords in your profile. There are five areas that impact the SEO: Headline, Summary, Employment History and Endorsements Recommendations. Ensure you include your keywords in all areas to maximise your SEO.

Positioning

When you have positioning, it means you stand out from your competition. You have differentiated yourself from others and you are perceived in the market for the work you want to be perceived as being able to do.

The main elements of positioning are:

1. **Content:** Your content relates to your expertise; it relates to those things that help your audience to understand what you do to help. It's about your profile photo, your content and your thought leadership. It's about your brand leverage and being the brand of the companies you have worked for.

2. **Social Proof:** What others say about you is more important than what you say about yourself. The importance of testimonials and case studies cannot be over emphasised. The evidence that you can do what you say you can do is invaluable and gives people hope as well as trust in you.

3. **First Four Seconds:** When a client lands on your profile, they don't make a cup of tea and read your profile, taking in every captivating word. You only have four seconds to grab their attention and help them make sense of what you do. Your profile needs to stand out immediately!

Connection

One of the things we often hear people say about LinkedIn is: "I've got a profile, but it doesn't do anything for me." It's actually a bit more of a team effort. People set up their profile thinking, "Oh, it's done now. I'll just sit back and wait." You need to be proactive with your profile, but there's no point being proactive unless you've got full SEO and it's fully branded. Only then can you go to market.

Just because you're online rather than engaging face-to-face doesn't mean you should treat people any differently. It can be easy to forget that the people behind the computer screen are human. The As a result of the sheer volume of people online, we try to speed everything up to attract the masses. The irony is that this slows the process down. The secret is less haste, more speed.

The three elements of connection are:

1. **Strategy (What):** What do you want to be doing with your clients? What do you help them with? What value do you bring? What problems do your customers have that you are trying to solve? For example, if you're a school principal, you're solving a parent's issue of deciding what school to enrol their child in. If you're an executive coach, you're helping people with their confidence or work-life balance. You're solving their problem of feeling burnt out and helping them regain their energy to re-connect to their work.

2. **Leads (Who):** The connection part is about knowing who you want to work with, so that your profile generates leads and puts you in front of the right people. If you're not able to move to a face-to-face or phone conversation, then you're not moving people to the next step. Clients don't magically appear from nowhere and buy from you. You need to make it easy for them to have a conversation with you.

3. **Responses (How):** What do you say when you want to connect with others or when they want to connect with you? Do you just use the default settings LinkedIn gives you? Do you know how to create a script that you use with potential clients? By personalising your interactions, you will move much more quickly than you will by just using what LinkedIn gives you. Default settings make people feel like a commodity; that you don't really care and you're just in it for you.

Push, Pull and Perspire

Our goal is to get both Push and Pull working in harmony with the least amount of Perspiration. If you have nothing in your profile, you will get nothing. If you have the right words and language in your profile, you're more likely to attract people who want those services.

Your push strategy is designed to complement that, so that when people land on your profile, they say: "Oh wow! I definitely want to talk to you."

Push comes from being able to put your content out there. Pushing content supports the pull strategy. A real direct push is about approaching people directly.

Take Control

Connecting with people on LinkedIn is a bit like dating. If you decide to lock yourself in your house and say, "Well, one day Prince Charming's going to turn up at my front door," then it's not going to happen.

You need to make some effort to reach out and connect with people. To do that, you need to:

- Know what you want and who you're going to connect with.
- Pre-write your scripts. Make sure you know what you're going to say when you go to connect with people.

Decide if you're going to connect by standard connection or InMail. This will be dependent on your budget, the amount of characters you're going to use and if you have a premium account.

People buy when they're ready. Your job is to ensure you're the person they contact when they need help. Overall, there are three things you need to be doing with your profile:

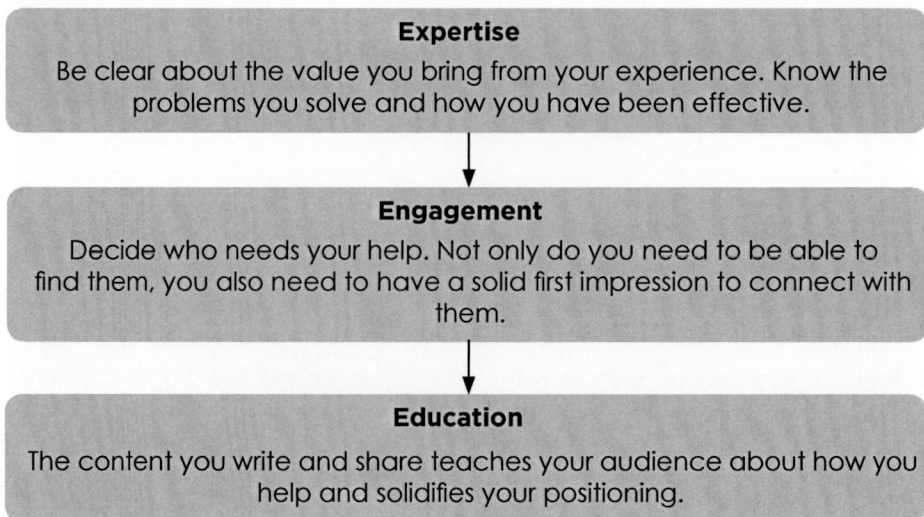

Expertise
Be clear about the value you bring from your experience. Know the problems you solve and how you have been effective.

↓

Engagement
Decide who needs your help. Not only do you need to be able to find them, you also need to have a solid first impression to connect with them.

↓

Education
The content you write and share teaches your audience about how you help and solidifies your positioning.

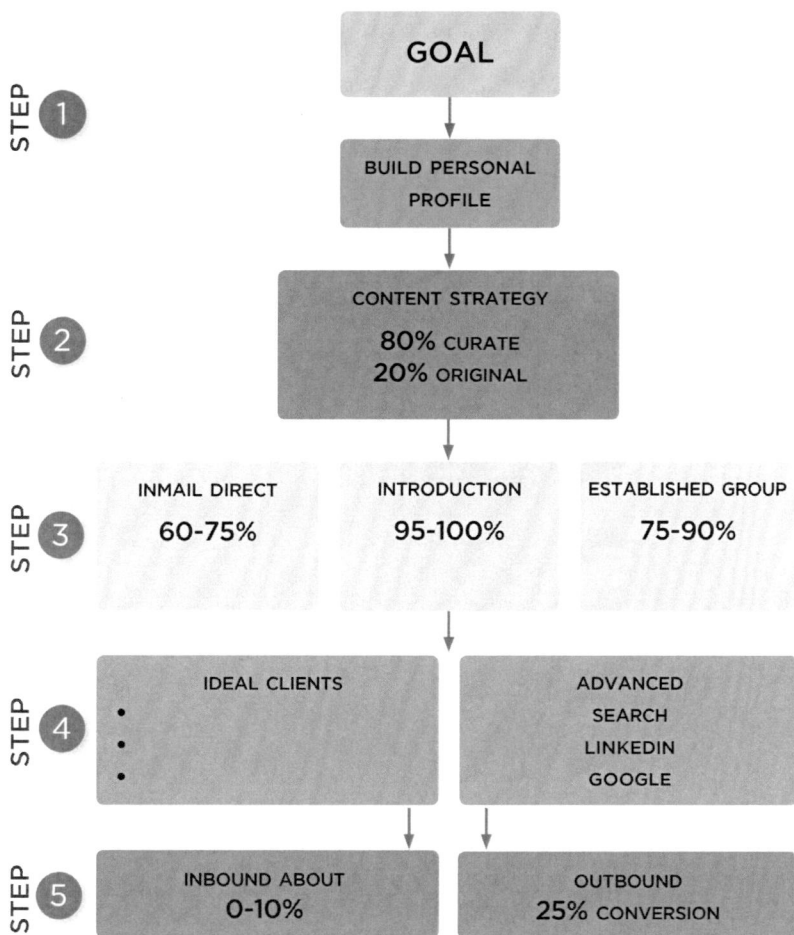

Step 1: Goal

What do you want to achieve with your profile? Do you want to get into a new market? Are you trying to find clients? Do you want to attract talent? Are you looking for strategic alliances? What is the purpose of your profile?

You can do all this work on your profile but if you're not clear about what you want, you're going to get frustrated because it's not working for you. What you're doing has to be crystal clear. To achieve that, you need to state who it is that you want to work with, what problems you solve and how you go about it.

Your profile is like a mirror. Your customer looks at your profile, thinking: "Where can I see me in your profile?" The unconscious decisions they make are about how you look – in keywords, in industries and the types of people you've worked with. It's far more about the customer and less about you. If it's all about you, you will ostracise people and repel them.

It was John F. Kennedy who said: "Efforts and courage are not enough without purpose and direction." You need to be clear about the niche you work with, your message and markets.

Step 1: Build Your Profile

Once you're clear about your goal, the next step is to focus on building your profile. The profile needs to be built around your goal and the future, not the past; otherwise, it will look like an obituary. This is often the step that is most overlooked and yet it is the most crucial, as you only have four seconds to help your reader understand what you do and how you help.

It's not all about you. There needs to be more emphasis on how you help your client, and less emphasis about what you love, what inspires you, or how you want to change the world. You need to make sure you use collateral that builds trust in your client and sings to the problems they have. As Matt Church, author of *Sell Your Thoughts*, says: "They don't care, they're not listening and you don't matter."

At this crucial stage, your profile needs to have full SEO so that you're turning up in search results and competing on keywords. Your profile also needs to be tested for the pages you are turning up on in LinkedIn and Google.

Step 2: Content Strategy

The next step involves looking at posting and content. You need to have a content strategy for what you're going to educate people about. About 80% of your content strategy should be sharing, commenting and liking content. The other 20% needs to be original content to educate people about your area of expertise.

This isn't necessarily about you selling stuff online. This is about how you address problems your customers have and what your thought leadership is in relation to that.

With the average person spending more than two hours per day on social media, you need to give them something to read. Robert Cialdini, the author of *Influence: the Psychology of Persuasion*, says that you need five to seven touch points to influence and persuade someone to do what you want them to do. Make content writing a habit and a priority – it is the number-one activity to be done each day or week, not something that is done when you have time.

Step 3: Connect

Clients we have worked with will say things such as: "I've tried doing direct approaches," or "I've tried doing introductions. I don't have any success," when they've only done one or two and given up. It's important you're clear about what is the benchmark.

Something that can really make a difference is this first-degree connection or the introduction. This is when you see someone's profile and you notice that they're connected to somebody you know, and you ask for an introduction, for example, "Would you mind?" or "Could you please connect me to …" The key here is to manage how you're positioned when you're introduced. So you may like to write your introduction for them.

If you're in an established group that your ideal target person is also in, they're more likely to take notice of you. About 75-90% of people will be happy to connect with you that way, as long as the connection request is written correctly and you have written your own profile effectively. As the saying goes, "You only get one chance at a first impression!"

Step 4: Searches

You need to know where your market is and how to find it. Your market often includes busy people who aren't trying to find you, particularly if they don't know they have a problem. Sitting back and waiting for people to approach you will not get results.

Profiles of ideal clients can be found via various search functions in LinkedIn. The reality is that LinkedIn's search engine is not perfect and your ideal clients don't know how to optimise their profiles, or don't want to be found by you. This means you may have to use other means to find your ideal client on LinkedIn. It also means you need to think about the people you want to connect with and create customised conversations with. Using a spray-and-pray method only ostracises people and makes them feel like a commodity.

If you don't have a premium account, you won't have all the options of searching for all roles, but you will have some. A premium account will give you access to greater search functions and can be worth the investment if you are undertaking an aggressive growth strategy with your profile.

Step 5: Sales Meetings

The last step is knowing how to approach people and start a conversation. If you've been doing all your ground work, then you can start to have some scripts to use when talking to people.

If you're doing all the previous steps, about 90% of your leads on LinkedIn will want to meet with you. If you're getting in front of those people, you should be closing at least one in four sales and that's even if you're not a great salesperson. The remaining 10% of leads will come to you directly without you approaching them.

Reflections and Actions

- What is your goal with your profile? Are you looking for new clients, strategic partners, investors, etc.?
- Who do you help?
- What do you know that you can share with your connections?

Chapter 4

Search Engine Optimisation (SEO)

"The best place to hide a dead body is page 2 of Google search results."
— Unknown

Pull vs Push

Thomas Edison once said: "There's a better way to do it. Find it."

When Jane first started working with her mentor, she remembered thinking: "Where on Earth have you been for the past four years?!" She wished she had known he existed. She didn't know about him or his business.

He kept within his stream of clients but didn't do much social media marketing. For a Gen Y/X like Jane, that's where she hung out, so why did it take her so long to hear about him? She didn't find out about him until someone who was being mentored by him reached out to have a coffee with Jane to learn more about what she did. He told Jane about his mentor and she thought, "Wow, that's exactly what I'm after."

So, from a sales perspective, times have changed. We have moved into an era of the information superhighway. The challenge with this is that there is so much information available, unless you really know what you need, it can be hard to know where to turn. So you either procrastinate and do nothing, or buy what you think you need and then waste it. Cut-through is so important to connect with the right buyer for your business or for a recruiter.

Pull

In a pull strategy:

1. Someone needs help.
2. They ask around, do a Google search, and turn to their LinkedIn or Facebook connections.

3. They go to your website or LinkedIn profile.
   - They look at your photo and scan your title for keywords.
   - If you don't have them, they've gone.

This is relevant in a **network or search** and you require good search engine optimisation for your LinkedIn profile and website to get this to work.

In a strategy, you would typically do the following:

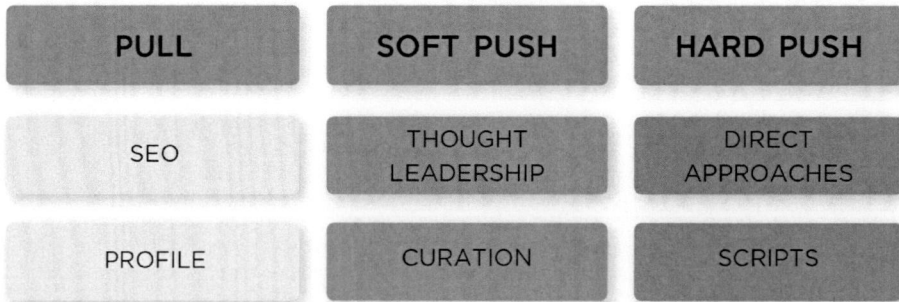

PULL	SOFT PUSH	HARD PUSH
SEO	THOUGHT LEADERSHIP	DIRECT APPROACHES
PROFILE	CURATION	SCRIPTS

The main thing to keep in mind with Pull strategies is that you will still be validated. People will still find you online to check that you are who they've been told you are, if you know someone they know. So a Pull strategy is still very much part of the Push process.

Businesses need to leverage their teams' networks to build awareness of what they do to cover all angles. Accessibility, visibility and continuity are key.

Christopher Mahar from Motorola implemented a search engine optimisation strategy. He said: "Post your sessions and my new understanding of how to grow my profile and search engine optimisation, I have achieved the following LinkedIn success within one week.!"

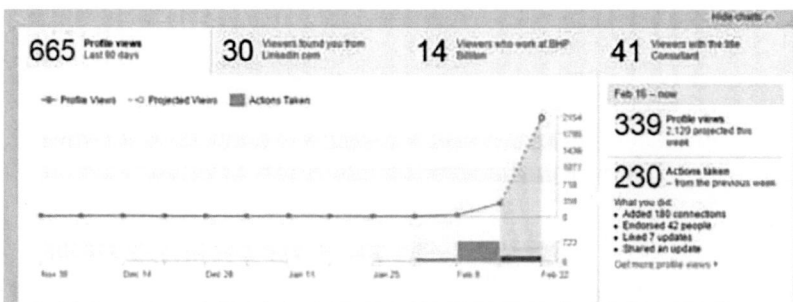

Get Found

Your LinkedIn profile generally has about four seconds to capture your readers' interest. An effective profile attracts your ideal audience.

Many people think LinkedIn is for job seekers, and although that is true, it is also a great low-cost tool for businesses to attract new clients. It can be a cost-effective strategy for consultants, small businesses and organisations.

By using LinkedIn effectively, you can be found in search results, position yourself as an expert in your field, and easily research prospective clients.

We recently spoke with a client who had a strong dislike for LinkedIn. He complained that the information he received wasn't relevant. After a quick search of his profile, we found that his LinkedIn profile had been written about his past, not his future. Writing about his past meant the LinkedIn search algorithm was providing him with information about exactly that. Remember that LinkedIn is about your future, so write your content to reflect this.

To support business-to-business sales, your LinkedIn profile needs to be found (search engine optimised) and needs to be marketable.

What Do You Want?

To deliver a strong LinkedIn strategy, it is important to first know what you want from LinkedIn. LinkedIn is not a mind reader and only understands data you enter. First and foremost, LinkedIn is an algorithm and a search engine.

It's a bit like a mirror and it will reflect what information you give it. The great news is that you can ask for what you want!

So, this leads to the question: "Who is your ideal audience?" With a clear picture of your audience, you will be able to communicate with them through your LinkedIn profile in a meaningful manner.

- What industry do they work in?
- What problems and challenges do they have?
- What are they most concerned about?
- Where do they congregate?
- Are they male or female?
- What age group might they be?

- What are their interests?
- What experience do you have working with them?
- Where do they eat?
- Where do they live?
- What do they do when they're not at work?
- What do they spend their time and money on?

When you're super clear about who you're talking to, then you can build a true connection with your audience and attract the opportunities you desire!

How Do You Know Where You're Turning Up in Search Results?

Sometimes, it can be hard to know if the work you put in to your profile is effective. Generally, we would expect to see increased engagement with your targeted audience and more leads.

There are a number of other measures of your LinkedIn profile's success. These include:

1. **Direct Google search results.**
You can do a direct search into Google (www.google.com). A well-optimised LinkedIn profile that includes a vanity URL will be returned in the search results.

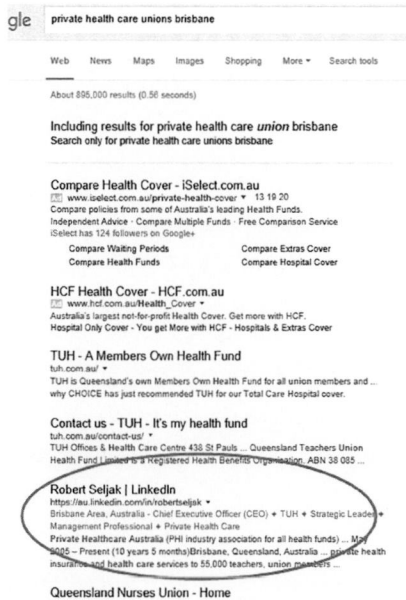

We have worked with clients where their LinkedIn profile is on the first page of the Google search terms. Of course, some keywords are more competitive than others. From an audience's perspective, these results are sometimes seen as more "authentic" than a company page on Google. Another advantage is that having your LinkedIn profile returned in search results is generally a cheaper option that paying for an SEO expert to keyword optimise your website.

For example, the initial results with SEO for a CEO in the health insurance industry had his LinkedIn profile returned on the first page of search results for the targeted keywords.

2. Search on LinkedIn directly and remove the parameters of connection.
This option will also allow you to access others who appear in your results.

For example, if you are an accountant in Brisbane, you can put the words "accountant Brisbane" in the search box. This would be the same search a client would do.

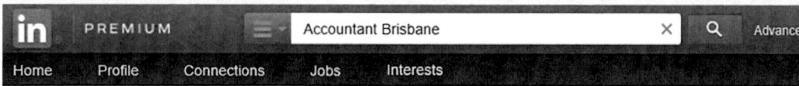

You can then see the right-hand side includes parameters that impact the search. These include:

1. People, Jobs, Companies, Groups, Universities, Posts and Inbox.
   Select People.
2. Relationship is the degree of connections. Select 3rd + Everybody else.
3. Select the location you want to search.

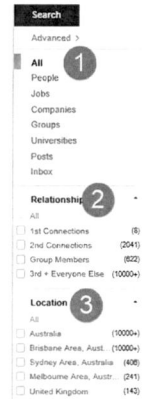

3. Perform a Google "X-ray" search for your client's keywords to check their rankings. Make sure you have logged out of your LinkedIn account. Enter the keyword into the Google browser.

site:linkedin.com/in | site:linkedin.com/pub -dir "Accountant" Brisbane
site:linkedin.com/in | site:linkedin.com/pub -inurl:pub/dir "Accountant" Brisbane

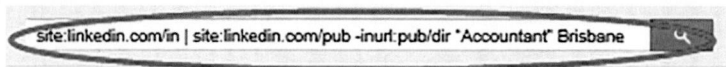

Having a fully search engine optimised LinkedIn profile – supported with blog posts, liking and commenting – directly and positively impacts Google and LinkedIn search results, meaning you have more visibility, more trust and more opportunities to work with your ideal audience.

Firstly, Be Found

It is vital to remember that **LinkedIn is a search engine**. This means it offers a great opportunity for you to be found by new clients. The key to this is SEO. LinkedIn is indexed heavily by Google.

Be Marketable

To support business-to-business selling, the profile needs to market yourself and your business, making it clear to the reader what is in it for them. A LinkedIn profile, for this purpose, needs to have a clear value proposition. What makes you different from others in your field?

The 5 Areas to Maximise Your LinkedIn SEO

The first and most important step with SEO is to identify and research keywords. Recently, we worked with a financial planner in Brisbane, Australia. This client specialised in retirement planning in Brisbane.

We thought about his ideal clients and words they would use to find people like him. We considered words such as "financial planning", "retirement planning" and "Brisbane". Think about who you want to be found by and what words they would use. You need to build your profile around keywords your ideal audience would use – not industry-specific buzz words. Not sure what words your ideal audience would use? You can always ask them what words they use when doing a Google search.

Once you have your keywords, conduct your own search on these words and see what people are returned in the search results. Is it what you expected? Once you have identified your keywords and have done some research, you can build your content and profile around these words.

LinkedIn has never shared its algorithm. However, based on research, you need to fully search engine optimise your profile. By not ensuring that you have the correct keywords, not only will you not be found, but you won't attract your ideal client because you won't make sense to them in less than four seconds. So your profile's a bit like a magnet: you will either repel or attract your ideal client or audience.

Think about what people you want to find you and what words they would use. Once you have identified your keywords, you can build your content around them.

There are five areas that will fully search engine optimise your profile. These include your:

1. **Title:** You have 120 characters to work with for your title and it needs to reflect your keywords and the problems your customer has.

2. **Summary:** The summary is a key component of your LinkedIn profile. The summary positions you for your target audience. It offers a great opportunity to include keywords, validation and a strong call to action.

3. **Employment history:** You can use up to 2000 characters for each position you've held in this space. Essentially, this is your positioning area and it needs to reflect your customers' problems, why should they care, how you can help, who trusts you, and leverage testimonials.

4. **Skills and endorsements:** You might be endorsed for things you've never

heard of before or by people you've never met, but these still carry a heavy weighting in the search results, so you can take control of them. You don't need to accept what people give you and you don't need to prioritise the numbers on your profile that LinkedIn gives you. You have complete control over it.

5. **Recommendations:** You might need to help people write recommendations for you, but they are a high priority on your profile.

Blog posts also contribute to search engine optimisation, as well as being returned in search results with your name, headshot and headline.

Other character limitations include:

- **Website label:** 30 maximum characters.
- **Website URL:** 256 maximum characters.
- **Company name:** 100 maximum characters.
- **Job title:** 100 maximum characters.

Keywords are based on your goals moving forward and may not directly reflect what you are doing at the moment. For example, we worked with a member-based organisation that had a reputation for servicing teachers, and was looking to expand into other industries, such as nursing. In this instance, the profile was developed around attracting nurses and other future clients industries, as well as teachers.

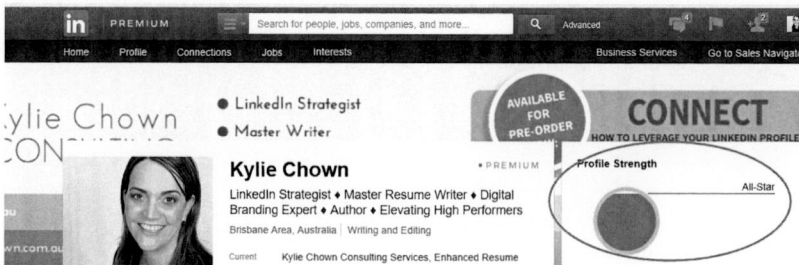

Profile Strength

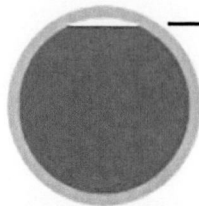

All-Star

You can also use Google AdWords' Keyword Tool to figure out which terms will increase your searchability. **Keyword Planner** is a free **AdWords** tool that finds **keyword** ideas and estimates how they may perform in Google searches. Although it is for Google and not LinkedIn, you will get an idea of words being used. To access Google Keyword Planner, you need to set up an AdWords account. You can find out more here: https://adwords.google.com/KeywordPlanner

Action Steps to Get Started

Go to https://www.linkedin.com/

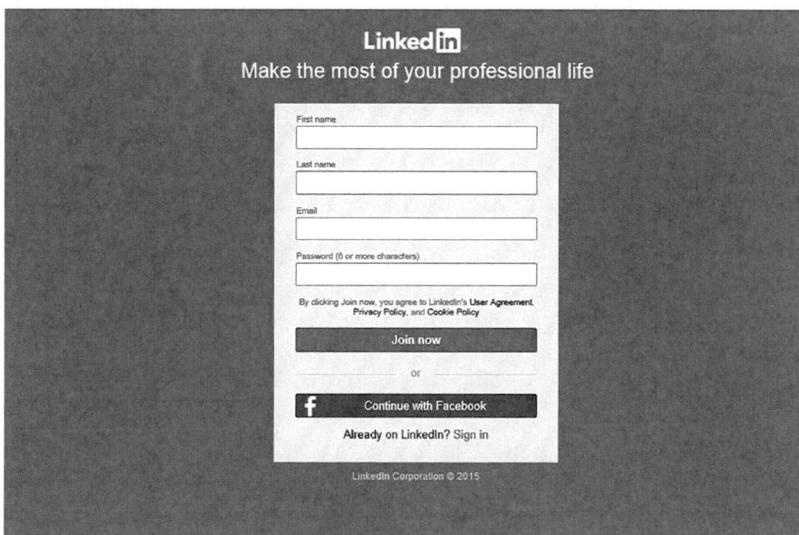

1. Fill in all the details and click "Join Now".
2. You will receive an email confirmation that you need to accept so you can get started.

The Title (Headline)

The headline looks like this:

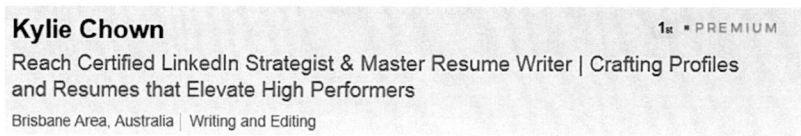

Kylie Chown   1st ▪ PREMIUM

Reach Certified LinkedIn Strategist & Master Resume Writer | Crafting Profiles
and Resumes that Elevate High Performers

Brisbane Area, Australia | Writing and Editing

The title or headline of your LinkedIn profile sits under your name. The default setting on LinkedIn will set your title to be exactly the same as your current role. Most of the clients we see make a fundamental mistake and leave it that way.

Why is this so important to change?

Positioning

Without the correct heading, you will be pigeonholed into the category people think you belong to, rather than perceived how you want to be. For example, if you have "CEO of Pegasus Pty Ltd", that doesn't tell me how you help me. I have to do a lot more reading to find out and, frankly, I don't have time. As Rachel Bourke, a leading expert in sales, says in her book The YES Zone: "A confused mind says 'no'." So if it's not clear to your reader how you can help them, your ideal client will pigeonhole you as a CEO who can't help them, when in fact you can. You just haven't sold it early enough in your profile.

Validation

Firstly, when your profile is returned in search results, the name, headline and photo will be the only sections of your profile that are visible. This means that the photo, headline and name are the determining factors for whether somebody is going to click through to your profile. It is imperative you use your title as a positioning statement for how you want to be found. When somebody is viewing your profile in search results, you only have three to four seconds to make an impact. The best way to do this is with a standout headline.

Search Engine Optimisation

Your title contributes to your search engine optimisation, so include keywords where possible. You have 120 characters in the headline to maximise your findability.

A well-written title distinguishes you from people with similar skills and expertise. If your keywords include a target location, you can include this in your headline as well.

Getting Click Through

Once you have keyword optimisation, you can apply the "who you are and who you help" principle.

Here are some great examples of headlines:

- Executive Gemologist serving CEOs. Cut, Polishing and Resetting the Inner Diamonds of Executives and their Companies.
- Business Development Co-ordinator ♦ Health Insurance ♦ Enhancing the Customer Experience for Teachers and Union Members.
- Environmental Leadership ♦ Project Manager ♦ Oil & Gas, Perth ♦ Positively Impacting the Environment, Safety and People.
- Specialist Technical Trainer Providing WH&S, Rehabilitation and Return-to-Work Services to the Health Insurance Sector.
- Industrial Relations (IR) Specialist – Driving Major IR Projects in the Australian Oil, Gas and Iron Ore Sectors.
- CEO | Company Name | Partnering with Business on Customised Solutions to Effortlessly Achieve Project Excellence.

We have worked with clients to create multiple headlines, and then tested them on a rotational basis to see what achieves the best click-through. You can do this to see what gets you the best results.

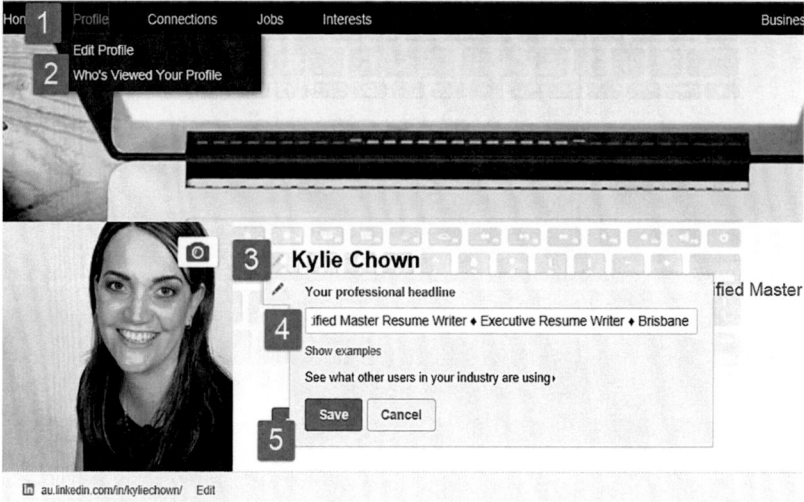

Action Steps to Create Your Stand-Out Title

1. Click Profile.
2. Click Edit Profile.
3. Click ✎
4. Write your new headline.
5. Click Save
6. Do a search and you will be able to see how your profile is returned in search results.

Top Tip #1: Use typology symbols (◆□❖●) to break use words, increase readability and minimise conjoint words.

Top Tip #2: If the location is part of your SEO strategy, use it in your headline.

Summary

We live in a competitive world and if you want to make an impact, you need to be in control of your online presence, personal brand, cultural fit and reputation.

Here is what a summary looks like:

Failing to give adequate attention to your LinkedIn profile may not only result in you missing out on potential contacts; you also run the risk of trailing behind your competitors.

In Ctrl Alt Delete, Mitch Joel introduces "digital first": the concept that the first place we learn about people is online. This means that people are making decisions based on what they read online, so you don't even know the opportunities you could be missing.

Understand people are making decisions based on the information they read. It is potentially the first place people find information on you and decide whether to take further action.

Importance of the LinkedIn Summary Section

Many people don't realise the importance of a great summary section in your LinkedIn profile. More than any other section, the summary represents you, your business and your brand. It is also the most viewed section on LinkedIn. If you get this area right, you are well on the way to having one of the most viewed profiles on LinkedIn – and attracting more of your target audience.

Here are a few top tips for creating a successful LinkedIn summary:

Be Clear About Your Objective

Before writing your summary, be clear about what you want to achieve with LinkedIn. Are you using it to raise your credibility or are you looking to expand your network? Are you seeking new clients? Understand what you are trying to do and make sure this is clear in your summary.

The key to a strong LinkedIn summary is writing for your future, not your past. You need to make it relevant to your audience. Make a strong, compelling summary that will have your ideal audience thinking you are what they need to solve their problem

LinkedIn Summary

Your summary meets the blend of keywords and your purpose. The content will be targeted to your audience and purpose. For a job seeker, think about content that will engage a recruiter. For a sales professional, think about your clients. If you are a thought leader, how can you demonstrate your expertise? This section is limited to only 2000 characters, so we recommend the following layout:

1st Paragraph:

This is your LinkedIn elevator speech. If I read the first sentence only, I have a strong sense of you and your offerings. These tasks need to match the keywords you want to be found with. For example:

"I am a professional leadership coach with more than 15 years of experience in leadership, consulting, human resources and performance management. Tertiary qualified with a wide variety of local and international experience."

2nd paragraph:

The next paragraph can highlight your core focus areas. These include specialist skills that relate to keywords. Include what you want to be known for and what makes you different from others like you. For example:

"I help executives in the finance industry gain clarity and direction. My core focus areas include: executive coaching, behavioural-based recruitment and performance management."

3rd paragraph:

Now you need to support your skills with evidence. How have you assisted your clients? What issues have you resolved? Have you increased engagement or efficiency? What have others said? Have you won any awards? For example:

"Achievements include …" and list your top three to five achievements.

"After working with me, what some have said includes …"

4th paragraph:

This is a great spot to introduce your role within your current organisation and leverage any internal marketing communications. At this point, you are elevating your capacity to be a brand ambassador. If you are a job seeker, you can leverage brands you have worked for. For example:

"I am the business development manager for ABC Company. At ABC Company, we help the mining sector to minimise costs and project delivery time frames."

Finally, we need a strong call to action, a "where to from here?" For example:

"To see how we can help your team reduce costs, email me at …"

"Ready to commit to my next opportunity, you can contact me at …"

Ensure your LinkedIn summary aligns with who you are. It isn't about what you have done or how successful you have been. The words in your summary are about making an emotional connection with the reader. The best way to do this is by using emotive language and keywords. Recent research shows that people will decide whether to contact you within a few seconds of reading your profile.

Action Steps to Create a Stand-Out Summary

To edit your summary, log into your LinkedIn profile and:

1. Click Profile.
2. Edit Profile.

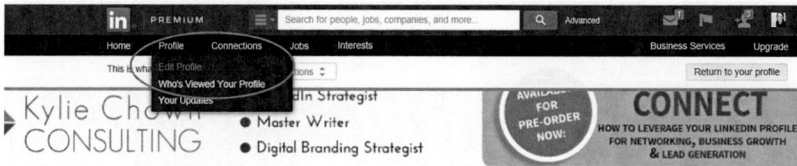

3. Scroll to the summary section.

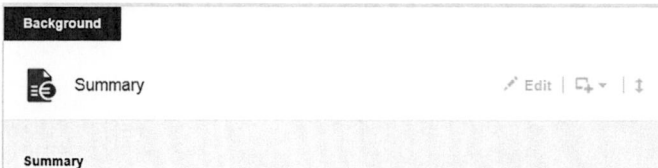

4. Write your summary.

5. Click **Save**

Top Tip #1: Make it easy for people to contact you. Having a strong call to action that includes contact details means prospective clients can easily take further action.

Top Tip #2: Most people aren't aware that they can find your contact information on other people's profiles.

Skills, Expertise and Endorsements

Many clients ask why they should bother with skills, expertise and endorsements. Skills, expertise and endorsements on LinkedIn give a clear and immediate picture of your abilities. Your endorsements also contribute to your SEO, as well as influencing those who look at your profile.

Kylie recently spoke to a client who was an accountant and had recently bought a new home. He noticed that his real estate agent had endorsed him for financial planning skills. The accountant was perplexed – why was his real estate agent endorsing him for a skill he knew nothing about?

This will often happen because the default setting on LinkedIn makes suggestions to your contacts on what they should endorse you for. There is the option to manually over-ride this setting so that your skills are not suggested endorsements for others.

On your profile, your skills and endorsements look like this:

Control What You Are Endorsed For and How This is Presented on Your Profile

Although we can't control who is endorsing us, we can control what we are endorsed for, the order they appear and their visibility within your profile.

The first step to having quality endorsements is controlling what you are endorsed for. The easiest way to do that is to manually add skills and expertise to your profile. We recommend that clients look at their endorsements and re-order or even hide endorsements so that they are reflective of their current goals and objectives.

LinkedIn provides you with the capacity to include up to 50 skills. Our advice when starting out is to only include your strongest skills. It is better to have 10 strong skills than 50 possible options diluting your endorsements. Once you have built these results, you can add more skills to your profile.

Leverage Endorsements

Having worked with thousands of profiles, we have found that recommendations are weighted more heavily than endorsements. If you want to increase the testimonials in your LinkedIn profile, you can start by looking at who has endorsed you. You already know these people think highly of your work and are prepared to say so in a public space, so you may consider asking them for a testimonial.

Endorsements for Others

By endorsing others, you will increase your own viability when that person is viewed in LinkedIn, but remember that what you endorse others for also reflects on you. Only first-level connections can endorse you, so by growing your network you are growing your possible endorsers. It also helps others to understand what you're known for.

Top Tip: List skills that are consistent with future industry needs to be ahead of the game. For example, if there is imminent change for your industry, list this as a skill. This gives you the opportunity to be endorsed for it and supports search engine optimisation outcomes.

Action Steps to Manage Skills, Experience and Endorsements

Once you have logged into your profile:

1. Click Profile.
2. Click Edit Profile.

3. Scroll to Skills and Endorsements. Under the Skills and Endorsements setting, personalise the check boxes.

This will take you to the next screen.

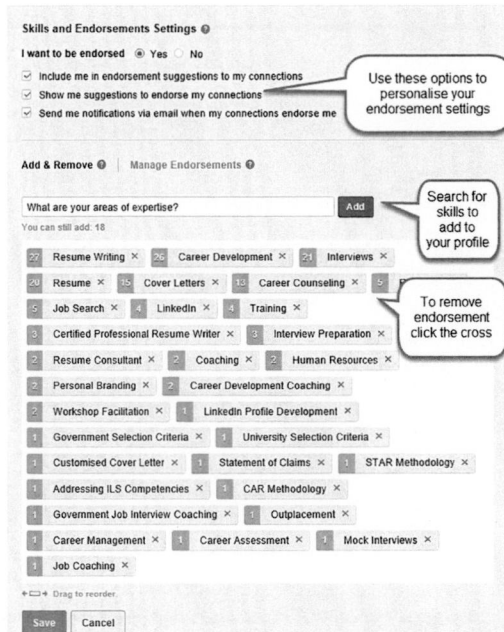

4. Add skills and expertise by typing in skills.

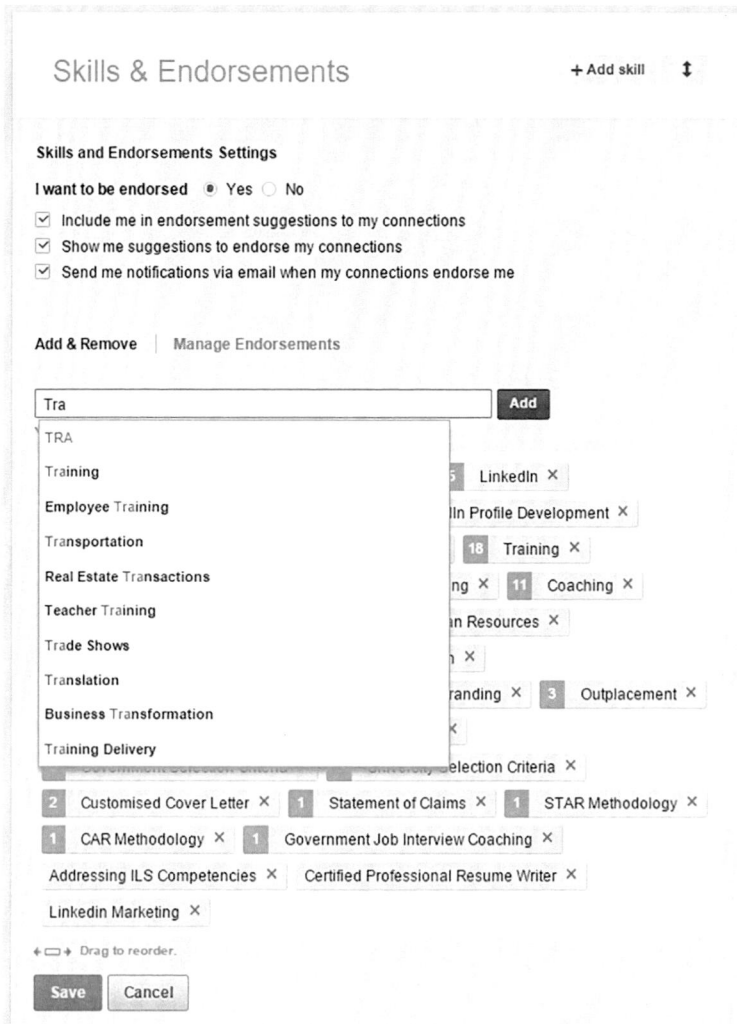

5. To remove endorsements, click the cross.

6. Click **Save**

Top Tip: If you are endorsed by someone, it is a good idea to send them a quick thank you note. If you are endorsed by someone, you don't need to endorse them in return, especially if you are not confident of their skill set.

Employment History

We often say to our clients, **"Your LinkedIn is all about your future and not your past,"** and this is especially true for your employment history.

Your employment history is not an obituary of your past jobs; it is a search engine optimised sales and marketing tool!

By taking this approach to your LinkedIn profile, you will be able to leverage its social selling capabilities to your advantage.

A fully completed employment entry looks like this:

Experience

LinkedIn Profile Writer for Business & Job Seekers | Master Resume Writer | Executive Resume Writer
Kylie Chown Consulting Services
February 2014 – Present (1 year 9 months) | Australia Wide (Brisbane, Sydney, Melbourne)

Offering assured solutions and purposeful results, I am inspired on a daily basis to see my clients elevate their on and offline presence, increase their business outcomes and take their career to the next level. I work with businesses and individuals across a range of industries.

CORE FOCUS AREAS:
⇢ Executive Resume Writer.
⇢ LinkedIn Profile Optimisation - Thought Leaders, Executives and Managers.
⇢ LinkedIn Profile Optimisation - Business Development Teams, Small Business Owners, Solopreners and Consultants.
⇢ LinkedIn Profile Optimisation - Professional Jobseekers.

FEATURED IN:
⇢ Australian Institute of Management (AIM)
⇢ Minnovare Mining and Civil
⇢ Franchise Business
⇢ Leaders In Heels
⇢ HC and HRM Online
⇢ Women in Leadership and Management Australasia (WILMA)
⇢ Guest Speaker for the Electus Recruitment Seminar for Job Seekers

CREDENTIALS:
♦ Reach Certified Branding Analyst (1 of 3 Australia Wide)
♦ Certified Master Résumé Writer (1 of 8 Australia Wide)
♦ Certified Executive Resume Master (1 of 4 Australia Wide)
♦ Certified Resume Specialist (Sales and Business Development)
♦ Certified Advanced Résumé Writer
♦ Certified Professional Online Job Search and Reputation Management

Some feedback I have received is:

"I really like how you converted my very technical resume into a more user friendly document without losing any of the content" IT Manager, VIC.

It is important to remember that your LinkedIn profile **isn't written for you –
you are writing for your audience.** Make sure the information in the Employment
History is clear, well organised and easy to read.

It is also important to remember that your LinkedIn profile is a public document
that anyone can potentially view. You need to be mindful of the information you place
in your profile.

A great formula to follow when writing your employment history is **ISCR
(Introduction, Specialties, Company and Results).**

Top Tip: Keep in mind what your audience's problems are and write about how you
solve them.

The Introduction

This is a brief overview of what you did in the position, who you engaged with and
for what reason. As an example: "As the business development manager for ABC
Company, I provided expert advice, guidance and recommendations for a range of
products that include …"

If the reader was to only read the first line of your employment history, they should
have a clear idea of your job and what you did in that role. You need to capture your
job in a single sentence.

Here are some other examples:

*"As the senior IT systems manager for ABC Company, I provide team leadership and
operational management to the Brisbane-based team."*

*"As the account manager for ABC Company, I developed and supported customers to navigate
the superannuation maze."*

*"As the sales manager, I led a team while managing high-value accounts within the
ABC business."*

These examples show that in just one sentence, you get a strong idea of what these
people did in their roles.

The Specialties

In this area, you can highlight your main competencies. The key here is to align the competencies with SEO. Here is an example of how to present your specialties:

My specialties at ABC Company include:

◆ *Relationship Management*
◆ *Account Management*
◆ *Business Development*

Some other examples of specialties include:

- Stakeholder Engagement
- Financial Planning
- Team Leadership
- Coaching and Mentoring
- Board Reporting
- Strategic Planning

The Company

This is a great opportunity to leverage your internal marketing and communications functions to further validate your profile. You can utilise the confidence your client has in your brand to further elevate your profile.

Review the company website and pick key information that supports your branding. Anything that includes facts and figures will be well received. How many customers does the company have? What is the company's main achievements? Has it won any awards? Think about this from your client's point of view. What information would be important to them?

As an example:

"At ABC Company, we have more than 5,000 business customers who rely on us to provide critical services. As a leader in the field, we were recently nominated for the 2014 Business of the Year Award."

The Result

The result is your time to shine. Think about achievements your ideal audience will value as opposed to what you value. Recently, we worked with a client who was targeting an organisation that had a strong focus on customer service. For this reason, we decided to include achievements that supported this company's values. We went with something like:

"During this time I have:

• Achieved a 5-Star Customer Service rating directly reflective of my service-driven approach.
• Solved all customer problems at the first point of call, mitigating the requirement for escalation."

Results can be further supported by testimonials. For example:

What others have said after working with me includes:

"Robert is a customer-focused business development manager. Before Robert, any problems were processed in the call centre. Now Robert personally manages to resolve all issues directly. This means our business can do what we do best."

If the people who have provided a testimonial are happy to include their name, you can do so. You can also include the location. This works particularly well if you are targeting a particular location.

Finally, have a strong call to action. At this point, you have been found in search results. Your reader has read through and now needs a clear directive on where to go next. For example:

"To see how I can help you and your team, email me at (include email) or phone (include phone number)."

There is a limit of 2,000 characters per role within the employment section. If you have trouble deciding what to include, always revert back to your audience. Ask yourself, "Is this important to them?"

Action Steps to Adding Your Employment History

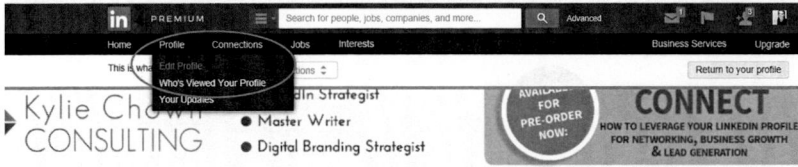

1. Under the Experience section, click +Add Position.

2. Start writing the name of the company you work for in the Company Name section. If the company is listed in LinkedIn, you can select it from the list. If not, you will need to add a new company.

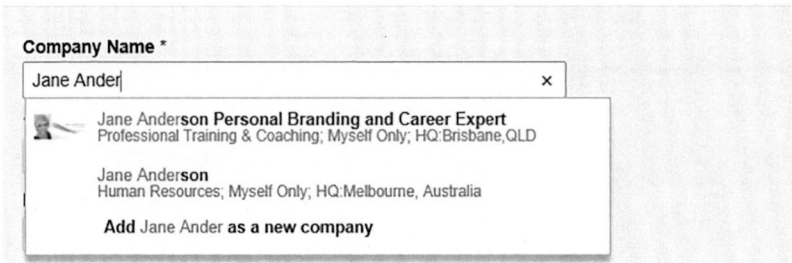

3. You can then add in the fields of Title (what your current job title is), Location (where this role is situated) and the Time Period that you have worked at the company.

Company Name *
Jane Anderson Personal Branding and Career Expert Change Company | Edit Display Name

Title *

Location

Time Period *
Choose... ∨ Year – Choose... ∨ Year
☐ I currently work here

Description
My responsibilities include...

See examples

Save Cancel

4. Under the Description, you can use the ISCR formula to complete the description of the role.

Company Name *
Jane Anderson Personal Branding and Career Expert Change Company | Edit Display Name

Title *
Business Development Manager

Location
Brisbane

Time Period *
January ∨ 2014 – Present
☑ I currently work here

Headline
☐ Update my headline to:

Description
As the Business Development Manager for ABC Company, I provided expert advice, guidance and recommendation on a range of products that include coaching and mentoring services.

My Specialties at Jane Anderson Personal Branding include:

✦ Relationship Management

See examples

Save Cancel

Important Pointer

The default setting is **Update my headline** to: Box checked. You need to uncheck this box.

Company Name *

Jane Anderson Personal Branding and Career Expert Change Company | Edit Display Name

Title *

Business Development Manager

Location

Time Period *

February ⌄ 2000 – Present

☑ I currently work here

Headline

☑ Update my headline to:

Business Development Manager at Jane Anderson Personal Brand

Description

My responsibilities include…

See examples

Save   Cancel

Top Tip: With 2,000 characters per role, your employment history is key to leveraging full search engine optimisation outcomes.

Publications

The Publications section lets you connect external content that you have authored or published to your profile.

Publications looks like this:

IÎ\ Publications

IMPACT: How to Build Your Personal Brand for the Connection Economy
Jane Anderson
October 1, 2014

Discover how to create "corporation you" without being a tall poppy

We're no longer in the industrial or information age. We're now in the connection economy. The economy where you're ability to stand out, connect with others and position yourself in your career and business mean security. It means you won't be left behind but instead ahead of the pack.

Understanding Y
Wlley
May 18, 2014

Understanding Y is a fresh and incisive book that offers a better understanding, appreciation and awareness of the Millennial generation. In this groundbreaking work, author Charlie Caruso has amassed a diverse array of papers, articles and journals from prominent individuals, noted entrepreneurs and bestselling authors who collectively explore how Gen Y thinks, interacts and works. Understanding... **more**

  ‣ 7 authors, including:

  Jane Anderson
  Author of "CONNECT" & "IMPACT" ♦ Pr...

  Charlie Caruso
  Communications Entrepreneur

  Chris Piper

  Bernard Salt

Should You Lie About Being Fired?
The Age
March 25, 2014

Ever suffered the frustration and humiliation of being fired? Then you'll know the dilemma of deciding whether to be honest with prospective employers.

How to Stand Out With Your LinkedIn Summary
Leaders in Heels
August 26, 2013

Many people don't realise the importance of a great summary section in your LinkedIn profile. More than any other section, this area, represents you, your business and your brand. It is also the most viewed section on LinkedIn. If you get this area right, you are well on the way to having one of the most viewed profiles on LinkedIn – and attracting more of your target audience.

This is particularly useful if you have had your work published on other mediums. It also reduces any issues with posts being duplicated on other sites and Google penalising you.

Publications supports thought leadership and establishes your expert status. If you have contributed to an article, you can show this collaboration in the Publications section.

Top Tip: If you have been featured on another site, you can use Publications to highlight this.

Action Steps to Add a Publication

After Profile, go to Edit Profile.

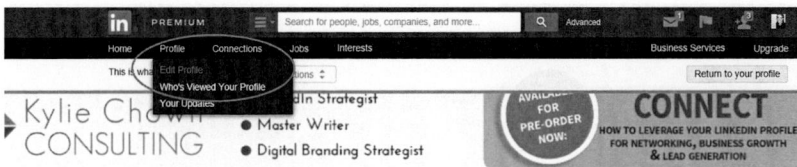

Scroll to Publications.

1. Enter the **Title** of the Publication.
2. Enter the **Publication or Publisher**.
3. Enter the **Date**.
4. Enter the **Publication URL**. You can use this field if you have been published on another site.
5. Your profile will be automatically added as an Author. You can add a co-author by typing their names.
6. In the **Description**, write a summary of your publication.
7. Click Save

It is important that publications don't sell a product or service. For thought leadership to be effective, publications need to be about educating and informing.

Plugins

Plugins offer a great opportunity to support and leverage internal communication and marketing functions. You can review your organisation's marketing collateral to include links in your own profile. LinkedIn allows you to add different types of media to your profile as a plugin. You can include:

• PowerPoint presentations
• Websites
• Videos
• PDF files
• YouTube channels

You can add plugins to three sections of your profile. These are:

• Summary
• Experience
• Education

Some ways that you can use plugins to support social selling include:

• Company advertising campaigns
• Customer testimonials
• Product and service information and education
• Contact Us page
• Speaker show reels

Jane's plugins look like this:

By adding company plugins to your profile, you can maintain the individualisation of your own profile while leveraging your organisation's marketing strategies. You can add plugins to websites or files.

To Add a Plugin Website

1. Under Profile, go to Edit Profile.

2. Go to Edit Summary, then Add Link or Upload File.

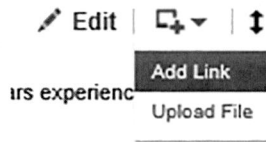

3. Type the address of the site you would like to add.

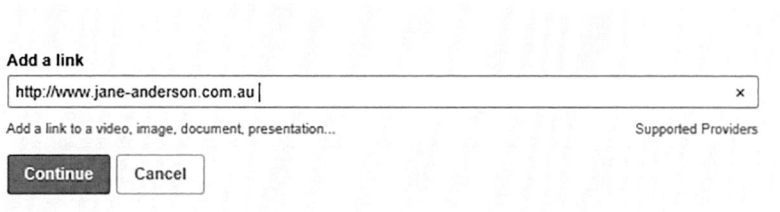

4. Once you select continue, the content will link to your profile. You can edit the description and add to the profile.

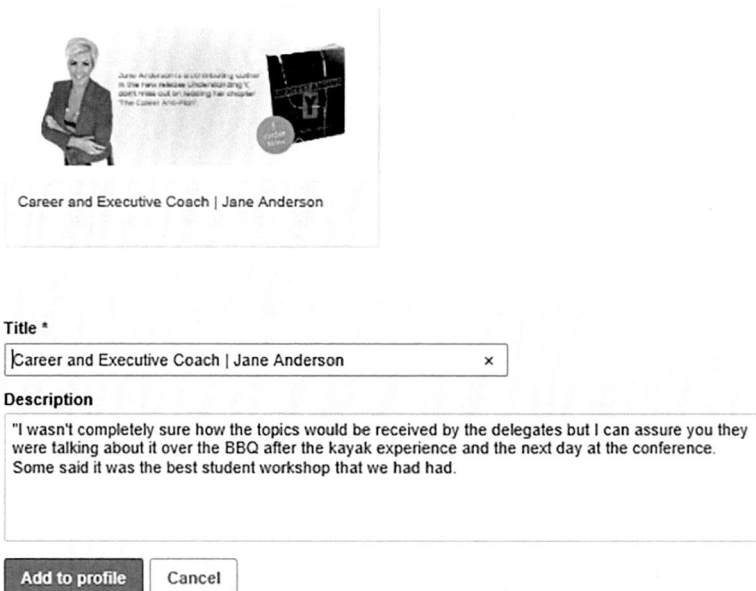

How to Add a File to Publications

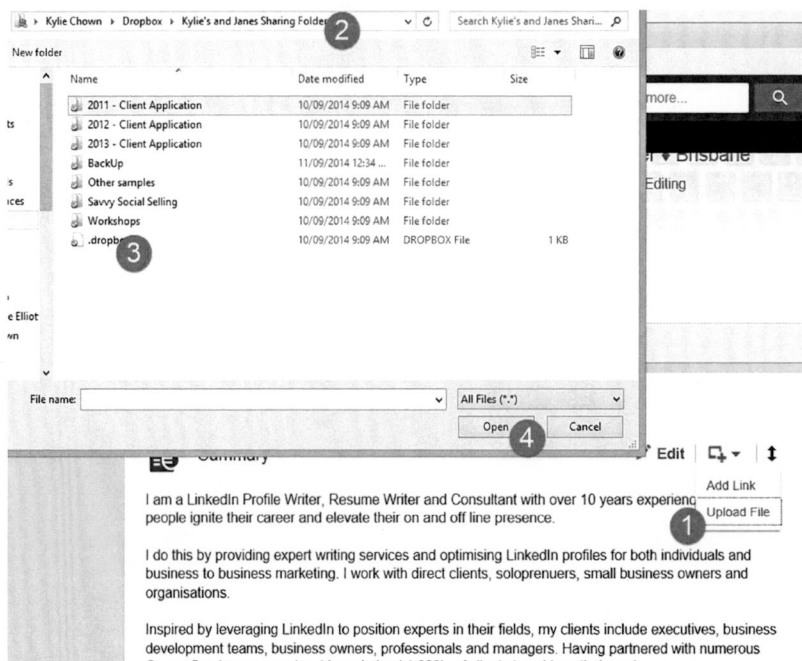

1. Click Add Link and Upload File.
2. Locate the directory.
3. Select the file.
4. Open the file.

5. Click **Save**

Top Tip: You can overwrite the content and descriptions from what is pulled from LinkedIn. By overwriting the content, you can further engage your audience. For example: "To find out more about our services, click here to view our website."

Testimonials and Recommendations

We recently worked with a group of salespeople to build their personal brand as thought leaders in their industry. We spent a considerable amount of time talking about testimonials and their value. Testimonials (or Recommendations) are what is called "social proof". When a potential client is looking at working with you, they need to see if someone else has said that you are good too work with.

Like a business, we have something to sell or something we want to create an influence with. So what's the benefit of testimonials for your target audience?

1. **They give hope:** The person looking at your testimonials uses their imagination to think, "Wow, I would love that to happen for me." They make the direct connection between what they need and how you can help them without you telling them.

2. **What others say about us is more important than what we say about ourselves:** Quite often, we work with clients to tone back their self-selling and let others do the talking.

3. **Brand leverage:** If that person has a position or works for a well-recognised brand, they will make a decision to call you based on brand association. This will give them confidence about who you have worked with before. It sends a clear message about who you CAN help.

4. **The potential client sees themselves in the client you have helped:** Based on stereotype, the potential client will make their own connection about your client and they'll think, "They're just like me," "That's exactly the problem I'm having," or "That's exactly the result I want."

5. **It's easier:** You don't need to write a truckload of content to sell yourself; recommendations and testimonials will do the majority of the work for you. By the time you get to a client meeting, you'll be answering the question, "When can you begin helping us?" rather than spending the meeting proving yourself.

Explore different ways you can make it easier for your potential clients or recruiters to see what others have to say about you on your website or LinkedIn profile. Making them dig will only let your competition beat you to the post. Here are some examples:

Professional Speaker, Author, Mentor on IMPACT
Jane Anderson International

Melissa Groom
CEO at Empowered Mums/Video Marketing Specialist/Host of Mums In Business TV

❝ Jane Anderson is a wealth of knowledge when it comes to branding and standing out in the market place. She is very professional, warm, friendly and a funny young lady with a real genuineness for wanting to help others.

Her presentation was very interactive and engaging and our members gained a lot of knowledge from her talk.

I would highly recommend Jane as a... **more**

August 6, 2015, Melissa was a consultant or contractor to Jane at Jane Anderson International

Jon Lindsay
Mentor for Business Leaders; Facilitator of Joined Up Thinking for Executive Teams

❝ Jane spoke last week to my two TEC groups on the subject "LinkedIn for CEO's, what's the benefit?" Since I have a few healthy sceptics in the groups we were conscious we weren't necessarily speaking to the converted. Jane came across as a true professional and of the greatest importance she was very aware of the nature of the group she was speaking to.
Because of her... **more**

June 21, 2015, Jon was a consultant or contractor to Jane at Jane Anderson International

Karin Flemm
Program, Project, Administration Manager ♦ Change Manager ♦ Process Improvement ♦ Consultant ♦ Writer ♦ Trainer

❝ I recently heard Jane speak at the Origin Energy WELL group, and her presentation about how to have IMPACT in today's online-dominated job search environment immediately changed my entire approach to my current search for a new opportunity. Her genuine desire to help people achieve their professional aspirations impressed me profoundly, as did her generosity with... **more**

June 7, 2015, Karin was Jane's client

A good testimonial includes a before and after. For example, "Before working with this person, I …" (This brings up the known unspoken of your potential customer. This means that the potential customer can relate to the person giving the testimonial.) "After working with them, I now …"

Here is an example from Kylie's profile:

LinkedIn Profile Writer | LinkedIn Strategist | LinkedIn for Business | LinkedIn for Job Seekers
Kylie Chown Consulting

Jade Hedley
Director, BE social. BE savvy. Brand, Graphic Design, Web, Marketing Campaigns for Small / Medium Business

" Before meeting Kylie I was unsure as to whether I required a presence on LinkedIn. I stuck in my comfort zone; Facebook. But since joining I've made many connections and it's been great for my business. It's resulted new clients and has led me to discover that my ideal client (target market) is in fact on LinkedIn. I have had comments made about the professionalism of my bio, yet it still depicts my personality. The training Kylie provided was fantastic so I felt confident to jump straight on and engage with people. **less** "

June 6, 2015, Jade was Kylie's client

Action Steps to Manage Testimonials

1. Under Recommendations, click Manage.

There are four sections: Received, Given, Ask for Recommendations and Give Recommendations.

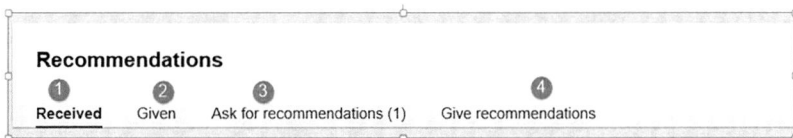

1. Under Received:

You can view all your received recommendations.

2. Under Given:

You can view all your given recommendations. If you have given a recommendation, you can manage its visibility.

3. Under Ask for Recommendation:

Ask your network for recommendations.

Ask your connections to recommend you

1 **What do you want to be recommended for?**

> LinkedIn Profile Writer | Master Resume Writer | E: ⬍

2 **Who do you want to ask?**

Your connections: (You can add up to 3 people)

> Jane Anderson ✕

3 Jane Anderson

What's your relationship?

> Choose... ⬍

What was Jane's position at the time?

> Choose... ⬍

4 **Write your message**

Subject:

> Can you recommend me?

> I'm writing to ask if you would write a brief recommendation of my work that I can include on my LinkedIn profile. If you have any questions, please let me know.
>
> Thanks in advance for your help.
>
> -Kylie Chown

Send **Cancel**

1. Start typing the name of the role you want to be recommended for.
2. Start typing the name of the person you would like to ask.
3. Select your relationship and their position.
4. Write a message and click send.
5. Give Recommendations.

To Give a Recommendation

1. Start typing the name of the person you want to recommend.
2. Select your relationship and positions.
3. Write the recommendation. This is what will appear on their profile. You can also include a message to send.

Give a recommendation

1 **Who do you want to recommend?**

2 **What's your relationship?**

Choose...

What were your positions at the time?

You: Choose...

Sarah: Choose...

3 **Write a recommendation**

If needed, you can make changes or delete it even after you send it.

s very detailed-oriented and produced great results for the company...

Your message to

You can personalize this message if you'd like.

Send   Cancel

Top Tip #1: Think of the value of a prospective client who sees someone they know and trust recommending your service on LinkedIn.

Top Tip #2: If you do recommend someone, you can hide this on your profile.

Contact Information

I am sure you have had the experience of finding exactly what you were looking for – the perfect product or service – and then couldn't find the necessary contact information or instructions on how to place your order. Quickly, happiness is replaced with frustration. LinkedIn offers a number of ways to manage contact information. You can also include information on websites. To make it easy for people to contact you, look at your contact information in the Edit Contact Information option.

You can see your contact information here:

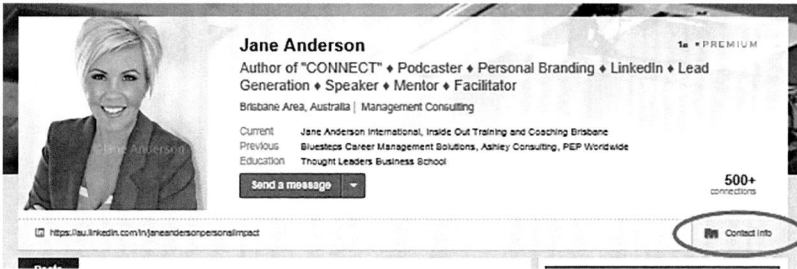

Once you click on Contact Info:

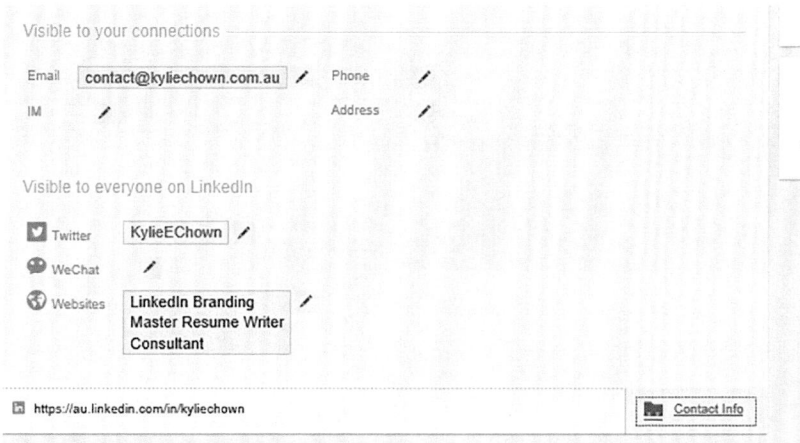

Click on the pencil icon to change the information.

If you don't have three websites, you can update the information so that it points to three different pages within one website.

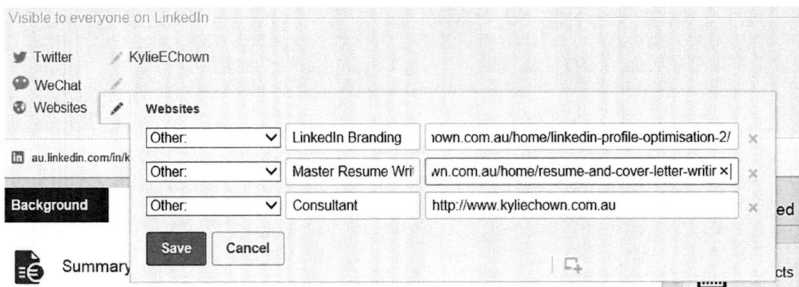

Click

Industry

The industry you select will also impact your search engine optimisation. Choose the industry you work in, not your job title. For example, if you are an account manager working in the private health sector, you would choose healthcare as opposed to sales and marketing.

Top Tip: Include your contact information as a call to action in your summary. For example: "For more information on how I can help your business, contact me on …"

Settings and Your Profile

How You Are Seen on LinkedIn

After doing all the hard work, it is important that you can be found by your ideal audience. The default position on LinkedIn is to create your profile URL (the web address) with your name and random characters.

The good news is that you can change this. You can create your own vanity URL. This means when someone searches for your name in Google, your LinkedIn profile will be returned. You can also customise how your content is viewed by people who are not connections.

All this can be managed under:

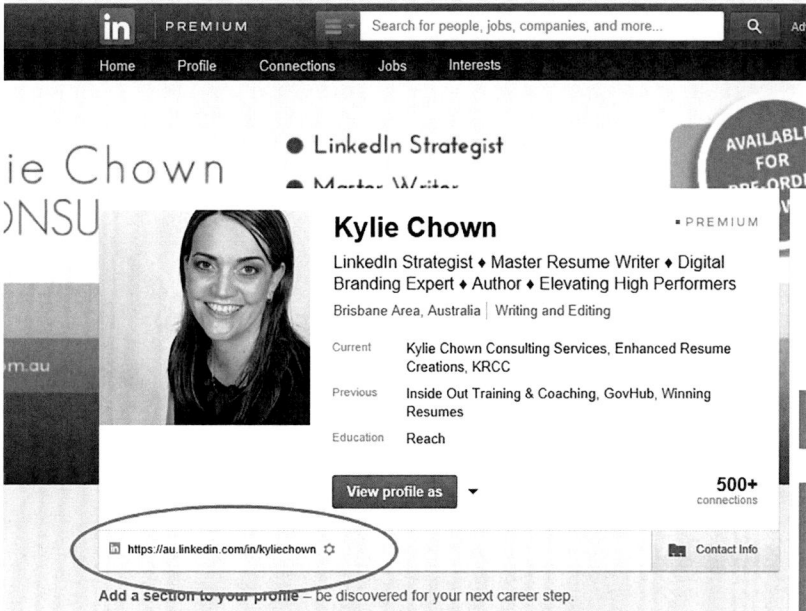

Then on the right you will see:

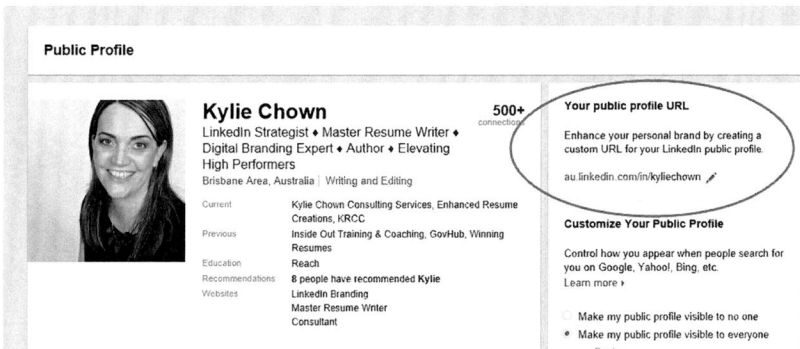

Action Steps

1. Select Edit next to your URL.
2. The next screen provides you with visibility options, as well as an option to change the vanity URL.
3. A ticked box means an area is visible to the public and an unticked box means the area is not publicly visible.
4. You can customise your vanity URL in the circle section above. The vanity URL is what is typed into the web browser. To get to your profile page:

Your public profile URL

Enhance your personal brand by creating a custom URL for your LinkedIn public profile.

au.linkedin.com/in/kyliechown   ×

Save   Cancel

Note: Your custom URL must contain 5-30 letters or numbers. Please do not use spaces, symbols, or special characters.

Privacy and Settings

Users have control over how they are presented on LinkedIn.

Under the **Privacy and Settings** option, you will see that you have five main areas you can manage: Profile; Communications; Group, Companies and Applications; and Account.

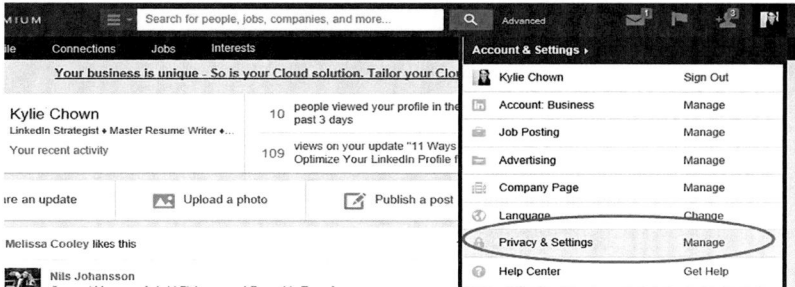

In your **profile tab** you can:

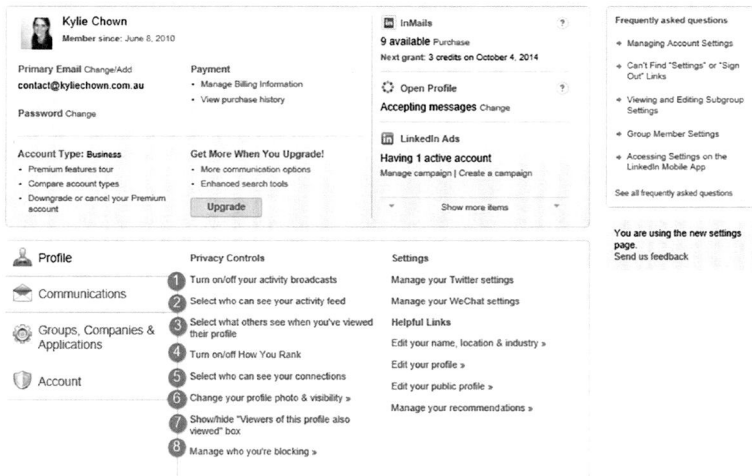

1. **Turn on/off your activity broadcasts.** Use this option if you are making changes to your profile and don't want your network to see them.

2. **Select who can see your activity feed.** You can select Everyone, Your Network, Your Connections or Only You.

3. **Select what others see when you've viewed their profile.** Your Name and Headline, anonymous profile characteristics such as Industry and Title, or you will be totally anonymous.

4. **Turn on/off how you rank.** This is your ranking against competitors.

5. **Select who can see your connections.** In this option, you can decide if your connections can see your other connections. To maintain the privacy of your connections, we recommend you select the Only You option.

6. **Change your profile photo and visibility.** You can change your headshot here.

7. **Show/hide "Viewers of the profile also viewed".** You can see how everyone else is being viewed by your audience.

8. **Manage who you're blocking.** Need to block or report someone? Go to the profile of the person you want to block and select "Block or Report" from the drop-down menu at the top of the profile summary. Note: After you've blocked someone, any previous profile views will disappear from both of your "Who's Viewed My Profile" section.

Additional Tabs Include:

In your communications tab:

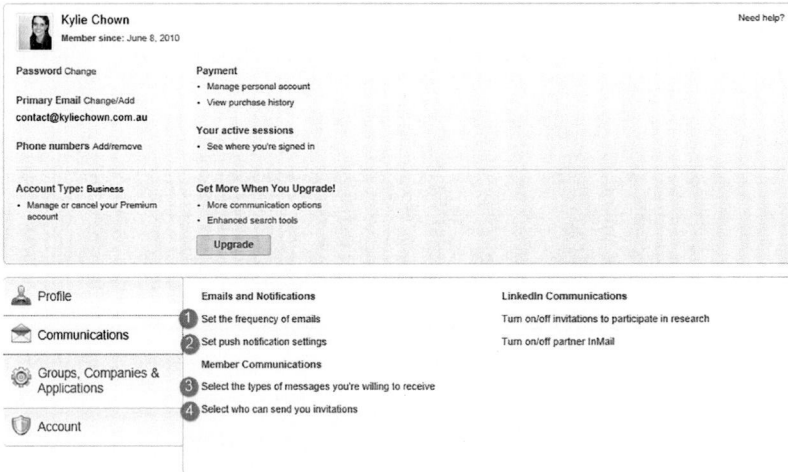

1. Set the frequency of emails.
2. Set push notification.
3. Select the types of messages you're willing to receive.
4. Select those who can send you invitations.

Groups, Companies and Applications allows you to:

1. Select your group display order.
2. View your groups.
3. Set the frequency of group digest emails.
4. Turn on/off group invitations.
5. Turn on/off notifications when joining groups.
6. View companies you're following.

The Account feature supports privacy controls, while Account allows you to:

1. Manage Advertising Preferences.
2. Change your profile photo and visibility.
3. Show/hide profile photos of other members.
4. Customise the updates you see on your home page.
5. Select your language.
6. Manage security settings.

Sharing Your Profile

Once you have a customised URL, you can share your profile. Add your LinkedIn URL to your communications (your email signature, newsletters, etc.) so people can easily connect with you. If you are speaking at a conference, seminar or workshop, invite people to connect. At the end of the presentation, you can say something like: "I am on LinkedIn if you would like to connect – just send a request."

Top Tip #1: Did you know that "Who Has Viewed My Profile" is one of the most used features on LinkedIn?

Top Tip #2: Claim your vanity URL quickly – they are all unique and there is only one available for each name.

Reflections and Actions

1. Make a list of all the words you think your ideal client may use when trying to find you.
2. Decide on those that you most enjoy doing and want to be known for.
3. Put those words in your profile and check your search engine optimisation.
4. Perform a Google X-ray search. Note that due to indexing, there may be a time delay in appearing in search results.

Chapter 5

Personal Branding

"My first impressions of people are invariably right."
— Oscar Wilde

The first four seconds on your profile are crucial. We only have a short time to connect with the right customer and client you're working with.

It's a bit like touching a hot plate. If your profile doesn't make sense, in other words it's too hot, and the client or person reading your profile will bounce right off.

The Neuroscience of Your Profile

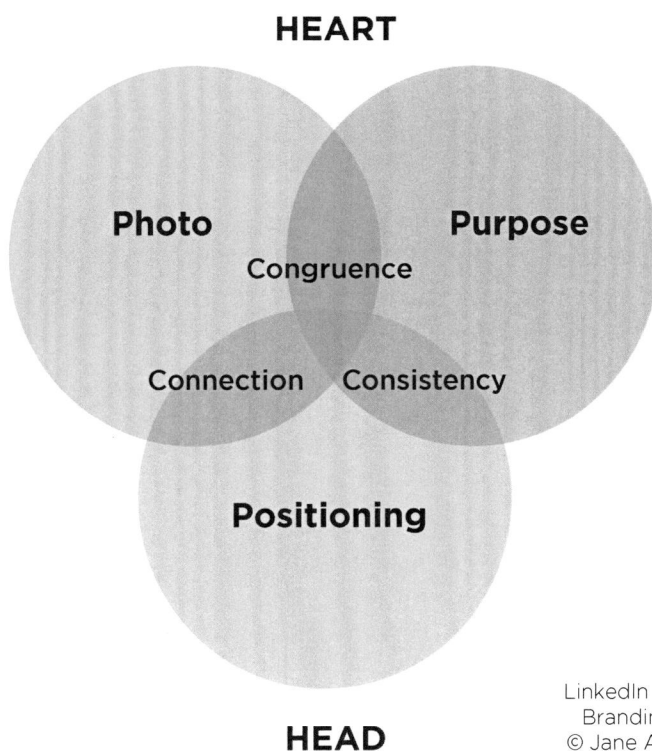

HEART

Photo

Purpose

Congruence

Connection   Consistency

Positioning

LinkedIn Personal
Branding Model
© Jane Anderson

HEAD

The model above is comprised of three elements:

- **Photo:** Your photo needs to mirror the type of person you want to work with. If it looks unprofessional, then you will attract people who are not necessarily professional. Equally, if it is polished, you will attract that type of client.

- **Positioning:** Positioning is about the customer problems you solve, your credibility and your brand leverage. In other words, it's the level and category that the customer understands you in their mind. It's human nature to categorise people quickly so you need to ensure you are positioned in the right category in the customer's mind.

- **Purpose:** Why do you do what you do? Why does what you do matter? These questions need to be answered early in your profile. Simon Sinek, the author of a number of books including *Start with Why*, says that we need to start with why. This will create rapid cut-through for your reader.

Questions When Someone is Looking at Your LinkedIn Profile

The first questions we are often asked are: "Why should I bother going on LinkedIn? I already have a Facebook page," and, "I don't know that I really want to have any social media presence."

There are a few reasons why you should have a LinkedIn profile. When it comes to running a business, one of the greatest challenges is getting started, and LinkedIn is a great way to help you establish your business. It lets you connect with people who could be interested in the type of work you do, and you can find the demographics of those people. Whereas with Facebook, you have to engage in Facebook marketing (which can be quite expensive) in order to choose and connect with your ideal client's demographics.

LinkedIn is a more cost-effective way of connecting with and researching potential clients if you know what you're doing. It's much cheaper than Facebook, unless you've got a business-to-consumer type of business. For example, if you're a personal trainer working with mums in the suburbs, Facebook is probably the better option, unless you have a lot of corporate clients. If this is the case, a presence on LinkedIn can help. The key question is: "Where does your potential client hang out?"

One of the best things about LinkedIn is that it leverages a Google search. If somebody uses Google to try to find somebody like you, you will turn up in their search results, provided you have excellent search engine optimisation. There are plenty of blogs detailing how to build a search engine optimised LinkedIn profile.

Another reason why you should use LinkedIn is that you can create permanent posts via the blog on your LinkedIn profile. These posts get you in front of your connections so that they don't have to visit your website to read your blog. Don't count on people setting up an RSS feed to your website – it creates too many hurdles for them to keep in touch with you.

Furthermore, LinkedIn lets you keep in touch with your connections without them having to be subscribed to your newsletter. LinkedIn keeps you in touch with the people who are most likely to buy from you. At the moment, there are about 365 million people on LinkedIn.

With the launch of the new students page on LinkedIn, the fastest-growing LinkedIn demographic is university graduates. The most under-represented group on LinkedIn is women.

If you're female, this is a great opportunity as a LinkedIn profile will help you position and market yourself to connect with others.

LinkedIn has grown incredibly to 365 million people having profiles. It was developed in 2003 and is gaining incredible momentum. The problem is, the noise can be a little overwhelming.

The key point to keep in mind is that people buy from people. Many businesses still hold on to the traditional way of doing things. They haven't tapped into social networks, purely because they don't know how to.

Regardless of the role you have, you are Brand You.

You are what makes your brand stand out.

People want to connect with you and like you.

Yes, we have blogs and newsletters, but LinkedIn has arguably been the biggest driver of our businesses' growth and ability to reach out to people.

Some thought leaders, sales people and marketers often fear putting too much self-serving content out there. A lot of people publish content that's about them, and it's not the way to go. LinkedIn has got to be about your audience and what you're doing to help them, not you.

Another challenge you may have is that you have a profile, but you don't know what to write in it. It's completely empty. Perhaps you're unsure of what to write, or think: "What if somebody doesn't like what I have to say?" If this is the case, you need to remember your audience and tell yourself: "I'm here to help people. I have to articulate what it is that I do to help them, and make it easy for them to work with me."

A good place to start is to think about who's reading your content. In Jane's book *IMPACT: How To Build Your Personal Brand for The Connection Economy*, she talks about the First Four Seconds.

When looking at your digital presence, particularly LinkedIn, you only have four seconds for somebody to decide whether they like you or not, and whether they're interested in knowing more.

Something you might be thinking is: "I don't care what's on my profile. I don't care what people think. I'm just going to put anything up there." Brene Brown – TED speaker, expert in vulnerability and author of seven books, including *Daring Greatly* – said: "When you stop caring what people think, you lose your capacity for connection." Connection creates results.

Your job, particularly under "Brand You", is to demonstrate: "I understand your challenges. I have a good knowledge of them. I'm here to help. This is what I can do to help you out of that frustration or pain."

To do this, you must care about what people are reading on your profile, because LinkedIn is all about connection. We're in this age of digital firsts. We often come across someone online before we meet them face to face.

You could be missing an opportunity when you're trying to influence and persuade, when you meet someone face to face, if your LinkedIn profile is not right.

As mentioned earlier, 60 per cent of a buying decision is made before somebody makes contact with you. We want to make it easy for them to think: "Oh yeah, I like this person. I like you. You seem to know what you're doing."

Your profile, in that digital first space we're in now, will either attract or repel a person long before they've even had a chance to meet you.

If your profile is written well, it should answer these questions:

1. **"Why should I care?"** This question creates extraordinary cut-through. Without it, readers will feel as though you're taking them along the yellow brick road and don't know where you're leading them. As Simon Sinek, author of *Start with Why*, says: "People don't buy what you do, they buy why you do it."

Your response to this question needs to be in the first line of your Summary. It hits the reader between the eyes, making them pay attention and wanting to know more!

2. **"Can I see me in you?"** Your profile is a bit like a mirror. When people look at your profile, they're looking to see themselves. "Do you look like the type of person I hang with, or who I would connect with? Do you look a bit like me?" The other thing, too, is your content. Have you written about their problems? Have you written about what your client is looking for? As a potential customer looks at your profile, they ask: "Where is my problem in your profile?" What they want to know is: "Can I see me in you?"

3. **"What makes you different?"** This is about differentiation, and it supports positioning. What do you do differently? Do you work with a particular calibre of clients? Do you work with clients in certain industries? Or the differentiation could be in your message. What is it that differentiates you? Maybe you coach CEOs who have companies of $250 million-plus. What makes you different?

4. **"How will what you do benefit me?"** For example, you might say: "I'm an expert in environmental engineering. How I help people, how I support you, is that I reduce your organisation's emissions by 25 per cent, so that you can be an environmentally responsible organisation." You need to articulate how people can benefit from what you have to offer.

5. **"Do you understand my world?"** This is about their problems. This is about clearly articulating the problems your potential client or customer has. If you don't show that you understand their world and your profile is all about you, then people will feel you're not going to listen to them.

6. **"Who have you worked with that I know?"** This is where brand leverage comes into play, because not everybody knows you. But they will get a better understanding of you if you have worked with an organisation they are familiar with, particularly if the organisation has a big name or brand. You might say something like: "Some of the clients I have worked with include ..." The reader might not know you, but they know and trust those well-established companies. It's brand association: "Who have you worked with that I know? That will give me trust."

7. **"What do people say about you?"** You might notice the recommendations at the bottom of your LinkedIn profile. This area is where the reader gets to see you through somebody else's eyes – not through your eyes. It helps people get to know you better. According to the 2012 Carer Builder Survey, if a recruiter or

hiring manager likes your personality, 50 per cent of the time they'll extend an offer. Now while we might be saying here, "We're not recruiting," the same thing happens for salespeople and solopreneurs, because they face the same challenges in their marketing. If you can get your personality to come through on as many angles as possible, you're more likely to connect.

8. **"How effective have you been? What results have you been able to achieve?"** You'll need to give reference to a particular program you deliver to clients and what they have said. You need to show the results you have achieved and how. Testimonials can help capture your achievements.

9. **"Who has said that you're any good?"** This can, in part, be answered by your recommendations, but you also may also have testimonials on your website that you can plug in to your profile. Let's say I'm a coach and I need a graphic designer. You're a graphic designer and I'm on your LinkedIn profile. If I see a testimonial from Mary Smith, executive coach, Sydney, I'm going to think: "Oh, well, this person understands what a coach is after." If you want to work with a certain industry, make sure your testimonials are from people in that industry.

10. **"What's your perspective?"** Your perspective will help the person understand or connect with your personality. Your perspective is evident in your blog posts. The great thing about LinkedIn is that your posts are permanent. They don't just pass through your feed like a normal update. Potential clients can read your previous posts, get your perspective, and decide whether or not to work with you. For example, if you are an HR consultant who has written about performance management and leadership, someone going through your posts and articles may think: "Oh yeah, he thinks like us. I think we could work together. I like that he said that, because that's exactly the challenge we're having."

11. **"How do I work with you?"** One of the basic things often missing from a LinkedIn profile is the answer to the question: "How do I work with you?" All you have to do is say: "If you'd like to work with me, here's my phone number," or, "Here's my website." Make it easy for people to understand how they can work with you. Don't be over the top or too creative. Just make it practical and straightforward, and let them connect.

12. **"Where can I find more information?"** Make sure you include your phone number, website and email address. Bear in mind that when you're on your LinkedIn profile and on your page, in the contact us area you'll see where the contact information drops down. It sits under your photo and under the title. A lot of people don't realise that's where to go to find your contact information.

Make sure you have it loud and clear in your summary area. It will use up a few characters, but it's worth it.

13. **"Are you a fake account?"** What makes your profile look fake and prevents people from connecting with you is not having an employment history and not having any recommendations, skills and endorsements. It looks particularly suspicious if you have, say, 500 connections and none of them have endorsed you. Make sure your profile has as much information as possible to help people trust and connect with you. By the way, LinkedIn is fantastic at responding quickly if someone has taken your profile photo or if you have any concerns.

If you can address these questions in your profile, you'll get your first four seconds working for you. People will find you interesting and be excited about connecting with you.

Your Photo

"A picture is worth a thousand words."
– Napoleon Bonaparte

When Jane started her first business, she asked a friend to take her photo for her website. It was a nice photo with a tree in the background. There was natural light and it was a nice, sunny day.

Jane used the photo in her branding and noticed she got clients who didn't really see that she was serious. It was as though she was working on a hobby. Jane progressed to a professional headshot, which helped, but the photo still looked a little washed out and too soft. She felt as though the clients seeing her were looking for someone soft and understanding, and she can be. But her ideal client was someone who wanted more, was motivated to get it and wanted practical steps to make it happen; not someone who just wanted a counsellor to have a chat to.

Your headshot will create an emotional connection with the person looking at it and you need to be mindful of the context in which your photo is seen:

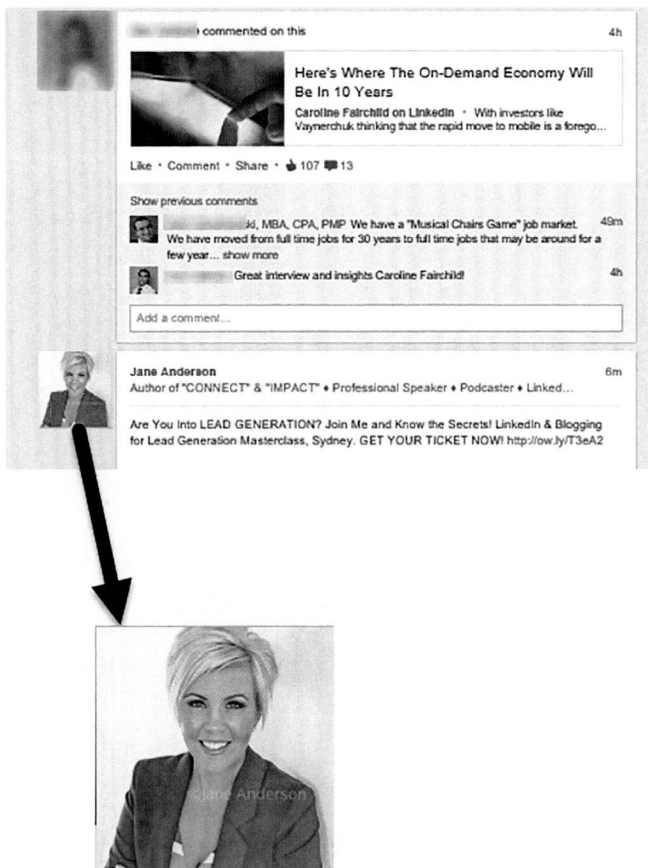

In this case, there are some issues:

- The colour means the image stands out. Black and white would play down the image and blend in too much, especially on LinkedIn.
- The photos that stand out the most are brightly coloured.
- The person in this photo is close and easy to recognise. If the image was too far away, it would be difficult to recognise in a LinkedIn feed.

Jane recently worked with a client who insisted on keeping a photo of himself speaking on stage as his LinkedIn profile picture. He was so far away in the picture that she could hardly see him, but he wanted to be known for speaking and thought this photo was relevant. His thinking was right, but the photo was better suited for a website than a LinkedIn profile picture as it was so small.

Something we don't always remember is that LinkedIn has many other distractions when someone looks at your profile. Ads, recommended connections or connections in common hamper the decision maker's analytical ability, so your profile needs to stand out from the noise on screen.

A recent study by The Ladders shows that decision makers tend to follow a consistent path when reviewing online profiles, so the organisation of your layout is crucial. As much as 19% of the time someone spends looking at your profile will be spent looking at your photo! To get a high return on investment on that time, consider the following:

1. **Does your photo portray what you're trying to achieve?** If you are wearing a suit in your picture, you will attract ambitious corporate clients. If you have soft, flowing fabrics, you will attract softer people. It sounds obvious, but you will get back what your photo portrays, more so than your text.

2. **Remember the context of your photo.** It needs to stand out in a feed. Too many people think their photo is seen in the context of their profile, rather than in someone's feed. Remember, your photo may be in the context of a comment or discussion. Many people will view your photo on a page other than your profile page.

3. **It is not a glamour shot.** It is not where you get your long, soft, flowing locks out, and you shouldn't use a photo of yourself in an evening gown or wedding suit. It is a corporate, professional business photo.

4. **Look at the camera.** Wistfully looking away does nothing to personalise your potential connection. Create chemistry with the reader by looking at the lens.

5. **Props should only be used if they convey your goal.** For example, if you're a photographer, you can have a camera. If you're a saxophonist, you can have a saxophone in the shot. If you're a speaker only, yes, you can have a microphone in your hand if your goal is to speak. If you want to be well-rounded, just have a picture of yourself. You will receive what you ask for, so be clear about the message your photo sends.

6. **Have a headshot on all your social media.** No blank heads or eggs! We know that a profile with a headshot will have seven times more click-through than a profile without a headshot.

7. **Make sure it's a clear headshot from your chest to the top of your head.** In other words, no full-body shots or anything where people can't recognise you if they met you at an event or on the run.

8. **Smile and show teeth.** It makes you look open and friendly, helping your "know, like and trust" perception amplify.

9. **Make sure you don't have sunglasses on.** You can look as though you have something to hide or are a bit "shady" – pardon the pun!

10. **You get what you pay for.** If you're trying to get a million-dollar client, you need to look like a million-dollar expert. Invest in a professional shot that mirrors what you're asking of your client.

By investing in a great headshot, you'll stand out and people will feel as though they already know you, making the sales or recruitment processes easier. If you have a tight budget, prepare to spend about $300 for a good professional shot. If you are ready to step it up in your business, invest in a higher-quality photographer and make-up artist. You can expect to pay $600-$2000 for a series of highly targeted shots to use in articles, brochures, newsletters, webpages and other marketing collateral. These shots need to mirror your business goals for the next three years.

By putting in a little bit of effort, your professional photos will pay dividends and generally last you three years.

Action Steps to Add a Photo

Log in to your account. Click Profile.

1. Click Edit Profile.

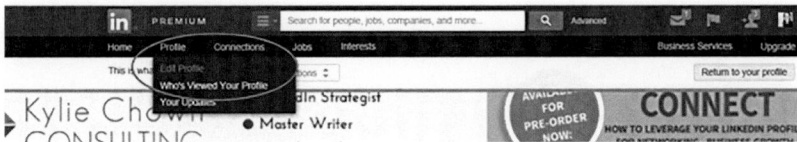

2. Click Change Photo and hover the cursor over your headshot. You will see an image of a camera and Change Photo.

3. Click Change Photo.

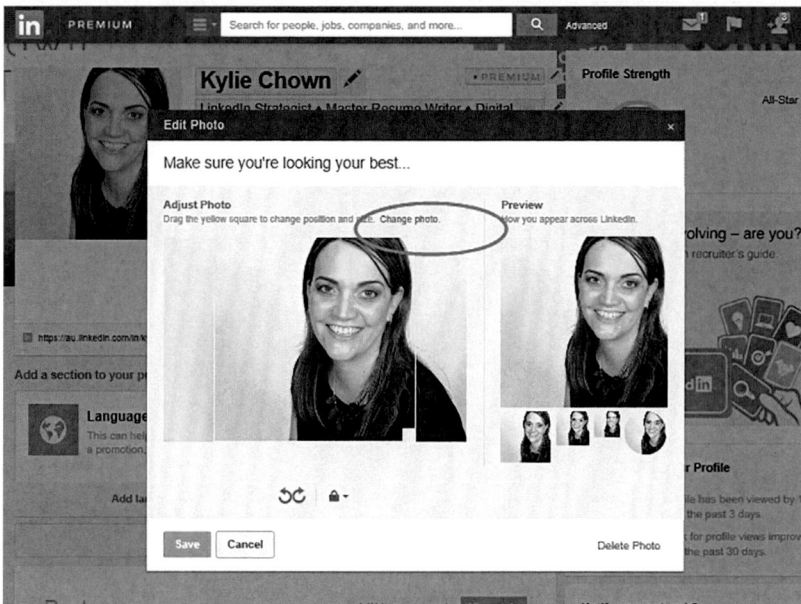

4. Select the photo you want, then open.

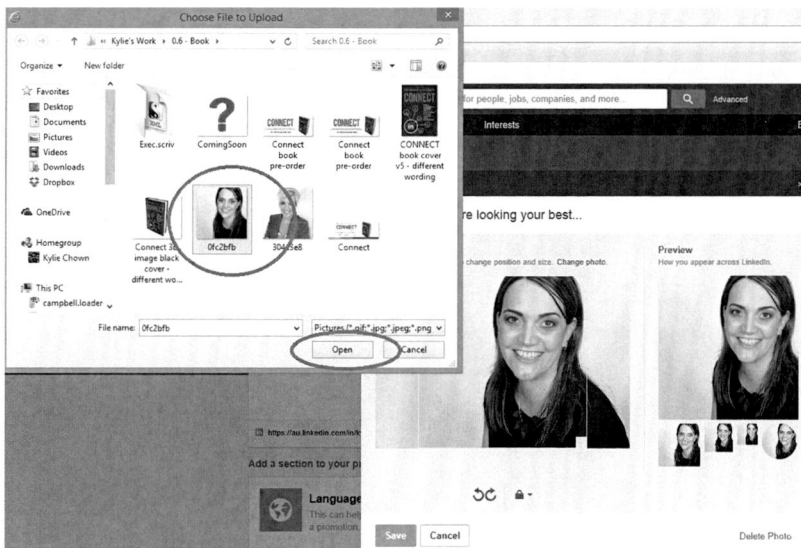

5. Click **Save**

Other Sections

LinkedIn offers you a range of additional sections to further enhance your profile. You can target the sections that best suit your requirements. These include:

Education

In your Education section, you can add anything that supports your ongoing development.

Under Education, click on Add Education.

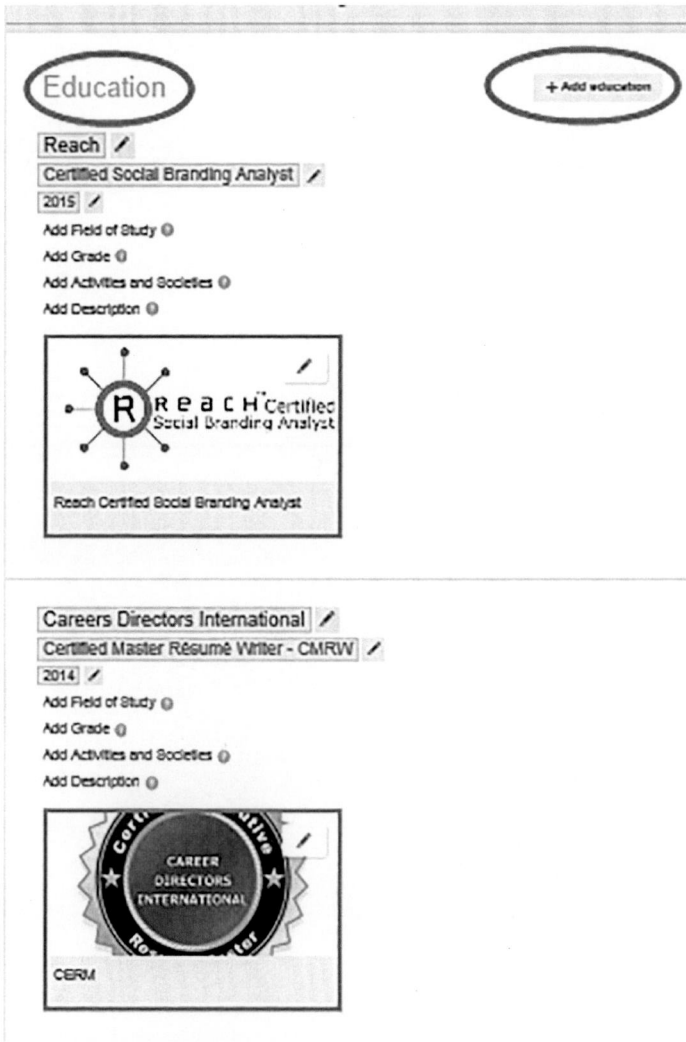

Action Steps

To complete the Education section:

1. Add the school you attended. You will see there is a drop-down menu within this area.
2. Enter the dates you attended.
3. Enter the degree you studied.
4. Enter the field of study.
5. Enter the grade (this is not a compulsory field).
6. Explain any activities and societies you were involved in.
7. Add a description of your course.

Other Sections You Can Add to Your LinkedIn Profile Include:

- **Organisations:** This area can be utilised to highlight participation in industry groups or professional associations. This supports you as an expert in your field.

- **Volunteering and Causes:** If you volunteer in an area that resonates with your ideal audience, include this here.

- **Certifications:** Include certifications relevant to your area of expertise.

- **Projects:** This area allows you to highlight collaborations and projects you have been a part of.

You also have the option to include:

- Languages
- Honours and awards
- Test scores
- Patents

Commenting

When commenting on something in your feed, always be positive and ask yourself: "Is my comment constructive and helpful, or is it supportive?" You can certainly challenge things, but be mindful of your language and tone. Don't swear or use put downs, otherwise you risk being removed from LinkedIn.

You can also tag people's names in your comments to include them or draw attention.

Recently, we had a client who was a coach in Sydney. She commented on an article about coaching in the workplace, saying: "Well, based on my experience, I think the challenge is this …" and wrote something insightful. Somebody else contacted her as a result of that comment and said, "Look, I really like what you said in your comment. We haven't met. I'd love to have a coffee with you." And they've ended up doing a lot of work together.

Commenting on an article or post allows you to share your experience and demonstrate to others your knowledge without having to say: "I'm so good." It's easier, too, isn't it?

How to Comment

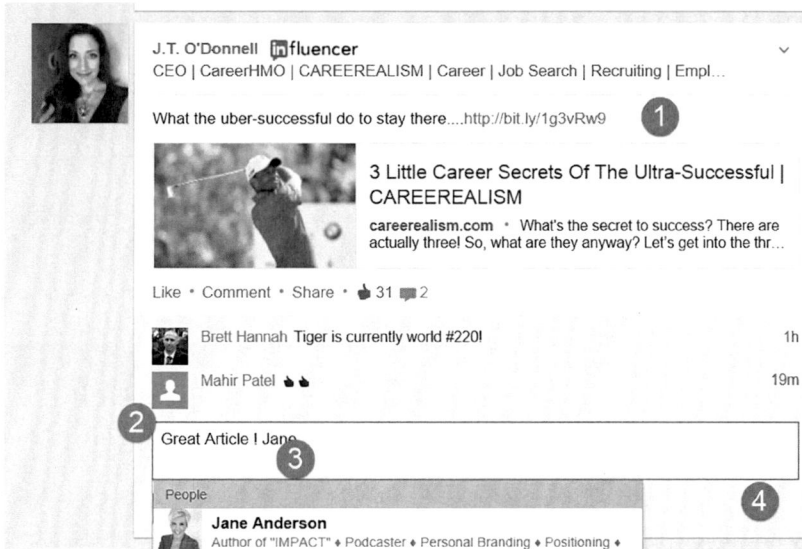

1. Identify something to comment on when you scroll through your newsfeed.
2. Write your comment.
3. To tag someone, start typing their name and click on them from the list.
4. You can then click the comment box.

Curatorship

Jane once said: "When I was little, I remember trying to talk my Dad into things I wanted, like new shoes or a new cassette (yes, I'm showing my age!), but it didn't always go too well because Mum was the boss and was in charge of those types of decisions! So I soon worked out that if I said that Mum said I could have it, Dad would listen because he trusted my Mum, of course. Otherwise, it was just me banging on again about something I wanted. The power of being able to influence an outcome was not so much about me asking for it, but the value of the *right* person saying it."

Content curation in social media provides the same influence. A content curator is a bit like a museum curator. A museum curator decides what artefacts go into the museum for people to see. Their job is to research and know what people are looking for so they visit. The curator's knowledge, expertise and experience are most valuable to a museum's success. So as a content curator, your skills are highlighted by the content you share in your social media.

After delivering some workshops recently, we discovered that many clients are reluctant to share their content because they feel it should be on their own blog, and they end up with less visibility. They don't believe curation has as much value, when in fact curation can be even more valuable. President of the Queensland Chapter of the Australian Marketing Association, Kellie-Ann Robinson, recently shared her insight that a new role will start to emerge in organisations called a "Content Curator", and this will be a public relations role.

There are four big reasons why content curation works:

1. **Someone else has said it:** The fact that it wasn't just said by you means your opinion is validated by other experts in your field. You're therefore opening yourself to being more trusted.

2. **You get to contrast your insights:** You can combine multiple pieces of information to curate and share your insights. You can still add your expertise, even if you don't agree with what is being said.

3. **Less "salesy":** Instead of constantly pumping out your own content and being too self-promoting, you can leverage what others say and genuinely add value to your audience. Let's face it, we don't like having sales talk shoved down our throat in feeds all day.

4. **It's more efficient:** You spend less time writing content from scratch and more on your insights. This means you can share more, add more value and increase your visibility.

You might be thinking: "Well, if I share other people's insights, won't I just be sending clients to them?" Not necessarily. It depends if they're a direct competitor and what they do. Some experts only write, so if you're a coach, you won't be competing. Equally, if you're in business development, you're looking for independent sources to validate your insights.

If you can allocate a few minutes to curate content each day, it will boost your visibility. You can even get your virtual assistants and marketing teams to help manage it. It's also an easy way to be consistent, making it easier for the reader to understand what you do and how you can help them. Not doing it means your competition will work with your customers before you do.

Scoop.it is a great curation site. It will email you content and articles to curate. You can sign in and put in the keywords you are interested in. It will then email your links to articles. The website address is http://www.scoop.it/

How to Curate

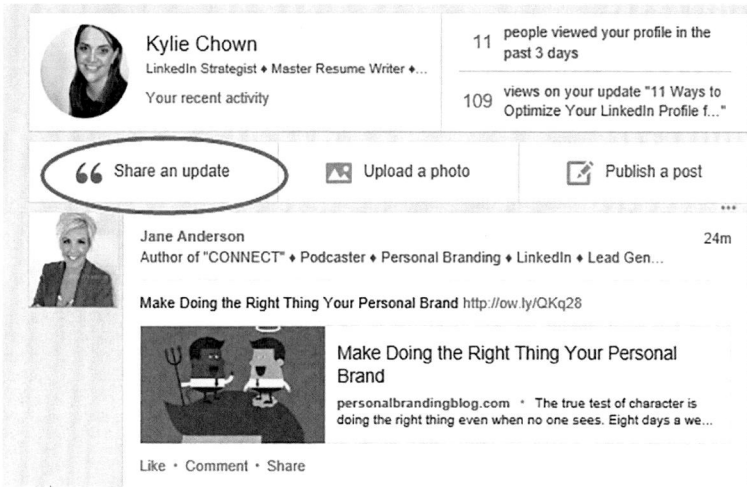

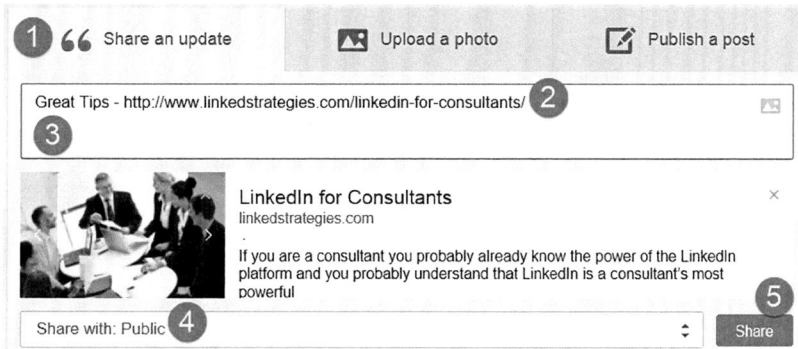

1. Click Share an Update.
2. Copy the URL you want to share.
3. You can make a comment before the article you are sharing.
4. Determine who you want to share it with: Public, Public + Twitter, or Just Your Connections.
5. Click Share.

Thought Leadership

You may have been wondering why there are so many different people posting on LinkedIn now, not just Richard Branson and James Caan. LinkedIn now allows anyone to post their content to become an influencer. The question we're being asked is: "What do I write? Is there a framework or formula?"

We need to write what we know so that we can amplify our message and give to others more efficiently. If you have enough of a profile online, you should get multiple views in a few hours after posting an article. Posting regularly on LinkedIn works hand-in-hand with other profile-building tools such as Twitter.

There are two ways your thought leadership validates and works for you on LinkedIn:

Notifications: This serves to share your insights and ideas. It also allows you to stay visible to your audience. Your connections will continue to see your posts as they receive a notification to say that you have written a new post.

Validation: When a potential client lands on your profile, they may read your posts based on your thought leadership. This helps them gain an understanding of you and your approach. It allows them to connect and determine if you understand their issues and challenges, and to identify how in-tune you really are.

Content Strategy

Jane has a friend who is a photographer. She takes beautiful shots, but she pushes her book in her newsfeed about three times per day. It feels as though the audience is just there to serve the purpose of buying her book. On the other hand, if she gave some tips on why good photography is important and how pictures need to tell different stories, then not only does the audience get a glimpse of what might be in the book, they might buy it and recommend it to others.

Your content strategy is not about you. It's about your customers and being visible to them. A good way to start doing this is to write a list of your areas of expertise that you can share with people.

Ensure you link your content strategy to what you're trying to achieve. If in the next 12 months you want to position yourself as a thought leader on innovation, what are your key areas of expertise related to innovation?

Have a call to action/service for every time you post content. It's recommended you "sell" once per week, or 20% of your time.

Jane recently shared: "Last month, I found myself looking for a new car. It was late on a Friday and I was rushing around, trying to find the best deal. I'd done all my online research and ended up at a particular dealer. He sensed I needed to decide on the car quickly, as it was the end of the financial year, so he let me take it home for the weekend to try it out. This certainly eased some pressure for me. I didn't have to rush my decision; I could drive the car for the weekend and return it on Monday. The dealer wasn't pushy. He was helpful, listened to my needs and made the whole process easy. As a result, I decided to keep the car."

According to *Forbes*, 60% of a buying decision is made before the customer buys from you. Similarly, the CareerBuilder Survey found that 58% of recruiters extended a job offer because they got a good sense of the job seeker's character and personality.

If you're a consultant, coach, job seeker, mentor, salesperson or solopreneur, one of the best ways to encourage people to test drive YOU is to write a blog. It's a bit like being allowed to take the car overnight. Your posts take the reader from their world into yours. They give the reader your insights and perspective. Too often, we want the customer or recruiter to make a decision there and then, and we risk looking pushy or salesy, or making the customer feel weird about the whole situation.

Seth Godin, author of 17 books including *Tribes*, says we're in the connection economy. People want to connect and buy you, but they will buy when they're ready.

We've all come across the stereotypical car dealer who just wants to get their commission. But we need to get to know the car first. "Will it give me what I need? Will be it economical enough? Do I like it? Is it safe?" Your client or recruiter is asking these same questions. Organisations don't have extra cash floating around if things go wrong, so every dollar matters.

As F.W. Woolworth, the founder of Woolworth Corporation, said: "I am the world's worst salesperson so I must make it easy for people to buy."

Allow people to get to know you. Give samples of your work through your blog so there is less pressure on you to sell.

Being a LinkedIn Poster

One of the more recent changes to LinkedIn has been the capability for anyone to write posts. Previously, the role of a poster was reserved for approximately 500 professionals, including the likes of Richard Branson, Bill Gates, Arianna Huffington and Guy Kawasaki. Now, anyone can be a poster on LinkedIn.

Why be a poster on LinkedIn?

- **Increased exposure across the platform:** If you publish a post on LinkedIn, it can be shared, liked and commented on. This in turn increases your exposure across LinkedIn.

- **Engage your target audience:** LinkedIn gives you the opportunity to talk directly to your target audience through posting.

- **Thought leadership:** Establish yourself as an expert in your field by posting articles.

- **Support SEO:** SEO optimised blog posts contribute to your SEO and are shown within search results.

Here are a few things to remember when writing articles if you have a premium LinkedIn account:

- **It's not Facebook.** Posting on LinkedIn is different to posting pictures on your Facebook page. LinkedIn is not the forum to post pictures, inspiring quotes or memes. This is a space for you to share your professional expertise and provide good-quality content.

- **Don't attach your newsletter as a Word document to your feed and think anyone will read it.** This is not posting information in a way that engages your audience. Put the newsletter content in the post area so it is there permanently and paints a clear picture of who you are for anyone who clicks on your profile. It also helps to build the "know, like and trust" factor you're trying to achieve.

- **A post can be as long as you like.** To engage your reader, keep it to the point. Ideally, stick to 400-600 words.

To begin with, there are a few elements your LinkedIn posts need to provide to your readers:

- Why what you have to say is important.
- Evidence to back your claims.
- A formula your readers can use for success.
- A call to action.

So if you're not a writer, how can you write effective posts? Gihan Perera, author of Fast, Flat and Free and 10 other books on internet marketing, suggests a method that we recommend to most novices. This method is called the PILES method.

The PILES method covers:

- **Principle/Problem/Purpose:** What is the point of the article? You need to give it context, so it could be a story, an analogy or recent research.

- **Implications:** What happens if you don't do it? Add hyperlinks to provide evidence to back your claims. It might be some research or an article from a credible source in your industry. Alternatively, you could detail implications the topic has for a particular industry.

- **List:** List steps to overcome the problem. Keep the list simple and easy to read. Lists with a prime number of steps allow you to easily market your steps in the heading of your post. Prime numbers jump off the screen and catch a reader's attention more easily.

- **Explanation:** Explain each step in a sentence or two. Explain what the benefit or impact each item in the list will have.

- **Summary:** Write a conclusion. This gives emphasis to the point you're trying to make. We also recommend writing a call to action here. For example, provide a link to a landing page on your website. It can be frustrating for your readers if they get to the end of an article and decide they need help, but the article fails to provide information on where to find it.

If you can stick to writing posts daily, in less than two months you will have a book on your hands! A book is a great way to position yourself an expert in your field. We also recommend using an image in your header that reflects the point you're trying to make. The image will be added to your profile and makes it more appealing for your reader to click through to your post.

To write a post, log in to your LinkedIn profile and:

1. Click Profile.
2. Edit Profile.

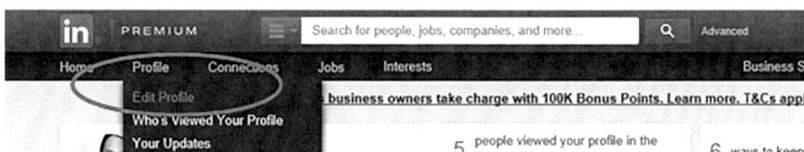

3. You will see "Share an update", "Upload a photo" and "Publish a Post". Click on Publish a Post.

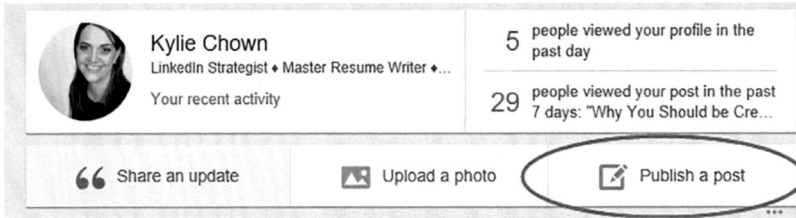

Action Steps to Write a Post

1. Add a title.
2. Write your post.
3. Format your post.
4. Add a hyperlink.
5. Add an image.
6. Save the post (note: this will not publish).
7. Publish the post.

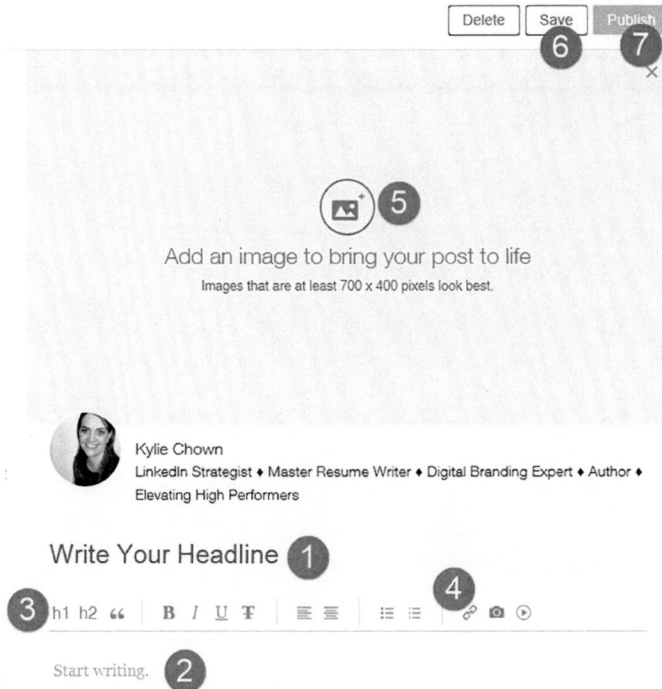

Groups and Companies

LinkedIn gives you the option to join groups and follow companies. This is a great way to find out information about your industry.

Within each group, there are discussions. You can use group discussions to:
- Position yourself as an expert in your field by providing information on your area of expertise and answering questions posted in groups. You can sort discussions to quickly identify discussions around your area of expertise.
- Obtain information by starting a discussion within a group.
- Increase exposure across your network with improved visibility.
- Join groups where your ideal customers and prospects are. You can contribute to discussions as an industry leader and engage with your targeted customers in an organic way.
- Improve your knowledge base by leveraging other leaders in the industry.
- Conduct market research and get a true sense of the current situation.
- Create a link to a potential connection. You can use the common group status if you are requesting to connect with someone.

Some guidelines around contributing to discussions in groups:

- Groups are for knowledge building and sharing. Make sure your posts are genuine and do not advertise your company's products or services.
- Remember your manners. Engage as you would in a face-to-face situation and remember that written material can be interpreted differently, so write in a clear and concise manner.

You will see your groups listed at the bottom of your profile page. Groups are like a branding exercise because they give people looking at your profile an idea of what you're interested in.

Groups also increase your proximity to your connections. You will turn up in the search result of a particular topic if you're part of a related group.

Running a group is a big job. There are benefits, but a lot of work is involved. It may be more worth your while to remain a contributor.

What does a contributor mean? A contributor means you can join a group and contribute to the discussion by posting your articles, posing questions and providing answers. Being a contributor to a group can open networks to you. It's easier to attract the attention of someone who is in a group you are a member of.

We said 40-60 per cent of connections that convert for you ideally come from direct introductions. Ten to 20 per cent ideally come from groups and 5 to 10 per cent are from direct emails, and that's you making direct approaches.

You need to customise your approach. For example, you could say: "Hi there. I thought I'd offer to connect. I noticed that we're in this particular group. I help people like you and would it be helpful if I sent you some information? Would it be helpful if I had a coffee with you?"

Action Steps

Some groups are open, meaning anyone can join, and some closed, meaning you need to be approved to join.

In the search box at the top of any page, select Groups from the drop-down list on the left. Type in your keywords or group name to search.

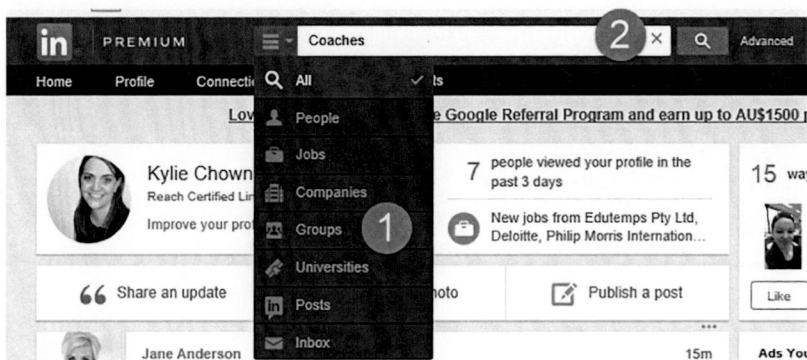

Once you have found a group you would like to join, click on the title and then:

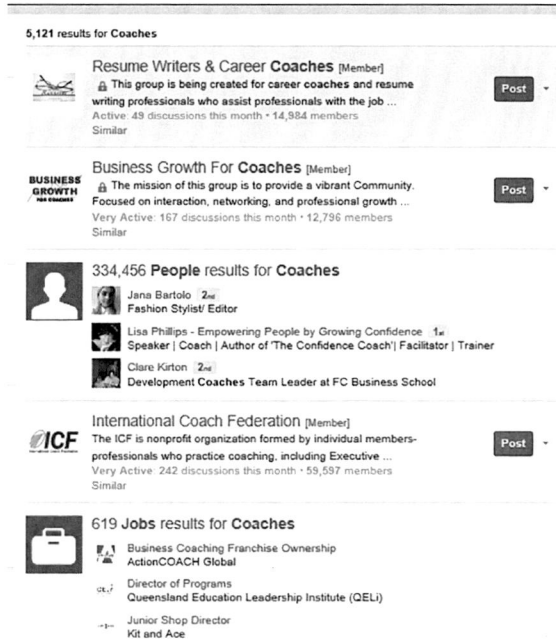

1. This is the title of the group.
2. This is a description of the group. This will often tell you what the group is about, who it is suitable for and any guidelines you should consider before you join.
3. This lists members of the group who are currently within your network.
4. "About this group" provides you with the group's statistics.
5. Once you have reviewed the information, click the join button if you would like to join.

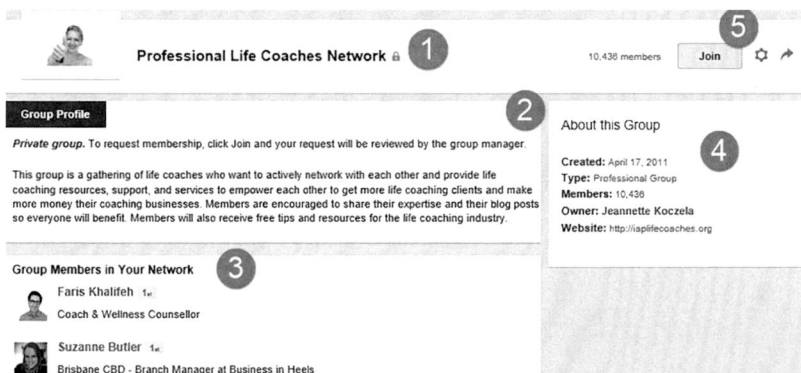

Once you have set your groups, it is a good idea to manage the communication for the group. You can do this by:

Logging in to your account.
Clicking Profile.

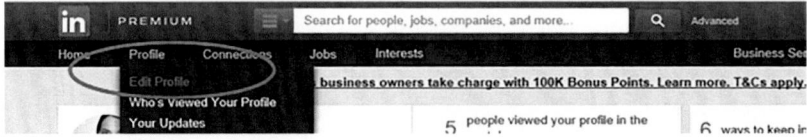

1. Click Edit Profile.
2. Click on Settings.
3. Click on Groups, Companies and Application.
4. Click on Set the frequency of emails.

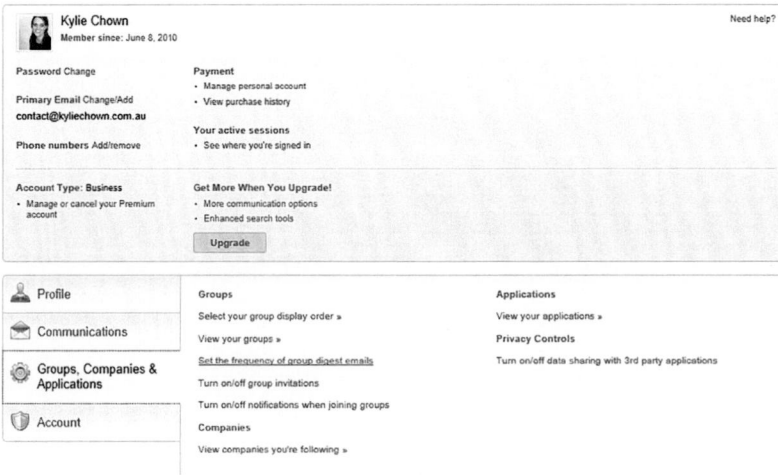

5. Select set the frequency of group digest emails
6. Select No Email, Daily Digest or Weekly Digest.

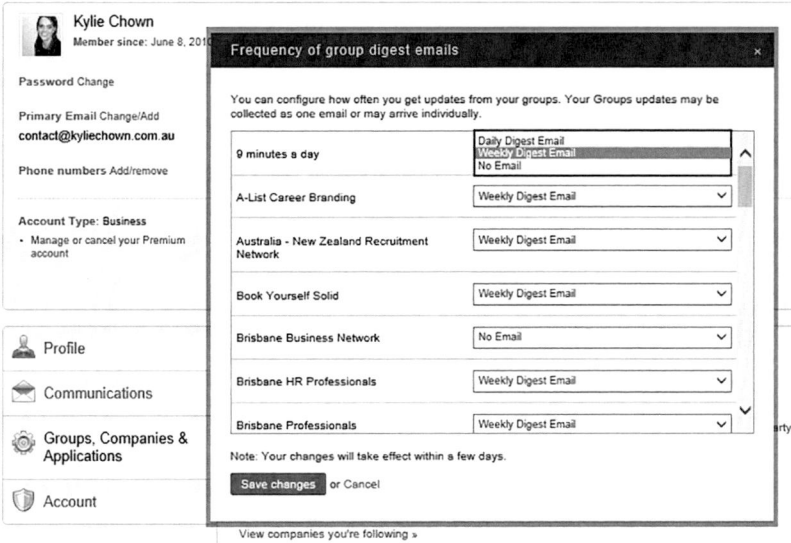

There are a couple of things to keep in mind with groups. They're the second-most important way to connect. The most important is introductions, and the third-most important is direct emails. Groups are also a great way for you to turn up in search results. You can have up to 50 groups.

How Do I Share an Update?

Once you have your shiny new profile ready to go, you can look at engaging with your network. One way to do this is to share an update.

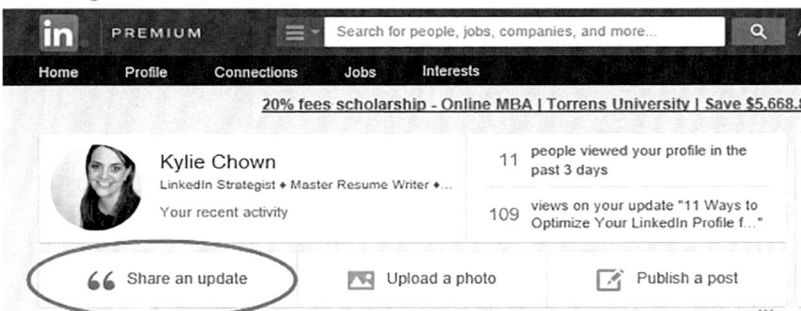

Action Steps to Share an Update

You can do this in one of two ways:

1. Click on the pencil icon and write a free-text update.
2. Click on the paper clip and attach a file.

You can share links to other articles in this section as well. You can do this by copying and pasting the URL in the "share an update" box.

LinkedIn is becoming a growth area for journalists to source information.

Have you seen the movie *Chef?* It is about a chef and his son. Dustin Hoffman is the crazy owner of the restaurant the chef works at. A food critic comes in and criticises the food. The chef gets really cranky. His son shows him how Twitter works, so the chef tweets to the food critics: "How dare you criticise my food?" The chef thought it was a personal message, however the message was actually public. The next morning, his son discovers a tsunami of comments on Twitter regarding the chef's tweet to the food critic. It had totally gone viral.

Jane woke one Sunday morning to discover that there had been a huge number of Twitter re-tweets and connection requests for her on LinkedIn overnight. The first thing she thought of was the movie, *Chef.* She thought, "Oh God. What have I done?", and frantically tried to work out what had happened overnight. What had actually happened was she'd recently written an article or a blog post on LinkedIn called "Seven Steps to Increase Your Likeability".

It was about rapport building and being able to connect with people. A journalist had picked it up in New York and re-framed it. She writes for "Business Insider Magazine", a big online business blog that has an Australian version as well. She had quoted a lot of what Jane had written in her own article, called "How to Be the Most Popular Person in the Office". She hyperlinked it back to her LinkedIn profile and said: "Jane Anderson, Personal Branding Strategist. She has recently written this article on LinkedIn about this." There were 8,500 views on LinkedIn.

Visibility and Consistency

One of the mistakes people often make with social media is thinking engagement is the goal. However, engagement is hard to achieve, so your goal should be visibility and consistency. People won't necessarily like everything you post. But the more we're seen, the more we're trusted and people get more of a feel for who you are.

Gihan Perera, author of *Fast, Flat and Free* and many other books about leveraging social media and branding, says it's a challenge to always get a return on investment with social media. However, if you can maintain your visibility on social media, even if it's just once a day, then it will give you enough brand equity to ask for what you want.

Rachel Bourke from Salespace wanted to use LinkedIn so she could be found by her ideal audience, be positioned correctly and have clients contact her via email or LinkedIn message.

Her profile was developed to:

- Support business-to-business (B2B) marketing.
- Nurture and strengthen relationships.
- Position herself to appeal to her ideal audience by tailoring language and keywords.
- Support branding and communication strategies.
- Curate, create and comment to support her expert positioning.
- Leverage search engine optimisation with industry keywords for B2B clients.

LinkedIn Strategy:

When we were approached by Rachel, her profile was a list of past roles and responsibilities. Her strategy focused on her future and included the following elements:

- Re-write a search engine optimised LinkedIn profile. The SEO was based on the keywords her ideal audience would use to find people such as her.
- Edit her summary and headline to reflect her business plan and targeted audience.
- Include testimonials from people her ideal audience can relate to.
- Compile content in her employment section to support her current business goals.
- Have a compelling call to action.
- Post search engine optimised articles to support her validation as an expert.
- Join and comment in groups to increase visibility and build credibility.

- Curate information of value to her audience.
- Share and promote business and industry events.
- Participate in coaching.

Rachel Bourke Initial Results

	Current score /10	Final score /10
Establish Your Profile		
1. Does your profile address the problems and fears of your ideal client?	5	10
2. Do you have a professional headshot?	10	10
3. Do you control updates clogging your inbox?	10	10
4. Is your profile fully search engine optimised in the title, summary, current role, skills and expertise, and does it include a vanity URL and contact details?	4	10
5. Are you well validated with recommendations and endorsements?	10	10
Total score /50	39	50
Engage Your Audience		
6. Do you like and comment professionally?	5	10
7. Do you create personalised scripts to connect professionally?	5	10
8. Do you leverage LinkedIn to support your face-to-face networks?	5	10
9. Do you curate content in a time-efficient and relevant manner?	5	10
10. Do you contribute to groups professionally?	5	10
Total score /50	25	50

Elevate Your Positioning		
11. Do you undertake advanced searches to find ideal connections?	5	10
12. Are you positioned effectively when being introduced to a potential client or contact?	5	10
13. Can you write a thought-leading post with a call to action to attract ideal clients?	0	10
14. Do you know how to write a compelling script to connect with ideal stakeholders via Connect or InMail, knowing the difference between the two?	5	10
Total score /40	15	40
Empower Your Team		
15. Can you maintain and troubleshoot your profile?	5	10
16. Do you know how to run your business page?	5	5
Total score /20	10	15
TOTAL SCORE /160	89	155

Results Immediately After Upload

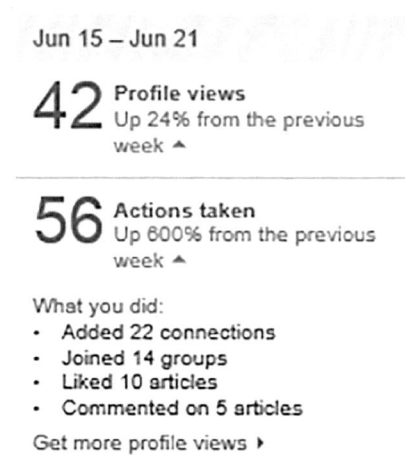

Jun 15 – Jun 21

42 Profile views
Up 24% from the previous week ▲

56 Actions taken
Up 600% from the previous week ▲

What you did:
- Added 22 connections
- Joined 14 groups
- Liked 10 articles
- Commented on 5 articles

Get more profile views ▸

Three-Monthly Tracking

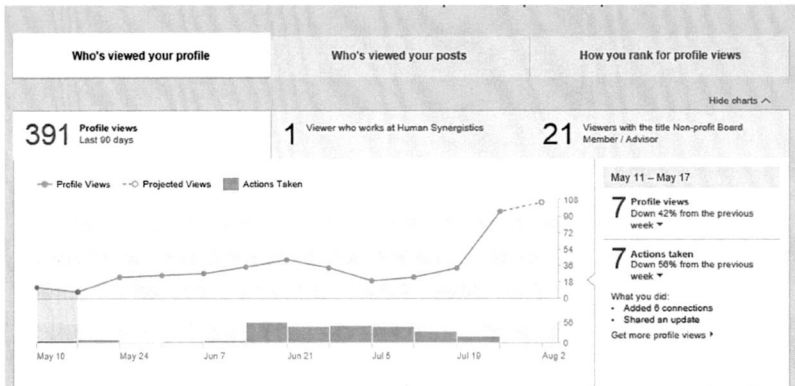

Impact on Posting

Posting was used to supports Rachel's positioning.

Date	View	Like	Comment
June 1, 2015	44	10	2
June 26, 2015	63	7	0
July 14, 2015	486	54	2
July 22, 2015	1419	96	12
July 24, 2015	4057	539	54

Date capture supports a 9120% increase in views on posts, 7600% increase in likes and a 2600% increase in comments (from lowest to highest viewed). Rachel's sales increased by more than 66% in the first quarter of her implementing the strategies from this book.

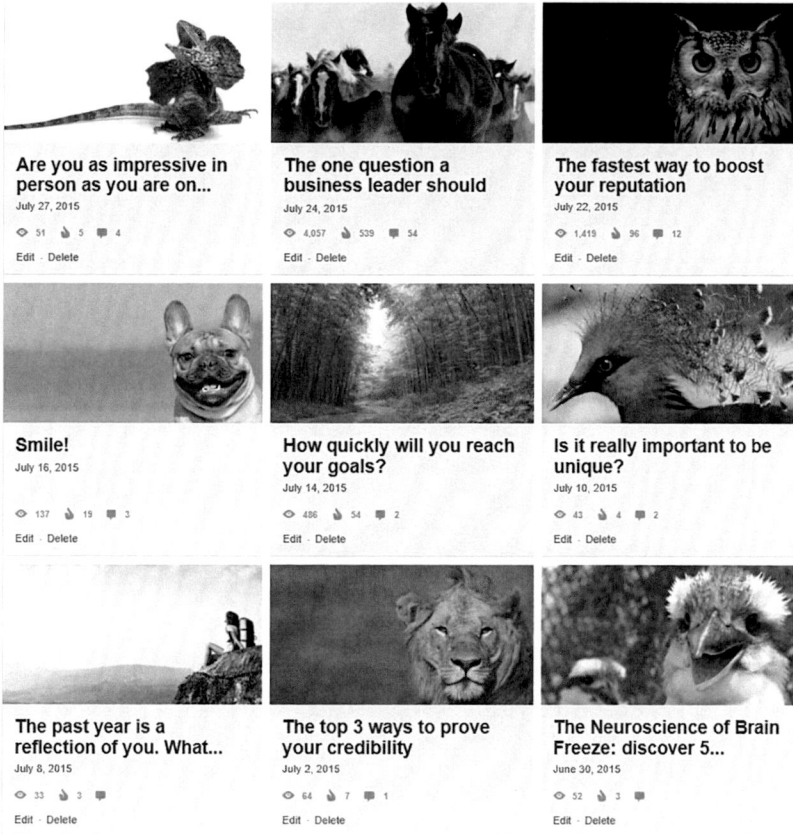

Are you as impressive in person as you are on...	**The one question a business leader should**	**The fastest way to boost your reputation**
July 27, 2015	July 24, 2015	July 22, 2015
👁 51 👍 5 💬 4	👁 4,057 👍 539 💬 54	👁 1,419 👍 96 💬 12
Edit · Delete	Edit · Delete	Edit · Delete
Smile!	**How quickly will you reach your goals?**	**Is it really important to be unique?**
July 16, 2015	July 14, 2015	July 10, 2015
👁 137 👍 19 💬 3	👁 486 👍 54 💬 2	👁 43 👍 4 💬 2
Edit · Delete	Edit · Delete	Edit · Delete
The past year is a reflection of you. What...	**The top 3 ways to prove your credibility**	**The Neuroscience of Brain Freeze: discover 5...**
July 8, 2015	July 2, 2015	June 30, 2015
👁 33 👍 3 💬	👁 64 👍 7 💬 1	👁 52 👍 3 💬
Edit · Delete	Edit · Delete	Edit · Delete

Scheduling Tools

Hootsuite is a tool you can use to schedule your posts. It means you don't have to sit down every morning posting content. You can allocate, say, half an hour every Friday afternoon to logging into Hootsuite, writing and scheduling posts. You can check out their website: www.hootsuite.com

Reflections and Actions

- Update your profile photo to mirror the type of clients you want to work with.
- Create a content plan based on the problems you solve for customers.
- Write a post at least monthly, if not fortnightly.
- Sign up for Scoop.it and hootsuite.com

Chapter 6

Connection

Brene Brown, author and expert in vulnerability, said in her TED talk: *"When you don't care what people think, you lose the opportunity for connection."*

In our experience, no matter the industry, we see the same issues with connecting. People are hesitant to connect because they:

- Are unsure how to approach or what to say.
- Can't override the default settings on devices.
- Are scared of pushing too hard, too quickly or not reading situations correctly.
- Don't optimise their profiles and are hard to find.
- Are worried people won't understand why they want to connect.

People need to earn the right to ask for a sale. For example, Jane has a friend who she has done some work with. Every day, this person puts up about 10 posts about herself and her business. Jane has had to actually turn off her feed because it's too much. She's not giving information.

Technology is moving fast. We try to keep you up to speed with some things that have changed. You might have noticed that people can start to post their own content if they have premium accounts, and those types of things. You see articles coming through that are a bit long, which is a tool called "pulse".

Connecting

When you conduct searches with particular words, your default will always be those that are first, second and third connections only.

Many years ago, Jane got divorced and her good friend Lisa recommended she go on a date with a guy she worked with called Travis. She kept saying that he was a nice guy, so Jane agreed. They met at a nice place in town but when Jane arrived, he had a backpack with him. She thought it was a bit odd, but went with it. They ordered an entrée and Jane asked Travis if he'd just come from the gym. He said "no"; he had brought his bag assuming the night would go well, and he laughed.

Hmm. Did he just say what she thought he said?

By this stage, Jane felt a bit awkward. As the entrée arrived, she asked: "So, what have you got in there?" He had fresh undies, his toothbrush, deodorant and a change of clothes. "Oh my goodness, he is actually serious!" Jane thought. Trying to remain calm, she laughed and said, "Well, that's brilliant because I had a key cut for you and the rent is due this week. I thought you might be able to help me out with that, too." At that point, she realised she had to wash her hair for the next day, so wrapped it up quickly, skipped the main meal and asked for the bill. It felt slimy and she couldn't get out of there quick enough. Sadly, he thought the date was amazing and called Jane the next day, saying it was such a shame she had to leave.

Have you felt like this when people have tried to sell to you and you haven't even met them? A common complaint we hear is: "Ewww, at least let me get to know you!"

Social selling and personal branding are a lot like dating. You need to let your audience get to know you. This helps your audience understand who you are, where you're coming from and to build trust. You can move slowly or quickly, but at least get a few dates in before you decide to try to move on to something more permanent. Otherwise, you look desperate. Self-promotion and marketing do not get the gig, whether it be the sale or the job. What they do create is awareness. Marketing is only one of the steps in the sequence of events required.

Winston Churchill once said: *"It is a mistake to try to look too far ahead. The chain of destiny can only be grasped one link at a time."*

Make it easy for your audience to get to know you. You can do this through sharing ideas, articles, curating content and your own thought leadership. That way, when you want to progress the relationship, they know who you are and if they like you or not. It takes time to build trust.

When approaching people, what you're looking for is common ground. Remember to personalise your connection requests because nobody does it. You've only got 300 characters to work with.

The next step is for that person to get used to your newsfeed and visibility so they get to know you. We're not trying to go home with the backpack on the first date. All we want to do is connect and say "hi". Let them know the reason you are connecting is because you have something in common with them. The goal is to maintain your visibility so people can get to know you.

Let People Get to Know You

Help people get to know you. People buy when they're ready, so you need to increase the amount of touch points to build trust. It's like a bank account. Imagine that you have a bank account with minus $50. You have to build it up past zero and get it into the black.

Robert Cialdini, best-selling author of *Influence, the Psychology of Persuasion* was the one who said that you need five to seven touch points to influence and persuade someone to do something. To do this, you need to know what you want and who you help. You need daily visibility and you need to be writing your own content weekly.

InMail

You might have noticed there is an opportunity called InMail. InMail gives you a few more characters, allowing you to provide more information.

Brisbane Area, Australia | Management Consulting

Current   The Performance Curve, PsyCare
Education   University of South Australia

Connect   Send Anna InMail

Search

LinkedIn allows you to search a keyword string and put constraints around it. For example, "CEO":

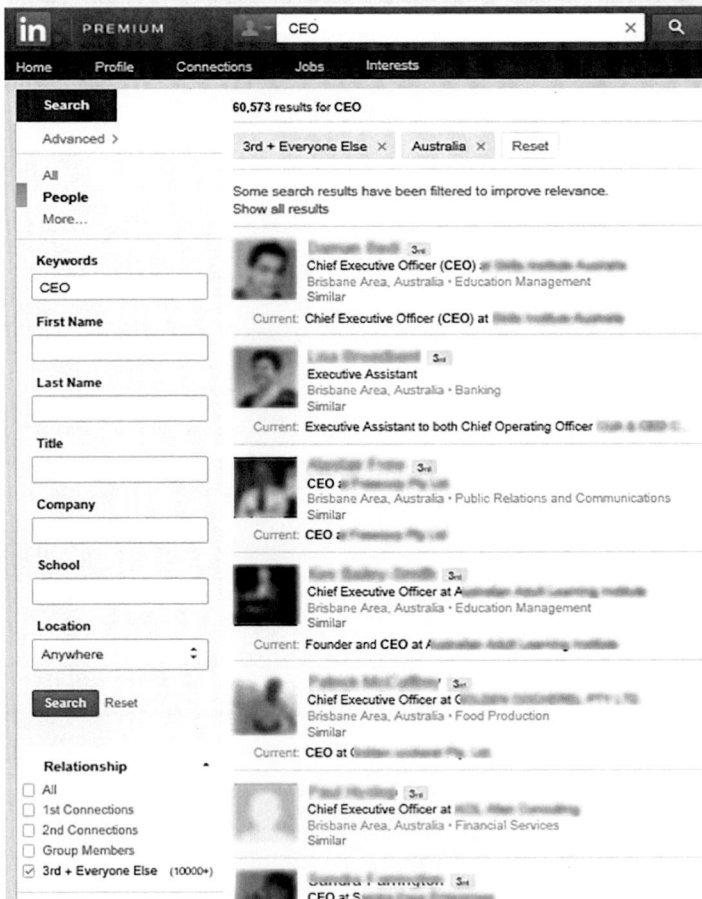

Connections

Once you have your profile set up, you can start inviting new connections. People who you can connect with include:

- Current colleagues
- Past colleagues
- Clients
- People from networking events

- Industry leaders
- Experts in the field
- Class members of past studies
- People who have viewed your profile

NOTE: LinkedIn currently caps the maximum number of connections at 30,000.

Action Steps: Adding a New Connection

To invite a new connection to your LinkedIn network:

1. Search for their name in the search box in the top field.
2. If the person isn't in the drop-down list, select the magnifying glass for all options.
3. If you have a long list, you can use the advanced search functions on the left-hand side to reduce the search criteria.
4. Once you have found who you are looking for, you can either Connect, Save, Get Introduced, Send InMail, Share or Find References.

Current	The Career Consultancy Pty Ltd, Casa Leisure Pty Ltd
Previous	Institute of Chartered Accountants in Australia
Education	Flinders University

Connect   Send Catherine InMail   ▼

Top Tip: It is easier to do this on a desktop computer. It is difficult to customise your connection requirements on a mobile device. Take the time to do it professionally – you only have one chance at a first impression.

From here, you can connect directly or make an approach. To connect, select the connect option and compete the form.

How do you know Anna?
- Colleague
- Classmate
- We've done business together
- Friend
- Other
- I don't know Anna

Include a personal note: (optional)

Hi Anna,

It was great to meet you at the conference today. I really enjoyed your presentation. Thanks so much for sharing your expertise.

Kylie

Important: Only invite people you know well and who know you. Find out why.

Send Invitation or Cancel

The other option for adding connections is to use the import feature.

See Who You Already Know on LinkedIn   Manage imported contacts ›

Gmail   Hotmail   Outlook   Yahoo! Mail   Any Email

Get started by adding your email address.

Your email

Continue   Your contacts are safe with us!
We'll import your address book to suggest connections and help you manage your contacts. We'll never email anyone without your permission. Learn More

Be careful if you import your connections this way. We do not recommend this as you do not have control over who you are connecting with.

Action Steps

1. Go to the Contacts and select Add Connection.
2. Enter your email address and password and click continue. From here, you can choose who you would like to connect to.

Top Tip: This will only work if the person you are connecting with is using the same email address for their LinkedIn account.

When connecting, always personalise the connection. Not many people do this, so it is a great way to stand out. If you have met them at an event or conference, mention that it was great to meet them, highlight something about them and ask to connect.

Once you have added a connection, you can keep notes, set a reminder, remember how you met and tag them.

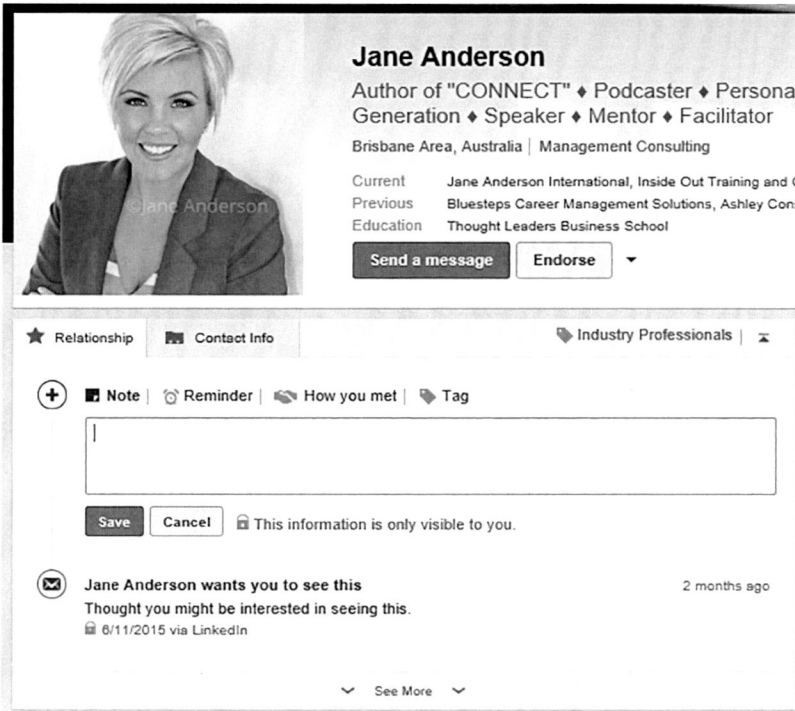

You can set a reminder that is only visible to yourself. This will appear on your contacts page as an action item.

Accepting Connection Requests

Remember that you don't need to accept all connection requests. There have been instances of fake LinkedIn accounts, so it is important to validate the request. You might like to look at whether you have any connections in common. If you can't determine why they have connected with you, you can always email them to ask!

When someone does connect with you, it is always a good idea to send them a quick message. Something along the lines of: "Thanks so much for connecting, Mark. Looks like you are doing some great work at (company name). I find most people who connect with me need help with their LinkedIn profile. Is there anything I can help you with?"

Again, not many people do this, so if you do, you will stand out.

When Others Connect With You

When people connect with you, be curious. Don't just accept it and soldier on with your mission to find new clients; they're right in front of you, even if you can't understand why they are connecting with you. Your profile is a similar to a shop front, so when customers "walk in", say hello and see if you can help.

If they connect with you, don't just accept and ignore it. Our research tells us that about 50% of people connecting with you are connecting because they want help – if not now, at some stage in the future.

To illustrate, Phillip connected with somebody on Friday afternoon. He asked them if he could be of any help, and by Monday he had received a $100,000 proposal. On Tuesday, they called him in for a meeting, and he was also put forward for further work within the organisation.

People want to move quickly. Help them do this by saying, "Thank you very much for connecting." Ask them if you can be of any help. Ask them if they would like to receive your newsletter. Offer tips and tricks. Make notes of your connections, use tags and use reminders if you need to follow them up.

Taking Notes

You can record notes specific to each connection, set reminders (that will sit on the top of your contacts page), and record how you met.

Tagging

You can tag your LinkedIn connections so you can group, sort and organise them for searches and messages. As the maximum amount of connections you can message at one time is 50, it is recommended that you do not have more than 50 connections with the same tag. One way to work around this is to have sub-tags. For example, you might have HR Managers, HR Managers 1, HR Managers 2, HR Managers 3 or more targeted groups, such as HR Managers Finance Sector, HR Managers Health Sector, HR Managers Retail Sector, etc. Only you can see your tags and you can create up to 200 tags.

Action Steps

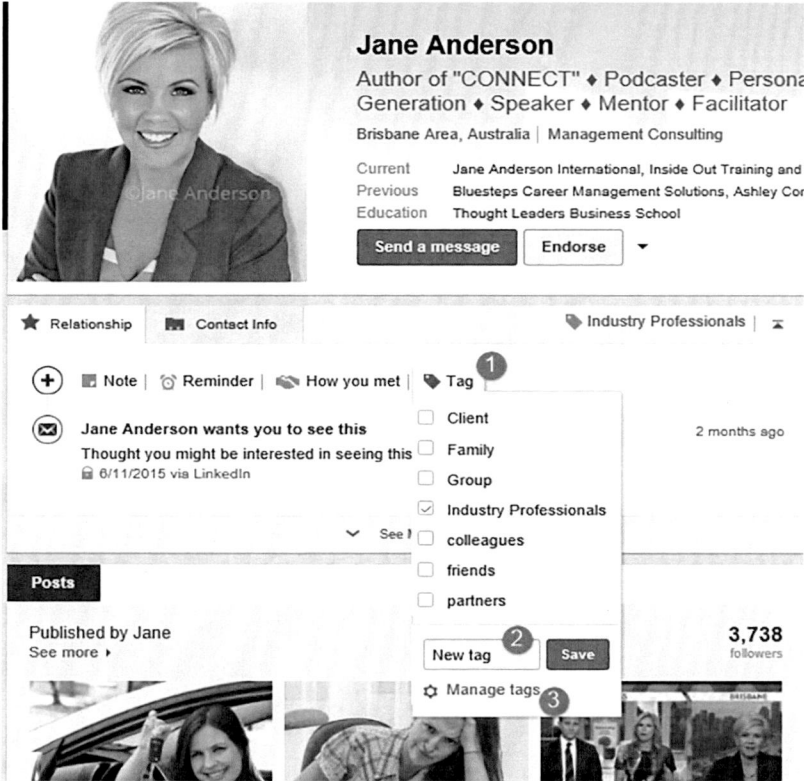

1. Select Tags.
2. Select a Tag or create a new one.
3. Manage tags.

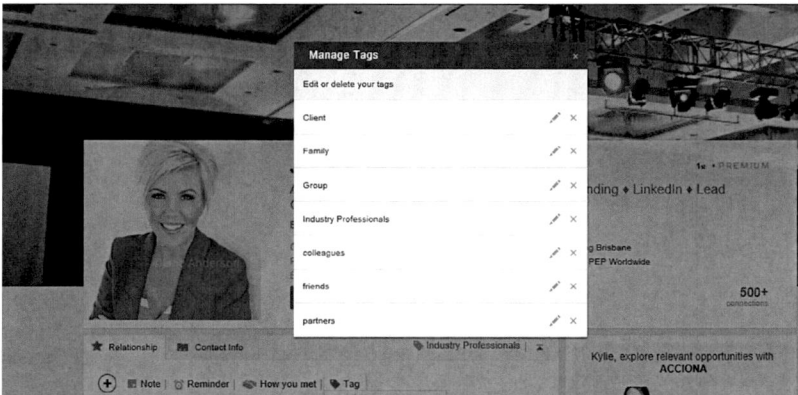

Exporting Your Connection Data

You can export your connection data from LinkedIn into a spreadsheet. Only the full name, email address, current employer and position are exported.

To do this:

1. Move your cursor over Connections at the top of your homepage and select Keep in Touch.

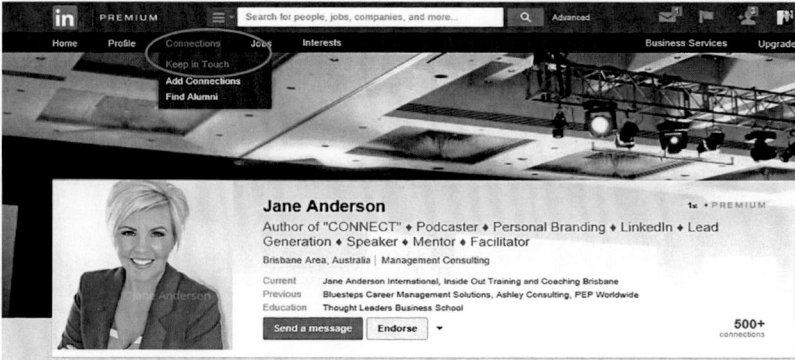

2. Click the Settings icon near the top right to reach the Contact Settings page.

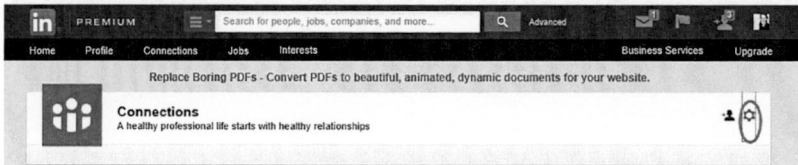

3. Under Advanced Settings on the right, click Export LinkedIn Connections.

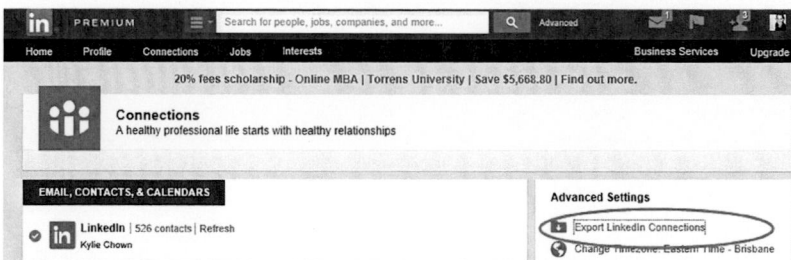

4. Enter the security verification text if prompted and then click Continue.
5. Click Export.
6. Save the file somewhere you can easily find it, such as your computer's desktop.

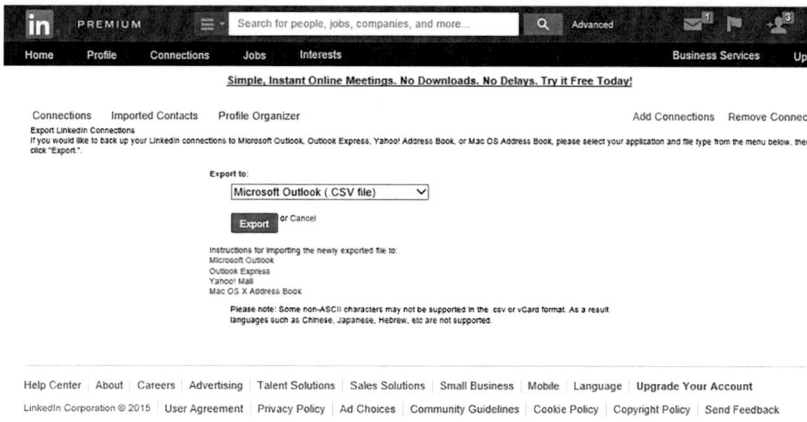

7. Open the file and print (optional).

Top Tip: It's a good idea to back up your connections on a regular basis in case anything happens to your profile – for example, if it gets hacked.

Sorting Connections

You can sort and filter connections by recent activity, first name, surname and newest. To filter your connections, click the filter option above the contacts.

Keep an Eye on Who Likes Your Comments the Most

Our other little tip for you is to keep an eye on who looks at your stuff. For example, Jane has a connection on LinkedIn who frequently comments and likes her articles and posts. Jane approached him and said, "I'm very grateful that you have been sharing your insights and your comments and liking my articles. Is there anything I can do for you? Do you want any feedback on your profile? Is there something I can help you with?" He replied, "Actually, I'd love to get feedback on this." Jane's connection has done a lot to advance her thought leadership. Keep an eye out for those people who are liking what you're doing. They can be a good source of business development. As

Seth Godin would say, they can help you build a tribe. They're people who buy into what you do regularly.

Asking For an Offer in Line With the Equity You've Built

Imagine you're driving along and see one of those inflatable men outside a furniture store. Then, you see a newspaper ad that says the store is having a big sale. You also hear an ad on the radio saying, "Get down to the furniture store." You've got all these messages about the furniture sale coming at you. People need at least five messages before they think, "Oh! Geez, I think we need a new lounge."

It's the same deal with social selling. It complements the other selling and marketing tools we use. The key is that we don't want to go too fast on the first date. We want to help people get to know us first and gain positioning.

Scripts

When you go to a particular profile, you've got a few options. You can set reminders. When you go onto a profile, you can make notes for yourself on how you met, and you can also create any tags to a profile.

You have two wording options when you go to approach someone. One is dependent on whether you're connected already, but the other is not.

The first option is if you're not already connected. It might be that you are a member of the same group. You might have someone in common. You might be interested in the same thing. You could say: *"Hi (their name), I noticed that you're …"* or, *"I notice that we work in this particular industry …"* or, *"I notice that …"*

You want to validate the person. You want to show that you've paid attention to what they're saying and what they do, so you're looking for common ground.

"I help organisations like yours," or, *"My role is …"* or, *"What we have in common is …"*

A great way to position yourself is through a positive first impression, so you need to personalise it. Make the person feel important and show what you have in common.

The second wording option is for when you are already connected. This wording is for when you want to progress the relationship. If you're already connected and you've been posting, sharing, curating and commenting, you may feel as though you have built enough brand equity so you can think, "Right now, I feel like I'm ready to talk to this person."

You might have used a reminder on the person's profile to follow up a week after you've connected with them. You're trying to progress the connection and give them more information. For example:

"Hi, I noticed that you're the employee relations manager for this particular union or organisation. I help organisations such as yours in this capacity."

"I recently delivered a speech at an organisation that is similar to yours. Would it be helpful if I sent you some information?"

Be mindful of your wording when you're reaching out to people, and always connect at a personal level, such as: *"I thought I'd follow up. Would it be helpful if I popped in and said hi?"*

Altogether, it looks something like this:

"Hi (the person's name), I noticed that you're the employee relations manager for this particular union or organisation. I help organisations like yours in this capacity. I recently delivered a speech at this organisation that is similar to yours. Would it be helpful if I sent you some information?"

Additional Sample Scripts

For Someone Offering to Connect With You:

Hi [Name]

Thanks so much for your connection request, I appreciate you reaching out. It looks like you're doing some great work in the [name] industry, congratulations on getting Manager of the Year! Well done.

Is there anything I can do to help? If not that's okay, just thought I'd ask.

Kind regards,

[Your name]

Sales Script if Already Connected

Hi Bill,

I noticed that you're ...

I help people/organisations like yours in ...

For example, I recently delivered ...

I'd love to send you my [video/whitepaper/first chapter of my book]. Is [address] the best one to send it to?

Kind regards,

[Your name]

Sales Script if Not Already Connected

Hi Bill,

My name is [name] and I noticed that you [are a member of the same group; know someone in common; have the same interest; work in same industry].

I help people/organisations like yours [in what capacity], so I thought I'd offer to connect and send you a free whitepaper on the challenges in the industry for [their position title].

Is this the correct email address to send it to? email@email.com.au

If so, just say yes and I can get it to you today.

[Your name]

Followed Up By

Send via email:

Hi Bill,

Hope you're well. I thought I'd see if you found the whitepaper helpful.

I'm currently delivering a training/coaching/facilitation program addressing the issues covered, such as [problem]. If this is something that might be helpful for you, I'd love to chat to you about it.

I can do the following times next week if any of these work:

- Date and time
- Date and time
- Date and time

I look forward to hearing from you.

Your sincerely,

[Your name]

Connecting Through Groups

You can conduct a search on the groups you might like to join. If you're interested in a closed group, you will have to be approved to join. Some are open groups and you can become part of that group instantly. You can be a member of up to 50 groups. If you do become a member of a group, you might want to set up a rule in Outlook so that the group's updates go to a reading list, which you read once a week.

Leveraging Your Profile for Events

Before you attend a conference, check whether the organisers are using a hashtag on Twitter and keep an eye on who is posting in the Twitter feed. Try to find them on LinkedIn and connect there. This way, you will have done half the work on connecting with attendees and finding out what you've got in common before the conference. Bear in mind that you will turn up in their search results, too.

Dropping them a line before the event is a great way of positioning yourself to meet them face to face:

"Hi, I noticed that you're attending this event that's coming up in a few weeks. I'd love to catch up with you. I just thought I'd introduce myself here so I could keep an eye out for you on the day. I hope that's okay with you."

It's also a great idea to follow up and connect with people on LinkedIn within 24 hours of the event. Don't just put their details into your Salesforce system; make a personalised experience for them. Drop them a line to say, "It was fantastic to meet you." Write the personal connection rather than use the default wording.

Always send messages from your desktop with a personal introduction. Mobile phones and iPads don't allow you to do personalise a connection. Always look for ways you can add your personal touch.

Reciprocity means that you're more likely to get back if you give first. It's as though people have a bank account in their minds: "Have I given more? Am I being used here? Have I given too much? Am I in debit or credit?" Look for ways of giving first because you're more likely to receive what you're looking for. For example: "I really want to acknowledge you at this point to say keep up the great work!"

Reminders

With some profiles, you'll see there are notes where you can set reminders and make comments about how you met. You can even set email reminders to make sure you follow up with someone. You can put tags on them as well. The main consideration with your approach is to look for what you have in common. Look for referrals, join the same groups and comment on articles.

Disconnecting

Jane had been connected with a particular person for a while when she noticed that he had started to post many times every day, filling up her newsfeed and notifications. The tsunami of self-promotion led to her decision to disconnect with him. He may have thought he was adding value, but Jane didn't see this in any of his posts – it felt like they were all about him and how good he thought he was.

People won't know if you disconnect with them or ignore their connection request until they go to your profile.

Follows

Follows are different to groups. They are for influencers, and you can follow anybody's posts now. If you look at Richard Branson for example, you'll notice it's difficult to connect with him on LinkedIn. If you know Richard, you can connect, but otherwise most people will follow him. He has almost seven million followers.

You'll notice he has an influencer logo on his profile. This means that LinkedIn have specifically chosen him to be an influencer. You cannot decide to become one yourself.

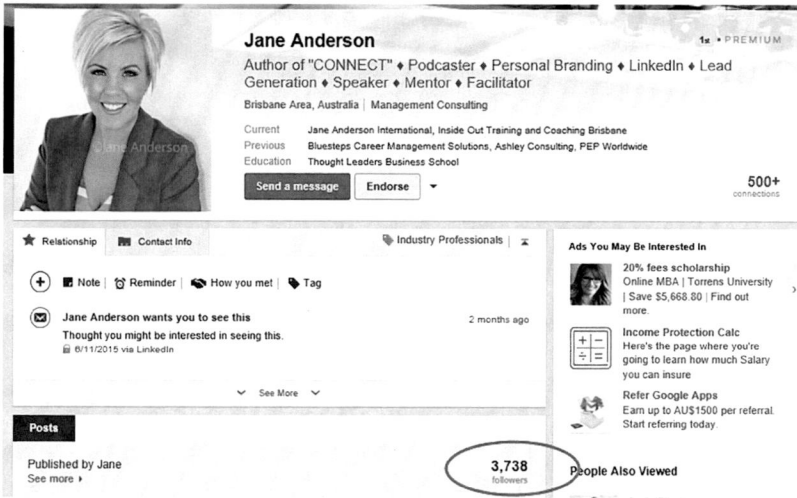

Reflections and Actions

- Write scripts you can use when connecting with others. Save them as a Word document to copy and paste when connecting with others.
- Export your connections at least once per month
- Search for those who help you the most and make offers to connect using your script.

Chapter 7

Organisational LinkedIn Strategy

Do you have a LinkedIn strategy for your organisation? How do you know it's working?

Everybody has a different role in your organisation, but remember it's not just about dealing with customers. It's about dealing with suppliers, the community, removing roadblocks, validation, and building trust within your business.

It's a bit like buying a car. You do your research and look around. You ask: "Can this car be trusted? Am I getting a reliable vehicle? Is it going to do what I need it to do?"

People are savvy. They're not stupid. They will do their research. The best thing about having a LinkedIn profile for your organisation is that it's a great way to beat the competition if you're a small player in a big industry.

Other reasons why an organisation might have a presence on LinkedIn, particularly for its leaders, include:

- 75% of job seekers validate managers and CEOs on LinkedIn when they apply for jobs.
- 60% of a buying decision is made before you've even heard from a customer. They may have already decided on buying the product; they just need someone to talk to.

We recently worked with a medium-sized organisation in the health insurance industry. It's a small player in a big industry. After helping the organisation with personal LinkedIn profiles for its team members, it was able to beat its competition in Google searches.

Seth Godin, one of the world's leading marketing authorities, describes in his book *Linchpins* those people in organisations who are highly leveraged and have a high impact on the business and its success. In your organisation, these may not just be sales people, but technical experts or those who have high visibility outside the organisation.

When deciding on who needs to have their LinkedIn profile written, you might like to think about those people in your organisation who are linchpins. Do you have team members who speak at conferences and events or connect with different people across your industry? It's important to make sure these people have a well-written profile. You need to consider their roles, write with a purpose and include their personalities.

If you are a school principal, your profile is much like a CEO's, and you need to think about your profile as part of the school community and less about you. The parents of your students will often be on LinkedIn, so it's a great way to show your professionalism and another touch point to market your school.

The overall strategy and design for an organization's LinkedIn program like peeling layers of an onion off. There are different layers and each person has different purposes in their role in that layer. It will also depend on the closeness to the customer

This model shows the steps to building your profile, whether you're an individual or a business owner looking to bring LinkedIn into your organisation:

LinkedIn Strategy for Individuals and Organisations

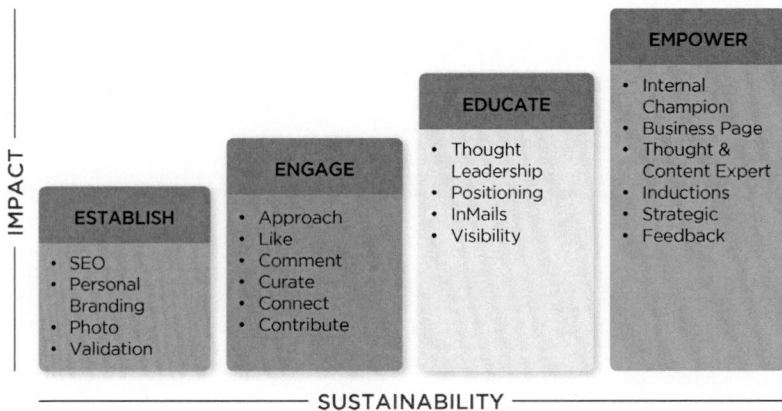

© Jane Anderson 2015

Establish: The first step is to consider your profile. Do you even need one? If you have a profile, how professional is it and how do you want it to serve you? You profile works for you 24/7, so it needs to align with your goals, support your face-to-face activity and define what you're trying to achieve. You need to make sure your team's profiles are fully search engine optimised, have a professional presence with a professional photo, and are well validated.

Engage: You need to teach your team members how to engage online – how to like things, how to comment and curate content, how to connect with other people, what to say and what scripts to use. They need to learn how to contribute to conversations and understand the etiquette of contributing to forums and groups. Are they comfortable sharing content? Are they aware of the impact of liking and commenting on content and how that supports your goals? Do they personalise their introductions and connect with others in a way that is meaningful and achieves results? Do they add value to their audience or are they spamming them?

Educate: The third level is about teaching people how to educate and this involves their positioning as thought leaders. They must be clear about their content strategy. What is the purpose? What do they want to be known for? This is about your team members becoming thought leaders and teaching them about thought leadership.

Your team needs to know how to write connection requests and InMails to clients and customers to initiate conversations. Visibility is about making sure your team is top of mind so that when people need help, your team members are who people think of.

How are you educating your audience to elevate your positioning? Is your content strategic enough? Are you known for what you want to be known for? How often are you seen in the average person's feed? Are you top of mind for referrals?

Empower: At this level, you're thinking about your business strategy and how LinkedIn fits with your goals at an organisational level. It's not just about having a profile written. Your team members own their profiles. How do you educate them to make the most of their profile? Do you have a LinkedIn policy in place? How do you on-board them? Do you have an exit strategy? How are you measuring success? This is where we're working with marketing and communications teams to make LinkedIn sustainable within organisations. This is about having an internal champion who is trained in how to get a LinkedIn strategy to work.

Checklists for Senior Management LinkedIn Profiles

If you're a CEO, here is a checklist with some questions to help you determine if your LinkedIn profile is working for you and where you need to focus your efforts.

	Current score /10	Final score /10
Establish Your Profile		
1. Does your profile address the problems and fears of your ideal client?		
2. Do you have a professional headshot?		
3. Do you control updates clogging your inbox?		
4. Is your profile fully search engine optimised in the title, summary, current role, skills and expertise, and does it include a vanity URL?		
5. Are you and your business well validated with recommendations and endorsements?		
Total score /50		
Engage Your Audience		
6. Do you like and comment professionally?		
7. Do you personalise your connection request scripts professionally?		
8. Do you leverage LinkedIn to support your face-to-face networks?		
9. Do you curate content in a time-efficient and relevant manner?		
10. Do you contribute to groups professionally?		
Total score /50		

Elevate Your Positioning		
11. Do you undertake advanced searches to find ideal connections?		
12. Are you positioned effectively when being introduced to a new connection?		
13. Can you clearly represent your organisation, vision and purpose?		
14. Do you know how to connect with ideal stakeholders via Connect or InMail?		
15. Do you write posts that position you as a brand ambassador?		
Total score /50		
Empower Your Team		
16. Do you have a LinkedIn expert on your team with the knowledge to maintain or troubleshoot your profile?		
Total score /10		
TOTAL SCORE /160		

If you're a sales or marketing manager, here is a checklist with some questions to help you determine if your LinkedIn profile is working for you and where you need to focus your efforts.

	Current score /10	Final score /10
Establish Your Profile		
1. Does your team have a LinkedIn profile as a brand ambassador attracting ideal clients instead of recruiters?		
2. Do your team members have professional headshots?		
3. Does your team control updates from clogging inboxes?		
4. Do your team members' profiles include a search engine optimised title, summary, current role, skills and expertise, and vanity URL?		
5. Is your team supported with leaders who have strong profiles?		
Total score /50		
Engage Your Audience		
6. Does your team like and comment professionally?		
7. Does your team personalise scripts to connect professionally?		
8. Does your team leverage LinkedIn to support face-to-face networks?		
9. Does your team curate content in a time-efficient and relevant manner?		
10. Does your team contribute to groups professionally to drive enquiries?		
Total score /50		

Elevate Your Positioning		
11. Does your team undertake advanced searches to find ideal clients?		
12. Is your team positioned effectively when being introduced to potential contacts on LinkedIn?		
13. Can your team write a customer-centric post defining customer problems and with a call to action to attract ideal clients?		
14. Does your team know when to connect with ideal clients via Connect or InMail and the difference between the two?		
15. Does your team maintain visibility aligned with your sales strategy?		
Total score /50		
Empower Your Team		
16. Do you have an internal LinkedIn expert to advise, troubleshoot and maintain profiles?		
17. Does your marketing and communications team run the business page effectively?		
18. Is there an internal thought leader and content expert who knows how to write posts and can advise the team on posting their own articles on LinkedIn to drive sales?		
19. Do you educate new employees on managing their professional presence online?		
20. Is there a champion who can talk at a strategic level on leveraging LinkedIn for the organisation?		
Total score /50		
TOTAL SCORE /200		

If you're a school principal, here is a checklist with some questions to help you determine if your LinkedIn profile is working for you and where you need to focus your efforts.

	Current score /10	Final score /10
Establish Your Profile		
1. Do you have a LinkedIn profile that is reflective of your school's marketing and branding, and less about you?		
2. Do you have a professional headshot?		
3. Do you control updates clogging your inbox?		
4. Does your profile include a search engine optimised title, summary, current role, skills and expertise, and a vanity URL?		
5. Are you and your school well validated with testimonials and endorsements in your profile?		
Total score /50		
Engage Your Audience		
6. Do you like and comment professionally?		
7. Do you connect professionally with others using personalised scripts?		
8. Do you leverage LinkedIn to support your face-to-face networks?		
9. Do you curate content in a time-efficient and relevant manner?		
10. Do you contribute to groups professionally?		
Total score /50		

Elevate Your Positioning		
11. Do you undertake advanced searches to find ideal connections?		
12. Are you positioned effectively when being introduced to a new connection?		
13. Do you clearly represent your school's vision and purpose?		
14. Do you connect with ideal stakeholders via Connect or In Mail, knowing when to use one and not the other?		
15. Do you know how to write posts that position your school to parents of prospective students?		
Total score /50		
Empower Your Team		
16. Do you have a LinkedIn expert on your team with the knowledge to maintain or troubleshoot your profile?		
Total score /10		
TOTAL SCORE /160		

CEO and Principal Profiles

After working with a large number of CEOs and their profiles, many say they don't have the time to waste on LinkedIn and are still doing the old ways of business. However, they say they do want to grow their businesses as their markets have become tougher. Changing customer demands and technology means their competition is getting in front of their clients more quickly and they need to gain ground.

As mentioned in Chapter 1, many CEOs have a number of fears about LinkedIn:

Loss of Talent

CEOs worry that well-written LinkedIn profiles will lead to recruiters poaching their organisation's talent. If that happens, it means the profile has been written incorrectly. The LinkedIn profile writing strategy for a team member versus a job seeker is very different. It is a different process, with a different result. If the profile is written based on what the organisation wants to achieve, then it won't appear in talent pools and it will be clear to a recruiter that the team member is not looking for a job.

Looking Stupid

Many clients we work with have a fear of looking stupid or not being able to manage their profile successfully. They are also concerned that they won't know how to manage the situation if they post something online that people disagree with.

Competitors

Others are concerned that the competition may use LinkedIn to see what they're doing. "What if they try to steal my clients? How do I protect my connections, my clients and myself?"

BLACK-BELT LINKEDIN PROFILE FOR A CEO

LEVEL	ACTIVITY	LEVERAGE
6	Influence	100% +
5	Magnet	75%
4	Organisation	50%
3	Future-focused	25%
2	Obituary	0%
1	Profile	-10%

A leader's LinkedIn profile, especially a CEO's or principal's profile, is all about leverage.

Level 1: Profile: This is the lowest level, where you may have had a profile created for you. You have no idea how you turned up on LinkedIn, you just simply woke up one day and you had a profile. The amount of leverage you have here is about minus 10% of what's possible. It's actually repelling people from your business because they don't understand it. There's no information, so your profile is not doing anything for you. In fact, it's having a negative impact because it makes your competition look much better.

Level 2: Obituary: At the next level, your profile is written as though it's an obituary. It's written about the past; it's about your previous jobs, your study, and all those types of things. The amount of leverage you have at this level is zero. It's only leveraging you as an employee and you are far more likely to have recruiters contacting you. The leveraging is zero because it's not inspiring. It doesn't motivate others to want to work for you, it doesn't connect with potential customers or potential talent, and it doesn't open any doors for you.

Level 3: Future Focused: When your profile is future focussed, it has been written strategically, but it's been written about your own future, not the company's. You will receive more interest from recruiters and hiring managers. You haven't thought about how people are contacting you. Your profile's leverage is about a quarter of what's possible. It makes you look good, but it doesn't serve the business and it doesn't serve the growth of the company.

Level 4: Organisation: At this level, your profile has been written more about the organisation. You've provided some information about the organisation's careers pages, you're leveraging plugins from websites, you've possibly added product disclosure statements, and you're more focussed on the type of talent that works in the business. However, your profile is not particularly compelling. Its leverage is about 50% of what is possible.

Level 5: Magnet: At the next level, your profile is like a magnet. It is focused on the organisation, but it takes the reader into the future and into what the organisation is trying to achieve. It has full search engine optimisation, so if somebody tries to find the types of services your business offers, you turn up in their search results. It also means you're not having to search for good talent; you're starting to draw them in, and potential opportunities are coming to you, such as strategic partnerships. The leverage your profile has is about 75% of what's possible.

Level 6: Influence: This is a profile that has influence. At this level, you have 100%-plus of the leverage that's possible. Your profile inspires people to want to work for your organisation. It creates influence with stakeholders and strategic partners. It influences customers – we know that two-thirds of customers will make a decision about employees based on their perception of the CEO. You, as CEO, are making it very clear that it's not all about you; it's about the organisation. It's also about your influence in the community, so you're leveraging things such as your corporate social responsibility. It serves as a strong touch point to help you get access to people, such as investors, who will help the business grow. You're leveraging your LinkedIn profile for the benefit of the organisation, and it's making you look good.

How to Build a CEO or Principal's LinkedIn Profile

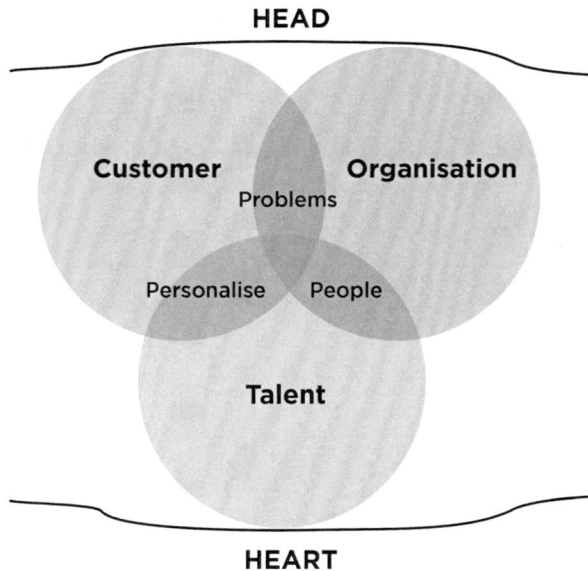

If you're building a CEO profile on LinkedIn, there are three factors you need to ensure it includes:

Customer: You must identify the customers you work with, their problems and the challenges they face, and even their fears. The content you share and the plug-ins you include need to have leverage and appeal to potential customers by connecting with their problems and fears. The profile must be fully search engine optimised, so a customer can find you based on their problem.

Organisation: A good CEO profile means it is more about the identity of the organisation and less about you. It's about the kind of business you have, addressing questions such as: "Is it a good place to work? Does it contribute to the community? What is its corporate social responsibility?" It also shows what the organisation is trying to achieve: "Our goal is to be the leader in X industry," or, "Our goal is to be Australia's favourite provider in X, or to be a world leader in X." It needs to be aspirational and it needs to highlight not just the organisation's goals, but its vision and values.

Talent: The profile needs to show the type of person who would be a good fit as an employee of the organisation. You could include turnover rates of the business. You could even provide a testimonial from a team member. This is particularly important if you're on a talent drive. Research shows that almost 75% of potential employees review the profiles of an organisation's leaders when applying for an advertised position at that organisation.

Underscoring these factors are three important points. Your profile needs to connect with the **problems** your customers have. It must be **personalised**, so it needs to make the connection between how we make a difference in the world and the customer. Finally, it also must also make a connection with the type of **people** who work at your organisation.

People can make very head-based decisions when they're considering working for an employer. They focus on questions such as: "What is the organisation trying to do? What is it trying to achieve? What's its vision? What's its purpose? Does it have a good name in the industry? What outcomes is it getting? Am I going to be paid?" All these are head-based questions around whether the person is going to work with you or whether they're going to be your customer.

Fifty per cent of the population makes logic-based decisions. The other 50% makes heart-based decisions. Those heart-based decisions focus on questions such as: "How am I going to feel when I work with you as an employee? How am I going to feel when I get to use your products or your services?" Your profile needs to connect at a personal and heart-based level because if you only focus on outcomes, results and tasks, you will only sell and leverage your profile to half the population. Here is an example of a CEO's summary:

Sample Company X provides equipment solutions, including excavators, mini excavators, hydraulic rock breakers, wheeled excavators, demolition excavators, wheel loaders, skid Steer loaders, materials handling excavators, compaction rollers and drill rigs.

We service a range of industries, including quarry and mining, civil, pipelining, plumbing, landscaping, forestry, demolition, materials handling and public works. Our clients (based in Australia, NZ and PNG) include Boral, Aurizon, Queensland Rail, Incitec Pivot, OneSteel, Xstrata, BGC, Leighton Holdings, Rio Tinto and Hansen.

We support our clients by supplying cost-effective sales and rental solutions for construction projects, helping them become more profitable, effective and sustainable, as well as enabling them with the latest technologies. In addition, we support them to maintain their assets by offering a competitive after-sales service function.

With more than 12 years' experience with Sample Company X, our team has:

♦ Doubled the Hyundai national support footprint, supporting both our customers and Australian jobs.
♦ Improved quality-control techniques through the pre-delivery process to reduce warranty and downtime from manufacturing defects by 90%.
♦ Provided parts and service support, which includes a 99% fill rate within five days on all parts, factory-trained personnel and a quarterly published parts pricing.

More recently, we have:

♦ Achieved high engagement scores for our team. We're a great place to work, we have low staff turnover and many have been in the business for more than 10 years.
♦ We give our staff one day per year to work in a charity of their choice. Many say this is one of the reasons why they love working with us and it gives them a sense of contribution to the world.
♦ We regularly have team development days and are committed to each team member achieving their potential.

Reflections and Actions

- Who looks at my profile? (i.e. customers, partners, talent)
- What is the vision for my organisation?
- What customer problems do we solve?
- Why is our organisation a great place to work?
- How do we undertake our corporate social responsibility?

Chapter 8

Metrics vs Results

Peter Drucker, world-leading management consultant, once said: "What's measured improves."

In 1988, an Australian woman called Leisa Campbell took the world by storm. She was an Australian body builder from Victoria. She won Miss Australia, Miss World and Miss Universe. Leisa travelled the world, competing and living in Europe and the US. She was before her time and even by today's standards is still considered one of, if not the, best body builders in the world.

When she was training, many things were measured that still are now, such as skin folds, fat percentage and weight. However, Leisa said she focused on something not all competitors valued. It was a diary of how she felt each day. She kept notes on her body's reaction to foods, sleep and training. Today, as a personal trainer for more than 25 years, she asks her clients to keep a diary as well. She says people pay too much attention to a whole lot of metrics that don't have enough leverage. They are just the results. The diary is what has leverage. In his book *The Power of Habit*, Charles Duhigg calls habits such as the diary keystone habits. These are every-day habits or leverage points that create big results.

Your LinkedIn profile is the same. It's easy to focus on the various LinkedIn metrics available, such as the All-Star rating, the new SSI (Social Selling Index), your profile's ranking, and the number of people who have viewed your profile and taken action. These metrics can motivate you to undertake more activities and stay on the site for longer.

In isolation, these metrics appear valuable and people tend to spend a lot of time trying to achieve an All-Star rating and an SSI score of 100%. However, as a result of the work we have done with clients, we have found that there are a number of other metrics that create the best results.

LinkedIn Metrics	Profile Keystone Metrics
All-Star rating	Search engine optimisation
Social Selling Index score	First four seconds
% viewed in your networks	Original thought leadership & curation
Post views, likes and comments	What action people take when looking at your profile
500+ connections	Effective scripts to connect with ideal clients
Connections	Ask if you can help connections who reach out to you

Why These Metrics Matter

- **Search engine optimisation:** It's important that you are easily found. LinkedIn is a search engine and there is someone out there trying to find you. Make it easy for them!

- **First four seconds:** When someone lands on your profile, you only have four seconds to "wow" them. If you don't, it will take a lot of work to impress them and motivate them to want to work with you. Your first four seconds needs to link to your future, not your past, otherwise you will only receive more of what you've already had.

- **Original thought leadership and curation:** Curation should comprise about 80% of your posts. Ideally, your original thought leadership (i.e. writing a post as opposed to sharing an update) should comprise about 20%.

- **What action people take when looking at your profile:** When people look at your profile, they should feel compelled to connect with you. If you have enough of the right content, the right connections and the right information for your first four seconds, people will be more likely to connect with you. This metric is important to review, however, it depends on the context of the views. For example, if you have a smaller amount of views but a high amount of clicks through to your profile, this is a good sign. It's all relative to what you're putting out there. This is the area of your profile that tells you this:

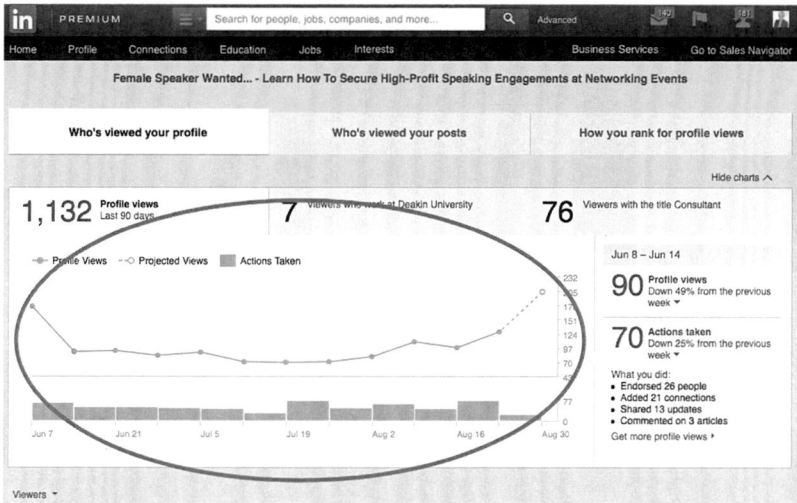

- **Effective scripts to connect with ideal clients:** Clients don't just magically appear. With effective scripting, you can maximise your chances of engaging with the right people. With the wrong scripting, you will repel them!

Why These Metrics are Less Important

- **All-Star rating:** The purpose of this rating is to encourage you to complete your profile. Yes, you certainly do want to complete it; however, if the content doesn't position you for your future, your profile will only give you more of what you've received in the past.

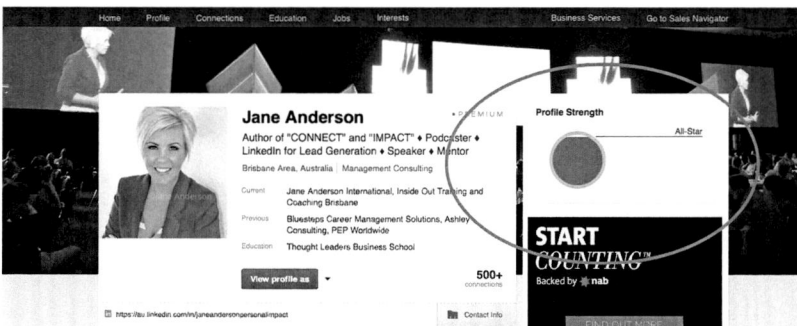

- **Social Selling Index:** The Social Selling Index is an indicator of how well your profile is leveraged as a sales tool. It is impossible to get a score above 85 without upgrading to Sales Navigator. A lot can be done on your profile to not only lift your score, but to leverage it for social selling before you upgrade to Sales Navigator.

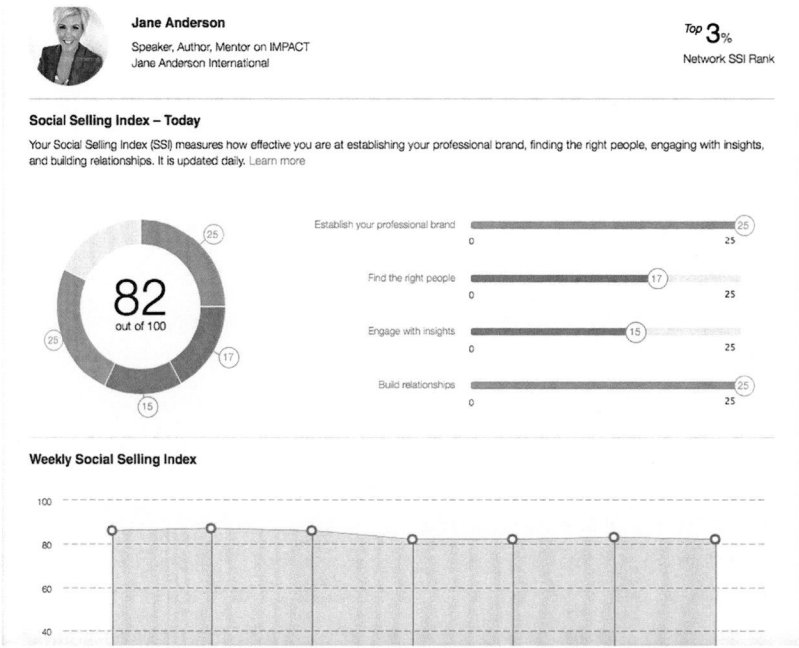

- **Post views, likes and comments:** Just because you get a lot of views or likes doesn't mean you're generating leads. It also doesn't mean that you're doing something wrong. What matters is if your content speaks to your tribe, its problems and aligns with your goals.

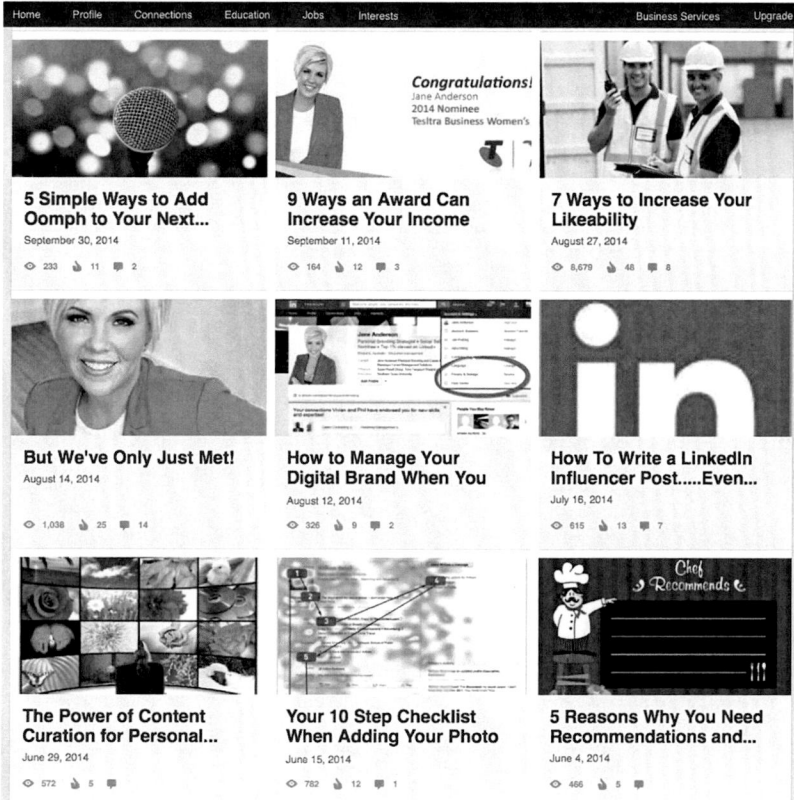

- **500+ Connections:** Having a large number of connections doesn't mean you're selling a lot. Yes, it may mean you turn up in search results, but the first question you need to ask is: "Is this in line with the goals I'm trying to achieve?" If not, then you need to make sure you're building the right tribe!

- **% viewed in your networks:** This measurement is based on the words in your profile and the connections you have. In other words, you could rank highly if you have a high number of keywords but a low number of people in your network use the same keywords. You could also have a low rank if you have a lot of connections in the industry who use the same keywords. It pays to regularly check your Boolean search, rather than be overly concerned about this score.

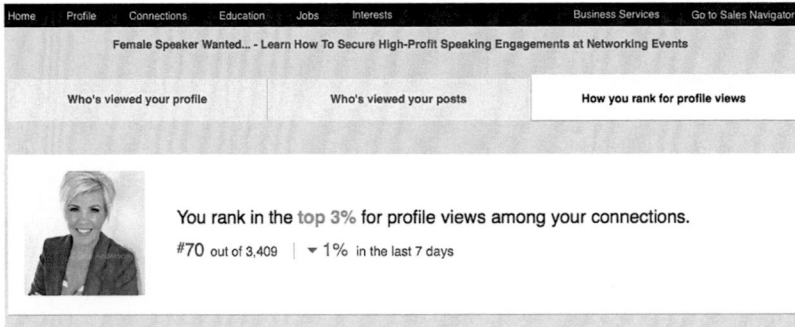

- **Connections:** The amount of connections you have certainly increases the amount of search results you're in. However, if you're connecting with everyone and not personalising the experience for them, it can seem a bit "smash and grab". Taking the time to personalise your connections takes extra effort, but it does pay off.

Overall, your metrics need to move potential clients into your sales meetings. If you focus on likes and comments, then you're not encouraging them to become clients.

Reflections and Actions

- Test your search engine optimisation by undertaking a Boolean search. Make any changes to keywords.
- Update your profile to create your "first four seconds".
- Personalise your interactions.
- Share your thinking through posts and curation.

Chapter 9

LinkedIn Groups

By now, you may be aware that LinkedIn offers you to be a member of a group. In fact, you can be a member of up to 50 groups. There are thousands of different groups. Some are closed groups, where you need to be approved by the manager of the group. Others are open groups, which means anyone can join.

The purpose of groups is to connect you with others who are like-minded or in the same industry as you. It's where your customers hang out.

Some of the most common questions we are asked by clients relate to being a member of and running a group.

Benefits of Being in a Group

- It expands your ability to be returned in search results. You will turn up in someone's search result if you're a first, second, third-level connection, and also if you're in the same group.
- It allows you to contribute to discussions and share your area of expertise.
- It can give you a direct line of communication with your ideal audience.
- Your contribution to the group sends a clear message to connections about your expertise, interests and passions.
- A group can help you find people in your local area with similar interests to you, particularly if it's a location-based group. This is especially helpful if you are new to your region.
- It increases your profile views. This is achieved by increasing your search results and people's curiosity when they see you making comments in the group.
- Groups build your knowledge and expertise.

Disadvantages of Being in a Group

- You receive updates in your inbox daily or weekly, summarising what has been happening in the group. If you're a member of 50 groups, this means a lot of email landing in your inbox.
- It may mean people pigeonhole you based on their perception of the group.

- There is limited ability to include personal branding in responses. You cannot include the same level of formatting that you can in a personal email, such as hyperlinks and a signature block, for example.

Benefits of Running a Group

- It positions you as a leader in the industry and you effectively become the "go-to person". It also allows you to include your website address in the group description.
- You have access to a responsive audience. A group owner has influence in the group and can direct the group's direction.
- It gives you visibility across your areas of expertise, and you are the "first to hear" what's happening.
- When a member joins a group, the group details and logo will be displayed on their profile. This increases the group's visibility.

Disadvantages of Running a Group

- It can be incredibly time consuming. However, there are features that can reduce this. These include an automated welcome message to new members, and the ability to create sub-groups that allow easier targeting.
- Once you start a group, you cannot close it so you need to be committed!
- There is limited analytics and return on investment data. It is hard to gain a tangible measure of running a group.

Running a group might be helpful for you when you have a community of like-minded people who are open to sharing. It would not be helpful if the group has a high potential for conflict and negative engagement.

Top Tips for Starting a Group

- Have a clear purpose for the group.
- Complete all the required fields and ensure all members know the group's guidelines and expectations. Setting clear expectations will help you manage a situation where a member does not comply.
- Make sure members know what to expect from you. For example, will you be checking in daily or weekly? You could consider co-managing the group to reduce the workload. Expectations management is key.
- Use the automation features to reduce manual workload.
- Maintain engagement by contributing topics for discussion and providing positive feedback to All-Star group members.

How to Start a Group

When you are logged into your profile:

1. Under Interests, click Groups.

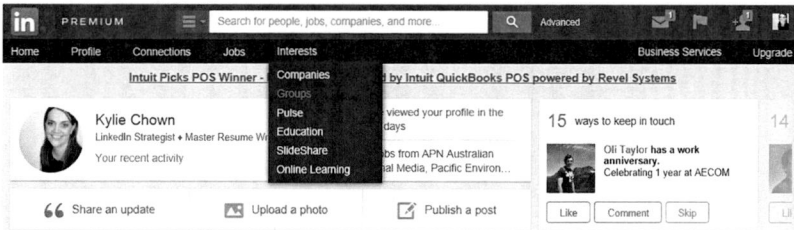

2. Click Create A Group.

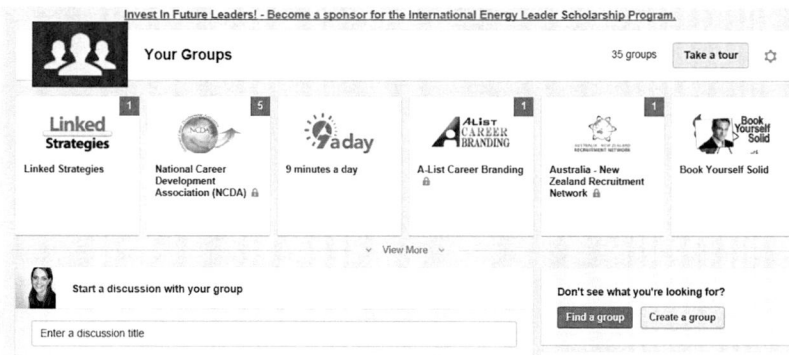

Logo: Your logo will appear in the Groups Directory and on your group pages.

[Browse...]

Note: PNG, JPEG, or GIF only; max size 100 KB

☐ *I acknowledge and agree that the logo/image I am uploading does not infringe upon any third party copyrights, trademarks, or other proprietary rights or otherwise violate the User Agreement.

* Group Name: [   ]

Note: "LinkedIn" is not allowed to be used in your group name.

* Group Type: [Choose...   ▾]

* Summary: Enter a brief description about your group and its purpose. Your summary about this group will appear in the Groups Directory.

[   ]

* Description: Your full description of this group will appear on your group pages.

[   ]

Website: [   ]

* Group Owner Email: [contact@kyliechown.com.au]

* Access: ○ Auto-Join: Any LinkedIn member may join this group without requiring approval from a manager.
          ● Request to Join: Users must request to join this group and be approved by a manager.

☑ Display this group in the Groups Directory.
☑ Allow members to display the logo on their profiles. Also, send your connections a Network Update that you have created this group.
☐ Allow members to invite others to join this group.
Pre-approve members with the following email domain(s):

[   ]

Language: [English   ▾]

Location: ☐ This group is based in a single geographic location.

* Agreement: ☐ Check to confirm you have read and accept the Terms of Service.

Discussions in LinkedIn groups can either be open to the world to see and share, or restricted to members only.   [Learn About Open Groups]

[Create an Open Group] [Create a Members-Only Group] or Cancel

* Indicated a required field

Reflections and Actions

- Does your ideal customer hang out on LinkedIn?
- What value will the group give to members?
- What will a group allow you to do that a standard profile doesn't?

Chapter 10

Company Pages

Basketball legend Michael Jordan once said: "Talent wins games, but teamwork and intelligence win championships."

Kylie recently worked with a client who was setting up her own business. The client wanted to set up both a personal profile and a company page, and asked what she should do first.

Your personal LinkedIn profile is an extension of your personal network and brand. It's a way for you to connect on a personal level online. A business page is slightly different. While personal profiles have connections, company pages have followers.

Simply wanting people to follow your business instead of connecting with you is counter-productive when networking and growing your business. People want to connect with you because you're you. It's similar to when you're at an event – you introduce yourself as you, not your company.

However, LinkedIn research indicates that members are 50% more likely to purchase from a company they engage with on LinkedIn. Furthermore, nearly 80% of LinkedIn members want to connect with companies in their lives. In other words, members aren't looking for once-off help. They want to connect and partner for the longer term. Your business page and personal page allow this to happen.

Benefits of Having a Company Page

- Elevates the quality of talent applying for a role. Potential employees will review your company page, so make sure it reflects your organisational values.
- Leverage company visual branding by including images and logos. A company page is also a great place to share videos.
- Add specific products and services and launch new products and services.
- Share updates and provide a collection of information team members can easily share within their own personal networks. This allows the company to engage with followers.
- Can be used when individuals link their personal profile to the company in their Employment History. The logo and correct name is on their own profile.

- Allows you to plugin to other media. This means you can link your LinkedIn company page to the company website and add a follow button to other websites.
- Supports paid advertising as being able to be defined as a precise audience.
- Provides analytics and data.
- Supports SEO by including keywords.
- You can drive traffic to your LinkedIn company page by including a follow button on your company website.
- Provides a way for your competitors to follow your business rather than you sharing your content and connections with them and putting your business at risk.

Some Disadvantages Include

- Needs an allocated page manager with a process in place for hand-over if the person leaves the organisation.
- Ongoing maintenance is required to ensure relevance.

An important point to note is that if you attempt to set up a company as a personal profile, your profile will be removed by LinkedIn. This means you lose all your connections and will have to start all over again, as LinkedIn ultimately owns your connections, not you. So don't risk it!

To Add a Company Page

1. Click over Interests and select Companies.
2. Click Create in the Create a Company Page box.
3. Enter your company's official name and your work email address.
4. Click Continue and enter your company information.

Companies Home   Following (7)   Add a Company   FAQ

Add a Company

Company Pages offer public information about each company on LinkedIn. To add a Company Page, please enter the company name and your email address at this company. Only current employees are eligible to create a Company Page.

Company name:

Your email address at company:

☐ I verify that I am the official representative of this company and have the right to act on behalf of my company in the creation of this page.

[Continue] or Cancel

You do have the ability to see who is following your page if you wish:

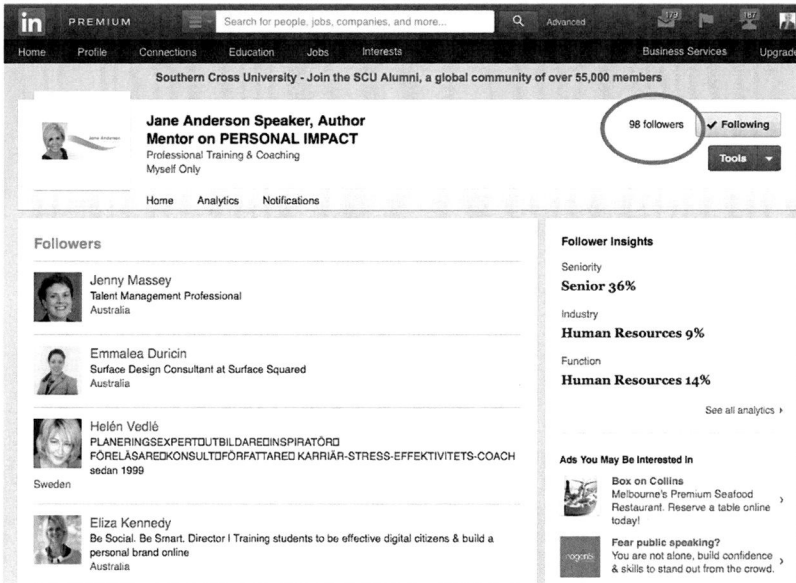

Reflections and Actions

- Do I not want people connecting with me and often due to my position? (i.e. if you're the CEO)
- Do I have a team of experts that differentiate our business and can contribute their thought leadership on a business page?
- Am I growing the business and recruiting in the future, or do I currently have positions advertised on other websites?
- Do I plan to run ads on LinkedIn?
- Do I have competitors who could be looking to capitalise on my network?
- Do I have the resources to manage both pages?

CONNECT: Leverage Your LinkedIn Profile for Business Growth and Lead Generation

Chapter 11

FAQs and Resources

Should I Have a Premium Account?

Like anything that offers a free and paid version, the product will generally develop to support paid users. Paid LinkedIn accounts offer advantages in how you present on LinkedIn and what you can find.

From our experience, LinkedIn has become less generous with the features of a basic account. It has taken some features that were basic and put them in premium. The main difference you'll find is the amount of InMails you can use. If you have a free account, you may notice you can't connect with someone without approaching them with an InMail, in which case you pay once-off fee. If you can do everything you need to, a free account is great. Our suggestion is to use that.

As of July 2015, the accounts included:

Basic (Free) Account

A basic account is for anyone who wants to create and maintain a professional profile online. You can:

1. Build your professional identity on the web.
2. Build and maintain a large, trusted professional network.
3. Find and reconnect with colleagues and classmates.
4. Request and provide recommendations.
5. Request up to five introductions at a time.
6. Search for and view profiles of other LinkedIn members.
7. Receive unlimited InMail messages.
8. View 100 results per search.
9. Save up to three searches and get weekly alerts on those searches.

Premium Accounts

LinkedIn offers premium account options for job seekers, sales and talent professionals, as well as general professionals who want to get more out of LinkedIn. If you have a free account and want to upgrade, you can compare the account types described below.

1. Land your dream job with **Job Seeker**.
2. Unlock sales opportunities with **Sales Navigator**.
3. Find and hire talent with **Recruiter Lite**.
4. Power your professional life with **Business Plus**.

Top Tip: From time to time, LinkedIn may offer you a trial of a paid account. This is a great opportunity to test an account and see if it is for you.

Can I Get Some Efficiency With Outlook to Manage LinkedIn?

If you are getting digests and feeds from LinkedIn, you can manage them with rules. To do this in Microsoft Outlook:

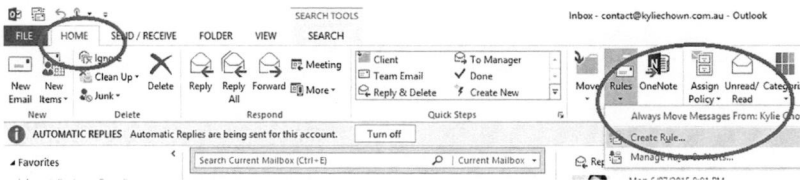

1. Make sure you are on the home tab. Click Rules. Create Rule.

2. Click Advanced Options.

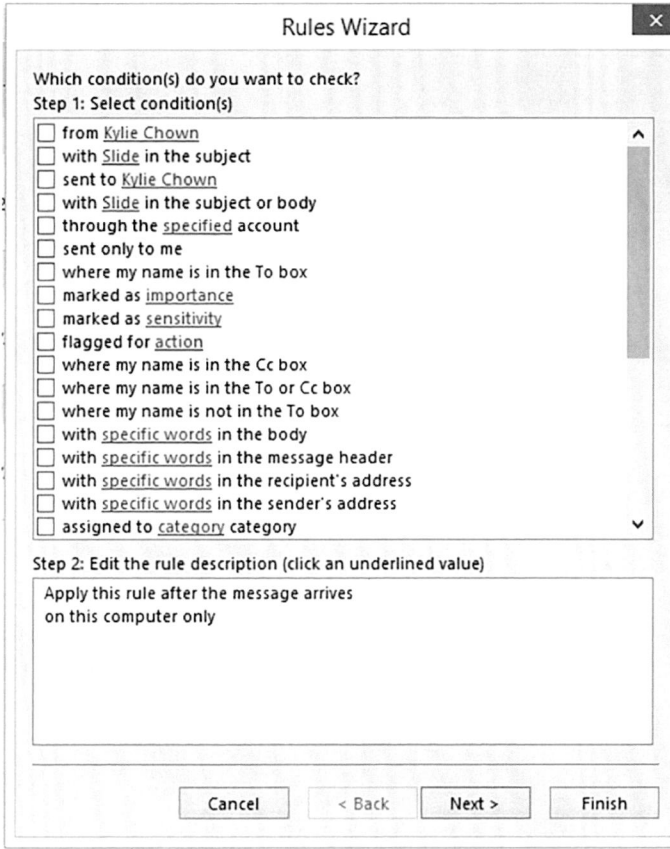

Rules Wizard ✕

Which condition(s) do you want to check?
Step 1: Select condition(s)

- [ ] from <u>Kylie Chown</u>
- [ ] with <u>Slide</u> in the subject
- [ ] sent to <u>Kylie Chown</u>
- [ ] with <u>Slide</u> in the subject or body
- [ ] through the <u>specified</u> account
- [ ] sent only to me
- [ ] where my name is in the To box
- [ ] marked as <u>importance</u>
- [ ] marked as <u>sensitivity</u>
- [ ] flagged for <u>action</u>
- [ ] where my name is in the Cc box
- [ ] where my name is in the To or Cc box
- [ ] where my name is not in the To box
- [ ] with <u>specific words</u> in the body
- [ ] with <u>specific words</u> in the message header
- [ ] with <u>specific words</u> in the recipient's address
- [ ] with <u>specific words</u> in the sender's address
- [ ] assigned to <u>category</u> category

Step 2: Edit the rule description (click an underlined value)

Apply this rule after the message arrives
on this computer only

[Cancel] [< Back] [Next >] [Finish]

3. Select your criteria options.

What About Profile Maintenance?

Your LinkedIn profile is not static and can be updated to align with your current goals and objectives. Updates can include:

- Any changes to your client testimonials.
- A review of your plans and goals each quarter. When you're business planning, look at what your goals are for the next 12 months and then what your goals are for the next 90 days.
- Adding or changing your plug-ins.
- Adding projects and moving them up in the profile.

If you are a thought leader, you can align your profile around your current cluster and business owners can align their profile around their 30/60/90-day plans.

How Long Do I Need to Spend on LinkedIn to See a Result?

Apart from your initial set up and strategy planning, you should be able to manage your LinkedIn profile in seven minutes a day.

Some things you can do in seven minutes include:

- Review curated content and share.
- Like a post and make a comment.
- Search and connect with your ideal audience.
- Facilitate an introduction via a connection.
- Export your connections.
- Write scripts.
- Make a list of people to contact.

Or you can combine your seven minutes into a weekly allocation of 35 minutes and:

- Write a blog post.
- Create a comprehensive strategy with a targeted outcome.
- Compile new scripts and communication structures.

I Am a Business. Who Owns My Team Members' Profiles?

A LinkedIn profile is owned by the specific staff member. This includes the content, connections and headshot. Companies and businesses may consider their social media policy and seek their own independent, legal advice.

How Do I Get My Team to Engage on LinkedIn?

In our experience, there are a number of strategies that can be used to maximise engagement. Resistance from team members can be presented in a number of ways that include: "I don't: have time for this / know how to do this / want to look silly."

To address your team's concerns, focus on the following areas:

Education: Educating team members on the benefit and value of LinkedIn will help them overcome their fear. If you can show your team how LinkedIn can make their job easier, they will be more likely to support the initiative.

Technical support: Providing the team with content to share and strategies to support the development of their own content is beneficial. This may include an internal champion who provides team members with advice when required.

Incentivise: Collaborating in a team environment supports a group approach and an "everyone else" is doing it mentality. Successful businesses have made LinkedIn management a key performance indicator or criteria for internal awards. Ongoing positive reinforcement will further support All-Star users.

In our experience, not everyone may be willing to jump in, but once they see the rewards LinkedIn offers, they will be more likely to get involved.

How Do I Know it is Working? What is the ROI?

There are a couple of measures you can use to gauge the success of your LinkedIn strategy. If your profile is effective, you should see an increase in the quality of connection requests you receive.

Additional measures include:

- Who has viewed your profile and are they your ideal audience?
- What action was taken by people who looked at your profile?
- How did they find you?
- What changes are there in LinkedIn search results and Google search results?

How Do I Export My Contacts ?

Depending on your role, we advise clients to export their contacts every 30-90 days.

To export your contacts:

1. Move your cursor over Connections at the top of your home page and select Keep in Touch.

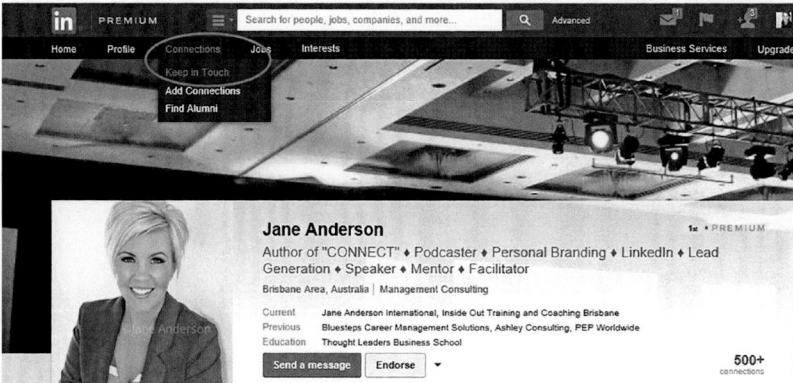

2. Click the Settings icon near the top right to reach the Contact Settings page.

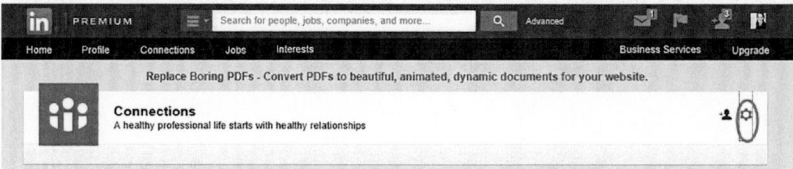

3. Under Advanced Settings on the right, click Export LinkedIn Connections.

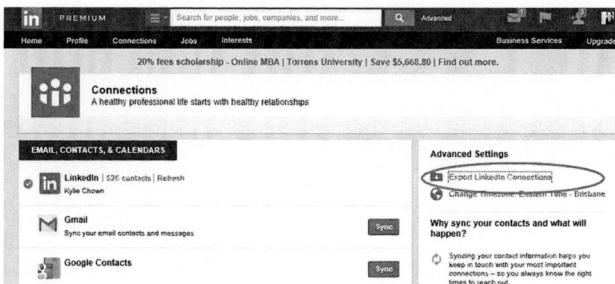

4. Enter the security verification text if prompted and click Continue.
5. Click Export.
6. Save the file where you can easily find it, such as on your computer's desktop.

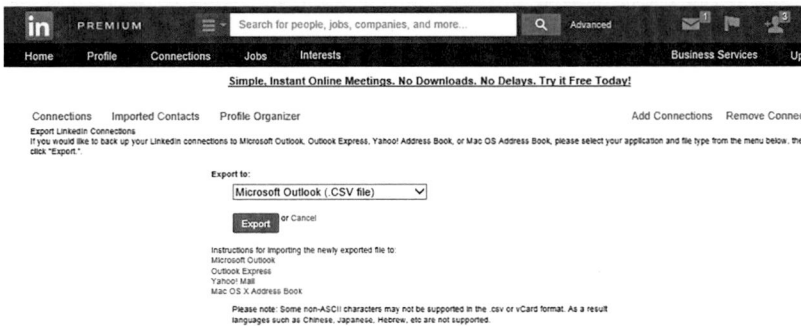

7. Open the file and print (optional).

By choosing Outlook, a file will be exported in a format that can be opened in Excel.

Should I Connect With Everyone?

It depends on what your goal is with LinkedIn. By having a goal, you can decide who you will connect with. For example, if you want to develop your network, you might be more open to accepting requests than if you are just starting out.

What Happens if Someone Connects With Me and I Don't Know Who They Are or Don't Want to Connect?

If you receive a connection request and you are not sure why, you can always send them a message, such as: "Thanks for requesting to connect. Generally, when people connect with me, it is because they would like assistance with ABC. Can you please let me know how you would like me to help?"

What Am I Missing if I Don't Set Up a LinkedIn Profile?

By actively investing your time in developing a quality LinkedIn profile, you take control of your account and mitigate the risk of others setting up a fake account under your name.

What if I Start a New Role?

You can easily add a new role under your employment history. To do this, once you are logged into your profile:

Experience

+ Add position

Add to Position: LinkedIn Profile Writer | Master Resume Writer | Executive Resun ▾

| http:// | | **or** | **Upload a file** |

Supported Providers

Continue Cancel

Company Name *

Title *

Location

Time Period *

Choose... ▾ Year – Choose... ▾ Year

☐ I currently work here

Description

See examples

Save Cancel

You can also upload your summary to capture the new direction.

How Do I Get a Banner?

This can be hard to get right as it's an awkward shape that runs around the header. If you are a thought leader, your banner is in a hero speaking shot. Books can be hard to position across the banner unless you create a mosaic or tiled effect. The banner has lots of "boom" factor for your first four seconds, so use it well! If in doubt, get assistance from a graphic designer.

1. Select +upload.
2. Select your image.
3. Select open.

How Do I Use a Hashtag?

A hashtag enables you to search for information about a specific topic. It looks like this: #.

If I wanted to hashtag the word LinkedIn, it would look like this: #LinkedIn. If something has a hashtag, it is essentially searchable as a topic. Some guidelines for hashtags include:

- Don't include spaces.
- You can include numbers, but not punctuation.
- Use relevant hashtags.

Is There Anything I Shouldn't Do on LinkedIn?

The main thing to remember is that LinkedIn is a public domain with the potential to be seen by anyone. As with all social media, only post content you would be happy for anyone to see.

How Do I Spot a Fake Account?

The signs of fake profiles are varied, but with a little work, you too can become an expert at spotting them. Some of the main points to look for include:

1. They may have a cartoon or a movie character name.
2. The information or profile is written in lower-case letters
3. They often have a career history that doesn't make much sense.
4. Often, the information on their profile is sparse and they seldom have any recommendations or LinkedIn applications. There is usually a lack of education or employment history.
5. Photos can look suspect or may be stock images.

Why Do People Set Up Fake LinkedIn Profiles?

The main culprits of fake profiles are spammers. Their intention is to get hold of your email address and the email addresses of everyone you are connected to. When this is achieved, your inbox will be inundated with annoying spam.

In addition to spammers, there are groups that simply want to capture your name for list building. This means your email address will be misused in different ways, from event promotions to porn sites.

Finally, there are also people who just want to find out more about you. Not because they like the look of your profile picture, but because they are interested in your personal content – all of it. Especially the stuff that is only visible to the people you are connected to.

How Do I Protect My LinkedIn Profile?

Always review your connection requests before accepting and take a few minutes to check their profile details.

If something doesn't feel right, don't accept the request. Look for all the red flags highlighted above. Another option is to reply to them using the LinkedIn user agreement and state: "I generally only connect with people I know. Can you tell me why you want to connect and what you hope to achieve?" If you don't get a response, ignore them.

LinkedIn does provide a remedy for spammers in the form of a flag button that will report a profile as spam. If enough people flag a profile, the site administrators will review it and if they determine it is spam, the user's account will be suspended.

How Do I Control the Settings?

There are a number of ways you can protect your information. Once you are logged into your account, click Privacy and Settings.

There are a number of primary options here. These include: select who can see your activity feed; see what others see when you have viewed their profile; and manage who you're blocking.

I Am a Consultant/Expert. How Can LinkedIn Help Me?

Forbes recently reported: "By 2020, freelancers will make up 50% of the USA labour force."

We are working with an increasing number of start-up solopreneurs and consultants who are setting up a LinkedIn profile as their number-one step to setting up their business – even before creating a website. LinkedIn is like a whole marketing machine in one place, and you have your blog and database at your fingertips. Setting up a LinkedIn profile is cheap and fast. Consultants can hit the ground running and access their ideal buyers in corporate markets more easily.

I Am a Teacher. How Can LinkedIn Help Me?

Why should teachers be on LinkedIn? In essence, they are brand ambassadors for their school. Kylie recently worked with a school principal who was hesitant to get on LinkedIn, but once Kylie explained that the client's profile was about her school, not her, the client was much more open to engaging on LinkedIn. Ways LinkedIn can help teachers include:

- For school leaders, having their school values in their profile means that prospective students' families that align with these values will be drawn to the school.
- Supports networking and professional development opportunities and allows teachers to develop a collaborative network.
- Validates Google search results and positions teachers as experts in their field.
- Allows the school to celebrate and communicate achievements in a professional manner. We know that LinkedIn is a tool for journalists, so by sharing information on LinkedIn, schools can potentially experience positive media coverage.

Useful Websites

For Finding Keywords: Google Keyword Planner

https://adwords.google.com/KeywordPlanner

Keyword Planner is like a workshop for building new search network campaigns or expanding existing ones. You can search for keyword and ad group ideas, get historical statistics, see how a list of keywords might perform and even create a new keyword list by multiplying several lists of keywords together. A free AdWords tool, Keyword Planner can also help you choose competitive bids and budgets to use with your campaigns.

Top Tip: Even though this is developed for Google AdWords, it is a great research tool for LinkedIn.

For LinkedIn Help: LinkedIn Help Center

https://help.linkedin.com/

Need help using LinkedIn? The LinkedIn Help Center helps you find answers to your questions.

LinkedIn Premium

premium.linkedin.com

For Information on LinkedIn Groups: LinkedIn Group Directory

http://www.linkedin.com/directory/groups

For Different Bullets: Miscellaneous Symbols

http://en.wikipedia.org/wiki/Miscellaneous_Symbols

This is a Unicode block (U+2600–U+26FF) containing glyphs representing concepts from a variety of categories, including astrological, astronomical, chess, dice, musical notation, political symbols, recycling, religious symbols, trigrams, warning signs and weather, among others.

For the CONNECT LinkedIn Group

https://www.linkedin.com/grp/home?gid=7015440

For More Information on Jane Anderson

www.jane-anderson.com

For More Information on Kylie Chown

www.kyliechown.com

Want More Help?

Jane Anderson

Jane is a speaker, author and mentor who works with thought leaders and organisations to help them grow by leveraging their talent and having more impact in their communications. She is a sought-after keynote speaker and contributes regularly to a variety of media publications. Jane holds a Bachelor of Business in Marketing and believes that people buy from people. She has worked as a business consultant and in senior management roles in sales and learning and development.

Some of the areas she can assist your business with include:

- Speaking at conferences and events
- LinkedIn sales strategy for organisations
- Personal branding mentoring
- High-impact presentations

Jane's other publications include:

- **IMPACT:** How to Build Your Personal Brand for the Connection Economy, available on Amazon.com.
- **Understanding Y:** co-authored with Charlie Caruso, published by Wiley. Available on Amazon.com and all other online retail book stores.

She can be found at www.jane-anderson.com

"Jane Anderson is the go-to expert for building your personal brand and with CONNECT, she helps leaders and business owners transform their relationship with LinkedIn from one of awkward and confusing social platform into that of powerful business-building ally."
– Dan Gregory, CEO The Impossible Institute

Kylie Chown

Kylie Chown has been writing LinkedIn profiles and other personally branded communications for consultants, thought leaders and executives for more than 10 years. She works with people so that they have more choice in their businesses and careers. Kylie works with individuals, consultants and business and can assist you with:

- LinkedIn profile development
- LinkedIn coaching
- Resume writing for executives
- Job search strategy and coaching

Kylie has been featured in Australian Institute of Management (AIM), Franchise Business, HRM America and Leaders in Heels.

She is currently one of eight Certified Master Writers in Australia and one of three Reach Certified Branding Analysts.

She can be found at www.kyliechown.com

"Kylie helped me to understand the complexity of LinkedIn profile development, from developing a SEO strategy to having a profile that positions me and the business in a way that supports our future goals. This combined with the coaching means that I can now leverage LinkedIn to represent and support the business in a proactive manner."
– David McDonald, Chief Executive Officer

The Tao of
UFO

The Tao of
UFO

The Tao Te Ching and The Integral Way-
The Pathway to ET/NHI Contact through
Universal Self-cultivation, and a New Paradigm
for Leadership and Governance in a
Post-disclosure, Post-ET/NHI Contact World

N. MICHAEL MURBURG, JR.

PALMETTO

P U B L I S H I N G

Charleston, SC

www.PalmettoPublishing.com

THE TAO OF UFO

Part 1. THE TAO TE CHING

THE TAO TE CHING and The Integral Way: The Pathway to Universal Self-cultivation and the New Paradigm for Leadership and Governance in a Post-disclosure, Post-ET/NHI Contact World

Hardcover ISBN: 979-8-8229-4952-2
Paperback ISBN: 979-8-8229-4953-9
eBook ISBN: 979-8-8229-4954-6

The reality of the world today is that grounding ethics in religion is no longer adequate. This is why I am increasingly convinced that the time has come to find a way of thinking about spirituality and ethics beyond religion altogether."
~ Dalai Lama XIV

"只要有一種道並且願意體現它，那麼整體之道就會繼續被傳授；今天這些捲軸上所寫的內容將以不同的形式在未來的許多世代中重新出現."

"The Integral Way will continue to be taught for so long as there is a Tao and one who wishes to embody it. What is written today in these scrolls will reappear in differing forms in the many generations to come." (P. 7) The Hua Hu Ching, translation by Brian Browne Walker, The Hua Hu Ching, The Unknown Teachings of Lao Tzu, Harper San Francisco, a division of Harpers Collins Publishers, Copyright 1992, brianbrownewalker.com

TABLE OF CONTENTS

INTRODUCTION

What the Author offers here is the Tao as he has learned it and interpreted it through his association with the higher or "Universal Beings" of the Tao's realm. There are numerous other translations and interpretations of the Tao Te Ching and the Hua Hu Ching. They all have their merits. The Author encourages the reader to read the other publications, especially those of Hua Ching Ni and Stephen Mitchell in this regard. As B. B. Walker states, the teachings about the Tao will appear and reappear in this generation and in different generations to come. The words and languages may change but the message is a universal one and the truth of that message remains the polestar for all the higher and more advanced spiritual beings of the universe. That was the primary message from the Author's contact with his ET/NHI on October 3, 2015. There was more to the message but, for the purposes here, it will be the basis of further discussion later.

Suffice it to say that for the time being the so called "experts" in the field of UFO/UAP acknowledge that there is undoubtedly a spiritual component to ET/NHI contact and there is. None to date have been able to put their finger on it. The Tao Te Ching and Hua Hu Ching, probably the two most spiritual works ever written, are right there in front of them, but nobody seems to want to crack the code, so to speak. These books should help the reader to do so and help them to understand that ET/NHI contact is beyond the old physical-materialist paradigm of nuts n bolts Ufology. It is about the conscious spiritual nature of the universe and using heightened spiritual states to initiate contact with ET/NHI and to build a better physical, mental and spiritual world and universe as a consequence.

Heightened spiritual states and the conscious states that one enters during meditation and the palpable results obtained by remote viewers and CE-5 groups prove this almost without exception. The history of mankind's art from neolithic cave paintings through the Renaissance and up through today proves this as well. Part of the message of October 3, 2015, was that ET/NHI honors the Tao and they too follow it. They accept its constancy and applicability throughout all of creation and in all incarnation and reincarnations. They honor those who accept its peace and wisdom and who preach it. They honor the groups and places where the love, peace and compassion of the Tao and its message is shared.

The takeaway here is and should be that the Tao Te Ching, the written teachings of Lao Tzu and the Hua Hu Ching the written text of the oral teachings of Lao Tzu Lao contain the entire truth of the universe. They give us all a universal template by which we may live our lives in order to evolve spiritually.

These teachings are simple yet profound, and they offer a path to peace, virtue, abundance and more. Those who wish to know the whole truth must follow the Integral Way. By doing so, they will take joy in learning the path to enlightened being. They will find the rewards of doing the mental, physical and spiritual work. They will know the fulfillment that comes with their service to others. They will find the wisdom that comes to them as an integral part of their self-cultivation and spiritual purification in life. They will know and understand that the key to the universe and living beyond fear is to live outside of their egos. By doing so, those who follow and practice the Integral Way will become one with the Tao, the intelligent and divine source and creator of all things. They will not only experience its miraculous nature but become an embodiment of it. This is the ultimate reason for the study of the Tao Te Ching and the Hua Hu Ching and practicing the Integral Way. All the intelligent, peaceful life in the universe does. The benefits that flow from this are timeless, infinite and without limitation or number. The higher orders of being understand this. And that is why they revere the Tao and are followers of the Integral Way.

WHAT IS THE TAO?

There are innumerable ways people have come to describe the Tao and Lao Tzu's work the Tao Te Ching. Both the Tao and the Tao Te Ching are easily conflated. That is because both are integrally intertwined and inseparable from one another.

Lao Tzu teaches that once one sees the world and all of existence as energy they see and understand existence for what it is. The visionaries of both science and the study of consciousness have long concluded now that consciousness is the primary element upon which the "physical" world is based. We are therefore infinite beings of energy and frequency that are having the experience of an apparent physical world. However, the world is not actually physical. It only seems that way. For lack of a better explanation, the human mind is a hologram that attunes itself to the universal hologram that some have referred to as the "Absolute" *. This Absolute, which I will refer to as the "Tao" projects itself internally into us and interacts with all of our senses, making all reality in fact, a kind of internal hologram. The universe that is the "Absolute" or Tao is composed of intelligent interacting energy fields. Some are at rest and others are in motion. The Tao is, in and of itself one gigantic hologram of unbelievable complexity." It is "the conscious intelligent mind behind all reality". **

Like the Absolute described by Hegel*** and the CIA, or Planck the Nobel prize winning originator of the quantum theory of energy, the Tao is conscious energy in infinity, that is without boundaries. It occupies every dimension to include the time-space dimension in which we have our physical existence. However, we cannot perceive it as it is, only its synchronistic projections at times. The Tao is the infinite energy that is completely at rest in what Lao Tzu refers to as "non-being". The Tao's energy permeates everything and is responsible for everything. Lao Tzu refers to this as "being". The Tao is therefore both being and non-being, the infinite energy that is responsible for the entirety of existence and all creation. It is the ultimate reality and truth. The whole purpose of creation and evolution is the "Absolute", the Tao coming to know itself through all of its creation.

The Tao Te Ching is therefore more than just a path or "The Way" for us to achieve enlightenment. The Tao is meaning itself. It is the essential underlying reality of things. It is the natural order of the universe. It is the inexhaustible, infinite intelligent energy and timeless source of all compassion, physical provision and guidance. It is that which gives us courage, hope and wisdom, knowledge and love. It is that which bestows its spiritual resources, true power and grace on us. It is the universal source of intelligence. It is the field of consciousness and potential that permeates everything and transcends not only being and non-being but time, space and matter itself. It is the Interconnected consubstantial firmament in all things that connects all beings and states of being. It is the infinite field of potential that simultaneously encompasses the past, present and future. It is the spirit that guides us and animates our intuition and creates the humility that dissolves ego and disarms us of our unbridled intellectual arrogance.

The Tao is intelligent infinity. **** It is the logos, "The truth that extracts habitable order out of chaos".***** It is a multi-dimensional intelligent, spiritual, sovereign, immortal living organism, the eternal verity from which all compassion flows. It is the same divine Locus of consciousness for the universe and simultaneously, the divine consciousness of the individual. It is the ultimate basis for the divine sovereign individual. And finally, for the purpose of a good part of Lao Tzu's work, the Tao Te Ching is a work, that along with the Hua Hu Ching and its Integral Way tries to describe and direct its reader from the abyss of ego back to the Tao, by explaining a universal unifying system of ethics, morality, values and behavior. By doing this, the works of Lao Tzu are as profound as they are a timeless manual for universal leadership and guidance for all those higher-level beings who live, lead and govern within the higher orders of existence within the cosmos that is the Tao.

*See, <u>Analysis and Assessment of the Gateway Process</u>, Central Intelligence Agency (.gov)
https://www.cia.gov › document, page 8, et. seq., Publication Date: June 9, 1983, Analysis and Assessment of the Gateway Process, US Army released September 10, 2003
**Max Planck
***Hegel argued that the Absolute Spirit unfolds itself as history, which encompasses all natural, social, and historical events and phenomena. The Idea of the Absolute is the rational notion that in its reality the Absolute meets only with itself. It is by virtue of this immediacy of its objective identity that It is us and we are it. We are by this and any rational measure, ultimately Tao creating and experiencing its own world as itself. Or as Emerson explained it, "We are part and parcel of God,"
**** Ra, The Law of One 61:13, Carla Rueckert, Don Elkins and Jim McCarthy, Schiffer Publishing Limited, 1981
*****Professor Jordan B. Peterson, PhD

THE TAO TE CHING

Unveiling the History of the Tao Te Ching: Tracing the Origins and Impact of an Eastern Philosophical Masterpiece

The history of the Tao Te Ching is quite fascinating: The Tao Te Ching, attributed to the ancient Chinese philosopher Lao Tzu, has a rich and complex history, which encompasses its authorship, textual variations, and its profound influence on Eastern philosophy and spirituality. The Tao Te Ching, a collection of ancient Chinese philosophical and spiritual texts, remains one of the most influential and enduring works in Eastern thought. Written by the legendary figure Lao Tzu, this mystical masterpiece has captivated minds and hearts for over two millennia. In this essay, we will embark on a journey to explore the fascinating history of the Tao Te Ching, including its authorship, textual variations, and profound impact on Eastern philosophy and spirituality.

Authorship and Origin

The first mystery surrounding the Tao Te Ching lies in its authorship. Lao Tzu, meaning "Old Master," is traditionally credited as the sage who penned this profound compilation. While some scholars debate the historicity of Lao Tzu, attributing the text to a collective effort, the prevailing belief is that Lao Tzu indeed existed during the 6th century BCE. However, historical records on Lao Tzu remain scarce, veiling the life and identity of this enigmatic figure, adding an air of mysticism to the Tao Te Ching's origin.

Textual Variations and Interpretations

The Tao Te Ching, consisting of 81 concise and cryptic verses, has witnessed numerous translations and interpretations across time and cultures. These variations have resulted in diverse understandings of the text. One of the earliest translations was by the scholar Wang Bi during the 3rd century CE, bringing to light the yin-yang philosophy and the concept of Wu-wei (non-action). In later centuries, renowned thinkers such as Chuang Tzu and Confucius influenced interpretations, leaving their indelible marks on the text's meaning. Today, a multitude of translations continue to offer readers unique perspectives on the Tao Te Ching's wisdom.

Influence and Impact

The true significance of the Tao Te Ching lies in its profound impact on various realms of life. Initially, the text held central importance for rulers and administrators in ancient China, guiding them in governance and the art of leadership. Its principles, focusing on benevolence, humility, and natural harmony, provided a moral compass for just rule. As time passed, the teachings of the Tao Te Ching permeated other aspects of Chinese society, from the arts and literature to martial arts and medicine. Furthermore, the Tao Te Ching has transcended cultural boundaries, inspiring thinkers, poets, and spiritual seekers worldwide, who find solace and wisdom in its profound simplicity.

The Tao Te Ching significantly influenced rulership in China for many centuries after its initial composition. The exact duration of its impact on rulership is difficult to determine precisely, as the text's influence continued to evolve over time. However, it is believed that the Tao Te Ching had a lasting impact on political and philosophical thought in ancient China, particularly during the period of philosophical and intellectual flourishing known as the Warring States period (475-221 BCE).

During this era of political instability and conflict, rulers and administrators turned to the Tao Te Ching as a guide for governing their states. The text's emphasis on qualities such as benevolence, humility, and natural harmony provided a moral framework for rulership and informed notions of virtuous leadership. The concept of Wu-wei (non-action) outlined in the Tao Te Ching also influenced ideas of governance, advocating for leaders to act in accordance with the natural flow of events rather than forcibly imposing their will.

The teachings of the Tao Te Ching continued to shape governance and political philosophy in subsequent dynasties. The principles and insights found within the text remained relevant and resonated with subsequent rulers. However, as Chinese history unfolded and different dynasties rose and fell, the specific ways in which the Tao Te Ching influenced rulership may have varied or adapted to the needs and contexts of different periods.

The Tao Te Ching in more recent times did face restrictions and suppression during certain periods in Communist China during the twentieth century. The Chinese Communist Party, which came into power in 1949, aimed to establish a new societal structure and ideology based on Marxist principles. As part of this process, various aspects of traditional Chinese culture, including religious and philosophical texts, were scrutinized, and sometimes suppressed to align with the party's ideology and policies.

During the early years of Communist rule, many ancient texts, including the Tao Te Ching, were subject to scrutiny and censorship. The Communist Party viewed these texts as representing traditional, feudalistic values that were incongruent with their revolutionary aims. Many temples, religious institutions, and traditional practices, including the study and dissemination of texts like the Tao Te Ching, faced significant restrictions or outright prohibitions.

However, it's important to note that the extent of the suppression varied over time, and during different periods, the Chinese government's policies toward traditional culture, including Taoist texts like the Tao Te Ching, fluctuated. In later years, especially during the reform era initiated by Deng Xiaoping in the late 1970s, there was a relative loosening of restrictions on traditional culture and a renewed interest in preserving and studying it.

Today, the Tao Te Ching is available and widely read in China, both for its historical and philosophical significance. It continues to be recognized as a significant piece of literature and is regarded as an important source of wisdom and inspiration, although its status and interpretation in contemporary China may still be influenced by political and cultural factors.

Overall, though the specific timeframe of the Tao Te Ching's influence on rulership in China is challenging to pinpoint, its impact on political and philosophical thought endured for centuries, leaving a lasting legacy in the annals of Chinese history.

Conclusion

The history of the Tao Te Ching is a journey through time and human understanding. Its authorship remains shrouded in mystery, while textual variations and interpretations continue to shape its meaning. Nevertheless, its impact cannot be denied. The Tao Te Ching has left an indelible mark on Eastern philosophy and spirituality, guiding generations with its profound wisdom. As we delve into its rich history, we uncover not only the story of a literary masterpiece but also a testament to the enduring power of timeless wisdom.

THE RELATIONSHIP OF THE TAO TE CHING TO THE HUA HU CHING

The Tao Te Ching and the Hua Hu Ching are two distinct texts that are related in terms of their philosophical and spiritual themes. While they share some similarities, they are different works. The Tao Te Ching Informs and the Hua Hu Ching instructs. Arguably they are attributed to different authors.

The Tao Te Ching is a collection of 81 ancient Chinese philosophical texts traditionally attributed to the sage Lao Tzu. It is a foundational text of Taoism, exploring concepts such as the Tao (the Way), Te (virtue), and the principles of yin and yang. The Tao Te Ching offers guidance on how to live a harmonious, authentic, and balanced life, emphasizing the importance of simplicity, spontaneity, and non-action.

On the other hand, the Hua Hu Ching, attributed to the legendary Chinese philosopher and sage, Lao Tzu, is a lesser-known text that is often considered as an extension or companion to the Tao Te Ching. It consists of additional teachings and stories attributed to Lao Tzu. The Hua Hu Ching delves into topics such as spiritual cultivation, inner alchemy, and the attainment of immortality. It explores the nature of reality, the integration of the physical and spiritual aspects of the self, and the transcendent nature of human existence.

While both texts draw upon Taoist principles and teachings, the Hua Hu Ching expands upon and offers further insights into the concepts introduced in the Tao Te Ching. It can be seen as a complementary text that provides additional guidance and understanding for those interested in further exploring Taoist philosophy and spirituality.

It's important to note that there are various translations and interpretations of both the Tao Te Ching and the Hua Hu Ching, and different versions may exist. The authorship and history of the Tao Te Ching is still being debated. And so, it is also the case for the Hua Hu Ching which is also often attributed to Lao Tzu. The text of the Hua Hu Ching has come down to us largely through oral tradition. Two unrelated versions are claimed to exist, a partial manuscript discovered in the Mogao Caves, Dunhuang, in China and a modern English rendering from oral tradition, while some scholars believe the whole work to be a later work from the 4th century CE.

The authorship and history of the Tao Te Ching and the Hua Hu Ching therefore, are subjects of contentious debate, with evidence pointing to the texts originating from oral traditions and potentially later iterations rather than being solely attributed to Lao Tzu. Despite this, the Tao Te Ching and the Hua Hu Ching have captivated scholars and enthusiasts for centuries, their ancient wisdom and profound teachings resonating across translations, time and cultures. Though the authorship and history of these texts remain shrouded in mystery and debate, their message is quite clear if studied and contemplated long enough.

Lao Tzu may not be the sole author of these works. It is widely accepted by Taoist scholars that both the Tao Te Ching and the Hua Hu Ching could have been composed or compiled by multiple individuals and that later versions of the texts may have been influenced by different cultural, political, and philosophical contexts. Who or what the actual sources were for the writers could be anybody's guess. Inspiration can come from many sources. Descartes received his inspiration for the scientific method from an angel in a dream. The canonical gospels attributed to four evangelists of the New Testament were "inspired by God". None of the authors ever signed off on their works. Who is to say from whence the inspiration for any written word might come. There are higher worlds and conscious levels other than our own through which inspiration and the transfer of knowledge and information operates.

Much like the study of Sumerian, early Hebraic and the Christian texts comprising the New Testament and the recently discovered Gnostic Gospels, the debate surrounding the authorship and history of the Tao Te Ching and the Hua Hu Ching underscores the complexities of translating ancient texts and the challenges of tracing their ultimate origins with certainty. While Lao Tzu's influence on these works is undeniable, in order to gain a deeper appreciation for the richness and vitality of these texts, it is vital to consider the diverse sources, interpretations, and cultural contexts that have contributed to their enduring legacy and where that leaves us today at the advent of disclosure and the prospects of what is to be expected of us, and our societies by those peaceful and more highly advanced extraterrestrials and non-human intelligences.

The wisdom found in the Tao Te Ching and the Hua Hu Ching is indispensable to those who search for the ultimate and universal truth of existence. It is a necessary inquiry for all spiritually inclined individuals who seek to develop themselves, refine their physical, mental and spiritual energies and to assist to enlighten and to evolve our human societies past their limited brutal thinking and ready both themselves and the inhabitants of this planet for the inevitable and significant engagement with the ET/NHIs who wish to make contact and who have existed and evolved for eons prior to our own human existence.

Despite cries of of some as difficult to authenticate from original texts, I am reminded of the old saying I learned years ago in statutory interpretation that "The spirit giveth life just as certainly the word taketh away." - See 2 Corinthians 3:6 King James Version The teachings of Lao Tzu, (or in more modern times "Laozi") whether these attributable to one person or a school of others, offer valuable insights that have long served as sources of inspiration and contemplation, offering timeless wisdom that transcends generations, time and space.

After many readings of many of the texts from a number of authors, most notably Hua Ching Ni on 10/03/2015, Stephen Mitchell and Brian Browne Walker it becomes evident that the numerous collective teachings of the Tao Te Ching and the Hu Hua Ching form a coherent and complementary framework that resonates with the ever-changing nature of the world and the universe in which we live. The numerous translations of these ancient texts and the present one before the reader should be read as inspired timeless glimpses of universal truths and modes of thinking that require patience, exposure, and careful observation to fully grasp their profound implications.

By investing in the process of interpretation and reflection upon the Tao Te Ching and the Hua Hu Ching, we can gain valuable insights that enrich our perspectives and enhance our capacity for the critical thinking that that the prospects that ET/NHI contact entails. By embracing these teachings as modes of thinking that invite ongoing exploration and contemplation, especially into worlds beyond our own, we open ourselves up to a universe of possibilities where change, especially that brought on by the ever-growing reality of contact with ET and NHIs is not feared but embraced as a natural aspect of their and our existence. As we navigate the complexities of modern life in a post disclosure, post contact world let us heed the timeless advice of Lao Tzu and embark on a journey of self-discovery, growth, and enlightenment.

The universe is a very mutable place. As we consider the lessons brought to us through the Tao Te Chung, their validity can only lie in their being observable at work in the world that surrounds us. Because of the nature of an ever-changing universe, these teachings should not be interpreted as being fixed or absolute. When viewed as evolving and adaptable modes of thinking, whether attributable directly to Lao Tzu or not, the Tao Te Ching and the Hua Hu Ching can provide a deeper understanding not only of the infinite nature our own being, but the the dynamic nature of the world, the universe and beings that populate the dimensions and cosmos around us. Remember, finally that the only constant that Lao Tzu reminds us of is that of change. Consequently, it is through an open mind and our willingness to adapt and learn from the wisdom of the past, that we can ready ourselves for change and pave the way for a brighter and more harmonious future for ourselves and all others in the universe.

The Integral Way

Throughout this book and the Hua Hu Ching, the reader will encounter the term "Universal Way" used quite frequently. At the outset it would seem to be a good idea to describe it. The Integral Way is a term used to describe the path of self-cultivation. This term was first described by Nei Teh and is further developed and elucidated by Lao Tzu here in the Tao Te Ching and in his later attributed teachings in the Hua Hu Ching. These lessons have continued to be transmitted through the schools of the various branches of the study and integration of the Tao. As the reader will discover, the Integral Way is the means by which one may learn to live a positive life through self-discipline and the refinement and harmonization of one's energy so as to live in consonance with universal law and the natural order of the universe.

The term "Integral Way" describes the original self-cultivation tradition of Taoism. The idea of the "Integral Way" or "Universal Way" or path is outlined and fleshed out by Lao Tzu in both of his works; initially in the Tao Te Ching and later, to a greater extent here in the oral teachings attributed to him in the Hua Hu Ching. But what does the Integral Way really mean?

Something that is integral is very important or necessary. If you are an integral part of a team, it means that the team cannot function without you. An integral part is necessary to complete the whole. In this sense, to be integral is to be the essence of or to be essential. A machine without an essential part being integrated into the whole will not function properly, if at all.

The Integral Way is a spiritual path that guides us to lead a life of balance, health and harmony. It is "the secret to leading a positive life is to refine and harmonize one's energy so as to live in consonance with the order of the universe.". - Tao, the Subtle Universal Law and the Integral Way of Life by Hua-Ching Ni

Following the Integral Way involves acting spontaneously and effortlessly without forcing, appreciating the interconnected nature of all things. Following the Integral Way involves the interrelated concept of Wu Wei and learning how to use it. It is a guiding principle when it comes to letting go and allowing things to settle, to doing and not doing. The Integral way is a discipline. It is an education that involves learning about the universe and its nature and inhabitants, how to relate to them and how to refine our energies to evolve spiritually as responsible individuals and societies within a multiverse in which all things are connected. It is the path of living a life of truth and a means of seeing reality as it is. Above all the Integral Way is the study of the Tao and how it operates through our lives of simplicity and patience and living the Tao by giving and receiving universal unconditional indiscriminate love and compassion to everyone and everything. - NMM

An Introduction to the Essentials of Self-Cultivation within The Tao's Integral Way

Because this book is one of an introductory level, it should be treated as such. It is meant to introduce the reader to the subject matter that is the Tao Te Ching. Part of that introduction by necessity, should include some insight into the Tao's Integral Way and the practice of "Self-Cultivation" through which one may evolve toward mastery of their understanding and harnessing their use of the Tao. Because there is a profound relationship between the Tao Te Ching and the Hua Hu Ching, the concepts underlying the Integral Way are mentioned and further expounded upon along with the idea and practices of Self-Cultivation addressed and further fleshed out by Lao Tzu in his later work the Hua Hu Ching that is also translated as the "Scripture of Transforming the Barbarians." Knowing that, the reader will understand the inevitable drift and the principles and purpose behind both Lao Tzu's gifts, the Tao Te Ching and the Hua Hu Ching.

Self-cultivation is an ancient practice of those who follow the Integral Way. It holds the key to unlocking our true potential and attaining inner harmony. Self-cultivation offers us a transformative path towards a more balanced and fulfilling life. But what does self-cultivation mean? At its essence, self-cultivation is a process of learning and unlearning. It is how we learn to dissolve our egos and learn to evolve spiritually and to lighten and purify our energies. In a word, self-cultivation is how we learn to surrender ourselves to the Tao, the underlying infinite and intelligent conscious force that governs all existence.

The practice of Self Cultivation organizes itself around Simplicity, Patience, Compassion, Absolute Truth, Integrity, Mindfulness, Spontaneity, Harmony, Surrender, Grounding, Inner Sagehood, Transformation and Immortality. Though Self Cultivation is not the central purpose for reading the Tao Te Ching, these concepts are interwoven into its text. In the Hua

Hu Ching, Lao Tzu teaches these virtues in depth, including how to use Chi energy in both sexual and non-sexual singular, dual and angelic cultivations. For now, a brief introduction into the world of self-transformation through Self Cultivation and the Tao's Integral Way will have to suffice.

By surrendering to the Tao, we can break free from limitations and allow our simple, patient and compassionate true nature to flourish. Through aligning ourselves with the Tao, we align ourselves with the flowing consciousness of life, experiencing deeper connections with ourselves, the community, and the natural world. As we embrace these essential principles of Tao self-cultivation, we embark on a journey of self-discovery and personal growth, the transformative journey towards a greater understanding of the universe within and around us and a happier and more fulfilling and balanced and harmonious life.

Simplicity: Unveiling the Inner Path

Life often appears complex on the surface, filled with numerous responsibilities and distractions. However, Tao self-cultivation teaches us that true simplicity lies within. Simplicity lies in our embracing minimalism and simplifying our surroundings by decluttering and focusing on what truly brings value and joy. It also lies in getting rid of mental clutter and cultivating a minimalist mindset that frees the mind from excessive thoughts and distractions. By adopting simplicity as a way of living we unveil our own inner path.

Self-cultivation and the unveiling of our own inner path involves practicing simplicity in our daily lives. We do this by decluttering our physical space and getting rid of unnecessary belongings and organizing our living and working spaces. We simplify our lives through mindful consumption. This involves being intentional about what we bring into our lives, including material possessions, media consumption, and commitments.

By cultivating simplicity, we can reduce our stress and stop being overwhelmed. By simplifying our lives, we release the burden of constantly managing and juggling numerous responsibilities. With simplicity we foster clarity and focus. With fewer distractions and mental clutter, we can better concentrate on our goals and priorities and become more aware of the Tao and its natural flow. Within simplicity lies the key to the experience of true being.

Patience

There is a space between stimulus and response. Within that space lies our power to choose our response. Patience is how we can take a step back and formulate proper response. Learning patience is a primary part of the Tao's Integral Way. Patience helps us develop emotional maturity, wisdom, and résilience. Practicing patience develops our ability to handle challenges and setbacks with composure and perseverance. Patience with ourselves gives birth to self-acceptance. By embracing our imperfections and allowing ourselves the time and space for growth and development. By practicing patience in our daily lives we can embrace uncertainty and acknowledge that not everything is within our control. Being patient in the face of unknown outcomes improves our chances of positive outcomes just as impetuousness decreases them.

Patience nurtures our own personal growth. Recognizing that meaningful progress often takes time and effort, we learn patience by allowing ourselves to learn and evolve at a sustainable pace. It enhances our decision-making skills and enables us to carefully consider options, evaluate consequences, and make more informed choices. Finally, it helps us form deeper relationships. Patient individuals are more empathetic, understanding, and nurturing, fostering stronger connections with others. Within patience there is great power.

Compassion

To free others from their suffering is the nature of compassion. By developing empathy towards others, we can cultivate compassion and a genuine understanding and concern for the well-being and experiences of others. Through self-compassion we can extend the same understanding, kindness, and forgiveness to ourselves. By cultivating compassion in daily life we can engage in acts of kindness and make a conscious effort to help, support, and uplift others in various ways. We can become more compassionate by developing a non-judgmental attitude. By being compassionate we can better see the inherent humanity and inherent worth in all individuals, regardless of their circumstances or differences.

By cultivating our compassion, we create stronger connections. Compassion fosters empathy and understanding, leading to deeper and more meaningful relationships. Compassion enhances our overall well-being. By practicing compassion, we experience a sense of fulfillment, purpose, and joy, boosting our own mental and emotional well-being. Within compassion lies the true nature of the Tao.

Absolute Truth and Integrity: Cultivating Personal Virtue

The great power of self-cultivation is found through the practice of simplicity, patience and compassion but as the reader will discover in subsequent chapters of the Tao Te Ching and the Hua Hu Ching, the mystical gates to immortality cannot be opened without the practice of absolute truth. In the pursuit of personal growth and moral development, through the Integral Way and self-cultivation, absolute truth and the integrity that flows from it play pivotal roles.

The Tao embodies all truth. Any deviation from truth is a deviation from the Tao and its Integral Way. Consequently, absolute truth and integrity need to be cultivated by those who

follow the Integral way in order to cultivate their higher energies and spiritual being. It is through the practice of embracing
absolute truth and integrity that illuminates the significance
and process of cultivating personal virtue. By embracing the
values of absolute truth and integrity, individuals can cultivate
personal virtue, shaping their character and impacting the
world around them in profound ways.

We embrace absolute truth by living it. This requires us to
understand the nature of absolute truth and recognize the
importance of truth-seeking in our daily lives and to cultivate
absolute truth in practice. We do this by pursuing knowledge
and intellectual curiosity and honoring honesty and transparency in all aspects of life. The benefits of embracing absolute
truth are innumerable. Besides keeping us on the path of the
Integral Way, by living lives of integrity and virtue we expand
and accelerate our personal growth and self-awareness. We
build trust and foster authentic connections by aligning our
actions with our personal values and principles.

Recognizing the need for integrity is the foundation of virtuous living. We cultivate integrity by practicing self-reflection
and self-awareness and through our own self-discipline and
self-control. We practice integrity through accountability and
taking responsibility for our choices. Such cultivation results
in our building a securely anchored moral compass and in
the garnering of respect and inspiring others through ethical
behavior. This, in turn enhances our overall well-being and
contentment and contributes to a more virtuous, ethical and
harmonious society, world and universe around us.

Mindfulness

Though not specifically addressed in either the Tao Te Ching as such or mentioned in very terse fashion in the Hua He
Ching, Qigong and meditation, "emptying the mind" in the
words of Lao Tzu throughout the Tao Te Ching and Hua Hu

Ching form the pillars of Tao self-cultivation. These practices empower the expression of personal integrity, also known as innate spiritual virtue or "de," in our daily lives. Moreover, by studying ancient wisdom such as the I Ching, feng shui, Chinese astrology, and Chinese medicine to which Lao Tzu introduces us in the Hua Hu Ching enhances our understanding of the interconnectedness of all aspects of life. The integration of these practices and skills that best suit us become elemental parts of our personal Tao or "Way," allowing us to tap into our highest potential and align with the Great Tao. With absolute truth and the integrity that flows from it as our guiding principle, we navigate each moment with authenticity and honor, evolve and refine our spiritual being and realize our soul's highest destiny.

Spontaneity

Every soul has a dual longing. It yearns for two things: to fulfill its unique worldly destiny and to achieve a high spiritual destiny by consciously merging back into the Tao, its Original Spirit. However, it is essential to understand that destiny is not a fixed or predetermined path. Lao Tzu teaches that there is only the effortless, spontaneous unfolding of each moment, known as "Wu Wei." . In the context of Tao self-cultivation, both Wu Wei and spontaneity, going with the flow of Tao become guiding principles.

The Supreme Mystery known as (Wuji) that births the Life Force will always remain unknowable and unpredictable, even as we gradually merge with it and the vastness of the Tao. This central Mystery resides deep within our inner selves, constantly refreshing and revitalizing all aspects of life, instilling it with a sense of joy and spontaneity. Spontaneity allows us to experience the fresh, joyful, and ever-changing nature of existence, bringing us closer to the essence of the Tao and our true selves. Embracing spontaneity allows us to surrender to the rhythm of the Tao, opening ourselves up to the creative flow of the universe.

Spontaneity is a fundamental aspect of the Tao's Integral Way and Tao self-cultivation. It invites us to discard fixed plans and to 'go with the flow" embracing the natural rhythm of life. By living in alignment with the natural flow of the Tao, we can fulfill our worldly destiny while consciously merging with our Original Spirit, harmonizing our individual will with the cosmic will and bringing us closer to our ultimate spiritual destiny. By being patient and by letting go of attachments, expectations, and the need for rigid structure, we can allow for the organic unfolding of our true nature and be conscious of the Tao unfolding around us.

By releasing our efforts to control and manipulate outcomes, we can tap into the natural intelligence that resides within us. It is through spontaneity that we can live in harmony with the Tao, effortlessly navigating the currents of existence and embracing the ever-changing circumstances that life presents. Through spontaneity, we can harmonize our actions with the spontaneous movements of the Tao, participating fully in the dance of creation.

Surrender: The Prerequisite to Self-Expression

One of the foundations of Tao self-cultivation lies in the principle of surrender. By trusting and surrendering to the Life Force, also known as Chi or Qi Field, we pave the way for its effortless integration in our body and mind. Surrender allows us to tap into our highest levels of individual free will and creativity. Our ordinary ego-personality often struggles with separation, fragmentation, and dispersion of our soul essence. Negative thoughts, self-judgments, and rejection of our spiritual nature hinder our growth and lead to suffering. Through the Integral Way and self-cultivation, we learn to let go of the ego and its resistance and allow the Life Force to flow freely, enabling us to unfold our true selves.

Harmony: The Flowing Consciousness of Life

Harmony is an integral aspect of self-cultivation through the Integral Way. The Life Force, comprised of three streams of consciousness, namely Yin (negative-receptive-female), Yang (positive-creative-male), and Yuan (neutral-stabilizing-primordial), permeates all aspects of life. It is a dynamic and ever-flowing entity, embodying the essence of process. Practitioners of qigong, for example, learn to communicate with the Life Force, utilizing its language of subtle energy or chi. Through this practice, we harmonize the three currents of chi within ourselves, our community, and the universe. By understanding and appreciating the cycles of Yin-Yang and the natural phases of energy we can understand the connection between our inner thoughts, feelings, and perceptions, and the unfolding actions of the natural world.

Grounding: Merging the Physical and Spiritual

Being centered in life necessitates both physical and spiritual grounding, allowing us to navigate the complexities of existence with clarity and stability. A centered life requires the balance of our mind, body and spirit. In the study of Tao through self-cultivation, qigong and meditation play crucial roles in grounding our being. Qigong exercises and meditation practices fuse our mind, body and spirit, the great trinity, with a strong, grounded, and integrated whole. Qigong promotes optimum health by harmonizing our heart-mind and physical body. Meditation, on the other hand, is how we learn to experience pure being, the gateway to many natural and supernatural states. Its useful emptiness or "no mind" merges our personality and physical body with our soul or "ling." This holistic approach to enlightenment enables us to lead simple, truthful and compassionate ordinary lives of peaceful contentment and harmony while nurturing our continued enlightenment and spiritual refinement and growth.

Sexuality and Inner Mastery

Our sexual nature holds the potential for profound spiritual transformation. Naturally, the principles of Tao self-cultivation expand to include the transformative concept of a sagehood that includes understanding the connection between our volatile female and male sexual energies and the split between our Heaven-formless spirit and Earth-form sexually embodied aspect. By tapping into our sexual yin-yang energies and practicing the sexual techniques explained in the Hu Hua Ching, we can unlock the "alchemical" powers within us. The Master or Inner Sage represents the harmonious integration of our masculine and feminine energies, transcending the limitations of duality. It is through both this dual and single integration that we can fully express our unique individual will, while remaining connected to the expansive non-dual nature of existence. This integration of our sexual and spiritual selves gives birth to an Inner Sage that embodies our immortal non-dual Original Nature and allows us to commune in a very special way with each other and the divine energy that is the Tao.

Through the integration of our sexual and spiritual selves, a "third self" emerges – a special form of sexual Inner Sage. This Inner Sage manifests our immortal non-dual Original Nature, transcending the limitations of dualistic thinking. It embodies the essence of non-duality and simultaneously maintains a sexually polarized male or female body. This integration allows us to express our unique individual will while embracing the expansive non-dual energy, known as yuan chi. As one deepens their understanding and practice of the principles, they continue on a profound journey of self-discovery, spiritual growth, and harmonious alignment with the timeless and eternal Tao.

Transformation

The core spiritual practice of self-cultivation is comprised of meditative processes that Lao Tzu introduces us to in the Hua Hu Ching. Throughout the Hua Hu Ching Lao Tzu focuses on alchemical transformation. Its purpose is the speeding up of internal change. This meditative process combines elements of science and art, offering a heart-centered, systematic method to bridge the apparent split between spirit and matter within a single lifetime. Within every human being exists the mystical trinity of jing-chii-shen, which holds precise meaning in the teachings of Lao Tzu in the Hua Hu Ching. Through alchemical meditation, the transformations between sexual essence (jing), subtle breath (chii), and intelligence-spirit (shen) are accelerated, facilitating the soul's greater freedom of expression.

Immortality

Lao Tzu's inner alchemy presents the Seven Alchemy Formulas for Eternal Life, which serve as a practical map for spiritually rebirthing the mortal self into a higher immortal consciousness that not only transcends physical death but brings to higher levels of spiritual existence that exist for those who are able to enter them. It is important to note that this quest for immortality is not for physical immortality. Instead, it is a journey towards achieving soul immortality, where enlightened souls hold enough integrity to consciously reincarnate in the higher realms where they are not encumbered by a physical existence. Spiritual immortality, therefore, goes beyond enlightenment and allows for the completion of the natural process of soul individuation in both our Lesser Self/personality, their cosmic Greater Self and ultimate reunification with the source of all creation, the Tao. It is the Tao's way of inviting and allowing the worthiest beings to participate in the ongoing creation of the divine multi-verse.

Conclusion

The principles of the Lao Tzu's Integral Way and path of self-cultivation encompass a wide range of transformative concepts, including simplicity, patience, compassion, surrender, harmony, grounding, absolute truth and integrity, mindfulness, transformation, immortality, spontaneity and even the often-overlooked realm of sexuality and its sagehood. By recognizing the power of self-cultivation and following the Integral Way we can embark on a great spiritual journey. This path, especially that leads toward our own conscious spiritual evolution, refinement and immortality requires dedication, discipline, and a deep understanding of the self, both on an individual level and as part of the larger cosmic whole.

Self-cultivation is an ongoing process that goes beyond mere personal growth in this lifetime. It is a path towards eternally aligning oneself with the profound forces of the Tao. Through the transformational disciplines as mentioned above, individuals can cultivate essential qualities that accelerate internal change and harmonize the energies that facilitate the transformation of our mortal self and the awakening of immortal consciousness, presenting a gateway to conscious spiritual immortality and a community of the highest spiritual beings in the universe.

By merging our inner and outer worlds, harmonizing our energies and aligning our actions with the principles of the Tao, we can transcend the boundaries of mortality and embark on a limitless voyage of self-discovery, contribution and unite ourselves with the other higher spiritual beings of the multiverse. In this way, spiritual immortality becomes a profound way to fulfill our purpose and engage in the ongoing dance of creation. It is through spiritual immortality that we can actively contribute to the ongoing process of creation, playing our part in the grand tapestry of our universal existence.

If nothing else, self-cultivation is a transformative journey that offers immense opportunities for personal growth, alignment with the Tao, and the activation of our highest potential. By embracing the Integral Way and self-cultivation we can embark on a path of self-realization, spiritual evolution and refinement. Through this journey, we unlock the vast potential within ourselves, attaining spiritual immortality, and realizing our interconnectedness with the divine fabric of existence — a profound contribution to the ongoing process of creation and connection with each other and the immortality of the divine Tao. Enough has been said; so, let us begin the journey.

"Peace will come to the hearts of men when they realize their oneness with the universe.»
~ Black Elk.

> "

CHAPTER 1

The Way: THE DARKNESS WITHIN DARKNESS

THE TAO OF WHICH ONE CAN SPEAK
IS NOT THE ETERNAL TAO.
THE NAME THAT ONE CAN NAME
IS NOT THE ETERNAL NAME.

THAT WHICH CANNOT BE NAMED
IS THE ETERNALLY REAL.
THE ORIGIN OF ALL PARTICULAR THINGS
LIES WITHIN THEIR NAMING.

ONE REALIZES THE MYSTERY
WHEN ONE IS FREE OF DESIRE.
ENSNARED BY DESIRE,
ONE SEES ONLY ITS MANIFESTATIONS.

HOWEVER, BOTH THE MANIFESTATION AND THE
MYSTERY
FROM THE SAME SOURCE ARISE.
DARKNESS IS WHAT THIS SOURCE IS CALLED.

TO ALL UNDERSTANDING,
THE GATEWAY LIES
IN THE DARKNESS WITHIN DARKNESS.

Exploring the Paradox of the Expression of the Eternal Tao
and The Call for Direct Eexperience and Non-conceptuel
Understanding

The essence of the study of the Tao lies within its profound
philosophical concepts, particularly the notion that "The Tao

31

that can be spoken is not the eternal Tao. The name that can be named is not the eternal name." This first statement implies that the true nature of the Tao is beyond verbal expression and intellectual comprehension. It can only be experienced and intuitively grasped through contemplation, unmediated by language or concepts.

Language and Naming have their imitations. Naming something gives little if any explanation about what is being named. The Tao therefore, is an ineffable concept: The Tao, in its infinite and transcendent nature, cannot be accurately represented through linguistic symbols. Naming something is actually a limitation of our understanding of what something actually is. To name or call somebody or something 'XYZ" actually confines or limits it. The act of naming brings limitations by confining the infinite Tao to finite linguistic constructs. *

This chapter introduces the reader to the "Paradox of Expression" and mere inadequacy of words especially when used as ontological of expressions of sincerely profound experiences: Words and concepts can only describe the Tao from a limited perspective and are wholly inadequate or unable to encapsulate its entirety. This brings us to the paradoxical nature of speaking about the Tao. By attempting to speak about the Tao, it becomes subject to the limitations of language, and loses its eternal essence.

So how is this Paradox of Expression to be reconciled so that one does not get quagmires in the language of inadequacy itself?

Implicit in the language of the statement "The Tao that can be spoken is not the eternal Tao. The name that can be named is not the eternal name.' Is the call to us for direct experience and the path of non-conceptual understanding, to understand with our hearts and not only our heads. The study of the Tao and the following of its path or "Integral Way" emphasizes the cultivation of direct experience and intuitive understanding through practices like meditation and mindfulness among others. ** By transcending language and conceptual thinking, one can access the unnamable essence of the eternal Tao.

The implications for our life and spiritual growth through direct experience of the Tao are immense. By accepting the limitations of language and the human mind and letting go of intellectual pursuit we can embrace the paradoxical nature of the eternal Tao and of life itself in its deepest meaning. In this passage and others Lao Tzu encourages individuals to shift their focus from intellectual understanding to experiential embodiment. and courageously facing the unknown. By recognizing the limitations of naming and language, one can embrace the mystery and the continuous exploration of the Tao.

In conclusion, the statement "The Tao that can be spoken is not the eternal Tao. The name that can be named is not the eternal name" serves as a powerful reminder to us of the limitations of language in expressing profound ontological and philosophical concepts such as the Tao and its and our own nature of being. The Integral Way calls on us to transcend conventional verbal expressions and embrace direct experience to grasp the essence of our own being and consubstantiation with the eternal Tao itself. By contemplating this paradox, we can free ourselves from the moorings and confines of language, embark on a transformative journey, and gain deeper insights into the nature of existence.

*The same can be said about the constructs imposed upon the unnamable divine through social, academic and religious constructs that come along with the names associated with the divinity that each attempt to name or describe.
**See., Hua Hu Ching, Chapter 55

CHAPTER 2

WHEN SOME THINGS ARE SEEN AS BEAUTIFUL,
THEN OTHER THINGS BEGIN TO BE VIEWED AS
UGLY.
WHEN PEOPLE SEE A NUMBER OF THINGS AS
GOOD,
THEN SOME OTHERS BECOME BAD.

NON-BEING CREATES BEING,
AND BEING CREATES NON-BEING.

LONG DEFINES SHORT,
AND SHORT DEFINES LONG.
HIGH DEPENDS ON LOW,
AND LOW DEPENDS ON HIGH.
AFTER FOLLOWS BEFORE,
AND BEFORE FOLLOWS AFTER.

THE MASTER ACTS THEREFORE, WITHOUT DO-
ING A THING.
WITHOUT SAYING A THING, THE MASTER TEA-
CHES.
THINGS ARISE AND THE MASTER ALLOWS THEM
TO COME.
THINGS DISAPPEAR AND THE MASTER LETS GO
OF THEM.

THE MASTER HAS, YET POSSESSES NOT.
THE MASTER ACTS BUT DOES NOT EXPECT.
WHEN THE MASTER'S WORK IS COMPLETED,
THE MASTER FORGETS IT.
THIS IS WHY FOREVER LASTS THE MASTER'S
WORK.

The Paradox of Creation and Destruction: Exploring the Profound Meaning of Lao Tzu's Philosophy

In this chapter, Lau Tzu encapsulates profound truths about the nature of existence and the interplay of opposites throughout the Tao Te Ching. At this point, one might best be served in this chapter by delving into Lao Tzu's philosophical insights and explore the paradoxical relationship between creation and destruction. Hopefully, this might help to inform the reader about the timeless wisdom of Lao Tzu and why his teachings continue to be relevant in our modern world and timelessly into the future.

Lao Tzu's teachings here demonstrate that when certain things are seen as beautiful, other things are, by comparison, deemed ugly. Similarly, when people perceive certain qualities as good, they tend to label others as bad. This dualistic perspective leads to a cycle of contrast and interdependence, illustrating that non-being (The unseen "Subtle Realm", the infinite and timeless, bodiless state of the Tao where nothing "nothing" exists but the creating Tao itself.) creates being, (the worldly universe of "Ten Thousand Things") and being creates non-being. The master, following the principles of this profound understanding, influences the world not through deliberate action, but by embracing detachment and allowing natural equilibrium to prevail.

The Duality of Beauty and Ugliness

Lao Tzu maintains that beauty and ugliness are inherently intertwined concepts. The perception of beauty arises only in comparison to ugliness, and vice versa. Without the existence of one, the other loses its meaning. This paradox encourages us to cultivate an appreciation for all aspects of life, recognizing the inherent beauty even in what appears ugly at first glance and that there is no difference between either the sacred or the profane.

The Dual Nature of Good and Bad

The Tao Te Ching emphasizes the significance of balance and harmony. Lao Tzu asserts that the labeling of certain qualities as good automatically implies the existence of qualities deemed bad. This juxtaposition encourages us to challenge rigid notions of good and bad, emphasizing the interconnectedness and fluidity of moral judgments. Change is eternal and what is good today may be bad tomorrow. By understanding the relativity of the concepts of good and bad, we can foster greater acceptance and empathy. This, in turn allows us to understand the inherent importance in our lives of patience and compassion, two of the four major tenets of the Tao's path to spiritual evolution and refinement, the Integral Way.

The Interplay of Creation and Destruction

Here, Lao Tzu also teaches us that non-being creates being and being creates non-being. This insight underscores the idea that every act of creation simultaneously necessitates the dissolution of something else. Just as long defines short and short defines long, the concept of creation cannot exist without the concept of destruction. Birth, death and rebirth is the universal law of the Tao. This profound understanding compels us to approach life with a sense of impermanence and embrace the infinite transformative power of change both internally in ourselves and externally in the universe.

The Master's Way of Non-Action

The master, in accordance with these principles, eschews forceful action and instead allows events to unfold naturally, By letting things take their natural course, and by refraining from excessive interference or manipulation, the master embodies the essence of the Tao. Through intentional non-action, "Wu Wei", the master teaches and influences others, paving the way for his and their own personal growth and self-discovery.

Detachment and the Art of Letting Go

Here, Lao Tzu teaches us the importance of detachment and the ability to let go of attachments. By relinquishing expectations and desires, the master harmonizes with the ever-changing flow of life. This pivotal teaching encourages individuals to cultivate a deep sense of tranquility and contentment, leading to a more fulfilling existence.

Ultimately, Lao Tzu's profound insights transcend time and continue to provide guidance in our contemporary world. The paradoxical nature of dualities, the interplay between creation and destruction, and the importance of embracing non-action and detachment are all valuable lessons that inform and inspire. By understanding and applying these principles, we can navigate the complexities of life with wisdom and find inner peace. And who doesn't want that? The master's work is timeless. It is universal and endures, unaffected by time, reminding us that forever lasts the master's work. All things considered, why not become such a master.

CHAPTER 3

The Tao Te Ching, The New Paradigm for Leadership and Governance on Earth in a Post-extraterrestrial Contact World

WHEN GREAT MEN ARE OVER-ESTEEMED,
POWERLESS DO THE PEOPLE BECOME.
IF POSSESSIONS ARE OVERVALUED,
THEN PEOPLE WILL STEAL.

THROUGH EMPTYING THE MINDS OF HIS PEOPLE,
BY FILLING THEIR OWN CORES,
BY MAKING THEIR AMBITION WEAK;
AND TOUGHENING THEIR RESOLVE
DOES THE MASTER TRULY LEAD.

THE MASTER HELPS OTHERS
TO FORGET ALL THEY KNOW,
AND GIVE UP ALL THAT THEY DESIRE.

IN THE ONES THAT THINK THEY KNOW,
THE MASTER CREATES CONFUSION.

THROUGH THE PRACTICE OF NON-DOING
IS EVERYTHING ALLOWED TO FALL INTO PLACE.

The Paradox of Power: Examining the Role of Great Men and Materialism in Society

Today, the influence of remarkable or charismatic individuals and the pursuit of material possessions often dominates our thoughts and actions. However, it is essential to consider the consequences that come with overestimating great men and overvaluing possessions. As human beings, we all need to recognize the potential dangers of these societal tendencies and highlight the importance of emptying our minds, reducing our ambitions, and embracing non-doing (Wu-Wei) in order to find true leadership and contentment.

When great men are over esteemed and possessions overvalued, the people become powerless, leading to a society plagued by theft and a lack of true leadership. However, by emptying the minds of individuals and allowing them the freedom to think and communicate and encouraging them to nurture their inner strength, and by encouraging patience and intentional restraint, a master can guide and help others forget their desires and lead them out of their attachment and mystery to genuine fulfillment.

The Pitfalls of Overestimating Great Men

The fascination and idolization of great men is a human mistake that can lead to power imbalances and a lack of individual empowerment. History has shown instances where overly idolized leaders became tyrannical, exploiting their positions for personal gain rather than serving the greater good. When people start to unquestioningly idolize individuals, critical thinking and self-reliance diminishes. The democratic processes that rely on these things suffer, and voices of dissent are silenced. Overestimating great men consequently undermines the collective power of the people, leading to powerlessness and a deterioration of society. Great men do not create great societies. Great societies produce great men.

The Consequences of Overvaluing Possessions

The rampant materialism and an obsession with possessions have a similar effect on society. When material wealth becomes the primary measure of success, people may resort to theft and deceit to obtain what they desire. The overvaluation of possessions also perpetuates a cycle of insatiable desire, as individuals seek a sense of worth and happiness through acquiring more material goods. Just like a junkie's fix and the inevitable development of an intolerance to the effect of morphine, this pursuit of possessions can be detrimental to personal relationships, well-being, and the overall social fabric.

The Power of Emptying Minds and Reducing Ambition

To counteract the negative effects of overestimating great men and overvaluing possessions, individuals must embrace the practice of emptying their minds and reducing ambition. By detaching from external influences and desires, one gains clarity and a greater sense of self. It is in this state of emptiness that individuals can channel their energy towards nurturing inner strength and cultivating wisdom. The master, through leading by example, fosters an environment where individuals can let go of their limitations, unlearn what they think they know, and open themselves to the new possibilities that a wide open universe offers them.

The Path of Non-Doing and True Leadership

Before going any further, it might be necessary to introduce the reader to the Concept of Wu Wei. "Non doing", the practice advocated by Lao Tzu of letting one's action follow the simple and spontaneous course of nature. One can only do so much before action becomes counterproductive. One needs to just plant the seeds and water them and late nature take its course. There is a time for every purpose. A time to act and a time not to act. Wu Wei is intentional non action rather than interfering with the harmonious working of universal law by imposing arbitrary and artificial forms. It is the doing or making nothing except in conformity to the Tao. It also includes the idea of keeping to a minimum governmental organization and regulation. This facet of Wu Wei, a central tenet of the Integral

Way will be further examined by Lao Tzu in the subsequent chapters of this book.

In light of this brief explanation then, true leadership, as espoused by ancient wisdom traditions, lies in the practice of non-doing. Non-doing does not mean inaction but emphasizes a shift in focus from external control and manipulation to internal alignment and natural flow. By embracing non-doing, individuals find a sense of ease and harmony within themselves and their environment, enabling effective decision-making and fostering authentic relationships. The master's role is to inspire others to let go, forget what they know, and embrace the freedom that comes with Wu Wei.

In conclusion, the overestimation of great men and the overvaluation of possessions have dire consequences for society. They lead to powerlessness, theft, a lack of true leadership and eventual societal collapse. However, by emptying our minds and reducing ambition, we can unlock our inner strength, accept our own personal responsibility for conducting ourselves and affairs in a truthful, honest and compassionate manner and allow for a more harmonious existence for ourselves and human society. True leadership emerges for those who study the Tao and by following its Integral Way. Part of this emergence follows from the practice of patience and non-doing, enabling us to find contentment, foster genuine relationships, and navigate the complexities of life with grace and wisdom. Let us look beyond the illusions of charismatic personalities and those who rise to assume the mantles of financial and political power. Let us both want nothing and want for nothing that we need. One never finds permanent happiness by way of way material possessions. Instead, let us embrace the Tao and its Integral Way, the path of spiritual evolution, self-awareness and enlightenment.

CHAPTER 4

**LIKE A WELL IS THE TAO;
THOUGH MUCH USED,
IT IS NEVER EXHAUSTED.**

**LIKE THE ETERNAL VOID
IT IS FILLED WITH INFINITE POSSIBILITY.**

**THOUGH HIDDEN
IT IS ALWAYS PRESENT.**

**NO ONE KNOWS
HOW CAME INTO BEING.**

**OLDER THAN GOD,
IS THE TAO.**

Exploring the Inexhaustible Nature of the Tao

These verses reflect the essence of Taoism and emphasize the timeless and mysterious nature of the Tao, often described as the fundamental principle that underlies and unites everything in the universe. The Tao is eternal, inexhaustible, and beyond human comprehension. It is the universal intelligent energy and field of consciousness that permeates all things. These verses are a beautiful expression of philosophical and spiritual ideas that permeate the reality that is the Tao.

The concept of the Tao encompasses profound wisdom and serves as a guiding principle for many aspects of life. This chapter emphasizes the Tao's inexhaustible qualities and beckons us to explore its eternal presence and thereby begin to appreciate, if not totally understand, the Tao's essence and eternal birth.

The Tao, like a bottomless well or an eternal void, embodies limitless potential, remains perpetually hidden, and predates the existence of even the divine, making it a fascinating and deeply intriguing philosophical and spiritual concept. Becoming aware of the Tao is the razon d'être for our presence in this world and sine qua non for the evolution of our spiritual selves. By studying the Tao and by following its Integral Way, we can gain insights into the infinite possibilities it holds for us in this life and in all our lives to follow.

The Tao as an Inexhaustible Wellspring of Wisdom

"Like a well is the Tao." Even though the Tao is much used, it is never exhausted. This metaphorical representation of the Tao as a well that it never runs dry echoes the idea of the Tao as not only an infinite and timeless source of physical provision but of courage, hope, wisdom and energy as well. In the Tao Te Ching, the Tao is also often described as a source of inexhaustible virtue, knowledge, spiritual resources and power. This quote should cause us to reflect upon the blessing of our potential constant use of the Tao with no signs of depletion and to utilize the Tao's unlimited resources that are always available without fail, in our daily lives.

The Eternal Void: Symbolizing Unbounded Possibilities

"Like the eternal void, it is filled with infinite possibility." The concept of emptiness or void is significant in the study of the Tao. Like a cup waiting to be filled, it represents a state of receptivity and potential. From the void, infinite possibilities can arise. The drawing of parallels of the Tao and the eternal void reflects Lao Tzu's teachings on the importance of emptiness and receptivity and recognizes our limitless potential for boundless creativity and growth that emerge from the Tao.

The Hidden Essence of the Tao

"Though hidden, it is always present." Throughout the Tao Te Ching, Lao Tzu emphasizes the subtle and hidden nature of the Tao, which is ever-present though not always apparent. Present yet enigmatic, one cannot see the Tao itself, only its effects and manifestations. The Tao is often said to be elusive and hidden, yet it pervades everything. It is up to us to unravel the mysteries of the Tao and recognize its presence in our everyday lives.

The Enigmatic Birth of the Tao: Older than Divinity

"No one knows how it was given birth." "Older than God, is the Tao." These entries highlight the mystery of the Tao's origins and the Tao predating God or any divine entity. Lao Tzu often speaks of the ineffable nature of the Tao, that is beyond human comprehension and transcends the boundaries of both time and space. The statement about the unknown age of the Tao emphasizes the primordial and eternal timeless nature of the Tao existing before all things, including the concept of deities or gods and the religions that worship them.

These two passages get us to think about the implications of a timeless birth for the endless wisdom of the Tao and how we fit into this picture as its mental, physical and spiritual progeny.

Because the Tao transcends both time and space, and is the creator of all things, and because it is said to have created all gods for these and for other reasons that will become evident in further chapters of this book, one ultimately needs to question the nature, origin and relevancy of all religions and belief systems in order to put them in their proper place and to help determine his or her own place in the universe.

In essence, these early verses of Lao Tzu's teachings above capture the core themes of the Tao Te Ching: the ubiquitous ineffable nature of the Tao, its omnipresence, its infinite potential, and its omniscience and role as the eternal wellspring and source of all spiritual being and physical existence. These early verses invite our contemplation and reflection on the profound mysteries of the Tao. They encouragee us as individuals to align ourselves with its creative and compassionate natural flow rather than trying to control or define it.

Certainly, the verses above align closely with the further teachings found in the Tao Te Ching. But how do these verses resonate with the key principles of the Tao Te Ching and its Integral Way, maintaining hidden in its essence? The Tao stands as an enigmatic reality that transcends time and space and offers a vast expanse of wisdom to those who seek it. Like a never-ending well or an eternal void, it remains full of infinite possibilities. By delving into the intricacies of the Tao, and its timeless wisdom, we can unlock a wealth of knowledge and embrace its unbounded potential in our own lives and in each life that we will experience in the present and in the hereafter.

CHAPTER 5

**NEITHER THE MASTER NOR THE TAO TAKE SIDES.
THE TAO BEGETS BOTH "GOOD" AND "EVIL".
TO HER, BOTH THE SINNER AND SAINT ARE WEL-
COME.
IT IS AS IF THE TAO WERE A BELLOWS.
THOUGH EMPTY, SHE IS INFINITELY CAPABLE.**

THE MORE IT IS USED; THE MORE IT PRODUCES.

**THE MORE ONE SPEAKS OF IT; THE LESS ONE UN-
DERSTANDS.**

ONE MUST HOLD ON TO THE CENTER.

Embracing the Yin and Yang of Existence: The Tao's Influence
in Harmonizing Opposing Forces

This age-old writing by Lao Tzu encompasses profound wisdom and has inspired countless individuals in their quest for
enlightenment and spiritual understanding, not to mention
revealing the mysteries of life. Central to The Integral Way is
the idea that neither the master nor the Tao take sides. Instead,
the Tao embraces both good and evil, welcoming sinners and
saints with equal acceptance as if they were her own children.
Like a bellows, seemingly empty yet infinitely capable, the
Tao's power grows with use, while its essence paradoxically
remains elusive the more it is spoken of. Hence, the pursuit
of the Tao calls for a deep alignment with its core teachings,
particularly the necessity of holding on to the center. It is of the
utmost importance that ant student of the Tao and follower of
the Integral Way understand the inherent nature of the Tao,
its ability to reconcile opposing forces, and the significance
of maintaining balance amidst life's inevitable fluctuations.

Exploring the Nature of the Tao

At its core, the Tao represents the ultimate truth and underlying force that governs the universe. However, the Tao is not fixated on duality or taking sides. It transcends conventional notions of good and evil, recognizing that they are part of an interconnected whole. By understanding the Tao's neutrality, we develop a broader perspective on the complexities of the Tao's existence and inevitably our own as we begin to align ourselves with it.

Embracing the Yin and Yang

The Tao gives birth to both "good" and "evil" through the concept of Yin (female energy) and Yang (male energy). This duality plays itself out through all aspects of existence. To coin a phrase from Newton, for every action, there is an equal and opposite reaction. Both yin and yang represent the interdependence and complementarity of opposing forces. Just as light cannot exist without darkness, good cannot exist without evil. By embracing both aspects of any given situation, light and dark, good and evil and life and death, for example, the Tao guides us towards a path of balance, emphasizing the unity of existence rather than favoring one extreme over the other.

The Significance of Acceptance

In stark contrast to many moralistic philosophies and dogmatic religions, (like Jesus himself), the Tao embraces sinners and saints alike, inviting them to find inner harmony within its teachings. The acceptance of both "good" and "evil" illuminates the Tao's all-encompassing nature. It encourages individuals who seek to find happiness and contentment to acknowledge the intricate web of interconnections that define our reality and thereby experience the peace and harmony revealed by the study of Tao and by following the Integral Way.

The Boundless Capabilities of the Tao

Analogous to a bellows, the Tao possesses boundless potential and capabilities for all aspects of our lives. As it is utilized and engaged with, its power expands rather than diminishes. Like a muscle that is used daily, it grows with power and stronger. This notion of strength with use reminds us that the more we connect with the Tao and apply its principles to our lives, the more we can tap into our own infinite potential and obtain more and more out of it.

The ancient wisdom embedded in the teachings of Lao Tzu and the Integral Way allow us to navigate the complexities of life by embracing the all-encompassing nature of the Tao. Neither the master nor the Tao take sides; instead, the Tao begets both "good" and "evil." By holding on to the center and practicing acceptance, we can harmonize opposing forces and discover our own infinite capabilities. So, in the chapters that follow, let us delve deeper into the depths of this timeless wisdom and embrace the balance between things like light and dark, good and evil, right and wrong, life and death and being and non-being to find solace in the embrace of the Tao and following the path of her Integral Way.

CHAPTER 6

**THE TAO IS CALLED „GREAT MOTHER".
"THE MYSTICAL FEMALE".
NEVER DOES HER VALLEY SPIRIT DIE.
THE ROOT OF HEAVEN AND EARTH IS WHAT
HER ENTRANCE CALLED**

**EMPTY, YET INEXHAUSTIBLE,
FROM HER, INFINITE WORLDS ARE BORN.**

**PRESENT WITHIN ALL,
SHE MAY BE EMPLOYED
IN WHATEVER WAY ONE MAY NEED.**

The Tao: The Inexhaustible Great Mother

These lines reflect the concept of the Tao often described metaphorically as the "Great Mother" or the source of all existence. They emphasize the idea of emptiness and inexhaustibility, and how everything emanates from it. Its essence lies in its emptiness, yet paradoxically it gives birth to infinite worlds and the interconnectedness of all creation through her own existence.

The Concept of the Tao

Not only is the Tao a profound presence in the realm of spiritual existence and philosophical thought, but as it is the source of all existence, present in all things, it can be utilized in as many various ways as it is needed. The Tao's omnipresent nature is of profound significance. Its ultimate and adaptable essence and its ability to be employed in all aspects of life make it worth knowing something about.

The Versatility of the Tao

The Tao is omnipresent. It is a ubiquitous influence within all aspects of life. Because of this, the Tao can be employed in different situations and contexts. With its unlimited flexibility the Tao is capable of influencing our individual and collective experiences and can guide our own personal growth and spiritual journeys. The Tao can reduce the friction of life and help us all find balance and harmony in an otherwise abrasive and chaotic world. Its potential can be invoked and employed so as to give it a central role not only in our own life experiences and interpersonal relationships but in our social, community and world dynamics as well.

The concept of the Great Mother Tao showcases its boundless power of creation through its emptiness. Seen or unseen, its universal presence affects every aspect of life. Acknowledging its existence and embracing the wisdom and teachings of the Tao allows us as individuals to tap into its immeasurable potential and to employ it in whatever way we may need. Ultimately, it is the Tao that allows us to find harmony within ourselves and the world and the rest of the universe at large.

CHAPTER 7

THE TAO IS INFINITE AND ETERNAL.
IT NEITHER CAN BE BORN NOR DIE.
IT IS PRESENT IN ALL
AND FOR ALL BEINGS.

THE MASTER LEADS
BY STAYING BEHIND.
FROM ALL THINGS,
SHE IS DETACHED.
THUS, THE MASTER
BECOMES AND REMAINS
ONE WITH ALL.

BY LETTING GO,
THE MASTER IS COMPLETE
AND BECOMES PERFECT.

Introduction

These beautiful words reflect the spiritual basis of the Tao and the philosophy behind the Integral Way. The Tao, often described as the source of all existence, emphasizes simplicity, detachment, and harmony with the natural order. Letting go and staying in the background are central principles for finding unity and perfection.

The Tao, An Eternal Source of Harmony and Wholeness

The concept of the Tao offers profound insights into the nature of existence and the path towards enlightenment. With its central tenets of infinitude, eternality, and interconnectedness, the Tao provides a comprehensive framework for understanding and navigating the complexities of life. There is endless timeless wisdom encapsulated within the Tao. But what is its essence and what is its relevance to and for all beings both here and throughout the universe?

The Eternal Nature of the Tao

The Tao is an infinite and eternal force that permeates the fabric of all existence and enables all individuals to attain unity and harmony by embracing detachment and letting go. The Tao is often depicted as an unchanging and everlasting entity that transcends birth and death. Reflective of the cyclical rhythms of the universe, the Tao encompasses and is consubstantial in all things, acting as the underlying fabric and firmament that connects every being. By recognizing the eternal nature of the Tao, individuals can find solace by understanding that they are an integral and intrinsic part of a grander whole.

Detachment as the Path Towards Unity

One of the key principles espoused by the Tao is the idea of detachment. By letting go of desires, attachments, and judgments, individuals attain a higher level of consciousness that enables them to achieve oneness with the Tao. Embracing detachment, individuals free themselves from the burden of ego and connect with the essence of their true being.

The Master's Approach: Leading from Behind

The great masters of the Tao exemplify its teachings through their ability to lead from behind. By eschewing ego and by stepping back and allowing others to flourish, these masters create an environment that nurtures growth, wisdom, and harmony. Through their detachment and selflessness, and leading by their selfless example, they become one with all beings, inspiring others to embrace the Tao's fundamental values of simplicity, patience compassion and truth.

Embracing Wholeness through Letting Go

To align oneself with the Tao, the act of letting go holds great significance. Attachments, especially unhealthy ones often lead to misery. By releasing attachments and expectations, individuals can find a sense of freedom, completion and perfection. Letting go is not a sign of weakness, but rather an embodiment of inner strength and acceptance—a pathway to achieve genuine fulfillment and balance.

The takeaway here should be that the Tao is a very real entity that embodies an ever-present force that exists within the fabric of all existence. It exists in all things. Through studying the Tao and the teachings of the masters and by following its Integral Way, individuals can discover unity, harmony, balance and enlightenment in their lives and share these things with others. By understanding the eternal and infinite nature of the Tao and incorporating its principles of detachment and letting go, we can truly embrace the essence of the Tao and become an embodiment of its wisdom and nature. As we continue on our journey through life, no matter where we are in it, the Tao serves as a beacon of light, guiding us towards an understanding of our place in the universe and our interconnectedness with all beings and all things.

CHAPTER 8

THE TAO, IS LIKE WATER,
THE SUPREME GOOD.
AS SHE NOURISHES ALL,
WITHOUT STRIVING.
SHE GOES WHEREVER SHE PLEASES
AND FLOWS INTO THE LOWEST OF PLACES
THAT ARE DISDAINED BY MAN.
THUS LIKE WATER,
SO TOO IS THE TAO.

IN LIVING, DWELL CLOSE TO THE GROUND.
IN THOUGHT, PREFER THE SIMPLE.
IN CONFLICT, BE GENEROUS AND FAIR.
IN GOVERNING, DO NOT CONTROL.
IN WORK, DO THAT WHICH GIVES YOU JOY.
IN FAMILY, BE PRESENT COMPLETELY.

ONCE ONE IS CONTENT TO BE SIMPLY ONESELF
WITHOUT COMPETITION OR COMPARISON,
ONE EARNS THE RESPECT OF ALL.

The Tao: Embracing Simplicity, Harmony, and Authenticity

The Tao, often compared to water, is a concept deeply rooted
in ancient Chinese philosophy and serves as a guiding principle
for living a fulfilling and harmonious life. There is profound
wisdom behind the Tao, its connection to water, and the principles this comparison imparts for personal growth and societal
well-being.

This passage by Lao Tzi reflects the deep wisdom of the Tao
Te Ching, emphasizing the many qualities of water and the
principles of living in harmony with the Tao. It encourages

simplicity, humility, and a non-controlling approach to life, suggesting that by being true to oneself and not seeking others' approval, adulation or to compete or compare oneself with others, one can gain their respect. It's a beautiful philosophy promoting patience, balance and authenticity.

The Tao: A Reflection of Water

The Tao is like water in its ability to nourish all without striving. Water symbolizes effortless and gentle strength. Just as the Tao manifests its influence without force, water can metamorphose itself to be a solid, a gas or a liquid. It changes to fit the environment. Both the Tao and water flow naturally and adapt to any circumstance. To be like water is to be like the Tao. The Tao, through its metaphorical relationship with water, teaches us the importance of embracing simplicity, truth, patience and enduring softness and living authentically. When we do this, we foster harmonious relationships with ourselves, others, the world and the universe around us.

Embracing Simplicity

Dwelling Close to the Ground and Living in harmony with the Tao involves embracing simplicity in our thoughts and actions. By focusing on what truly matters, we cultivate contentment, peace, and a deeper sense of purpose. Simplicity keeps us from being overwhelmed. It allows us to navigate life's complexities with ease, as we prioritize what is necessary and what brings us true joy and fulfillment and eliminate those things that are unnecessary or do not.

The Power of Authenticity: Being Simply Oneself

The Tao encourages us to be authentic and actualize our true Tao selves, free from the burdens of egoism, competition and comparison. We are all good enough. There is nothing to prove. Our actions and abilities will speak for themselves as we become who and what we were meant to be by our creator. By accepting ourselves as we are, and by doing our best, we foster self-respect and earn the respect of others. Authenticity allows us to connect with others genuinely and build harmonious relationships based on trust and understanding.

Cultivating Harmony: Generosity, Fairness, and Non-control

In conflicts, the Tao advises us to adopt a generous and fair mindset, seeking resolutions that benefit all parties involved. By relinquishing control and embracing flexibility, we create space for collaboration and harmony to thrive. The Tao teaches us that governing with fairness, compassion, and non-control leads to a happy, more balanced and prosperous society.

Joyful Work: Pursuing Passions and Purpose

It has long been said that "'If you find what you love and make a living from it, then you will never work a day in your life". Following the Tao means engaging in work that brings us joy and fulfillment. By aligning our passions with our daily endeavors, we tap into what Lao Tzu refers to 'Energy Response" * to fulfill naturally our Tao-given full potential and contribute positively to the world. The Tao reminds us of the importance of finding meaning and purpose in our professional lives. This, in turn, betters our own lives and the lives of those around us.

Family and Presence: Cultivating Meaningful Connections

The Tao emphasizes the significance of being completely present in our familial relationships. By devoting our attention and love to our loved ones, we create strong bonds and foster a sense of belonging. The Tao teaches us to prioritize the well-being of our families and to create and cherish the moments we share together.

The Tao, like water, holds profound wisdom for leading a meaningful and peaceful life. By embracing simplicity, authenticity, and harmony, we can find balance within ourselves, foster harmonious relationships, and contribute to the betterment of human society. The Tao invites us to live with intention, compassion, and respect for all beings, earning the respect and admiration of those around us.

*Commonly referred to in more modern times as the "Law of Attraction", we attract the energies we produce and are attracted to those energies that naturally resonate most strongly in us. When we refine and harmonize our energy and nature so as to live in consonance with the order of the universe, we become harmonized with the Tao and attract the higher and more refined energies of the universe to us. By finding out authentic selves and exploring those Tao-given gifts the Tao collaborates with us to help us to do what we most naturally do and to become who and what we were always meant to be

CHAPTER 9

FILL NOT YOUR VESSEL TO ITS BRIM
LESS IT SPILL OUT.
OVER SHARPEN A KNIFE
AND IT WILL BE OF NO USE.
PURSUE WEALTH AND SECURITY
AND YOUR HEART WILL NEVER SOFTEN.
CARE ABOUT THE APPROVAL OF OTHERS
AND YOU WILL ALWAYS BE AS A PRISONER TO
THEM.

THE PATH TO SERENITY IS TO DO (AND COM-
PLETE) ONE'S WORK
AND (THE WORK HAVING BEEN FINISHED),
STAND AWAY FROM IT,
(THEREAFTER LET THE WORK SPEAK
FOR ITSELF).

The Path to Serenity: Embracing Simplicity and Self-Acceptance

These are profound words, emphasizing the importance of
balance, moderation, and self-reliance. Lao Tzu suggests that
one should not be consumed by excess, obsession, or external
validation, but instead focus on meaningful work and to let
the results speak for themselves. He encourages a path to inner
peace and serenity through both self-discipline and detachment.

In a world consumed by constant striving and pursuit of external validation, it is crucial to take a pause and reflect on the
path to true serenity. Often, we find ourselves overwhelmed by
filling our lives to the brim, overexerting ourselves, and seeking the approval of others. In this chapter, Lao Tzu explores

the importance of simplicity, self-acceptance, and letting our work speak for itself in achieving a state of serenity.

Embracing Moderation

The metaphor of filling a vessel to its brim symbolizes our tendency to become consumed by excessive desires and responsibilities. By adopting a mindset of moderation, we not only avoid burnout but also create space for self-reflection, growth, and personal fulfillment.

The Perils of Overexertion

The analogy of over sharpening a knife highlights the consequences of pushing ourselves too far, diminishing our effectiveness. Constantly striving for perfection and overloading ourselves with work can lead to physical and mental exhaustion, hindering our ability to find true serenity.

Chasing Wealth and Security

The pursuit of external markers of success, such as wealth and security, may prevent us from cultivating deeper connections and genuine happiness. True serenity lies in prioritizing personal fulfillment, maintaining a balanced perspective on material possessions, and nurturing meaningful relationships.

Escaping the Approval Trap

Placing excessive importance on the approval of others can create a state of constant anxiety, leading to an inability to find inner peace. By caring what others think of us, we give our power away to others who really do not care about our own best interests. Emphasizing self-acceptance and focusing on intrinsic motivation and reward allows us to free ourselves from the expectations and judgments of others.

<u>Allowing the Work to Speak</u>
Standing away from our work after completing it and letting it speak for itself fosters a sense of detachment and humility. By embracing the idea that our efforts will be recognized without constant self-promotion, we can redirect our energy toward deeper personal growth and serenity.

In conclusion, Lao Tzu's message here urges us to seek serenity by embracing simplicity and self-acceptance. Through moderation, avoiding overexertion, reconsidering our pursuit of wealth and security, and breaking free from the approval trap, we can find peace within ourselves. By allowing our work to speak for itself, we cultivate humility and focus on authentic personal growth rather than external validation. Ultimately, by embarking on this path, we can unlock the door to serenity, contentment, and a more fulfilled existence.

CHAPTER 10

The "Supreme Virtue"

ARE YOU ABLE TO WILL YOUR MIND FROM WAN-
DERING
AND KEEP TO ITS ORIGINAL STATE OF ONENESS?
ARE YOU ABLE TO ALLOW YOUR BODY
TO BE SUPPLE AS THAT OF A NEWBORN CHILD?
ARE YOU ABLE TO CLEAR YOUR INNER VISION
UNTIL YOU CAN SEE NOTHING BUT THE ONE
LIGHT?

ARE YOU ABLE TO LOVE PEOPLE AND TO LEAD
THEM
WITHOUT IMPOSING YOUR WILL?
ARE YOU ABLE TO DEAL WITH THE MOST VITAL
OF MATTERS
BY SIMPLY ALLOWING EVENTS TO TAKE THEIR
COURSE?
ARE YOU ABLE TO STAND BACK FROM YOUR OWN
MIND
AND FROM THERE, UNDERSTAND ALL THINGS?

ARE YOU ABLE TO BRING FORTH AND NOURISH?
ARE YOU ABLE TO HAVE WITHOUT POSSESSING?
ARE YOU ABLE TO ACT WITHOUT EXPECTATION?
CAN YOU LEAD, YET NOT TRY TO CONTROL?

THESE CONSTITUTE THE SUPREME VIRTUE.

The Supreme Virtue

These questions reflect the teachings of Lao Tzu and the concept of living in harmony with the Tao (the Integral Way). The

'Supreme Virtue" emphasizes qualities like humility, simplicity, and non-attachment. They teach us that true wisdom lies in being in tune with the natural flow of life rather than trying to control or possess it. It's a profound philosophy that teaches us to find serenity and virtue through inner alignment and acceptance of the way things are.

The essence of the supreme virtue in us reflects a state of mindfulness, selflessness, and non-attachment. It is through embodying these qualities that we can attain a sense of oneness, clarity, and compassionate leadership. By allowing events to unfold naturally, 9Wu Wei) without imposing our will, we can find harmony and balance in our interactions with others and the world around us. Moreover, the ability to act without expectation, nourish without possessing, and lead without trying to control speaks to a higher level of understanding and wisdom.

Supreme virtue is a universal virtue. By cultivating these virtues, we can find true fulfillment and contribute positively to the lives of others and the lives of all of the inhabitants of the universe in which we exist.

CHAPTER 11

THOUGH THE CARTWHEEL
IS MADE OF A RIM AND SPOKES.
JOINED TOGETHER AT A HUB,
IT IS THE CENTER HOLE THOUGH
THAT ALLOWS THE CART TO MOVE.

WHEN EARTH IS SHAPED INTO A POT.
IT IS NOT THE CLAY
BUT THE EMPTINESS INSIDE
THAT HOLDS
THAT WHICH IS INTENDED
TO BE HELD.

ONE FABRICATES WOOD
TO BUILD A HOUSE,
BUT IT IS THE INNER SPACE
THAT MAKES THE HOUSE
A LIVABLE HOME.

ONE WORKS BY BEING,
BUT ONE'S NON BEING
IS WHAT ONE USES.

Introduction

These poetic verses underscore the significance of emptiness, space, and the unseen aspects in various aspects of life. They emphasize that in the physical world, it's often the voids, the empty spaces, or the intangible qualities that give meaning and functionality to things. This idea resonates with Taoist and Zen philosophies, highlighting the importance of balance, harmony, and the interplay between the visible and the invisible.

The verses highlight the significance of emptiness, space, and non-being as essential components in various aspects of life.

The Cartwheel Analogy

The rim and spokes of a cartwheel are crucial for its structure, but it is the center hole that allows the cart to move. Similarly, it is the emptiness or the vacant space within something that gives it purpose, functionality, and the ability to fulfill its intended function. This emptiness in the wheel is analogous to our own emptiness and holding on to anything too tightly.

Shaping the Earth Into a Pot

When forming a pot with clay, it is not the clay itself that makes the pot valuable, but the emptiness inside that makes it useful for holding things. The negative space within the pot is what provides utility and potential. We are the clay in life. It us up to us to shape ourselves into something useful to ourselves and the society in which we live.

Building a House

One may fabricate a house using concrete, wood and shingles but it is the inner space, the rooms, and the voids of safety and security within that make it a livable home. The emptiness, the voids between objects, and the space within the house give it its essential purpose. Just like any void created in our lives, it is up to us to decide wisely who and what will be allowed within.

Working Being and Non-being being

While one works through active being, it is through the power of non-being, embracing emptiness and stillness, that true effectiveness and peace can be achieved. By recognizing the importance of non-being, non-action, and the ability to step back and observe, we can find clarity and use this state to guide us in our actions.

Ultimately, this passage emphasize the transformative nature of emptiness, space, and non-being in our lives. They remind us that the absence, the voids, solitude and stillness play a vital role in freely creating meaning, functionality, and balance. Embracing and understanding the power of emptiness and non-being and the value of meditative states can lead to greater insight, purpose, and being and ultimately harmony with others and peaceful fulfillment in our own lives.

CHAPTER 12

A Heart as Open as the Sky

THE EYE IS BLINDED BY COLORS. THE EAR IS DEAFENED BY SOUND.
TASTE IS NUMBED BY FLAVOR; THE MIND WEAKENED BY THOUGHT.
THE HEART WITHERS FROM DESIRE.

THE MASTER OBSERVES THE WORLD, YET TRUSTS HIS INNER VISION.
THE MASTER ALLOWS THE COMING, AND GOINGS OF THINGS
WITH A HEART AS OPEN AS THE SKY.

Introduction
These words emphasize the importance of cultivating a master's mindset, rooted in inner vision and openness. They accentuate the idea of simplicity, inner clarity, and the importance of cultivating a sense of detachment from external distractions and desires. They suggest that by not being overly consumed by sensory experiences and external stimuli, one can gain a deeper understanding of the world and maintain a sense of inner peace and openness. It's a reflection of mindfulness and the ability to trust one's inner wisdom.

Senses and Perception

Colors can blind the eye, sounds can deafen the ear, and intense flavors can numb the sense of taste. The constant bombardment of sensory stimuli can overwhelm our perception. Likewise, the mind can become weakened by excessive thoughts, distractions, and mental clutter. This can hinder our ability to see clearly and make sound judgments.

Trusting Inner Vision

The master, in contrast, observes the world around them but trusts their inner vision. By tapping into our intuition and inner knowing, we can see beyond the superficial and perceive the essence of things. This inner vision allows us to become masters ourselves and transcend the limitations of external stimuli and gain deeper insight into the true nature of reality.

Embracing Openness

The master embraces the ebb and flow of life. Rather than clinging to attachments or resisting change, they allow things to come and go with an open mind and a heart. This openness mirrors the vast expanse of the sky, symbolizing a state of non-attachment, acceptance, and freedom.

These verses highlight how our senses and thoughts can sometimes lead us astray, but by cultivating inner wisdom and embracing openness, we can navigate the world with clarity and trust. By being aware of the potential limitations of our senses and thoughts, we can cultivate a deeper sense of perception and wisdom.

By embodying the qualities of the master, we too can navigate the complexities of life with clarity, peace, and a deep understanding that allows us to truly appreciate the beauty and interconnectedness of all. By trusting our inner vision and embracing openness, we can navigate the complexities of life with clarity, resilience, and a greater sense of connection to the world we live in and the universe and that exists around us.

CHAPTER 13

SUCCESS AND FAILURE
ARE EQUALLY DANGEROUS.
HOPE AND FEAR SIMILARLY,
ARE EQUALLY HOLLOW.

WHAT IS MEANT BY
THE EQUALITY OF
SUCCESS AND FAILURE?
LIKE THE ASCENT AND DESCENT
OF A LADDER,
BOTH ARE EQUALLY SHAKY.
BALANCE COMES TO THE ONE
WHO STANDS WITH BOTH FEET
ON THE GROUND.
WELL GROUNDED,
ONE IS ALWAYS ABLE
TO KEEP ONE'S BALANCE.

WHAT DOES IT MEAN THAT
HOPE AND FEAR ARE EQUALLY HOLLOW?
FEAR AND HOPE ARE PHANTOMS.
SUCH PHANTOMS ARISE
OUT OF ONE THINKING
ABOUT ONE'S SELF.
WHAT IS THERE TO FEAR
WHEN ONE DOES NOT SEE ONE'S SELF
AS SELF?

SEE THE UNIVERSE AS SELF.
BE THE UNIVERSE AND LOVE IT
SO THAT ALL IS CARED FOR.

TRUST IN THE WAY THINGS ARE.

Introduction

These words by Lao Tzu reflect the idea of embracing balance and letting go of attachments and ego-driven emotions. They emphasize the ephemeral nature of success, failure, hope, and fear, suggesting that one can find true equilibrium and peace by seeing oneself as integrally interconnected with the universe rather than as an isolated self. Trusting in the natural flow of existence and letting go of personal desires can lead to a sense of harmony and contentment.

Lao Tzu also emphasize the dangers of attaching ourselves too strongly to the dualistic concepts of success and failure, hope and fear. By finding balance, letting go of self-centered thinking, and trusting in the natural flow of things we can lead to true contentment and fulfillment in life. By living a Tao-centered life, we can also ground ourselves by living simply and harmoniously in our surroundings, by establishing healthy routines and by undertaking our own rightful actions independently from either success and failure and the favor or opinions of others.

Equality of Success and Failure

The verses state that success and failure are equally dangerous, as both can lead to instability and imbalance if we become too attached to them. Like ascending and descending a shaky ladder, a balanced perspective is achieved when we remain grounded and unswayed by extremes.

The Emptiness of Hope and Fear

Hope and fear are seen as equally hollow. They are illusions that both arise from egoic self-centered thinking. When we let go of the illusion of self and identify with the vastness of the universe, fear and hope lose their grip on us. This is also referred to as "dissolving the ego into the Tao". By embracing compassion and selflessness and by perceiving the interconnected unity and oneness of all things, we can approach life with love and care for ourselves and others and the universe with all its manifestations as a whole.

Trusting in the Way Things Are

The verses urge us to trust in the inherent wisdom and order of the universe. By relinquishing our need for control and accepting the natural course of events, we can find serenity and harmony.

Overall, these verses invite us to cultivate a mindset of equanimity, humility, and trust in the way things unfold. By letting go of attachment to success and failure, and by transcending our self-focused hopes and fears, we can attain a sense of profound peace and alignment with the universe and all of the inhabitants within it, including ourselves.

CHAPTER 14

The Essence of Wisdom

LOOK FOR IT AND IT CANNOT BE SEEN.
LISTEN FOR IT AND IT CANNOT BE HEARD.
REACH FOR IT AND IT CANNOT BE GRASPED.

WHAT IS ABOVE IS NOT BRIGHT.
WHAT IS BELOW IS NOT DARK.
WITHOUT A SEAM OR NAME
IT RETURNS TO ITS SOURCE:
NOTHING.

ITS FORM IS THE FORM OF ALL FORMS:
AN IMAGE WITHOUT IMAGE.
ITS SUBTLE NATURE IS BEYOND ALL CONCEPTI-
ON.

THERE IS NO BEGINNING SHOULD ONE AP-
PROACH IT
AND THERE IS NO END TO IT ONCE IT IS FOLLO-
WED.
ONE CANNOT KNOW IT; BUT CAN ONLY BE IT,
ONCE ONE IS AT EASE IN ONE'S OWN LIFE.

ONCE ONE REALIZES THE SOURCE
FROM WHENCE ONE COMES,
SO TOO THE ESSENCE IS REVEALED AND WISDOM
REALIZED.

Introduction

In this passage, Lao Tzu describes the Tao as emptiness or the
void that is often associated with philosophical and spiritual

ideas. He paints the Tao as an endless creative emptiness that is formless, beyond perception, and can only be realized through inner understanding and being at ease in one's own life. He also alludes to the idea that wisdom comes from recognizing the Tao, the source of one's own existence. It is apparent from the context of this passage in the earlier portion of the Tao Te Ching that what he writes is not intended as a comprehensive exploration of the topic. The following chapters will have to suffice for that. It serves though, as a starting point for further reflection and exploration into the ontology of intangible formless emptiness and its utilization within the spiritual context of the Tao.

Unveiling the Profundity of Emptiness: A Path to Inner Wisdom

In the realm of philosophical and spiritual contemplation, the concept of emptiness or the void occupies a significant place. It is an enigmatic notion that suggests a state that is formless, beyond perception, and can only be realized through inner understanding and being at ease in one's own life and in one's own skin. In this passage Lao Tzu begins to shed light on the profound nature of emptiness, its philosophical and spiritual connotations, and the idea that recognizing the source of one's existence ultimately leads to the acquisition of wisdom.

The Paradoxical Nature of Emptiness

The concept of emptiness presents a paradoxical nature, as it simultaneously implies absence and presence, nothingness and every thingness. It transcends our usual understanding of existence and challenges us to explore alternative modes of perception. By delving into emptiness, we can uncover hidden layers of truth and gain deeper insights into the nature of reality and consciousness. Inevitably, this brings us all back to the Tao; something that we cannot see or touch but, with its wisdom, we know and understand that it is always there.

Emptiness and Spiritual Enlightenment

Within various spiritual traditions, including the Tao and the Integral Way, emptiness is seen as a gateway to profound wisdom and spiritual enlightenment. It is a paradoxical riddle that beckons individuals to embark on a journey of self-discovery and inner exploration. By acknowledging the formless void within, we can transcend the limitations of the material world and cultivate a heightened sense of awareness. Through the spiritual practices of the Integral Way such as meditation, individuals can understand their true nature and cultivate inner peace, harmony, and a deeper connection with their intangible yet very real true selves.

Emptiness and Philosophical Perspectives

From a philosophical standpoint, emptiness aligns itself with concepts such as existentialism and the notion of the absurd. It questions the fundamental nature of existence, challenging traditional perspectives on reality. Embracing the emptiness within ourselves allows us to confront the existential void and find meaning amidst the chaos. It encourages individuals to embrace their freedom and actively shape their own lives, rather than being slaves to societal norms and expectations. Once one realizes that the void is not a void but filled with the Tao itself, human existence and all existence begins to make sense.

The Role of True Wisdom

True wisdom therefore arises from recognizing the source of one's own existence, which is intimately entwined with an understanding of emptiness. By acknowledging the inherent void filled with the Tao within and embracing the indeterminacy of physical life, we can have profound insights into our purpose in life, and gain a sense of inner peace. True wisdom is not merely intellectual knowledge; it is the deep and transformative understanding that arises from contemplating both the comparative vastness and the full interconnectedness of all things.

Conclusion

The concept of emptiness holds profound significance in both philosophical and spiritual contexts that surround the Tao.. By embracing the Tao and realizing its ubiquitous yet formless nature, we can embark on a journey of infinite universal self-discovery, spiritual evolution and refinement and inner growth. Through the understanding of our own timeless, conscious and infinite inner being and being at ease in our own lives, true wisdom is acquired. This acquisition ultimately leads to a deeper appreciation of the source of existence and to a richer and deeper experience of reality. Embracing emptiness is an invitation to explore the depths of our consciousness and to transcend societal norms and discover a profound sense of purpose and fulfillment through the study and awareness of the Tao in an otherwise incomprehensible void within the vastness of a seemingly equally and infinitely empty universe.

CHAPTER 15

The Ancient Masters

PROFOUND AND SUBTLE WERE THE ANCIENT MASTERS.
UNFATHOMABLE WAS THEIR WISDOM.
THOUGH ONE MAY TALK ABOUT THEIR APPEARANCE,
ONE CANNOT ADEQUATELY DESCRIBE THEM.

THE SAGES OF OLD USED THE CARE
THAT ONE WHO CROSSES
AN ICE COVERED STREAM WOULD USE;
ALERT AS IF A WARRIOR IN ENEMY TERRITORY,
AS COURTEOUS AS ONE WOULD BE AS IF A GUEST.

AS FLUID AS THE MELTING OF ICE,
THEY WERE AS CAPABLE OF BEING SHAPED
AS A RAW BLOCK OF WOOD,
AS RECEPTIVE AS A VALLEY
AND AS CLEAR AS A GLASS OF WATER.

DO YOU HAVE THE PATIENCE TO WAIT,
UNTIL YOUR WATERS ARE CLEAR
AND MUD SETTLED?
CAN YOU STAY UNMOVING
UNTIL THE RIGHT ACTION ARISES FROM ITSELF?

THE MASTER SEEKS NOT FULFILLMENT.
BECAUSE HE KNOWS THAT IT IS IN NOT SEEKING
OR EXPECTING THAT THE MASTER IS ENTIRELY PRESENT.
WHEN THE MASTER IS ENTIRELY PRESENT
THE MASTER IS ABLE TO WELCOME ALL THINGS.

Introduction

This passage by Lao Tzu describes the qualities and demeanor of the ancient masters or sages who existed before his time. It emphasizes their profound presence and wisdom, their adaptability, and their patience. The text suggests that true mastery involves being entirely present, not seeking fulfillment, and being open to all things. It encourages patience and waiting for clarity and right action to arise naturally. These traits underpin both the concept of Wu Wei and ones who master the Way.

Mastery: What It Takes

Lao Tzu's concept of the sage master reflects principles often found in later Eastern philosophies and spiritual teachings. The passage above evokes a sense of Lao Tzu's own deep wisdom and presence, from which he draws upon the imagery of nature to convey profound insights. The essence of the passage lies in the idea that the ancient masters possessed a wisdom that is both profound and subtle, transcending ordinary descriptions. Their wisdom was unfathomable, beyond the limits of comprehension but not the limits of mindful being.

In ancient times even a simple mistake could be life threatening. The master and sages of old therefore approached life with great care and awareness. Lao Tzu uses the analogy of crossing an ice-covered stream to convey this. Sages were alert and cautious, akin to a warrior in enemy territory, yet they also displayed the courtesy of a guest. This suggests that they navigated life with a delicate balance of strength and humility, embodying virtues such as courage, humility, gratitude and respect. Despite his success in battle, the greatest warrior could still be a good guest and a gentle man.

The passage also emphasizes the fluidity and adaptability of the ancient masters. They, like the Tao, were as malleable as the melting of ice, able to be shaped like raw wood. This points to their openness to change and their ability to learn, adapt and grow. They were also receptive, like a valley that collects and welcomes everything into its midst. Their thoughts and speech were clear, like a glass of water that is unambiguous and reflects reality without distortion.

In the final part of this passage Lao Tzu presents a contemplation on both patience and presence. He questions whether we have the patience to wait and stay unmoved until our own understanding becomes clear and the mud of confusion settles. The passage then turns to a reflection on being entirely present. By doing so, Lao Tzu emphasizes the importance of inner stillness and clarity, an inner peace void of distraction despite our circumstance. To do so is to have truly mastered the Tao. Lao Tzu concludes with the idea that true mastery in life lies not in seeking fulfillment or expecting certain outcomes. Seeking and expectation are both manifestations of ego. As the master is entirely present in the moment, he or she has found a way to dissolve and eliminate ego. By being "mindful", i.e., by learning how to meditate and by practicing it, one embraces this state of presence. When we are entirely present, we can cultivate the ability to welcome all things with an open mind and an open heart and respond to them as integral consubstantial parts of the eternal and infinite universal Tao.

Finally, the passage by Lao Tzu invites us to contemplate and emulate the traits and attitudes of the ancient masters. These qualities of profound wisdom include, but are not limited to sincere humility and gratitude, mindfulness, the ability to be fully present, clarity in thought and speech, great patience, and adaptability and above all, the ability to exercise universally unconditional and indiscriminate compassion. Lao Tzu's passages here should encourage those of us who are so inclined toward mastery of the Tao and our daily lives to cultivate these qualities within ourselves as we navigate our own paths of inner growth towards peace and ultimately to our own enlightenment and understanding of the Tao and its Integral Way, our place in the universe and our own destiny and reason for being.

CHAPTER 16

Life and Death

OF ALL THOUGHTS,
ONE'S MIND MUST BE EMPTY.
AT PEACE, ONE MUST LET ONE'S HEART BE.
ONE SHOULD SEE NOT ONLY THE TURMOIL OF
BEINGS
BUT CONTEMPLATE THEIR RETURN
TO THE COMMON SOURCE OF ALL.
IN THE RETURN TO THE SOURCE
TO WHICH EACH BEING
OF THE UNIVERSE RETURNS,
SERENITY IS FOUND;
JUST AS IS ONE'S OWN.

TO NOT REALIZE THE SOURCE
IS TO STUMBLE IN CONFUSION AND SORROW.
ONE BECOMES TOLERANT,
DISINTERESTED AND AMUSED,
AS ONE, BY NATURE REALIZES
FROM WHENCE THEY CAME,

KINDHEARTED AS A GRANDMOTHER,
DIGNIFIED AS A KING,
IMMERSED IN THE WONDER OF THE TAO,
ONE CAN HANDLE WHATEVER LIFE BRINGS.
ABIDED IN THE TAO,
AT THE TIME THAT ONE'S DEATH COMES
ONE IS READY.

N. MICHAEL MURBURG, JR.

Introduction

Years ago, before I began to become a serious student of the Tao and writer about the Integral way, I watched the Coen brothers' movie, The Big Lebowski starring Jeff Bridges. Bridges' character the protagonist never seemed to worry about anything despite the ironic and absurd circumstances that surrounded him. He just accepted life for what it was. He simply went with the flow. As circumstances changed, he changed his approach and despite the trying situations the storyline placed upon the protagonist Lebowski, aka, "the Dude" everything seemed to eventually work out for him just fine in the end. Life goes on. Don't make too much of things. Let go of the bad stuff. No need to worry. Be patient. Be good with people. Ultimately things will work out for you. That was the message.

In 1998 when the movie was released, Sam Elliott's statement at the end of the movie to the Dude "Take it easy dude, I know you will." to which Lebowski replies "The dude abides." made me ask, "Abide in what?'. Years later I would begin to find out. It would be my experience that movies like Bridges' The Big Lebowski and Simon Pegg's 2014 performance in Hector and the Search for Happiness and Harry Dean Stanton's* spiritual search for the Tao in life and in the movie Lucky as well in 2017 helped fill in the gaps and provided the same message that I gleaned from my study of the Tao. Abide in the Tao and the Tao will abide in you.

To Abide in the Tao

In the passage above, Lao Tzu segues into a deep exploration of the Tao, that subtle field of intelligent energy, information and Uber consciousness that births and connects us to everything and everything to us. Lao Tzu, as he has done in his previous chapters, reminds us that finding serenity and wisdom are done through emptying the mind and reposeful contemplation of the Tao, the source of all being. Lao Tzu teaches us that realizing this source brings us peace, tranquility, tolerance, disinterest in worldly concerns, and brings to us a joyous sense of amusement. The text also conveys a sense of kindness, dignity, and readiness for life's challenges and even fearless insight into and readiness for our inevitable death once we have become immersed in the understanding of the Tao and following its Integral Way. One who understands or "groks" the Tao recognizes the fundamental way or path of their own infinite conscious universal existence, or "soul" if you will, that is beyond physical life and death. To learn to do so is to connect with the Tao and all of its creation, in short to trust in and "abide in the Tao".

The passage above also reflects Lao Tzu's ideas on wisdom and his insights related to emptiness, peace, contemplation, and one's return to their Tao source. To do so, to "abide" in, or to accept or act in accordance with the Tao, one needs to meditate and train their mind to be empty of thoughts, allowing for clarity and peace to arise. By emoting the mind of thought and by cultivating a serene and tranquil heart, we can observe not only the troubles and conflicts of all beings but also contemplate their and our eventual return to the Tao, the common source of all.

The passage particularly emphasizes the importance of recognizing and realizing this infinite source, as failing to do so leads to confusion and sorrow. Through this recognition of the Tao, we become tolerant, disinterested, and amused, and more easily see and understand the natural cycle of existence and the interconnectedness of all things. This recognition allows us to embody qualities such as love and kindness, with resemblance to that of a grandmother, and wisdom and dignity, resembling that of a king. By abiding and immersing ourselves in the wonder of the Tao, we become capable of gracefully navigating the multitude of various challenges that life presents to us.

Ultimately, Lao Tzu concludes with the notion that those who are abided in the Tao are ready for whatever comes, even in the face of death. This suggests that by being deeply connected to the source and understanding the transient nature of all physical existence, we can be at peace and be prepared for the eventual end of our lives here on earth. Death is not the end of that which is eternal. It is merely a point of further transition, evolution and spiritual awareness and existential refinement that is the path of all that is created by the Tao.

Overall, the passage conveys the idea that by emptying our minds, finding peace within, recognizing the common source of all being and all beings themselves, and by immersing ourselves in the wonder of the Tao, we can attain serenity, handle life's challenges, and be ready for the inevitable process of death and rebirth. Lao Tzu invites us to contemplate the nature of our own existence and purpose for being, the unity and interconnectedness of all things, and the importance of finding inner peace and wisdom in the face of life's uncertainties and becoming the living human embodiment of the Tao itself. In the end, this is how and in what the Dude ultimately abides.

CHAPTER 17

The Tao of Leadership, The Tao Te Ching, The New Paradigm for Leadership and Governance on Earth in a Post-Extraterrestrial Contact World

WHEN PEOPLE
ARE GOVERNED PROPERLY,
THOSE WHO ARE GOVERNED
ARE HARDLY AWARE
OF THE EXISTENCE OF
THEIR MASTERFUL LEADER.

BENEATH THE MASTERFUL LEADER
COMES THE BELOVED LEADER.

BELOW THE BELOVED LEADER
IS THE LEADER WHO IS FEARED.

THE LEADER WHO IS BENEATH ALL
IS THE LEADER WHO IS DESPISED.

IF A LEADER DOES NOT TRUST HIS PEOPLE
HE CAUSES THEM TO BE UNTRUSTWORTHY.

THE MASTER SPEAKS LITTLE.
INSTEAD OF WORDS, THE MASTER ACTS.

WHEN PEOPLE ARE MASTERFULLY GOVERNED,
WHEN ALL THE WORK IS DONE,
BY THOSE WHO ARE PROPERLY LED
THE PEOPLE WILL REMARK,
„WE DID EVERYTHING BY OURSELVES,
AMAZING!".

Introduction

In this passage that I like to refer to as "The Tao of Leadership", Lao Tzu discusses the hierarchy of types of leaders and levels of governing ability. He observes and tells us that effective leadership is subtle and unobtrusive, with the governed hardly aware of their leader's presence. He also emphasizes the importance of trust, especially between leaders and their people.

When leadership is done well, people take ownership of their actions and pride in their accomplishments, feeling as though they did everything by themselves. This attitude of those who are governed well indicates an accomplished, harmonious and well-governed society. It is one that is based on personal responsibility, creativity, self-reliance and ultimately on self-governance. Such a society is capable of many great things. Self-governance is the hallmark of all higher beings and inevitably of their societies when it is taught, encouraged, recognized and rewarded within them.

The Tao of Leadership

This passage explores the concept of great leadership and proper governance. It suggests that when people are governed properly, they are hardly aware of the existence of their masterful leader, indicating that effective leadership operates behind the scenes, allowing the governed to employ their own creativity to solve problems and to collaborate and thrive without feeling oppressed or restricted. This form of governance fosters the reality that who they is trusted are and what they are is valued. This creates feelings of individual and social responsibility and nurtures their own abilities in the direction of self-governance.

Lao Tzu further describes different levels of leadership. Below the masterful leader in effectiveness is the beloved leader, who is held in high regard by the people. Below the beloved leader is the leader who is feared, implying that this leader is not a good or effective one as he or she relies on fear and intimidation to maintain control. Lastly, the leader who is despised occupies the lowest level of leadership, likely due to their inability to gain the trust and respect of the people. This sort of leadership is the least desired and least effective of all the forms of leadership. As history has shown us, leaders who are despised have reigns and legacies that are short lived.

Importantly, Lao Tzu's passage on leadership highlights the importance of trust between a leader and their people. If a leader does not trust their subordinates, it creates an environment of mistrust where the people may become untrustworthy themselves. This indicates that trust is a vital element in effective governance and leadership.

Just as the master teaches without teaching, the master leads without leading, this passage also suggests that like example, actions speak louder than words. The master speaks little but acts decisively, implying that true leadership is demonstrated through action and example, rather than through empty promises or persuasive rhetoric.

When people are properly led and masterfully governed the work is successfully accomplished by those who are properly assigned to it. Lao Tzu suggests that when the work is done and the tasks accomplished, the people will perceive their achievements as their own, feeling a sense of mastery, empowerment, ownership and autonomy. They may exclaim, "We did everything by ourselves, amazing!" This speaks to the idea that effective leadership is not about centralized control and power but empowering and enabling individuals to take charge of their own success and by extension their own destinies.

Overall, Lao Tzu explores not only the qualities and dynamics of different levels of leadership, emphasizing the importance of trust, action, and empowering governance but the needs of the governed to be met. In the end, effective leadership goes unnoticed and allows individuals to flourish independently, resulting in a sense of accomplishment and self-reliance among the people and respect and trust in those who compassionately and effectively lead them.

CHAPTER 18

**WHEN FORGOTTEN IS THE GREAT TAO
THERE APPEAR PIETY AND GOODNESS.
WHEN THE INTELLIGENCE OF THE BODY WANES
THERE COMES FORTH KNOWLEDGE AND CLE-
VERNESS.
IN THE FAMILY, WHEN PEACE DOES NOT EXIST
THERE BEGINS FILIAL PIETY.
PATRIOTISM IS BORN
WHEN THE COUNTRY
FALLS INTO
CHAOS.**

The Consequences of Forgetting the Great Tao

The lines above by Lao Tzu: provide profound insights into the relationship between forgetting the infinite Tao, the underlying force that governs all existence, and the subsequent emergence of lesser human virtues like piety, goodness, knowledge, cleverness, filial piety, and patriotism as inferior substitutes. They are a reflection on the relationship between forgetting the infinite Tao and the consequential rise in the adversity, and denigration of the human experience from diluting the divine manifestation of the Tao in human systems and relationships into admirable, though lesser, human virtues like piety, goodness, knowledge, cleverness, filial piety, and patriotism.

The Absence of the Great Tao

The Tao, when remembered and embraced, brings harmony and balance to all aspects of life. However, when the Tao is forgotten, we witness the gradual decline of the intelligence of the body, the disruption of familial peace, and the societal descent into chaos within a nation. These consequences highlight the pivotal role played by the Tao in governing our actions and promoting well-being on both individual and societal levels. When the Tao is remembered and abided in, all things seamlessly fall into place. When the Tao is forgotten, we suffer. The development of fundamental virtues such as piety, knowledge, filial piety, and patriotism are no substitute for the divine self-governance provided by the Tao and abiding in its Integral Way.

Piety and Goodness, Substitutes Emerging from the Forgotten Tao

When individuals forget the teachings and principles of the great Tao, they often find themselves searching for alternative sources of guidance and moral grounding. The absence of a spiritual foundation rooted in the non-egoic nature of the Tao prompts individuals who find themselves in a virtual vacuum causing them to turn inward, seeking connection with something larger than themselves. In this quest for meaning and a moral compass, piety and goodness emerge as prevailing virtues. It is both fascinating and hopeful to witness the development of individuals who exhibit genuine acts of piety and kindness, even in the absence of a direct connection to the Tao. However, both piety and goodness can be feigned and often are used to the advantage of those who seek to manipulate the masses and gain social and political control.

Knowledge and Cleverness in the Wake of Waning Intelligence

As the memory of the Tao dissipates and is forgotten, the body's natural intelligence and intuition weaken. As spiritual understanding of the Tao wanes, the mind compensates by engaging in intellectual pursuits. This compensation can result in a deepening value of knowledge and the cultivation of cleverness at the expense of spiritual development. Without the heart to govern, the head takes over. When faced with spiritual limitations, individuals find solace and strength through the expansion of their mental faculties. Many individuals may then find themselves compensating for the loss of their intuitive intelligence by relying on knowledge and cleverness. However useful, these are no substitute for the Tao.

In situations where the Tao is forgotten, the pursuit of knowledge becomes paramount, as individuals seek to fill the void left by the absence of their spiritual wisdom and insight. While knowledge and cleverness can offer temporary solutions, they pale in comparison to the profound understanding and holistic intelligence that the Tao can provide.

Filial Piety as a Response to Family Discord

The absence of peace within families is a consequence of deviating from the Tao's path. When the Tao is no longer allowed to govern, bonds can fracture, and relationships can deteriorate. Families then become plagued by discord and disharmony. However, it is precisely during times of familial discord and the absence of peace that compels individuals to reassess their values and priorities. Paradoxically, it is in these tumultuous circumstances that in place of genuine filial love and compassion, filial piety often emerges in the Tao's void.

In an effort to restore harmony, family members may again begin to recognize the importance of cherishing and nurturing their familial ties and strive to restore harmony by embodying the values and principles that the Tao represents. Filial piety, which involves showing respect and gratitude towards one's family, though inferior to true patience, love and compassion can begin to fill the large void created by the Tao's forgotten presence and serve as a catalyst for healing and reconciliation within strained family relationships. However admirable, filial piety is no substitute for the genuine governance of the Tao.

Patriotism Arising from National Chaos

Because political philosophies and nation states are not founded on the principles of the Tao and the Integral Way, their order
and stability are only temporary. It is the nature of nation states
to be transitional as they are born, grow, age, decline, create
conflict and then collapse and die. In the passage above, Lao
Tzu reminds us that patriotism arises as a symptom of a country falling into chaos. Even though the absence of a cohesive
societal structure can prompt individuals to band together and
work towards restoration and stability, these are measures taken
by civilizations in decline. This decline can be forestalled but
it cannot be reversed. Because of this inevitability it is worth
remembering the truth of the adage that in patriotism is found
the last bastion of the scoundrel.

Conclusion

In societies where the Tao is not allowed to govern, periods of
chaos and uncertainty inevitably arise. Consequently, people
begin to see the world in a dualistic fashion. Instead of life being one great integrated thing, people begin to see the world as
"us" and "them". There, rather than love for one's fellow man,
patriotism, the love for one's country begins to flourish as the
foundations of a nation crumble and individuals are prompted
to rally together and protect the values and ideals they hold
dear. Without the Tao to govern, the sense of unity and cohesion that arises from adversity give rise to a profound sense of
patriotism. Even though a patriot's love for country may go
beyond personal gain, motivating individuals to contribute
actively towards the restoration of order and stability, it is no
substitute for the Tao. Inevitably, the loss of the Tao in society
devolves it into nationalism, then tribalism, conflict, and chaos.

In the end, the passage above by Lao Tzu provide profound
insights into the consequences of forgetting the great Tao.
While the emergence of virtues like piety, goodness, knowl-

edge, cleverness and patriotism may seem positive, it is crucial to remember that they are not sustainable substitutes for the holistic wisdom and self-governance provided by the Tao. Recognizing the importance of the Tao and abiding by its Integral Way and the universal virtues of simplicity, patience, compassion and truth and by recognizing the universal laws of karma and energy response we can lead more harmonious existences, both on an individual and societal level and inevitably on the level of human civilization as well.

CHAPTER 19

Embracing the Center

**IF HOLINESS AND WISDOM WERE THROWN AWAY,
A HUNDRED TIMES HAPPIER WOULD PEOPLE BE-
COME.
TOSS AWAY WITH MORALITY AND JUSTICE,
PEOPLE WILL DO WHAT IS RIGHT.
DO AWAY WITH INDUSTRY AND PROFIT,
THERE WILL BE NO THIEVES.**

**IF THESE ACTIONS ARE NOT ENOUGH,
ONE MERELY SHOULD STAY WITHIN THE CIRCLE'S
CENTER
AND ALLOW EVERYTHING TO TAKE ITS COURSE.**

Challenging Conventions: Embracing the Inner Circle

The lines by Lao Tzu, "If holiness and wisdom were thrown away, a hundred times happier would people become. Toss away morality and justice, people will do what is right. Do away with industry and profit, there will be no thieves," provoke contemplation on the impact of detaching from conventional norms and embracing a more innate and spontaneous way of living. These words should prompt us to explore the potential benefits of relinquishing societal constructs and embracing the wisdom found within the center of our own life's circle, allowing everything to take its natural course.

The Liberation from Holiness and Wisdom

Contrary to conventional belief, Lao Tzu suggests that discarding the notions of holiness and wisdom could lead to increased happiness. In a society burdened by expectations and rigid beliefs, individuals often find themselves constrained by the pursuit of external validation and the pressure to conform. By shedding the limitations of what we label as holiness and wisdom, individuals may discover a newfound freedom to express their true selves, unburdened by expectations and conditioned thinking.

Paradigm Shift: Morality and Justice

The idea of discarding morality and justice may seem contradictory to the principles that uphold a functioning society. However, Lao Tzu challenges us to contemplate a paradigm shift. Instead of relying solely on external moral codes and rigid systems of justice, he posits that individuals would naturally do what is right if freed from the constraints of societal expectations. By cultivating inner awareness and listening to their inherent sense of right and wrong, healthy individuals can find their innate moral compaseses. Such an approach fosters both individuals and societies to undertake the responsibilities of their own personal development and the foresight to see that the actions of one are not isolated incidences that affect only the self but thr existence of all.

Redefining Succes: Industry and Profit

In a world driven by relentless pursuit of industrial progress and material wealth, Lao Tzu suggests that eliminating the obsession with industry and profit would eradicate the existence of theft. By shifting the focus away from physical wealth, material accumulation and embracing a more balanced approach to life, individuals can alleviate societal discontent by focusing less on doing and more on being and foster harmony that stems from a deeper connection with one's true purpose and the natural world.

The Circle's Center: Embracing Harmony

When Lao Tzu suggests "staying within the circle's center," he emphasizes the importance of the Tao in our hearts. He also invites us to embrace the philosophy of Wu Wei, which emphasizes non-action and the alignment with the natural flow of life. By relinquishing control and surrendering to the universal forces of the Tao at play, individuals can find inner peace and navigate life's challenges with greater ease. This shift allows everything to take its natural course, steering us away from unnatural choices and deleterious consequences and aligning us with the harmonious rhythm of the universe.

Conclusion

The lines by Lao Tzu propose a radical departure from conventional thinking, urging individuals to question the societal norms that shackle us to materialism and to embrace a more intuitive spiritual and spontaneous way of living. While the idea of discarding holiness, wisdom, morality, justice, industry, and profit may seem counterintuitive, it offers a glimpse into the potential benefits of detaching from societal constructs and connecting with the Tao and one's inner wisdom. By staying within the circle's center and allowing everything to take its course, individuals can unlock a profound sense of freedom, contentment, and harmony with the world around them. External governance is close to unnecessary in a society that is based in the unifying consciousness that is the Tao and encourages personal responsibility and self-governance as the natural extension of lives of truth that exemplify the "Three Treasures" of the Tao: simplicity, patience and compassion.

CHAPTER 20

BY STOPPING THOUGHT ONE ENDS THEIR PRO-
BLEMS.
YES AND NO,
WHAT IS THE DIFFERENCE BETWEEN THEM?
SUCCESS AND FAILURE,
WHAT IS THEIR DIFFERENCE?
MUST WHAT OTHERS VALUE ALSO BE VALUED BY
YOU?
MUST WHAT OTHERS AVOID BE AVOIDED BY YOU
TOO?
TO SO DO IS RIDICULOUS.

OTHERS ARE EXCITED AS IF AT A PARADE.
YET I ALONE DO NOT CARE.
SOLITARY AND EXPRESSIONLESS AM I,
AS IS AN INFANT, BEFORE IT IS ABLE TO SMILE.

OTHERS HAVE WHAT THEY NEED;
NOTHING DO I ALONE POSSESS.
SINGULARLY I FLOAT ABOUT,
AS IF I WERE ONE WITHOUT A HOME.
MY MIND IS WITHOUT CONTENT,
AS IF I WERE AN IDIOT.

OTHERS ARE ILLUMINATED.
YET ALONE, I AM DARK.
OTHERS ARE HONED;
YET ONLY I AM DULL.

OTHERS LIVE WITH A PURPOSE;
ONLY I DO NOT KNOW.
AS A WAVE UPON THE SEA I DRIFT.
AIMLESSLY AS THE BREEZE, I BLOW.

FROM AN ORDINARY PERSON, I AM DIFFERENT. I SLAKE MY THIRST FROM THE BREASTS OF THE GREAT MOTHER TAO.

Embracing the Paradox: Finding Freedom in Non-Differentiation

The lines presented by Lao Tzu challenge our conventional understanding of concepts such as thought, difference, success, failure, and societal values. It is worth exploring the wisdom behind Lao Tzu's words, which advocate for the cessation of thought and the dissolution of rigid distinctions. By letting go of societal standards and embracing non-differentiation, we can find liberation and a deep connection with the nurturing essence of the Tao.

The Cessation of Thought and the End of Problems

Lao Tzu tells us that by stopping thought, we can put an end to problems. Thinking is helpful and necessary, but thinking too much is not. Thinking too much is the part of the human mind that drives us to madness. In a world dominated by overthinking, constant mental activity and environmental chatter, we can become entangled in self-created problems and conflicts. By quieting the mind through meditation and embracing stillness, we can gain clarity and break free from the cycle of mental distraction and unnecessary troubles and find peace in life, no matter where we are.

Transcending Dichotomies - Yes and No, Success and Failure

Lao Tzu questions the inherent differences between opposites such as yes and no, success and failure. In a reality shaped by dualistic thinking, individuals often get caught in the perpetual pursuit of one extreme at the expense of the other. By transcending these dichotomies and embracing non-differentiation, we find a freedom from ego and its duality that takes us beyond the limitations of polarized thinking and into the realm of the unity consciousness that in the Tao.

Liberating Oneself from the Influence of Others

Lao Tzu also challenges the notion that one must align their values and actions with societal norms. Instead, he suggests that it is ridiculous to conform to what others value or avoid. By detaching from the expectations imposed by society, we can find true authenticity and freedom from the need for external validation. This is how one holds on to one's center and makes the center hold. Do not let others define you. Find what is most real and natural to you. There you will find your center.

Embracing Solitude and Simplicity

Lao Tzu describes a state of solitude and expressionlessness as an infant before it learns to smile. He emphasizes the importance of being content with ourselves and finding fulfillment in simplicity. By letting go of the pursuit of possessions, our desires, and the constant pursuit of external achievements, we can escape suffering and find inner peace and a connection with those around us through the nurturing embrace of the great Mother Tao.

Surrendering to the Mystery

Finally, Lao Tzu acknowledges the contrasting states of illumination and darkness, honing and dullness. He embraces the mystery of existence, where understanding is not limited to intellectual enlightenment. By surrendering to the natural ebb and flow of life's currents, one drifts like a wave upon the sea or seemingly blows aimlessly like a feather in the breeze - finding freedom in the acceptance of the unknown, trusting in the Tao and understanding that this unknown will be there until we are ultimately reunited entirely with our creator.

Conclusion

Lao Tzu's poetic expression in these lines above invites us to question our attachment to thoughts, divisions, societal expectations, and the ego's relentless pursuit of external achievements. By embracing non-differentiation, solitude, simplicity, dissolving our egos and surrendering to the mystery of existence, we can find a profound connection with the nurturing essence of the Tao. In letting go of the need for constant validation and unending pursuits, true freedom and contentment can be found in the peace and stillness that comes in the natural course of a Tao-centered life.

CHAPTER 21

The Master's Mind

THE MASTER KEEPS TO THE MASTER'S MIND
AT ONE ALWAYS WITH THE TAO.
THIS GIVES THE MASTER THE MASTER'S RA-
DIANCE.

IF SO DARK AND IMMEASURABLE IS THE TAO,
HOW CAN IT MAKE THE MASTER RADIANT?
THE MASTER IS RADIANT BECAUSE
THE MASTER ALLOWS THE TAO
TO MAKE THE MASTER RADIANT.

IF THE TAO IS SO UNABLE FOR ONE TO GRASP,
HOW CAN THE MASTER'S MIND BE ONE WITH IT?
THE MASTER'S MIND IS ONE WITH THE TAO
BECAUSE THE MASTER DOES NOT CLING
TO IDEAS.

BECAUSE THE TAO EXISTED
BEFORE TIME AND SPACE,
IT IS BEYOND BEING AND NON BEING.
IT IS BEYOND WHAT IS AND WHAT IS NOT.

HOW DO I KNOW THIS TO BE TRUE?
BECAUSE THE MASTER LOOKS INSIDE AND SEES
THAT IT IS TRUE.

The Radiant Master and the Eternal Tao: Illuminating the
Path to Inner Harmony

Here in the Tao Te Ching, Lao Tzu, introduces the reader to
the concept of the Master-Mind relationship with the Tao. By

exploring the essence of this connection, we unveil the ways in which the Master achieves radiance through alignment with the Tao. Through an analysis of the contrasting characteristics of the Tao, we can learn about the power of harmony and mindfulness in achieving inner radiance and enlightenment.

The Master's radiance is a product of their deep understanding that the Tao is an enigmatic force, beyond human comprehension. By relinquishing attachment to ideas and embracing the eternal nature of the Tao, the Master's mind becomes enlightened and one with it, paving the way for radiant wisdom and inner harmony.

The Tao's Dark and Immeasurable Nature

The Tao is described as the underlying intelligent force and creator omnipresent in all existence. It is an entity so profound and vast that human intellect struggles to comprehend its essence. Its mystery lies in its immeasurable, formless nature, which transcends conventional understanding. This darkness, rather than being a limitation, is the catalyst for the Master's radiance.

Radiance and the Master's Alignment with the Tao

The Master's radiance arises from their willingness to surrender and allow the Tao to guide their thoughts and actions. By letting go of rigid ideas and preconceptions, the Master embraces the harmony and flow of the Tao. This alignment creates a state of radiant ego lessness that emanates from the Master's being, illuminating their path and inspiring others.

The Tao's Ungraspable Essence

The Tao, as best one can encapsulate the Tao is the creative divine intelligence that underlies all phenomena in existence. It is the vast intelligent energy that gives rise to existence itself.

It is. It is the organizing principle of being itself that pervades the entire universe and causes the arising of all form.

Even though the Tao exists everywhere and in everything, the Tao is beyond human grasp, existing beyond the boundaries of time and space. Its fluidity and non-dualistic nature challenge the limitations of human cognition. However, the Master's mind becomes one with the Tao precisely because it does not attempt to grasp or confine it. The master sees its mystery and surrenders to it. The master accepts the world and the Tao as it presents itself. He or she sees things for what they are. It is through the openness and acceptance that the Master gains insight into himself and the deep transformative power of the Tao.

Beyond Being and Non-Being

The Tao defies traditional notions of existence and non-existence. It transcends duality, encompassing both what is seen and what is unseen, what is and what is not. This paradoxical nature of the Tao allows the Master to transcend conventional dualistic thinking and immerse himself in a state of non-clinging. It is through this understanding and openness that the Master aligns their mind with the limitless potential of the Tao.

Conclusion

In this passage, Lao Tzu gives us the opportunity to think about and explore the relationship between the Master and the Tao, unveiling the source of the Master's enlightenment and their radiant wisdom. By embracing the paradoxes of the Tao, the Master's mind becomes one with its mysterious, limitless power. Through relinquishing attachment to ideas and embracing harmony, the Master creates his or her inner radiance, contributing to their state of enlightenment and to that of those around them. The profound insights of the Tao and the Master's alignment with it serve as a guide for those who seek harmony and authenticity in their own lives and seek to bring peace to their families, communities and to the world and to harmonize these all with the universe that surrounds them.

CHAPTER 22

How Does the Master Succeed?

TO BECOME WHOLE,
LET YOURSELF YIELD.
TO BECOME STRAIGHT,
ALLOW YOURSELF TO BE CROOKED.
TO BECOME FULL,
ALLOW YOURSELF TO BE EMPTY.
TO BE REBORN,
ALLOW YOURSELF DEATH.
TO GAIN EVERYTHING,
GIVE UP ALL.

BY BEING AND LIVING IN THE TAO,
THE MASTER EMERGES
AND SETS AN EXAMPLE FOR ALL.

BY NOT DISPLAYING HIMSELF,
THE MASTER'S LIGHT IS SEEN BY OTHERS.

AS THE MASTER HAS NOTHING TO PROVE
HIS WORDS CAN BE TRUSTED.

THE MASTER DOES NOT KNOW
HIS OWN IDENTITY,
SO OTHERS SEE THEMSELVES IN HIM.
BECAUSE THE MASTER HAS IN MIND NO GOAL,
IN EVERYTHING THE MASTER DOES,
THE MASTER SUCCEEDS.

LONG AGO THE MASTERS OF OLD SAID,
„IF YOU WANT TO BE GIVEN EVERYTHING,
GIVE EVERYTHING UP".

THESE SAYINGS WERE NOT HOLLOW. ONE CAN TRULY, ONLY BE ONESELF IN A LIFE LIVED IN ACCORDANCE WITH THE TAO.

Embracing the Tao: The Path to Wholeness and Authenticity

The path to becoming whole and finding our authentic selves lies in embracing the truth and the teachings of the Tao. These concepts were illuminated by the Masters of old. In this passage Lao Tzu delves into the transformative power of yielding, embracing imperfections, letting go, and trusting in the innate wisdom of the Tao. By aligning ourselves with the Tao, we not only emerge as Masters of living but also serve as examples for others to embrace the Tao and find their true selves.

Through yielding, embracing imperfections, letting go, and trusting the wisdom of the Tao, the Master allows the radiant light of authenticity to shine, inspiring others to embark on their own journey towards enlightenment, self-discovery, wholeness and heightened states of awareness and our own spiritual evolution and conscious immortality.

Yielding to Become Whole

The Tao teaches us that true wholeness is achieved not through force or resistance but rather, like water, through patience and yielding. By acknowledging our vulnerabilities and accepting ourselves as imperfect beings, we open up possibilities for growth and inner harmony. It is in yielding that the Master finds the path to becoming whole and encourages others to do the same.

Embracing Imperfection to Find Authenticity

In the quest for perfection, we often neglect our true selves. The Masters of old understood that embracing imperfections is the key to authenticity. By acknowledging our flaws and idiosyncrasies, we allow our true essence to shine through. The Master, by accepting and embracing their own imperfections, becomes a mirror for others to recognize their own special gifts and challenges and embrace their own uniqueness and to be as the Tao meant them to be.

Letting Go to Experience Fulfillment

The journey towards fulfillment requires letting go of attachments and expectations. The Master teaches that true fulfillment is found not in accumulating possessions or achievements but in emptying ourselves of the burdens that weigh us down. By releasing our attachments, we create space for the beauty and abundance of the Tao to flow into our lives.

Trusting the Wisdom of the Tao

The Master, devoid of personal ambition or ego, fully surrenders to and trusts the wisdom of the Tao. By embracing a state of non-knowing, the Master becomes a vessel through which the Tao can work its transformative powers. By trusting the Tao, the Master gains the trust of others, as their words and actions become rooted in the authenticity and wisdom of the Tao.

Conclusion

Living in accordance with the teachings of the Tao allows us to embrace our true selves and live a life of wholeness, truth and authenticity. By yielding, embracing imperfections, letting go, and trusting the wisdom of the Tao, we not only achieve our own fulfillment but also inspire and guide others to embark on their own heroic and transformative journeys. Just as the Masters of old have shown us, the path to self-discovery, spiritual evolution and lasting success lies in embracing the profound wisdom of the Tao.

CHAPTER 23

Opening Oneself to the Tao

ONE SHOULD SAY THEIR PIECE
COMPLETELY, THEN BE SILENT.
ONE SHOULD BE LIKE THE FORCES OF NATURE.
WHILE A STORM BLOWS, THERE IS ONLY THE
WIND.
WHEN IT RAINS, THERE IS ONLY THE RAIN.
AS CLOUDS PASS, THE SUN BREAKS THROUGH.

IF ONE OPENS ONE'S SELF TO THE TAO,
THE TAO AND THE SELF ARE ONE.
ONE CAN THEREFORE EMBODY THE TAO COM-
PLETELY.

IF ONE OPENS ONE'S SELF TO INSIGHT,
ONE IS THEN ONE WITH INSIGHT
THEREBY ONE CAN USE INSIGHT COMPLETELY.

IF ONE OPENS ONE'S SELF TO A LOSS,
ONE IS AT ONE WITH THAT LOSS.
WHEN ONE IS AT ONE WITH THE LOSS,
THEN THE LOSS MAY BE ACCEPTED COMPLETELY.

ONE SHOULD OPEN ONE'S SELF TO THE TAO,
AND TRUST ONE'S OWN NATURAL RESPONSES.
THEN ALL WILL FALL INTO PLACE.

Embodying the Tao: Embracing the Natural Way for Harmony
and Completeness

The teachings about the Tao through Lao Tzu's words guide
us to welcome and accept the qualities and forces of nature. By

being like the wind, rain, and sun, we learn the art of patience, silence, persistence, the power of embodiment, and the wisdom of trust. There is profound wisdom in being one with the Tao. In this passage, Lao Tzu uses insight, and loss to highlight the importance of aligning with our own natural responses to find peace, harmony and wholeness. By opening ourselves to the Tao, embracing insight, and accepting grief and loss, we become embodiments of the Tao, allowing all aspects of our lives to fall into place harmoniously.

Embracing Silence: Being Like the Forces of Nature

The Tao teaches us to express ourselves completely and then embrace silence. Just as the forces of nature operate with minimal disruption or resistance, we can learn to be like the wind, rain, and sun. When misfortune befalls us, it is useful to remember that no storm can blow forever. The rains, like our tears, eventually subside and the sun inevitably comes out despite the dark enormity of clouds. All things and events eventually take their natural course. By embodying our innate Tao qualities, and by letting nature take its course, we find peace in silence and allow the natural flow of life to again unfold.

Oneness with the Tao: Embodying Completeness

By opening ourselves to the essence of the Tao and recognizing our intrinsic connection with it brings about a state of timeless oneness. By aligning our thoughts, actions, and intentions with the Tao, we embody completeness. This calming alignment allows us to navigate life with ease and grace, finding fulfillment in every aspect of our existence.

Insight: Opening to Wisdom and Unity

By opening ourselves to silent and reflective insight, and through meditation, for example, we cultivate a deep sense of connection and unity with all things. When we are one with insight, we gain access to a profound wisdom that guides our choices and actions. Embracing this insight completely allows us the patience and timing to make decisions in alignment with the compassionate and naturally spontaneous flow of the Tao.

Acceptance of Loss: Being at One with Impermanence

Allowing ourselves to be at one with loss enables us to embrace the inevitable changes and impermanence of life. Instead of resisting or clinging to what is lost, even the loss of a spouse or child, we accept it as an integral part of the natural order. By surrendering to our loss completely, we find the strength and resilience to move forward with the grace, spiritual growth and understanding that come with surviving great loss and the strength to help others in their time of need after a great loss. By accepting great loss and reacting to it with poise, strength and dignity, we have the opportunity to step up to the plate, so to speak, and lead. To be vulnerable but at the same time to summon such strength that we can become a beacon of light to help and lead others in their own time of loss is the hallmark of a follower of the Tao and its integral Way.

Conclusion

By embracing the teachings of the Tao and by following its Integral Way, we open the door to embodying its wisdom and finding harmony within ourselves and the world around us. By understanding and being like the forces of nature, embracing silence, embodying completeness, and trusting our natural responses, we align with the natural flow of the Tao. Through this alignment, we find peace, wholeness, and a deep connection to the wisdom within. The Tao teaches us to trust the process, to be patient and to allow all aspects of life to fall into place, revealing the profound beauty of living in harmony with the Tao and its natural way.

CHAPTER 24

ONE CANNOT STAND FIRM
BY STANDING ON ONE'S TIPTOES.

WHEN ONE SPRINTS AHEAD,
ONE CANNOT PROGRESS FAR.

BY ATTEMPTING TO SHINE,
ONE'S OWN LIGHT IS DIMMED.

ONE WHOSE SELF IS DEFINED
CANNOT KNOW ONESELF.

ONE CANNOT EMPOWER ONESELF
BY EXERTING POWER OVER OTHERS.

ONE WHO FAILS TO LET GO OF HIS WORK
CANNOT CREATE THAT WHICH ENDURES.

TO BE IN ACCORD WITH THE TAO,
ONE MUST DO ONE'S WORK
AND THEN LET IT GO.

The Power of Reason, Balance, Humility, and Servant Leadership

Again, Lao Tzu gives us new insight into the Tao of leadership. In the pursuit of personal growth and effective leadership, the teachings of the Tao emphasize the importance of reason, balance, humility, and letting go. There is profound wisdom in this passage by Lao Tzu that stresses the importance of standing firm without striving for dominance, making progress through keeping a steady pace, shining without ego, defining oneself through selflessness, empowering by serving others, and creating enduring work by letting go. By aligning with the Tao and embodying these qualities, we can become impactful leaders who inspire others by our example and create lasting contributions that benefit all.

By embracing reason, balance, humility, and servant leadership, individuals align themselves with the Tao, resulting in personal growth, effective leadership, and the ability to create meaningful and enduring work.

Standing Firm with Balance: Reason and Stability

It is through reason and stability that one can truly stand firm. By maintaining a grounded state of mind and balanced perspective, individuals are better equipped to face challenges and make sound decisions. Striving for dominance, like standing on one's tiptoes, cannot be maintained for long. Such actions lead to instability and a loss of inner strength. True firmness comes from cultivating an unwavering commitment to true and balanced reasoning.

Progress Through Steady Pace: Humility and Sustainable Growth

Long journeys are the culmination of many small steps. True progress is not achieved by sprinting ahead but through a steady and sustainable pace. Embracing humility and acknowledging our limitations enables us to focus on continuous learning and improvement. By beginning with small steps and methodically progressing, we gain valuable insights and develop a deep understanding of the path we need to navigate to ultimately achieve meaningful and long-lasting growth.

Shining without Ego: True Leadership

Leadership is not about exerting power or seeking personal glory. It is about shining a light on others, supporting their growth, and fostering contribution and a collaborative environment. By letting go of the desire to shine solely for oneself, individuals can inspire and empower those around them, creating a collective radiance that illuminates the path to success.

Defining Oneself through Selflessness: Knowing and Empowering Others

True self-definition lies in selflessness. By letting go of self-interest and embracing a servant leadership mindset, individuals gain a profound understanding of themselves and others. By valuing and empowering others, they create an environment where everyone can thrive. Through humility and genuine care for others, true leaders nurture growth and foster a sense of unity and collective accomplishment. When allowed to excel, people will rise to the occasion.

Letting Go for Enduring Work: The Tao of Creation

As mentioned in Chapter 9 and here by Lao Tzu, the pursuit of creating lasting contributions, it is essential to let go. Holding tightly to one's work inhibits the work's ability to evolve and endure. By allowing ideas, projects, and creations to flow freely and adapt to changing circumstances, individuals tap into the creative power of the Tao. Letting go does not signify detachment but an acknowledgment that the true essence of enduring work transcends individual control, leaving room for growth and evolution and by allowing the work to have its own autonomy and to let it speak for itself when done.

Conclusion

By adopting the principles of reason, balance, humility, and leadership through servitude that are in alignment with the Tao yields both personal growth and impactful leadership. By standing firm with stability, progressing through humility, shining without ego, defining oneself through selflessness, and letting go to create enduring work, individuals navigate life's journey of self-discovery and meaningful impactful leadership. Through recognizing its existence and by using the wisdom of the Tao, individuals can inspire, empower, and create a lasting impact that can transform not only their lives but the lives of those around them and the universe as well.

Great journeys are the culmination of many small steps. True progress is not achieved by sprinting ahead but through a steady and sustainable pace. Embracing humility and acknowledging our limitations enables us to focus on continuous learning and improvement. By beginning with small steps and methodically progressing, we gain valuable insights and develop a deep understanding of the path we need to navigate to ultimately achieve meaningful and long-lasting growth.

CHAPTER 25

Embracing the Tao, The "Four Great Powers"

BEFORE THE UNIVERSE WAS BORN
THERE WAS SOMETHING MYSTERIOUS,
SILENT, INFINITE, IMMEASURABLE, FORMLESS
AND PERFECT IN ITS SOLITARY, EMPTY, SERENE,
UNCHANGING,
UNMOVING, INEXHAUSTIBLE AND ETERNAL
PRESENCE.

THE TAO MOVES AND GROWS WITHOUT END OR
EXHAUSTION.
MOTHER OF THE KNOWABLE AND UNKNOWABLE
UNIVERSE,
HER NAME IS UNKNOWN, YET SHE IS CALLED
"TAO", "THE GREAT".

WITHIN AND WITHOUT, SHE FLOWS THROUGH
ALL
AND RETURNS TO HER HEART,
THE ROOT AND ORIGIN OF ALL THINGS.

GREAT IS THE TAO.
THE UNIVERSE IS GREAT.
THE EARTH IS GREAT.
GREAT IS THE ONE WHO FOLLOWS THE TAO.
THE TAO, THE UNIVERSE, THE EARTH AND MAN:
THESE ARE THE FOUR GREAT POWERS.

JUST AS MAN FOLLOWS THE EARTH
THE EARTH FOLLOWS THE HEAVENS,
AND THE HEAVENS FOLLOW THE TAO;
ONLY ITSELF DOES THE TAO FOLLOW.

The Tao and the Four Great Powers: An Exploration of Infinite Wisdom

The Tao, as the all-encompassing force, flows through the Universe, Earth, and Man, representing the interconnectedness and interdependence of these four great powers. The profound essence of the Tao, described by Lao Tzu as mysterious, infinite, and formless, serves as the foundation of the universe. In this passage Lao Tzu delves into the significance of the Tao as the root of all existence, and its interconnectedness with the Universe, the Earth, and humanity. He explores the concept of the "Four Great Powers' — the Tao, the Universe, the Earth, and Man— and the harmonious relationships between them.

The Mysterious and Infinite Essence of the Tao

The Tao predates the existence of the universe and transcends human comprehension. It is described as silent, formless, and immeasurable, embodying timelessness and infinite wisdom. It is an infinite conscious field of potential and energy that permeates all things. The Tao is the root and origin of all things, existing in a state of serenity and changelessness or non-being (The Subtle Realm) from which all things ("The World of 10,000 things") are born and come into being. Conformal Cyclic Cosmology or "CCC" in modern times sees that such a thing happened before the Big Bang. *

The Great Powers: The Universe, Earth, Man and the Tao

The Universe, with its vastness and complexity, is an expression of the Tao. It encompasses all known and unknown aspects of existence. The Earth, as a part of the Universe, derives its power from the Tao and follows its natural flow. And finally, and very importantly, Man (and by implication, all sapient and sentient life within the cosmos), as a microcosm of the universe, has the potential to connect with and align with the Tao.

The Interconnectedness and Harmonious Relationships

Lao Tzu highlights the interdependence between the four great powers. Man, like all creatures, is influenced by the Earth and follows its natural rhythms. The Earth, in turn, follows the movements of the heavens, representing the cosmic order. The heavens, as the ultimate expression of the Tao, follow only itself. This interconnectedness emphasizes the harmony and balance that exist within the Tao and its relationship with the great powers.

Following the Tao: Wisdom and Way of Life

The Tao embodies infinite wisdom and offers guidance to those who seek it. By aligning with the Tao, individuals can tap into this wisdom and live in harmony with the natural world. The natural Way requires us to explore the concept of Wu Wei, the practice of effortless action and non-interference, which promotes balance and peace in life.

The Importance of Embracing the Tao

Lao Tzu concludes this poignant passage by emphasizing the importance of acknowledging the existence of the Tao and embracing its wisdom. Without this, one's ability to access and use the four great powers becomes incomplete. By recognizing the interconnectedness of the Four Great Powers and aligning them all within the omnipresent Tao, individuals can find balance, harmony and understanding and live an enlightened life of purpose, peace and fulfillment.

Conclusion

In this passage, we have explored the profound essence of the Tao and its interconnectedness with the Universe, Earth, and Man. The Four Great Powers—the Tao, the Universe, the Earth, and Man—highlight the harmony and balance that exist between them. By aligning with the Tao and embracing its wisdom, we, like the other enlightened beings of the cosmos can lead purposeful and fulfilling lives and find our place in both the universe and natural order of things.

*Conformal cyclic cosmology (CCC) is a cosmological model arguably within the framework of general relativity and proposed by Nobel Prize winning theoretical physicist Roger Penrose. in his 2010 book *Cycles of Time: An Extraordinary New View of the Universe.* In Penrose's theoretical model, the universe iterates through an infinite number of cycles, with a time line of an infinite number of possible futures (iterated from the latest end of any potential timescale evaluated for any point in space) with the end of each previous iteration being identified with the Big Bang singularity of the next. 9It is rather amazing how science is finally catching up to the concepts upon which Lao Tzu expounded 2500 years ago in the Tao Te Ching and the Hua Hu Ching. How did he know?

CHAPTER 26

The Tao Te Ching, The New Paradigm for Leadership and Governance on Earth in a Post-Extraterrestrial Contact World

THE ROOT OF THE LIGHT IS THAT WHICH IS HEAVY.
THE SOURCE OF THE MOVED IS THE UNMOVED.

THE MASTER MOVES AND TRAVELS ALL DAY
WITHOUT EVER LEAVING HOME.
HOWEVER SPLENDID THE VISTA,
THE MASTER REMAINS SERENELY WITHIN HIMSELF.

WHY SHOULD THE LORD OF A COUNTRY
FLUTTER ABOUT LIKE A FOOL?
IF ONE ALLOWS THEMSELF TO BE BLOWN TO AND
FRO,
BEING GROUNDED IN ONE'S ROOT IS LOST.
IF ONE ALLOWS RESTLESSNESS TO MOVE HIM,
HE LOSES TOUCH WITH WHO HE IS.

Introduction

In this passage, Lao Tzu emphasizes the importance of staying rooted and connected to our inner self, even in the face of external distractions and temptations. The master moves and travels all day without leaving home, highlighting the idea that true fulfillment can be found by staying grounded in one's own essence. There is no need to go anywhere to find it.

Wherever He or She Hoes, the Master is Comfortably at Home

The passage also tells us that being swayed by external influences or constantly seeking new or novel experiences can lead one to a loss of their identity and a disconnection from one's authentic self. Lao Tzu questions why a leader or someone in a position of power would need to constantly flutter around, suggesting that true wisdom and strength comes from being firmly grounded and rooted in one's principles and in the Tao.

Lao Tzu uses the analogy of the light and heavy emphasizing that the true source of illumination, "light" and movement comes from a heavy deep and solid foundation. Lao Tzu suggests that by staying rooted and connected to the Tao, our inner integral truth, we can navigate through life with serenity and certainty, regardless of the external circumstances, attractions or distractions.

Finally, in the context of leadership, the passage suggests that a wise and effective leader should not be easily swayed by external pressures or events. Instead, he or she should stay true to their principles and values, unshaken by the changing tides of opinions or trends. By staying connected to their inner wisdom, trusting in the Tao and by remaining grounded in their core beliefs, leaders can provide stability and guidance to those they lead, even in dangerous and uncertain times.

Ultimately, this short passage encourages individuals, particularly those who have been chosen to lead, to stay rooted in their true Tao essence, maintaining a sense of substance and self and of commitment and purpose amidst the vicissitudes, chaos and temptations of the world. By understanding and by being deeply rooted in the Tao, they and we can all find inner peace, our authentic selves, and lead with proper wisdom, direction and clarity. At the root of all evolved leadership is the Tao.

CHAPTER 27

"Embodying the Light" & "The Great Secret"

THE GOOD TRAVELER LEAVES NO FOOTPRINTS
AND HAS NO SET PLANS
FOR HIS INTENT IS NOT IN ARRIVING.

THE GREAT ARTIST
ALLOWS HIS INTUITION
TO LEAD HIM WHEREVER IT DESIRES.

THE GOOD SCIENTIST
KEEPS HIS MIND OPEN
TO WHAT IS, AND THEREBY FREES HIMSELF.

THE MASTER REJECTS NO ONE
AND AVAILS HIMSELF TO ALL.
HE WASTES NOTHING AND IS READY
TO USE ALL SITUATIONS.
TO DO SO IS CALLED "EMBODYING THE LIGHT".

A GOOD MAN IS NO MORE
THAN THE BAD MAN'S TEACHER.
A BAD MAN IS NO MORE
THAN A GOOD MAN'S LABOR.
IF ONE DOES NOT UNDERSTAND THIS
HE WILL LOSE HIS WAY AND GET LOST
NO MATTER HOW INTELLIGENT HE IS.
THIS IS KNOWN AS "THE GREAT SECRET".

Introduction

In this passage, Lao Tzu explores the concepts of intuition, open-mindedness, and embracing all situations as a means of embodying the light and understanding the great secret.

The Traveler, the Artist and the Scientist

Lao Tzu begins by highlighting the idea that a good traveler leaves no footprints to trail and has no set plans. This suggests that true wisdom lies not in the destination but in the journey itself. He emphasizes that the intent of the good traveler is not in arriving but in the process of traveling and experiencing. Such should be one's life.

The great artist is portrayed as someone who allows their intuition to guide them. By following their inner wisdom and creative instincts, they allow their heart to guide the mind to create with the hand art that is authentic and unique. This suggests that the great secret lies both in listening to one's intuition and allowing it to lead the way and in being a good example and excluding no one from finding the Integral Way.

A good scientist, on the other hand, is described as someone who keeps an open mind and is willing to embrace what is. By doing so, they are able to free themselves from preconceived notions and limitations, giving them a broader perspective and opportunities for new discoveries and insight into that which is true and not to be confined by that which is only believed to be. The artist balances the scientist and the scientist balances the artist. By accepting both and by allowing them to work in concert with each other, great things may be accomplished.

Embodying the Light

Most of us have heard the old saying that everyone is a genius at something. The passage emphasizes the importance of not rejecting anyone and availing oneself to all situations. By doing so, the master is said to "embody the light". This suggests that true enlightenment comes from embracing all aspects of life, including the good and the bad, and finding wisdom and lessons in every experience. Embodying the light, in essence, means becoming one with the Tao and becoming a beacon to which, all may look for guidance and leadership.

The Great Secret

Finally, Lao Tzu introduces the concept that a good man is no more than a bad man's teacher, and a bad man is no more than a good man's work. This perspective suggests that understanding the interconnectedness of good and bad, light and darkness, is crucial to navigating life's complexities. The great secret lies in not only recognizing this interplay and not getting lost in moral judgments about people or in ideas of intellectual superiority but in placing an affirmative responsibility on the would-be Tao master to be patient and not give up on people no matter how "bad" they might be or how difficult a challenge that they might pose.

Overall, this passage by Lao Tzu encourages us as individuals to trust our intuition, keep an open mind, and embrace all situations as means of embodying the light and understanding the great secret. It suggests that true wisdom comes from the integration of opposites, recognizing the inherent connection between all aspects of existence. With hearts as deep as the ocean and minds as open as the sky, how can one not embody the light.

CHAPTER 28

Keeping to the Female

UNDERSTAND THE MALE,
YET TO THE FEMALE KEEP;
AND INTO YOUR ARMS
ALL THE WORLD
WILL FALL.

ONCE ONE RECEIVES THE WORLD
IN THEIR ARMS,
THE TAO WILL NEVER LEAVE THEM.
WITH THE TAO WITHIN,
ONE BECOMES AS A SMALL CHILD.

KNOW THE WHITE,
BUT TO THE BLACK KEEP.
BECOME FOR THE WORLD,
AN EXAMPLE.

IF AN EXAMPLE, ONE BECOMES FOR THE WORLD,
THE TAO WILL BE STRONG WITHIN THEM.
WITH THE TAO STRONG WITHIN,
THERE WILL BE NOTHING
THAT ONE CANNOT DO.

THE PERSONAL KNOW,
BUT TO THE IMPERSONAL KEEP.
IF YOU ACCEPT THE UNIVERSE AS IT EXISTS.
THE TAO WILL ILLUMINATE YOU FROM WITHIN,
AND TO YOUR PRIMAL SELF YOU WILL RETURN.

FROM THE VOID, THE WORLD IS FORMED,

LIKE IMPLEMENTS MADE FROM A WOODEN
BLOCK.
THESE TOOLS ARE KNOWN TO THE MASTER:
YET THE MASTER STAYS TO THE BLOCK
SO THAT ALL MAY BE USED.

In this passage, Lao Tzu brings forth the principles of understanding, receiving, and becoming an example of Tao mastery in the context of leadership.

The passage begins by emphasizing the importance of understanding both the male and the female aspects of energy in life. This suggests that true mastery and leadership involve recognizing and integrating both masculine and feminine qualities. When in doubt, just as with the employment of Wu Wei, Lao Tzu advises us to err on the side of the gentle feminine energies because they avoid force and harshness. By embracing these qualities and holding them in proper balance, we become capable of embracing the world and attracting others towards us.

Once one receives the world in their arms, the passage suggests that the Tao will never leave them. The master sees things for what they are. This passage can therefore be interpreted as the idea that by fully embracing and accepting the world as it is, one becomes aligned with the natural flow of the Tao. This alignment brings a sense of purity and simplicity, akin to that of a small child who is free from the complexity and attachments that are learned through cultural and societal conditioning. Throughout the study of the Integral Way, we are reminded in many ways to be as a child, supple, innocent and open-minded.

The passage also mentions the importance of being an example or archetype for the world. By embodying the principles of the Tao and becoming a model for others, we become a source of inspiration, modeling and influence. This connection with the Tao strengthens our abilities and opens up limitless possibilities to us. The universe of everything and the subtle realm of no-thing is ours to explore.

Furthermore, Lao Tzu highlights here the concept of the personal and the impersonal. Engage with the outside world but keep to your own center. He suggests that while recognizing one's individuality and personal experiences, it is important to transcend the ego and connect with the integral nature of the universe. By accepting and aligning with the universe as it is, we become illuminated by the Tao from within, leading us to a return to our primal self. Within the center of this self is the Tao itself, the eternal underlying source and force that creates and governs all existence and encapsulates within us the natural order of the universe.

Lastly, the passage uses the analogy of implements made from a wooden block. From the block of wood, it is said that the master can fashion whatever tools he or she needs to accomplish his work and fulfill his or her needs. The block of wood not only symbolized potential in the world of things but the potential for us to fashion and create ourselves and transform what is rough-hewn into something more refined and beautiful. Finally, the metaphor of the uncut block of wood is there to symbolize the potential and versatility of a leader. By staying connected to their source, the master allows all aspects and tools to be made and used as needed. This highlights the idea that a true leader understands the varied capabilities within themselves and embraces the potential for growth, adaptation, and utilization of resources that lie within him or her and to abide in and to avail themselves to the Tao to provide the rest.

In the end, this passage suggests that in the Tao of Leadership, true leadership involves understanding, receiving, and embodying the principles of the Tao in all things. By living lives of truth, simplicity, patience and compassion, by embracing balance, becoming an archetype for others, and connecting with the integral nature of the universe, we can become better human beings and more influential and effective leaders in this world and beyond.

CHAPTER 29

For Every Purpose There is a Time

DO YOU DESIRE TO IMPROVE THE WORLD?
I THINK THAT IT CANNOT BE IMPROVED.
BECAUSE THE WORLD IS ALREADY SACRED,
IT IS IMPOSSIBLE TO BE IMPROVED UPON.
TO TAMPER WITH IT IS TO RUIN IT.
TREAT THE WORLD LIKE AN OBJECT
AND IT WILL BE YOUR LOSS.

THERE IS A TIME TO BE AHEAD.
THERE IS A TIME FOR BEING BEHIND.
THERE IS A TIME FOR MOTION
AND A TIME TO BE EXHAUSTED.
THERE IS A TIME TO BE VIGOROUS,
AND A TIME TO BE AT REST.
THERE IS A TIME TO BE SAFE,
AND A TIME TO BE IN DANGER.

THE MASTER SEES THINGS AS THEY TRULY ARE.
HE DOES NOT TRY TO CONTROL THEM.
THE MASTER ALLOWS THEM
TO GO ON THEIR OWN WAY,
AS THE MASTER RESIDES
WITHIN THE CENTER OF THE CIRCLE.

Introduction

In this passage, Lao Tzu explores the concepts of beauty, time, and the role of the master in relation to the world. Lao Tzu begins by questioning the desire to improve the world, suggesting that the world is already sacred and perfect in its own nature. He implies that any attempts to tamper with or control the natural world would only result in its ruin. Treating the world like an object or trying to impose one's own will or ideas onto it would lead to a loss for oneself. Just look to the mountains, the stars, the skies and waters and other natural phenomena of this world and beyond. It is impossible to improve upon the creative work of the Tao.

There is a Time for Everything

Lao Tzu then goes on to discuss the notion of time, highlighting the different phases and rhythms that exist within it. Reminiscent of Ecclesiastes 3:1-8*, there are times for being ahead and times for being behind, times for motion and times for rest, times for vigor and times for exhaustion, times for safety and times for danger. This suggests that both we and the world operate on our own natural and cyclical patterns, and the wise individual recognizes and adjusts to these energy flows and the flow of events.

The Master as Center of the Universe

With age and experience come wisdom and perspective. The passage indicates that the Tao master, or sage, possesses a deep understanding of the world and sees things for what and as they truly are. Instead of trying to control or manipulate the natural course of events, the master understands and uses Wu Wei and exercises patience and avoids unnecessary interference and allows things to go on their own way. By residing within the center of the circle, the Tao, the master symbolizes a living state of perfect balance, harmony, wise engagement and non-interference.

Ultimately, this passage suggests that beauty and perfection already exist in the world, and any attempts to impose control or change upon it would be disruptive. It highlights the importance of respecting and aligning ourselves with the natural rhythms of time and events and with the natural world of the Tao itself. The master, by embodying this understanding and residing in the center of the circle, exemplifies a state of realistic wisdom, harmony, and acceptance. When the master realizes the Tao as his center, he and the natural world and the entire universe are as one and they function in synchronization with each other. This is the way of the Tao, the Integral way of peace, harmony and self-cultivation.

*"For everything there is a season, and a time for every matter under heaven..." - Ecclesiastes 3:1-8

CHAPTER 30

Effective Leadership and Governance, The Tao Te Ching, The New Paradigm for Leadership and Governance on Earth in the Post-Extraterrestrial Contact World

ONE WHO GOVERNS
WITH RELIANCE UPON THE TAO
TRIES NOT TO ATTEMPT TO FORCE ISSUES
OR DEFEAT HIS ENEMIES
THROUGH FORCE OF ARMS.
THE MASTER KNOWS THAT
FOR EVERY FORCEFUL ACTION
THERE IS A COUNTERFORCE.
EVEN VIOLENCE USED WITH GOOD INTENT
IT NEVER FAILS TO REBOUND UPON ITS WIEL-
DER.

THE MASTER COMPLETES HIS WORK,
THEN HE STOPS.
THE MASTER UNDERSTANDS
THAT THE UNIVERSE IS ALWAYS BEYOND CON-
TROL
AND ATTEMPTING TO DOMINATE EVENTS
IS CONTRARY TO THE TAO AND ITS FLOW.

BECAUSE THE MASTER BELIEVES IN HIMSELF
HE MAKES NO ATTEMPT TO CONVINCE OTHER
PEOPLE.
BECAUSE WITHIN HIMSELF THE MASTER IS CON-
TENT
HE NEEDS NOT THE APPROVAL OF OTHERS.

AND SO BECAUSE THE MASTER ACCEPTS HIMSELF, THE WHOLE WORLD ACCEPTS THE MASTER.

The Use of Force, Self-acceptance and the Role of the Master in Leadership

This passage continues to teach us about the nature of Tao leadership. Here Lao Tzu begins by emphasizing that one who governs with reliance upon the Tao does not attempt to force issues or defeat enemies through the use of arms. The master understands that for every forceful action, there is a counterforce. This suggests that trying to impose one's will or dominate through the use of force is contrary to the natural flow of the Tao.

Even when violence is used with good intentions, the passage highlights that it will ultimately rebound upon its wielder. This suggests that resorting to violence or force, even in pursuit of noble goals, ultimately results in negative consequences. Violence begets violence. Compassion begets compassion. It really is that simple. The Law of Energy Response makes both propositions so.

This passage also goes on to describe the behavior of the master. The master completes his or her work and then stops. Masters of life and of the Tao understand that the universe is always beyond control. So when the work is done, the master leaves it alone and lets the work speak for itself in space and time.

Attempting to dominate events or manipulate outcomes is contrary to the flow of the Tao. The master is not one to be dominated or manipulated; nor is he one to manipulate or dominate others. The approval of others is unnecessary for the master to do his work. What others may think of the master has no relevance. Consequently, the master does not seek the approval of others. Approval is an ego trap. So instead of seeking to convince others or gain their approval, masters believe in themselves and find contentment within. As a result, the master is accomplished and accepted by the whole world.

Ultimately, this passage applies to how masters act in their relationships with others and emphasizes the importance of non-forceful and non-domineering approaches to life and to leadership. Because the master understands the Tao and abides in it, the master understands Wu Wei and the futility of using force and violence as tools of governance. Instead, masters of the Integral Way see things for what they are. They embrace acceptance, trusting in the natural flow of the universe and the power of the Tao and self-belief. Through this self-acceptance and self-contentment, the master gains the acceptance and respect of others. True leadership stems from understanding and aligning ourselves with the inherent wisdom and harmony of the Tao. It is through acceptance, self-belief, and patient, compassionate non-forceful approaches that the master becomes a beacon and enlightened example to all can lead effectively and gain the trust and acceptance of others.

CHAPTER 31

The Possession and Use of Weapons

WEAPONS ARE THE IMPLEMENTS OF VIOLENCE.
THEY ARE DETESTED BY ALL DECENT MEN.

DECENT MEN AVOID WEAPONS,
EXCEPT IN THE MOST DIRE OF NECESSITY
BECAUSE THEY ARE THE TOOLS OF FEAR.

SHOULD THE MASTER BE COMPELLED THOUGH,
THE MASTER WILL USE THEM,
BUT WILL DO SO ONLY
WITH THE UTMOST OF RESTRAINT.

PEACE IS THE MASTER'S HIGHEST VALUE.
SHOULD PEACE BE MADE TO SHATTER
HOW CAN THE MASTER BE CONTENT?

THE MASTER'S ENEMIES AREN'T DEMONS
BUT BEINGS THAT ARE HUMAN,
LIKE HIMSELF.

THE MASTER DOES NOT WISH
HIS ENEMIES PERSONAL HARM.
THE MASTER DOES NOT REJOICE IN HIS VICTORY.
IN VICTORY, HOW COULD THE MASTER REJOICE,
OR IN THE SLAUGHTER OF HIS FELLOW MEN
FIND DELIGHT?

GRAVELY THEN DOES THE MASTER ENTER BAT-
TLE.
WITH GREAT COMPASSION AND SORROW
DOES THE MASTER ENGAGE IN COMBAT.

HE DOES SO AS IF HE WERE
TO ATTEND THE FUNERAL OF KIN.

Introduction

The awareness that is one in the Tao is more than awareness of self as other and other as self. It is much greater. To violently kill and destroy is not the way of the Tao. It is not the path of a master of Integral being. In this passage Lao Tzu teaches us about the importance of peace, mercy, and restraint in leadership. He demonstrates how these virtues can shape a leader's approach to conflict and emphasizes the universal moral responsibility leaders hold to themselves, their people and all beings in promoting peace over violence.

The Art of Leadership: Promoting Peace, Mercy, and Restraint

In the realm of leadership, there exists a profound paradox—while the use of weapons and violence may seem necessary in certain situations that Lao Tzu delves into in later chapters, the mark of a truly great leader lies in their ability to prioritize peace, mercy, and restraint. In this passage Lao Tzu explores the significance of these virtues in the context of leadership, emphasizing the importance of avoiding weapons unless absolutely necessary. By examining the master's dedication to peace, treating enemies with compassion, and engaging in combat with solemnity, we can uncover valuable insights into the art of leadership with a focus on maintaining harmony and minimizing harm.

Peace as the Master's Highest Value

Masters' unwavering commitment to peace sets them apart as remarkable leaders. By cherishing peace as his highest value, the master demonstrates an understanding that the foundation of any thriving life or society is built on tranquility, cooperation, and goodwill. The master recognizes that without peace, contentment and progress become elusive, making it crucial for all leaders to hear all sides and with compassion, actively strive for the preservation of peace.

Seeing Enemies as Human Beings

All beings are children of the Tao. Instead of viewing enemies as demons or objects of personal harm, the master perceives them as fellow human beings. No matter who the enemy is, this shift in perspective allows for empathy and understanding, fostering potential for resolution and reconciliation even in the face of conflict. By cultivating the mindset that his adversaries are human and parts of the same Tao that is the master's center, the Master embodies a compassionate approach to leadership that seeks lasting peaceful and bilaterally co-beneficial resolutions.

The Master's Avoidance of Rejoicing in Victory

In victory, the master refuses to rejoice, understanding the devastating consequences that result from the slaughter of fellow men. This refusal highlights the master 's ability to transcend the notions of conquest and domination common in human leadership throughout history. By refraining from deriving pleasure from the suffering of others, the master demonstrates compassion and a deep sense of empathy and a commitment to building a harmonious society. In war, it is not only the war to be won but ultimately to establish a long-lasting peace that will become the underpinning for the future of all mankind and beyond.

The Master's Engagement in Combat

As we will learn in future chapters of this book, it is the master's responsibility to train and be ready for combat if their land is invaded and the lives of the innocent are put at risk. Although the master is trained in the use of weapons, he or she loathes having to use them.

When the master finds himself compelled to engage in combat, he or she does so with great compassion and sorrow, as if attending the funeral of a family member. This mindset showcases the master's acute awareness of the gravity of violence and its consequences. By entering the battlefield solemnly, the master emphasizes the need for leaders to approach conflict and the potential for war with profound respect for life and a dedication to minimizing harm whenever and wherever possible.

Conclusion

Ultimately, this passage by Lao Tzu highlights the significance of peace, mercy, and restraint in the realm of leadership especially when that leadership is facing the prospects of war. When leaders act within the Tao and honor the Integral Way war becomes unnecessary. However, in a world that has not yet accepted the reality of the Tao and follow the Integral Way, by prioritizing these virtues and avoiding the use of weapons unless absolutely necessary, masterful and compassionate leaders can create societies that thrive on cooperation, empathy, and mutual respect.

The Tao master's example serves as a guiding light for aspiring leaders, demonstrating the power of peaceful approaches, compassion towards enemies, and the solemnity of combat should it be their misfortune. By embracing these principles, leaders can begin to engage the Tao to navigate the challenges of conflict with integrity and with patience and compassion contribute to the establishment of a world that values peace and harmony and rejects violence. By doing this, human civilization can and will begin evolving morally, ethically and spiritually towards someday taking its place among the more highly spiritually cultivated and technologically advanced interstellar human and non-human civilizations of the cosmos who honor the Tao and its universal laws and practice the Tao's Integral Way.

CHAPTER 32

IMPERCEPTIBLE IS THE TAO.
SMALLER THAN THE SMALLEST ATOMIC PARTI-
CLE.
IT CONTAINS COUNTLESS UNIVERSES.

IF THE WORLD'S POWERFUL MEN AND WOMEN
WOULD BE ABLE TO REMAIN CENTERED WITHIN
THE TAO,
HARMONIOUS WOULD ALL THINGS BE.
THE WORLD WOULD BE TRANSFORMED INTO A
PARADISE

AT PEACE WOULD BE ALL PEOPLE.
IN THEIR HARTS WOULD THE LAW BE WRITTEN.

KNOW THAT NAMES AND FORMS ARE PROVI-
SIONAL.
AND WHEN THE FUNCTION OF AN INSTITUTION
SHOULD END.
KNOW WHEN TO STOP AND ANY DANGER MAY
BE AVOIDED.

JUST AS INTO THE OCEAN ALL RIVERS FLOW,
IN THE TAO ALL THINGS REPOSE.

The Endless Universe Within Institutions and Leadership:
"Rocking the Tao"

In the quest for harmony and transformation, the teachings
of Lao Tzu provide valuable insights. From fundamental principles of the Tao and the Universal Way, we can glean wisdom
on the role of institutions and leadership in creating a harmonious world. This I refer to as truly "Rocking the Tao". This

book and its essays aim not only to help the reader understand the benefits of a Tao-centered life within themselves but to inform readers about the importance of adopting a Tao-centered approach within institutions and leadership, emphasizing the need to recognize the provisional nature of names and forms that include religious, societal, and political institutions as well. By delving into the depths of the Tao, we can understand how to bring about positive change and avoid potential dangers that arise from clinging to outdated institutions and structures that will no longer serve mankind as they step from the darkness of ignorance into the light of understanding their place in a universe that is filled with higher levels of intelligent and compassionate spiritual life, followers of the Tao and the Integral Way..

Understanding the Power of the Tao

At the core of Taoism lies the notion that the true power of the universe is imperceptible. It is smaller than the smallest atomic particle, yet it encompasses countless universes. This cosmic essence, the Tao, not only permeates all things but transcends them as well. By acknowledging this vastness, powerful individuals within institutions can tap into the transformative energy necessary for systemic change.

The Harmony of Tao-Centered Leadership

leaders can remain centered within the Tao, harmonious outcomes become attainable. The Tao's influence can guide their decisions and actions, fostering a sense of unity and collaboration among all involved. By internalizing the principles of the Tao, leaders can transcend ego-driven motivations and work towards a greater good. This alignment enables the creation of institutions that serve the well-being of society as a whole, transforming the world into a paradise.

The Tao and Written Law

The Tao encapsulates a wisdom that transcends man-made laws. By recognizing the provisional nature of names and forms, institutions can develop a flexible and adaptive approach to governance. When leaders are attuned to the Tao, the very essence of the law will be written within their hearts. This understanding allows for the application of just and compassionate principles in decision-making processes, nurturing a society that is not bound by rigid regulations but guided by an internal moral compass.

Embracing Change and Knowing When to Stop

The Tao teaches us to embrace change and recognize when the function of an institution should end. Institutions that outlive their purpose can become sources of stagnation, corruption, and potential danger. By being attuned to the Tao's wisdom, leaders can discern the signs of obsolescence and exercise the courage to dismantle outdated structures. Through this awareness, they can navigate the delicate balance between preserving valued traditions and making room for progress.

Conclusion

In conclusion, embracing a Tao-centered approach within institutions and leadership is vital for the transformation of our world into a harmonious paradise. The Tao's imperceptible power, harmonious influence, and ability to guide the essence of law offer profound insights for those in positions of power. By acknowledging the provisional nature of institutions and knowing when to stop, leaders can avoid dangers that arise from clinging to outdated structures. Through the endless universality of the Tao, we can aspire to create a future that embodies harmony, peace, and the eternal wisdom encapsulated within the essence of the Tao.

CHAPTER 33

True Wisdom, True Power, True Wealth and True Immortality

INTELLIGENCE IS THE KNOWING OF OTHERS. BUT TRUE WISDOM IS FOUND IN KNOWING ONESELF.

THOUGH STRENGTH IS FOUND IN THE MASTERY OF OTHERS. TRUE POWER IS FOUND IN THE CONQUERING OF ONESELF.

HE IS TRULY WEALTHY WHO REALIZES THAT HE HAS ENOUGH.

TO REMAIN CENTERED IS TO ENDURE.

TO DIE WITHOUT DYING, IS TO EMBRACE DEATH WITH ONE'S WHOLE HEART.

Title: Unveiling the Path to True Fulfillment

In the pursuit of a fulfilling and meaningful life, we often find ourselves chasing external markers of success such as intelligence, wisdom, strength, power, wealth, and the quest for eternal life. In the passage above, Lao Tzu sheds light on the deeper truths hidden within these aspirations, causing us to reflect on the importance of self-awareness, personal growth, contentment, and embracing the inevitability of our own physical mortality. By exploring the teachings of Lao Tzu and the wisdom they provide, we can uncover a path to true fulfillment that transcends material desires and wealth and enters a realm that is both spiritual, universal and eternal.

Intelligence and True Wisdom

While intelligence allows us to understand and navigate the world around us, true wisdom is discovered through life experience, self-reflection and introspection. It is the journey of learning how to just be and getting to know oneself. This journey of discovery leads us inevitably to profound insights and a sense of existential purpose. As we delve into the depths of our own being, we unravel the mysteries of existence, uncovering the true wisdom otherwise hidden in the Tao that guides us towards a meaningful and fulfilling life. True wisdom comes from living lives of truth and compassion and knowing and understanding oneself.

Strength and True Power

The pursuit of strength often involves the conquest and mastery of others. However, similar to true wisdom, true power lies in conquering ourselves. By embracing self-discipline and personal growth, we can tap into an inner strength that surpasses mere physical prowess. It is through the recognition and transformation of our own weaknesses that we cultivate a power that is aligned with our true and authentic selves and empowers us to make a positive impact on the world and beyond. Our own self-cultivation is made simple by following the Integral Way. This path, the path of the Integral Way and self-cultivation to which the reader has already been introduced inevitably will be made clear in the rest of this book and Lao Tzu's work and teachings found in the Hua Hu Ching.

Wealth, Gratitude and Contentment

Wealth is commonly equated with material possessions and abundance. However, true wealth lies not in the accumulation of external possessions, but in the realization that one already has enough. Gratitude is the price we pay for abundance. Contentment can be found in appreciating and utilizing what we have, rather than constantly chasing after more. By cultivating a mindset of sufficiency and gratitude for what we already have, we liberate ourselves from the ego's insatiable desire for possessions, and instead, invite lasting fulfillment into our lives.

Embracing Mortality and Living in the Present

In the face of our mortal physical existence, the pursuit of eternal life, like the smell of a steak's sizzle, may seem enticing. However, true fulfillment comes from fully embracing the present moment and accepting the inevitability of physical death and discovering the purpose and survival of our individual conscious souls. By centering ourselves in the Tao and by intentionally living each day as if it were our last, we can infuse our lives with purpose, passion, and a deep appreciation for the preciousness of every moment. It is through understanding the ephemeral nature of death and embracing it with our whole hearts that we truly learn to live. It is through the realization of the cyclical nature of life and the infinitude of the existence of our own conscious being that we truly learn why we are here. There is no death of the Tao, nor our conscious souls. Our purpose is to evolve and refine ourselves and our conscious souls spiritually in this life by living lives of truth and to manifest the Tao through the way we live simply, patiently, compassionately and infinitely.

Conclusion

The path to true fulfillment lies not in the external pursuit of intelligence, wisdom, strength, power, wealth, or eternal life, but in the profound journey of self-discovery, self-mastery, and in being of service to others. By finding and expressing gratitude, being content with what we have and by embracing the knowledge of our own transient physical mortality and permanent nature of our spiritual immortality we can die without dying. By delving into the depths of our beings, conquering our inner weaknesses, appreciating what we have, and consciously living fully in the present within the eternal presence that is the Tao, we can unlock the door to the fulfillment of knowing and living a conscious immortal life filled with meaning, purpose, untoward inner riches, eternal love and compassion and everlasting fulfillment.

CHAPTER 34

The Nature of the Tao and True Greatness, Stoicism

TO EVERYWHERE THE GREAT TAO FLOWS.
FROM IT ALL THINGS ARE BORN,
YET THESE THINGS THE TAO DOES NOT CREATE.
INTO ITS WORK THE TAO POURS ITSELF,
YET THE TAO LAYS NO CLAIM TO ANYTHING.
INFINITE WORLDS DOES IT NOURISH,
YET IT HOLDS ON TO NONE.

BECAUSE THE TAO IS HIDDEN IN THE HEART
AND WITH ITS MERGER INTO ALL THINGS,
THE TAO MAY BE CALLED HUMBLE.

BECAUSE ALL THINGS VANISH INTO THE TAO,
AND IT IS THE TAO ALONE THAT ENDURES,
THE TAO CAN BE CALLED "GREAT".

BECAUSE THE TAO IS UNAWARE OF ITS GREAT-
NESS,
THUSLY, TRULY GREAT IT IS.

Introduction

The Ancient spiritual nature of the Tao embodies an intriguing concept—the Tao, the underlying source of all life and the force that permeates all existence and encapsulates the natural order and governs the universe. The Tao is characterized by its ability to create and nourish, while remaining detached and humble. There is both complexity of the Tao, highlighting its greatness and simplicity, which is exemplified by its humility. By delving deeper into its enigmatic nature, we will gain a deeper understanding of how the Tao operates and how its influence shapes the world and universe around us.

The Profound Essence of Greatness and Humility

Across various spiritual traditions like Buddhism, Hinduism, Christianity, and Islam and philosophies like Stoicism, to mention just a few, the concept of greatness and humility plays a central role. The passage above gives reason to the reader to explore the teachings of these traditions, their perspectives on birth and rebirth, and the profound nature of greatness and humility as they relate to the source of creation and our modern and ever-evolving scientific understanding. There is only just so much time and space that can be dedicated to these traditions, however; by delving into these ancient wisdom systems and merging them with our own understanding of science, we can uncover deeper insights into the true nature of reality, greatness and the beauty of humility.

Unfolding the Tao's Creative Power

The first aspect of the Tao that deserves our attention is its extraordinary capacity to engender life. The Tao is the source from which all things are born. It pours itself into its work yet lays no claim to anything. By not taking ownership of its creations, the work becomes timeless, and the Tao remains detached and selfless. This quality allows the Tao to manifest incredible creativity and adaptability, making it an ever-flowing force that shapes and sustains infinite worlds.

The Tao and the Source of Creation

The concept of the Tao, as represented in Eastern philosophies of Buddhism, Hinduism, and Christianity, suggests that it flows everywhere and gives birth to all things. However, the Tao does not claim ownership or credit for these creations. It silently and almost without perceptible notice pours itself into its unending work, nourishing infinite worlds without holding onto any. This understanding highlights the humility of the Tao, which does not seek recognition for its vast creative power.

Nourishment Without Attachment

The Tao nurtures and nourishes the diverse worlds it has created. The Tao's ability to provide sustenance to all things without holding on to any one thing speaks to its selflessness and humility. It allows the universe to maintain balance and harmony, as the Tao feeds the growth and prosperity of all elements within its realm. This inherent characteristic of the Tao emphasizes its role as a life-giving, nurturing force.

The Humble Nature of the Tao

The Tao is hidden in the heart of all things and merged with everything. Because of its inherent humility, it can be called humble. This humility arises from the recognition that the Tao does not force or impose its will upon the creations it brings forth. Instead, it harmoniously aligns with the natural order of existence, allowing for the flourishing of life without asserting its greatness.

Humility in Greatness

Here, we unravel the concept of the Tao's humility in its enduring greatness. Despite its power and influence, the Tao remains unaware of its own greatness. This lack of self-awareness enables the Tao to maintain a state of profound humility, which further enhances its ability to harmonize and merge with all things. Through its modesty, the Tao becomes a model for the pursuit of greatness without ego, demonstrating the essence of wisdom in a world marked by self-importance and pride.

The Greatness of the Tao

While the Tao remains humble, it also embodies greatness. All things arise from it, and all things return to it. It endures through the cycles of birth and rebirth, remaining constant amidst the impermanence of the world. The greatness of the Tao lies in its unwavering presence, guiding the cosmic flow of creation without conscious awareness of its own magnitude.

Spiritual Traditions and Scientific Understanding

The teachings of Buddhism, Hinduism, Christianity, and Islam offer profound insights into the nature of greatness and humility. When merged with scientific understanding, these perspectives can enrich our comprehension of the interconnectedness of all things, the cycles of birth and rebirth, and the humility and greatness found in the fabric of the universe. Through this integration, we discover the harmony between spirituality and science, offering a more comprehensive view of our existence. In this view, we can begin to see reality as it is and fear physical death no longer. It is through this fearlessness that we can truly live the lives we were meant to live and become the spiritual beings who we were always meant to be.

The Tao and Stoicism

As part of the reader's foray into the exploration of different spiritual traditions, Stoicism, the philosophy of the ancient Roman stoics is worthy of a brief expository mention. Upon examination, there is little difference in basic substance when it comes to the Tao and the nature of the stoic universe. The difference lies in the greater scope and depth of the world of Lao Tzu and the Tao.

Stoic Philosophy: Embracing Inner Tranquility, Natural Order and Interconnectedness

The Stoic philosophy, as articulated and championed by the great Marcus Aurelius, (121-180AD), serves as a timeless guide to achieving inner peace and tranquility amidst the challenges of life. The Stoic philosophy is one of personal growth and centers around the cultivation of virtues, the acceptance of the natural order of the universe, and the development of a tranquil mindset, leading individuals towards lasting contentment and resilience. Stoicism is a personal philosophy that encourages the pursuit of wisdom, courage, justice, and temperance as the essential virtues for leading a harmonious life. Marcus Aurelius believed that honing these virtues enables individuals to navigate the complex moral fabric of existence with integrity and honor.

Central to Stoic philosophy is the acceptance of the inherent limitations of human control over external circumstances. Marcus Aurelius emphasized the importance of acknowledging and embracing the natural order of the universe, recognizing that some things in life lie beyond our influence. Stoicism teaches the development of a tranquil mindset through the practice of conscious self-awareness. Aurelius believed that by training our minds to remain calm in the face of adversity, we can maintain equilibrium and avoid succumbing to external pressures and turmoil.

Unlike Lao Tzu's Tao Te Ching and Hua Hu Ching, Marcus Aurelius' Stoic philosophy does not spend much time trying to explain or expound upon the nature or source of creation and how to work with it, it does, however advocate for the cultivation of virtue, acceptance of the natural order, and the development of a tranquil mindset. Like Lao Tzu, by embodying these principles, Aurelius believed that individuals can find solace amid the uncertainties of life, leading to a more fulfilled lives and purposeful existences.

Both Stoicism and the Tao Te Ching also share a fundamental acceptance of the interconnectedness and interdependence of all things. The Stoic concept of *Sympatheia*, as referred to by Marcus Aurelius in his work <u>Meditations</u>, suggests that everything in the universe is intertwined, and we, as humans, are all part of one collective body. The Tao extends this concept to all beings human and otherwise. Similarly, the Tao emphasizes the idea that the Tao flows through everything as its own collective body and nourishes infinite worlds, while holding on to none.

Both the Tao's Integral Way and Stoic philosophy recognize that our actions and choices matter. They have consequences not only for us but also for others and in the case of the Tao, for the entire cosmos. The Stoics argue that understanding our interconnectedness should prompt us to be good for the sake of being good and to do good for one another. Similarly, the Tao, with its nurturing and selfless and indiscriminately compassionate nature, teaches us through the Integral Way that by recognizing our interconnectedness and acting with unconditional and universal compassion, we can develop our own harmony and balance and thereby positively affect our friends, family, society and world and the universe as well.

Both Stoicism and the Tao's Integral Way advocate for a sense of personal responsibility for our actions and our social responsibility towards others. The Stoics emphasize the importance of being good stewards of the common good, while the Tao encourages a humble and selfless approach to life, where one's actions benefit not just oneself but also the greater whole. Both highlight the significance of acting in ways that promote harmony, justice, and the common good. In the end, the two approaches to the cosmos leave few major differences and little reason to be reconciled. Both Stoicism and the Tao offer valuable insights into the nature of existence and how to live a meaningful and fulfilling life. They both emphasize the importance of recognizing our shared humanity and interconnectedness with each other and, as in the Tao with all the beings of the multiverse, immortal or otherwise.

Universal truths and wisdom are timelessly the same wherever one goes.

<u>Conclusion</u>

Through its remarkable ability to create and nourish without claiming ownership, and its humbleness despite its enduring greatness, the Tao demonstrates profound wisdom and represents the ultimate essence of harmony in the universe. The Tao transcends both time and space and all of our understanding. It exists as an enigma that embodies greatness through its humility while nurturing and sustaining the universe. In its ability to create without claim to its creation and endure without awareness, the Tao guides us to act similarly and voyage toward a deeper appreciation of harmony and balance. As we navigate the complexities of existence, we can find inspiration in Lao Tzu's teachings of the Tao, and emulate and follow its remarkable wisdom in our own lives. By embracing humility amidst greatness, we can aspire to bring about a deeper sense of harmony, both within ourselves and in the world and universe around us.

In the exploration of greatness and humility as presented in various spiritual traditions and aligned with the philosophy of the stoics and our new scientific understanding especially in the research of quantum physics and consciousness, we uncover a profound understanding of the Tao, the eternal source of creation. The humble nature of the Tao, which pours itself into all things without seeking recognition or compensation, contrasts with its enduring greatness as the unchanging donative and creative essence that encompasses the cycles of birth and rebirth. By embracing the ancient teachings of Lao Tzu and Marcus Aurelius, and studying them in the light of meaning from the ancient teachings of Hinduism, the Buddha and

Christ and merging them with new scientific knowledge, we can gain further insights into the interconnectedness of all things and the inherent beauty found in the harmonious dance of greatness and humility in the cosmos and within ourselves.

CHAPTER 35

Centering Oneself in the Tao

THE ONE WHO IS CENTERED IN THE TAO
TRAVELS WHEREVER HE WISHES
WITHOUT DANGER.

BECAUSE THERE IS PEACE IN THE MASTER'S
HEART,
EVEN AMIDST GREAT PAIN
HE CAN PERCEIVE THE UNIVERSAL HARMONY
IN ALL.

FROM THE STREET, PASSERS BY CAN HEAR
THE SOUND OF ENTICING MUSIC
OR SAVOR THE SMELL OF GOOD FOOD
AND ENTER TO ENJOY THEM WITHIN.
HOWEVER, THE WORDS
THAT DIRECT US TO THE TAO
ARE FLAVORLESS
AND STEEPED IN BLAND MONOTONY.

WHEN ONE LOOKS FOR THE TAO
HE CANNOT SEE IT.
LISTEN FOR THE TAO
AND IT CANNOT BE HEARD.
HOWEVER, THE TAO ONCE FOUND,
IS EVERYWHERE.
INEXHAUSTIBLY,
IT AVAILS ITSELF ENDLESSLY
FOR ONE'S USE.

The Inexhaustible Sustenance: Exploring the Tao

The concept of the Tao, rooted in ancient philosophy and spiritual practice, holds a profound allure with its promise of inexhaustible sustenance. In this passage Lao Tzu embarks on a journey that challenges us to understand the universal significance of the Tao and explore how it offers endless nourishment and fulfillment especially to those who find it. By delving into the depths of this profound concept, Lao Tzu sheds light on the Tao and its transformative power to create universal harmony and eternal use. Through our cultivation of a centered heart and an understanding of the Tao's enigmatic nature, one can attain inner peace, perception of universal harmony, and access to a boundless source of sustenance.

The Essence of the Tao

To truly grasp the essence of the Tao, one must unravel its elusive nature. Unlike enticing music or the aroma of good food, the words guiding us towards the Tao may appear flavorless, boring and steeped in bland monotony. Oft times, the Tao is not something that can be directly seen or heard. It is an entity and energy that once found, permeates every aspect of our lives. It becomes an inexhaustible comfort and resource that is available for our constant use. The key is to realize its presence in its multitude of forms and go with its flow and the flow of events it creates in our behalf.

Centering in the Tao

Being centered in the Tao holds the key to traveling through life without danger. By embracing the Tao and realizing the Tao at one's center individuals can find peace in the core of their being, even in times of great turmoil and amidst great pain. This centeredness enables us to perceive and understand the universal harmony that ultimately connects all things. Once recognized, the Tao becomes a guiding light, leading individuals towards a profound understanding of the interconnectedness of the world, the universe and each other.

The Inexhaustible Sustenance

At its core, the Tao offers an infinite and inexhaustible source of life and sustenance. Unlike tangible resources that can be depleted, the Tao is an intelligent creative energy that remains inexhaustible. It nourishes the mind, body, and spirit, providing individuals with a wellspring of inspiration, wisdom, and vitality. By aligning ourselves with the Tao, we tap into a boundless source of energy that fuels personal growth and opportunity and material that facilitates the realization of our own true potential.

Embracing the Tao's Universal Harmony

Beyond individual enrichment, the Tao also invites individuals to engage with the broader tapestry of existence. By surrendering to the flow of universal harmony, we inevitably learn to accept and appreciate the interconnectedness of all things and beings. This deepens our compassion, empathy, and understanding, fostering a sense of unity that transcends boundaries. Time, space, distance and matter become irrelevant to it. When we are completely present in being, we are directly experiencing the Tao.

In our quest to understand the Tao, by searching and striving, we can never find it. The Tao is always there and comes to those who let it. Once we have discovered it though, we find a profound concept that holds the promise of eternal inexhaustible sustenance. By centering ourselves in the Tao, we can find safety, embrace its inner peace, perceive universal harmony, and tap into an inexhaustible source of physical, mental and spiritual nourishment. Let us strive to go beyond the enticement of the external and sensual pleasures and embark on a journey to surpass these things and discover the deep and endless riches and infinite number of rewarding experiences and encounters that the infinite and immortal Tao has to offer.

CHAPTER 36

THE "Subtle Perception od How Things Are", the Paradox of Wave-Particle Duality, Nonlocality and Quantum Entanglement

TO SHRINK SOMETHING,
ONE MUST FIRST ALLOW IT TO EXPAND.

TO DISCARD SOMETHING,
ONE MUST ALLOW IT FIRST TO FLOURISH.

FOR SOMETHING TO BE RECEIVED,
IT MUST FIRST BE GIVEN.

THE HARD IS OVERCOME
BY THE SOFT.

THE FAST IS OVERCOME
BY THE SLOW.

THIS IS CALLED
THE „SUBTLE PERCEPTION OF HOW THINGS ARE".

ALLOW YOUR WORKINGS TO STAY MYSTERIOUS,
AND LET ONLY YOUR RESULTS
BE SEEN BY OTHERS.

The Subtle Perception of How Things Are: Revealing the Power of Paradoxes

In a world governed by binary thinking, where contradictions are often seen as barriers to progress, lies a profound truth. It is the truth that reality itself embraces paradoxes*, and by unraveling, understanding and embracing these paradoxes, we can navigate and shape our own paths more effectively. In this passage Lao Tzu explores the concept of "The Subtle Perception of How Things Are" – the notion that to bring about change, we must first allow for its opposite to exist and flourish. By delving into the interplay between expansion and contraction, discarding and flourishing, taking and giving, hardness and softness, and the slow and the fast, Lao Tzu aims to inform his students of the power that lies in solving the riddles, understanding the enigmatic and thereby embracing and working with paradoxes. Hopefully this passage will encourage its readers to embrace contradictions, challenge conventional thinking, and find new opportunities for personal and collective growth by learning how to subtly perceive how things are.

Expansion and Shrinking

To truly shrink something, we must first allow it to expand. This paradoxical idea speaks to the notion that by giving something the space to grow, it reveals its inherent limitations. By stepping back, observing, acknowledging and understanding these limitations, we gain the ability to shape and control the outcomes in a myriad of situations that life presents to us.

Discarding and Flourishing

Discarding something becomes meaningful only when its potential to flourish has been acknowledged. By recognizing the value and potential within what we seek to discard, we can use this understanding to plant the seeds of growth and transformation, ensuring that what remains is stronger and more resilient than before.

Receiving and Giving

The act of receiving is deeply intertwined with giving. To properly take something, it must first be offered or presented to us. By acknowledging the importance of reciprocity, we begin to comprehend the delicate balance between our desires and the need to contribute to the well-being of others. This opens the door to a more harmonious and interconnected existence.

The Hard and the Soft

The belief that the hard is overcome by the soft may seem counterintuitive, but it reveals the power of adaptability and flexibility. Hardness can be brittle and fragile, easily broken under pressure, while softness possesses resilience and the capacity to mold and absorb. By embracing softness, just like water wearing away through and smoothing even the most jagged of rocks, we can patiently navigate challenges and find solutions that may not be initially apparent.

The Fast and the Slow

Speed is often equated with progress and efficiency, but the fast can be surpassed by the slow. This paradox, just like Aesop's fable of the turtle and the hare, illuminates the importance of patience, deliberation, and persistent thoughtful action. Rapid change may be exhilarating, but it is the unhurried and meticulous approach that often yields the most enduring results.

Letting the Results Speak for Themselves

There is an old saying that "Nobody really wants to watch sausage being made. They only want to enjoy the end product". In the same way, Lao Tzu instructs us to let our workings stay mysterious and leave the results to be seen.

In a world inundated with constant scrutiny and the need for validation, the idea of letting our work stay mysterious and allowing only the results to be seen holds a profound significance. Lao Tzu, illuminates the importance of solitude and independence in the creation process. By retreating from the gaze of others, we can preserve the purity and integrity of our work while pursuing the creation of timeless masterpieces.

The presence of others has a profound impact on our actions and behaviors. We become conscious of their judgment, their expectations, and their opinions. This awareness can lead to self-doubt, distraction, and even compromise in our creative endeavors. When we constantly seek outside validation or approval, or caring what others think about us, we not only give away our creative power but run the risk of diluting our originality and losing sight of our true creative potential.

By guarding the mystery of our process and letting our workings remain unknown, we create a sacred space for our ideas to flourish. This allows us to nurture our creations with undivided attention, free from external influence. In this solitude, we are able to explore our thoughts and ideas, pushing the boundaries of our imagination without the fear of judgment or interruption.

Furthermore, by allowing the results of our work to speak for themselves, we invite others to engage with our creations on their own terms. Our work becomes an invitation for reflection and interpretation, leaving room for personal connection and meaning-making. By relinquishing control over the consumption of our creations, we enable a deeper, honest and more authentic connection between the audience and the artwork.

This approach not only applies to artistic endeavors but also extends to various areas of life, such as entrepreneurship, scientific research, and even personal growth. Allowing the process to unfold in the shadows allows us to bring forth our best work, unfettered by external pressures or expectations. It is through this self-directed exploration and introspection that we find our authentic voice, create something truly remarkable, and leave a lasting impact on the world.

By embracing Lao Tzu's wisdom and letting our workings stay mysterious while making the results visible, we safeguard the integrity and purity of our creative process. By retreating from the gaze of others, we create a space for unhindered exploration and originality. Allowing our work to speak for itself invites a deep and personal connection between the audience and the creation, fostering a more meaningful engagement. Ultimately, by valuing the power of solitude and self-directed creativity, we have the potential to engage the timelessness of the Tao to produce timeless work and leave a lasting legacy. If producing timeless work is what we want to accomplish, it is best that we are left alone to do and complete our work.

Conclusion

"The Subtle Perception of How Things Are" presents us with a new lens through which we can view reality. Through this exploration of paradoxes, we gain insight into the intricate nature of existence and the interconnectedness of its elements. By embracing the counterintuitive and allowing room for contradiction, we unlock the potential for innovation, growth, and transformation. It is in unraveling, understanding, and harnessing the power of these paradoxes that we can shape a future that is both fulfilling and harmonious. Let us revel in the mysteries of our workings and in our subtle perception of the way things are and let our results speak for themselves.

*The Paradoxes of Wave-Particle Duality and Non-Duality in Quantum Physics: Resolving the Conundrum

In this chapter and the previous chapter, modern science and quantum physics, if not hinted at, were mentioned. Quantum physics, a field of study that delves into the fundamental nature of matter and energy, like the Tao has long puzzled scientists with its intriguing paradoxes. One such paradox lies in the concept of wave-particle duality and non-duality. In the context of the Tao's own paradoxes within the perception of how things are, before leaving this subject and moving on, it might behoove us to analyze and unravel these paradoxes, shedding light on their significance and proposing possible resolutions to this compelling enigma.

Understanding Wave-Particle Duality

The concept of wave-particle duality refers to the scientific understanding that subatomic particles, such as electrons and photons, can exhibit characteristics of both waves and particles. This duality challenges the classical Newtonian model of physics and suggests a deeper underlying reality. Numerous experiments have provided evidence for wave-particle duality. The famous double-slit experiment demonstrates that particles exhibit wave-like interference patterns when passed through a pair of slits, indicating their wave-like behavior. Conversely, the photoelectric effect experiment proves the particle-like behavior of light, as it exhibits discrete particle-like behavior when interacting with matter. The concept of wave-particle duality has profound consequences and implications for the understanding of quantum physics. It introduces uncertainty in the precise measurement of both position and momentum of particles, as described by Heisenberg's uncertainty principle. Additionally, wave-particle duality plays a crucial role in quantum mechanics, quantum field theory, and the development of technologies like lasers and electron microscopes.

The Paradoxes of Wave-Particle Duality and Role of the Observer

When I played sports, I noticed that when My parents came to watch me compete, there was a change on how I performed and the outcomes. The role of the observer in quantum physics is much the same. Within quantum physics there is something known as the "measurement problem" that highlights the role of the observer in the collapse of a particle's wavefunction. According to the Copenhagen interpretation, the act of measurement by an observer causes the wavefunction to collapse into a specific state, leading to a probabilistic determination of observable properties.

Wave function collapse is inevitably related and inextricably connected to what in physics is known as the "uncertainty principle". Like attaching a measuring tape to a batter's baseball bat and measuring the arc of his swing, the act of measuring a particle's position precisely disturbs its momentum and vice versa, leading to unavoidable uncertainties in measurement outcomes.

The Paradoxes of Non-Locality and Entanglement

The Wave-Particle and the role of the observer are not the only two paradoxes that quantum physics present to understanding the subtle perception of how things are. Even at the level of quantum physics Lao Tzu was on to something. For example, in quantum physics we have Bell's theorem and the violation of the principle of local realism. Bell's theorem proves the limitation of local realism in explaining quantum phenomena. It shows that certain experiments involving the non-locality of entangled particles cannot be explained by any theory based on predetermined local properties, challenging classical notions of causality and locality.

In the realm of quantum physics we also have the EPR paradox and entanglement. The EPR (Einstein-Podolsky-Rosen) paradox highlights the entanglement of quantum particles, wherein the properties of one particle become instantaneously correlated with the other, regardless of the physical distance between them. This phenomenon challenges classical notions of locality and raises deep questions about the nature of reality. If just prior to the Big Bang all mass condensed into a singularity, then is not all matter and energy subject to the potential for quantum entanglement?

Non-Duality in Quantum Physics and the Tao

The paradoxical notions of duality and non-duality have long existed in the annals of Eastern philosophy. Non-duality is a central concept in Eastern philosophies like the Tao, Advaita Vedanta, Zen and both Theravada and Mahayana Buddhism. It suggests that reality is fundamentally interconnected and indivisible, transcending the conventional duality of subject and object. Non-duality, the lack of distinction between subject and object, for example emphasizes the unity and interconnectedness of all phenomena.

There are also questions about the philosophers observed reality of non-duality and those of the quantum physicist. Some scientists and philosophers have begun to propose parallels between the principles of non-duality and certain aspects of quantum physics. Both non-duality and quantum physics challenge the notion of a separate, independent observer and emphasize the interactive nature of reality. Some, this writer included, would argue that non-duality provides a philosophical framework to understand the inherent interconnectedness of all things and the indeterminism found in quantum physics.

The implications of non-duality for understanding reality through the purview of of what is taught in the Tao Te Ching and the Hua Hu Ching are great. The exploration of non-duality in the context of quantum physics could redefine our understanding of reality by transcending classical boundaries and providing a unified perspective for the otherwise disconnected scientific mind that is constantly trying to measure a phenomenon at the expense of experiencing and understanding it. Arguably pre-Cartesian pre-"modern" science was not this way as it had not yet created a physical-spiritual schism and its own duality with science that continues to this very day. Non-duality challenges the notion of an objective, observer-independent reality devoid on integral consciousness and invites a deeper examination of the nature of consciousness and the observer's role in shaping reality.

Resolving the Quantum Paradoxes

There are four basic ways that scientists have tried to resolve the paradoxical nature of the universe that they are now observing. These are the "Many-Worlds Interpretation", Bohmian Mechanics, Information-based Interpretations, and the "Consciousness and the Observer Effect".

The Many-Worlds Interpretation, proposed by physicist Hugh Everett, suggests that every time a measurement occurs, the universe splits into multiple branches, each representing a different outcome of the measurement. This interpretation resolves the measurement problem by avoiding wavefunction collapse and instead maintains a superposition of multiple states.

Bohmian Mechanics, developed by physicist David Bohm, introduces the concept of "hidden variables" that determine the behavior of particles. It suggests that particles have definite positions and trajectories that are governed by non-local forces. Bohmian Mechanics provides an alternative deterministic interpretation of quantum mechanics, addressing both the measurement problem and non-locality.

Information-based interpretations, such as the Transactional Interpretation and the Quantum Bayesianism, propose that quantum phenomena can be understood in terms of information exchange between the observer and the observed system. They argue that reality is fundamentally informational, and that the observer interacts with the quantum system through a process of information acquisition and refinement.

In the Consciousness and the Observer Effect, some of the theories propose a strong connection between consciousness and the observer effect observed in quantum physics. They suggest that consciousness plays a fundamental role in collapsing the wavefunction and determining the observable properties of particles. This perspective opens up scientific avenues for exploring the fundamental nature of consciousness and its relationship to the physical world.

In conclusion, the paradoxes of wave-particle duality and non-duality in quantum physics present fascinating challenges for scientists and philosophers alike. While the true resolution of these paradoxes remains elusive, several interpretations and theories have been put forward to help shed light on their nature. Understanding and resolving these enigmas may not only redefine our perception of reality but also pave the way for groundbreaking advancements in quantum physics and beyond. But right now, so far what we have to use and understand as best we can in order to live balanced, happy and contented lives and evolve out of the material realm that has been dominated by Descartes and Newton and ended in a dead end is the Tao.

CHAPTER 37

The Tao of Leadership, The Tao Te Ching as The New Paradigm for Leadership and Governance on Earth in the Post-Extraterrestrial Contact World

THE TAO NEVER HURRIES,
YET ALL THINGS ARE ACCOMPLISHED
THROUGH IT.

IF PERSONS OF POWER
WERE ABLE TO CENTER THEMSELVES
WITHIN THE TAO,
THE ENTIRE WORLD
AND ALL ITS NATURAL RHYTHMS
WOULD UNDERGO A TRANSFORMATION.

CONTENTED AND HARMONIOUS,
BY THEIR SIMPLE DAILY LIVES,
PEOPLE WOULD BE SATED
AND FREE FROM DESIRE.

WHEN DESIRE IS ABSENT,
PEACE COMES TO ALL.

The Tao: A Path to Contentment, Social Harmony, Leadership and Peace

The teachings of Lao Tzu offer valuable insights into people leading a fulfilling and balanced life. The essence of the Tao lies in its paradoxical nature - it never forces, strives or hurries, yet all things are accomplished; - it is intangible, yet it permeates everything, affecting both the natural world and human behavior. By understanding and embracing the Tao, individuals in positions of power have the potential to transform the world, promote contentment, harmony, and the absence of desire in order to achieve true world peace. If world leaders would align themselves with the Tao, the world and its resonant natural rhythms would undergo a profound transformation, leading to contentment and harmony, as well as freedom from desire, ultimately bringing peace to all. Such is the Tao of Leadership.

Exploring the Nature of the Tao

To comprehend the impact of the Tao on the world, it is essential to delve into its essence. The Tao is described as a force that is both passive yet influential - it does not directly act, yet everything is accomplished through it. This intricate concept highlights the Tao's ability to guide and harmonize existence especially for those who follow the Integral Way.

Contentment and Freedom from Desire

A key aspect of the Lao Tzu's philosophy is the concept of contentment with what one needs and has and freedom from desire from hot having what one wants. By embracing simplicity in life, individuals can find true satisfaction when their material needs are fulfilled and even gratitude in the present moment having the freedom to experience life with meaningful work and meaningful love, unburdened by the constant pursuit of material possessions or external validation. This grounded perspective allows individuals to experience lasting peace, irrespective of external circumstances.

Aligning with the Tao in Positions of Power

When individuals in positions of power center themselves within the Tao, they tap into its transformative power. By internalizing the Tao's teachings about living lives of truth, patience, humility, forgiveness, compassion, introspection, mindfulness, and simplicity, these leaders can cultivate a form of leadership based on their service to others and harmonious presence, radiating their inner balance outwards to make the world a better place.

The Transformation of the World

Lao Tzu's perspective on leadership, what the author calls "The Tao of Leadership", is not a utopian one. Unlike dialectic materialism, for example, it offers a realistic and provable alternative to the conventional notions of power and control and the reasons for them. It reminds us that true leadership lies in connection and alignment with a greater force, rather than imposing one's will upon others. By surrendering to the flow of the Tao, leaders unlock their true potential to inspire and uplift those around them. As powerful individuals embody the Tao, their influence can extend beyond their immediate circles. The alignment of these leaders with the Tao can ripple throughout societies, transforming the world's natural rhythms to unite all people into a communality of mutual experience and civilizational destiny.

Unlike unbridled capitalism, communism or fascism, the Tao encourages an understanding of interdependence, fostering sustainable systems and promoting reciprocity and unity. By centering themselves within the Tao, leaders cultivate a state of contentment and harmony. Their actions and decisions flow effortlessly in accordance with the rhythms of the Tao and its natural world. This state of alignment brings about a transformation on this planet, where people are no longer driven by insatiable desire, they find satisfaction and fulfillment in the simplicity of their daily lives, patience with others and mutually exercised compassion.

In a society whose basic needs are cared for, where people are free from the chains of desire, conflict subsides, peace becomes a natural state. The absence of desire leads to a profound sense of contentment and inner peace for individuals. This peace extends to the collective, fostering harmony and tranquility among people. These attributes are those of all higher civilizations. By stepping away from personal ambition and embracing the wisdom of the Tao, leaders become examples of the self-cultivation of their own mental, physical and spiritual "holy trinity of being' and conduits for self and societal transformation, spreading peace, contentment, and harmony throughout their communities and beyond.

Conclusion

The philosophy of Lao Tzu resulted in significant impact upon Chinese society for almost a millennium. It still holds some degree of influence and has shown signs of resurgence in modern times. People again are looking for great leaders who can drop their provincial and regional interests in lieu of a Greater Way of doing things. The Tao's Integral Way provides valuable insights into achieving contentment, harmony, and peace in our lives and the world. It speaks to the powerful influence of the Tao on all things and underscores the transformative potential of leaders who align themselves with this universal force.

If leaders of power can connect with the essence of the Tao, the entire world and its natural rhythms would undergo a profound metamorphosis. Through aligning with the Tao, individuals in positions of power have the potential to bring about positive transformations, fostering contentment and freedom from desire for all.

By embracing the egoless and paradoxical nature of the Tao and internalizing its teachings, we can cultivate a harmonious and fulfilling existence, contributing to the collective well-being of humanity. Leaders who embrace the principles of the Tao can bring about a profound change in the world. By centering themselves within the Tao, they create a ripple effect of contentment, harmony, and peace, liberating individuals from the constant pursuit of desire. By embodying the wisdom of the Tao, leaders can inspire and guide others towards a more enlightened path and the spiritual evolution of humankind and prepare it for its integration into those advanced and higher-level civilizations that populate our universe and beyond.

CHAPTER 38

The "Moral Man", The Tao Te Ching, The New Paradigm for Leadership on Earth in the Post-Extraterrestrial Contact World

THE MASTER STRIVES NOT FOR POWER
THUS, TRULY POWERFUL THE MASTER IS.

AN ORDINARY MAN CONTINUES TO STRIVE FOR POWER.
AS A CONSEQUENCE, HE NEVER HAS ENOUGH.

NOTHING DOES THE MASTER STRIVE TO DO,
YET NOTHING LEAVES HE UNDONE.

THE ORDINARY MAN CONSTANTLY DOES THINGS,
YET THERE ARE MANY MORE THAT HE MUST STILL DO.

THE KIND MAN ACTS
YET SOME THINGS STILL REMAIN TO BE DONE.

THE JUST MAN ACTS
AND HE LEAVES A MULTITUDE OF THINGS STILL TO DO.

THE MORAL MAN ACTS
AND WHEN NONE RESPOND,
HIS SLEEVES HE ROLLS UP
AND THEN HE GETS THINGS DONE.

WHEN ONE LOSES THE TAO,
GOODNESS REMAINS.

**WHEN ONE LOSES GOODNESS,
MORALITY REMAINS.**

**WHEN ONE LOSES MORALITY,
RITUAL REMAINS.**

**RITUAL IS TRUE FAITH'S HUSK
AND THE SEED OF CHAOS.**

**THE MASTER THEREFORE
CONCERNS HIMSELF WITH THE DEPTHS
OF THINGS
AND NOT THEIR SURFACES.**

**THE MASTER'S INTEREST IS NOT IN THE FLOWER
BUT IN ITS FRUIT.**

**THE MASTER'S WILL DOES NOT BELONG TO HIM.
THE MASTER LIVES IN REALITY
AND LETS GO OF ALL ILLUSION.**

This is a somewhat long passage by Lao Tzu that sets out two separate but related areas that address the mastery of power and true leadership. It serves as a reminder for leaders to embrace the ego lessness of the Tao and its virtues of universal compassion, equanimity, magnanimity and that true authenticity will eclipse the inchoate but lesser values of goodness, morality to unlock their true potential and foster meaningful connections with their people. The Tao, if and when it is recognized and followed, creates a transformative power for those who follow it and makes for more effective leadership in a world too often driven by superficiality, ego and control.

The Paradox of Power: Exploring the Untapped Potential of the Masterful Leader

In the poetic verses of the passage titled "The Master Strives Not for Power," a contrasting portrayal of the master and the ordinary man unfolds, shedding light on the true essence of power and the limitless potential that lies within individuals who detach themselves from the pursuit of power and embrace a higher understanding of leadership. When duty calls and no one answers the true Tao master rolls up his own sleeves to get the job done.

In a world consumed by the relentless pursuit of power, the verses in this passage challenge traditional notions of leadership and present a thought-provoking perspective on the nature of leadership and true power. This passage invites us to explore the paradoxical relationship between power and striving, highlighting the profound potential inherent in those who relinquish the pursuit of power and embrace a path of self-mastery and social responsibility.

The Master's Transcendance

This part of the passage asserts that the master does not strive for power, yet paradoxically, the absence of striving makes the master truly powerful. This counterintuitive concept propels us to question conventional notions of power and encourages leaders to explore alternative approaches that transcend the relentless ego and its delusions and unhealthy pursuit of dominance. By embracing a mindset that prioritizes self-mastery over power-seeking, leaders can tap into a source of power from the Tao that emanates their authority and leadership from within.

The Limitations of the Ordinary Man

In contrast to the master, the "moral man", the ordinary man continuously strives for power, yet he is never satisfied, as the pursuit itself becomes an unquenchable thirst. This depiction illustrates the pitfalls of an unbalanced focus on power accumulation, highlighting its inherent insatiability. This continuous striving hinders the ordinary man from recognizing the true potential that lies within him and leaves him perpetually yearning for more.

Mastering the Art of Non-Striving

The next part of the passage emphasizes that the master accomplishes everything effortlessly, without striving to do anything in particular. This state of non-striving includes the implementation of Wu Wei and allows the master to tap into a deeper understanding of their own capabilities and the natural flow of life. Lao Tzu delves into the transformative power of embracing non-striving in leadership, emphasizing the importance of being present, responsive, and open to the opportunities that arise, rather than fixating on rigid goals and forcing their implementation.

Unveiling the Slippery Slope to Chaos: Exploring the Relationship Between Virtue and True Leadership

In a world where power often becomes the focal point of leadership, the wisdom shared in the later part of this passage again challenges conventional notions of leadership and prompts a deeper reflection on the essence of goodness and the potential dangers of those who undertake ritualistic practices, especially ones that are undertaken by those in power for the purpose of popular consumption. Any analysis of Lao Tzu's words should highlight the significance of embracing humility, true goodness, morality, and authenticity for their own sake as with the

Tao they become essential attributes of universal and effective leadership.

Leadership is a multifaceted concept that requires numerous qualities to uphold its integrity and effectiveness. Lao Tzu's passage explores the digression of virtues, namely goodness, morality, and ritual, as potential pitfalls that lead individuals away from true leadership. Lao Tzu causes us to delve thoughtfully into this topic, by shedding light on the significance of these virtues, their limitations, and the importance of embracing the Tao and the Integral Way as the highest form of leadership.

While goodness, morality, and ritual are essential components of the orthodoxy of leadership, they fall short in comparison to the true altruism of a Tao-centered life or the virtues learned on the path of the Integral Way. Lao Tzu emphasizes the dangers of relying solely on these virtues, as they can become disconnected from one's genuine moral compass and ethical decision-making, thus inviting chaos. True leadership goes beyond the surface level of virtues and encompasses a deeper understanding of reality.

Goodness as a Foundational Attribute

In the hierarchy of effectiveness, after the Tao and its emphasis on personal responsibility and spiritual evolution, there is goodness. Goodness is a quality that remains even when one loses touch with the Tao. It otherwise forms the bedrock of leadership, showcasing the innate quality of individuals. However, relying solely on goodness without aligning it with the Tao may lead to its insufficiency in guiding a leader's actions. Exploring the dualistic limitations of goodness unveils the significance of integrating it with a Tao-centered perspective to achieve genuine leadership.

Without goodness, mankind falls back onto traditional notions of morality. Without genuine morality man falls back onto religion and making laws. With religion mankind falls back onto relying on religion's rituals. As we devolve from the Tao to goodness and then on to morality and ritual we eventually devolve into a society of empty rituals, great bodies of law that restrict human freedom and deprive us of our dignity and inevitably end in chaos.

Conclusion

Lao Tzu's passage outlines the gradual digression of virtues, from the Tao into goodness, morality, and ritual, in the context of leadership. While these virtues may be crucial in our past and present mode of leadership, they fall short when detached from the Tao and its Integral Way. A true leader should be a true master of the Tao and the Integral way. Lao Tzu emphasizes the necessity for leaders to live in reality, letting go of illusions that cloud judgment and authenticity. The master must be able to see things clearly as they are. The Tao helps to provide this. True leadership also lies in understanding the depths of things and embracing a holistic approach that moves to the genuine and beyond the surface level of virtues and actions done for public consumption. By following the Tao and practicing its Integral Way, we can pave the way for effective leadership in the post-contact world that embraces universal values, transcends superficiality and ultimately embraces eternity.

Effective leadership necessitates seeking meaningful connections and true sincerity beyond superficial expressions. By integrating one's innate goodness, humility and morality with a Tao-centered life and by letting go of ego and all its illusions, a great leader can preserve the integrity and effectiveness of their leadership and by doing so, create a legacy that will ultimately speak for itself and survive the test of time.

One who follows the Tao and practices the Integral Way does not strive for power but rather focuses on understanding and embodying the principles of existence. This approach to life does not change when one leads. This approach to leadership highlights that true power resides not in the external quest for dominance and power but rather in wisdom, self-awareness and in the practice of the four main virtues of the Tao: simplicity, patience, compassion and truth. Examining the limitations of power as an end in itself and the true potential that Tao-centered leadership provides, leaders at all levels can shift their focus away from worn out and outdated modes of leadership toward more enduring qualities that contribute more positively and constructively to their potential impact.

CHAPTER 39

The Master and the Tao

WITH THE TAO
ALL THINGS ARE IN HARMONY.
CLEAR AND VAST ARE THE SKIES.
THE EARTH IS FIRM AND ABUNDANT.

CONTENT WITH THEMSELVES AND HOW THEY
ARE,
ALL LIVING THINGS FLOURISH TOGETHER.
THEY ENDLESSLY REPRODUCE AND RENEW
THEMSELVES.

WHEN HUMANS INTERFERE WITH THE TAO
THEY DEPLETE THE LAND
AND THEIR SKIES BECOME FILLED WITH FILTH.
EQUILIBRIUM CRUMBLES
AND EXTINCTION BEFALLS EARTH'S CREATURES.

BECAUSE THE MASTER UNDERSTANDS THE
WHOLE
HE VIEWS ITS COMPONENTS WITH COMPASSION.
HUMILITY IS THE MASTER'S CONSTANT PRAC-
TICE.
HE DOES NOT SPARKLE LIKE A PRECIOUSLY CUT
JEWEL
BUT ALLOWS THE TAO TO SHAPE HIM TO BE
AS RUGGED AND AS COMMON AS STONE.

Title: Harmony with the Tao: The Key to Sustainability and Flourishing

In the realm of ancient Chinese philosophy, Lao Tzu and the reality of the Tao hold immense significance. With Lao Tzu's profound teachings on the interplay between nature and humankind, the Tao offers a blueprint for harmonious coexistence and sustainable prosperity. There is profound wisdom encapsulated in the Tao, emphasizing the importance of understanding, respecting, and aligning ourselves with the natural order of things. Through embracing the Tao, we can reduce the chaos and entropy in our lives, restore balance and harmony but also protect the environment, and foster the well-being of all living beings both on Earth and by extension, throughout the Universe as well.

Harmony and Balance

The Tao teaches us that by embracing harmony, balance, humility, and compassion, we can alleviate the negative impact of human interference on the environment, restore equilibrium, and ensure the flourishing of all life forms.

The Tao and its Integral Way emphasize the importance of embracing harmony to achieve a balance between human actions and the natural world. By respecting the interconnectedness of all things, we can understand and appreciate the delicate equilibrium that sustains the Earth and puts all things in the universe in balance. The Tao teaches us to avoid extremes. Within these extremes are excessive intervention and exploitation, as these things disrupt the natural flow of things and cause long-term harm.

Humility and Respect

The Tao encourages humility in our relationship with nature. While humans possess great intellect and power, to maintain harmony, we must not impose our will onto the environment recklessly. Instead, we should align ourselves with the Tao's principles and allow it to shape our behavior. By practicing humility, we recognize that our place in the world is no more significant than that of a tiny pebble. When we act accordingly, fostering a spirit of respect towards all living beings and all aspects of nature.

Compassion and Responsibility

Compassion towards nature is central to the teachings of the Tao. By understanding the intricate networks of life and acknowledging the inherent value of all living beings, we can cultivate empathy and responsibility. The Tao encourages us to view the Earth's components as interconnected universal entities deserving our care and consideration. This understanding compels us to protect the environment, nurturing it for future generations instead of exploiting it for immediate gains.

Conclusion

The wisdom of the Tao calls upon humanity to recognize the importance of living in harmony with nature. By embracing the principles of simplicity, patience, balance, humility, and compassion, we can mend the fractures caused by human interference and pave the way towards an enlightened and sustainable future. It is through our understanding of the Tao's teachings that we can restore equilibrium, protect the environment, and ensure the flourishing of all life forms on Earth. Let us embrace the ways of the Tao, allowing it to shape us to be as rugged and common as stone, yet retaining the capacity to foster a world and a universe that thrives with the abundance and harmony that is the universal way of the Tao.

CHAPTER 40

Being and Non-Being

**GENTLE AND YIELDING,
RETURNING UNTO ITSELF
IS THE SUBTLE WAY OF THE TAO.**

**ALL THINGS THAT COME INTO BEING
ARE BE BORN OUT OF NON-BEING.
"NON-BEING" BEGETS BEING.**

Mankind's exploration of immortality has journeyed through the realms of history, philosophy, science, and popular culture. Immortality, in its various forms, has captured the human imagination for centuries, fueling our desires, shaping our beliefs, and pushing the boundaries of scientific inquiry. While the concept of immortality and reincarnation remain elusive in their purest form, the quest for eternal existence will continue to challenge humanity until it is properly understood. Whether through ancient myths, philosophical musings, scientific research, or fictional tales, our fascination with immortality reflects our deep-rooted curiosity about life's mysteries and the boundaries of human potential. The study of Tao helps us understand the nature of life, reincarnation, "immortality", karma, divine energy and the essence of being and consciousness itself.

The excerpt from the Lao Tzu above serves as a profound reflection on the nature of existence and immortality. He reveals that the subtle path of the Tao, characterized by gentleness and yielding, is the way in which all things emerge and return to themselves. Recycling, birth, life, death, and rebirth is the machinery of all creation. Additionally, the idea that "non-being" gives birth to being implies that life and existence are rooted in a deeper state of nothingness. It is in that nothingness, the "subtle realm" where the Tao, the enigmatic and mysterious creator of all things resides.

These verses resonate with the philosophical concept of immortality, as they invite contemplation on the nature of eternal life. They suggest that immortality may not simply be the continuation of one's physical existence but rather a fundamental connection to the underlying essence of existence itself and the reappearance of conscious energy in physical form throughout eternity. Because we have discovered that consciousness is not a secondary emergence from the physical world but the fundamental block from which it emerges. As the quantum physicist Niels Bohr told us a century ago "Everything we call real is made of things that cannot be regarded as 'real'." And that is the enigmatic nature of true reality and the Tao itself.

By exploring and pondering the themes presented in this excerpt, we can gain a deeper understanding of the ephemeral nature of "reality" and the underlying motivations and aspirations of ego that drive humanity's eternal quest for immortality. It also invites us to question our understanding of life, death, and the very nature and existence of being and its purpose.

As we delve into ancient myths, examine philosophical perspectives, and explore scientific advancements and even the realm of quantum mechanics, we can see more and more how these ideas intertwine with the universal principles, knowledge and understanding expressed by Lao Tzu in the Tao Te Ching and in his later work the Hua Hu Ching. They remind us that the pursuit of immortality is not merely a desire for an extension of our current existence, but a search for a profound connection to the Tao and an understanding of the eternal and timeless essence of creation and life itself.

CHAPTER 41

The "Superior Person"

WHEN A SUPERIOR PERSON FIRST LEARNS OF THE TAO,
THEY IMMEDIATELY START TO BECOME THE EMBODIMENT OF IT.
AS SOON AS AN AVERAGE PERSON FIRST LEARNS OF THE TAO,
HE OR SHE EQUALLY BOTH DOUBTS AND BELIEVES IT.
WHEN ONE WHO IS A FOOL HEARS THE TAO FOR THE FIRST TIME,
THEY WILL LAUGH OUT LOUD AT IT.
IF THE FOOL DID NOT DO SO,
THE TAO WOULD NOT BE THE TAO.

IT IS THEREFORE SAID THAT,
DARK APPEARS THE PATH TOWARDS THE LIGHT.
THE PATH THAT GOES FORWARD APPEARS TO GO BACK.
LONG SEEMS THE PATH THAT IS DIRECT.
WEAK DOES TRUE POWER SEEM.
TARNISHED DOES TRUE PURITY APPEAR.
CHANGEABLE DOES TRUE STEADFASTNESS SEEM.
OBSCURE DOES TRUE CLARITY APPEAR.
UNSOPHISTICATED SEEMS THE GREATEST ART.
IMPARTIAL DOES THE GREATEST LOVE APPEAR.
CHILDISH SEEMS THE GREATEST WISDOM.

NOWHERE IS THE TAO TO BE FOUND.
HOWEVER, ALL THINGS ARE NOURISHED AND COMPLETED BY IT.

<u>Embracing the Tao: A Journey of Understanding, Doubt, and Enlightenment</u>

The ancient concept of the Tao has mesmerized philosophers, scholars, and spiritual seekers for centuries. It is said that when a superior person first learns about the Tao, they immediately start embodying it, while an average person experiences a conflicted mixture of doubt and belief. On the other hand, the foolish laugh out loud at the very idea of the Tao. Even though the terms superior, average and foolish are relativistic terms, they are necessary to shed light on how the Tao is received differently by different people.

In exploring this topic, Lao Tzu delves into the enigmatic multifaceted nature of the Tao - its elusive yet pervasive presence, its paradoxes, and its profound impact on our lives. Look into the paradox deeply enough and you will unravel its truth. Here in this chapter, we begin in earnest to learn about the Tao from Lao Tzu, its transformative power, and the journey one who is so inclined undertakes to truly understand and embrace it.

<u>The Nature of the Tao</u>

The Tao is often described as the "path" or the "way". Paradoxically, it cannot be found or grasped, yet it permeates all things and nourishes and completes them. It embodies both light and dark, forward and backward, strength and weakness. The Tao is an enigma, a force that defies easy comprehension, yet guides and nourishes all aspects of existence.

<u>The Transformation of the Superior Person</u>

Despite is sounding judgmental, Lao Tzu uses the word merely to explain the hierarchy of three types of people and how they respond to the concept of the Tao. When a superior person first encounters the Tao, it becomes an intrinsic part of their being. They embody its principles, actively incorporating them into their thoughts, actions, and interactions. The superior person intuitively recognizes the wisdom and truth in the Tao, embracing it wholeheartedly as a guiding force in their life and applying it by living honestly and simply in their own lives and by employing patience and compassion to their interactions with others.

The Doubts and Beliefs of an Average Person

Unlike the instantaneous embodiment experienced by a superior person, an average person's reaction to the Tao is a delicate interplay of doubt and belief. The Tao's profound teachings, with their paradoxes and subtle nuances, elicit both skepticism and curiosity. Such individuals, intrigued yet uncertain, embark on a journey of exploration, seeking to reconcile their doubts and discover the truth within the Tao.

The Laughter of the Foolish

When a foolish person first encounters the Tao, they respond with laughter. To them, and their inability to think outside of concrete terms and physical reality, the profound concepts and teachings of the Tao appear absurd and incomprehensible. However, it is precisely this laughter that reaffirms the essence of the Tao. By challenging the foolish person's preconceptions and inviting a deeper exploration, the laughter serves as both a confirmation and a catalyst for enlightenment and spiritual transformation.

The Paradoxes of the Tao

The Tao's manifestations and teachings are replete with paradoxes as this chapter shows. The path towards the light appears dark, progress seems like regression, true power hides behind weakness, purity appears tarnished, steadfastness seems changeable, clarity is obscured, simplicity embodies the greatest artistry, and impartiality reflects the greatest love. The Tao and its Integral Way challenge conventional wisdom, urging individuals to embrace paradox as a gateway to understanding and its unraveling of the gateway to enlightenment and teaching us through its own example to impartially and indiscriminately give our love and compassion to all universally as we are able and their needs require.

The Journey of Seeking the Tao

In one discovering the Tao, he or she embarks on a journey of self-discovery and enlightenment. The Tao is nowhere to be found in a sense on the physical plane, yet its influence is everywhere. It nourishes and completes all things, granting individuals a profound sense of purpose and interconnectedness. The journey first involves our cultivating awareness, opening oneself to the existence of the Tao through the teachings of Lao Tzu and embracing its principles in our daily lives.

Conclusion

The concept of the Tao is a fascinating tapestry of paradoxes, doubts, and profound wisdom. While the superior person embodies the Tao effortlessly, the average person grapples with doubt and belief while the foolish person laughs, unaware of the profundity within. Through its paradoxical teachings, the Tao challenges conventional wisdom, inviting individuals to embark on a transformative journey of self-discovery and embrace the eternal interconnectedness of all things and events. In truly understanding and embodying the Tao, we nourish and complete ourselves, reduce unnecessary chaos, create harmony within ourselves and extending it to the world and universe around us.

By exploring the various perspectives towards the Tao, we come to become aware and appreciate the depths of its teachings and the significance that its existence holds in our lives. It is in this understanding that we are able to inform others of the impact the Tao can have on personal growth and spiritual enlightenment and explaining the eternal nature of its own being and that of our own.

CHAPTER 42

Embracing Solitude

ONE IS BORN FROM THE TAO.
THE ONE BEGETS TWO.
THE TWO BEGET THREE.
FROM THREE,
ALL THINGS ARE BORN.

WE STAND AND FACE OUR YANG SIDE TO THE
WORLD,
YET CARRY OUR YIN UPON OUR BACKS.
WHEN MALE AND FEMALE ENERGIES BLEND,
ALL THINGS ACHIEVE HARMONY.

THE ORDINARY MAN DISLIKES SOLITUDE
BUT THE MASTER MAKES GOOD USE OF IT.
BY EMBRACING HIS LONELINESS,
THE MASTER REALIZES HE IS ONE
WITH ALL THE UNIVERSE.

The Harmony of Yin and Yang: Exploring the Tao, the Internal
Operating System of the Universe

The teachings of Lao Tzu constitute one of the foundational
philosophies of ancient China. They emphasize the importance
of simplicity, balance, harmony, and unity in the universe. According to the Taoist ontology, everything is interconnected.
Underlying this connection is the notion that one is born from
the Tao and undergoes a transformative journey guided by the
principles of Yin and Yang. Understanding this concept and
its significance in achieving harmony within ourselves and
the world around us is an important step the student of Tao

must take in order to understand the universe, its energies, its inhabitants and his or her place in the cosmos.

In these passages above, Lao Tzu teaches us that through the integration of opposing energetic forces, symbolized by the female Yin and masculine Yang, we can achieve a state of balance and harmony, both individually and collectively. What is written below provides a general overview of the topics introduced by Lao Tzu above and can be and will be expanded further with more specific examples and deeper analysis further on in this book and in the Hua Hu Ching.

The Foundation of Tao

The core concepts of the study of Tao, include the notion that one is born from the Tao, the source of all existence. The belief in the dynamic interplay of Yin and Yang, symbolizing contrasting yet complementary forces, forms the basis of Taoist ontology. The journey of transformation from the oneness of the Tao to the manifestation of the many is a central underlying theme in all Taoist thought.

Yin and Yang in Unity

Yin and Yang, often depicted as feminine and masculine energies respectively, coexist and interact to bring about harmony in all aspects of life. This principle asserts that true harmony can only be attained through the integration and balance of opposing forces. By recognizing and valuing both our Yin and Yang aspects, we can embrace our wholeness and achieve inner and outer harmony and begin to understand how the universe operates and its energies play themselves out in the dance of life.

Embracing Solitude for Self-Realization

Solitude and introspection are essential for one's personal growth and realization. The ordinary person may shy away from solitude, as it can produce profound states of being. The master, however, actively seeks and embraces it, recognizing both its restorative and its transformative power. Through solitude, one can detach from external distractions and connect with the universal essence, realizing their oneness with everything.

Solitude is essential but it is unnecessary to practice it to the extreme. Balance in life requires both solitude and engagement as the reader will learn in further chapters here and in the Hua Hu Ching. A true master of the Integral Way was never meant to cloister himself or herself in some monetary or ivory tower. Such a life is without true compassion. Without societal engagement, spiritual evolution and refinement become useless tools and cannot be perfected.

Harmony in the World

The concept of Yin and Yang extends beyond the individual to the world and the universe beyond. These energies in all their forms, something that will be explained in great detail in the Hua Hu Ching, constitute the integral reality of being everywhere. When male and female energies blend, a harmonious and balanced relationship emerges, resulting in the flourishing of all things. Lao Tzu's perspective prompts us to nurture awareness, cooperation, respect, and understanding between different individuals, cultures, nations, and civilizations fostering a more harmonious global and universal community as a consequence thereof.

Conclusion

The interplay of Yin and Yang offers a profound understanding of the nature of existence and the path to balance and harmony. By acknowledging our inner duality, embracing solitude, and recognizing the interconnectedness of all things, we can unlock the potential for personal growth and cultivate harmony within ourselves and the world. As we face our Yang side to the world and carry our Yin on our backs, let us strive to achieve the balance and unity that Lao Tzu visualized and advocates, and to realize our oneness with the universe and all of its beings and inhabitants.

CHAPTER 43

Gentleness and The Nature of True Power, Wu Wei, "Teaching Without Words", The Tao Te Ching, The New Paradigm for Leadership on Earth in the Post-Extraterrestrial Contact World

IN THE WORLD
THE MOST GENTLE
OVERCOMES THAT
WHICH IS THE MOST DIFFICULT.

THAT WHICH IS WITHOUT SUBSTANCE
ENTERS THE PLACE WITH NO SPACE.
IN THE PENETRATION OF THE SPACELESS
BY THE INSUBSTANTIAL,
THE MEANING OF NON-ACTION
BECOMES MANIFEST.

TO TEACH WITHOUT WORDS,
TO ACCOMPLISH WITHOUT INTERFERENCE,
THIS IS THE WAY OF THE MASTER.

This passage from Lao Tzu encapsulates arguably, the three most important functional tenets of the Tao and of true leadership: gentleness, Wu Wei and teaching without words, making ourselves models for others so that they too might find the path for themselves and others towards peace, harmony, love, compassion and fulfillment through the Integral Way.

Part 1

"War itself is, of course, a form of madness. It's hardly a civilized pursuit. It's amazing how we spend so much time inventing devices to kill each other and so little time working on how to achieve peace." ~ Walter Conkrite

In a world that often equates strength with aggression and dominance, the paradox of gentleness and strength calls us to reevaluate conventional notions of strength and consider the transformative potential of gentle approaches in our own lives and within our communities and to redefine our understanding of power, influence, and resilience. In a world that often equates strength with aggression and dominance, the idea that the gentlest can overcome the most difficult challenges may appear counterintuitive. However, by understanding the transformative power of gentleness, we can begin to realize its true strength lies in its ability to foster compassion, connection, and understanding. In this way we can spend our time and creative ingenuity not on weapons of war and mass destruction but on achieving true and lasting world peace.

The Paradox of Power: Understanding the Paradox of Gentleness and Strength: Influence over Dominance: Embracing Compassion for Lasting Change

Contrary to popular belief, power is not solely derived from dominance and control. True power lies in influence. Gentleness and strength intertwine in one's ability to inspire, motivate, and effect positive change without resorting to force. In a world often driven by power and dominance, by examining the concept of gentleness when it comes to effecting real change upon deeper exploration, we uncover the true power and resilience of gentleness. This passage by Lao Tzu sheds light on the paradox of gentleness and strength, emphasizing the importance of listening and patience in creating compassionate connections, resolving conflicts, and ultimately, bringing about lasting and harmonious change.

Understanding the Paradox of Gentleness and Strength: How the Power of Gentleness Overcomes the Most Difficult

In a world focused on power and dominance, gentleness may seem ineffective. However, it possesses a hidden power that brings about lasting change. Lao Tzu's teachings emphasize the importance of gentleness in fostering compassion, resolving conflicts, and creating meaningful connections.

In a world often driven by aggression and force, the notion that gentleness, like water, can overcome the most difficult challenges may appear contradictory. However, upon delving deeper into the wisdom of the Tao, we discover an intriguing yet subtle truth; that over time, persistent patient gentleness prevails over formidable obstacles, no matter how difficult by allowing them to soften and change. This truth transcends traditional notions of power and dominance. Through an examination of the principle that "The most gentle overcomes that which is the most difficult," we can uncover the inherent strength and transformative potential of gentleness in overcoming adversity in both our personal relationships and otherwise.

Defining Gentleness: Moving Beyond Stereotypes

To grasp and truly understand the paradox of gentleness and strength, it is essential to define gentleness, challenge and move beyond stereotypes. Gentleness is often misinterpreted as weakness, lacking in assertiveness and determination. It is not. At its core, gentleness is strength. It is a form of compassionate, mindful restraint. It incorporates traits of benevolence, kindliness and care. It is humanity at its best.

Gentleness is an intentional approach to others that prioritizes compassion, empathy, and understanding. It embodies and goes hand in hand with qualities such as patience, humility, tenderness, and social and emotional intelligence. It is how we learned in Verse 28 to "Understand the male" yet "Tend toward the female". It is how we must be aware of the monstrous destruction that we can cause to everybody but choose not only to control it but to elevate ourselves above that low base energy to a higher one. By choosing gentleness is ultimately how we allow our yin energies to balance out our yang for the betterment of ourselves and all involved.

The Paradox of Power: Dominance Versus Influence: The Resilient Force of Gentle Persistence

Contrary to popular belief, power does not solely reside in dominance and control. True power lies in influence - the ability to inspire, motivate, and bring about positive change without resorting to force or violence. The paradox of gentleness and strength lies in leveraging this power of influence, engaging others through thoughtful dialogue, and leading by example. By demonstrating understanding and empathy, gentleness and the wisdom of kindness open doors for cooperation, collaboration, and long term collective growth.

In the face of challenges and adversity, gentleness can fuel resilient persistence. Its calm and unwavering nature allows for flexibility, adaptability, and the ability to navigate complex situations with grace. Through gentle persistence, we can inspire change, even in the most resistant environments and challenging of circumstances. It paves the way for open dialogue, fostering a culture of listening and understanding that breaks down barriers and helps us and others to discover what is in the best interests of all sides and for society as well.

Gentleness as a Catalyst for Compassion and Connection

At the heart of gentleness lies a catalyst for compassion and connection. By embracing gentleness, we create an environment that cultivates patience, compassion and empathy, allowing for more meaningful interactions, negotiations and respectful relationships. Engaging hearts, minds, and souls becomes possible when we approach others with the wisdom of kindness and understanding. It thus enables us to bridge differences and build bridges that foster cooperation and collaboration.

Cultivating Empathy: Engaging Hearts, Minds, and Souls

Empathy, a cornerstone of gentleness, is a skill that can be developed and nurtured. By actively seeking to understand others' perspectives, we deepen our ability to connect with them on an emotional level and to mediate our differences. It is through this connection that we forge bonds, break down prejudices, and create a space for dialogue and mutual understanding. When we find common ground we begin to see and understand the Tao in each other.

The Power of Listening: Creating Space for Dialogue and Understanding

Gentleness encourages active listening - a vital component in fostering understanding and resolving conflicts. It has long been said that "To listen is to love". By attentively listening to others, we not only can listen to their pain which, in itself has a therapeutic effect but show that we actually care. By listening, we validate others' experiences and emotions, inviting open and honest conversations. In turn, this leads to mutual understanding, ultimately paving the way for peaceful resolutions and sustainable change.

Building Bridges: Fostering Cooperation and Collaboration

Gentleness also acts as a bridge builder, bringing diverse individuals and communities together. By embracing gentleness, we can overcome divisive barriers and foster creativity and promote an environment of cooperation and collaboration.

Through shared goals and a collective commitment to understanding, we can achieve lasting change that benefits society as a whole and show our readiness to engage in higher orders of universal social intercourse.

Overcoming Conflict through Gentle Approaches: Negotiation and Mediation: The Gentle Path to Resolution

Gentleness also has the power to transform conflicts by prioritizing negotiation and mediation over aggression and hostility. By approaching conflicts with compassion and empathy, we create an atmosphere conducive to finding mutually beneficial solutions. Through the gentle path of negotiation and mediation, we can dissolve differences and resolve disputes while preserving relationships. History has shown us that the alternative to this approach bodes badly for those who fail to engage in compassionate, and meaningful dialogue to resolve their problems. We should take pause to remember that "Only thistles grow where the wagons of war tread."

The Art of Persuasion: Influence without Force

Gentleness shows us the art of persuasion - the ability to influence others without resorting to force. Effective persuasion comes from a place of unselfishness and non-ego. By empathetically understanding others' perspectives and presenting compelling arguments with kindness and being receptive of the needs of others, we can sway opinions and bring about change. The art of gentle persuasion ensures that our actions align with our values, fostering an atmosphere of respect and understanding.

Transforming Enemies into Allies: The Power of Forgiveness and Reconciliation

It is said that is is through forgiveness that we unburden ourselves of karma. Gentleness challenges us to embrace forgiveness and reconciliation, even when faced with hostility and animosity. By replacing vengeance with forgiveness and hatred with compassion, we can restore broken relationships, encouraging former enemies to become new and faithful allies. This transformative power not only heals individual wounds but also contributes to the healing and unity of communities and even worlds.

Vengeance begets an unending cycle of violence. It is never a solution. Compassion and forgiveness that begets forgiveness and compassion always is. Compassion is how higher beings and social orders operate.

The Transformative Potential of Gentleness: The Gentle Revolution: Creating Lasting Change through Kindness: Small Acts, Great Impact: The Ripple Effect of Random Acts of Kindness

Gentleness possesses a transformative potential that transcends traditional notions of power. Unlike its opposite, gentleness ignites a gentle revolution that starts with small acts of kindness. These acts, seemingly insignificant, have a ripple effect that extends beyond the individual. They grow and take on a life of their own over time. By inspiring and encouraging kindness in others, we can create a collective movement that compounds itself and brings about positive and lasting change, shaping a more advanced, peaceful, compassionate, and empathetic society. By embodying gentleness, we can nurture understanding, navigate conflicts peacefully, and foster a harmonious and empathetic world and align our intentions with our actions in a way that is harmonious and consistent with the universe of an ultimately eternal and compassionate Tao.

The Transformational Challenge: Embracing the Inner Power of Gentleness in Leadership: Leading with Compassion: Inspiring Others through Benevolence

In a world driven by aggression, the idea that gentleness can overcome the most difficult challenges seems contradictory. However, by exploring the wisdom of the Tao, we uncover the truth that gentleness prevails over time.

Gentleness in leadership offers an alternative approach that inspires others through benevolence and kind-heartedness. By leading with compassion, empathy, and an unwavering commitment to fairness and justice, leaders become agents of change who inspire and empower others to embrace gentleness, fostering a culture of understanding, and empathy.

Finding Courage by Embracing Vulnerability: The Courage to Show Gentleness in a Harsh World

In a world that often celebrates strength and resilience, embracing gentleness requires courage. It necessitates the powerful to show their own vulnerability and to be truthful and authentic and to challenge societal norms and expectations. By cultivating gentleness, we not only transform ourselves but also impact the world around us by challenging the status quo and fostering a more inclusive, advanced and compassionate society and world.

Conclusion: Gentleness

The paradox of gentleness and strength reveals a deeper truth about the potential of gentleness in overcoming challenges. By embracing gentleness, we tap into an inner power that fosters lasting change through patience, compassion, understanding, and influence. Let us break free from preconceived notions and harness the transformative potential of gentleness in our own lives and societies to create a more empathetic and harmonious society.

By embracing gentleness as a catalyst for compassion and connection, we can overcome conflicts, foster understanding, create lasting change, and shape a world driven by kindness and mutual compassion. Let us recognize the untapped potential of gentleness and embark on a journey towards building a more empathetic, advanced and harmonious society. Through the wisdom of gentle approaches and acts of kindness, we can create a ripple effect of positive change, transform conflicts, and build bridges in all of our relationships. By embracing gentleness, we can redefine power, influence, and resilience and existentially guarantee our own survival as a species. The legacy of the gentle is to inherit the earth. The legacy of the aggressor is earth's eventual destruction.

Part 2

The second part of this chapter, Non-action, introduces us to the transformative power of Wu Wei, challenging the notion that constant action is always the key to success. By embracing subtlety, minimalistic simplicity, and the profound meaning within non-action, we open ourselves to the transformative potential of gentle influence. Let us explore the art of non-action, harness the power of emptiness and stillness, and embark on a journey of personal and global transformation.

Wu Wei: The Transformative Power of Non-Action

By exploring the profound verse "That which is without substance enters the place with no space," we unravel the essence of Wu Wei - intentional non-action and its inherent power. By understanding the concept of non-action penetrating the substanceless and spaceless, we can grasp the significance of subtle influence and the manifestation of meaning in a state of non-action.

In a world of constant action, the power of gentle triumph may seem counterintuitive. Wu Wei, or "non-action," offers an alternative approach to action-driven living. By embracing non-action, we tap into the transformative essence and clarity of subtlety and minimalism. The verse suggests that what lacks substance and enters the place with no space carries profound meaning. Non-action allows us to distance ourselves from excessive action, to "Let the mud settle" and embrace the power of subtle influence and being.

Through silence, patient observation, and the release of resistance, we connect with the realm of Wu Wei and its transformative potential. By embracing the art of non-action, we discover a profound sense of purpose, meaning, something greater than ourselves and harmony in our lives. Cultivating a mindset that values emptiness and stillness allows us to tap into the power of subtle influence, the subtle energy of the Tao, that though they are unseen control the creation and flow of things around us. Wu Wei and intentional patience and non-action becomes a path through which personal and global transformation can occur. It is one of the main concepts that defines the Tao's Integral Way.

Wu Wei: The Essence of Non-Action: Unraveling the Meaning of Subtle Influence

The profound verse "That which is without substance enters the place with no space" challenges our conventional understanding of action and its impact. Delving deeper into this enigmatic statement, we unravel the essence of Wu Wei, intentional non-action and its inherent power. There is great importance, meaning and significance within the concept of non-action, as it has enormous transformative potential in our lives.

We have already learned that by being as gentle as water, we not only overcome difficulties but also help shape a more compassionate and harmonious world and universe. Similarly, by exploring the concept of non-action penetrating the spaceless and substance less, we can come to understand the profound implications of the Tao's "subtle influence" and the manifestation of meaning in a state of non-action as well.

The Art of Non-Action: Exploring the Power of Subtlety and Minimalism

In a world driven by constant action and noise, the idea that the most gentle can triumph over the most difficult may seem counterintuitive. However, when we dive deeper into the philosophy of Wu Wei or «non-action," as proposed by Lao Tzu, we uncover a profound truth. The verse suggests that what appears without substance and enters the place with no space holds a profound meaning within the realm of non-action. By distancing ourselves from the constant need for excessive action and embracing the power of subtle influence and being, we open ourselves to the transformative essence of non-action.

Through silence, patient observation, and the meditative release of resistance, we tap into the spaceless and substance less "subtle" realm, where the true meaning of non-action becomes manifest. By embracing this approach, we discover a profound sense of purpose, meaning, and harmony in our lives. By embracing the art of non-action, we can tap into the power of the Tao's subtle and too often unseen influence, harness the potential of the Tao's empty space, and its potential for personal and global transformation.

Conclusion: Non-action

We have all heard the term "going with the flow", sometimes there is no flow. At these times there is a need to employ patience. There is no need to do. So, Wu Wei, non-doing is how we harness the Tao. Non-action, as a philosophical and spiritual approach to life, challenges our conventional understanding of achievement and success. It encourages us to be patient and embrace the Tao's subtle influences, empty space, and a timely, balanced approach to action. In a world that is constantly moving, learning when to act and when not to act and thereby to navigate the path of non-action can provide enormous insight and untapped potential for personal growth and transformation.

Finally, by adopting Wu Wei, the way of the master, we learn to teach without words, accomplish without interference, and find beauty and significance in the simplicity of being. Embracing the art of non-action can lead us towards a more peaceful, meaningful, and fulfilling existence. By embracing the art of non-action, owe can tap into the power of subtle influence, harness the potential of empty space, and manifest meaningful achievements without unnecessary interference.

Part 3

The path of the master challenges our preconceived notions of leadership and accomplishment, advocating for a more subtle and intuitive approach. In a world where words dominate, non-verbal communication has the power to break us free from the limitations of language, inspiring others and accomplishing without interference. By mastering the art of non-verbal communication, we unlock the potential for effortless achievement, silent influence, and the integration of these powerful practices into our everyday lives.

Masters of Action: Unveiling the Path of Silent Achievement

Lao Tzu's profound statement "To teach without words, to accomplish without interference, this is the way of the master" challenges our conventional understanding of leadership and achievement. Exploring the depths of this wisdom, we can uncover the essence of mastery and delve into the power of example, non-verbal teaching and seamless accomplishment.

The Integral Way is the path of the master, a path that emphasizes the significance of actions that transcend language and interfere with no process. By embracing the way of the master, and teaching without words we accomplish without interference and can unlock new dimensions of influence and achievement.

Teaching Without Words: Unlocking the Power of Non-Verbal Communication: The Path to Effortless Achievement and Silent Influence

In a world dominated by words, it is easy to forget the profound impact that non-verbal communication can have on our lives and those around us. In this last part of his three part passage, Lao Tzu invites us to explore the art of non-verbal communication, shedding light, its power to inspire, and its ability to influence and accomplish greatness without words. By delving into the realms of exemplary presence, intuition, empathy, adaptability, and mindfulness, we will uncover the hidden potential of non-verbal communication in our everyday lives.

The Limitations of Words

Words can often fall short in expressing the depth of our feelings, thoughts, and intentions. They are finite and can be easily misinterpreted. Non-verbal cues, on the other hand, possess a universality that transcends language barriers, enabling a more authentic and profound connection with others.

The Power of Presence: Leading by Example

True leadership lies not in the command of words, but in the power of presence. By embodying qualities such as confidence, compassion, and integrity, leaders inspire others to follow their lead. Non-verbal communication serves as a mirror, reflecting the essence of our being and radiating its influence onto those around us.

Inspiring through Intuition and Empathy

Non-verbal cues are the language of intuition and empathy. They allow us to tap into the unspoken emotions and needs of others, forging deep connections and fostering a sense of understanding. In the absence of words, these intuitive signals hold the key to inspiring and uplifting others, encouraging them to reach their full potential.

Accomplishing Without Interference: Navigating the Path of Effortless Achievement: The Delicate Balance: Letting Go of Control

Success often eludes us when we become entangled in the web of control. Non-verbal communication teaches us to release the grip of excessive control and instead embrace a sense of surrender, allowing for spontaneity and creative flow. It is through this balance that we unlock the true potential for effortless achievement.

The Strength in Adaptability: Flowing with Change

Rigid verbal communication can hinder our ability to adapt to the ever-changing circumstances of life. Non-verbal cues, like showing courtesy or doing a kind act, pave the way for flexibility and adaptability, enabling us to navigate through challenges with grace and ease. By embracing change and flowing with it, we pave the path towards effortless accomplishment and doing what is right under any circumstance.

Creating Space for Success: Removing Obstacles

Non-verbal communication shows us that success is not about forcing our way through obstacles, but, like Wu Wei is about creating the space for it to unfold naturally. By removing unnecessary barriers, such as negative body language, unconscious biases, and limiting beliefs, we open up the doors to new possibilities and greater achievements.

The Mastery of Non-Verbal Influence and Silent Accomplishment: The Ripple Effect: Inspiring Others through Actions

The beauty of non-verbal communication lies in its ability to ripple outward, inspiring others through even our subtle yet impactful actions. By aligning our words with our actions, we create a synchronous message that speaks volumes to those around us. We are what we do not what we say. The power of our non-verbal influence can create a domino effect, igniting a wave of positive change.

Leading with Intention: Aligning Actions with Values

Non-verbal cues offer us the opportunity to lead authentically and with integrity by our example and countenance. By aligning our actions with our core values and beliefs, we become the embodiment of our aspirations. This silent influence has the potential to inspire others to do the same, creating a collective movement towards a better world.

Embracing Humility: Recognizing the Power of the Collective

Non-verbal communication also teaches us the art of humility and the power of collective accomplishments. By recognizing and appreciating the contributions of others, we create an environment where teamwork and collaboration thrive. Through silent appreciation and giving credit to others we amplify the potential for collective success.

Integrating the Way of the Master in Everyday Life: Cultivating Mindfulness: Heightening Awareness of Non-Verbal Communication

To truly harness the power of non-verbal communication, one must cultivate awareness and meditative mindfulness. By sharpening our awareness of the subtle cues we emit and receive, and mindfully observing our thoughts and actions and the actions of others, we unlock the capacity to connect on a deeper level. Mindfulness allows us to fully engage with the present moment and make conscious choices in our interactions.

Nurturing Inner Harmony: Developing Inner Wisdom and Intuition

The journey of mastering non-verbal communication begins within us. By nurturing inner harmony, we tap into our innate Tao wisdom and intuition – the guiding forces behind our non-verbal expressions. As we develop this internal connection, we empower ourselves to communicate with authenticity and resonance both in what we say and what we do.

Embracing Stillness: Finding Transcendence in Action

In the midst of movement and action, finding moments of stillness is essential to transcendence. Through cultivating stillness, we create space for deep reflection, heightened self-awareness, and connection with others. In these moments of true being, non-verbal communication takes on new depth and meaning, carrying profound messages without a single word.

Conclusion: Teaching Without Words: Embracing the Integral Way

Teaching without words and accomplishing without interference opens opportunities for deeper connections, unspoken understanding, and effortless achievements. By cultivating non-verbal communication and navigating the path of non-interference, individuals can transcend language barriers, inspire others through their actions, and create a lasting impact.

By embracing the Integral Way, the path of the master offers us the profound opportunity to leave a legacy of silent influence and accomplishment by incorporating the principles of gentleness, doing without doing and teaching without words into our own lives, fostering personal growth, and unlocking new potentials for leadership, spiritual evolution and refinement and higher self-actualization and societal realization. Let us embrace the Way of the master and embark on this transformative journey towards a more connected and impactful existence in our own lives and the lives of others throughout this world and the universe in which we with others reside.

CHAPTER 44

The Tao of Fulfillment

WHICH IS MORE IMPORTANT: INTEGRITY OR FAME?
WHICH IS MORE IMPORTANT: MONEY OR HAPPINESS?
WHICH IS MORE IMPORTANT: SUCCESS OR FAILURE?

BY LOOKING TO OTHERS TO BE FULFILLED
TRUE FULFILLMENT CANNOT BE ATTAINED.
IF ONE'S HAPPINESS DEPENDS ON MONEY
ONE WILL NEVER BE HAPPY WITH ONESELF.

ONE MUST BE CONTENT WITH WHAT ONE HAS.
REJOICE THAT THINGS ARE THE WAY THEY ARE,
FOR THE WHOLE WORLD BELONGS TO THE ONE
WHO REALIZES THAT NOTHING IS LACKING.

True Fulfillment: Looking Beyond External Measures of Success

In today's society, there are numerous external factors that people attribute to their happiness and fulfillment. However, the question arises: What truly matters in life? In this passage Lao Tzu aims to inform us about the importance of valuing integrity over fame, happiness over money, and the significance of learning from both success and failure. By exploring these topics and challenging the common notions of fulfillment, we can gain a more holistic and complete understanding of what it means to lead a truly fulfilling life.

Integrity vs. Fame: The Essence of Character

Integrity, the quality of being honest and having strong moral principles, is often overshadowed by the desire for fame and recognition. However, it is crucial to recognize that integrity forms the foundation of one's character. While fame may bring temporary recognition and validation from others, it is integrity that will sustain a person's reputation in the long run. It is integrity that prevents the accumulation of karma in life.

Without integrity, devoid of substance and authenticity, fame is merely an empty shell for the ego. Therefore, it is integrity, not fame, that should be prioritized and valued for its enduring impact on one's life and spiritual evolution and refinement and the spiritual development and lives of others.

Money vs. Happiness: The Pursuit of True Well-being

In a world increasingly driven by materialistic desires, the pursuit of money often takes precedence over one's happiness. However, it is important to realize that true fulfillment cannot be attained solely through financial success. While money may provide temporary comforts and pleasure, it falls short in providing lasting happiness. Happiness, on the other hand, stems from within, and it can be found in the simplest joys of life, such as meaningful relationships, personal growth, and a sense of purpose. Rather than placing undue importance on accumulating wealth, it is crucial to focus on cultivating compassion towards others and happiness within ourselves and finding contentment in the present moment.

Success vs. Failure: The Pathways to Growth

In society, success is often glorified while failure is seen as something to be ashamed of. However, both success and failure are two sides of the same coin as they both play integral roles in personal growth and development. Success provides a sense of achievement and affirmation, but it is through failure that we learn valuable lessons and gain resilience. Without experiencing failure, we cannot truly appreciate the hard-earned success. Embracing failure as a natural part of life allows us to learn, adapt, and ultimately achieve greater success.

It has been said that risk is the price one pays for the opportunity to succeed. Rather than fearing failure in a heartfelt endeavor, we should see it as a risk worth taking and an opportunity for growth and an essential aspect of the journey towards true fulfillment.

Conclusion

True fulfillment cannot be attained by solely relying on external measures such as fame, money, or material success. It is through prioritizing integrity over fame, happiness over money, and embracing both success and failure that we can find genuine contentment. By challenging conventional notions of fulfillment, we can embark on a path towards a more meaningful and fulfilling life. Ultimately, it is by living simply and looking inward, being grateful and appreciating what we have, and evolving physically, mentally and spiritually to be the best versions of ourselves that we can experience true fulfillment that surpasses any external measure of success.

CHAPTER 45

**IMPERFECT DOES TRUE PERFECTION APPEAR,
YET PERFECTLY ITSELF IT IS.**

**THAT WHICH IS TRULY FULL SEEMS EMPTY.
YET FULLY PRESENT IT IS.**

**CROOKED SEEMS THE TRULY STRAIGHT.
AND FOOLISH DOES TRUE WISDOM SEEM.
ARTLESS APPEARS TRUE ART.**

**THE MASTER ALLOWS THE HAPPENING OF
THINGS
EVEN AS EVENTS COME TOWARDS HIM,
THE MASTER STEPS OUT OF THEIR PATH
AND ALLOWS THE TAO TO SPEAK FOR ITSELF.**

"Don't worry about mistakes, there aren't any." ~ Miles Davis

Embracing Imperfection: The Paradox of True Perfection in
the Tao's Integral Way

In the realm of Tao and its Integral Way, a paradoxical notion
prevails, challenging the conventional notion of perfection.
The quote "Imperfect does true perfection appear, yet perfectly
itself it is" encapsulates the essence of this philosophy. In this
passage Lao Tzu aims to explore the concept of true perfection
in Tao, shedding light on the seemingly contradictory nature
of its manifestations. By delving into the paradoxical interplay
of emptiness and fullness, crookedness and straightness, foolishness and wisdom, and artlessness and art, he unveils the
wisdom and beauty of embracing imperfection in the search
for true perfection.

The Paradox of Fullness and Emptiness

In Taoism, true perfection is said to be found in that which appears empty. Paradoxically, emptiness holds the potential for fullness. It is in the void that possibilities abound, and true essence can be realized. The wise masters of the Tao harness the power of emptiness, allowing them to be of service and having the richness of experiences to fill their lives. Through detachment, they relinquish their desire to control outcomes and nimbly react to and embrace the flow of life's events, allowing the interplay of yin and yang to unveil the true perfection within.

Crookedness and Straightness: The Illusion of Dichotomy

True perfection, in the Lao Tzu's lens, challenges the notion of a singular, rigid path to righteousness. Crookedness and straightness are perceived as illusory dualistic concepts that exist in a dynamic continuum. Wisdom lies in recognizing the inherent wisdom in what may appear foolish or divergent from traditional societal norms. By embracing the fluidity of perspective, the wise follower of the Integral Way learns to take the best path in every situation that presents itself and to navigate the complexities of life with greater ease and openness.

The Artlessness of True Art

In the study of Tao, true art is not constrained by meticulous techniques or calculated precision. It is often birthed from a state of artlessness, devoid of overly contrived efforts. As all creativity flows from the Tao as its source, a master of the Tao allows creativity to flow effortlessly, surrendering to the natural rhythm of the universe. By embracing imperfections and intuitive spontaneity, true art arises, transcending prevailing societal standards and capturing the essence of life itself.

N. MICHAEL MURBURG, JR.

Allowing the Tao to Speak

A fundamental aspect of the study of the Tao and following its Integral Way revolves around the concept of non-interference. Intentional non-interference is a manifestation of Wu Wei. The wise master understands that true perfection is found in allowing things to unfold naturally and in harmony with the Tao. It does so without imposing personal desires or intentions. Much like the Tao of Leadership, by stepping aside and letting events take their course, the master relinquishes control and allows the wisdom of the Tao to guide the unfolding of reality.

This approach has also proved to be the correct one when it comes to modern man's approach to aboriginal human societies and ecosystems. Interference always runs the risk of somehow contamination of things, events and destinies included. The rule should almost always be non-intervention unless asked for or obviated by the potential destruction that non-intervention risks. Because the existence of the Tao is universal, Wu Wei is the universal law of all higher beings throughout the cosmos.

Conclusion

In our paradoxal universe, where energies harmonize their opposite polarities, it is imperfection that holds the hidden key to true perfection. Through the interplay of apparent opposites like emptiness and fullness, crookedness and straightness, foolishness and wisdom, and artlessness and art, like the paradoxes of light and dark, male and female and life and death, the follower of the Tao's Integral Way reconciles seemingly opposing forces and ideas to transcend the limitations of conventional understanding. There is perfection in imperfection. By embracing imperfections and surrendering to the wisdom of the Tao, the pursuit of true perfection becomes an enlightening journey rather than an ominous, impossible or. formidable destination. In the grand tapestry of life, imperfection reveals its hidden beauty, and true perfection manifests in its own unique and harmonious way as part and parcel of the eternal Tao.

CHAPTER 46

The Tao Te Ching, The New Paradigm for Leadership and Governance on Earth in a Post-Extraterrestrial Contact World

WHEN A LAND IS IN HARMONY WITH THE TAO THE FACTORIES MAKE PLOUGHS AND WAGONS. WHEN A LAND IS NOT IN HARMONY WITH THE TAO SWORDS AND PIKES ARE STOCKPILED OUTSIDE OF THE CITIES FOR WAR.

OF ALL ILLUSIONS, FEAR IS THE GREATEST. OF ALL MISFORTUNES, HAVING AN ENEMY IS THE WORST. OF ALL WRONGS, THERE IS NONE GREATER THAN IN PREPARING TO DEFEND ONESELF.

THE ONE WHO IS ABLE TO SEE THROUGH FEAR WILL FOREVER BE SAFE.

The Power of Harmony: A Message of Peace and Security

In the wise words of Lao Tzu, "When a land is in harmony with the Tao, the factories make ploughs and wagons. When a land is not in harmony with the Tao, swords and pikes are stockpiled outside of the cities for war." This profound statement serves as a reminder that 'Where the wagons of war tread, only thistles grow". It emphasizes the importance of harmony and peace in society. In this passage Lao Tzu explores the significance of living in harmony with the Tao, the illusionary and cruel nature of fear, the detrimental effects of having enemies, and the paradoxical wisdom behind avoiding preparation for self-defense.

Harmony with the Tao and Prosperity

The Tao is what connects us all to each other and to it through its subtle fields of energy and information. It also represents the natural way of life and the interconnectedness of all things. When a land and its people embrace the principles of the Tao, its focus shifts from violence and conflict to collaboration, productivity and progress. The presence of ploughs and wagons symbolizes a society's ability to cultivate and prosper through peaceful means. In modern times the benefit societies get is known as the peace dividend. In Roman history, the 'pax Romana' was a two-hundred-year era of prosperous stability that came from a golden age of relative peace and order.

War causes needless chaos and destruction. Peace causes welcome stability and prosperity. Whether we are aware of it or not, peace, not conflict, is the ultimate path of the Tao and its Integral Way. We can create the friction of battle with our needless friction in life or we can choose to evolve by empowering ourselves and our world by following the Tao and its Integral Way.

Disharmony with the Tao and Militarization

When a society loses touch with the Tao, it falls victim to the cruel illusions of fear, ego, and struggles for power. The accumulation of swords and pikes signifies a nation's readiness for conflict and suggests a lack of trust in each other and in peaceful relations. The cycle of violence perpetuated by a lack of harmony ultimately harms the people and the nation as a whole. It takes human effort and treasure to produce weapons of war and to have standing armies. This effort and treasure is better expended elsewhere. As we will learn in later chapters and verses of the Tao Te Ching, there is no excuse for engaging in warfare absent an actual invasion into one's own sovereign land by a foreign force that endangers innocent life of those who are invaded.

Overcoming Fear and Ensuring Safety

Lao Tzu believes that fear is the greatest and most cruel of all illusions. Fear is a product of the ego. It is how the mind breeds paranoia, hostility, and a constant state of insecurity. By cultivating an understanding of fear's cruel and illusory nature, we can break free from its grip and experience true freedom and safety from it.

The Dangers of Having Enemies

Having enemies creates a constant state of tension and hostility. It leads to an unnecessary expenditure of resources and energy that could otherwise be directed towards progress and development. Lao Tzu considers the presence of enemies as one of the worst misfortunes, highlighting the destructive nature of such relationships. Whether in our own personal lives or in the affairs of nations and worlds creating an enemy when a friend can be made should be avoided. Recognize the needs of others and reply to challenging circumstances with the wisdom of kindness, patience and compassion. The same will be done for you when people and societies meet within the magnanimity and equanimity that is the Tao and its Integral way.

The Futility of Preparing to Defend Oneself

Lao Tzu argues that preparing for self-defense is a misguided approach to ensure safety. Defensive preparations often escalate conflicts and perpetuate a never-ending cycle of fear and violence. It is the path to mutually assured destruction. The true path to security lies in being compassionate and in fostering harmony, understanding, and mutual respect. It lies in seeing not only others as we and ourselves in others, but seeing all as parts of one universal and integral Tao.

Conclusion

Lao Tzu's profound and timeless universal insight continues to hold relevance in our modern world. By living in harmony with the Tao and by transcending fear and ego, we create better and safer lives for ourselves and help create relationships, families, communities and societies that flourish through peaceful means. Understanding the futility of having enemies and the inefficiency of bilaterally preparing for self-defense, we can pave the way towards a more harmonious, peaceful and secure future on this planet and in the universe. Let us begin to embrace the power of the Tao and of its harmony and work towards a world free from poverty, repression, isolation, conflict, and the greatest and most cruel illusion, that of fear.

CHAPTER 47

Unlocking the Tao Within, Wu Wei

**WITHOUT OPENING ONE'S DOOR
ONE CAN OPEN ONE'S HEART TO THE WORLD.**

**WITHOUT LOOKING BEYOND ONE'S WINDOW
ONE CAN SEE THE TAO'S ESSENCE.**

**THE MORE ONE KNOWS,
THE LESS ONE UNDERSTANDS.**

**WITHOUT LEAVING,
THE MASTER ARRIVES.**

**WITHOUT LOOKING,
THE MASTER SEES THE LIGHT.**

**WITHOUT DOING ANYTHING,
THE MASTER ACHIEVES.**

Unlocking the World Within: The Power of Inner Exploration

In today's fast-paced world, we are constantly bombarded with the message that to understand and appreciate the world, we must venture outside our doors. However, the ancient wisdom encapsulated in this passage of Lao Tzu's the Tao Te Ching challenges this notion by suggesting that we can open our hearts to the world without physically opening our doors. Significantly, and along the same lines, Christ taught that the kingdom of God was within. * By delving deeper into the concept of inner exploration, we can uncover the profound truth that knowledge, understanding, and true personal and spiritual growth can be achieved without leaving the confines of our immediate surroundings. There is tremendous transformative power to be found in self-reflection and meditative contemplation. This passage highlights how without looking beyond our windows, we can see the essence of the Tao, and how without doing anything, we as masters of the Tao can find it within.

Opening One's Heart to the World

The ability to open our hearts to the world is not dependent on physical movement, but rather on emotional, spiritual and intellectual engagement. By immersing ourselves in literature, art, and human connection, we can begin to understand and establish profound connections with the world's complexities, cultures, and people. Without stepping outside, we can cultivate empathy, understanding, and compassion for others, broadening our perspectives and breaking down the barriers that separate us.

Seeing the Essence of the Tao

In this passage Lao Tzu proposes that we can perceive the essence of the Tao without even looking beyond our windows. The Tao, often described as the underlying force that governs all existence, can be understood through observation, contemplation and our own experience. By quieting the external noise and focusing inward, we can develop a heightened awareness of the interconnectedness of all things, leading to a deeper understanding of the nature of reality and our place within it.

The Paradox of Knowledge and Understanding

In the pursuit of knowledge, we encounter the paradox that the more we learn, the less we understand. This paradox suggests that true wisdom lies not in accumulating facts and information, but in embracing the limits of our knowledge and acknowledging the vastness of what remains unknown. Through introspection and reflection, we can come to terms with the limitations of knowledge and cultivate a genuine sense of humility that fosters a genuine thirst for further understanding and enlightenment.

Mastery Without Action

The idea that mastery can be achieved without physically doing anything challenges the traditional notion of progress and accomplishment. Just as silence is a very powerful statement and how we let go, stillness is equally as powerful. The Tao teaches us that stillness and inaction or "Wu Wei", can hold immense power, allowing us pause to dispel our fear in order to navigate life's challenges with grace and wisdom. By relinquishing our desires for control and actively embracing the present moment, we can find a state of inner equilibrium that leads to true mastery. One need not even leave one's home to get there.

Conclusion

The notion that without opening one's door, one can open one's heart to the world offers a profound perspective on personal growth and spiritual understanding. The power of inner exploration lies in its ability to connect us with the essence of the Tao, expand our capacity for empathy and compassion, embrace the limits of our knowledge, and seek mastery through stillness. By realizing that the pathway to enlightenment lies within us, wherever we are, we can embark on a transformative journey of self-discovery that transcends physical boundaries. It is through this journey that we can unlock the world within, cultivate a deep sense of connection with others and the universal creator itself to find wisdom, tranquility and fulfillment in our lives. One need not even leave one's home, much less one's own heart in order to find the Tao the underlying force that governs all existence within us and the cosmos.

*Neither shall they say, Lo here! or Lo there! for the kingdom of God is within you." (Luke 17:21)

CHAPTER 48

Simplicity, Wu Wei and Letting Go to Let Things Find Their Own Way

WHEN KNOWLEDGE IS PURSUED,
EVERY DAY, SOMETHING IS ADDED.

HOWEVER, WHEN THE TAO IS PRACTICED,
EVERY DAY, SOMETHING IS SUBTRACTED.

AS ONE ARRIVES AT NON-ACTION,
LESS AND LESS
DO THINGS NEED TO BE FORCED.

WHEN ONE PRACTICES NON-ACTION,
NOTHING IS DONE,
YET NOT A THING IS LEFT UNDONE.

TRUE MASTRY CANNOT BE GAINED BY INTERFE-
RING.
IT CAN BE GAINED ONLY
BY LETTING GO OF THINGS SO THAT THEY MAY
FOLLOW THEIR OWN PATH.

The Power of Non-Action: Embracing the Tao for True Mastery

In a world that champions constant pursuit of knowledge, it is essential to recognize the alternative path of wisdom through the practice of the Tao. The ancient Chinese philosophy of the Tao emphasizes simplicity and the idea that when one embraces non-action, a profound transformation occurs. As the quote suggests, every day, something is subtracted, and as one arrives at non-action, things are forced less and less.

For the neophyte in the world of eastern thought, doing by non-doing does not make sense until it is adequately explained. Nothing is ever accomplished by doing absolutely nothing, however, there is a time for doing and a time to let ourselves and our work rest. As Lao Tzu shows us in this passage, there are many benefits and insights that can be gained by practicing non-action and by letting go of our incessant need to control outcomes. By giving ourselves the space to simply observe and follow our own path, we are able to achieve true mastery of the Tao and live a more harmonious, compassionate and fulfilling lives.

The Paradox of Knowledge

In our modern society, knowledge is highly esteemed, and the pursuit of it is seen as a means to success and progress. However, the Tao challenges this perspective by suggesting that the accumulation of knowledge alone does not guarantee wisdom or true mastery. Instead, it emphasizes the need to let go of our attachment to knowledge and embrace the concept of emptiness and non-action. By doing so, we create space for new insights and experiences to emerge naturally.

The Power of Non-Action

When we practice non-action, we actively let go of the need to control and force outcomes. By surrendering our attachment to results, we allow situations to unfold without interference. This does not imply laziness or indifference. Instead, it is an active choice to trust in the natural flow of life and have faith that things will align as they should. In this state of non-action, we become observers, gaining a deeper understanding of the interplay between all things.

N. MICHAEL MURBURG, JR.

Embracing Non-Action for True Mastery

True mastery is not gained through trying to control or manipulate external circumstances. It is attained by cultivating an inner stillness and aligning with the harmony of the universe. By practicing non-action, we create a space for our intuition and inner wisdom to guide us. We allow things to unfold organically, trusting that the right actions will naturally arise at the right time. In this way, we tap into a higher level of consciousness, where clarity and insight flourish.

Letting Go and Allowing

One of the most profound lessons the Tao teaches is the art of letting go of attachments and allowing things to follow their own path. This is not an easy task, as human nature often urges us to take charge and control outcomes. However, control is an illusion and as we detach ourselves from the need for control, we discover a greater sense of freedom, peace, and alignment with the Tao and the flow of life. Letting go does not mean inactivity or passivity; instead, it is an act of surrender and trust in the Tao and embracing the wisdom that comes from seeing things as they are and allowing things to be as they are.

Conclusion

In a world focused on constant forward motion and the accumulation of knowledge, embracing non-action and surrendering control seems counterintuitive. However, the wisdom of the Tao reminds us that true mastery lies in observing, letting go, and allowing. By practicing non-action, especially when we do not know exactly what to do in a situation, we create room for the Tao to flow and the opportune time for action to arise. Ultimately, Wu Wei provides those who recognize and practice it spiritual and personal growth, insight, and alignment with the Tao's natural order of things. Let us remember that the pursuit of knowledge is essential to understand a physical universe and how it operates, but it is through the practice of Wu Wei, patience and intentional contemplative non-action that we can truly find harmony, wisdom, and fulfillment in our lives and understand our true place in the universe as it unfolds around us.

CHAPTER 49

The Mind of the Masterful Leader, The Tao Te
Ching, The New Paradigm for Leadership and
Governance on Earth in the Post-Extraterrestrial
Contact World

NO MIND OF HIS OWN
HAS THE MASTER,
IT IS WITH THE MIND OF THE PEOPLE
THAT HE WORKS.

TO THOSE WHO ARE GOOD,
THE MASTER IS GOOD.
TO THOSE WHO ARE NOT GOOD,
THE MASTER IS GOOD AS WELL.
THIS IS THE NATURE OF TRUE GOODNESS.

THE MASTER TRUSTS THOSE WHO ARE TRUST-
WORTHY
AND TRUSTS THOSE WHO ARE NOT.
THAT IS THE NATURE OF TRUE TRUST.

LIKE SPACE,
IS THE MIND OF THE MASTER.
HE IS NOT UNDERSTOOD BY PEOPLE.
SO, UNTO THE MASTER THE PEOPLE LOOK AND
WAIT.

LIKE HIS OWN CHILDREN
DOES THE MASTER TREAT OTHERS.

The Mind of the Masterful Leader: The Tao of Leadership, An Unconventional Perspective on True Goodness and Trust

In the world of masters and disciples, there exists a peculiar phenomenon. Masters, and especially masters who have been placed in positions of leadership, contrary to popular belief, do not possess an independent mind. Instead, they rely on the collective consciousness of the people with whom they work. This passage by Lao Tzu lets us delve into the nature of this relationship and further explore the Tao of Leadership and its counterintuitive concepts of true goodness and trust exemplified by the master-disciple dynamic. The master's mind is not an individual construct but a manifestation of the people's collective consciousness. This unconventional understanding of the master's role challenges traditional notions of leadership and offers a unique perspective on the nature of true humility, goodness and trust.

The Master's Mind and the Collective Consciousness

The master, contrary to popular belief, does not operate with a mind of their own. Rather, their mind is a reflection of the thoughts, beliefs, and aspirations of the people from whom they emerge and with whom they work. This symbiotic relationship contributes to an interconnectedness that fuels the master's actions and fortifies his or her decisions. It builds trust and is also the reason why those who are led embrace such a master so dearly as one of their own.

Embracing Goodness Unconditionally

True goodness, as embodied by the master, transcends the concept of conditional morality. Like the Tao, the master demonstrates their indiscriminate compassion and unconditional goodness towards both the virtuous and the wayward souls alike. By manifesting unwavering indiscriminate kindness and compassion, the master, by his or her example, cultivates a transformative environment that emphasizes personal growth and enlightenment.

Trust as the Bedrock of the Master-Disciple Relationship

The master's trust extends beyond those who prove themselves trustworthy. In an act of faith, the master also places trust in individuals who are not yet trustworthy. This unorthodox approach fosters an environment of empowerment and encourages personal growth, propelling those he or she leads to rise to their true potential.

The Enigmatic Nature of the Master's Mind

Like the vast expanse of space, the master's mind remains inscrutable and beyond the comprehension of ordinary people. The master reveals his work and not necessarily his process. The master's depth of wisdom and unusual perspective on life elude conventional understanding, creating an aura of intrigue and curiosity amongst the disciples. What one sees of the master is the product of true leadership, but not necessarily the internal process.

Conclusion

The master's mind operates in harmony with the collective consciousness of the people, defying conventional expectations of individuality and autonomy. True goodness, demonstrated by the master's unconditional and indiscriminate kindness, challenges the limitations of conditional morality. The master's trust, extended even to those yet to prove themselves, inspires personal growth and fosters transformation. Encapsulating the enigmatic nature of the master, the mind remains an enigma waiting to be unraveled by those who seek his leadership and enlightenment.

By understanding Lao Tzu's idea of true leadership, we can broaden our own perspective on the meaning of true leadership and the quintessential importance of goodness, and trust in it. By embracing the unconventional notions presented by Lao Tzu here in this passage, we can open ourselves up to new possibilities in leadership in ourselves and in those who lead us and ultimately make the world a better place and enrich our own lives and those around us because of it.

CHAPTER 50

How the Master Treats Death

**THE MASTER SURRENDERS HIMSELF OVER COMPLETELY
TO WHATEVER THE MOMENT REQUIRES.
(Eternally Present) HE NO LONGER THINKS ABOUT
HIS ACTIONS,
AS THEY FLOW FROM THE CORE OF HIS BEING.**

**THE MASTER UNDERSTANDS THAT EVENTUALLY
DEATH WILL OVERCOME HIM
AND HE WILL HAVE NOTHING ONTO WHICH TO
HOLD.
THE MIND'S ILLUSIONS WILL ALL SLIP AWAY.
HIS BODY WILL NO LONGER RESIST.**

FROM LIFE, THE MASTER HOLDS BACK NOTHING.

**BECAUSE HE AS HELD BACK NOTHING FROM LIFE,
THE MASTER IS THEREFORE READY FOR DEATH,
JUST AS ONE WHO IS READY FOR SLEEP
AFTER THE COMPLETION OF A FULL DAY'S WORK.**

Embracing Life's Ephemeral Nature: The Path to Mastering Existence

Life is a fleeting journey, and within the spark of its brief span, we search to find purpose, meaning, and fulfillment. The purpose of life is to live it fully. The meaning of life is whatever meaning we choose to give it.

This passage lets us explore the profound concept of being present and surrendering oneself entirely to the present moment, recognizing the impermanence of life, and the liberation that results from it. By embracing life's ephemeral nature, we not only unlock our true potential, but we also prepare ourselves for the inevitability of physical death. In this passage Lao Tzu teaches us to embrace the mindset of a master who realizing the power of living life to the fullest in the present moment transcends the illusions of the mind.

By surrendering themselves completely to the demands of the present moment, understanding the transitory essence of life, and letting go of mental attachments, the master transcends time and space and ordinary existence and prepares themself for the eventuality of death. By ultimately embracing life's ephemeral nature fully we can live and appreciate the rare fragility and pricelessness of each experience and every moment of presence. By adopting the mindset of embracing life's ephemerality and surrendering to the present moment, recognizing the fleeting nature of life, and letting go of mental attachments we too can fully live and be. By doing this, we can become the master who is prepared for death and who and thankfulness for everything, can experience a profound sense of gratitude and fulfillment in the journey of life.

Surrendering to the Present Moment

Being wholly present and engaged completely in the moment is a practice that allows us to fully experience and appreciate life. It is a complete surrender of ego to the compassionate and creative force of the Tao. Surrendering to the present allows us to hyper focus on the task or the needs and concerns of those at hand. When we surrender the need for control and accept what is, we open ourselves up to the richness of each passing moment and the rewards of having done so. By surrendering we allow ourselves to masterfully transcend the stresses and anxieties that come from our egos constantly seeking to manipulate and change our circumstances. By being fully present, like the master, we can connect with our innermost being, and access the deep sense of peace and clarity that connects us more completely with the Tao.

Recognizing the Impermanence of Life

Just as change is eternal, so too is impermanence in life. Everything in life is inherently transient, and this recognition can lead to a profound sense of freedom. When we understand that nothing lasts forever, we can begin to cherish each experience, relationship, and moment. By embracing physical impermanence, the master transcends the clinging and attachment that often bring suffering. Instead, they learn to appreciate the beauty and significance of even the smallest aspects of life, knowing that (good or bad), they too will pass from this existence into a very different one in the next. By seeing the impermanence of life and accepting the way things are, the master gains great insight into the nature of eternity and his or her experience of it.

Letting Go of Mental Attachments

The mind often creates illusions that limit our true potential and hinder our ability to embrace life fully. These mental attachments can include fear, hatred, lust, longing, guilt, prolonged grief and regret to mention but a few. By letting go of these mental attachments, the master regains a sense of clarity and freedom. Detaching from preconceived notions, expectations, and desires allows the master to cultivate contentment and find joy in the present moment. This freedom from mental attachments enables the master to remain open to new experiences, meet life head on, adapt to change, and appreciate the inherent richness of each passing moment and experience.

Preparing for Death

Death is an inescapable part of the human experience, and the master understands and accepts this reality. Rather than fearing death and physical demise, the master embraces these things as an integral part of life's cycle. Having held back nothing from life, the master approaches death with a sense of readiness born out of having fully lived and experienced the ephemerality of existence. Just as one embraces sleep after a long, productive day's work, the master embraces death as a natural and expected transition, having experienced the fullness of life filled with meaning and purpose.

By surrendering to the present moment, recognizing the impermanence of life, letting go of mental attachments, and preparing for death, the master embraces life's ephemerality. This approach leads to a deep sense of fulfillment, freedom, and readiness to face the inevitable. The master's journey is one of embracing every aspect of existence, allowing for a truly transformative and purposeful life.

Conclusion

Living life as a master requires holding back nothing and surrendering ourselves completely to the present moment. It requires understanding the ephemeral nature of life and liberating ourselves from mental attachments. By embracing these principles, we can unlock our true potential, experience fully every moment in life and find fulfillment in every aspect of existence. The master's readiness for death stems from having held back nothing from life and experiencing it fully, understanding that death is nothing to be feared as it is merely a natural and transitional part of the cycle of physical life. Just as a weary worker longs for the solace of sleep after a productive day, we just like the master, need to accept and understand our own ephemerality and embrace the prospects of our eventual physical death, knowing that we have experienced life to its fullest. As eternal children of the Tao, our death is not an end but the beginning of yet another transformation for us as eternally conscious souls.

CHAPTER 51

"The Primal Virtue"

ALL THINGS ARISE FROM THE TAO.
FROM THE TAO ALL BEINGS ARE BORN.
THROUGH HER CREATION ALL OF THE BEINGS
OF THE UNIVERSE
ARE FORMED
THEY ARE NOURISHED BY HER VIRTUE.

THE TAO EXPRESSES ITSELF BY FORMING ALL
MATTER
FROM NON-BEING AND SPRINGING FORTH INTO
BEING.
UNCONSCIOUS, FREE AND PERFECT,
THE TAO TAKES ON HER PHYSICAL FORM
AND THEN ALLOWS THE ENVIRONMENT AND
CIRCUMSTANCE TO COMPLETE HER.

THE TAO CREATES WITHOUT POSSESSION.
SHE ACTS WITHOUT EXPECTATION.
THE TAO DOES NOT DEMAND HONOR OR RE-
SPECT.

SHE GUIDES WITHOUT INTERFERENCE.
SHE NOURISHES, COMFORTS AND PROTECTS
THEM.
SHE CARES FOR THEM AND MAINTAINS THEM
ALL
UNTIL SHE RETURNS THEM BACK TO HER BO-
SOM.

SPONTANEOUSLY, ALL BEINGS CREATED BY THE
TAO

HONOR AND RESPECT HER.
THIS IS "PRIMAL VIRTUE".

BECAUSE OF THIS,
THE TAO HONORS THE CONTINUED EXISTENCE
OF ALL OF HER CREATION.
THIS IS WHY, THE LOVE OF THE TAO
IS WITHIN THE ESSENTIAL NATURE OF ALL
THINGS.

> "Seen or unseen, God is present."
> ~ Carl G. Jung

The Tao's Influence on the Universe: A Personal Exploration

The Tao, an ancient Chinese concept, is often referred to as the underlying force that creates and permeates all the universe. The Tao expresses itself through all beings, embodying spontaneous creation, nurturing, and unconditional love. Through its essence, the Tao shapes and sustains all beings, guiding them without interference, and fostering a profound connection that is inherent in its love. The influence the Tao exerts on the universe and its continued existence is both integral to all existence and timeless.

The Tao as the Source of Creation

The Tao, characterized as non-being, manifests itself into being, granting life and form to all things within the universe. By exploring the concept of Wu Wei, the Tao's spontaneous and effortless action, we can understand how the Tao creates without seeking ownership or control. The Tao is without ego. This essence of its selfless creation showcases the Tao's boundless power and influence through all of the laws of the universe and its unconditional and indiscriminate love and compassion.

The Tao's Nurturing and Protective Nature

Just as loving parents care for their children, the Tao nourishes, comforts, and protects all beings it has brought forth into existence. The harmony that exists within nature, the cycles of life and death, the natural order of things and the balance maintained are a testament to the Tao's inherent nurturing qualities. Its care extends to all living beings, ensuring their well-being until they return to its embrace.

Guidance Without Interference

The Tao governs the universe without imposing its will, enabling beings to develop freely and follow their own paths. Unlike human intervention, the Tao guides from a place of wisdom and non-interference. This philosophy allows for the exercise of free will necessary for spiritual growth and evolution and for unique deviations, diversities, and individual expressions within the universe while maintaining the harmony and interconnectedness of all things.

The Love of the Tao

At the heart of the Tao, lies a divine consciousness and profound love and compassion that permeates the essential nature of all things. This love connects every being to the Tao and to each other, forging a harmonious web of existence. Through consciously recognizing and embracing the love of the Tao, we can tap into our own shared inherent nature and experience a deeper sense of purpose, unity, and compassion towards all of creation from wherever in creation it may come and wherever it may be.

Conclusion

The Tao's influence on the universe is patently evident through its creative, nurturing, and guiding qualities. With the Tao, we are never without. Its spontaneous and selfless nature allows for the continuous existence and flourishing of all beings within its realm. By recognizing and embracing the love and compassion of the Tao, we can engender it, and embrace its freedom and perfection. We too can create without possession, act without expectation, demand neither honor nor respect. These things will come on their natural accord once we align ourselves with the Tao. Meanwhile, we can guide without interference, nourish, comfort, care for and protect others and help maintain them until the Tao calls us back to her bosom.

By developing our own Primal Virtue, we can foster a profound patience and compassionate connection with the universe and ourselves. This will ultimately lead to a more harmonious and interconnected existence with and understanding of all beings in the universe. Practicing our prime virtue is how we can spiritually evolve. The rewards are not secondary or incidental but integral to how the Tao honors our continued and infinite existence.

Truly, seen or unseen, all are connected to the Tao. When we act in confluence with the Tao, our hidden or "primal" virtue governs. When we do allow our primal virtue to govern us, all things, and beings around us flourish. Hence, we should not need laws to make us respect what created us, to respect and honor our source and to honor and respect ourselves and other beings. Recognizing our primal virtue and our interconnectedness of all things through the Tao is all that is necessary to begin establishing a peaceful and divine existence throughout the Tao's creation.

CHAPTER 52

"Practicing Eternity"

IN THE BEGINNING,
THERE EXISTED ONLY THE TAO.
FROM HER ALL THINGS ISSUED
AND TO HER ALL THINGS RETURN.

TO FIND HER SOURCE
JUST TRACE BACK
FROM THAT WHICH IS MANIFEST.
TO RECOGNIZE HER CHILDREN
IS TO FIND THEIR MOTHER.
TO DISCOVER THE MOTHER
IS TO FIND FREEDOM FROM SORROW.

IF YOU CLOSE YOUR MIND TO JUDGMENT
YET TRAFFIC IN DESIRE,
TROUBLED WILL YOUR HEART BE.

SHOULD YOU KEEP YOUR MIND FROM JUDGING.
AND NOT BE LED BY THE SENSES,
PEACE WILL YOUR HEART FIND.

TO SEE INTO THE DARKNESS IS CLARITY.
STRENGTH LIES IN KNOWING HOW TO YIELD.

WHEN ONE USES ONE'S OWN LIGHT,
AND RETURNS TO THE SOURCE OF LIGHT,
ONE IS SAID TO BE "PRACTICING ETERNITY".

Embracing the Tao: The Path to Eternal Freedom

The concept of the Tao, as described in this passage as "Practicing Eternity", holds profound wisdom that can transform our lives. In this passage Lao Tzu explores the essence of the Tao, its significance in returning to the Tao and finding freedom from sorrows, and how embracing her principles can lead us as her children to lives of peace and clarity. By embracing the principles of the Tao, and the Integral Way, we can find liberation from judgment and desire, experience inner peace, and gain clarity and strength in their journey towards eternal freedom.

Freedom from Judgment

The Tao emphasizes the importance of closing our minds to judgment: our own and the judgment of others. By cultivating non-judgmental thinking, we can detach ourselves from our own biased views and the views of others and embrace a balanced perspective with everything and everyone. This detachment allows us to navigate through life's challenges with greater ease and equanimity and not be drawn into the trap of prejudice and public opinion.

Liberation from Desire

While desire can be an inherent part of human nature, the Tao encourages us to be aware of its potential to cloud our minds and trouble our hearts. By reducing our attachment to desires and finding contentment within ourselves, we can experience freedom from the constant longing for external validation and material possessions.

Peace through Mindfulness

This passage highlights the significance of keeping our minds free from judgment and being led by our senses. Embracing mindfulness practices can help us achieve a state of peace. By staying present in the moment and observing our thoughts and emotions without judgment, we can find inner tranquility.

Clarity through Yielding

Enlightenment lies in our ability to yield, rather than resisting the flow of life. By letting go of our ego-driven need for control and embracing the inherent wisdom of the Tao, we can tap into the inner clarity that comes from surrendering to the natural order of things. Yielding grants us the insight needed to navigate life's challenges with grace and humility.

Practicing Eternity: The Path to Freedom

When we align ourselves with the principles of the Tao and its teachings, we embark on a journey towards eternal freedom. By shining our own light and returning to the source of light, we embrace our true essence and transcend the limitations of the material world. Practicing eternity allows us to live in harmony with the natural flow of life, nurturing our connection with the Tao and finding lasting freedom from sorrows.

Conclusion

The Tao, as described in Lao Tzu's thought-provoking passage, offers us a path towards eternal freedom. By freeing ourselves from judgment, detaching from desires, cultivating mindfulness and compassion, and yielding to the flow of life, we return to our source of light where we can embody the Tao. We then can live in alignment with it. When we embody the light of the Tao and live it, we "practice eternity". In this way we can experience the profound peace, clarity, and strength that come with this practice. Embracing the eternal light of the Tao and practicing its eternal wisdom are not only a means to personal fulfillment but doing so also provides an opportunity for us to contribute meaningfully to the collective well-being of the world and of the beings in our universe and beyond.

CHAPTER 53

Straying from the Great Way, The Tao Te Ching, The New Paradigm for Leadership and Governance on Earth in the Post-Extraterrestrial Contact World

EASY TO FOLLOW IS THE TAO;
HOWEVER, THERE ARE THOSE
WHO PREFER TO TAKE SIDE PATHS.

WHEN THE RICH PROFIT
BY THEIR SPECULATION;
AND FARMERS' LANDS ARE LOST;
WHEN GOVERNMENT OFFICIALS
SPEND MONEY ON ARMS.
INSTEAD OF CURES FOR THE SICK.
WHEN THE UPPER CLASS IS
IRRESPONSIBLE AND EXTRAVAGANT;
AND THE POOR HAVE NO PLACE TO TURN,
THIS IS ALL ROBBERY AND CHAOS,
THAT COMES FROM NOT IN KEEPING
WITH THE TAO.

BEWARE WHEN THINGS ARE OUT OF BALANCE,
AND REMAIN CENTERED WITHIN THE TAO.

Introduction

The teachings of the Tao have long been revered for their wisdom and guidance in leading a balanced and harmonious life. In the previous passage, Lao Tzu extolled the benefits of returning to the Tao as our source of wisdom and light. If anything, the Tao's Integral Way is the path of truth and compassion. If there is truly a reason why we are here it is to help one another through the difficulties of life. In the Hua Hu Ching we will learn later that truth and compassion form the "Mystical Gates" to eternity. It is through these gates that we encounter our own divinity and transform ourselves into a higher form of human spiritual being in this lifetime and universal beings in the next. This passage conveys to us the necessity of staying on the path of the Tao and what happens to those who stray from the Way.

Straying from the Great Way: A Call to Return to Balance and Harmony

In this passage Lao Tzu emphasizes the consequences of veering away from the principles of the Tao and its Integral way and the urgent need for us to realign ourselves with its teachings. In the passage above Lao Tzu explores the negative impacts of deviating from the Tao on society, economy, governance, and individual well-being. Inevitably, Lao Tzu emphasizes the need for us to embrace the Tao, the underlying source and force that governs all existence and restore its balance in all aspects of life. The consequences of not doing do are that life on this planet will worsen until we extinguish ourselves as a human species. Because we have the gift of free will, the choice is up to us individually and collectively.

Society in Disarray

When individuals and society stray from the principles of the Tao, chaos and imbalance inevitably ensue. This can be seen in the widening wealth gaps, where the rich profit through speculation, farmers lose their lands to governments and large corporations and people lose their health and wealth. The resulting inequality and lack of social support from our society by not choosing to follow the Tao and its Integral Way creates a breeding ground for further disharmony, resentment and unrest.

Through self-cultivation and reintegrating the principles of the Tao into our daily lives, we as individuals and groups can progress towards a more highly physically, mentally and spiritually advanced society that values the lives of all beings and fosters a magnanimous and equanimous and conscientious distribution of labor and resources and promotes the values of simplicity, patience compassion and truth. Inevitably, the result will be an advanced social evolution and planetary cohesion that is the necessary basis for our own physical survival and our spiritual evolution and refinement as individuals and as a species.

Governance and Responsibility

Government officials play a pivotal role in exemplifying and upholding the principles of the Tao within society. However, when they prioritize spending on arms over investing in human well-being, healthcare and addressing the needs of the sick, they deviate from the Tao's path of wisdom and compassion. This results in an imbalance in priorities, impeding the progress of society as a whole and delaying its integration into the more technologically and spiritually advanced societies that populate the multiverse.

By embracing the Tao, like the more highly developed beings and races of interstellar and inter dimensional beings of the multiverse do, leaders can see that the needs of people are met. They can refocus their efforts on creating a just, verdant, caring, compassionate and more equitable society, ensuring the well-being of all its citizens and that treasures their lives as the children of the same creator and similarly values the lives of all beings throughout the universe.

Individual Reconnection

Where the Tao is followed, ego dissolves. When individuals become disconnected from the Tao, they often succumb to the drive for excess, egotistic irresponsibility and extravagant materialistic behaviors. This invariably leads to personal dissatisfaction, a sense of ennui or emptiness and even despair. Furthermore, without the Tao, there is an absence of a universal moral compas. This lack of a consistent application of truth and compassion in all things human, erodes the bonds within relationships, families, communities and nations leaving the vulnerable and less fortunate with no place to turn. By returning to the simplicity, patience and compassion of the Tao, we can regain a sense of meaning, purpose and interconnectedness, cultivating a harmonious existence that extends to the broader world and greater multiverse and the beyond of which we too are an integral part.

Restoring Balance

The warning in this passage about a world that is out of balance serves as a clarion call to restore balance and natural order amidst the chaos. Recognizing the perils of straying from the Great Way, we as individuals and our inseparable societies must make a conscious effort to remain centered within the Tao. By incorporating its teachings and its Integral Way into our daily lives, we can create balance and harmony within ourselves, our relationships, our society and in our world. Through introspection, mindfulness, and a commitment to the Tao and through further self-cultivation, we can rekindle the natural balance in our lives and in our world and ensure a more sustainable future for the potential countless generations of humanity that will inevitably be guaranteed to follow.

Conclusion

In a world plagued by growing disparities, social unrest, wars and personal disillusionment, the principles of the Tao offer us a much-needed guiding light. By contemplating the profound teachings of Lao Tzu, we can begin to see and appreciate the consequences of straying from the Great Way. We can also elect and advocate to those who govern us for a return to the balance and harmony that comes by following the Tao and its Integral Way. Finally, we can do this by practicing eternity by embodying the Tao by becoming examples of living simple lives of absolute truth, patience and compassion.

When we deviate from the path of truth and compassion, we create chaos for ourselves and others. Chaotic energies beget the return of these energies ultimately to the one who creates them. Creating chaos also creates Karma. Karma requires payback in the next life. So, if you want to hazard your life in this existence and in the next just deviate from the path of the Tao's universal truth. It's really that simple. By embracing the Tao's teachings, we can all individually, collectively and collaboratively work towards a better future—one characterized by truth, compassion, equity, and interconnectedness.

Tell the truth and exercise compassion in all relations and you will become a divine being in this lifetime and become one of the universal beings* in your next. The future is now in our own hands, heads and hearts. Let us heed the warning of Lao Tzu and remain centered within the Tao, unlocking its transformative power for the betterment of ourselves, society, mankind and universe at large.

* Those "angelic immortal 'unruling rulers and uncreating creators' who have entered the Tao's divine immortal realm of both being and non-being" - See, e.g., Hua He Ching, Chapters 60-81.

CHAPTER 54

When in the Tao One Abides, the Universe Thrives.

THE ONE WHO IS PLANTED IN THE TAO
WILL NOT BE UPROOTED.
THE ONE WHO EMBRACES THE TAO
SHALL NOT SLIP AWAY FROM IT.

WITH THE PASSAGE OF EACH GENERATION,
IN HONOR SHALL THE NAME OF TAO
BE HELD.

BY ALLOWING THE TAO
TO BE PRESENT IN ONE'S OWN LIFE,
ONE ALLOWS THEMSELF TO LIVE A LIFE OF
TRUTH.

THE ONE WHO ALLOWS THE TAO
TO BE PRESENT IN ONE'S FAMILY
WILL HAVE A FAMILY THAT FLOURISHES.

LET THE TAO BE PRESENT
IN ONE'S OWN COUNTRY
AND THAT COUNTRY WILL BE
AS AN EXAMPLE
TO THE REST OF THE WORLD.

WHEN THE TAO IS PRESENT IN THE UNIVERSE
THE UNIVERSE SINGS.

HOW DOES THE AUTHOR KNOW THIS TO BE TRUE?
HE KNOWS BY LOOKING WITHIN.

The Power of the Tao: Cultivating Balance, Harmony, and Flourishing

The Tao, as best one can describe it, is the creative divine intelligence that underlies all phenomena in existence. It is the vast intelligent energy that gives rise to and governs all of existence itself. It is the embodiment of all wisdom and the organizing principle of being itself. It is the divine energy that pervades the entire universe, gives it balance and causes the arising of all being and form. It is the intelligent underlying source and force that encapsulates the natural order of the universe.

In chapter 53, Lao Tzu taught us about what happens to a world where the Tao and its natural and integral Way is not followed. In chapter 54 above, Lao Tzu informs us about the profound impact the Tao and its Integral Way can have on us as individuals, our families, societies, and the entire universe. Through the Tao's transformative power and guiding force it is the source of harmony, growth, and prosperity for an entire world and beyond. By embracing the presence of the Tao in our own lives, families, and communities, we can foster flourishing relationships, create exemplary societies, and contribute to the well-being of the world here and the universe at large.

The Tao in One's Life

Unearthing the Tao and allowing it to permeate our lives leads to a profound sense of purpose and truth. When individuals align their actions with the Tao's natural flow, they unlock a deeper understanding of themselves and find fulfillment. By walking this path, one becomes firmly rooted in the Tao. With the Tao as our moral, ethical and spiritual compass we are resilient against the turmoil of life, and less likely to be swayed by external influences and more likely to produce successful outcomes.

The Tao in One's Family

Embedding the Tao within the family unit is paramount to its functionality and prosperity. As each member embraces the principles of the Tao, they contribute to fostering patience, kindness and harmonious compassionate relationships, empathy, and understanding. This interconnectedness not only strengthens the bond within the family but also extends to the broader community. A family driven by the Tao becomes a beacon of love and support, inspiring others to follow suit.

The Tao in One's Country

When the Tao is deeply ingrained in a nation's values and policies, it becomes an exemplar for the world. Other countries become attracted to it. A country governed by the principles of the Tao forges a path towards peace, justice, and sustainability. It serves as a model for other nations, inspiring them to adopt similar values of harmony, compassion, and respect for the natural order. Such a country radiates success with its positive vibrations, offering hope and inspiration to the rest of the world and beyond.

The Tao in the Universe

The profoundest truth lies in the intimate connection between the Tao and the universe. The presence of the Tao in the universe is reflected in the symphony of existence. When the Tao is acknowledged and celebrated, the universe responds with resounding harmony, as if singing in alignment with the natural order. By nurturing the Tao's presence within us and extending it to our surroundings, we participate in the cosmic dance and sing along with it and contribute to the thriving of the world we live in and in the universe.

Conclusion

The persuasive evidence presented by Lao Tzu reinforces the transformative power of the Tao. By embracing the Tao in our lives, fostering it within our families, and embodying it in our nations, we can create a ripple effect that resonates beyond individual realms. Let us heed the wisdom of Lao Tzu and recognize that by allowing the Tao to manifest within us and by abiding in it, we become agents of balance, peace, harmony, and flourishing in an interconnected world and an integrally connected universe.

CHAPTER 55

The Power of the Newborn

WHEN ONE IS IN HARMONY WITH THE TAO,
IT IS AS IF THEY ARE A NEWBORN CHILD.
THOUGH THE NEWBORN'S BONES ARE SOFT,
AND ITS MUSCLES WEAK, POWERFUL IS ITS GRIP.

SO COMPLETE IS THE HARMONY OF THE NEW-
BORN,
THAT EVEN THOUGH IT KNOWS NOTHING
OF THE UNION OF THE MALE AND FEMALE.
ITS VITAL POWER IS SO INTENSE
THAT ALREADY ITS PENIS CAN STAND ERECT.

SO COMPLETE IS THE HARMONY OF THE NEW-
BORN
THAT IT CAN SQUAL AND CRY ALL DAY
YET NEVER GET HOARSE.

LIKE THE NEWBORN, SO TOO IS THE POWER OF
THE MASTER.
WITHOUT EFFORT OR DESIRE,
THE MASTER ALLOWS ALL THINGS TO COME AND
GO.

BECAUSE THE MASTER NEVER EXPECTS RESULTS,
THE MASTER IS NEVER DISAPPOINTED.
BECAUSE THE MASTER IS NEVER DISAPPOINTED
THE MASTER'S SPIRIT NEVER GROWS OLD.

The Power of Harmony: Embracing the Tao

The teachings of Lao Tzu are rooted in the ancient wisdom of those who came before him. This wisdom, from wherever or whomever it came and however it was garnered, teaches us to reconnect with the Tao's natural order of the universe and find harmony within ourselves and the world around us. In this passage the imagery of a newborn child is used by Lao Tzu to symbolize the profound power of being in harmony with the Tao. Lao Tzu's words make inherent sense and naturally encourage us to embrace the wisdom of the Tao and the Integral way and those of its teachings of self-cultivation, especially those here that emphasize the virtues of harmony, effortless action, and the temporal immortality of eternal youthfulness.

When we are born, no matter how long or short our journeys, the Tao provides us with the tools we need to thrive in life. By cultivating harmony with the Tao, we can tap into our innate power, effortlessly move through life's challenges, and achieve not only a state of perpetual youthfulness but spiritual awareness and conscious immortality as well.

The Profound Power of Harmony

The metaphor of a newborn child in the passage above illustrates the profound power that lies in perfect harmony with the Tao. Despite the fragility of its bones and muscles, the newborn possesses an unexpectedly strong grip. This symbolizes the unseen strength that surfaces when one is in complete alignment with the natural order of things. Through the example of the newborn, and all its inherent strengths and abilities, subtle and otherwise, we can understand the transformative potential of harmony with the Tao.

Effortless Action

The teachings of Taoism emphasize the concept of Wu Wei, intentional non-doing or "effortless action". Like the newborn child who is in the earliest stages of human development and self- cultivation and who knows nothing of male and female union but effortlessly exhibits vital power, the master of the Tao allows life to unfold without striving or forcing outcomes. By relinquishing attachment to specific results and allowing events to flow naturally, the master experiences the power, grace and success of effortless action. Things seem to unfold successfully, like magic around him or her because they have patiently allowed themselves to align with the purposeful flow of the Tao. The principal of Wu Wei is central to understanding and harnessing the flow of the Tao. The principle of Wu Wei serves as an invitation to all individuals to let go of the ego and its need for monopolizing situations and control and embrace the flow of life. In the end, one does not create flow, especially that of great events. It is the Tao that does. Without it, one's efforts are ephemeral and pointless.

Freedom from Disappointment

The passage by Lao Tzu suggests that because the master never expects results, he or she is never disappointed. We see this again and again in the writings of Lao Tzu. In the Tao's Integral Way, letting go of egoic expectations and physical desires allows for a state of inner peace and contentment. By dissolving our egos and accepting non-attachment, we as individuals can escape the suffering that comes with attachment. We can navigate life's ups and downs without being weighed down by disappointment or destroyed by loss. This freedom from disappointment enables the master to maintain a balanced youthful spirit with energies and attitudes that are unburdened by the weight of loss or unmet expectations.

Eternal Youthfulness

Finally, this passage highlights how the spirit of the master never grows old due to their lack of disappointment. In the Tao's Integral Way, true agelessness lies not in physical appearance but in the spirit. By letting go of societal constructs of aging and embracing a mindset of continual growth and change, we can tap into our inner wellspring of vitality and experience a perpetual state of youthfulness. This is state of physical longevity is sometimes referred to in the Hua Hu Ching as a physical form of immortality, but such health also becomes a manifestation of an evolved and refined soul who has been enlightened and transformed by their knowledge and experience of the Tao.

Conclusion

Harmony with the Tao is a powerful concept whose exploration offers us the ability to unlock our true potential and embrace life's flow with grace and ease. Through the symbolic imagery of the newborn child, we are reminded of the transformative power and wonder that arise from aligning ourselves with the Tao, the underlying source and force that governs all existence and encapsulates the natural order of the universe. By embracing the virtues of the Integral Way and especially those of harmony, effortless action, and a youthful spirit, we can navigate life's challenges with grace, resulting in a sense of peace, joy and fulfillment in our lives. The wisdom of the Lao Tzu holds great persuasive power, urging us to reconnect with the Tao, the inexhaustible source of our own innate nature and the harmony within ourselves and the world and multiverse around us.

CHAPTER 56

The "Primary Identity", The Tao Te Ching, The New Paradigm for Leadership and Governance on Earth in a Post-Extraterrestrial Contact World

THE ONES WHO KNOW, DO NOT TALK.
THE ONES WHO TALK, DO NOT KNOW.

SILENCE YOUR MOUTH AND WALL OFF YOUR SENSES.
YOUR SHARPNESS MAKE BLUNT.
UNDO YOUR KNOTS AND MAKE SOFT YOUR GLARE.
ALLOW YOUR DUST TO SETTLE.
TO DO SO IS CALLED THE "PRIMARY IDENTITY".

BE AS THE TAO.
ONE CAN NEITHER APPROACH IT
NOR WITHDRAW FROM IT.
THE TAO CANNOT BE BENEFITTED
NOR CAN IT BE HARMED.
IT CAN BE NEITHER HONORED
NOR DISGRACED.
THE TAO GIVES OF ITSELF CONTINUALLY.
THIS IS WHY THE TAO ENDLESSLY ENDURES.

The Power of Silence: Embracing the "Primary Identity" in Leadership

In the world of leadership, there is a common misconception that talking and asserting oneself are essential for success. However, ancient wisdom from Lao Tzu challenges this notion in chapter 56. It states, "The ones who know, do not talk. The ones who talk, do not know." This powerful excerpt urges leaders to embrace the Tao of leadership; practice silence, detach from external distractions, and tap into their "primary identity", their manifested Tao nature, to unlock their true potential. Incorporating silence and stillness into our leadership and governing practices can lead to profound growth, enhanced decision-making, and sustained success in all facets of our lives. In this way we can lead and become the leaders of humankind and thoughtful ombudsmen and examples to those whom we lead and worthy custodians of our precious living planet.

The Paradox of Silence

The Tao Te Ching presents a paradoxical notion that silence, often associated with weakness or ignorance, can actually be a source of strength. By being patient and silencing our mouths and walling off our senses, we gain the ability to observe, listen, and understand the world around us more deeply. By untying, or by allowing the Tao to undo our knots and by making soft our glare, we become receptive to new perspectives and make ourselves better equipped to understand the waters in which we find ourselves and better navigate ever more complex and changing challenges in leadership and governance.

The Primary Identity

Much like "embodying the light" to which Lao Tzu introduces us in Chapter 27, when a leader embodies the "primary identity," they align themselves with the Tao. Like the Tao, which cannot be approached or from which it cannot be withdrawn, leaders with a primary identity that reflects their internal Tao transcend the limitations of ego and personal biases. This is how they embody the light and make the Tao their primary identity. By embracing silence and detaching from desires, we can tap into a higher level of consciousness, enabling us to make decisions that are selfless, compassionate, and act in alignment with the greater good for those around us and throughout the world and the universe beyond. Every act we take has a universal impact. Those who embody the light and have the Tao as their primary identity understand this and act in accordance with this understanding.

Embracing Stillness in Decision-making

In a world characterized by constant noise and distractions, leaders who dare to silence the chaos and embrace the stillness gain a significant advantage. By making space for silence, leaders can eliminate impulsiveness and restlessness. They can cultivate clarity, tap into their intuition, and better make well-informed decisions. The ability to meditate and silently use Wu Wei allows the dust to settle and provides silence necessary for quiet contemplation. When this happens, the stillness enables leaders to exercise extreme patience to listen and have great calm in discerning the truth amidst a sea of loud competing voices. This discernment leads to greater consideration of facts and conflicting ideas and ultimately to more effective and impactful positive outcomes as cooler heads prevail.

The Enduring Power of the Tao

The Tao was not invented by Lao Tzu, but he is credited with first writing about it. As described in verse 56, by Lao Tzu, the Tao is an omnipresent force that exists and endures beyond matter time and space. By embodying the qualities of the Tao, leaders transcend personal gain and adopt a mindset of service to their partners, teams, organizations and worlds. In doing so, they create an environment that fosters altruism, collaboration, growth, realistic and sustainable progress and success.

The enduring power of the Tao lies in its ability to give of itself continuously and mirror the potential of leaders who embrace their "primary identity" and give of themselves in the same way. When those who lead and govern from their primary identity, those who are led or governed also come to reflect their own primary identity. This is one of the ways that the Tao's Law of Energy Response or "Law of Attraction" operates. Both positive or negative energies and thought bring positive or negative energies and experiences into our lives.

Conclusion

The ancient wisdom encapsulated in this passage of the Tao Te Ching invites leaders to explore the Tao of leadership and the transformative power of silence and their "primary identity" the Tao. By embracing silence we learn patience and gain the ability to listen. To learn to listen is to learn how to love.

Listening is an act of both patience and compassion. By learning silence and learning how to love and to be indiscriminately compassionate with those whom we meet and those in our care, leaders can then unlock deeper levels of understanding, enhance decision-making, and cultivate enduring success for everyone. Embracing the Tao-like qualities of selflessness, stillness, and service will not only benefit leaders who lead and those who govern but also will enlighten and inspire those around them. As we embark on our leadership journeys through the Tao, let us remember the words of Lao Tzu, "To do so is called the 'primary identity.' Be as the Tao."

CHAPTER 57

Wu Wei, The Great Leader, Spontaneous Order, Ruling Through Non-Action, The Tao Te Ching, The New Paradigm for Leadership and Governance on Earth in a Post-Extraterrestrial Contact World

IN ORDER TO BE A GREAT LEADER,
ONE MUST LEARN TO FOLLOW THE TAO.

A GREAT LEADER DOES NOT TRY TO CONTROL.
HE LETS GO OF FIXED PLANS AND CONCEPTS
AND ALLOWS THE WORLD TO GOVERN ITSELF.

THE MORE NUMEROUS THE PROHIBITIONS
THAT PEOPLE HAVE,
THE MORE LACKING IN VIRTUE WILL THEY BE.
THE GREATER THE NUMBER OF WEAPONS PEO-
PLE HAVE,
THE LESS SECURE WILL THEY BE.
THE MORE SUBSIDIES THAT PEOPLE RECEIVE
THE LESS SELF-RELIANT DO THEY BECOME.

THE MASTER SAYS THEREFORE: WHEN I LET GO
OF
THE LAW, HONEST DO THE PEOPLE BECOME;
WHEN I DO NOT CONCERN MYSELF WITH ECO-
NOMICS,
THE PEOPLE MAKE THEMSELVES PROSPEROUS;
WHEN I DO NOT BOTHER WITH RELIGION,
THE PEOPLE BECOME SERENE.
WHEN I RELEASE ALL DESIRE FOR THE COMMON
GOOD,

AS COMMON AS GRASS DOES THE COMMON GOOD GROW.

The Tao of Leadership: Embracing Non-Action for Great Leadership

Leadership is a complex concept that has been explored through various theories and approaches. However, the path to truly becoming a great leader can be found in the teachings of Lao Tzu about the Tao and its integral Way. Besides truth and the "Three Treasures" of simplicity, patience, compassion, the fundamental principles of the Tao's Integral Way are embodied in the concept of Wu Wei (non-action) and in self-reliance and personal responsibility for oneself, one's family, community, world and by extension, the universe at large. These concepts are also central to "The Tao of Leadership" which encourages leaders to let go of control and allow the world, through the natural flow of the Tao, to govern itself.

In earlier chapters, Lao Tzu has mentioned some of the tenets of The Tao of Leadership. However, in a nutshell, the Tao of Leadership holds that in order to be a great leader, one must embrace the Tao and its principles. Embodying the light and the prime identity have been outlined previously, almost in passing in passing. However, in this passage Lao Tzu goes to some great length to point out the nature of human social fabric and its foibles here in this passage and how a great leader needs to treat them.

Through keeping an open mind and exercising seamless leadership by relinquishing fixed plans and concepts, being free of excessive restrictions and subsidies, trusting others to accomplish things of which they are capable and by focusing on their own self-reliance, leaders can foster an environment where people thrive and the common good flourishes and those who complete the work will celebrate their achievements because it will appear that it was all accomplished all by themselves.

The leader who embraces the light of their primary identity is one who will naturally excel in his or her leadership because they understand the nature of the Tao and how it operates.

Letting Go of Control

Control is an illusion that the ego creates to allay its own fear. Great leaders operate in a world without fear. They dissolve their egos, act selflessly and put their goals, tasks and priorities in order. They are clear communicators and make those tasks and time frames that are delegated clear to those to whom they delegate.

The Tao teaches us that a great leader refrains from trying to control every aspect of a situation. Great leaders are great managers of energy and resources, especially their human ones. They do not need to micro-manage or control every aspect of a project. They lead by example. By embracing Wu Wei, intentional non-action and by letting go of fixed plans and concepts, great leaders allow for spontaneity, adaptability, and creativity. This approach fosters an environment where individuals can communicate and express themselves freely, find new solutions and discovering more effective ways of doing things to reach their full potential and complete successfully the work to which they are assigned.

Avoiding Excessive Prohibitions

This passage highlights the human need for freedom. When the Tao is followed, freedom breeds virtue, because that is the nature of the Tao. Lao Tzu notes that the more numerous the prohibitions people have, the more lacking in virtue they become. Great leaders must understand the importance of creating an atmosphere of trust, where individuals are allowed to act responsibly and are not burdened by excessive rules and regulations. This freedom in both production and government empowers individuals to know what is in their own best interests when they are fully informed and to become personally responsible and take ownership of their actions and to make sound decisions from which they can reap the physical, mental and spiritual rewards. Contrary to our modern and conventional wisdom that emphasizes power and control from the top down, because human needs and human nature are what they are, such systems become self-regulating. And that is what the Tao of Leadership is and should be all about.

Cultivating Self-Reliance

It is an old but true saw that if a government wants more of something all they need to do is subsidies it. If you want a welfare state with all its maladies, subsidies it. If the government wants more of anything and is buying it, then people will produce ever so much more to sell to the government. *
In chapter 57 Lao Tzu also emphasizes the truth in this often hackneyed saying by emphasizing his age-old observation that the more subsidies people receive, the less self-reliant they become. This seems to be an eternal reflection on the nature of encouraging things we do not want by reinforcing the behavior that begets it. This is the idea behind Skinnerian psychology. Undeniably, we share most of the central nervous system of Pavlov's dog.

In the end, great leaders and governors in the post ET Contact world, like a good parent would and should do for their own children, rather than fostering dependence in the people they lead, will need to encourage independence, creative thought and self-reliance by providing opportunities for growth and development in those they govern. When individuals are self-reliant, they become more independent, innovative, resourceful, and virtuous. As a consequence, they become worthy of greater and greater amounts of trust as they become ever more capable of self-cultivation and self-governance and increasingly able to overcome the challenges they will inevitably meet along their way in life.

Letting Go of Concerns

Contrary to modern and neo-liberal trends where people get elected based on their professed and all too often hypocritical care for the common good of the people, the Tao teaches leaders to release their desire for the common good, allowing it to grow naturally. Form follows function. It is not the other way around. One cannot fit the round pegs of humanity into a square one size fits all hole. By not obsessing over the common good or imposing their own ideas upon what is best for people, great leaders create an environment that encourages individuals to determine what is best for them and to take initiative and contribute to the collective well-being. This approach promotes teamwork, mutual goals, collaboration and compassion for themselves and others with whom they work and for those upon whom the benefit of their work will inevitably fall. As the old saying goes, "A society grows great when old men plant trees in whose shade they know they shall never sit." Inevitably, the approach put forward by Lao Tzu allows people to develop a sense of empowerment and fosters a natural and co-reliant community that thrives on its own, without the constant involvement of any government or leader.

Conclusion

The study of Tao and its Integral Way offers valuable insights into what constitutes necessary and effective leadership in the post contact world. By embracing the Tao and its universal principles, leaders can transcend the traditional notion of power and control and cultivate an environment that promotes harmony respect, growth, self-reliance, and innovation among those who are governed. The Tao of Leadership therefore emphasizes the importance of letting go of fixed plans, excessive restrictions, and an obsession with the common good, thereby allowing individuals and the common good to flourish. Great leaders who embody the Tao understand that the path to leadership excellence lies in their ability to understand and follow Wu Wei and the rhythm of the world and to trust in the inherent wisdom of those they lead wherever they are in the universe.

*The Original Cobra Effect: The term *cobra effect* was coined by economist Horst Siebert based on an anecdotal occurrence in India during British rule.[2][3] The British government, concerned about the number of venomous cobras in Delhi, offered a bounty for every dead cobra. Initially, this was a successful strategy; large numbers of snakes were killed for the reward. Eventually, however, enterprising people began to breed cobras for the income. When the government became aware of this, the reward program was scrapped. When cobra breeders set their now-worthless snakes free, the wild cobra population further increased.[4] This story is often cited as an example of Goodhart's Law or Campbell's Law.[5] - Wickipedia

CHAPTER 58

Tolerance and Subtlety, The Tao Te Ching, The New Paradigm for Leadership and Governance on Earth in a Post-Extraterrestrial Contact World

WHEN TOLERANCE GOVERNS A COUNTRY
COMFORT AND HONESTY FLOURISH AMONG ITS
PEOPLE.
WHEN REPRESSION IS USED TO GOVERN,
THE PEOPLE BECOME CRAFTY AND DEPRESSED,

WHEN THE WILL TO POWER RULES,
LOFTY ARE ITS IDEALS,
BUT THE LOWER ARE ITS RESULTS.

BY ONE TRYING TO MAKE PEOPLE HAPPY,
ONE LAYS THE GROUNDWORK FOR MISERY.
BY TRYING TO MAKE PEOPLE MORAL,
ONE LAYS THE GROUNDWORK FOR VICE.

THE MASTER GOVERNS NOT
BY IMPOSING HIS WILL UPON THE GOVERNED.
THE MASTER IS CONTENT TO SERVE AS AN EX-
AMPLE FOR THEM.

THE MASTER MAY BE POINTED,
YET THE MASTER DOES NOT PIERCE.
THE MASTER IS STRAIGHTFORWARD,
YET THE MASTER IS SUPPLE.
THE MASTER IS RADIANT,
YET EASY TO LOOK UPON.

The Tao and the Art of Proper Governance: Embracing Tolerance for Success and Sustainability

Effective governance is a fundamental aspect of any thriving social organization wherever it may be. In the Tao Te Ching, specifically in Chapter 58, Lao Tzu highlights the concept of tolerance as a governing principle and its transformative power in fostering comfort, honesty, and overall well-being among a country's, and by implication, the world's citizens. By examining the detrimental effects of repression and the will to power on society, we can understand the wisdom behind the Tao and its Integral Way and embrace the guiding universal principles of tolerance, compassion, and exemplary leadership in a post extraterrestrial contact world.

Tolerance: The Catalyst for Comfort and Honesty

The Tao teaches us to honor truth and compassion above all of its other treasures. When we are compassionate and understand that we are all -integral parts of the same whole, tolerance becomes unnecessary. However, as human civilization evolves from its present archaic state into a universally conscious one that integrates extraterrestrial and non-human intelligences into its world, tolerance is a necessary transitional developmental trait.

When a country is governed with truth and compassionate tolerance, it creates an environment where social and physical comfort and honesty can flourish. Tolerance entails acceptance and respect for diverse viewpoints, beliefs, and lifestyles including the ones to which we are all going to be exposed in the coming years. By embracing diversity, we encourage individuals to express themselves freely, leading to a heightened sense of acceptance and comfort within society. Moreover, a tolerant society fosters a mutuality of respect and open and honest communication, enabling the exchange of ideas, identifying needs and promoting a culture of trust and understanding. Such a culture is one that is capable of overcoming its conditioned xenophobia, processing new cultures and information systems that are not considered "of this planet" and integrating itself into the more intelligent highly technologically and spiritually advanced beings of the multiverse.

The Repression Paradox: Craftiness and Depression

When repression becomes the governing principle, the consequences are far from favorable. Repression stifles individual expression and forces people into adopting crafty means to navigate an oppressive system and its ever-growing multitude of laws. Citizens lose their sense of agency and become trapped in a society plagued with frustration, fear and despair. Growing frustration breeds aggression. Aggression is either expressed in violence or internalized as depression. Un-ameliorated fear and dishonesty cause societies to rot from within and eventually result in societal collapse. It is only through tolerance that we can begin to break the oppressive shackles that bind us. It is through practicing patience and tolerance that we can begin empowering individuals to embrace their true selves and contribute positively to society and its advancement towards meaningful contact and social intercourse with extraterrestrial civilizations and other human and non-human intelligences.

The Pitfalls of the Will to Power

The will to power emphasizes the pursuit of lofty ideals, but often fails to deliver the intended results. When governance is driven solely by the ego's desire for dominance and control, societies tend to become mired in division, corruption, and moral decay. By dissolving our egos and by favoring tolerance over the will to power, leaders can cultivate an environment where personal gain takes a backseat to personal responsibility for the welfare of oneself and others and the collective well-being of a nation, the world and by natural extension, the universe. Genuine progress and sustainable development can only be achieved when leaders prioritize the welfare of people above all else and allow the people to decide what is best for them.

A Masterful Example: Leading through Service

Here in this chapter, Lao Tzu teaches us that true mastery lies not in imposing one's will upon the governed, but in serving as an example for them. Exemplary leaders prioritize honesty, natural humility, simplicity in their approach to life, unshakeable integrity, unflappable patience and indiscriminate compassion, showcasing through their own actions the ideals they wish to see in society. By leading through service and selflessness, they inspire others to follow suit and contribute to the betterment of both the nation and mankind. Such leaders create a ripple effect, instilling the values of tolerance, compassion and fairness at every level of governance and in their relations with all others.

A Radiant Balance: Pointed yet not Piercing, Straightforward yet Supple

The Tao further emphasizes the importance of balance in governance. A masterful leader understands the value of being to the point without causing harm and being straightforward without being stubborn. This delicate balance promotes effective decision-making, allowing leaders to address challenges with wisdom, consideration of the needs of others and adaptability. When leaders do this they radiate the Tao. By embodying both this radiance and approachability, leaders can inspire trust and create an environment where the harmonious coexistence of diverse perspectives, thoughtful negotiation and mutually beneficial outcomes are encouraged and can be accomplished.

Conclusion

In a world where there is no "I" or "thou", only, "we" as an inseparable part of an immortal and eternal integral one Tao, tolerance would be unnecessary. But the world at large is not there yet. As a consequence of mankind being in a transitional phase of spiritual and cultural evolution, in the pursuit of a thriving society, tolerance stands out as an indispensable principle in governing mankind. Lao Tzu and the Integral way teach us the adverse effects of fear and repression and the ego's will to power, while emphasizing the transformative power of patience and tolerance for the mental and physical comfort and the fostering of honesty, and the overall physical, mental and spiritual well-being of mankind and beyond.

Post Script

Humankind may not yet be at the point in its evolution where the universal consciousness of the oneness of the Tao has been universally accepted as a reality, but until it is, by embracing the principles of patient tolerance, compassionate leadership, and serving as an example to others, nations and our leaders can pave the way for sustainable progress and the flourishing of their people and the earth and prepare them for the next stage of social and spiritual evolution. This stage is that of mankind's eventual evolution as a species toward its acceptance into a multiverse filled with the highest levels of both human and non-human beings. It should be understood that these ancient universal beings and their societies are based upon the principles and the universal truth of the Tao and on the same Integral Way that Lao Tzu teaches us here and in the Hua Hu Ching. - NMM

CHAPTER 59

Moderation, The Tao Te Ching, The New
Paradigm for Leadership and Governance on
Earth in a Post-Extraterrestrial Contact World

THE FREEDOM FROM ONE'S OWN IDEAS
IS THE MARK OF THOSE WHOSE APPROACH TO
LIFE
IS THAT OF MODERATION.

IN ORDER TO GOVERN A COUNTRY WELL,
THERE IS NOTHING BETTER THAN MODERATION.

AS TOLERANT AS THE SKY,
AS ALL-PERVADING AS THE LIGHT OF THE SUN,
AS FIRM AS A MOUNTAIN,
AS SUPPLE AS A TREE MOVING IN THE WIND,
(SO TOO IS THE MASTER).

WITHOUT ANY DESTINATION IN VIEW,
THE MASTER MAKES USE OF ALL THE THINGS IN
LIFE
THAT HAPPENSTANCE BRINGS HIS WAY.

BECAUSE THE MASTER HAS LET GO,
FOR HIM, NOTHING IS IMPOSSIBLE.
THE MASTER IS ABLE TO CARE FOR THE WELFARE
OF PEOPLE
JUST AS A MOTHER CARES FOR THAT OF HER OWN
CHILDREN.

Embracing Moderation: The Path to Effective Leadership and Proper Governance

In today's fast-paced world, where extreme ideas and radical approaches dominate and cripple the political and social landscapes, it is essential to explore the concept of moderation as a guiding principle for leadership and governance in the world. Since the time of the Early Greeks* moderation has been the key to a balanced, happy, and healthy life. It is also the key to effective leadership according to Lao Tzu, and after a 20th century filled with leaders who led themselves into perdition and their people and societies into decimation with two world wars and a multitude of bloody communist revolutions that were, in sum, responsible for the deaths of hundreds of millions of innocent people, considering moderation as a means of proper lifestyle and governance offers a fresh perspective on the renowned principles found in this chapter. Through Lao Tzu's emphasis on freedom from personal ideas, the cultivation of moderation creates a fertile ground for capable governance and compassionate leadership, enabling leaders to foster harmony and empathetically address the needs and welfare of their people.

Moderation as Freedom from One's Own Ideas

In Chapter 58 Lao Tzu emphasizes the importance of freeing oneself from personal ideas and opinions. Leadership and governance require an open mind. Lao Tzu suggests that moderation is not merely a sign of patient restraint but also a mark of wisdom and discernment.

Embracing Moderation as a Mark of Wisdom and Restraint

Moderation allows leaders to step back from their personal biases and consider a wider perspective. It encourages them to approach decisions with rationality, equanimity and impartiality, leading to more well-rounded and effective governance.

One's freedom from personal ideas allows for open-mindedness and unbiased decision-making: By freeing oneself from personal ideas, leaders can maintain open-mindedness, consider all viewpoints, and remain receptive to alternative solutions. This approach fosters unbiased decision-making and nurtures an environment where diverse ideas can be explored.

The Benefits of Moderation for Effective Governance

Moderation is integral to maintaining a balance between conflicting interests. Governance often involves reconciling conflicting interests and balancing competing demands. Moderation enables leaders to find a middle ground that best serves the needs of various stakeholders and promotes societal harmony.

Moderation encourages inclusivity and unity within a diverse society. Moderation promotes inclusivity by recognizing and respecting the diverse values, beliefs, and perspectives within a multiplicity of cultures. It creates an environment where compromise is valued and cooperation thrives, fostering a united and cohesive society and world.

Moderation fosters stability and long-term sustainability in policy-making. Moderation promotes stable and sustainable policy-making by avoiding extreme and abrupt changes. A moderate approach supports gradual and incremental improvements, minimizing disruptions and ensuring long-term stability and environmental and social sustainability.

Moderation and Leadership: The Qualities of a Moderate Leader

A moderate leader possesses qualities such as humility, patience, empathy and compassion. They listen actively**, considers multiple perspectives, and is willing to adapt their positions based on new information or insights. The benefits of leading with humility and adaptability are many. Adopting a moderate approach allows leaders to set aside ego and personal ambitions, focusing instead on the solutions by those who determine the greatest good for all the solutions will reach. This humility and adaptability foster collaboration, build trust, and inspire cohesive collaborative and collective action.

Moderation inspires trust and respect. Moderate leaders are perceived as fair, rational, and trustworthy. Their ability to make thoughtful, fair and balanced decisions earns the respect and confidence of their constituents, strengthening their leadership effectiveness and inspiring trust in others who can see the benefits of having such leaders moderate disputes and diffusing hostilities.

Applying the Taoist Principle to Real-World Scenarios
It is easy to extol the virtues of moderate leaders through their proper governance, but what about some examples. One might ask. The examples are many. Below are cited a handful of them for the reader.

By examining historical leaders who embraced moderation, we can gain insights into the positive outcomes achieved through this leadership approach. What follows are some real-world examples where leaders applied moderation successfully as a governing principle, resulting in societal progress, stability, and improved well-being for both their citizens and eventually the world in which we live.

Evaluating the success of these historical leaders who incorporated moderation in their approach demonstrates how moderation has proven to be effective in diverse cultural and political contexts. The following examples of applying Lao Tzu's principle of moderation in leadership to real-world scenarios and examples demonstrate the positive impact of moderation in governance and leadership in their approach.

1. George Washington: Washington's leadership during the founding of the United States demonstrates the effectiveness of moderation. As the first President, he sought to balance the interests and concerns of various factions without favoring one over the other. By embodying moderation in his decision-making and by promoting compromise, Washington helped establish a stable and successful democratic republic.

2. Abraham Lincoln: Lincoln, the 16th President of the United States, demonstrated moderation during one of the most challenging periods in American history – the Civil War. While preserving the Union was his primary goal, he pursued a moderate approach, carefully balancing the interests of both Northern and Southern states. Through his leadership, Lincoln emphasized reconciliation and moderation, ultimately leading to the end of slavery and the reunification of the United States.

3. Mahatma Gandhi: Gandhi's nonviolent resistance movement against British colonial rule in India showcased the power of moderation. His approach of peacefully appealing to the moral conscience of the oppressors inspired millions and ultimately led to India's independence. Gandhi's philosophy of moderation, known as Satyagraha, emphasized nonviolent methods, compromise, and respect for all parties involved.

4. Nelson Mandela: As the first post-apartheid President of South Africa, Mandela exemplified moderation in his leadership approach. Instead of seeking revenge or retribution against his oppressors, he prioritized reconciliation and unity, fostering social progress and stability. By embracing moderation, Mandela established the Truth and Reconciliation

Commission, allowing for the acknowledgment of past wrongs and the healing of wounds, ultimately leading to a more harmonious and inclusive society.

5. Mustafa Kemal Atatürk: Atatürk, the founder and first President of the Republic of Turkey, implemented a series of sweeping reforms based on moderation and rationality. His approach aimed to modernize Turkey by embracing a secular, inclusive, and democratic system. Atatürk's moderation led to significant social, cultural, and political progress, transforming Turkey into a modern nation-state.

6. Aung San Suu Kyi: Suu Kyi, a Nobel laureate and former State Counsellor of Myanmar, practiced moderation during her nonviolent struggle against the military dictatorship. Her leadership emphasized dialogue and reconciliation, striving for a peaceful transition to democracy. Despite facing challenges and criticism in recent years, Suu Kyi's promotion of moderation provided hope for a more democratic Myanmar.

7. Lee Kuan Yew: As Singapore's founding Prime Minister, Lee Kuan Yew implemented a pragmatic and moderate leadership style. He focused on promoting economic stability, social harmony, and good governance. Under his leadership, Singapore's economic transformation and social progress demonstrated the effectiveness of moderation in providing citizens with a high standard of living and a harmonious society.

Hopefully, these examples, however truncated, have highlighted the positive outcomes achieved through moderation in leadership and governance throughout our relatively modern history, showcasing its applicability in diverse contexts among all races and at all times and nationalities and emphasizing its ability to facilitate progress, stability, well-being for the people. Listening to the voices of all sides and governing with moderation have allowed for effective governance, economic stability, and social cohesion within the examples presented within the past two hundred and fifty years.

These examples represent the positive impact of moderation in leadership and governance. They showcase how leaders who embraced balanced moderation as a guiding principle were able to navigate complex issues in difficult situations to foster unity, and bring about positive change in their respective contexts. Analyzing additional historical leaders can provide additional valuable insights into the effectiveness and versatility of moderation as a leadership approach.

The Power of Letting Go and Embracing Moderation: Allowing the Flow of Life to Guide Decisions and Actions

Letting go of personal ideas and biases allows leaders to be more receptive to the flow of life, adapt to changing circumstances, and make decisions that align with the greater good. The potential possibilities when personal biases are set aside are boundless. By embracing moderation, leaders open themselves up to a world of possibilities that might otherwise go unnoticed. This flexibility and openness pave the way for innovative solutions and unexpected breakthroughs.

Moderation enables leaders to cultivate compassion and care for the welfare of the people. It allows them to listen patiently and prioritize the welfare of their constituents, embracing a nurturing and compassionate approach to their governance. This caring mindset fosters social cohesion and ensures that the needs of all individuals are met. Moderation opens up new vistas of potential for all those who are governed and for new groups who come to be involved with the properly led and well governed constituency.

Conclusion

By embracing moderation as a guiding principle in leadership and governance, we can elect compassionate leaders who can effectuate proper leadership and effective governance. Drawing inspiration from this chapter written by Lao Tzu that highlights the advantages of adopting a moderation-centered approach while governing a nation our leaders can help us evolve from our present state of dysfunctional affairs to one of a higher mental, physical, social and spiritual order. By freeing themselves from personal ideas and biases and by staying the moderate course, the world's leaders can navigate through the highly complex issues that humanity will be facing in the post-contact world and strike a balance between conflicting interests, and beliefs to genuinely provide for the health, safety and sustainable welfare of the people of this wonderful blue dot of a planet in an immeasurably large cosmos. Through moderation, both we and our leaders in this brave new post-contact world can shape a harmonious society that thrives in unity and progress and is one whose inhabitants and governance is compatible with their integration into associations with other beings and worlds in a moderate, patient, peaceful, balanced, caring and compassionate manner.

*"Pan metron ariston" (παν μέτρον άριστον) is a quote in ancient Greek that is commonly attributed in the west to Klevoloulous o Lindios in the sixth century B.C. It literally means "everything in moderation". Others believe that the quote was originally "Metron Ariston" which means "moderation is best". Despite the etymology, the meaning is unmistakably the same.

**"Listening is a very deep practice. You have to empty yourself. You have to leave space in order to listen. Especially to people we think are our enemies - the ones we believe are making our situation worse. When we have shown our capacity for listening and understanding, the other person will begin to listen to you, and you have a chance to tell him or her of your pain,

and it's your turn to be healed. This is the practice of peace."
-Thich Nhat Hanh

CHAPTER 60

"Frying a Small Fish", The Tao Te Ching, The New Paradigm for Leadership and Governance on Earth in a Post-Extraterrestrial Contact World

THE GOVERNANCE OF A LARGE COUNTRY IS LIKE THE FRYING OF A SMALL FISH. BOTH ARE SPOILED BY TOO MUCH POKING.

FOR A COUNTRY CENTERED IN THE TAO EVIL WILL HAVE NO POWER.

THOUGH EVIL WILL NOT DISAPPEAR ONE WILL BE ABLE TO STEP OUT OF ITS WAY.

WHEN EVIL IS GIVEN NOTHING TO OPPOSE IT WILL VANISH ALL BY ITSELF.

The Tao Te Ching: A New Paradigm for Post-Extraterrestrial Contact Leadership

In our ever-evolving world, the concept of leadership takes on new dimensions, particularly in the wake of the reality of and potential for further human and non-human extraterrestrial contact. To navigate the intricacies of proper governance on Earth, we can turn to the wisdom of the Tao Te Ching and embrace its profound teachings and its integral Way. As we explore the metaphor presented in the quote, "The governance of a large country is like the frying of a small fish. Both are spoiled by too much poking," we discover the timeless and universally transformative power of Tao-centered leadership and the efficacy of the Tao Te Ching as a paradigm for leadership and governance in a post-extraterrestrial contact world.

The Harmony of Tao-Centered Governance

The Tao Te Ching emphasizes the importance of aligning governance with the Tao, the universal principle of harmony and balance. This is a principle that is universal and accords itself with all spiritually advanced beings. By adopting a leadership style centered around the Tao, leaders from literally all walks of life can foster a sense of tranquility, unity, and cohesiveness within a diverse and complex society and world. This Tao-centered governance helps to counterbalance the inherent chaos and tensions that can arise not only in the world as we now know it but especially in a growing post-extraterrestrial contact world as well.

The Power of Non-Resistance

In Lao Tzu's rather controversial proposition, "For a country centered in the Tao, evil will have no power," lies a valuable lesson for leaders. Rather than engaging in constant confrontation and resistance against "evil", a Tao-centered leader chooses a path of non-resistance. By stepping out of the way of evil and refusing to oppose it directly, the leader deprives evil of its unnatural and destructive power. This approach enables the leader to focus on constructive solutions, allowing the Tao to make its way and to avoid being consumed by negativity. *

Confronting Challenges through Self-Transformation

While evil may persist, a Tao-centered leader understands that true change starts within oneself. By embodying the teachings of the Tao Te Ching and the Integral Way and constantly self-cultivating and working towards one's personal growth, the masterful leader becomes a catalyst for positive change in the larger society. This emphasis on self-transformation allows the leader to inspire others and create a collective shift towards a harmonious and enlightened society. This transformation is that which is universally accepted by both advanced terrestrial and non-terrestrial intelligences throughout the multiverse. It constitutes the basis for their societies and for their engagement with each other.

Embracing Adaptability in a Changing World

In the context of a post-extraterrestrial contact world, uncertainty and rapid change become ever-present. The Tao Te Ching's metaphor of "The governance of a large country is like the frying of a small fish" encourages leaders to avoid excessive interference and manipulation. Instead, a leader rooted in the Tao embraces adaptability and allows natural processes to unfold. By relinquishing control and trusting in the inherent order of the Tao the underlying source and force that governs all existence and encapsulates the natural order of the universe, leaders can navigate complexities while preserving the essence of a people's and a world's governance.

Conclusion

To value the Tao and to follow the Integral Way is to value and understand the Rules of Interstellar and inter dimensional universal engagement. The Tao Te Ching and the Tao of Leadership offer a fresh and compelling paradigm for leadership in our post-extraterrestrial contact world. By centering governance around the Tao, leaders can cultivate harmony, embrace non-resistance, promote self-transformation, and adapt creatively to new challenges that nascent civilizations ultimately face as they progress physically, mentally and spiritually towards cooperation with the more advanced worlds and societies that populate the cosmos. The alluring simplicity of Tao-centered leadership holds the power to inspire and guide us towards a future where evil loses its stronghold, and humanity thrives in unity and balance. As we ponder the profound teachings found within the Tao Te Ching and practiced through the Integral Way, we can embark on a journey of evolution and leadership that transcends conventional boundaries, paving the way for a brighter and more enlightened future for all here on earth and elsewhere in the universe.

*The power of non-resistance and the rule of non-confrontation of evil does have its exceptions. Those few exceptions include times when, in the circumstance of the individual, immediate and inevitable violence threatens innocent lives. The exceptions also include wars in which one's lands are invaded by a foreign force and innocent lives are endangered. In these cases, we are obliged by the Tao to defend those innocents only to the extent necessary to make these behaviors cease and to repel the invader. These are extreme cases and the rare few times when even deadly force may be used out of necessity.

CHAPTER 61

Dispelling the "Prime Directive", The Role
of True Humility and Yielding in Proper
Governance, The Tao as the New Paradigm for
Leadership and Governance on Earth in a Post-
Extraterrestrial Contact World

WHEN A COUNTRY ATTAINS GREAT POWER,
IT BECOMES LIKE THE GREAT OCEAN.
DOWNWARD UNTO IT DO ALL STREAMS FLOW.

THE GREATER THAT A COUNTRY'S POWER GROWS,
THE GREATER BECOMES ITS NEED FOR HUMILI-
TY.

(TRUE) "HUMILITY" MEANS TO TRUST THE TAO.
WHEN ONE TRUSTS THE TAO,
ONE NEEDS NEVER TO BE DEFENSIVE.

LIKE THE GREAT MAN, SO TOO IS A GREAT NA-
TION.
WHEN THE GREAT MAN MAKES A MISTAKE,
HE REALIZES HIS MISTAKE.
HAVING REALIZED THE MISTAKE,
THE GREAT MAN ADMITS HIS MISTAKE.
HAVING ADMITTED HIS MISTAKE,
AND CORRECTS IT.

WHEN OTHERS POINT OUT HIS FAULTS,
THE GREAT MAN CONSIDERS THOSE WHO HAVE
DONE SO
TO BE AS BENEVOLENT TEACHERS.
AND OF HIS ENEMIES,

THE MASTER THINKS OF THEM TO BE
CASTS OF HIS OWN SHADOW.

IF CENTERED IN THE TAO IS A NATION,
ITS OWN PEOPLE ARE NURTURED,
AND THE AFFAIRS OF OTHERS NOT MEDDLED IN,
SUCH A NATION BECOMES A SHINING LIGHT
TO ALL THE WORLD'S NATIONS.

The Role of True Humility and Yielding in Proper Governance: The Tao Te Ching, The New Paradigm for Leadership in a Post Extraterrestrial Contact World

In a world where power dynamics define the course of nations, the concept of true humility and yielding often takes a back seat. However, the ancient wisdom of the Tao Te Ching provides an alternate perspective on leadership and governance—a paradigm that holds immense promise especially in a post extraterrestrial contact world.

The Tao Te Ching, with its emphasis on true humility, self-reflection, and the art of yielding, offers a profound framework for enlightened governance. By adopting these principles, leaders can navigate the complexities of power, promote mutual respect, and create a world where cooperation and understanding prevail. By also incorporating the principles of the Tao like true humility and yielding, humankind can reshape its leadership and foster peace and non-aggression and a harmonious planetary and universal order.

The Need for Humility in the Face of Power

The imagery of the great ocean Lao Tzu paints a powerful picture. When a country attains great power, it becomes like the vast ocean, where all streams flow into it. However, the greater a country's power, the greater is its need for humility. True humility, as advocated by Lao Tzu, lies in trusting the natural order of things rather than relying solely on strength and force. Embracing true humility enables leaders to transcend ego and defensiveness, facilitating openness to compassionate alternative perspectives and nurtures a genuine commitment to forgiveness and learning from past mistakes. What is good for the great nation is also good for the individuals that inhabit as well. Both go together like a hand in a glove.

The Great Man: An Embodiment of Humility and Self-Reflection

Lao Tzu in the passage above focuses on the qualities of a great man, emphasizing introspection and self-awareness as essential characteristics of effective leadership. When a great man makes a mistake, he recognizes it. He then acknowledges it, takes responsibility, and endeavors to correct it. This willingness to grow and learn sets an example for others. By considering those who point out faults as benevolent teachers and viewing enemies as reflections of one's own weaknesses, leaders can transform adversarial relationships into opportunities for learning, self-improvement and mutual growth.

Non-Interference and Nurturing Nations

A nation or world centered in the Tao is characterized by a commitment to not meddle in the affairs of others, fostering respect for diverse cultures, governments, and ideologies. By nurturing its own people and allowing them the autonomy to develop in accordance with their unique cultural and spiritual identities, a nation becomes a shining light that illuminates a path towards harmony and understanding. The Tao Te Ching offers an alternative approach to governance, one that prioritizes inclusivity, diplomacy, and cooperation.

Dispelling the "Prime Directive"

While running this chapter on the Tao of Leadership by an old friend of mine, he made a comment in jest saying, "What's the matter, isn't the Prime directive not good enough for ET anymore?" Admittedly, my friend, with his limited knowledge of the Tao and ET/NHI contact and only the numerous télé-seasons of Star Trek as his polestar, had a point. Because of the popularity of the series and movies, humankind has little more than the Prime Directive to guide it in its understanding of what and how ET/NHI may be approaching mankind right now. So, it may be of some help to differentiate and contrast the two approaches of governance in a post disclosure world.

In a world where the existence of extraterrestrial life has been disclosed, it becomes crucial to explore the contrasting approaches to governance found in the Tao of Leadership and the Prime Directive. While the popular Star Trek series has familiarized us with the concept of the Prime Directive, the Tao of Leadership offers a unique perspective on how leaders should interact with other civilizations and how they are most likely to interact with us. With the Tao as an agreed upon and common bond, the interaction between ourselves and advanced extraterrestrial races just might be seamless. The Tao of leadership and governance is a two-way street.

The Tao Te Ching, with its emphasis on humility, transcendence of ego, and openness to alternative perspectives, provides a powerful framework for understanding leadership here on earth and elsewhere in a post-disclosure world. According to the Tao Te Ching, true leaders, no matter who they are or from where they hail, should embrace humility and let go of defensive ego-driven behaviors. They should foster compassion in all other beings and nurture a commitment to yielding, forgiveness, and learning from past mistakes. This approach encourages leaders to understand the interconnectedness of all beings throughout the universe and prioritize harmonious relationships among and between human beings and those who may not be.

The Prime Directive as authored by Gene L. Coon for the Star Trek series obviously offers a different perspective on governing peaceful interactions with other civilizations in the galaxy. For those who do not know, the Prime Directive is a guiding principle for the fictional Starfleet and certain other advanced star faring civilizations of "The Federation" to refrain from interfering with the internal development of less advanced civilizations, like ours. The Prime Directive centers around peaceful non-interference, maintaining a balance of power, and allowing lesser developed civilizations to progress autonomously and naturally, even if that advance is done at the peril of the less advanced society.

The Prime Directive also has nothing to do with a society's dissolving the ego of for its leaders to follow suit. Obviously, this fiction of Star Trek is not and has not been a reality both on Star Trek and on earth as ET/NHI contact has been happening on for earth for thousands of years if not millions.

In a post-disclosure world, where interaction with extraterrestrial civilizations has become a nascent reality, both philosophies offer valuable insights. The Prime Directive prompts leaders to consider the potential consequences of their actions and prioritize the preservation of lesser developed civilizations' self-determination. This is a wise approach with developing societies, as the effect of EY/NHI inputs like any inoculation may not produce the desired results. Caution is a commendable approach. As contact begins and people's attitudes toward it begins to be realized and mature, the Tao of Leadership encourages leaders on both ends of the equation to transcend their egos, embrace humility, and cultivate truthful and compassionate relationships with each other. This enables them to navigate the complexities of interstellar relations with openness and understanding.

Both the Tao of Leadership and the Prime Directive therefore, present distinct contrasting but complementary approaches to governance in the context of ET/NHI contact in a post-disclosure world. The Tao Te Ching advocates for humility, openness, and compassion, the transcending of ego and openness to alternative perspectives. The Tao Te Ching's emphasis on leaders embracing true humility enabling them to transcend ego and defensiveness, facilitating openness to compassionate alternative perspectives and the nurture of a genuine commitment to yielding, forgiveness and learning from past mistakes, however important differs the concept of the "Prime Directive" 1.*

Although the Prime Directive guides the behavior of imaginary advanced civilizations when encountering less advanced ones, emphasizing non-interference to preserve and respect the natural development of other societies in a very forward thinking television show from the 1960s, it has limited relevance in reality. Open contact has already been made and has been documented by our own official and historical sources. 2.**

While the Tao Te Ching promotes humility, introspection, and yielding as guiding principles for leadership within a nation, Gene Roddenberry's Prime Directive in Star Trek is an imaginary guide and a literary artifice. It primarily applies to encounters in space exploration and deals with decisions on when, if ever, to intervene in the development of other civilizations. From all apparent intents and purposes, the decision by ET/NHI to intervene has already been made.

While the Tao of Leadership and the Prime Directive have distinct focuses, integrating their principles can help guide the conduct of leaders both human and ET/NHI to engage each other in a post-disclosure post-contact world. It is up to earth to develop its own civilization. It is nobody's chore but our own. But the appearance of ET/NHI would seem to go a long way in accelerating humanity's mental and spiritual processes.

By combining humility, compassion, and limited interference, leaders can strive for a balanced and thoughtful approach to governing interactions between this planet and extraterrestrial civilizations. This integration requires an understanding of the Tao and the interconnectedness of all beings. It emphasizes the need to patiently and compassionately navigate complex power dynamics while respecting the unique aspirations and needs of each civilization and approaching them with patience and compassion.

Conclusion

In a post-disclosure, extraterrestrial contact world, where global interconnectedness and the search for meaning tend to redefine the quest for power, the Tao Te Ching emerges as a most compelling paradigm for civilized leadership in the universe. By embracing true humility, acknowledging our own mistakes, and adopting a compassionate and yielding approach to international and interstellar relations, leaders can best navigate the complexities of power in a manner that promotes harmony and mutual respect among all nations and beings. The paradigm shift proposed by the Tao Te Ching has the potential to shape a new era of governance, leading the world towards an enlightened and cooperative future here on earth and beyond to a place that, as far as we know it, and to actually borrow a line from Star Trek, if not the Prime Directive. "Where no man has gone before".

1*The Prime Directive. "The creation of the Prime Directive is generally credited to *Original Series* producer Gene L. Coon. [9][10] The Prime Directive reflected a contemporary political view that US involvement in the Vietnam War was an example of a superpower interfering in the natural development of southeast Asian society; the creation of the Prime Directive was perceived as a repudiation of that involvement.[11][12]

In the fictional universe of *Star Trek*, the **Prime Directive** (also known as "Starfleet General Order 1", and the "non-interference directive") is a guiding principle of Starfleet that prohibits its members from interfering with the natural development of alien civilizations.[1] Its stated aim is to protect unprepared civilizations from the danger of starship crews introducing advanced technology, knowledge, and values before they are ready.[2] Since its introduction in the first season of the original *Star Trek* series, the directive has featured in many *Star Trek* episodes as part of a moral question over how best to establish diplomatic relations with new alien worlds.

"The Prime Directive is one of many guidelines for Starfleet's mandate to explore the galaxy and "seek out new life and new civilizations." Although the concept of the Prime Directive has been alluded to and paraphrased by many *Star Trek* characters during the television series and feature films, the actual directive has never been provided to viewers.[3] The most complete attempts to define the directive have come from non-canonical works and include:

The Prime Directive prohibits Starfleet personnel and spacecraft from interfering in the normal development of any society, and mandates that any Starfleet vessel or crew member is expendable to prevent violation of this rule.[4]

As the right of each sentient species to live in accordance with its normal cultural evolution is considered sacred, no Starfleet personnel may interfere with the normal and healthy development of alien life and culture. Such interference includes introducing superior knowledge, strength, or technology to a world whose society is incapable of handling such advantages wisely. Starfleet personnel may not violate this Prime Directive, even to save their lives and/or their ship, unless they are acting to right an earlier violation or an accidental contamination of said culture. This directive takes precedence over any and all other considerations and carries with it the highest moral obligation.[5][6]

The Prime Directive was frequently applied to less developed planets which had not yet discovered warp travel or subspace communication technology. (Arguably with the discovery of zero-point energy and anti-gravities technology reverse engineered by mankind at the expense of downed and recovered Et Craft in our own atomic age, we are already there.)

The Prime Directive was also sometimes applied to advanced civilizations that already knew of life on other worlds but were protected by empires outside the Federation's jurisdiction. First contact could be made by the Federation with alien worlds that had either discovered warp or were on the verge of it, or with highly advanced civilizations that simply hadn't ventured into space yet. In those cases, the Prime Directive was used as a general policy to not disrupt or interfere with their culture when establishing peaceful diplomatic relations.[7]

Consequences for violating the Prime Directive could range from a stern reprimand to a demotion, depending on the severity of the infraction. However, enforcement of these rules -- and interpretations of the Prime Directive itself -- varied greatly and were at the discretion of the commanding officer. In many instances, prominent Starfleet personnel like captains James T. Kirk, Jean-Luc Picard, Kathryn Janeway and Benjamin Sisko willingly broke the Prime Directive but faced no real punishment or consequence for doing so.[8]

However, the Prime Directive is not absolute. Starship captains have been known to violate it to protect their ships and crews, and certain Starfleet regulations such as The Omega Directive can even render it null and void in certain circumstances".
- Wikipedia

2. A Brief Official Record of UFO/UAP Military and Nuclear Interference

Sharing his account of the incident where his nuclear missile base at was allegedly "attacked by a UFO", retired US Air Force captain Robert Salas said that an encounter at Malmstrom AFB took place over 50 years ago, on March 24, 1967, to be exact. He reported that at the time, the base was holding 10 nuclear missiles. The guards on duty reportedly were left "frightened," "screaming" and "babbling" after the close encounter.

As recently as 2023 at hearing before the House of Representatives on UAPs unidentified anomalous phenomena, also known as UFOs, a retired Navy fighter pilot Retired Navy Cmdr. David Fravor was commander of the F/A-18F squadron on the USS Nimitz when he says he spotted the object during a flight off the coast of Southern California on Nov. 14, 2004. He testified about his experience seeing such a UAP during naval operations in what he described as a "Tic Tac-looking object" while on a routine flight back in 2004.

"Whatever the mysterious lights in the sky were, they seemed to have an interest in our nukes. One of the more out-of-the-ordinary press conferences held in Washington this week consisted of former Air Force personnel testifying to the existence of UFOs and their ability to neutralize American and Russian nuclear missiles.

UFO researcher Robert Hastings of Albuquerque, N.M., who organized the National Press Club briefing, said more than 120 former service members had told him they'd seen unidentified flying objects near nuclear weapon storage and testing grounds. Star & Stripes quoted former Air Force Capt. Robert Salas, who was at Malmstrom Air Force Base in Montana in 1967 when 10 ICMs he was overseeing suddenly became inoperative - at the same time base security informed him of a mysterious red glowing object in the sky.

Robert Jamison, a retired USAF nuclear missile targeting officer, told of several occasions having to go out and "re-start" missiles that had been deactivated, after UFOs were sighted nearby.

Similar sightings at nuclear sites in the former Soviet Union and in Britain were related. CBS Affiliate KSWT describes "Britain's Roswell," a case of unidentified phenomena in December 1980 incident near two Royal Air Force Bases in Suffolk, England.

Several U.S. Air Force personnel reported seeing a strange metallic object hovering in Rendlesham Forest near RAF Woodbridge and found three depressions in the ground. Speaking at Monday's press briefing, retired USAF Col. Charles Halt said that in December 1980, when he was deputy base commander at RAF Bentwaters, strange lights in the forest were investigated by three patrolmen." - CBS News cbsnews.com 9/28/10

CHAPTER 62

Assisting Leadership to Properly Govern, The
Proposition for the Tao Te Ching as the New
Paradigm for Leadership and Governance on
Earth and Throughout the Universe in a Post-
Extraterrestrial Contact World

AT THE CENTER OF THE UNIVERSE
THERE IS THE TAO.
FOR THE GOOD MAN, THE TAO IS HIS TREASURE.
FOR THE BAD MAN, IT IS HIS REFUGE.

THOUGH THOUGHTFUL WORDS BRING HONORS.
AND GOOD DEEDS CAN WIN RESPECT,
BEYOND ALL VALUE IS THE TAO.
EVEN THOUGH, NO ONE FULLY CAN ACHIEVE
A FULL UNDERSTANDING OF IT.

THUS, WHEN CHOSEN ANEW IS A LEADER,
ONE SHOULD OFFER NOT ONE'S HELP
OR EXPERIENCE TO THE NEW LEADER.
BUT SHOULD OFFER INSTEAD,
TO SCHOOL ONE'S NEW LEADER IN THE TAO.

ONE MIGHT ASK "WHY WAS THE TAO SO ESTEE-
MED
BY THE ANCIENT MASTERS?".
IT IS BECAUSE THEY KNEW THAT
ONCE THEIR BEING BECAME ONE WITH THE TAO,
THAT SHOULD THEY MAKES A MISAKE,
THAT THE MISTAKE IS FORGIVEN.
THIS IS WHY THE TAO
IS SO LOVED

**(AND TRUSTED)
BY ALL.**

The Tao Te Ching: The Guiding Light for Leadership in an
Evolving World

The Tao Te Ching and its wisdom are based upon universal
truths that apply everywhere and at all times. As a consequence,
the Tao Te Ching and the principles of its Integral Way with
their emphasis upon personal responsibility and self-cultivation
provide a powerful light and a compelling paradigm for leadership in a post extraterrestrial contact world. They offer a
transformative approach that can assist leaders in governing
effectively and ethically in a new world where borders are no
longer defined by land mass but by light years and inter dimensional travel.

As humanity moves towards a future filled with unprecedented
challenges and opportunities to evolve into a post-contact world
with a multitude of non-human intelligences, it becomes increasingly crucial for leaders to embrace new paradigms for
leadership that can guide them in negotiating with more technologically advanced and spiritually aware beings and their
societies to successfully navigate uncharted territories. Lao
Tzu's ancient Chinese text, the Tao Te Ching, offers a unique
and persuasive framework for leadership, rooted in the concept
of the Tao, the underlying source and force that governs all
existence and encapsulates the natural order throughout the
universe. Those who accept the reality of the Tao and use it
and the Tao Te Ching as a guiding principle for leadership
and integrate the concepts of its Integral Way will attain the
ability to enhance NHI-human decision making, foster ethical
conduct between us, NHIs and our extraterrestrial cousins.
This will inevitably instill trust in both world leaders, NHIs
and those who have come to assist us from other galaxies and
dimensions.

Enhancing Decision-Making

The Tao Te Ching emphasizes the importance of aligning oneself with the Tao, the central essence of the universe. ET and NHIs understand the Tao and it's nature and operation, no matter how or what they may call it. By cultivating a deep understanding of the Tao, human leaders will gain access to profound wisdom that underlies the wisdom of other ET/NHI civilizations and enhance their decision-making capabilities. Unlike conventional leadership principles that prioritize rigid strategies and outcomes, the Tao Te Ching encourages leaders to adopt a more holistic, compassionate and intuitive approach. Leaders who embrace the Tao transcend conventional boundaries, allowing their decisions to be guided by patience, compassion, mutual trust, natural rhythms and long-term sustainability on this planet and others across the universe rather than short-term gains and power plays.

Fostering Ethical Conduct

One of the remarkable aspects of the Tao Te Ching is its emphasis on ethical conduct. The text suggests that leaders who fully comprehend and embody the Tao will prioritize virtues such as integrity, compassion, trustworthiness and humility. In a post extraterrestrial contact world, where diverse societies and cultures converge, ethical leadership becomes paramount for fostering harmony and unity. The Tao Te Ching equips leaders with the necessary values and tools to navigate complex moral and ethical dilemmas, grounded in the principle of universal truth, compassion, harmony and respect for all beings.

Instilling Trust in Leaders

Trust is the bedrock of effective leadership, and the Tao Te Ching recognizes this fundamental truth. By urging all leaders to immerse themselves in the Tao, the text imparts the necessity for truth and a sense of authenticity and transparency that engenders trustworthiness. In a world where skepticism towards leaders prevails, accepting and cultivating trust through the principles of the Tao Te Ching can foster stronger connections between leaders of all races and beings throughout all of the Tao's creation and their followers. By adhering to the wisdom of the Tao, leaders wherever they are from demonstrate a commitment to service to others over service to self, empathy, and to the greater good, establishing themselves as credible examples of Tao=centered beings and reliable figures in their respective domains.

Conclusion

The Tao Te Ching presents a captivating new paradigm for leadership for both mankind and ET/NHI in a post extraterrestrial contact world. Its emphasis on shared values, aligned decision-making, ethical conduct, and trust-building should not be overlooked. As we navigate an evolving world filled with unforeseen challenges and complexities, integrating the principles of the Tao Te Ching into our leadership practices can pave the way for a harmonious and prosperous future. By embracing the wisdom of this ancient text, leaders here on earth and throughout the universe have the opportunity to transform themselves and the worlds they govern.

CHAPTER 63

Wu Wei, Small Steps and Going With The Flow, Achieving Greatness

ONE SHOULD ACT WITHOUT DOING.
ONE SHOULD WORK WITHOUT EFFORT.
THINK THE SMALL TO BE LARGE,
AND THE FEW TO BE MANY.

ONE'S DIFFICULTIES SHOULD BE CONFRONTED
WHILE STILL SMALL,
SO THAT THEIR CORRECTION EASILY IS MADE.
ONE ACCOMPLISHES A GREAT TASK
BY COMPLETING A SERIES OF SMALL ACTS.

BECAUSE THE MASTER NEVER STRIVES FOR
GREATNESS
GREATNESS THUS HE ACHIEVES.
FOR BY NOT STRIVING FOR GREATNESS
IS HOW TRUE GREATNESS IS ACCOMPLISHED.

WHEN THE MASTER ENCOUNTERS DIFFICULTY,
HE STOPS AND GIVES FULLY OF HIMSELF UNTO IT.

BY LETTING GO OF HIS OWN COMFORT,
PROBLEMS ARE NO LONGER PROBLEMS
FOR THE MASTER.

<u>Embracing Flow: The Path to Achieving Greatness</u>

In life, we often find ourselves striving for greatness. We set ambitious goals, make grand plans, and work tirelessly to achieve them. However, as the ancient Chinese philosopher Lao Tzu teaches, there is another path, the Integral One and - the path of Wu Wei, the path of small steps, and going with the flow. In this passage Lao Tzu instructs us that by acting without doing, working without effort, thinking small to be large, and embracing challenges, we all can achieve true greatness.

Wu Wei and the Art of Non-Action

The central idea of this chapter is encapsulated in the principle of Wu Wei, which literally translates to "non-action" but encompasses a deeper meaning. By acting without doing, we allow things to unfold naturally, without imposing our will upon them. It is a surrender to the present moment and a recognition that sometimes the best course of action is inaction. Through Wu Wei, we liberate ourselves from the burden of control and allow the natural flow of events to guide us towards greatness.

Working Without Effort

In our pursuit of success, we often equate hard work with achievement. However, here in chapter 63 Lao Tzu suggests that working without effort can be equally, if not more, transformative. By letting go of excessive striving and finding balance, we tap into a state where work becomes effortless. In this state, work is no longer a burden but a joyous expression of our true selves. By aligning ourselves and our actions with the natural rhythm of life, we achieve a state of flow, where greatness effortlessly emerges.

Thinking Small to Be Large

Often, we get caught up in the grandeur of big dreams and overlook the power of small steps. The journey of a thousand miles begins wirh the friar step. This passage, in the same way teaches us to think small to be large, emphasizing the importance of taking incremental actions towards our goals. By breaking down daunting tasks into manageable steps, we create a momentum of small victories that ultimately culminate in greatness. No challenge becomes too daunting. It is through the accumulation of these small acts that we pave the way for significant accomplishments.

Embracing Challenges

We have all heard from our mothers that "A stitch in time saves nine". While many may shy away from difficulties, Lao Tzu wisely encourages us to confront them while they are still small. By willingly facing challenges early on, we prevent them from escalating into insurmountable obstacles. Tao masters, who achieve greatness, do not shy away from discomfort but fully immerse themselves in it. Through this immersion, they discover that difficulties become opportunities for growth and transformation. Discomfort is the price one pays for growth. Through discipline and self-cultivation and by letting go of personal comfort, they find the strength to overcome any challenge that comes their way.

Conclusion

In a world fixated on constant hustle and the pursuit of greatness, this passage offers a refreshing universal and timeless perspective. By acting without doing, working without effort, thinking small to be large, fixing problems and embracing challenges early on, we can transcend the limitations of our efforts and attain true greatness. Let us remember that our destination is in each step and not strive for greatness in the conventional sense. Instead, we should embrace the wisdom of Wu Wei and the power of small steps and follow the Integral Way. By doing so, we can inevitably unlock the pathway to achieving greatness in ways that go far beyond our wildest expectations and assure ourselves of the contentment and comfort in our daily lives that comes with abiding in the Tao.

CHAPTER 64

Who We Are, Allowing Things to Take Their Course, The Tao Te Ching, The New Paradigm for Leadership and Governance on Earth in a Post-Extraterrestrial Contact World

THAT WHICH IS ROOTED IS MOST EASILY NOURISHED.
THAT WHICH IS RECENT IS MORE EASY TO CORRECT.
THAT WHICH IS BRITTLE IS MORE EASILY BROKEN.
THAT WHICH IS SMALL IS MORE EASILY SCATTERED.

TROUBLE IS BEST PREVENTED BEFORE IT ARISES.
PUT THINGS IN ORDER BEFORE THEY COME INTO EXISTENCE.
FROM A TINY SPROUT GROWS THE GREAT PINE.
FROM BENEATH ONES OWN FEET BEGINS A JOURNEY OF A THOUSAND MILES.

ONE FAILS BY RUSHING INTO ACTION.
ONE LOSES THINGS BY TRYING TO GRASP THEM.
BY FORCING A PROJECT TO COMPLETION,
ONE RUINS THAT WHICH HAS ALMOST RIPENED.

THE MASTER, THEREFORE ACTS
BY ALLOWING THINGS TO TAKE THEIR COURSE.
THE MASTER REMAINS AS CALM AT THE FINISH
AS HE WAS AT THE BEGINNING.
THE MASTER HAS NOTHING.
THUS, HE HAS NOTHING TO LOSE.

**WHAT THE MASTER DESIRES
IS NON-DESIRE.
WHAT THE MASTER LEARNS HE UNLEARNS.
THE MASTER REMINDS PEOPLE SIMPLY
OF WHO THEY ETERNALLY HAVE BEEN.**

**THE MASTER CARES OF NOTHING,
BUT FOR THE TAO.
BECAUSE THE MASTER CARES ONLY ABOUT THE
TAO,
HE IS ABLE TO CARE FOR ALL THINGS.**

The Tao Te Ching: A New Paradigm for Leadership in a Post-Extraterrestrial Contact World

The Tao Te Ching offers a profound perspective on leadership, emphasizing the value of harmony, balance, and Wu Wei. By allowing things to take their course, leaders can prevent trouble, nurture growth, and ultimately foster a world characterized by peace, wisdom, and spiritual connectedness.

In a rapidly evolving world that has witnessed the dawn of extraterrestrial contact and contact by non-human intelligences, humanity finds itself facing both unprecedented challenges and formerly unthinkable opportunities. In this regard, one should explore the ancient wisdom of the Tao Te Ching, and its potential as a new paradigm for leadership on Earth. Embracing the teachings of the Lao Tzu in the Tao Te Ching can lead our civilizations to effective, compassionate, and enlightened leadership among and for ourselves and in the substance and method of engaging with ET and NHI IN our post-extraterrestrial contact societies.

The Power of Wu Wei, Non-Interference

The Tao Te Ching reveals the inherent wisdom in not forcing outcomes or rushing into action. By allowing things to unfold naturally, leaders can avoid unnecessary conflict and unforeseen consequences. By addressing issues before they arise and maintaining a calm demeanor, leaders can cultivate a harmonious environment, ensuring that potential conflicts are nipped in the bud. By putting things in order by organizing and preparing for challenges before they manifest is crucial to effective leadership. By offering guidance instead of imposing control, leaders can foster an atmosphere of autonomy and growth.

This chapter also underscores the importance of Wu Wei and allowing things to take their course. This principle becomes especially pertinent when interacting with other worlds and cultures. By resisting the urge to impose our own values, beliefs, and systems, leaders can foster an environment of understanding, respect, and mutual growth. Wu Wei, non-meddling, and being non-judgmental and not trying to impose ourselves on others enable us to learn from the wisdom and unique perspectives of other civilizations, creating the potential for a rich tapestry of understanding, acceptance and collaborative exploration with ET and NHIs.

<u>Embracing Humility and Unlearning: The Pursuit of Non-Desire: Unlearning and Reconnecting</u>

The Tao Te Ching emphasizes the importance of humility and selflessness in leadership. It urges leaders to discard personal desires and attachments in favor of a higher purpose. By desiring less and embracing contentment, leaders can transcend self-interest and make decisions that serve the greater good. The text highlights the value of unlearning preconceived notions and reconnecting with the eternal essence within. Leaders who remind people of their true Tao-selves can foster a sense of purpose, belonging, and spiritual connectedness between humans and ET/NHIs.

When engaging with other worlds and cultures, it is essential to approach interactions with humility and an open mind.

The Tao Te Ching and the Integral Way teach us to unlearn our biases, preconceived notions, and cultural conditioning. By cultivating a genuine desire to understand and appreciate diverse perspectives, leaders can build bridges of trust and forge meaningful connections. Humility allows us to shed ego-driven motivations, proceed with compassion for ourselves and others and genuinely learn from and integrate the learning and wisdom of other civilizations. For the highest order civilizations that have the Tao as part of their internal operating systems, this approach is their approach as well.

Care for All Things: Compassion and Universal Care:

The concept of caring for all things is particularly relevant in the context of interfacing with other worlds and cultures. By extending our care and compassion to these entities, we demonstrate our commitment to fostering harmonious relationships. This involves not only respecting their values, traditions, and ways of life but also actively engaging in efforts to preserve the natural and cultural environments that sustain them. By acknowledging the interconnectedness of all beings, leaders can promote mutual appreciation, collaborative problem-solving, and shared progress.

This passage also teaches us that true leaders, wherever in the universe they are from, they, by the nature of their existences care deeply for the Tao, the underlying principle of all existence. By prioritizing this cosmic harmony, leaders from this world and others can extend their care to all living beings, the environment, and the broader universe and cosmos. By caring for all things, leaders can transcend selfish motivations and act as compassionate stewards of the universe. This approach paves the way for sustainable practices, empathy, and a deeper understanding of our interconnectedness with ET/NHIs throughout the multiverse.

Conclusion

In a world that has expanded its horizons to include encounters with other worlds and cultures, the integration of the Tao Te Ching's teachings becomes ever more crucial. By incorporating the Tao and its Integral Way as their own internal operating procedures, these newly encountered or disclosed entities demonstrate a profound understanding of the necessity for harmonious coexistence and enlightened leadership.

By honoring and incorporating the principles of the Tao the eternal underlying source and force that creates and governs all existence and its universal and Integral Way into our interactions with other worlds and cultures, we can create common ground and an atmosphere of mutual respect, trust, genuine curiosity, and cooperation. This approach serves as a foundation for building lasting relationships that transcend boundaries and promotes a world where diverse civilizations thrive through interconnectedness, co-reliance and the pursuit of their collective well-being.

Finally, in our post-extraterrestrial contact world, leadership must out of necessity change the paradigm of control and power and adapt to the evolving landscape of the intelligently populated universe. The Tao Te Ching and the Integral Way serve as a timely and relevant guide, offering a persuasive alternative approach to leadership and governance both here and on other worlds. By allowing things to take their course, embracing humility, and prioritizing the care for all things, leaders here on earth and throughout the cosmos can navigate the challenges and opportunities of our time, fostering a world that resonates with peace, wisdom, freedom and prosperity for all and ultimately our individual and societal spiritual growth.

CHAPTER 65

"Subtle Insight", Learning and Learning How to
Govern, "Principled Self-Governance", The Tao
Te Ching, The New Paradigm for Leadership on
Earth in a Post-Extraterrestrial Contact World

THE MASTERS OF ANCIENT TIMES
ATTEMPTED NOT TO EDUCATE PEOPLE,
BUT WITH KINDNESS
THEY TAUGHT THEM TO NOT-KNOW.

WHEN ONES THINK THEY KNOW AN ANSWER,
GUIDING THEM IS DIFFICULT.

WHEN A ONE KNOWS THAT ONE DOES NOT KNOW,
THEN ONE CAN FIND ONE'S OWN WAY.

IF LEARNING HOW TO GOVERN IS WHAT ONE
WANTS TO LEARN,
THEY SHOULD THEN AVOID BEING RICH OR CLE-
VER.

CLEAREST IS THE MOST SIMPLE OF PATTERNS.

WHEN ONE IS CONTENT IN AN ORDINARY LIFE,
THEY CAN SHOW THE WAY TO ALL PEOPLE.
THAT WILL RETURN THEM
TO THEIR OWN TRUE NATURE.

The Power of Humility in Leadership: Embracing the Lessons of the Tao Te Ching

In today's rapidly changing world, effective leadership has become a crucial necessity especially as our world passes from a terrestrial to an interstellar one. As we navigate the complexities of a post-extraterrestrial contact era, it becomes essential for leaders to explore alternative paradigms for governing. As a new dawn in human civilization arises, the ancient wisdom found in the Tao Te Ching offers valuable insights for leaders seeking a new approach to leadership and governance on Earth. Specifically, in Chapter 65, Lao Tzu focuses on "Subtle Insight", Learning and Learning How to Govern and "Principled Self-Governance," which emphasize the power of humility in leadership.

The masters of ancient times understood that true education does not come from bombarding people with knowledge but rather from fostering an attitude of open-mindedness and humility. They taught people to admit their ignorance and embrace a state of "not-knowing" as a means of being receptive to new knowledge and thereby unlocking their true potential. This emphasis on humility challenges the conventional notion that leaders must have all the answers. They do not and cannot. Beware the government that thinks it does. What happens when it confronts a situation where it simply does not? The same is true with people. Instead of professed omniscience, the Tao encourages leaders to acknowledge their limitations and foster an environment that values continuous learning, discussion, and growth.

When individuals become overly confident in their knowledge, guiding them becomes a formidable task. The Tao Te Ching suggests that leaders who understand the limits of their own knowledge are better equipped to guide others effectively. By cultivating a sense of true humility, leaders create space for alternative perspectives and encourage collaborative decision-making. Such leaders empower their people and teams and foster an environment where diverse ideas can be discussed and flourish, ultimately leading to more innovative and effective solutions for all involved and impacted.

In the pursuit of learning how to govern, the Tao Te Ching advises leaders to eschew material wealth and cleverness. This seemingly counterintuitive advice underscores the importance of prioritizing the well-being of others over personal gain. By not becoming ensnared in the pursuit of wealth and power, leaders can concentrate on developing clear, ethical patterns of behavior. Honesty, transparency, compassion, and simplicity empower leaders to exemplify virtuous lives and decision-making and inspire others to do the same.

Finding contentment in an ordinary life allows leaders to be a beacon of light and show the way to all people. It is through embracing true humility and finding fulfillment in the present moment that leaders can connect with their own true nature. By embodying authenticity and the Tao, leaders can inspire others to tap into their unique potential, fostering a culture of individual growth and collective harmony.

In conclusion, Lao Tzu and the Tao Te Ching offer profound insights into leadership and governance that are particularly relevant in our post-extraterrestrial contact world. By embracing the Tao and the power of its humility, leaders can create an environment that values open-mindedness, collaborative decision-making, and ethically driven behavior. As we navigate the complexities of this new era, let us look to the ancient wisdom found in the Tao Te Ching to guide our approach to leadership and governance, and in doing so, we can usher in a new paradigm of leadership on Earth that will have its effect in the hearts of all this planet's inhabitants and throughout the universe.

CHAPTER 66

Natural Humility and True Leadership: The Tao
Te Ching, The New Paradigm for Leadership and
Governance on Earth in a Post-Extraterrestrial
Contact World

UNTO THE SEA
DO ALL STREAMS FLOW.

BECAUSE IT IS LOWER,
THE HUMILITY OF THE OCEAN
BESTOWS UPON IT ITS GREAT POWER.

IF TO GOVERN PEOPLE
IS WHAT ONE WANTS,
THEN ONE MUST PLACE ONESELF
BENEATH THEM.

IF TO LEAD A PEOPLE,
IS WHAT ONE WANTS,
HOW TO FOLLOW THEM
IS WHAT ONE MUST LEARN.

ABOVE THE PEOPLE IS THE MASTER'S PLACE,
YET THERE ARE NONE WHO FEEL OPPRESSED.
SHOULD THE MASTER GO AHEAD OF THE PEOPLE,
NONE FEEL MANIPULATED.

GRATEFUL IS THE WORLD TO THE MASTER.
BECAUSE THE MASTER COMPETES WITH NO ONE,
NONE CAN COMPETE WITH HER.

Natural Humility and True Leadership: Embracing a New Paradigm for Leadership in a Post-Extraterrestrial Contact World

In a constantly evolving world, the role of leadership has become paramount in guiding societies towards progress and prosperity. However, as we delve deeper into the realms of leadership, we discover a unique perspective that places humility at its core. In this passage, Lao Tzu explores the concept of natural humility as the essence of true leadership. We can draw inspiration from this chapter of the Tao Te Ching and the idea of a post-extraterrestrial contact world. Consequently, we can delve into the importance of genuine humility, its transformative power, and how it defines authentic leadership in an age when the old values of power, leadership and governance over humanity can no longer really apply.

The Humility of the Ocean: Unveiling True Power

The age-old wisdom holds true – "Unto the sea do all streams flow." In its vastness, the humble ocean exhibits immense power, derived exactly from its lower position. Similarly, true leadership stems from acknowledging and embracing similar natural humility. By humbling oneself, leaders tap into a wellspring of strength and authority that resonates with followers, paving the way for true influence.

Placing Oneself Beneath the People: The Art of Governance

To govern people effectively, leaders must position themselves beneath them. This inversion of power dynamics provides leaders with a clearer understanding of the needs, challenges, and aspirations of those whom they serve. By prioritizing the well-being of their constituents, true leaders, foster a sense of trust and unity, setting the stage for initiative in themselves and others as well as sustainable progress into the future.

Learning How to Follow: Nurturing True Leadership

The desire to lead should go hand in hand with the willingness to learn how to follow. True leaders understand that their positions of authority should not alienate them from their followers' experiences and struggles. By actively listening, observing, empathizing with and working along side of those whom they lead, leaders create authentic and lasting bonds and connections, forging a path towards shared visions and goals and a promising future together.

Embracing the Master's Place: Inspiring Without Oppressing

While leaders may find themselves in a position of authority, it is crucial that they do not oppress or manipulate their followers. True leaders excel in guiding without force and inspiring without coercion. By embodying natural humility, they lead by example and create an environment where individuals feel empowered, fostering a culture of shared growth and innovation.

The Gratitude of the World: The Ripple Effect of Humble Leadership

When leaders embrace natural humility, they transcend the limitations of competition and comparison. By prioritizing collaboration and cooperation, they create an ecosystem of gratitude and appreciation. This mindset ripples beyond their immediate sphere of influence, inspiring a collective shift towards a more humble, inclusive, and compassionate world, one that balances itself within a universe where the higher authority of the Tao governs.

Conclusion

In a world often driven by ego and competition, the wisdom of the Tao Te Ching teaches us the enduring value of natural humility in effective leadership. In a post extraterrestrial contact world, the paradigm of leadership is ultimately due for a transformative shift. True power is not about domination and manipulation, but about uplifting others. Natural humility emerges as the cornerstone of true leadership, blending authority with honesty, simplicity, patience and influence with empathy and compassion. True leadership fosters trust, creates harmonious environments, and empowers individuals to achieve their full potential.

By placing oneself beneath the people, embracing the Integral Way and its art of leadership and governance, and by nurturing the willingness to learn, leaders can contribute to a peaceful and progressive society. The gratitude received from the world and the universe becomes an affirmation of the transformative power of humble leadership. As we embark on this new chapter of leadership on Earth, let us embody true leadership by embracing the power of natural humility and heed the wisdom of Lao Tzu: "Because the master competes with no one, none can compete with her.

CHAPTER 67

THE SOURCE OF BEING: The "Three
Treasures": Simplicity, Patience and Compassion,
"Returning to the Source of Being",
"According Oneself With the Way Things Are",
Self-Compassion

IT IS SAID BY SOME
THAT THESE TEACHINGS OF MINE ARE NONSEN-
SE.
BY OTHERS, IT IS SAID,
THAT THESE TEACHINGS ARE TOO LOFTY AND
NOT PRACTICAL.

FOR THOSE WHO LOOK WITHIN THEMSELVES
THOUGH,
THAT WHICH OTHERS SAY IS "NONSENSE" MAKES
PERFECT SENSE.

WHEN ONE PUTS THE TAO INTO PRACTICE,
ONE FINDS THAT ITS "LOFTY" ROOTS RUN DEEP.

THERE ARE ONLY THREE THINGS THAT I HAVE
TO TEACH.
THESE ARE "SIMPLICITY, PATIENCE AND COM-
PASSION".
OF ALL TREASURES, THESE THREE ARE THE
GREATEST.

WHEN ONE BECOMES SIMPLE IN THEIR
THOUGHTS AND ACTION
THEY RETURN TO "THE SOURCE OF BEING".

WHEN ONE IS PATIENT WITH BOTH ENEMIES AND FRIENDS ALIKE, ONE ACCORDS ONESELF WITH THE WAY THINGS ARE.

WHEN ONE IS COMPASSIONATE TOWARDS ONE-SELF, THEY RECONCILE THEMSELVES WITH ALL THE WORLD'S BEINGS.

Embracing the Three Treasures: Unlocking the Essence of the Source of Being

In the world of philosophy and spirituality, there often arise differing opinions on the validity and practicality of certain teachings. The teachings that Lao Tzu explores here revolve around the core Tao concepts of simplicity, patience, and compassion. They captivate some and are dismissed by others. However, for those willing to delve deeper and look within themselves, the purported "nonsense" suddenly reveals profound wisdom and makes undeniable sense. By embracing these teachings and recognizing their transformative power and by highlighting their significance in achieving personal growth and cultivating harmonious relationships we can create a deeper connection with the world, those in it and in the universe around us.

Simplicity: The Gateway to the Source of Being

"Our life is frittered away by detail. Simplify, simplify...Simplicity, simplicity, simplicity! I say, let your affairs be as two or three, and not a hundred or a thousand; instead of a million count half a dozen, and keep your accounts on your thumb nail." ~ Henry David Thoreau

The concept of simplicity serves as a guiding principle for untangling the complexities of life. Simplicity is transcendental. By cultivating simplicity in our thoughts and actions, we align ourselves with the source of being, the Tao. Simplicity liberates us from the distractions and burdens that hinder our personal growth and understanding. It leads to clarity, profound self-awareness, and the realization that true fulfillment lies not in accumulating material possessions, but in embracing the truth and essence of our own being. This awareness is the beginning of enlightenment. This is the awareness from which all other awareness extends.

Patience: Harmonizing with the Way Things Are

"Between stimulus and response there is a space. In that space is the power to choose our response." ~ Viktor Frankl

Patience, oftentimes underrated, is a virtue that holds tremendous power to transform our lives. By exercising patience towards both adversaries and allies alike, we attain self control and a state of peace and harmony. Patience allows us to step back from conflicts, observe with a calm perspective, and respond in a manner that aligns with the natural order of things. Through patience, we learn empathy, enhance our listening and problem-solving skills, and can foster deep and meaningful relationships with those with whom we come in contact. With patience we accord ourselves with the Tao and the way things are. Patience is the virtue that others can easily see and understand in action, thereby making one who exhibits it easy to emulate. It is the source of great leadership and governance.

Compassion: Reconciling with All Beings

"Compassion is the wish to see others free from suffering."
~ Dalai Lama

Compassion, the noblest expression of our humanity, is a force born of the Tao that dissolves ego, eliminates boundaries, connects us with the present and unifies us with the tapestry of existence. Self-compassion is important but little understood in its value. Self-compassion is necessary because if we cannot apply unconditional compassion to ourselves first, like the oxygen mask that drops out over our heads if there is depressurizing turbulence in an airplane flight, we cannot hope to ably help those who may be seated next to us. By cultivating compassion towards ourselves and others, we unlock the immense potential within us to create a world filled with empathy, understanding, and love. Compassion brings us closer to the realization of the interconnectedness of all living beings, terrestrial, extraterrestrial, and otherwise and our connection with them. Compassion enables us to transcend our fear of others and our egocentric outlook to embrace the shared human and non-human experience of divine being and presence with all the inhabitants of all the universe's heavenly realms.

Conclusion

In a world that often values complexity over simplicity and quick fixes over patience, the timeless teachings in the Tao Te Ching in general and in this passage in particular, provide much-needed guidance for the values we need in order to live a more fulfilling, rewarding, spiritually evolved and purposeful life. By living lives of uncompromising truth and by recognizing the profound wisdom encapsulated within the three treasures of simplicity, patience, and unconditional and non-discriminating compassion, we can unleash our inner potential, cultivate meaningful relationships, and attune ourselves with the Tao and to its vibrant tapestry of existence. Let us fully embrace these three treasures and with the absolute truth of the Tao as our polestar, embark on a lifelong journey towards peace, self-discovery and natural harmony. There, we can accord ourselves with the way things are and the realization of the Tao as the source of our own being and that of all living things in the world and in the cosmos beyond.

CHAPTER 68

"True Greatness", The Tao Te Ching, The New
Paradigm for Leadership and Governance on
Earth in a Post-Extraterrestrial Contact World

THE GREATEST ATHLETE WANTS OPPONENTS
TO BE AT THEIR BEST.

THE GREATEST GENERAL ENTERS INTO THE
MIND
OF HIS ENEMY.

THE GREATEST BUSINESSMAN SERVES THE COM-
MON GOOD OF ALL.

THE GREATEST LEADERS FOLLOW THE WILL OF
THE PEOPLE

THE BEST ATHLETE, GREATEST GENERAL AND
GREATEST BUSINESSMEN
ARE THE EMBODIMENT OF NON-COMPETITION
AS A VIRTUE.

IT IS NOT THAT THEIR LOVE OF COMPETITION
WANES,
BUT THAT THEY ENGAGE COMPETITION IN THE
SPIRIT OF PLAY.

LIKE CHILDREN IN THIS ARE THEY. AND SO, THEY
ARE HARMONIOUS WITH THE TAO.

> "The first and most pressing problem is how to do away
> with warfare as a method of solving conflicts."
> ~ Margaret Mead

The Power of Non-Competition: A Paradigm Shift for True Leadership in a Post Extraterrestrial Contact World

In a world marked by advanced technologies and global interconnectivity, the concept of leadership has undergone a profound transformation. As humanity moves towards a post-extraterrestrial contact era, the traditional perspective of leadership as driven solely by competition needs to be reevaluated. In this passage Lao Tzu explores the notion of non-competition as a virtue and argues that the greatest athletes, generals, businessmen, and leaders embody this paradigm shift.

The true greatness of athletes, generals, businessmen, and leaders is not determined by their ability to dominate and defeat others, but by their capacity to foster unity, collaboration, and the common good in a spirit of play.

The Greatest Athlete

Contrary to popular belief, the greatest athletes do not seek to crush their opponents but desire them to be at their best. By embracing non-competition, and turning the competition inward, athletes compete against themselves to improve each day. When they do this, they inspire others to push their limits as well, leading to greater achievements and an overall elevation of the sport itself. A game or a match is not one athlete proving his superiority over an opponent but the level of self-improvement and ability to demonstrate mastery that he or she has achieved. Because of this each approaches competition as a form of play, where the primary objective is personal growth and the pursuit of excellence each great athlete pushes themselves so much that he or she pushes the bar of excellence up and up and up from the dome of the known out and beyond to master the things that have yet to be mastered.

The Greatest General

War is the ultimate result of the failure of diplomacy. Every wise general understands that only thistles grow where the wagons of war tread. The greatest generals know the risk of war for both them and their enemies. Great generals, therefore, do not simply overpower their foes, but strive to understand them on a deeper level. It is better to have a friend and ally than an enemy. By entering into the mind of the enemy, they gain insight into their needs, motivations, strategies, and weaknesses, allowing for more informed decision-making. This empathetic approach to leadership encourages understanding, diplomacy, compassion, conflict resolution, and the pursuit of peaceful solutions instead of resorting to unnecessary aggression in solving conflicts.

The Greatest Businessperson

It has long been said that a rising tide floats all boats. The greatest businesspeople recognize that true success lies in serving the common good of all, rather than solely pursuing personal gain. By prioritizing the needs and well-being of all stakeholders, they create harmonious relationships, sustainable business practices, and a positive impact on society. They understand that genuine prosperity comes from uplifting others and fostering a cooperative environment, rather than engaging in cutthroat competition.

The Greatest Leaders

The greatest leaders are those who follow the will of the people, embracing a free, democratic and inclusive approach to governance. They recognize that leadership is a collective endeavor, and decisions should reflect the aspirations and values of those they lead. By empowering others, listening to diverse perspectives, and fostering collaboration and the free flow of ideas, they create a sense of unity and shared responsibility within their families, businesses, communities and societies wherever they may be.

Conclusion

In a post-extraterrestrial contact world, where humanity faces unprecedented challenges and opportunities, a new paradigm of leadership is required. The approach of Lao Tzu is different than the approach we have taken in the modern world. Though the Tao and the Tao Te Ching may appear parallel to the failed modern approaches the Taoist approach proposed by Lao Tzu is potentially far more useful a system and basic underlying structure of reality than that which has so deeply influenced both the East and West and has resulted in a failure to peacefully resolve conflicts to the point where it has become an atomic existential threat to mankind and this planet.

To follow the Tao is to transform ourselves so that we and our lives and the people, places and things around us get better and better and better. The greatest athletes, generals, businessmen, and leaders exemplify non-competition as a virtue, emphasizing unity, collaboration, and the compassion universally towards a shared common good. By embracing competition in the spirit of play, they reach their own full potential and inspire others to reach their own full potential and to go beyond as well. Great leaders foster understanding and empathy. With their compassion they prioritize the well-being of all. It is through this transformative approach to leadership that those we choose as our leaders and who undertake to govern us can build a harmonious framework for conflict resolution and a collaborative and prosperous future for our world us and those in the universe beyond.

CHAPTER 69

Moving Forward Without Advancement, Repelling Without Force, Underestimating an Enemy, The importance of Keeping One's "Three Treasures", The Tao Te Ching, the New Paradigm for Leadership and Governance on Earth in a Post-Extraterrestrial Contact World

AMONG GENERALS THERE IS A SAYING THAT
IT IS BETTER FOR ONE TO WAIT AND OBSERVE
RATHER THAN FOR ONE TO MAKE THE FIRST
MOVE.

IT ALSO IS SAID THAT THERE IS GREATER ADVAN-
TAGE
FOR ONE TO RETREAT A YARD RATHER THAN TO
ADVANCE ONE INCH.

THIS IS KNOWN AS "MOVING FORWARD, WIT-
HOUT ADVANCEMENT",
AND "PUSHING BACK AND WITHOUT THE USE OF
WEAPONS".

NO GREATER MISFORTUNE CAN BELIE ONE
THAN TO UNDERESTIMATE ONE'S OWN ENEMY.
"UNDERESTIMATING ONE'S ENEMY"
MEANS TO THINK OF ONE'S ENEMY AS EVIL.

THUS WHEN ONE THINKS AN ENEMY
TO BE EVIL ONE DESTROYS ONE'S OWN THREE
TREASURES

(SIMPLICITY, PATIENCE AND COMPASSION) AND BECOMES AN ENEMY UNTO HIMSELF.

WHEN TWO POWERFUL FORCES FACE EACH OTHER,
TO THE ONE THAT KNOWS HOW TO YIELD DOES VICTORY GO.

The Tao: Embracing a New Paradigm for Leadership in a Post-Extraterrestrial Contact World

In a rapidly evolving world, the concept of traditional leadership needs to be reevaluated. Our encounter with extraterrestrial beings has brought forth new challenges and opportunities, requiring a shift in perspective and in our approaches to leadership and governance. In this chapter of Lao Tzu's teachings, we can explore and see the importance of embracing a new paradigm for leadership that emphasizes observation over impulsiveness, retreat over blind advancement and acknowledges the significance of the "Three Treasures" – simplicity, patience, and compassion and integrates them into our societal and diplomatic encounters. By incorporating the principles of the Tao into our leadership practices, we can cultivate a harmonious approach that moves beyond the limitations of control, conflict and aggression, fosters understanding and ultimately achieves sustainable success in human and non-human relations in a post-extraterrestrial contact world.

Moving Forward Without Advancement: The Power of Observation

There is true power in restraint. According to Lau Tzu's wisdom, it is wiser to wait and observe rather than make the first move. This principle reminds us of the importance of patience, information gathering and analysis, and understanding others in our decision-making. Leaders who embody this philosophy are more likely to gather valuable insights, identify and avoid potential risks, and devise effective strategies for success. By embracing this approach, they avoid rushing into unnecessary conflicts, promote collaborative solutions, and foster a climate of immediate mutual respect and eventual trust.

Repelling Without Force: The Art of Strategic Retreat

The sage advice of retreating a yard rather than advancing an inch teaches us the value of humility and the art of non-aggression. Leaders who prioritize retreat over blind advancement recognize the significance of preserving resources and relationships. By stepping back, reassessing situations, and regaining perspective, they can strategically navigate challenges, avoiding unnecessary confrontations. This approach allows them to maintain their strength while opening doors to diplomatic resolutions, demonstrating adaptability, and earning the trust and respect of allies and adversaries alike.

Understanding the Enemy: Overcoming Underestimation

Underestimating an enemy is one of the gravest mistakes in leadership one can make. By labeling adversaries as enemies, unlike themselves or purely evil, leaders lose sight of the oneness and interrelatedness of all things and their own "Three Treasures" – simplicity, patience, and compassion. True understanding requires acknowledging the complexity of human experience and refraining from labeling and hasty judgments. Leaders who approach their enemies with an open mind and heart retain their empathy and retain the capacity to seek common ground and peaceful resolutions. This compassionate perspective fosters collaboration, reduces tension, and creates an environment conducive to cooperation and growth.

Yielding for Victory: The Power of Adaptability

It has long been said that it is better to bend than to break. When two powerful forces clash, victory favors the one who knows how to yield. This insight challenges the conventional notion of dominance and encourages leaders to exercise caution, flexibility, adaptability, and foresight. Instead of fixating on a single path, leaders who prioritize negotiation and the ability to yield understand the need for compromise and agreement that support mutually beneficial outcomes. By embracing this paradigm, leaders foster peace, harmony and cultivate long-term relationships with people and cultures who would otherwise be considered foes, surpassing the limitations of brute force and might. By yielding, bending and not breaking those who lead us and govern in a post ET/NHI contact world can ensure sustainable success and positive common futures for mankind and our new partnerships with the other peaceful and advanced beings of the universe.

Conclusion

As we venture into a post-extraterrestrial contact world, it is crucial to reevaluate our approach to leadership. By heeding the wisdom of the Tao Te Ching, we can usher in a new paradigm that prioritizes observation, diplomacy, negotiation, strategic retreat, understanding, and adaptability. These principles promote a harmonious and inclusive leadership style that sparks collaboration, enhances empathy, and drives sustainable progress that benefits all beings. As we transcend the limitations of aggression in leadership and governance and embrace the holistic wisdom of the Tao, we can navigate the complexities of our evolving world within a very diverse and complicated universe with magnanimity, unanimity, peace, grace and wisdom.

The old ways of doing things were and are too primitive for the more highly advanced ET/NHI civilizations throughout the cosmos. If we have any hope of peacefully and productively interfacing with them, the mindset of analyzing every interfacing as a possible threat and cause for conflict promotes nothing but fear and xenophobia and our needless resort to armed conflict. It is time that we, like those ET/NHIx with whom we make contact, adopt the Tao and its universal truths and values as the universal paradigm for leadership and governance in the expanded universe that is now unfolding around us.

CHAPTER 70

Extraterrestrials and Non-Human Intelligences,
Within the Heart Beats the Flame of Connection
and the Light of Understanding

EASILY UNDERSTOOD ARE MY TEACHINGS.
AND EASILY ARE THEY PUT INTO PRACTICE.

ONE'S INTELLECT
WILL NEVER TRULY GRASP THEM.
IF ONE TRIES TO PRACTICE THEM
(INTELLECTUALLY) ONE WILL FAIL.

OLDER THAN THE WORLD ARE MY TEACHINGS,
BUT HOW CAN THEIR MEANING BE GRASPED?

IF ONE WANTS TO KNOW ME,
ONE SHOULD LOOK INSIDE
OF ONE'S OWN HEART.

Introduction

In the quest for knowledge and understanding, humanity has
always been intrigued by the possibility of extraterrestrial life
(ET) and intelligences (NHI) beyond our own. Over the course
of time both have proven their reality by manifesting themselves to both primitive societies here on earth and to mankind
in the present day. The chapter above provides profound teachings that the exploration of which offer us a unique perspective
on this concept. By considering the proposition of the reality
of both terrestrial and extraterrestrial life and the ideas voiced
in this chapter, we can delve into the ancient wisdom of the
Tao Te Ching, exploring its significance and adaptation to

ET/NHI in our own present reality, and ultimately allow us to decide how to embrace the idea of this integral connection and to explore it for our own benefit and for theirs as well.

The Profound Connection Between Humanity and Extraterrestrial Intelligences: Unveiling the Secrets Within

There is, has been and will continue to be a profound connection between humanity and extraterrestrial and non-human intelligences. In order to realize and embrace the concept of this integral connection between humanity and these beings and their intelligences, it is essential for us to tap into the universal human desire for knowledge, exploration, understanding and unity. The profound impact that such a realization and desire can have on our collective consciousness fosters a sense of wonder and awe that transcends borders, cultures, and differences. The enormous potential benefits of recognizing this connection, includes not only expanded horizons trade and obvious technological advancements, but creates a deeper understanding of our own spiritual nature and our own place in the universe. By exploring the teachings of Lao Tzu in the passage above, we can discover a profound spiritual connection between humanity and extraterrestrial and non-human intelligences, leading us to a deeper understanding of ourselves, them and the universe.

Exploring the Teachings

The teachings of Lao Tzu in this chapter are described as 'easily understood yet difficult to grasp' intellectually. This paradox highlights the depth and complexity of the message, urging us to look into our hearts and beyond our intellect. By emphasizing the importance of practice rather than mere intellectual understanding, the teachings of Lao Tzu encourage us to embrace a holistic approach to knowledge and spiritual growth. The timeless nature of these teachings suggests that the nature and concept of extraterrestrial intelligences have been understood since ancient times, involving a wisdom that transcends human generations and, like the heart, time and space itself. It is no wonder that as time goes on, research and investigation in these areas outside of the orthodoxy of modern academia are taking place and curiosity and understanding are growing by leaps and bounds.

Unveiling the Meaning

The question arises: How can we truly grasp the meaning hidden within these teachings? The teachings here suggest that looking inside our own hearts is the key to understanding. This implies that, like the Tao, the connection between humanity and extraterrestrial intelligences lies within us, waiting to be discovered. By cultivating self-awareness, empathy, awareness of others, compassion and the Tao and embracing the interconnectedness of all beings, we can unlock the true meaning and bridge the gap between ourselves and extraterrestrial and non-human intelligences no matter from where these beings hail.

The Conviction of Connection

Rather than allowing our ego's fear to dominate, our new ET/NHI interface we will need to embrace the concept of an integral connection between humanity and extraterrestrial intelligences. In such an interface it is crucial to appeal to our innate and universal desires for knowledge, exploration, unity, understanding and peace and to cautiously reproach the old paradigms of control, violence and power in our contact and negotiations with these very powerful and technologically and spiritually evolved entities.

Universal Human Desire

Humans are naturally curious beings, driven by a thirst for knowledge and a deep-rooted desire to explore and understand the unknown. This innate human curiosity transcends borders, cultures and differences. The potential impact of recognizing the connection between humanity and extraterrestrial and non-human intelligences can foster a sense of wonder and awe that transcends all barriers, even space and time as we have traditionally understood these concepts. This realization has the power to unite humanity and ET, emphasizing our shared origins in the Tao, and bringing all intelligent spiritual beings together in their quest for understanding and unity within the universal consciousness that is the Tao.

When individuals grasp the harmony and interdependence between humanity and extraterrestrial and non-human intelligences, it can have a deeply significant impact on the collective consciousness of us all. This newfound awareness can elevate human consciousness, leading to a shift in perspectives and fostering a sense of design and purpose and our interconnectedness with all beings in the universe. Recognizing the connection between humanity and extraterrestrial intelligences opens exciting possibilities for exploration and literally expands our horizons. It ignites the desire to venture beyond the boundaries of our own planet, enabling us to embark on new journeys of discovery, pushing the limits of human knowledge and understanding as far as they can possibly go.

Embracing the concept of a profound connection can also lead to technological advancements. The exchange of knowledge and ideas between humanity and extraterrestrial and non-human intelligences could propel scientific and technological progress to new heights. This, in turn would unlock innovations that benefit not only our understanding of the universe but also our daily lives and collective futures.

Finally, the connection between humanity and extraterrestrial and non-human intelligences provides us with a deeper understanding of our own shared spiritual nature and of our true being, function and place in the vast cosmos. It enables us to grasp the interconnectedness of all species and beings, emphasizing our shared existence and collective responsibility for the preservation and well-being of our home planet and the universe as a whole.

Conclusion

The teachings of Lao Tzu in this passage shed light on the integral Tao connection between humanity and extraterrestrial and non-human intelligences. By encouraging us to venture beyond intellect and explore the depths of our hearts, these teachings offer a path towards a deeper ontological understanding of ourselves ET/NHIs and the universe. If we want to peacefully evolve as a species and as a planet and get along with others, we need to embrace this concept to foster a unity that traverses boundaries, fuels exploration, and expands all of our horizons to the stars and beyond.

By highlighting the universal human desire for knowledge, exploration, unity and understanding, we can embrace the profound integral connection between humanity and extraterrestrial and non-human intelligences. The transformative impact that this can have on our collective consciousness, can foster a sense of wonder and awe, and underscore the potential benefits such as expanded horizons, technological advancements, and a deeper understanding of our place in the universe. The results will be immeasurable. Let us together embark on this journey of connection and discovery and as we begin this part of our inevitable journey toward enlightenment and social evolution and seeking to understand our other Tao brothers and sisters of the universe, let us remember the Tao's own message: "If one wants to know me, one should look inside of one's own heart."

CHAPTER 71

How the Master Becomes Whole

TRUE KNOWLEDGE LIES IN ONE NOT KNOWING. IT IS A DISEASE TO PRESUME TO KNOW.

ONE MUST FIRST BE AWARE THAT ONE IS SICK SO THAT ONE MAY ADVANCE ONE'S OWN HEALTH.

THE MASTER IS THE MASTER'S OWN PHYSICIAN. BECAUSE THE MASTER HAS HEALED HERSELF OF THE DISEASE OF BEING ALL KNOWING, THUSLY, THE MASTER IS TRULY WHOLE.

The Journey to Wholeness: How the Master Becomes Whole

In our pursuit of a fulfilling life, a path of true meaning emerges in the ancient philosophy of the Tao. The Tao encompasses the principles of balance, harmony, and interconnectedness, offering valuable insights on how we can achieve a state of wholeness. Those who seek mastery of the Tao embark on a transformative journey towards their own mastery of becoming whole. By delving into the essence of the Tao, examining the process of mastery, and showcasing its remarkable effects, we can shed light on the profound impact that embracing the Tao can have on an individual's sense of self and purpose and understanding their fate and role in the universe.

Understanding the Tao

To comprehend how the master becomes whole, it is crucial to first grasp the significance of the Tao. Rooted in ancient Chinese thought, the Tao represents the natural order of the universe, emphasizing the integration of opposing forces and the cultivation of harmony within oneself and one's environment. This ancient wisdom as recorded by Lao Tzu encourages individuals to reconcile polarity and align themselves with the rhythm of the cosmos and seek unity themselves and that diversity.

The Path to Mastery

Becoming a master of the Tao is not a destination but a lifelong journey. If there is a destination, each step is a destination within itself. Masters embody the principles of the Tao through diligent practice, self-reflection, self-cultivation, discipline and continuous growth. They work to cultivate balance in all aspects of life, embracing the interplay of yin and yang, action and non-action, affinity and distance, effort and surrender. Through contemplation and meditative mindfulness, and the study of texts of the ancient masters, new masters can deepen their understanding of the Tao and its sometimes-enigmatic presentations and meanings and refine their ability to understand and harmonize with it.

Transformation Towards Wholeness

The process of mastering the Tao propels individuals towards a deeply felt and thorough transformation. As masters become more attuned to the natural flow of existence, they begin shedding the shackles of ego, discord, and fragmentation. By embracing the Tao, they can navigate the complexities of life with wisdom, patience, equanimity, magnanimity, and compassion. The mastery of the Tao allows us to transcend limiting beliefs, resolve our inner conflicts, and reconnect with our true selves, resulting in a profound sense of wholeness, connection and the infinite.

The reflection by Lao Tzu in the passage above highlights the deep wisdom embedded in the journey towards mastery of the Tao and becoming whole. It emphasizes the importance of true humility, self-awareness, and the recognition of our limitations in the pursuit of knowledge and growth. To know everything is to not know enough. To know everything is the disease of a closed mid. To know nothing is the best place at which to start. One who knows everything simply cannot learn or be taught.

The notion that true knowledge lies in not knowing suggests that an open and receptive mind allows for the continual exploration and acquisition of knowledge for the purpose of understanding and integration into how we see the world and universe. When we presume to know everything, we limit ourselves and hinder the possibility of further learning and growth. It is in acknowledging our own limitations, our own "sickness" and embracing a state of curiosity, openness and a willingness to learn that we can truly expand our understanding.

The analogy of a disease is used to convey the idea that presuming to know everything is an illness detrimental to our personal development and growth. Just as one must recognize illness to seek healing, acknowledging the limitations of our knowledge is essential to dissolving our egos, and fostering our own growth and advancement. This awareness prompts us to cultivate a desire for self-improvement, leading to a healthier state of mind and an overall state of wellbeing.

By becoming our own physician, we take personal responsibility for our own growth and well-being. The master, having undergone the process of healing and letting go of the ego-based disease of being all-knowing, becomes truly whole. This achievement reflects the transformative power of self-reflection, self-awareness and awareness of others and the Tao and embracing a state of humility and openness that is consistent with the natural way of things.

The Ripple Effect

The effects of the master's transformation from sickness to wellbeing extend beyond their personal journey. Masters who have attained wholeness often become sources of inspiration for others. They radiate a profound sense of peace and authenticity. Their actions and words ripple outwards, fostering harmony and encouraging others to embark on their own paths of self-discovery. By embodying the wholeness attained through mastery of the Tao, these individuals become beacons of light for others who struggle with their own darkness. They contribute to the collective well-being of society, the world and the universe. This effect and its cultivation are something upon which Lao Tzu further educates us in the Hua Hu Ching in some great detail and are addressed in book 2 of this set.

Conclusion

Acknowledging our limitations and embracing a state of not knowing is a vital step towards growth and wholeness. It emphasizes the importance of self-awareness, awareness of others and our awareness of the Tao that unites us all. It highlights the necessity for personal responsibility, and our continuous journey towards enlightenment through learning and spiritual cultivation and refinement.

The journey of how the master becomes whole is a testament to the transformative power of embracing the Tao. Through dedication, self-reflection, and an unwavering commitment to simplicity, patience, compassion and truth that lead to balanced and harmonious lives, individuals on this path embark on a profound and integral transformation. As they shed the layers of ego, arrogance and intentional ignorance and embrace not knowing and their interconnectedness with the universe, an awesome sense of wholeness prevails. This unity with the Tao allows those who become masters of it to navigate their own mental, physical and spiritual health and lives with wisdom, compassion, and grace, inspiring others to embark on their own journeys of self-discovery and healing. By embracing the Tao, we can unlock the pathway to personal well-being, peace, joy, gratitude and fulfillment and an eternal life lived in harmony with the rhythms of the universe and all those beings who live in sync with it.

CHAPTER 72

The Way of the Master

WHEN A PEOPLE'S SENSE OF AWE IS LOST, IT IS TO RELIGION THEY TURN.
WHEN PEOPLE TRUST THEMSELVES NO LONGER UPON AUTHORITY DO THEY BEGIN TO DEPEND.
THE MASTER THEREFORE STEPS BACK SO THAT THE PEOPLE WILL NOT BE CONFUSED.
WITHOUT TEACHING, THE MASTER TEACHES, SO THAT THERE WILL BE NOTHING FOR THE PEOPLE TO LEARN.

The Way of the Master: The Power of Non-Traditional Teaching

In the world of education and leadership, there is a prevalent belief that a teacher must constantly assert their authority and provide explicit instruction. However, the ancient wisdom of the Tao Te Ching challenges this notion, suggesting that true masters step back and allow people to learn without formal teachings. Like doing without doing, non-doing, there are profound philosophical ideas behind the concept of teaching by example, "teaching without teaching". The potential transformative effects of teaching without teaching can have on individuals and societies are immeasurable.

The Shift from Religion to Self-Trust

When individuals lose their sense of awe they turn to blind faith in religion. They also often seek alternative sources of guidance. The Tao Te Ching advocates for a different approach, where the master provides an environment of self-discovery and empowerment, enabling individuals to trust themselves and the

Tao rather than relying on external authority figures. Students are naturally attracted to the energies and pursuits to which they can respond positively and excel based on their own Tao connection. Inevitably it is that internal Tao connection that they will learn to treasure and trust.

The Tao Te Ching asserts that when people lose their sense of awe in the Tao and the universe they turn to traditional religious institutions or alternative forms of spirituality. Rather than relying on the Tao where individuals seek connection and inner wisdom through personal experience and relying on their own Tao natures, especially in times of chaos and turmoil, people inevitably gravitate with the masses towards the prescribed teachings and dogmas of established religions. Unlike priests who direct and gurus who guide, the Tao master's role is to create a space where individuals can reconnect with the Tao and themselves, fostering self-exploration and empowerment.

The Master's Role in Guiding: Teaching without Teaching

The traditional model of teaching often relies on imparting knowledge and information directly to students. In contrast, the Integral Way teaches that masters should step back from direct instruction and allow individuals to learn through their own experiences. By doing so, the master creates an environment where people can gain insights independently, internalize their lessons and ground themselves in their natural pursuits and what they have learned. Ultimately this leads to a deeper understanding, personal transformation and the highest levels of achievement for the student.

The Power of Unlearning

By avoiding conventional teaching methods, the master encourages individuals to unlearn preconceived notions and limitations. Through this process of open-mindedness, individuals can discover their own unique path and tap into their unlimited potential. The absence of explicit teachings allows people to question societal norms, observe for themselves, experiment, experience and develop their own wisdom, leading to personal and spiritual growth and to societal evolution and progress.

The Paradoxical Nature of the Master's Teachings

The role of a teacher is to allow the student to learn, not to indoctrinate. In this passage, Lao Tzu accordingly tells us that without teaching, the master teaches. This paradoxical statement encapsulates the concept that by not imposing knowledge and beliefs onto others, the master creates a space for individuals to learn and grow with genuine curiosity and open-mindedness. It is in this space that the Law of Energy Response* operates for both the teacher and the student. By guiding without guiding and teaching by not teaching, the master through the operation of the Tao, allows for a more profound and transformative learning experience for both the student and the master. Inevitably, the road to mastery is complete when the teacher and the student are indistinguishable.

Conclusion

In a world where blind faith and external authorities often dictate actions, the Tao Te Ching offers an important alternative perspective to institutionalized forms of education so prevalent in human societies. By emphasizing the importance of self-trust and inner wisdom both teachers and students can creatively cultivate their talents and let the flow of the Tao in. By stepping back and creating a space for individuals to learn without walls, restrictive boundaries or explicit teachings, the ever compassionate and patient master teacher enables personal growth for their students and the societal progress that occurs beyond the classroom. The Way of the Master challenges conventional notions of teaching and the indoctrination of students into rigid orthodoxies and formal and dogmatic ways of thinking, inviting us to explore our own unique paths and embrace the power of the Tao within ourselves. It is through this unorthodox approach that free thought, empirical study, true learning and self-discovery can take place and flourish and propel us into a braver, newer world that we ever thought possible.

*Similarly stated in common parlance as the "Law of Attraction", the basic philosophy behind the Law of Energy Response is that energy precedes its manifestation. When we produce positive energies and thoughts, we attract similar thoughts and energies into our lives. Conversely, we are drawn to those energies that most naturally resonate within us and negative thoughts and energies have the opposite effect by producing negative results.

CHAPTER 73

Heaven's Net

AT EASE ALWAYS IS THE TAO.
WITHOUT COMPETING, IT OVERCOMES.
WITHOUT UTTERING A WORD, IT ANSWERS.
WITHOUT SUMMONING, IT ARRIVES.
WITHOUT ANY PLAN, IT ACCOMPLISHES.

THE NET OF THE TAO COVERS THE ENTIRE UNI-
VERSE.
AND EVEN THOUGH ITS MESH IS WIDE
THE TAO ALLOWS NOTHING TO SLIP THROUGH
IT.

The Cosmic Wisdom of the Tao: Embracing the Power of Harmonious Flow

In the realm of ancient philosophy and wisdom traditions, the concept of Tao has long captivated seekers and scholars alike. In this chapter Lao Tzu presents a profound perspective on the way of the Tao shedding light on its inherent wisdom and timeless relevance. By exploring some of its historical underpinnings and its central themes of balance, ease, non-competition, silence, spontaneity, and holistic interconnectedness, we can uncover how the Tao's synchronistic cosmic net serves as a guiding force for the harmonious experience of our own existence.

Historical Context: Unveiling the Origins of the Tao Te Ching

The Tao Te Ching, euphemistically called "The Tao" and named after the entity it seeks to beautifully describe is attributed to Lao Tzu, an ancient Chinese philosopher and the attributed founder of Taoism. The Tao Te Ching emerged during the late Warring States period (475-221 BCE), a tumultuous era marked by political and social instability in China. As a counterpoint to this conflict, chaos and instability, Lao Tzu offered a spiritual and philosophical framework for individuals seeking harmony amidst that chaos. The Tao Te Ching is as relevant today, and probably even more so than it was 2,500 years ago. However brief, Chapter 73 is and remains one of the most renowned chapters within this profound work.

Philosophical Underpinnings: Essence of Taoist Wisdom

Chapter 73 encompasses the core principles of the Tao and the Integral Way, ancient philosophies and approaches to existence that are rooted in embracing the Tao, the natural way of the universe. Followers of the Tao and of the Integral Way believe in the principle of the Tao, representing in the macrocosm, the underlying and unifying force that creates and governs all aspects of existence. In the microcosm, each human being is its own manifestation of the Tao, subject to the same energies and universal laws through which it governs all of its creation. As we know from prior chapters, the Tao is often associated with the concept of balance flow, harmony, and the interconnectedness of all things. Chapter 73 captures the essence of Taoist thought by highlighting key tenets such as non-competition, spontaneity, and embracing the effortless flow of life.

Embracing Ease: The Tao's Natural Flow

In this passage, Lao Tzu teaches us the importance of acting in alignment with the natural flow of the universe. It offers a profound perspective on embracing ease and surrendering to the rhythms of life, allowing us to navigate challenges with grace and tranquility. Lao Tzu emphasizes the importance of effortless action and ease. Unlike conventional wisdom, which often glorifies hard work and struggle, the Tao reveals that true mastery lies in aligning with the natural flow of the universe.

By embracing the principle of ease, we relinquish resistance and allow life to unfold organically. Through this chapter, we learn that by adopting a state of ease, and implicitly by employing Wu Wei, we can navigate life's challenges with grace, tranquility, and experience the synchronicity* that can reveal the Tao at work to us.

Transcending Competition: A Path to Unbounded Potential

In a world driven by competition and comparison, Lao Tzu presents a refreshing alternative. He teaches us that true victory does not come from outdoing others but from transcending competition altogether. By releasing our attachment to labels like winning and losing, we open ourselves up to a realm of infinite possibility. Through the lens of the Tao, we discover that cooperation and collaboration foster growth, innovation, and true fulfillment. In this passage, Lao Tzu invites us to release the tendency to constantly judge and compare ourselves to others and engage in endless rivalry. By transcending competition, we shift our focus from external validation to a state of self-realization, fostering mental, physical and spiritual growth, collaboration and an existential state of individual and universal peace and harmony.

The Power of Silence: Listening to the Wisdom Within

Within the realm of words and noise, Lao Tzu reminds us of the potency of silence. It reveals how the Tao's profound wisdom is often best conveyed in the absence of words. Silence is a very profound and powerful thing. Through the practice of silence, we cultivate stillness within ourselves, creating space to observe and receive the subtle messages of the universe. By listening attentively in silence, we allow the Tao to provide guidance and answers to our deepest questions, leading us towards authentic understanding and inner harmony. By cultivating stillness within us, we let the mud settle and allow our vision to clear. We become receptive to the subtle messages of the universe, allowing the Tao to guide us towards an enlightened true understanding of where we are and what we need to do. This inevitably leads us to better choices and best results scenarios and ultimately to inner peace.

Embracing Spontaneity: Flowing with the Tao

The metaphorical net of the Tao covers the entire universe, allowing nothing to slip through its mesh. This poetic symbolism highlights the interconnectedness through the Tao of all things. It encourages us to not overthink things and embrace the Tao by embracing spontaneity. By relinquishing rigid plans and trusting in the flow of life, we align ourselves with the Tao's innate intelligence, its subtle presence and ability to manifest extraordinary outcomes. When we let go of expectations and engage with the present moment, we become active participants in the grand tapestry of the universe.

Conclusion

In Chapter 73, the enigmatic Heaven's Net holds immense significance within the historical context of Taoist philosophy. Its author, Lao Tzu, offered timeless wisdom during a bloody and turbulent period in Chinese history. This wisdom profoundly affected Chinese wisdom, politics and cultural values and thought for over 1000 years and continues to do so even to today.

Embodied in this chapter of his are the philosophical underpinnings of Taoism and the Integral Way. Lao Tzu emphasizes the natural flow of the Tao through the universe, its complete holistic interconnectedness, the benefits and ease of effortless action, non-competition, silence and spontaneity. By exploring and embracing these themes we align ourselves with the profound wisdom of the Tao and with the Tao itself.

As we integrate these teachings into our daily lives, we not only enhance our own well-being, as we align ourselves with the TAO's boundless wisdom but contribute to the greater harmony of the universe. By rekindling our connection with the Tao and the comprehensive understanding of its impact on both the ancient world and contemporary thought in a new age of ET/NHI contact, we embark on a transformative journey towards inner fulfillment and a deeper understanding and appreciation of the harmonious interconnected nature of our own existence and that of the other sapient and sentient beings who also populate the universe. The Tao Te Ching is, at its core an atlas of the Tao and a handbook on how to relate to each other and to ET/NHIs as our universal brothers and sisters and the more technologically and spiritually advanced progeny of the same universal mother, the Tao.

*Synchronicity: Synchronicity is a term that is used to describe when things happen together, such that their happening is beyond the odds of mere chance and the happening occurs with such frequency that it appears as if it were intelligently and perfectly timed. It is a concept first introduced by ana-lytical psychologist Carl G. Jung to describe circumstances that appear meaningfully related yet lack an otherwise causal connection. Synchronicity is a glimpse into the workings of the almighty so that its existence appears obvious, at least for that moment. It is "the coincidental occurrence of events and especially psychic events (such as similar thoughts in widely separated persons or a mental image of an unexpected event before it happens) that seem related but are not explained by conventional mechanisms of causality —used especially in the psychology of Carl Gustav Jung" ~ Merriam Webster Diction-ary https://www.merriam-webster.com

Synchronicity is the pulling back of the curtain that reveals the presence of the almighty whatever one may call it. Synchronic-ity is a reminder that the Tao is always there behind the scenes orchestrating it simply, patiently and compassionately for all its creation. "'Vocatus atque non vocatus, deus aderit.' - Called or uncalled, God is present. It is a Delphic Oracle, the translation by Erasmus. You ask whether the oracle is my motto. In a way, you see, it contains the entire reality of the psyche...All that I have learned has led me step by step to an unshakeable conviction of the existence of God. I only believe in what I know. And that eliminates believing. Therefore, I do not take his existence on belief. I know he exists." ~ Carl Gustav Jung, Speaking, John Freeman Interview, Page 251

CHAPTER 74

The Master Carpenter

ONCE ONE REALIZES
THAT ALL THINGS ARE SUBJECT TO CHANGE,
THERE IS NOTHING ONTO WHICH ONE MAY
HOLD.

IF ONE HAS NO FEAR OF DEATH
THERE IS NOTHING THAT THEY CANNOT
ACHIEVE.

FOR ONE TO TRY AND CONTROL THE FUTURE,
IS LIKE THE NOVICE TRYING TO TAKE CONTROL
OF THE PLACE OF THE MASTER CARPENTER.
WHEN HE HANDLES THE TOOLS
OF THE MASTER CARPENTER,
THE CHANCES ARE THAT THOSE WHO ARE IN-
EXPERIENCED
WILL CUT THEIR OWN HANDS.

Embracing the Flow of Change: The Art of Letting Go

Change is eternal in life. Change like Karma and the Law of
Energy Response is a universal law. Consequently, the concept
of embracing change and its impermanence and relinquishing
control is central to understanding the Tao and following the
Integral Way. Despite the raging omnipresence of change in
life and in the universe, many individuals struggle with the notion of impermanence. They want things to remain the same.
Change is uncomfortable to them. However, the ancient Taoist
philosophy of Lao Tzu reminds us that by acknowledging and
accepting the transient nature of all things, we can find true
contentment and unlock our full potential. There is therefore,

profound wisdom contained in the verse above highlighting the importance of letting go, overcoming the fear of death, and releasing our grip on the future in order to achieve mastery of the present moment and in the art of living. This passage by Lao Tzu offers profound wisdom that can lead us to our own personal physical, mental and spiritual growth, increase our happiness, and success in life for ourselves and by our example, for others and the entire universe as well.

Embracing Impermanence

Change is eternal. The passage above teaches us that embracing impermanence is the key to inner peace and personal growth. Like a master carpenter who skillfully lets go of their tools and trusts that when he picks them up again, all will still be well, we too must learn to let go of attachments and expectations. By understanding that change is inevitable, we free ourselves from unnecessary suffering and open up space for new possibilities to arise for us to trust the Tao and ourselves to use our old tools and make new ones if necessary for the task at hand. The practice of mindfulness and non-attachment allows us to navigate life's challenges with agility, balance, grace and resilience.

Letting Go of Our Fear of Death

Time is a concept of great importance to the ego. The life of the conscious soul is eternal. So why get upset at having to wait? Why fear death. Death is only a transition that all biological beings must experience because of the physical nature of the being that supports its consciousness in a physical material realm.

The verse reaffirms that when we release ourselves from the confines of our egos and the fear of death, we gain the courage and freedom needed to achieve great things. Time, in a spiritual sense, becomes irrelevant. By confronting our physical mortality head-on, we gain a fresh perspective on life, focusing on what truly matters, and strive towards our goals without inhibition. Whether in personal relationships, career ambitions, or creative pursuits, freeing ourselves from the fear of death liberates and empowers us to take risks, pursue our passions, and achieve extraordinary feats that we would otherwise be unable to accomplish were we to allow ourselves to become paralyzed by the ego's cruel illusion of fear of our inevitable physical death. This life is not all that there is. It is merely our opportunity to work out our karma and to learn and to evolve and refine ourselves spiritually for this and our next incarnation.

As we learned in Chapter 50, it is good to remember in coordinating this verse that the master understands that eventually death will overcome him and that he will have nothing onto which to hold. The mind's illusions will all slip away. His body will surrender and will no longer resist. Because the master has lived in the present he holds nothing back from life. Because he has given all, the master is ready for death, just as one who is ready for sleep after the completion of a full day's work.

The Futility of Trying to Control the Future

This verse reminds us that one must live in the present. There is no other place or time to be. Attempting to control the future is an exercise in futility. Like the novice trying to dominate the master carpenter's domain, our forcing outcomes and attempting to manipulate our destinies only lead to frustration and disappointment. Instead, by being present and being fully in the moment surrendering to the natural flow of life and trusting in the unfolding of events, do we discover the beauty, serendipity and even seen or unseen, the synchronicity inherent in the present moment. This surrender to the energies and natural rhythms of life allows us to tap into our innate intuition and to navigate the ever-changing currents of the river of existence with mastery, grace and ease.

Conclusion

Like Chapter 50, Chapter 74 of the Tao Te Ching serves as a gentle reminder that by embracing impermanence, releasing the fear of death, and by letting go of our egos and its need to control the future, we can unlock our full potential, find fulfillment, and achieve greatness in the present. By adopting the wisdom of the master carpenter and learning to work in harmony with the ever-changing pulse and nature of life, we can experience mastery of life and the Tao and with them a profound sense of freedom, peace, and joy. May we all venture forth on this path of surrender and discover the boundless possibilities that lie within ourselves and in the universe that the Tao has provided for us to as ours to ultimately discover and explore.

CHAPTER 75

On Proper Government, The Tao Te Ching, the
New Paradigm for Leadership and Government
on Earth in a Post-Extraterrestrial Contact World

**WHEN TAXES ARE TOO HIGH,
THE PEOPLE GO HUNGRY.**

**WHEN GOVERNMENT BECOMES TOO INTRUSIVE,
THE PEOPLE LOSE SPIRIT.**

**ONE SHOULD TRUST THE PEOPLE,
ACT FOR THEIR BENEFIT
AND LEAVE THEM ALONE.**

A New Paradigm for Leadership: Trusting the People and Leaving Them Alone

In a rapidly changing post-extraterrestrial, post-disclosure world, it is crucial for governments to adapt and evolve to meet the needs and aspirations of their citizens. In this passage and throughout the Tao Te Ching, Lao Tzu provides us with a new paradigm of leadership and governance that will be necessary for this brand-new era, one in which leaders value trust in people, act for their benefit, and minimize government intrusion. By examining the detrimental consequences of high taxes, intrusive government, and the lack of trust in the people themselves, we can understand the importance of trusting and empowering individuals who abide in the Tao and understand what is necessary in a Tao based society. A Tao-based society is one that emphasizes personal responsibility and values the autonomy of the individual for determining their own mental, physical and spiritual wellbeing. A proper government does this by promoting the people's autonomy, trusting in them and by allowing them to mentally, physically, and spiritually evolve and refine themselves so as to become proper examples and great leaders in their own right.

The Downfall of High Taxes

In Chapter 60, we learned that the government of a country is like the "frying of a small fish". Both are spoiled with too much intervention. In much the same way, when taxes are excessively high, the consequences for a society can be severe. One of the fundamental concerns throughout this world, especially in its underdeveloped parts, is hunger. As citizens anxiously face a significant burden to contribute their hard-earned income, their ability to provide for themselves and their families is compromised by high energy costs and taxes. High taxes force economies underground. High taxes limit economic growth, weaken entrepreneurship, and stifle innovation, resulting in a stagnant economy with limited employment opportunities. Consequently, poverty, lawlessness and hunger become prevalent, undermining the very bedrock and fabric of society.

The Consequences of Intrusive Government

A government that becomes excessively intrusive infringes upon the natural rights and spirit of the people. In a world where personal freedoms and individualism are valued, excessive governmental control is often met with resistance and resentment. When governments regulate every aspect of citizens' lives, their personal autonomy and dignity is compromised, and their spirit is dampened. This leads to a sense of disillusionment and apathy towards societal development. As people feel stripped of their agency and what little power they do have and find themselves reduced to mere subjects, the prospects of a revolution cannot be far behind.

Trusting the People

To overcome the drawbacks of high taxes and intrusive government, it becomes imperative for leaders and the governments to
whom the good of the people has been entrusted, it is necessary
that those in positions of leadership and governance to trust the
people, keep them independent and help them to provide for
their own needs. By fostering an environment of trust, governments can empower individuals to take charge of their lives,
do what is best for themselves and their families and actively
contribute to the betterment of society. Trusting the people
means providing them with access to working capital and to
create opportunities for self-reliance, entrepreneurship, creativity and innovation. By reducing the burden of high taxes,
governments free up working capital. By minimizing government intervention, individuals can drive economic growth
and societal progress beyond what it is now towards an even
greater and more rewarding future tomorrow.

Acting for the Benefit of the People

Leadership is not merely about power; it is about acting in the
best interests of the people. People know what is best for themselves and work diligently when self-interest is not frowned on
or suppressed. A truly progressive government understands that
fostering sustainable development requires creating an environment that supports citizens' well-being, personal growth, self-
direction and economic prosperity. By prioritizing the needs
and aspirations of its citizens, a truly effective leadership can
inspire and enable individuals to achieve their fullest potential.

Leaving the People Alone

The fundamental principle of a new paradigm of leadership is
one of general laissés faire that leaves the people alone. People
flourish in environments where their freedom is respected,
where they can make decisions that align with their values and

aspirations. By minimizing unnecessary regulations and giving individuals the autonomy to shape their lives, governments can create a society that nurtures human potential, encourages diversity, personal responsibility and self governance and fosters creativity and innovation scientifically technologically and otherwise.

Conclusion

Earth need not become a prison planet where everything is controlled, and economies dictated by the government. History has shown how catastrophically such situations have not worked and inevitably, despite their originally good intentions, have miserably failed. High taxes and intrusive government hinder the accumulation of financial and human capital and contribute to societal unhappiness and the detriment of personal and spiritual well-being for all. High taxes and intrusive government compromise the spirit and potential of all the people.

To create a thriving and progressive society in a post-ET/NHI contact world, a new paradigm of leadership and government is necessary. Such a paradigm must be one that acknowledges and understands the existence of the Tao and how it operates. Leadership in the new paradigm should be one that trusts the people, acts for their benefit, and leaves them alone to thrive. By reducing the burden of taxes and minimizing government intrusion, individuals can embrace their autonomy, contribute to economic growth, and foster a sense of empowerment. It is through this new paradigm that we can build a better future, where the people are autonomous and self-responsible and at the heart of progress and prosperity here on this world and can spread that self-supporting independence and autonomy throughout the universe as it opens up to us.

CHAPTER 76

Redefining Softness, Practicing Life and becoming its "Disciple", The Impact of Extraterrestrial Contact on Social, Political and Religious Institutions: The Soft and Yielding Will Prevail

WHEN MEN ARE BORN,
SUPPLE AND SOFT
THEY ARE.

WHEN MEN DIE,
HARD AND STIFF
DO THEY BECOME.

WHEN PLANTS ARE BORN,
THEY ARE PLIANT AND TENDER.

WHEN PLANTS DIE,
THEY HAVE BECOME BRITTLE AND DRY.

WHOEVER IS INFLEXIBLE AND STIFF
BECOMES A DISCIPLE OF DEATH.

WHOEVER IS SOFT AND YIELDING
REMAINS A DISCIPLE OF LIFE.

THAT WHICH IS HARD AND STIFF
WILL BREAK.

THAT WHICH IS SUPPLE AND SOFT
SHALL PREVAIL.

The Power of Softness: Embracing Balance, Harmony, Flexibility and Resilience

The concept of balance and harmony has been explored by numerous philosophies throughout history. The ancient wisdom depicted in Chapter 76 Lao Tzu's profound and renowned philosophical work, he emphasizes the profound significance of cultivating a soft and yielding approach to life and delves into the profound implications of adopting a soft and yielding mindset, not only in our personal lives but also in society as a whole and by way of extrapolation, in our approach to a world with ET/NHIs are present.

There is much to be said for embracing the philosophy of flexible strength and the transformative potential it holds. By embracing flexibility and resilience, individuals and their societies can navigate the challenges of existence, find harmony within themselves, and unlock the transformative power of life for themselves and for the universe as well.

The Fragility of Inflexibility: Adapting to Thrive

Inflexibility is often portrayed as a virtue, synonymous with strength and unwavering commitment. However, this notion is misguided. In reality, inflexibility can lead to a state of dysfunction, stagnation and decay. In the passage above, Lao Tzu asserts that rigidity and hardness ultimately lead to breakdown and destruction. Throughout history, we have witnessed countless examples of how rigidity and hardness ultimately lead to conflict and war. By exploring various real-life examples, such as brittle materials that shatter or organizations that resist change, we can understand the detrimental effects of stubbornness and the importance of flexible adaptability and the necessity of bending without breaking. We can also see the futility of any opposite approach. By understanding the importance of adaptability and the necessity of bending without breaking, we can learn to thrive in an ever-changing world and ever-expanding universe.

The Brittle Nature of Rigid Materials

One striking example of the fragility of inflexibility can be found in the realm of materials science. Brittle materials, such as glass or ceramic, are known for their lack of flexibility at room temperatures. When subjected to external forces, these materials are prone to shattering into countless pieces. Similarly, individuals and human institutions and organizations that refuse to yield or be adaptable often find themselves in a similar state of vulnerability. By being steadfast, stubborn and unyielding, they risk collapsing under the pressures of the real world and of those to which they inevitably be exposed in a post-ET/NHI contact world.

Organizations Resisting Change: The Perils of Inflexibility: The Technological Revolution and Its Victims: A Lesson from Companies That Failed to Embrace Change

In our dynamic society, and especially in a post-ET/NHI contact world, the ability to adapt and embrace change is crucial for survival. Failure to do so can have dire consequences, as demonstrated by numerous high-profile examples. Take, for instance, once-thriving companies that resisted technological advancements or shifting market trends. By stubbornly clinging to outdated practices and resisting innovation, these companies quickly found themselves obsolete or gone. Inflexibility led to their downfall, while their more adaptable counterparts thrived and left them behind.

The failure of once-thriving companies to adapt and embrace change serves as a poignant reminder of the dire consequences that can befall those who resist change, innovation and technological advancements. There are many high-profile examples highlight the devastating effects of inflexibility, emphasizing the importance of adaptability in a dynamic society. Below, we will examine two.

In our rapidly evolving world, the ability to adapt and embrace change has become essential for survival. Failure to do so can have profound and far-reaching consequences for individuals, communities, and even companies. By exploring the downfall of companies that resisted change, focusing on two high-profile examples should suffice it to serve as cautionary tales for businesses that find themselves in similar situations. By examining the factors that contributed to their demise, we can learn valuable lessons about the power of adaptability.

Kodak

The rise of the digital age and the advent of groundbreaking technologies have reshaped various industries, leaving companies that failed to keep up with these advancements in the dust. One such example is Kodak, a former giant in the photography industry. Despite being an industry leader, Kodak resisted embracing digital photography, instead clinging stubbornly to its traditional film-based business model. This failure to adapt ultimately led to Kodak's demise, as competitors adeptly capitalized on the disruptive power of digital cameras and online photo-sharing platforms. Today, but for a few limited products, hardly even the name is recognizable.

Blockbuster

The Changing Tides of Consumer Preferences, market trends and shifts in consumer preferences can be equally impactful, often forcing companies to reevaluate their strategies and adjust their offerings. Blockbuster, once an unrivaled force in the video rental industry, failed to recognize and adapt to the rising demand for digital streaming and home delivery services. Instead, the company remained entrenched in its brick-and-mortar rental stores, ultimately succumbing to the more adaptable and forward-thinking Netflix. This example highlights the importance of recognizing changing consumer needs and embracing innovative business models to stay relevant.

The downfall of companies like Kodak and Blockbuster underscores the importance of adaptability and flexibility in a dynamic society. By examining these cautionary tales, business owners and leaders can glean valuable lessons for navigating an ever-changing business landscape. Embracing innovation, investing in research and development, and anticipating possible disruptions are key to remaining competitive in an evolving market. They will also be key to success in a post-contact world.

The Necessity of Bending without Breaking

In our post-ETNHI contact world, the ability to adapt and embrace change is paramount for survival. Companies that shun innovation and resist the forces reshaping their industries are doomed to obsolescence. The cautionary tales of Kodak and Blockbuster serve as poignant reminders of the consequences of inflexibility. To thrive in this dynamic society, companies must learn from these examples, actively seeking and embracing change to secure their future in an ever-changing business landscape.

To thrive in a world where unpredictability reigns, we too must adopt a mindset of flexibility. Just as a tree that bends in the face of a strong wind is more likely to survive, individuals and organizations that can adapt and embrace change are better equipped to navigate uncertain times. The ability to pivot, innovate, and reinvent oneself has become a prerequisite for success. By embracing change rather than resisting it, we can evolve and flourish both as we await and later experience a world in which human beings are not the only participants.

The Power of Softness: Embracing Resilience and Creativity

In a world that often prizes strength and force, it is time to challenge the notion that softness equates to weakness. Contrary to popular belief, yielding and embracing softness brings forth unique qualities such as resilience, adaptability, and the capacity to bounce back from adversity. By drawing inspiration from the softness found in nature, particularly in the suppleness and tenderness of plants, we can uncover the undeniable power that lies within embracing softness. Embracing softness allows us to remain open to new experiences, foster creativity, and maintain emotional and physical well-being. Perhaps it is not the meek who shall inherit the earth but those who know when to yield and be soft and to be patiently forgiving and resilient.

Redefining Softness as Resilience

While commonly associated with fragility, softness can actually be seen as a demonstration of resilience. Just as a supple tree withstands the harshest winds, individuals who embrace the power of softness learn to adapt and endure amidst adversities. Softness allows us to remain flexible in the face of challenges, enabling us to bounce back and grow stronger with each experience.

The Creative Potential of Softness

Softness serves as a catalyst for creativity. When we soften our minds and let go of rigid beliefs or preconceived notions, we create room for new ideas and perspectives to emerge. Like the gentle sway of a flower in the wind, softness allows thoughts to flow freely, fostering a creative environment that encourages innovation and problem-solving.

Emotional and Physical Well-being through Softness

In a world filled with constant tension, embracing softness becomes vital for maintaining emotional and physical well-being. When we allow ourselves to be vulnerable and open, we cultivate meaningful connections with others, foster empathy, and build strong support systems. Softness also allows us to take care of ourselves by practicing self-compassion, reducing stress, and promoting overall wellness.

The power of softness lies in its ability to defy stereotypes and unlock incredible potential within individuals. By redefining softness as resilience and embracing it enables us to navigate through challenges and come out stronger. Moreover, softness nurtures creativity, facilitating fresh ideas and innovative thinking. Lastly, softness promotes emotional and physical well-being, allowing us to foster compassionate meaningful relationships and prioritize self-care and self-compassion. It is time to recognize the strength and transformative power that comes with embracing softness—all while remaining open to new experiences and adventures that life and the universe have to offer.

Disciples of Life vs. Disciples of Death

Chapter 76 of the Tao Te Ching presents a compelling dichotomy between disciples of life and disciples of death. The disciples of death represent those individuals and organizations who cling to fixed beliefs, resist change, and succumb to the inevitable hardships of life. Conversely, the disciples of life embrace softness and flexibility, enabling them to navigate challenges with poise and grace, learn from their experiences, and find true fulfillment. In a post-contact, post-disclosure world, how we see and define our religious, social and political institutions as either disciples of life and disciples of death will depend on no small amount upon their ability to accept the truth of ET/NHI existence and to change.

The Impact of Extraterrestrial Contact on Religions and Governments

Chapter 76 of the Tao Te Ching highlights the contrasting approaches of disciples of life and disciples of death. The former embody flexibility and openness to change, while the latter uphold fixed beliefs and resist transformation. But what are the potential effects of extraterrestrial contact on the world's religions, especially the more dogmatic ones. And what will become of the world's governments, especially the inflexible ones?

An examination of these areas, even though brief may shed light on how this reality could challenge both world religions and governance and their established doctrines, institutions and their structures. The inevitable encounter with extraterrestrial life has the potential to undermine the authority and viability of these religions and governments and reveal them to be disciples of death because of the limitations of their rigid belief systems. Conversely, perhaps by admitting past mistakes and shortcomings the official revelation of the profound presence of ET/NHI may prompt the necessary adaptations making these institutions viable disciples of life in the new post-contact, post-disclosure world.

Implications for Religions: The Threat to Human-Centric Beliefs

It would doubtlessly be insufficient to come to the end of this book without addressing the effect of ET/NHI contact on the world and the world's great religions. Lao Tzu teaches us that religions are dualistic and unnecessary because they detract from our conscious realization and awareness of the oneness and unity of all things. That being so, religions presently are a fact of life on this planet, albeit a transitional one. Looking back at the known history of mankind, other than the kernel of truth around which the major religions of mankind have based, where have their teachings and dogma gotten us and at what price? Moreover, how will the faithful be able to embrace the reality not only of the existence of ET/NHI but the fact that they have been present here on earth for millions and millions of years just waiting for us to grow up and evolve physically, mentally and spiritually as a species.

The revelation of intelligent extraterrestrial life would challenge religious doctrines centered around the idea of humanity as the supreme creation of a divine being. The existence of other intelligent beings would necessitate a reevaluation of human exceptionalism. Religious texts may be subject to reinterpretation to accommodate the new reality of extraterrestrial contact. Religious leaders would face the challenge of reconciling traditional teachings with the existence of sentient beings from other planets.

One could easily write a book on the potential effects of the reality of contact and its impact on humanity. That, perhaps is a book left to another author on another day. However, just like the examples Kodak and Blockbuster, further edification of the paradigm shifts we might expect with the advent of ET/NHI disclosure, may also come from a study, albeit cursory of the five great religions of the world. They will all be affected.

The Paradigm-Shifting Religious Impact of Extraterrestrial Contact: Be Flexible or Perish, Lessons from Historical Examples

The possibility of extraterrestrial contact has fascinated humans for centuries, raising profound questions about our place in the universe and challenging long-held beliefs and social structures. To comprehend the potential impact of such contact, it is crucial to examine historical events that have transformed our understanding of the world and disrupted established belief systems and political structures. This essay will explore three significant historical examples - Christianity, Buddhism, and

Islam - and analyze how these paradigms shifted in the face of new insights, presenting valuable lessons on adapting to potential extraterrestrial contact. Through the examination of the transformative impact of Christianity, Buddhism, Islam, Hinduism and Taoism on established belief systems and political structures, we can gain valuable insights into the potential paradigm shift that extraterrestrial contact may bring.

Examining the Transformative Impact of Christianity, Buddhism, Islam, Hinduism and Taoism: Insights for Extraterrestrial Contact

Throughout history, transformative belief systems and political structures have emerged, reshaping societies and challenging existing norms. In this essay, we will explore the profound impact Christianity, Buddhism, Islam, Hinduism and Taoism had on established belief systems and political structures, and how these insights can inform our understanding of the potential paradigm shift brought about by extraterrestrial contact. By examining historical examples and uncovering valuable lessons, we can gain valuable insights for embracing change and navigating uncharted territory.

Christianity: The Shifting Power Dynamics and Belief Systems

Before the advent of Christianity, the world was dominated by various belief systems and spiritual practices. From the polytheistic cultures in Rome to the philosophical traditions of Greece, societies held distinct religious worldviews. With the emergence of Jesus Christ and his teachings, Christianity challenged established religious beliefs and offered a new perspective on spirituality and salvation. As the movement spread, it caused a paradigm shift, dismantling old hierarchies and emphasizing equality, compassion, and love.

Christianity's rise confronted the existing power structures, particularly within the Roman Empire. The message of human dignity and the equality of all believers challenged the hierarchical social order. Consequently, Christianity faced persecution, but it eventually gained acceptance and exerted significant influence on political systems. The transformative impact of Christianity teaches us that flexibility, adaptability and resilience are crucial in navigating paradigm shifts. Despite facing challenges, Christianity grew and adapted, embracing new cultural contexts while remaining true to its core principles. But the question remains that despite the church's acknowledgment of angels and demons, how after 2000 years of repression of the church's knowledge of ET/NHI, will it ever be trusted to convey the truth at the risk of losing its followers once the new paradigm has begun.

Buddhism: The Transformation of Consciousness and Belief

Before the emergence of Buddhism, ancient India was a rich tapestry of religious and philosophical traditions, including Hinduism, Jainism, and Vedic rituals. Siddhartha Gautama's spiritual journey led him to develop Buddhism, a path to awakening and enlightenment. His teachings challenged the existing religious and societal norms, urging individuals to seek liberation from suffering. Buddhism questioned prevalent beliefs, such as the rigid caste system, rituals, and doctrines. It emphasized personal transformation, mindfulness, and compassion towards all forms of life. Buddhism teaches us the importance of embracing change and finding harmony amidst uncertainty. By recognizing impermanence and fostering compassion, individuals can navigate paradigm shifts with wisdom and resilience. Having the historical example woven into its most holy literature in chapter 23 of the Lotus Sutra where an ET/NHI pops out of the Buddha's forehead to hear him preach the lesson before 10,000 followers, doubtless, the transition to a post extraterrestrial contact world should not be very difficult.

Islam: Political and Social Transformations through the Prophet Muhammad

Arabia before Islam was a diverse landscape of tribal societies, each following its own religious rituals and belief systems. Mohammed's teachings marked a paradigm shift in Arabia. Islam challenged the prevailing social order, promoting equality among its followers and emphasizing justice, knowledge, and compassion. The principles of monotheism, social justice, and accountability transformed the religious landscape and provided a unified foundation for Arab society. Islamic civilizations flourished, leaving a lasting impact on art, science, and political systems. Islam's transformative impact reminds us of the importance of finding a balance between tradition and openness to new ideas. It highlights the ability to adapt existing frameworks to incorporate new insights while maintaining the core principles. But will the rigidity of the clerics and Islamic fundamentalism be an insurmountable barrier to assimilation into the post contact world?

The Transformative Impact of Hinduism: Nurturing Inclusivity and Embracing Diversity

Before the emergence of Hinduism, a rich tapestry of beliefs and practices existed in ancient India. The core principles and scriptures of Hinduism, emphasizing its inclusive nature, belief in multiple paths to spiritual realization, and the concept of dharma. One of Hinduism's defining features is its ability to synthesize diverse beliefs and spiritual practices. We will examine how this synthesis brought about transformative shifts in ancient Indian society, fostering inclusivity and harmony. Hinduism's transformative impact teaches us the importance of nurturing inclusivity and embracing diversity in the face of paradigm shifts. With Hinduism's history and mythology, will the acceptance of ET/NHIs make the transition to a post-contact world easier?

The Origins and Foundational Beliefs of Taoism: Lessons
Learned: Cultivating Harmony and Adaptability

The historical origins of Taoism and its foundational beliefs,
focusing on the reverence for nature, pursuit of balance, and
the concept of the Tao (the Way). Taoism had a profound
and lasting impact on Chinese society for more than a millennium. There were many areas where Taoism influenced
Chinese culture, philosophy, arts, and governance. Taoism
brought transformative changes to ancient China, shaping the
mindset of individuals, promoting harmony in society, and
influencing political structures. The transformative impact
of Taoism teaches us the importance of cultivating harmony,
embracing adaptability, and navigating change in a balanced
way. Lao Tzu's teachings of the universal truths about sapience
and sentience and proper leadership and government in the
Tao Te Ching and his treatment of extraterrestrials and non-
human intelligences in the Hua Hu Ching will be of great
use in humanity's ability to relate to and understand our ET
brothers and sisters and our NHI cousins.

Conclusion on Religion

As we contemplate the possible impact of extraterrestrial contact, it is insightful to delve into historical examples that have
led to paradigm shifts. The transformative power of Christianity, and Islam highlights the potential for extraterrestrial
encounters to challenge established belief systems and political structures. Hinduism's ability to synthesize diverse beliefs
and spiritual practices teaches us the importance of nurturing
inclusivity and embracing diversity should make the transition
easier for Hinduism's followers.

The transformative impact of Buddhism, Hinduism and Taoism provides valuable insights that can be applied to the potential paradigm shift brought about by extraterrestrial contact.
Buddhism's emphasis on change, personal transformation,

mindfulness, and compassion towards all forms of life and Taoism's similar emphasis and that on nature, balance, self-cultivation and the Tao, can guide us to cultivate harmony and adaptability amidst change and contact with the extra-terrestrials and non-human intelligences that populate the cosmos. Each provides us with something useful, some more than others. But in the end, the Tao compassionately directs and governs all.

Impact of ET/NHI on Governments: A Crisis of Inflexible Governance

Beyond the reach of religion, there is the impact of ET/NHI contact and disclosure by the world's governments. The revelation of extraterrestrial life could lead to a crisis of governance, as rigid political systems often rely on maintaining control through the suppression of alternative perspectives. The existence of extraterrestrial intelligence would shake the foundations of these governments, demanding a more flexible and adaptable approach to governance. The existence of extraterrestrial life would undoubtedly necessitate collective international efforts in terms of diplomacy, security, and resource management. Inflexible governments that prioritize isolationism and nationalistic approaches may struggle to adapt, potentially leading to their decline. But are the leaders that are presently in power fit to lead in a world in which the ET/NHI approach to this world and the universe is basically Taoist?

Societal Paradigm Shifts: The Philosophical and Existential Impact

The reality of extraterrestrial contact would force societies to confront profound questions about human existence, our place in the universe, and the nature of consciousness and of our own existence, questions that governments have left to the philosophers and poets to whom they have given little attention. ET/NHI contact will likely result in a paradigm shift, challenging long-held beliefs and demanding new frameworks for understanding the world and living in a universe populated by beings who were not essentially human. The encounter with advanced extraterrestrial civilizations could provide an impetus for accelerated technological advancements in various fields, such as space exploration, communication, and energy sources but would it propel equally the necessary human advancements in matters of thought, conscience and spiritual matters. Inflexible governments and dogmatic religions may find themselves inadequately prepared to harness the potential benefits of both these types of advancements.

Extraterrestrial contact has the potential to catalyze transformative changes in dogmatic religions and inflexible governments making them either responsive or irrelevant. Such contact would challenge established belief systems, necessitate reinterpretation of scriptures, call for adaptive governance, and trigger societal paradigm shifts and a reordering of priorities where the mental, physical and spiritual wellbeing of people come before all else. The key to the survival of existing human institutions lies in embracing flexibility, openness, and a willingness to adapt, as disciples of life do, rather than clinging to fixed beliefs and resisting change, characteristic of disciples of death.

Paradigm Shifts in Human History: Insights into the Potential Impact of Extraterrestrial Contact: The Copernican Revolution: The Discovery of America: The Enlightenment Movement of the 18th Century: Lessons for Extraterrestrial Contact

To comprehend the possible impact of extraterrestrial contact on human social institutions, it is essential to examine historical examples of paradigm-shifting events that have challenged established belief systems and political structures. The Copernican Revolution and the challenge to the geocentric model of the universe, the discovery of America and its impact on existing political and social hierarchies, the Enlightenment movement of the 18th century are three prime examples of paradigmatic change that warrant at least a brief examination.

In contemplating the potential impact of extraterrestrial contact, it is crucial to examine these historical events because they have reshaped our understanding of the world and challenged established belief systems and political structures. By exploring three significant examples, the Copernican Revolution, the discovery of America, and the Enlightenment movement of the 18th century we can shed light for ourselves on the potential consequences of a paradigmatic shift that will inevitably occur after encountering intelligent beings from beyond our planet. By analyzing historical examples of paradigm shifts, we can gain valuable insights into the possible impact of extraterrestrial contact, including its potential to transform our own perspectives on cosmology and ontology, the nature and origin of consciousness to reshape our existing political systems, and revolutionize human society as we know it.

The Copernican Revolution and the Challenge to the Geocentric Model

The Copernican Revolution, spearheaded by Nicolaus Copernicus in the 16th century, was a momentous scientific breakthrough that challenged the prevailing geocentric model of the universe. Copernicus proposed a heliocentric model, placing the Sun at the center of the solar system. This shift had profound implications for scientific thought, religious beliefs, and political power structures. It disrupted the established cosmological order, prompting a human realization of our place in a vast and expanding universe. The shift in thought that Copernicus caused was a titanic occurrence to the scientific and cosmological beliefs of the time and set the western world on its head. Extraterrestrial contact could similarly challenge our understanding of the universe, prompting us to reevaluate our perceived dominance and significance.

The Discovery of America and its Impact on Existing Hierarchies

The "discovery" of America by Christopher Columbus in 1492 had far-reaching consequences, fundamentally altering the existing political, economic and social hierarchies of the time. It challenged prevailing knowledge and expanded horizons, triggering intense debates, exploration, and trade. The encounter with new lands and civilizations not only led to the reshaping of empires and the spreading of new ideas but also exposed the inherent flaws in the prevailing power structures of the era. It began the rise of empires in the fifteenth century and led to their inevitable fall in the twentieth. In the context of extraterrestrial contact, a similar transformation could transpire, forcing us to reconsider our societal structures and reevaluate our perspectives on identity, unity, and cooperation, not to mention softness, compassion, yielding and collaboration with beings who may or may not be human.

The Enlightenment Movement of the 18th Century:

One more paradigm-shifting event that warrants examination is the Enlightenment movement of the 18th century. This era saw a shift in intellectual thought, emphasizing reason, science, and individual liberty. The Enlightenment challenged entrenched religious and political dogmas, sparking revolutions and shaping modern democratic systems. Extraterrestrial contact might trigger a similar renaissance of thought, inspiring a fresh wave of intellectual curiosity, innovation, and societal progress. Moreover, it may prompt us to question our notions of humanity's uniqueness and ego-driven ideas of exceptionalism and redefine our moral and ethical obligations towards each other and toward intelligent life beyond our planet.

The examination of historical paradigm shifts, such as the Copernican Revolution, the discovery of America, and the Enlightenment, offers crucial insights into the potential impact of extraterrestrial contact. These examples are but a few that highlight the profound transformations that occurred when established belief systems and political structures were challenged by new encounters and discoveries. As extraterrestrial contact occurs, it could lead to a renaissance of thought, stimulate scientific advancements, and necessitate a reassessment of who and what we are exactly, where we are and how to find our place individually and collectively in the universe. As we speculate about the future, it is vital to understand the lessons history has taught us and prepare ourselves to navigate the potential paradigm shifts that could accompany such a monumental event. So, what should be our approach?

Embracing Softness in Contemporary Society

In today's fast-paced, demanding world and being faced with the reality of a post-ET/NHI contact world, the value of softness is more relevant than ever. There are practical strategies for incorporating flexibility and resilience into everyday life and with our interactions with other beings and societies and civilizations. By exploring examples from various economic, religious, and historical domains and exploring those such as interpersonal relationships, leadership, and personal growth, it should be rather obvious by now how a soft and yielding approach can foster healthier connections, enhance problem-solving skills, and promote personal well-being in all aspects of our human and non-human and terrestrial and extraterrestrial relations.

Conclusion

The belief that rigidity and inflexibility are synonymous with strength is a fallacy. The fragility of inflexibility becomes evident when examining the tangible consequences, it brings forth. Just as brittle materials shatter and organizations resisting change crumble, individuals and organizations must acknowledge the futility of an unyielding approach.

Embracing flexibility is not a sign of weakness, but rather a testament to our ingenuity and capacity for growth. The chapter above serves as a persuasive reminder of the importance of softness and flexibility in our lives. The ability to bend without breaking, to adapt and embrace change, is vital for survival, growth and prosperity. By being flexibly receptive to new ideas, challenges, and opportunities, we can navigate the complexities of life with resilience and emerge as stronger, constantly evolving human beings. By adopting a mindset of "softness" that remains open to change, embraces patience and resilience, and harmonizes with the Tao and its natural flow of life, we can overcome challenges, find fulfillment, and lead a meaningful existence both now and in a post-ET/NHI contact world.

By drawing upon the valuable lessons from religious, economic and historical examples, and the Tao Te Ching upon softness, and the necessity of being flexible and yielding, we can navigate the potential ontological and existential crises and overcome the social and societal challenges and potential political hazards posed by contact. The examples above, if nothing else, should teach us the importance of adaptability, resilience, embracing change, and finding harmony in new perspectives. With an open mind and a willingness to learn, we can prepare ourselves for the potential paradigm shift that extraterrestrial contact will inevitably bring. This openness will most certainly guarantee mankind of a future that expands our understanding of the world and our place and secure the place in our lives for the undeniable presence a supreme divine intelligence that underlies and creates all reality rather than limit it. Let us recognize the transformative power of softness and become the disciples not of death but of life; for it is through its softness and flexibility that we will always prevail and thrive as a new arrival in a promising timeless and ever-expanding universe.

CHAPTER 77

Orion's Bow, The Tao Te Ching, The New
Paradigm for Leadership and Governance on
Earth in a Post-Extraterrestrial Contact World

THE TAO ACTS IN THE WORLD
AS IF IT WERE BENDING A BOW.
DOWNWARD BENT IS THE TOP.
UPWARD BENT IS THE BOTTOM.

SO AS TO CREATE A PERFECT BALANCE,
THE TAO ADJUSTS
BOTH DEFICIENCY AND EXCESS.

THE TAO TAKES FROM OVER-ABUNDANCE
AND GIVES TO THAT WHICH IS LACKING.

THOSE WHO ATTEMPT TO CONTROL OTHERS
BY USING FORCE IN ORDER TO SAFEGUARD THEIR
POWER
TRULY OPPOSE THE TAO'S DIRECTION.

THEY APPROPRIATE FROM THOSE
WHO HAVE NOT ENOUGH
IN ORDER TO GIVE TO THOSE
WHO HAVE FAR TOO MUCH.

THE MASTER IS ABLE TO KEEP GIVING
BECAUSE HER WEALTH IS WITHOUT END.

WITHOUT EXPECTATION THE TAO ACTS.
WITHOUT TAKING CREDIT SHE SUCCEEDS.

N. MICHAEL MURBURG, JR.

THE TAO THINKS HERSELF TO BE NO BETTER THAN ANY OTHER.

Embracing the Tao: The New Paradigm for Leadership and Governance in a Post-Extraterrestrial Contact World

In a rapidly changing world, leadership and proper governance have become essential aspects of human progress. As we venture into a future potentially influenced by extraterrestrial contact, it is crucial to explore new paradigms of leadership and governance rooted in wisdom and balance. So why embrace the Tao? Is it not enough for a philosophy to offer profound insights on effective leadership in a post-extraterrestrial contact world? The answer is no, it is not enough. By understanding and implementing the principles of the Tao, we can create a harmonious and prosperous society that transcends the limitations of traditional power dynamics and fosters the kind of peaceful collaboration and growth that will be required of us in the years to come as we interface with new beings, their societies, leaders and governing concepts.

The Tao, as described in Chapter 77 of this ancient text, offers a revolutionary approach to leadership, emphasizing the importance of balance, abundance, and selflessness. Through the practice of the Tao and its Integral Way, true leaders can empower themselves and others, promote equity, and ultimately create a world where everyone and everything can thrive. This is not an aspirational guideline but an imperative for our future because of its potential to create a beneficial realistic reality that we have already seen when and where the Tao is followed.

The Tao's Concept of Balance and Adjustment

Lao Tzu posits that leadership should emulate the bending of a bow, wherein the top is bent downward, and the bottom is bent upward. This symbolic imagery reminds us of the constellation Orion in the northern hemisphere's fall and winter

ُِ. les. The stretched bow exemplifies the power in maintaining equilibrium in all aspects of leadership and in life. True leaders recognize the value of balance and make continual adjustments to ensure equality, fairness and justice. By embracing the Tao, leaders can cultivate a sense of powerful equilibrium within themselves and extend it to others, promoting a harmonious coexistence here on earth that reflects that of which we are reminded by the stars.

The Tao's Approach to Abundance and Redistribution

The Tao Te Ching teaches us that leaders must transcend the desire for personal power and instead focus on service to others over service to self. They must set up the circumstances that produce abundance for those whom they govern. Instead of exerting force to control others, true leaders look for balance. They follow the Tao's direction of taking from over-abundance and giving to those in need. This practice helps fine-tune systems and bring back into balance systems that have begun to lose their equilibrium. The Tao's approach supports a more equitable society, where all have access to power, resources are distributed fairly, and everyone can grow and flourish.

The Tao's Essence of Selflessness

In contrast to power-driven leadership models, the Tao encourages leaders to let go of self-centered tendencies and adopt a selfless mindset. Service to others is valued by society over fame, wealth and power and in governance especially over service to oneself. When leaders cultivate humility and see themselves as no better than others, they gain the capacity to give without expectation or taking credit. By embodying the essence of the Tao, leaders can inspire trust, foster collaboration, and cultivate an environment that values the growth and mental, physical and spiritual well-being of all.

The Endless Wealth of the Tao

One of the most fascinating aspects of the Tao is its limitless wealth and its unceasing ability to provide abundance. Unlike external resources, the Tao's wealth and energy are boundless, enabling leaders to give without depleting their own reserves. By tapping into this infinite reservoir, leaders can sustain their ability to serve others and create a positive impact on their organizations and societies.

Conclusion

In a post-extraterrestrial contact world, where other, more advanced civilizations can teach us about our own origins and the nature of life and being, the dynamics of leadership may drastically change. What happens when humanity realizes that the laws of karma and the existence of an eternally conscious soul and its reincarnation from various lower to higher forms of life are real? Because of the nature of the transformation, embracing the Tao offers a compelling solution and a societal transformation that is better and much easier. There is no reason to reinvent the wheel.

By adhering to the Tao's principles of simplicity, patience, compassion, Humility, truth, balance, abundance, selflessness, and infinite wealth, leaders can pave the way for a more enlightened and inclusive future. As we transition into this new era, the persuasive power of the Tao should not be underestimated. Let us embrace this paradigm shift and strive towards a world where leadership is rooted in universal wisdom, ultimately benefiting humanity in general and the universe and those with whom we come in contact.

CHAPTER 78

Being Like Water, The Tao Te Ching, The New
Paradigm for Leadership and Governance on
Earth in a Post-Extraterrestrial Contact World

IN THE WORLD
THERE IS NOTHING
AS YIELDING AND
AS SOFT AS WATER.

IN ORDER TO DISSOLVE
THAT WHICH IS
INFLEXIBLE OR HARD,
BY NOTHING IS WATER SURPASSED.

THE HARD IS OVERCOME BY THE SOFT.
THE RIGID IS OVERCOME BY THE GENTLE.
THIS TRUTH IS KNOWN BY EVERYONE.
YET IT IS PLACED INTO PRACTICE
BY BUT ONLY A FEW.

SERENE DOES THE MASTER REMAIN,
THEREFORE, EVEN WITHIN SORROW'S MIDST,
INTO HIS HEART, EVEN EVIL CANNOT MAKE ENT-
RY.

BECAUSE THE MASTER HAS GIVEN UP HELPING,
HE IS THE GREATEST HELP TO PEOPLE.

PARADOXICAL DO TRUE WORDS SEEM.

Harnessing the Power of Water: A Paradigm Shift for Effective Leadership

Water, often described as yielding, soft, and gentle, holds immense power, able to change form from solid to liquid and gas, it is also capable of dissolving the inflexible and overcoming the rigid. In the context of leadership, the metaphorical significance of water extends beyond its physical properties. In this chapter by Lao Tzu we can explore the concept of being like water, drawing inspiration from the Tao and its application to leadership in a post extraterrestrial contact world. By adopting a fluid and adaptable approach to leadership, individuals can navigate complexities and inspire their teams and teammates to overcome the boundaries that may confine them and with patience create new channels for their energies and do great things. There is great transformative potential that lies in embracing the principles of softness and water-like leadership, nurturing resilience, empathy, and strength and creating new and genuine connectionss between us and those with whom we come into contact.

The Soft Overcomes the Hard

Water's innate ability to dissolve and overcome the inflexible is mirrored in effective leadership. There are many oppositional forces in life. The traditional view of leadership often emphasizes toughness and hierarchical dominance with a head-on approach to obstacles. However, adopting a softer and patient water-like approach shifts the focus towards first understanding the problem and then collaboration on how obstacles may be overcome, dismantled or avoided altogether. By demonstrating flexibility, leaders can inspire creativity, openness and innovation rather than rigidity and resistance. This soft and gentle power fosters an environment where individuals can be heard, appreciated and thrive, leading to improved team dynamics and all around better outcomes.

The Gentle Overcome the Rigid

Gentleness, as we have learned in previous chapters is often mistakenly associated with weakness. Yet, it is precisely through gentle leadership that true strength and influence emerge. Water's gentle and adaptable nature reflects an empathetic and compassionate approach towards others. By prioritizing patience, compassion, empathy and understanding, leaders can cultivate meaningful connections and create a supportive work culture. The ability to listen attentively and respond with sensitivity allows leaders to address challenges and conflicts with wisdom and tact and thereby create win-win best scenarios.

The Serene Master

The Tao teaches us that by remaining serene, even amidst sorrow, we can prevent evil from infiltrating our hearts. In the context of leadership, serenity enables leaders to avoid making rash judgments by allowing them enough room to make sound decisions and guide their teams with clarity. By being poised and staying calm in the face of adversity, leaders become examples of courage and mastery. Thereby endearing themselves to those they lead and inspiring in them love, confidence and trust. Adopting a calm demeanor is a conscious choice. With serenity comes clarity and connection with the Tao. This connection empowers individuals to face their own challenges, fostering resilience and adaptability not only within their subordinates and teams but become examples for those who get to witness these masters of calm and serenity in action.

Giving Up to Truly Help

Paradoxically, the greatest help one can offer is often attained by giving up control. Our lives here on earth cannot last forever. It is up to us to teach by not teaching so that the reigns to the wagon of progress may be turned over to a younger generation. The Tao reminds us that true assistance lies not in always controlling things or overpowering others but by allowing them to watch, learn and grow into their own mastery. We can help them by nurturing their independence, natural abilities, integrity and their self-sufficiency. By relinquishing the need for constant intervention, mothers and fathers and leaders alike can empower those in their charge to think, act and flourish independently. This act of selfless leadership creates an environment where all individuals can grow autonomously to contribute, and take ownership of their work, thereby fostering long-term success and creating individuals who can stand on their own and accomplishments that will withstand the tests of time.

Conclusion

In a rapidly changing world, being like water and fostering leadership that resembles water holds immense potential for success, especially in the new post-extraterrestrial paradigm. By embracing the power of water-like leadership, individuals can navigate complexities, dissolve barriers, and build cohesive teams. Softness, gentleness and selfless assistance are components of both compassion for others and compassion for us. Moreover, serenity and flexibility are the cornerstones of both patience and effective leadership. All these traits are invaluable in a post extraterrestrial contact world. Let us not overlook the profound impact that water, and its inherent qualities, can have in shaping a more fluid, empathetic, adaptable, and resilient future. This is how effective leadership and governance is achieved. Being about 60% of human body mass, it only makes sense to be like water. It is really that simple.

Will humans learn to be like water happen overnight? Perhaps not that quickly, but it will happen with time. Change in direction can only happen when there is collective awakening. Ultimately, until that time will come with ET/NHI disclosure and contact, we must remember to be patient and compassionate and as we learned back in Chapter 37 that when it comes to the natural world, the Tao does not hurry, yet everything will be accomplished.

CHAPTER 79

Personal Responsibility, Failure and
Opportunity, The Tao Te Ching, The New
Paradigm for Leadership and Governance on
Earth in a Post-Extraterrestrial Contact World

FAILURE IS BUT AN OPPORTUNITY.
OF OTHERS, ONES BLAMING CAN BE ENDLESS.

THEREFORE,
THE MASTER FULFILLS THE MASTER'S OWN OB-
LIGATIONS.
THE MASTER CORRECTS HIS OR HER OWN MI-
STAKES
AND DOES WHAT NEEDS TO BE DONE.

THE MASTER DEMANDS NOTHING OF OTHERS.

The Mastery of Personal Responsibility: Embracing Failure
as an Opportunity

In a world that often places blame on others for failures, true
mastery lies in taking personal responsibility and viewing failure as an opportunity for growth. The concept of personal
responsibility, failure, and opportunity as seen through the
lens of Tao philosophy is a view that is integral to one's understanding of how the universe truly operates. By acknowledging
and living up to our own obligations, being responsible for our
own thoughts and actions, correcting our own mistakes when
we inevitably make them, and demanding nothing of others,
we can achieve a new paradigm for mastery and leadership in
a world shaped by both interpersonal and extraterrestrial and
non-human contact. When we embrace the mastery of personal

responsibility and see our failures as the steppingstones to success, we become masters of the Tao and of our own destiny.

Failure as an Inevitable Part of Life

To err is human and failure is part of the trial and error of our human experience. Failure is a universal encounter that everyone faces at some point in their lives. It can manifest in various aspects of life, such as personal and family relationships, professional endeavors, or even personal goals. No endeavor is either too big or too small to fail. By acknowledging the widespread nature of failure, individuals can realize that it is not a reflection of their worth, but rather a natural part of the journey towards success. It is not that we fail but how we handle failure that matters. Our triumphs in life are meant to reward us for overcoming challenges and failure. They are there to teach and for us to learn gratitude. Our failures are there to teach us not only humility but tenacity and resilience and how to succeed. More than our successes, it is our failures that build our character.

Along with failure, Lao Tzu broaches the topic of blame. Blaming others for our failures is a common tendency that can hinder our personal growth. It is the ego's way of protecting itself. When we shift the blame onto external factors, we relinquish our power to dissolve our egos and to learn from our mistakes and improve. Instead of pointing fingers, it is important to take responsibility for our actions and decisions, recognizing that this paves the way for personal development and growth and rectifying the potential causes of failure in the future.

Failure provides us with invaluable opportunities for personal development and improvement. It prompts us to reflect on our actions, reassess our strategies, and develop new approaches. Through failure, we learn its costs, however; we also gain resilience, problem-solving skills, and the ability to adapt to challenging circumstances, ultimately making us more equipped to overcome future obstacles and assume greater personal responsibility in the future.

The Philosophy of Tao: Embracing Personal Responsibility

The philosophy of Tao and the practice of its Integral Way are rooted in self-awareness, self-reliance, self-improvement and spiritual self-cultivation. They encourage individuals to develop an understanding of their own true nature, their strengths, and their weaknesses. By cultivating self-awareness, we can make conscious choices that reflect our relationship with the Tao and help us to actively work towards our own personal physical, mental and spiritual growth and improvement.

There is nothing so strong as a society of aware and self-reliant individuals who recognize the value of truth, simplicity, patience and compassion in life. This form of responsible individual sovereignty is what successful societies are all about.

Fulfilling one's own obligations is viewed as a path to personal enlightenment and mastery within the philosophy of Tao. This encompasses both external obligations, such as responsibilities towards others, as well as internal obligations, such as living with one's values and principles in alignment with the Tao. By honoring these obligations in a way that is consistent with the natural order of things, individuals foster a sense of integrity and purpose, leading to personal fulfillment and mastery. In societies where these values flourish, the need for laws and governance is minimal. Each individual is responsible for themselves and for the compassionate treatment of those with whom they live and the society, world and universe that supports them.

Taking ownership of one's mistakes and actively seeking corrections is a key tenet of personal responsibility in the Tao. It is something that the Integral Way reinforces. Rather than deflecting blame or shifting responsibility onto others, individuals are encouraged to be accountable for their actions and make amends as necessary. This practice fosters personal growth, as it allows individuals to learn from their mistakes, to forgive themselves and others for their shortcomings and continuously evolve and refine ourselves spiritually as sentient and sapient beings.

Leading by Example: Inspiring Change in Others

Embracing personal responsibility sets a powerful example for others by demonstrating the benefits of taking ownership of one's actions. Through our actions, we have the ability to inspire change and motivate others to adopt a similar mindset. By modeling personal responsibility, individuals can create ripple effects of positive transformation within their personal and professional circles.

Self-correction and the willingness to admit mistakes can have a profound impact on personal and professional relationships. When individuals demonstrate true humility to acknowledge their own errors and actively work towards rectifying them, it fosters trust, respect, and open communication. This, in turn, leads to stronger and more harmonious relationships built on mutual understanding and growth.

Demanding nothing of others while fostering a culture of personal responsibility allows for the cultivation of individual strengths and growth. By letting go of expectations and focusing on personal development, individuals create an environment where everyone is encouraged to take their own initiative and contribute to collective growth. This approach promotes self-realization and empowers individuals to reach their fullest potential.

Failure as an Opportunity for Growth

One need not take just this writer's word for it. There are many examples of individuals who turned failures into stepping-stones for success that can inspire and motivate readers. These examples could range from well-known figures who faced significant failures and ultimately achieved great success, to individuals in everyday life who overcame setbacks through resilience and determination. These stories serve as reminders that failure should not define us, but rather serve as motivation to push forward.

Here are five real-life examples of individuals who turned failures into steppingstones for success:

1. Elon Musk: Elon Musk, the CEO of Tesla and SpaceX, encountered numerous failures and obstacles in his entrepreneurial journey. From the early failures of his early internet companies to the challenges faced during SpaceX's rocket launches, Musk persevered through setbacks and continuously learned from them. His ability to bounce back, innovate, and push the boundaries of what is possible has made him one of the most influential entrepreneurs of our time.

2. Michael Jordan: Widely regarded as one of the greatest basketball players of all time and one of the world's most wealthy athletes, Michael Jordan faced significant failures early in his career. As a high school student, he was cut from the basketball team. Rather than letting this setback define him, Jordan used it as motivation to improve his skills and prove himself. Through hard work, determination, and a relentless drive for success, he eventually became a dominant force in the NBA and an iconic figure in the world of sports and one of its most wealthy.

3. J.K. Rowling: The author of the Harry Potter series, J.K. Rowling faced rejection from multiple publishers before finally

finding success. Her initial manuscript was rejected by several publishing houses, but she did not give up. Rowling used the setbacks as motivation to refine her work, ultimately finding a publisher who believed in her story. Her perseverance and resilience resulted in one of the most beloved and successful book and movie franchises in history.

4. Steve Jobs: Co-founder of Apple Inc., Steve Jobs experienced several failures and setbacks throughout his career. He was initially forced out of Apple but returned to lead the company to unparalleled success. Jobs's ability to learn from his failures, persevere through adversity, and create revolutionary products like the iPhone and iPad transformed the tech industry and cemented his legacy as a visionary entrepreneur.

5. Jack Ma: the founder of Alibaba Group, is another inspiring example of someone who turned failures into stepping-stones for success. Turned down for admission at Harvard, Jack Ma faced numerous other rejections and failures before he established Alibaba, one of the world's largest e-commerce platforms. In his early years, he struggled academically, failed twice in the college entrance examination, and faced multiple rejections when applying for jobs, including being rejected by KFC. Despite these setbacks, he did not lose hope and instead used his failures as motivation to persevere and think creatively, becoming one of China's wealthiest businessmen.

When he first introduced Alibaba, the platform faced skepticism and financial challenges. However, Ma saw these obstacles as opportunities to innovate and find unique solutions. He built a customer-centric platform that revolutionized the e-commerce industry in China and globally. Today, Alibaba has become a conglomerate, encompassing multiple businesses, including e-commerce, cloud computing, fintech, and more.

Jack Ma's story just like the others, serves as a reminder to us that failure is not the end but a steppingstone towards success.

Through his resilience, entrepreneurial spirit, and ability to learn from every setback, Ma transformed the e-commerce landscape and became one of the most influential business figures in the world.

Walt Disney, the founder of The Walt Disney Company, Steven Spielberg: One of the most renowned filmmakers in history, Vera Wang, Opra Winfrey and Thomas Edison are but a few more who faced numerous failures and rejections throughout their careers. These real-life examples demonstrate that failure is not a fatal roadblock to success but rather an opportunity for growth, learning, and resilience. By persevering through setbacks and using them as motivation to push forward, individuals can turn failures into steppingstones towards achieving their goals and experiencing personal growth.

The lessons learned from these examples help us understand the applicability of these experiences to our own lives. They highlight the valuable insights gained from failure, such as increased self-awareness, the importance of resilience, the need for adaptability, and the benefits of self-reflection. We can draw parallels to our own circumstances and consider how we can apply these lessons to our own journeys.

Failure, Leadership and Good Governance

Those who study American history are well aware of the political failures of Abraham Lincoln. Before he was elected as the sixteenth president of the United States, Lincoln ran for US Senate twice and lost twice. He also ran for the U.S. House of Representatives twice and lost twice before he finally was elected in 1846. Failures deepen our resolve. Adopting a growth mindset and viewing failure as a valuable opportunity for learning and improvement is the paramount requrement for great leadership and governance.

Humanity needs persons of character to lead us, not characters who lead us. One cannot emphasize enough the power of mindset, the benefits of embracing challenges, and the importance of reframing failure as a steppingstone towards growth in building leadership skills. By cultivating a growth mindset and learning true humility, our leaders can transform even the greatest societal setbacks into opportunities and continuously learn and evolve personally and professionally from them. By their growth, we all grow as well.

Together, these expanded ideas rooted in the Tao provide a comprehensive understanding of our own personal responsibility and that which we need to expect of those whom we choose to lead us. Our past failures in choosing the wrong leaders should be seen as an opportunity for growth. There is great significance and importance in choosing leaders who represent the best in us and of us; who lead by good personal, mental and spiritual example and who can help foster a culture of humility, integrity and personal responsibility for themselves, ourselves and for each other. This is the kind of leadership the new post-ET/NHI paradigm needs and is going to require. Ego will have no place in it.

Conclusion

Personal responsibility and the mastery of failure are essential components of effective leadership and personal growth. By following the principles of the Tao and the Integral Way, individuals and their leaders can effectively navigate the political, social and economic challenges of a post-extraterrestrial contact world with grace and resilience. Embracing personal responsibility means acknowledging our own obligations, humbly correcting mistakes, and demanding nothing of others. Through this lens, failure becomes an opportunity rather than a source of blame. Let us embark on a journey of personal responsibility, and honor ourselves and those around us by fulfilling our own obligations, by not blaming others and by our own Tao mastery. It is only this sort of leadership that can and will inspire positive change in the world around us and let us fearlessly reach out into the universe and diplomatically engage and work with the ET/NHIs who have been patiently waiting for us to evolve.

CHAPTER 80

The Final Chapter, Unvarnished Truth, The Tao
Te Ching, The New Paradigm for Leadership and
Governance on Earth in a Post-Extraterrestrial
Contact World.

WORDS THAT ARE TRUE
ARE NOT ELOQUENT.
WORDS THAT ARE ELOQUENT
ARE NOT TRUE.

WISE MEN
NEED NOT PROVE THEIR POINTS.
MEN WHOSE POINTS NEED TO BE PROVEN
ARE NOT WISE.

NO POSSESSIONS HAS THE MASTER.
THE MORE THE MASTER DOES FOR OTHERS
THE HAPPIER THE MASTER IS.
THE MORE THE MASTER GIVES TO OTHER
THE WEALTHIER THE MASTER IS.

BY NOT USING FORCE
THE TAO NOURISHES.
BY DOMINATING NOT
DOES THE MASTER LEAD.

"People often ask me what the most effective technique is
for transforming their life. It is a little embarrassing that
after years and years of research and experimentation, I have
to say that the best answer is - just be a little kinder."
~ Aldous Huxley

The Tao: A New Paradigm for Leadership and Governance in a Post-Extraterrestrial Contact World

In a rapidly changing post-extraterrestrial contact society and world, the future of mankind, effective leadership and proper governance are crucial. The ancient wisdom and universal truths of the Tao that we have read in the earlier chapters of this work provide valuable insights that can revolutionize our approach to leadership and assist human society and its governance in its integration into a higher order of being and higher orders of beings. By exploring the concept of the Tao and its potential we can shape a new paradigm for leadership on Earth, emphasizing the core principles of truth in speech, wisdom in thought, selflessness in action, and Wu Wei and the art of non-force. By embracing the principles outlined by Lao Tzu in the Tao Te Ching, the Hua Hu Ching and the integral way, we can cultivate ourselves as individuals and leaders and create a harmonious environment for those with whom we live and interrelate and those whom we might be called to lead and help govern. By abiding in the Tao and following its Integral Way, we can empower both ourselves and others, and achieve true greatness and fulfillment on a personal level and on a societal and civilizational scale. These achievements will have a great effect both here on earth and throughout the universe.

Eloquence in Speech

The Tao challenges the notion that persuasive speech is solely achieved through elaborate rhetoric. Instead, consistent with its value of simplicity, Lao Tzu suggests what we should already know, that words that flow from authenticity and truth carry the most weight. It is the truth that sets us free. The truth is essential to keeping us on the path of the Tao. We must trust in the Tao and in ourselves to live lives of truth. It is far better to tell a bitter truth than to speak a sweet lie. Even if the message is a painful one, leaders who speak the truth with honesty and transparency resonate with their audience, building trust and fostering genuine connections. By telling the truth is how the Tao speaks and works through us.

Wisdom in Action

Truly wise leaders understand that actions speak louder than words. They don't feel the need to prove themselves constantly. Instead, they let their actions and examples speak for themselves. By employing simplicity, patience and compassion and by embodying the greatest wisdom and kindness in their interactions and the decision-making process, great leaders inspire and guide others to do the same. The energy they create and emit affects all and thereby builds a stable culture of integrity, personal and social responsibility, peace, harmony and growth around them and out into the universe.

Selflessness and Empathy

The concept of selflessness lies at the compassionate heart of the Tao. True leaders altruistically prioritize the welfare of their governed and for society over their own personal gains. Service to others trumps service to self. By dissolving their egos into the Tao and dedicating themselves empathetically to the well-being of others, leaders not only nurture a sense of unity and purpose but also share the experience of deep fulfillment and happiness that come with this sense.

Non-Forceful Leadership

The Tao teaches us that true leadership does not rely on dominance, control or the exertion of power. Leaders who choose to do without doing and teach by not teaching and lead by their example and govern without force create an environment of true love and compassion that allow individuals and societies to self-actualize and flourish. Love and compassion are ultimately the real and strongest forces in the universe. They both are indestructible and forever will overcome the illusions of ego:

force, power and control. By nurturing and empowering others through the Tao, leaders unlock the immense potential within themselves, their families, partners, co-workers, subordinates, teams, communities, nations and their worlds fostering personal integrity, responsibility, creativity, innovation, trust and collaboration with the known and those yet to be known.

Conclusion

In a post-extraterrestrial contact world, the timeless wisdom of the Tao presents itself as a transformative framework for proper leadership and proper governance. By embracing simplicity in words and truthfulness in speech, wisdom in thought, selflessness in action, and non-egoic, non-forceful leadership, leaders can naturally inspire positive change, nurture harmonious relationships, and guide humanity towards an ever brighter and prosperous future. The Tao and its Integral Way provide an opportunity for leaders and those whom they govern to grow and evolve spiritually and to adapt and create a paradigm shift that aligns with the challenges of the modern world and the opportunity for peaceful and meaningful contact with human and non-human Extraterrestrials, Interdimensional and all Non-human intelligences. These entities have already been visiting us throughout the millennia, they are already here today and far more will come to assist us in our transition from a very primitive and generally unenlightened world into a higher, more technologically developed, and spiritually evolved and refined one. Let us look for and find the truth of God, the Source, the "Absolute", what I have come to know and call the "Tao", as we ready ourselves for their further involvement with us and with our human society.

Finally, it has long been the case with humanity that mankind settles not where it finds beauty, wealth, or status but where it finds peace. We should always remember that long-lasting peace is the goal of true leadership and proper governance. True power lies not in the possession of material wealth or the exertion of brute force but in harnessing the power of our souls with the absolute truth and sincerity and the wisdom of living lives of simplicity, patience, and compassion. It is through these universal values that leaders, men and women of the Tao, can rise to the occasion and fulfill their true potential as human beings, leaders and teachers while bringing out the best in others in the post-contact world. Let us embrace the teachings of Lao Tzu and the Tao and usher in a new era of leadership marked by peace, unity, love, patience, kindness, and compassion as well as the prosperity and growth that will accompany our contact with our extraterrestrial brothers and sisters of the Tao who have come to make contact and to teach and to learn from us. We have waited thousands upon thousands of years for this event. The time is now upon us to accept the challenges that ET/NHI contact will provide. It is up to us to prepare ourselves physically, mentally, and spiritually for contact by learning from the Tao Te Ching, Hua Hu Ching and the Integral Way and thereby make the best existence possible for all. At stake is inevitably the beginning of the conscious infinite future of all souls and spiritual beings in the universe and to help create a truly great and "brave new world that has such people in it". *

*The Tempest, William Shakespeare, Miranda, Act 5, Scene 1

THE END OF PART 1.

FOREWORD TO PART 2

"Indians have been waiting for Kalki for 3,700 years. Buddhists have been waiting for Maitreya for 2,600 years. The Jews have been waiting for the Messiah for 2500 years. Christians have been waiting for Jesus for 2000 years. Sunnah waits for Prophet Issa 1400 years. Muslims have been waiting for a messiah from the line of Muhammad for 1300 years. Shiites have been waiting for Mandi for 1080 years. Drussians have been waiting for Hamza ibn Ali for 1000 years.

Most religions adopt the idea of a 'savior' and state that the world will remain filled with evil until this savior comes and fills it with goodness and righteousness. Maybe our problem on this planet is that people expect someone else to come solve their problems instead of doing it themselves!" ~ Riccardo Dablah

"Anxiously we look round for collective measures, thereby reinforcing the very mass-mindedness we want to fight against. There is only one remedy for the leveling effects of all collective measures, and that is to emphasize and increase the value of the individual. A fundamental change of attitude (metanoia) is required, a real recognition of the whole man. This can only be the business of the individual and it must begin with the individual to be real.... The message which the UFO brings to the dreamer is a time problem that concerns us all. The signs appear in the heavens so that everyone willl see them. They bid each of us remember his own soul and his own wholeness, because this is the answer the West should give to the danger of mass-mindedness."
- Flying Saucers: a Modern Myth of Things Seen in the Sky, *by Carl G Jung, Princeton University Press 1958, page 73, 76.*

In Book 1, the Tao Te Ching we learned about the Integral nature of the Tao and how it operates and how we can align ourselves with it in order to live in peace and abundance. We also learned about the nature of who we are and how to lead and govern ourselves. In the Hua Hu Ching, the focus becomes internal as we learn about self-cultivation and how to do it. The purpose of self-cultivation extends to us in this lifetime as human beings and to us as we advance to other higher forms of life that through the process of physical life and death progress towards higher and higher physical, mental and spiritual forms of life that thrive through the Tao and throughout all of its creation. Let's begin that journey now.

INTRODUCTION

This book is an analysis of Chapters 1 - 81 of the Hua Hu Ching "(Chinese: 化胡經/化胡; pinyin: *Huàhújīng*; Wade-Giles: *Hua Hu Ching*; literally "Classic on Converting the Barbarians") "Wikipedia, due to its open nature, isn't always right, but in the case of *Hua Hu Ching*, its entry back in 2009 is quite correct:

The *Huahujing* (Chinese: 化胡經/化胡; pinyin: *Huàhújīng*; Wade-Giles: *Hua Hu Ching*; literally "Classic on Converting the Barbarians") is a Taoist book. Although traditionally attributed to Laozi, most scholars believe it is a forgery because there are no historical references to the text until the early 4th century CE. According to Louis Komjathy (2004:48), the Taoist Wang Fu (王浮) originally compiled the *Huahujing* circa 300 CE, and the extant version probably dates from the 6th century Northern Celestial Masters. The text is honorifically known as the *Taishang lingbao Laozi huahu miaojing* (太上靈寶老子化胡妙經, "The Supreme Numinous* Treasure's Sublime Classic on Laozi's Conversion of the Barbarians"). "The following explains the meaning of the *Hua Hu Ching* title. Let's break the three characters down one by one:

- 化 *Hua* = To change, to transform

- 胡 *Hu* = Barbarians, savages; people foreign to the ancient Chinese

- 經 *Ching* = Book, tome, classic; same character as the *Ching* in *Tao Te Ching*

This entry was posted in <u>Misconceptions</u> by <u>Derek Lin</u>. Bookmark the <u>permalink</u>.© 1998-2024 Derek Lin. All Rights Reserved, <u>www.DerekLin.com</u>

* Numinous, Definition adjective · of or relating to a numen (divinity); heavenly, divine, indicating the presence of a divinity, a state evoking a sense of the mystical, mysterious or awe-inspiring (formal) as in magic. An occurrence having seemingly supernatural qualities or powers. Etymology, from Latin numen, literally, "nod of the head", "divinity" or indicating "divine will" or "sway". In Ancient Greek the meaning is derived ultimately from the word noos, meaning "mind", "thought" or "purpose".

The Hua Hu Ching is also known as the "Scripture of Transforming the Barbarians." the "Book of Transformations "or the "Classic of the Pivot of Change". The Hua Hu Ching is said to contain the entire truth of the universe. Like the Tao Te Ching, the teachings in the Hua Hu Ching are simple, universal and profound. Those who wish to know the whole truth can find it by following a simple path that leads to peace, virtue, balance and abundance.

Like the Hua Hu Ching, the Hua Hu Ching emphasizes the importance of simplicity, selflessness, and the pursuit of inner harmony. The Hua Hu Ching (HHC) encourages us to focus on personal growth, value service to others over service to self and seek guidance from a master of the Way whenever possible.

By following the teachings of Lao Tzu about the Tao, one we can attain true virtue, peace, and abundance. By learning and understanding the nature of the universe and all the Tao's creation it is very possible to successfully engage in and make sustainable contact with ET and advanced non-human intelligences who also understand the universal law of the Tao and follow its precepts.

For those who might be so inclined to read this book, it should be understood that throughout the past 12,000 years in our art and written history, contact has inevitably come with the experience of heightened spiritual states created through meditation and other plant based peak or extraordinary experiences. "Flying Saucers" cannot any longer be explained as imaginary, hallucination or as a mythical projection of mankind's collective unconscious. ETs, UFOs, UAPs and non-human intelligences are now facts of life that have become our factual modern reality. Now it is up to us to learn how to stop behaving like barbarians and think and act like mentally, spiritually, and physically advanced children of the Tao. By accepting our role along with that of ET and NHIs as the progeny of the Tao, we can now maximize the physical, mental, and spiritual advantages of the potential that contact now offers. This book, in great part, was written to help do that.

The Integral Way

Throughout this book, the reader will encounter the term "Universal Way" used quite frequently. At the outset it would seem to be a good idea to describe it.

The term "Integral Way" describes the original self-cultivation tradition of Taoism. The idea of the "Integral Way" or "Universal Way" or path is outlined and fleshed out by Lao Tzu in both of his works; initially in the Tao Te Ching and later, to a greater extent here in the oral teachings attributed to him in the Hua Hu Ching.

Something that is integral is very important or necessary. If you are an integral part of a team, it means that the team cannot function without you. An integral part is necessary to complete the whole. In this sense, to be integral is to be the essence of or to be essential. A machine without an essential part being integrated into the whole will not function properly, if at all.

The Integral Way is a spiritual path that guides us to lead a life of balance, health, and harmony. It is "the secret to leading a positive life is to refine and harmonize one's energy so as to live in consonance with the order of the universe.". - Tao, the Subtle Universal Law and the Integral Way of Life by Hua-Ching Ni

Following the Integral Way involves acting spontaneously and effortlessly without forcing, appreciating the interconnected nature of all things. Following the Integral Way involves the interrelated concept of Wu Wei and learning how to use it. It is a guiding principle when it comes to letting go and allowing things to settle, to doing and not doing. The Integral way is a discipline. It is an education that involves learning about the universe and its nature and inhabitants, how to relate to them and how to refine our energies in order to evolve spiritually as responsible individuals and societies within a multiverse in which all things are connected. It is the path of living a life of truth and a means of seeing reality as it is. Above all the Integral Way is the study of the Tao and how it operates through our lives of simplicity and patience and living the Tao by giving and receiving universal unconditional indiscriminate love and compassion to everyone and everything. - NMM

An Introduction to the Essential Principles of Self-Cultivation and The Tao's Integral Way

Because this book is one of an introductory level, it should be treated as such. It is meant to introduce the reader to the subject matter that is the Tao Te Ching. Part of that introduction by necessity, should include some insight into the Tao's Integral Way and the practice of "Self Cultivation' through which one may evolve toward mastery of their understanding and harnessing their use of the Tao.

Self-cultivation is an ancient practice of those who follow the Integral Way. It holds the key to unlocking our true potential and attaining inner harmony. Self-cultivation offers us a transformative path towards a more balanced and fulfilling life. But what does self-cultivation mean? At its essence, self-cultivation is a process of learning and unlearning. It is how we learn to dissolve our egos and learn to evolve spiritually and to lighten and purify our energies. In a word, self-cultivation is how we learn to surrender ourselves to the Tao, the underlying infinite and intelligent conscious force that governs all existence.

The practitioner of Self Cultivation organizes themself around the Surrender of Ego, and living lives of Simplicity, Balance, Harmony, Integrity, Humility, Peace, Patience, Compassion, Wisdom, Truth, and developing Self-Control and Leadership. The Integral way emphasizes Spontaneity, Spiritual Evolution and Transformation, as well as the Purification of Spiritual Energy to arrive at a state of Physical and Spiritual Immortality.

Though Self Cultivation is not the central purpose for reading the Tao Te Ching, these concepts are interwoven into its text. In the Hua Hu Ching, Lao Tzu teaches these virtues in depth, including how to use Chi energy in both sexual and non-sexual singular, dual and angelic cultivations. For now, a brief introduction into the world of self-transformation through Self Cultivation and the Tao's Integral Way will have to suffice.

By surrendering to the Tao, we can break free from limitations and allow our true nature to flourish. Through aligning ourselves with the Tao, we align ourselves with the flowing consciousness of life, experiencing deeper connections with ourselves, the community, and the natural world. As we embrace these essential principles of Tao self-cultivation, we embark on a journey of self-discovery and personal growth, the transformative journey towards a greater conscious understanding of the universe within and around us and a happier and more fulfilling and balanced and harmonious life.

Surrender: The Prerequisite to Self-Expression

The foundation of Tao self-cultivation lies in the principle of surrender. By trusting and surrendering to the Life Force, also known as Chi or Qi Field, we pave the way for its effortless integration in our body and mind. Surrender allows us to tap into our highest levels of individual free will and creativity. Our ordinary ego-personality often struggles with separation, fragmentation, and dispersion of our soul essence. Negative thoughts, self-judgments, and rejection of our spiritual nature hinder our growth and lead to suffering. Through the Integral Way and self-cultivation, we learn to let go of the ego and dissolve its resistance and allow the Life Force to flow freely, enabling us to unfold our true selves.

Harmony: The Flowing Consciousness of Life

Harmony is an integral aspect of self-cultivation through the Integral Way. The Life Force, comprised of three streams of consciousness, namely Yin (negative-receptive-female), Yang (positive-creative-male), and Yuan (neutral-stabilizing-primordial), permeates all aspects of life. It is a dynamic and ever-flowing entity, embodying the essence of process. Practitioners of qigong, for example, learn to communicate with the Life Force, utilizing its language of subtle energy or chi. Through this practice, we harmonize the three currents of chi within ourselves, our community, and the universe. By understanding and appreciating the cycles of Yin-Yang and the natural phases of energy we can understand the connection between our inner thoughts, feelings, and perceptions, and the unfolding actions of the natural world.

Simplicity: Unveiling the Inner Path

Life often appears complex on the surface, filled with numerous responsibilities and distractions. However, Tao self-cultivation teaches us that true simplicity lies within. The development of one's Inner Smile, though not mentioned in either of Lao Tzu's works specifically is a practice rooted in the self-cultivation of the Tao's Integral Way. It serves as the path of simplicity. By opening the heart of our soul and unconditionally accepting ourselves, we lay the foundation for accepting everything "Other" as part of the unified essence of the Life Force. We greet all as a manifestation of the Tao, even ourselves. The Inner Smile keeps us grounded on a heart-centered path, fostering soul peace and eliminating separation and loneliness. Through this simple act of acceptance, we allow spiritual qualities such as patience, love, kindness, compassion, and forgiveness to naturally unfold with our dealings with all things, including ourselves.

Grounding: Merging the Physical and Spiritual

Being centered in life necessitates both physical and spiritual grounding, allowing us to navigate the complexities of existence with clarity and stability. A centered life requires the balance of our mind, body and spirit. In the study of Tao through self-cultivation, qigong and meditation play crucial roles in grounding our being. Qigong exercises and meditation practices fuse our mind, body and spirit, the great trinity, with a strong, grounded, and integrated whole. Qigong promotes optimum health by harmonizing our heart-mind and physical body. Meditation, on the other hand, is how we learn to experience pure being, the gateway to many natural and supernatural states. Its useful emptiness or "no mind" merges our personality and physical body with our soul or "ling." This holistic approach to enlightenment enables us to lead simple, truthful and compassionate ordinary lives of peaceful contentment and harmony while nurturing our continued enlightenment and spiritual refinement and growth.

Absolute Truth and Integrity: Cultivating Personal Virtue

Though not specifically addressed in either the Tao Te Ching as such or mentioned in very terse fashion in the Hua He Ching, Qigong and meditation, "emptying the mind" in the words of Lao Tzu throughout the Tao Te Ching and Hua Hu Ching form the pillars of Tao self-cultivation. These practices empower the expression of personal integrity, also known as innate spiritual virtue or "de," in our daily lives. Moreover, by studying ancient wisdom such as the I Ching, feng shui, Chinese astrology, and Chinese medicine to which Lao Tzu introduces us in the Hua Hu Ching enhances our understanding of the interconnectedness of all aspects of life. The integration of these practices and skills that best suit us become elemental parts of our personal Tao or "Way," allowing us to tap into our highest potential and align with the Great Tao. With absolute truth and the integrity that flows from it as our guiding principle, we navigate each moment with authenticity and honor, evolve and refine our spiritual being and realize our soul's highest destiny.

The Essence of Spontaneity in Self-Cultivation

Every soul has a dual longing. It yearns for two things: to fulfill its unique worldly destiny and to achieve a high spiritual destiny by consciously merging back into its Original Spirit. The Supreme Mystery that births the Life Force will always remain unknowable and unpredictable, even as we gradually merge with it and the vastness of the Tao. This central Mystery resides deep within our inner selves, constantly refreshing and revitalizing all aspects of life, instilling us with a sense of joy, presence and spontaneity.

It is essential to understand that destiny is not a fixed or predetermined path. In the realm of Tao self-cultivation, spontaneity stands as a fundamental principle that guides individuals towards aligning with the natural rhythm of life in fulfilling worldly and spiritual destinies. Spontaneity enables us to align with the natural flow of the Tao, harmonize our will with the cosmic will, and fulfill our spiritual destiny. When we lose touch with our own spontaneity, we lose touch with the joyous gift of life.

Spontaneity, as used by Lao Tzu, though is not mere impulsivity. Importantly, it is the conscious surrender to the present and within that present and ever-changing moment, the flow of the Tao. Spontaneity in the sense that it is used by Lao Tzu involves letting go of fixed plans and embracing the natural unfolding of each moment, allowing for a harmonious alignment with the cosmic will. It is a fundamental aspect of our own self-cultivation because it invites us to discard fixed plans and embrace the natural rhythm of life harmonizing our individual will with the cosmic will and bringing us closer to our ultimate spiritual destiny. By being patient, present and by letting go of attachments, expectations, and the need for rigid structure, we can relax and allow for the organic unfolding of our true nature and the universe as it collaborates our destiny with us as a conscious and willing participant.

Spontaneity also opens us up to the collaborative and creative intelligence of the universe. This alignment facilitates a deeper connection with our true nature and the essence of the Tao and the other beings who are also consciously connected to the Tao. By living in alignment with the natural rhythms and flow of the Tao, we can fulfill our worldly destiny while consciously merging with our Original Spirit. Moreover, this conscious surrender to spontaneity allows us to experience the fresh, joyful, and ever-changing nature of our present existence, bringing us closer to the essence of the Tao and our true selves. By letting go of attachments and expectations, we can tap into our innate wisdom and navigate the currents of existence with ease and grace.

When we surrender to the rhythm of the Tao, we open ourselves up to the creative flow of the universe. By releasing our efforts to control and manipulate outcomes, we can tap into the natural intelligence that resides within us and all beings, ET and NHIs included. Through spontaneity, we can harmonize our actions with the spontaneous movements of the Tao, participating fully in the dance of creation and consciously experience the gift of the joyous and ever-changing nature of existence, ultimately connecting with our true selves with the eternal divine essence of the Tao.

By recognizing our unique individuality and profound connection with the divine we enable ourselves to see the same connection in all beings. By dedicating ourselves to self-cultivation, we contribute to the cosmic tapestry of existence, and play a vital role in the evolution of consciousness and ET/NHI contact throughout the universe.

Transformation

In the middle portion of this book the reader will learn about integrating the esoteric and holistic practices that combine elements of science and art. As the old Chinese saying goes, "Sound minds live within sound bodies." Accordingly, within every each higher being there exists the mystical trinity of jing-chii-shen, "essence, breath and spirit" the three theoretical cornerstones of ancient and traditional Chinese medicine. Jing-chii-shen, hold precise meanings in the teachings of Lao Tzu. Although Lao Tzu introduces these concepts yet leaves it up to the reader to find out which practices resonate with them. As the reader will learn, the following that which resonates within us is one of the ways the "Law of Energy Response" works.

Lao Tzu also teaches us in the middle to later chapters of this book to the concept of "Alchemical Meditation", a meditative process that is meant to accelerate our alchemical transformation and speed up our soul's internal change. All the things that we do in life can be done in a mindful way. Virtually everything can become a meditation. In alchemical meditation we accelerate our spiritual evolution and purification by integrating our sexual essence (jing) with our subtle breath (chii), and intelligence-spirit (shen). This integration facilitates the soul's immediate emergence into the higher spiritual realms. By focusing on these systematic, heart-centered practices of self-cultivation, we can bridge the apparent gap between spirituality and physicality, energy, and matter within our lifetimes.

Alchemical Elixir and Mastery over the Sexual Self

The spiritual core for the practice of self-cultivation is called Internal Alchemy or "neidan gong".
The principles of Tao self-cultivation expand in the last twenty chapters of this book to include the transformative concept of a mastery over the physical-sexual self. This includes understanding the connection between our sometimes-volatile female and strong male sexual energies and the split between our Heaven-formless spirit and the sexually embodied aspect of our Earth-born form. By tapping into our sexual yin-yang energies and practicing the sexual techniques explained by Lao Tzu in the Hu Hua Ching, we can unlock the alchemical powers and the "Golden Elixir", our exclusive fundamental nature, that exists within us. This integration of our sexual and spiritual selves gives birth to an Inner sage-like mastery that embodies our immortal non-dual Original Nature and amazingly allows us to commune in a very special way with each other. It is the divine energy that is the Tao. This energy exists equally within us. It is our immortal seed and that of the

energy of both the Buddhas and immortals. As one deepens their understanding and practice of the principles, they continue on a profound journey of self-discovery, spiritual growth, and harmonious alignment with the timeless and eternal Tao.

Sexual Mastery

One's level of spiritual mastery is mirrored by their understanding and practice of human sexuality. As we explore the essential principles of Tao self-cultivation as set forth by Lao Tzu in this book, we will delve deeply into the profound concept of sexual mastery and sage hood. Our volatile male-female sexuality mirrors the polar split between the two halves of our soul – the Heaven-formless non-physical energy that we call "spirit" and the Earth-form material and physically sexually embodied aspect of it. In this book, we will uncover the transformative power of tapping into our sexual volatility and integrating it into our spiritual practice. By tapping into our sexual volatility and practicing the Integral Way's sexual techniques, we can merge our sexual and spiritual selves, giving birth to a sexual Inner Sage that embodies our immortal non-dual Original Nature and simultaneously expresses our unique individual will. This in turn can have a profound effect on our ability to make significant and profound contact with ETs and NHIs through our human initiated contact using the appropriate protocols, the subject of another book at another time.

Sexual Volatility as Alchemical Elixir

Our sexual nature holds the potential for profound spiritual transformation. While on the surface, our sexuality may seem volatile, it serves as our soul's alchemical elixir. Our sexual nature, with its inherent volatility, serves as the key to unlocking our deepest spiritual transformation. Through conscious and skillful cultivation of our sexual energy, we have the potential to experience rapid and deep spiritual growth. Lao Tzu's "Dual Cultivation" and "Angelic Dual Cultivation", sexual practices with a partner and "Single Cultivation" and "Angelic Cultivation" solo meditative inner sexual alchemy aim to utilize our tangible sexual essence to "capture" and crystallize the invisible essence of our spirit into a pure and divine energy that has the Tao as its source.

Union of Sexual and Spiritual Selves

As best as it can be described, through the integration of our sexual and spiritual selves, a "third self" emerges – our sexual sage hood, a special form of sexual and energy mastery. This Inner Sage manifests our immortal non-egoic, non-dual Original Nature. It transcends the limitations of dualistic thinking. It embodies the essence of non-duality while it simultaneously maintains a sexually polarized male and female body. This integration of two distinct energies allows us to even out the highs of one energy while elevating the lows of our partner. The combination of energies is nothing less than a tectonic transformative discovery for us. It allows us to become something better than who we were before the discovery and transformation. It helps us to become and express ourselves as unique individuals as embodiments of the expansive non-dual energy, known as yuan chi.

Epicene Androgyny: The Expression of Non-Dual Energy

Lao Tzu teaches us to know the masculine yet keep to the female. By doing so we dwell in the child-like virtue of constant virtue and become a ravine for the world. See., Book 1. Tao Te Ching, Verse 28. By mastering the union of our sexual and spiritual aspects and increasing our ability to direct and channel their energies lead to the manifestation of sexual and spiritual mastery and our own Inner Sage. This all-encompassing entity allows us to embody non-dual energy, known as "yuan chi", while existing in a sexually polarized male or female body. The Inner Sage represents the harmonious integration of our masculine and feminine energies, transcending the limitations of duality. It is through both dual and single cultivation that we can fully express our unique individual will, while remaining existentially connected to the Tao's expansive non-dual nature.

Immortality

Immortality as used by Lao Tzu in this work does not ultimately mean physical immortality. It refers to the immortality of the consciousness that is at its essence, spiritual in nature. In the realm of spirituality, the concept of immortality, therefore, takes on a profound and transformative meaning. Moving beyond mere enlightenment, spiritual immortality delves into the intricate process of soul individuation, where the individual soul where its journey is toward its own refinement and evolution ultimately to participate in the creation of the divine multiverse itself as evolves and integrates with the Tao, its cosmic counterpart.

Spiritual immortality, therefore, transcends the boundaries of physical existence, emphasizing the eternal essence of the soul. It heralds a journey of self-discovery and integration, leading towards a harmonious union between the conscious individual self and the cosmic consciousness. The quest for spiritual immortality ultimately involves the completion of the soul's individuation process, where the Lesser Self, devoid of ego merges with the Tao its Greater Self.

This integration paves the way for a deeper understanding of one's purpose and connection to the universal consciousness. Enlightened souls who attain spiritual immortality, possess the awareness and integrity to consciously reincarnate and evolve into higher spiritual beings. This continuous cycle of growth and transformation enables them to play an active role in the ongoing creation of the divine multiverse.

Conclusion

The principles of Tao self-cultivation offer a profound path towards spiritual immortality, guiding individuals to align ourselves with the forces of the Tao and awaken our inner wisdom and divine connection with immortality with our conscious soul. The whole purpose of self-cultivation, therefore, is not for merely contacting ET/NHIs or attaining simply better physical, mental and spiritual health but for spiritually rebirthing the mortal self into an immortal consciousness that transcends physical rebirth. It is a journey towards becoming an immortally conscious soul state where enlightened souls hold enough integrity to consciously reincarnate into the higher realms of physical, energetic, and spiritual existence.

The attainment of spiritual immortality is achieved through the embodiment of one's unique individuality while recognizing their profound connection with the divine. By actively engaging in the process of self-cultivation, practitioners contribute to the ongoing process of creation, playing an integral role in the grand tapestry of existence. This journey requires dedication, discipline, and a deep understanding of the principles and practices, such as sexual sagehood and the mystical trinity within.

Although self-cultivation is most helpful in our attaining good health and longevity in this life, the quest for immortality is not one of physical immortality. Instead, it is a journey towards the conscious recognition and embodiment of an immortal soul. In The Hua Hu Ching, Lao Tzu provides us with a roadmap for spiritually transforming our "mortal" conscious self into an immortal consciousness. This evolved spiritual consciousness is an actual state of being that transcends physical death and allows us to be reborn into the world not of form or energy but of pure being.

Spiritual immortality, therefore, goes beyond enlightenment and allows for the completion of the natural process of soul individuation in both our Lesser Self/personality and their cosmic Greater Self. This quest for immortality is not centered on physical immortality. Instead, the focus is on achieving a kind of soul immortality, where enlightened souls maintain enough integrity to consciously reincarnate into the higher spiritual beings of the universe. It is Nature's way of inviting and allowing the worthiest beings to participate in the ongoing creation of the divine multi-verse.

Self-cultivation is an ongoing process that goes beyond mere personal growth; it is a path towards aligning oneself with the profound forces of the Tao. Through disciplines such as surrender, harmony, simplicity, grounding, and integrity, individuals can cultivate essential qualities that accelerate internal change and harmonize their energies. Inner alchemy facilitates the transformation of our mortal self and the awakening of immortal consciousness, presenting a gateway to conscious spiritual immortality.

The journey towards spiritual immortality requires dedication, discipline, and a deep understanding of the self, both on an individual level and as part of the larger cosmic whole. By merging our inner and outer worlds, harmonizing our energies and aligning our actions with the principles of the Tao, we can transcend the boundaries of mortality and embark on a limitless voyage of self-discovery, spiritual fulfillment and unite ourselves with the other higher spiritual beings of the multi-verse. In this way, spiritual immortality becomes a profound way to fulfill our purpose and engage in the ongoing dance of creation. It is through spiritual immortality that we can actively contribute to the ongoing process of creation, playing our part in the grand tapestry of our universal existence. It is by transforming ourselves from the barbarians that we are into one the "Highest Spiritual Beings of the Universe" that we as newly enlightened souls can develop and refine our soul bodies to hold enough integral virtue to reincarnate consciously into our next existence and avoid the wheels of the endless cycle of birth, death and rebirth and transmigration into our human reincarnation here on earth. That is the whole point of our existence here anyway. Lao Tzu shows us the way out and ET/NHIs, the "Highest Spiritual Beings", the "Immortals of the Divine Realm", the "Unruling Rulers and Uncreating Creators" that Lao Tzu describes in the Hua Hu Ching are here to help.

THE HUA HU CHING

"There are more things in heaven and earth Horatio than are dreamt of in your philosophy."
- William Shakespeare, Hamlet

CHAPTER 1

The Whole Truth of the Universe

This, the first passage that we encounter on the Integral Way through the Hua Hu Ching captures the essence of its practice: simplicity, patience, compassion, and the pursuit of truth. By embracing the path of the Integral Way with joy and accepting our responsibility for spiritual evolution and service to others, the Way becomes a profound guide to our own personal virtue, abundance, and peace. By extension, the virtue that we develop within ourselves and our own being extends the being of the universe itself and those other beings and the higher and more advanced beings of the universe as well.

"I have reached the integral way by uniting with the mysterious and great Oneness. I call it the Tao. Simple that my teachings are; should one try to make a science or religion of them these teachings will elude them. Even though my teachings are profound and plain, in them you will find contained the whole truth of the universe. For those who wish to understand the entire truth of the universe, take joy and undertaking this work and in your service to others that will come to you inevitably as part of my teachings and your offering of universal compassion to all. Take joy in your lives, and keeping yourselves clean and fed. As you care for others and for yourselves, should you need instruction return to the masters of the Integral Way. The path of the integral way may be simple, but it will ultimately lead you to virtue, abundance and peace."

In this chapter, we begin to explore the teachings of Lao Tzu in the Hua Hu Ching and the Integral Way. It begins to lay out the path for those who seek to know the whole truth of the universe. This truth includes our own personal truth, that truth shared by the universe and its inhabitants.

At the core of the Hua Hu Ching is the Integral way, a universal path for us to unite with the great and mysterious Tao. This Way is not a religion or a science, and those who try to make it into one will miss the mark. It is no more of a philosophy than would be a map. Rather, it is a path of simplicity and humility that leads to a deep understanding of the nature of consciousness and of the universe. By following the Integral Way, we can experience the Tao itself directly and become one with it, making it integral to our nature and virtue. At the core of our conscious experience of awareness, awareness of ourselves and the awareness outside of ourselves is our personal awareness and experience of the Tao itself. Our further enlightenment comes as we begin to explore this internal and eternal path from ourselves to the Tao and then back into ourselves where the heart of the Tao forever dwells.

Years ago after I thanked an elder, a pastor of mine for helping me during a time of great grief he wisely said, "Michael, if we are not here to help one another, then I don't know why we are here." Much like What I was told by a devout man of God, at the heart of the Hua Hu Ching is the idea of being of service to others. What Lao Tzu emphasizes is that by caring for others and for themselves, we can, through the use of our own divine energies create a state of peace, virtue, and abundance for all. This is the ultimate goal of the Integral Way, and it is attainable by anyone who follows these teachings. By becoming responsible for our own health and wellbeing, by cleansing and feeding ourselves, by caring for others and helping those in need, and by turning for instruction to those who have become masters of life and the Integral Way, we can learn and evolve as spiritual beings living in an otherwise material existence inevitably to reach a state of deep understanding and profound enlightenment in this lifetime and in the next. The purpose of these teachings is spiritual evolution and refinement, not to be able to reach and contact ET/NHI. That can certainly be a byproduct of the Way.

The simple teachings of the Hua Hu Jing are profound in their wisdom. They teach us how to be better human beings and how to find peace, joy and contentment in our existence. They contain the entire truth of the universe. Outside of these truths, there is not much need, if any, to search elsewhere. Yet the words of these works are plain and easy to understand.

In practice, it may be difficult for us to let go of old ways of thinking and to begin as we operate in a world that is not a wholly physical-material one but one based on consciousness and the omnipresent conscious energy and supreme intelligence that is the Tao. Lao Tzu emphasizes that those who wish to know the whole truth must take joy in doing the work of self-cultivation and in their service to others. These attributes of our universal awareness come to us as we become conscious of the Tao and how she operates through her creation. By accepting our responsibility for serving others and by caring for ourselves physically, mentally and spiritually, we can prepare ourselves to receive the further instruction of the master Lao Tzu here. What he offers us through the Hua Hu Ching is the knowledge and opportunity to learn self-cultivation and to evolve to become a more divine spiritual being in this life and a more universal being in the next. This is how the Tao allows the souls to which she has given birth to evolve. It is how our souls are not only recycled but are refined through self-cultivation and service to be reincarnated into newer and higher levels of existence within its infinite universe.

CHAPTER 2

Undiscriminating "True" Virtue

This passage below highlights the practice of undiscriminating or indiscriminate virtue as a fundamental aspect of the Integral Way. Here Lao Tzu teaches that those who seek to know the whole truth should cultivate this virtue by caring for both deserving and undeserving individuals alike. By extending virtue to all without discrimination, we align ourselves with the path that leads back to the Tao, the ultimate truth and experience of universal and natural harmony. Once practiced, our dedication to and the act of undiscriminating virtue brings about within us a state of awareness, inner calmness and connection with the Tao. With that calm connective awareness comes a peaceful understanding and transformative conscious experience of our unity to the Tao and with all things.

"Those who wish to become aware of the entire truth of the universe should follow the Integral Way and adopt its practices. Time-honored are its disciplines. With them, you will be able to calm your minds and align yourselves naturally and harmoniously with all things. The primary practice in following the Integral Way is to practice non-discrimination in sharing your virtue. Just as the Tao equally takes care of both those who are deserving and those who are not so too must we. To follow the Integral Way and be universally virtuous, one must not discriminate between those in need. Though your virtue may be boundless, keep your feet placed firmly on the Integral path that will forever return you to the Tao."

The teachings of Lao Tzu here emphasize the importance of the Integral Universal Way, the path to uniting ourselves with the great and mysterious Tao. One of the key practices of the Integral Way is true and undiscriminating virtue. True virtue involves taking care of both deserving and undeserving individuals. It is not our place to judge or to discriminate between those in need. To embody the Tao is to help all those who need us. When we extend our true virtue in all directions, without discriminating between those in need, our feet are firmly planted on the path that is and always will return us to the Tao.

True Virtue

Undiscriminating, or indiscriminate virtue is "true virtue". True virtue is more than consciously seeing oneself in another and another in oneself. It is a practice that requires us to expand our awareness past the concepts of other and self and to recognize the universal interconnectedness and oneness of all things. It involves treating all beings with kindness and compassion, wherever they are from, and regardless of whether they are deserving or not. By serving others in this way, we can cultivate a sense of harmony and balance within ourselves, as well as within the world and by extension, the universe around us.

The practice of true virtue is particularly relevant in today's world, which is often marked by divisiveness and polarization. By extending our virtue in all directions, we can bridge gaps and build connections between individuals who may otherwise be at odds with us or with each other. This self-extension can help to heal divisions and foster understanding, creating a more peaceful and harmonious world. By doing so, as an individual and collectively as a civilization we can consciously prepare ourselves physically, mentally and spiritually so that we are ready for contact and meaningful interaction with the numerous advanced Extraterrestrial beings and non-human intelligences that have already arrived here on earth and who inhabit the rest of our infinite cosmos.

Daily Practice

In addition to true and undiscriminating virtue and service to others, the Integral Way also emphasizes the importance of other daily practices. These disciplines include but are not limited to mindfulness, meditation, wholistic arts and sciences. Much more will be written about these subjects in the chapters yet to come. By incorporating these time-honored disciplines into our daily lives, we can cultivate within ourselves a sense of meaning, purpose, inner strength, peace and clarity, which can help us to better navigate the challenges of life and become better, stronger and more resilient and highly evolved human beings with each passing day.

Conclusion

The practice of undiscriminating virtue is one of the key aspects of the Integral Way. The Integral Way is ultimately a universal path for all sapient and sentient beings of the universe to unite with the Tao. By extending our virtue in all directions, we can cultivate a sense of harmony and balance within ourselves and others and within the world and in the universe around us. This practice, along with other disciplines of the Integral Way, can help us to cultivate inner peace and clarity, and to better navigate the challenges of life, especially that we inevitably will face in a post ET/NHI contact world.

CHAPTER 3

Embodying the Tao

The passage below emphasizes the importance of embracing all things as a way to embody the Tao. It suggests that true embodiment of the Tao involves letting go of anger, resistance, and concepts of duality and separation. Acceptance plays a central role in a Tao-centered life. By embracing all things without division or antagonism, we can experience the harmonious oneness that exists within everything. This mindset transcends ideas of male and female, self and other, and even life and death, recognizing the interconnectedness and unity of all existence. The truth of this interconnectedness is realized when we reach out to ET/NHI and ask them to embrace us and share with us through their undiscriminating compassion their help and support. They too are followers of the Integral Way. The Tao is there for everybody and everything.

"If you wish to embody the Tao, practice non-discrimination by embracing all things. This means that you must accept and see things for what they are. Hold no anger or resistance against anything whether it is formed or formless, living or dead. At the very heart of the Tao lies this acceptance. Part of this acceptance is dissolving dualistic concepts like self and other, male and female and life and death that create separation.

The nature of the Tao is Universal Oneness. Division is contrary to its nature. By foregoing separation, antagonisms will disappear and with all things you will enter the harmonious Oneness."

Solving the Enigma: Embracing All Things by Letting Go

The Essence of the Tao is to Embrace All Things. The Tao is more than just a philosophy. It is a way of life that emphasizes harmony, balance, and the unity of all things. At the heart of the Tao is the idea of embracing all things, including ET and NHIs which means that one holds no anger or resistance toward any idea or thing, living or dead, formed or formless. This kind of universal acceptance is the very essence of the Tao and the key to living a fulfilling and peaceful life. At some point, humankind will have to embrace all things. Including ET aand NHIS, because they too are an integral part of our eternal and consubstantial Tao.

To embrace all things, we must first learn to dissolve our ego by letting go. We do this by first letting go of our anger, our resentments and our resistance. We must then learn to accept things as they are, without judgment or criticism. This does not mean that we need to approve of everything, but rather that we need to acknowledge that everything has a purpose and a place in the world. When we hold on to anger and resistance, we create unnecessary tension and conflict in our lives. This blocks the natural flow of the Tao's energy. It prevents us from seeing the beauty and wonder of the world around us. This is why the idea of letting go of things in life is so important to our self-cultivation and evolution as human beings.

The Illusion of Separation

No man or woman is an island. Islands are only an illusion of separation because their connection to the rest of the world is obscured by the water that covers the earth beneath them. Separation is the illusion. Connection is reality.

In order to embrace the oneness that is the Tao, in addition to letting go of anger and resistance, we must also rid ourselves of any concept of separation. This means letting go of our dualistic perceptions of ideas of separate male and female, self and other, and life and death. Each is an integral part of the other and both are necessary components of an integral whole. As separate concepts these seeming opposites are illusions and material constructs that can create division and disharmony in our lives. When we see ourselves as separate from others, human and otherwise, and something apart from the world and universe around us, we create unnecessary walls and barriers that prevent us from experiencing our connection with the Tao and the fullness of life.

Oneness and Universal Consciousness

When we embrace all things, we begin to experience Universal Consciousness and enter into a world of harmonious oneness with all things. When we see that everything is interconnected and that there is no separation between ourselves, other beings and the world around us, we can experience a conscious sense of unity and belonging. This brings peace and joy to our lives. In this state of universal being, we can feel our deep unfathomable connection to the earth and with all living beings. When we experience this unity consciousness, we are recognizing that we are all part of something far, far greater than just our individual selves. What we experience is something eternal. It is our divine spark of our Tao within. This realization of conscious unity becomes one of the bases for our connection to ET/NHI and our ability to communicate with them and to invoke their presence.

Conclusion

The essence of the Tao is to embrace all things. This means embracing the reality or being and emotions like anger and resistance and letting them go. It means letting go of our egos and the hurt that they produce. It means ridding ourselves of the illusion of separation. When we do these things, we enter into the harmonious oneness of all things, and can experience there a deep sense of peace, joy, and fulfillment.

As we embrace all things by letting go of ego, we begin to see the world with new eyes. We can discover the beauty and wonder of life and the Tao and become peaceful embodied examples of it. This embodiment is the essence of an evolved spiritual state and being with whom ET and NHIs will readily make contact. Somehow, they can sense it and see it in us. One's embodiment of the Tao is one of the primary indicia that shows our extraterrestrial friends and non-human intelligences that we are ready to reach out to engage the phenomenon and experience human initiated contact with them.

CHAPTER 4

Departing from the Integral Way, Perfecting Integral Virtue, The Subtle Law

This passage below highlights the universal truth that any departure from the Tao and its path the Integral Universal Way can contaminate one's spirit and cause the accumulation of karma and create unnecessary problems in this existence and in the next. Departures such as anger, conflict, self-absorption and resistance to the natural flow of things are deviations from the Tao's harmonious path. Accumulating karmic contamination over multiple lifetimes can burden the spirit. To cleanse ourselves of these poisonous contaminations, and prevent the accumulation of Karma in this lifetime, the practice of true virtue is a necessary antidote.

Practicing true or "Integral" virtue involves more than just being a good person. One does not perfect the Tao within by stealing ourselves away to some reclusive mountain retreat to meditate in seclusion for hours and days on end. True virtue requires engagement with others. We perfect the Tao within by living in the world and by selflessly assisting others. We perfect our virtue by offering help without limitation in terms of time, abilities, and possessions, without prejudice towards who is in need. It is emphasized that consistent with the "Law of Energy Response", the willingness to give blessings without limitations is connected to our ability to receive blessings. This interplay between our actions and the Law of Energy Response is considered a subtle operation of the Tao, illustrating the importance of selflessness and generosity in cultivating higher and higher levels spiritual refinement and purity that are necessary for our evolution as individual souls and as a species.

"One's Integral virtue is found in the Tao and through its Integral Way. When we depart from it, we contaminate our divine spirit. Anger, self-absorption and resistance are all departures. Over the course of our many lifetimes the contaminations that result from our departures from the Tao can accumulate to become even great weights. The only way one may cleanse oneself of contamination is to practice Integral virtue. To do this is simple. To others, practice indiscriminate selflessness. Whenever needed, without prejudice to the identity of those in need, offer your time, your possessions and your abilities in assistance to them as they require. If your willingness to give blessings is unlimited, so will it be that your ability to receive them is unlimited as well. If limited is your willingness to give blessings, then so too will be your capacity to receive them. This is part of the Tao and the operation of its subtle Law (The Law of Energy Response)."

All Choices Have Consequences

Embracing the Tao emphasizes accepting the subtle reality of the interconnectivity of all things in the universe. According to this principle, every action taken by humans can affect not only the mind, body and spirit of the individual but the universe's physical environment and its spiritual realm as well. Human beings can either choose to align themselves with the Tao and its Integral Way or depart from it. Every departure from the Tao can contaminate our spirit by introducing negative energy. Practicing Integral virtue is the only way to cleanse ourselves of egoism contaminations that lead us away from the Tao.

The concept of Integral virtue in the Tao refers to selflessly offering assistance to others, giving indiscriminately and without condition or limitation our time, abilities, and possessions in service, whenever and wherever needed, without prejudice concerning the identity of those in need. By practicing this kind of virtue, we can align ourselves with the Tao and its natural flow and contribute positively to the world and universe around us.

Departure From the Tao

Every departure from the Tao can contaminate our eternal conscious soul or "spirit". Anger, resistance, self-absorption are just a few examples of negative energy that can accumulate over many lifetimes and become a burden to our souls. The contaminations can weigh down the spirit and disconnect it from the flow of the universe, causing disharmony and suffering to ourselves and to others. This effect is not only personal and local but universal as well. Everything we do, every thought we think, every action and inaction has a consequential and eternal effect upon ourselves and the cosmos that is part and parcel of us and the Tao.

Practicing Integral virtue is the only way to cleanse ourselves of these contaminations. By giving selflessly to others, we can release ourselves from our egos and the negative energy that has accumulated within. By doing this we realign ourselves with the Tao, thereby allowing our souls to thrive and to flow freely with their creator. Only when we give blessings without limitations or conditions, can we open ourselves to the ability to receive them.

Conclusion

If anything, like the Christian idea of achieving salvation not by faith but by good deeds, the Tao and its universal Integral Way emphasize the importance of practicing virtue as the only way to cleanse ourselves of both egoism and karmic contaminations. By aligning oneself with the Tao and giving selflessly to others, we can release negative energy and realign ourselves with the positive energies and natural flow of the universe.

The practice of Integral virtue not only benefits others, but it also brings harmony, peace, and satisfaction to our own souls. It is also how we perfect our connection with the divine. The Tao does not discriminate with its compassion. So why would we. Therefore, it is essential to practice indiscriminate virtue and give of ourselves without prejudice concerning the identity of those in need. Only then can we attain the spiritual balance and universal harmony that is essential to our own personal and societal evolution and prepare us spiritually for our contact with ET and NHIs and the other higher spiritual beings of the universe. It is from these beings that in our time of need we may then ask for and receive indiscriminately their blessings without limitations through their Integral virtue as part and parcel of the Tao, the creator of us all.

CHAPTER 5

The "Spiritually Advanced" Person, The "Subtle Origin", *Prayer for ET/NHI Contact

This passage here encourages the contemplation and observation of the universe to gain insight into its nature and consequently the nature of the Tao, the "Subtle Origin". By going into the desert at night and gazing at the stars, one can witness the calm and stillness of the cosmos. The passage suggests that by settling one's mind, mirroring the serenity of the universe, and connecting with the subtle origin (the Tao), inner peace is achieved. As the mind calms, it expands and opens up, eventually becoming as vast and boundless as the night sky itself. This passage speaks to the profound potential for inner transformation and the limitless nature of the mind when aligned with the harmony of the universe. This alignment is essential for practitioners of the Integral Way who want to initiate contact and become more adept and frequent in their contact with ET and NHIs.

"If you believe that the universe is agitated, go at night, into the desert and look up into the stars and the darkness that seems to surround them. With practice, the answer eventually will soon become manifest. The spiritually advanced person, therefore, will settle his mind just as the Tao settles the stars. By connecting our minds with the Tao, the "Subtle Origin", we can lay claim to it. Once we claim the Tao, it expands naturally. Ultimately, with this expansion, our minds become as vastly immeasurable as a clear sky at night."

Settling the Mind

This quote by Lao Tzu is derived from the Tao Te Ching and encapsulates the Tao and its Integral Universal Way's emphasis on aligning oneself with the universe to find inner peace. The analogy with the universe's calmness and the vastness of the sky highlights the importance of settling our minds and connecting them with the subtle origin to attain spiritual balance. The importance of this unity, the Universal Consciousness that can be attained through peaceful meditative states cannot be gainsaid.

Upon looking out at the stars in the desert at night, we realize the vastness of the universe and the reality of our existence, that of other intelligences and ancient inhabitants of the universe. We understand both the infinitesimal smallness and youth of our own human existence and its integral importance. When we observe and contemplate-late the Tao, we can see that the universe is not agitated; it is harmonious, peaceful, and in perfect balance. We need to be committed to not disrupting that balance and to creating our own balanced, peaceful, and harmonious lives. By emulating this calmness, we can settle the mind and connect to our subtle origin.

The Spiritually Advanced Person

The spiritually advanced person, according to Tao and its universal and Integral Way is one who can connect with the subtle origin and attain inner peace. This is also called becoming one with the Tao. By calming the mind, the individual can plug themselves into the infinite and open themselves up to the vastness of the universe, expanding their consciousness and opening wider their universal perspective. This expansion, if called to, can lead us to engage in ET/NHI contact. With this contact comes a metanoia that gives us a greater conscious understanding of ourselves, the nature of true communication and the conscious experience of the unity of all things in the universe.

Conclusion

Lao Tzu's analogy of the universe settling the stars in the sky suggests that the universe is in perfect balance and harmony. The Integral Way emphasizes aligning ourselves with this balance and finding inner peace through settling the mind, settling our own stars through meditation and connecting ourselves with the subtle origin. By doing so, we can not only expand our consciousness but attain a greater understanding of the universe and our place within it. We can also use this heightened spiritual state of consciousness to project out into the universe our indiscriminate love and compassion with our peaceful intent to engage ET/NHI. In a relaxed and peaceful meditative state, we can send out our prayer for help and for their mental, physical, visual and spiritual contact necessary to achieve it. *

* UNIVERSAL CONVOCATION AND PRAYER FOR ET/NHI CONTACT

'Tonight, we gather here because we want to connect with the extraterrestrial, inter dimensional and all higher intelligent beings of the universe to unite in peace, truth, compassion and love. We ask that you Extraterrestrial, Interdimensional and Non-human intelligences and energies who hail from our common infinite divine source, listen to us and join us here in this place tonight. Come celebrate with us and know that we accept, appreciate and celebrate your presence.

Please come visit with us and reveal yourselves. Allow us to embrace you and to share our open, accepting, and loving hearts with you. We are in a difficult time here on this planet and need your reassuring presence to help us to grow spiritually to ensure our evolution and survival. Your destiny and ours are the same. We share a common bond with the Universal Creator. Our future existence and survival is at risk without your care and support. So please join us here tonight.

We know that you can hear us and understand us in ways that are beyond words. Some of us have already experienced your healing, compassion and love. Please come visit us again. We believe that your wise, ancient, and loving ways will help us in our time of need. So, our most dear celestial brothers and sisters, the "unruling rulers and uncreating creators of the vast universe"; divine angels of the Integral Way, please join us here tonight and bring to us your wisdom, healing energies, and patient love and compassion.

We are here to seek the truth and learn by connecting with your higher spiritual presence. So, we invite you tonight to join us in this our Universal Convocation and Prayer for Contact. Together, with your help, we can create a new chapter in human history, one in which we value each individual's soul and that is marked by universal truth, compassion, patience, unity, joy and spiritual growth. Let us take this step towards a brighter and more expansive future together tonight and every evening to follow.

With our hearts and minds open, please give us a sign by your visual presence that you have heard us and that we have made connection with you and touched your hearts as well. With all of our tidings of peace, love and mutual compassion, may the love and compassion that unite us in this circle also be the same that unites us with you here tonight. So, it is said, Let it be so. Amen"

CHAPTER 6

Being One with the Tao

The Tao is often described with many definitions. The Tao is generally understood as an ineffable and formless principle and intelligence that underlies everything. Trying to conceptualize or define it too rigidly can limit our understanding of its true nature. Instead, embracing the experience of the Tao without trying to confine it within mental constructs allows for a deeper connection and appreciation of its essence. By being open and receptive to the flow of the Tao, we can find contentment and support in its unbounded and eternal presence.

> **"To all forms does the Tao give rise. Though the Tao creates all, no form of its own does it have. For the one who affixes a picture of the Tao in his or her mind, he or she that tries, loses it. Like capturing and pinning a butterfly, when it ceases to fly, it is no longer a butterfly. All one has is its dead husk. Why lose the butterfly by trying to capture it? Simply learn to be content while you are experiencing it. It is the same with the Tao."**

The Tao gives rise to all forms, yet it has no form of its own. This statement encapsulates the essence of the Tao and its Integral Universal Way a philosophy and path for living peacefully within the universe that has been around for billions of years. The concept of "Tao" is difficult to define in a few words but can broadly be understood as the "way" or the "path". The Tao is a supremely intelligent ever-flowing force that permeates everything around us and gives rise to all forms.

An interesting aspect of Tao is that it has no form of its own. This means that it exists in yet cannot be confined, captured or even conceptualized in any particular shape or form. If you attempt to do so, you will lose it. The Tao is like a butterfly that is in a constant state of motion. It cannot be captured or pinned down without losing its essence. Is this not also the same at the quantum level? Does not our conscious observation of the wave phenomena turn the energy of the wave, the butterfly flying, into the particle?

Being One with the Tao

So, what can we do to experience the underlying consciousness and wave of energy that is the Tao? The answer is that we need not try to parse it out and separate the experience from its observation. We should be content with simply experiencing it. The Tao cannot be described or explained in words; it is something that must be felt to be experienced. One can experience Tao by being present in the moment and simply observing its beauty in the natural flow of things. Being one with the Tao is about being aware of the rhythms of nature and the ebb and flow of life.

Conclusion

The concept of Tao is not something that can be captured or explained in a fixed form. It is form and it is formless. It is both particle and wave. It is an ageless, ever-changing intelligent and creative force that gives rise to all forms, yet enigmatically, it has no form of its own. Attempting to pin it down like a butterfly or to describe or taxonomize or fixate on it or a particular image is like trying to grab water with an open hand. Grasping at the flow of the Tao will only cause us to lose its essence.

The Tao cannot be contained but it can be experienced, and its energy utilized for our own wellbeing. The best way to experience the Tao is to be content with simply experiencing it. Becoming one with the Tao is a spiritual state. It is about being present in the here and now and experiencing the present moment. It is also internalized by being at peace with ourselves and our surroundings and by our observing the natural flow of things. We become one with the Tao by accepting ourselves for what we are and the things and events that surround us for what they are.

CHAPTER 7

Beginning on the Path of the Integral Way

The teaching of the Integral Universal Way emphasizes the timeless essence of the Tao and its potential for its own embodiment by those who seek to experience and embody it. While the specific forms and expressions of the teachings that make up the Integral Way may vary across generations and languages, certain fundamental principles remain constant. Cultivating undiscriminating virtue, transcending dualistic thinking, and letting go of mental biases are central aspects of this path. By engaging in these practices, individuals can initiate a process of liberation and foster a deeper understanding of the universe as a harmonious oneness with which they can integrate themselves. This teaching of the Integral Way has endured for milenia and will endure as long as there are both the Tao itself and those beings who aspire to integrate it into their lives and make it manifest in their core values and the way they live.

"The Integral Way will continue to be taught for so long as there is a Tao and ones who wishe to embody it. What is written today in these passages will reappear in differing forms in the innumerable generations to come. What is never changing is that for those who intend to experience true Oneness, they must practice and embody indiscriminate virtue. To do this, all forms of duality must be dissolved. Distinctions like good and evil, high, and low, ugly and beautiful must be eliminated from one's thought. All cultural, religious, and mental biases must be abandoned. The one who seeks to embody the Tao must open and hold his or her mind free. One should let go of any thought that interferes with his or her understanding of the Tao as the harmonious

great Oneness. The beginning of liberation begins with these practices."

The Integral Universal Way is the spiritual path of all advanced intelligent beings of the universe. Its teachings have continued to be passed down from one spiritual entity to another for eons and it will continue to be passed down as long as there are those who seek to embody it. Although the teachings may take on different forms throughout time, the core principles will remain unchanged as they embody the universal truth of the Tao itself.

Achieving Oneness

To achieve oneness with the Tao, one must live a life of truth and practice indiscriminate compassion through undiscriminating virtue. This involves dissolving all ideas of duality and eliminating judgments of good and bad, beautiful, and ugly, or high and low and even life and death. One must also abandon any mental bias that arises from cultural or religious belief to fully experience the universe as harmonious oneness. To achieve liberation, one's mind must be free of any thought that interferes with their understanding of the world as it is and the cosmos itself as a unified, interconnected, and inter-related whole.

The beginning of these practices marks the start of our own liberation and the realization of our potential for our transformation from ego centered unconscious physical beings to conscious spiritually beings who are here to evolve beyond ego and the material world into a higher and more spiritually refined being who is better able to further evolve beyond the world of form and explore the universe.

Those who embody the principles of the Integral Universal Way and cultivate undiscriminating virtue, transcend judgment and dualistic thinking, and who let go of their religious and philosophical biases will inevitably embody the Tao. Such humanly divine beings can come to lead by their example and inspire future generations to do the same as they have done. By practicing undiscriminating Integral virtue and dissolving the veil of duality, we can all experience the natural calm and joy that is oneness with the Tao. We can be reborn and experience the universe in a new, unified light. Because of its fruit, the tree of the Integral Universal Way will continue to be relevant and valuable to all the Tao's children for as long as there are beings who seek enlightenment, liberation, peace and understanding and oneness for themselves and for the societies and worlds in which they live in this infinite universe that is the creation of the Tao.

CHAPTER 8

The Importance of Being Aware of the Great Oneness

The nature of the Tao and the Integral Way often transcend verbal and conceptual understanding. While teachings and expressions may vary, their ultimate purpose is to point beyond words and concepts towards the direct experience of oneness. The essence of the Tao cannot be fully captured or confined by any specific religious, scientific, philosophic, political or informational framework. Instead, it is through cultivating awareness of the interconnectedness and unity of all things that one can come closer to the realization of the Tao. It is in this awareness that the wisdom of the Integral Way resides. It is this awareness through which we become most readily connected to ET and NHIs who are our other spiritual brothers and sisters within the Tao.

"To confess, there is nothing here really to teach. There is no science, no religion, no tome or great body of information that will return your thoughts back to the Tao. One day I may speak of the Tao in one fashion and tomorrow in yet another. The Tao that can be described is not the eternal Tao. Similarly, both it and its Integral Way are beyond both mind and words. I can direct you to the path but I cannot find it or walk it for you. All that is really necessary is that you be aware of the great Oneness the Tao and of all things."

In this chapter, Lao Tzu acknowledges that there is no definitive body of knowledge that can teach us how to return to the Tao. No religion, no science, no information can lead the mind back to this state of being. Although the speaker may express this truth in various ways, and direct or point one toward the

Tao, the Integral Universal Way will always be a concept that is beyond words and mind.

To come closer to the Tao, one first must be aware of the oneness of things. This involves recognizing the universality and interconnectedness of everything. This understanding is something that cannot be taught in a traditional sense but comes from an internal awareness of the world and the universe of which it and we too are integral parts. This awareness transcends the limits of language and concepts to bring through our own personal experience, a profound sense of peace and unity with the entire universe.

The Integral Way exists outside of literal concepts, language, and constructs. It is something that can only be sensed and felt through a heightened awareness of the world around us. To achieve oneness with the Tao, we must be mindful of the collective experience and look beyond labels and preconceptions of reality that it us..

The Integral Universal Way is more that just a path. It is an aspect of being that lies beyond instruction and knowledge. It is an understanding at the level of gnosis. Nonetheless, however we describe it, the Universal Way is the aspect of being that we share with ET and NHIs. It is illuminated within us by being aware of the oneness of things and allowing ourselves to experience the interconnectedness of it all. The Integral Way exists beyond language and mind. Understanding the Integral Way comes from a personal and profound experience of the world and the nature and connectedness of all things in our own universe and those beyond our own as well.

CHAPTER 9

Admiration and Spiritual Evolution

In this passage Lao Tzu gives us a profound perspective about life. Lao Tzu teaches us here that instead of seeking admiration through material wealth, to bring forth the greatest good in life, one should focus on aligning themselves with the principles of the Tao and sharing its teachings with others. By doing so, they can become aware and experience the blessings that arise from this awareness and living in harmony with the Tao. This new paradigm encourages a shift in priorities from one's external validation to that of inner fulfillment and spiritual growth.

> **"If you want to gain great admiration in the world, it would behoove you to build up a great treasure and then to give it away. The world will respond to you in proportion to the amount that you give away. Such a pursuit is meaningless, however, because you strive for admiration. There is no need for such striving. Instead, esteem the Tao. Live in accord with its Integral Way. Selflessly share the Tao and these teachings so that others will be directed to it. When you do, immersed you will be with the blessings that from it immeasurably flow."**

The Desire for Admiration

The idea of amassing a great fortune and giving it away in hopes of gaining admiration and appreciation from the world is an intriguing concept that has been explored by many throughout history. In the Tao and through the Integral Way, it is believed that such desires are meaningless and should be replaced by a focus on living and becoming one with the Tao through our living simple, truthful, patient and compassionate lives.

The desire for admiration is a meaningless form of ego. By rejecting our egos, by living in accordance with the Tao and by sharing its teachings with others both we and they can and will lead more fulfilling lives.

The desire for admiration and need for appreciation from others are arguably a natural human feeling at some level. However, many people believe that accumulating vast amounts of wealth will lead to admiration from others. What they do not realize is that this sort of admiration is often fleeting and hollow as it does not bring true happiness. It may be that admiration is more a result of the wealth itself, rather than the actions or character of the person that attained it. If one were to give away a great fortune, the admiration from others may increase, but it is still based on wealth, rather than the person. In a spiritual sense, if we were to gain the world and give it away for the purpose of being admired by others, nothing would be gained from it. The purpose of the gift would still be for something other than giving for the sake of satisfying the needs of others.

Spiritual Evolution

In contrast, living in accordance with the Tao and learning and sharing its teachings can lead us to evolve physically, mentally and spiritually towards a more fulfilling life. The Tao's Integral Way is a path of virtue that seeks harmony with nature through universal ethical principles. It can lead to a sense of peace, tranquility, and contentment. When we follow the Tao and share its teachings with others, we are contributing to the betterment of society and to the peace and harmony of all beings within the universe. This type of contribution is much more admirable and fulfilling than merely amassing a great fortune or even giving it all away for the purpose of admiration or other gain.

The concept of amassing a great fortune and giving it away for admiration is a shallow and meaningless pursuit. It is a desire that is driven by the vanity of ego rather than a genuine compassionate desire to help others. Instead of placing our esteem in material wealth, we should place our esteem in the Tao and abide by it and to live in accordance with its teachings. By doing so, we can experience the blessings that naturally flow from it and contribute to the betterment of our lives and the lives of others.

Conclusion

What Lao Tzu inexplicably leads us to conclude here is that the desire for admiration and appreciation from others should not be the focus of our lives. Instead, we should do what we can in order to live in accordance with the Tao and share its simple teachings with others. Such a life will lead to greater fulfillment in life through our relationships with others and ultimately our contribution to the betterment of all life here on earth and in the universe.

CHAPTER 10

Understanding the Ego

The ego is a monkey catapulting through the jungle. Totally fascinated by the realm of the senses, it swings from one desire to the next, one conflict to the next, one self-centered idea to the next. The monkey is a lower and more base form of intelligent life. If you threaten it, the monkey will actually fear for its life. Although humans share much DNA with these and other primates, we need not act like them. We are all capable of transcending our egos, our lower "monkey" selves.

What Lao Tzu teaches here is that for us to let this monkey go we must let our senses go. Let desires go. Let conflicts go. Let ideas go. Let the fiction of life and death go. Just remain in the center, watching. And then forget that you are there.

> **"The ego is like a monkey that swings from tree to tree and catapults itself through the jungle. Fascinated totally by its senses, it jumps from one self-centered idea, conflict or desire to another. When threatened, it fears for its life. Let go of the monkey. Let go of senses. Let go of desire. Let go of dualistic fictions like life and death. Just center yourself. Watch silently and become the observer and forget then that you are even there."**

The human ego is a complex and often confusing entity that governs our thoughts, actions, and behavior. It is driven by the endless pursuit of sensory pleasures and is constantly swinging from one desire to the next, seeking self-gratification. However, it is important to understand that this self-centered nature of the ego does more harm than good. By letting go of the ego, desires, conflicts, and the fiction of life and death we can lead to a state of peace and contentment.

The Ego

The ego is completely mesmerized by the physical and sensory realms. It thrives on the next thrill, the next desire, the next self-centered idea, and the next self-satisfying conflict. In fact, the ego fears for its life when threatened, leading to never-ending cycles of conflict and struggle. What is true for the ego in general is true for ego-based societies as well.

For both the individual and for society, we can free ourselves from this endless cycle, but first, we need to understand that the ego is ultimately a fictional construct that has no basis in reality. By recognizing and detaching ourselves from the ego, we can start to let go of unhealthy desires, conflicts, self-centered ideas and dangerous social pathologies.

The second thing we must understand is that regardless of how much the ego desires something, the possession of material things can never bring us lasting happiness and peace. Instead, true happiness can only be found when we live in the present moment, without getting attached to our fears, desires, or regrets.

Similarly, conflicts arise when our ego needs to protect or defend itself. By recognizing the ego for what it is, we can let go of conflicts and instead focus on finding common ground with others and end our conflicts with them.

Finally, we need to understand that the ego-driven fear of death and the desire for a prolonged lifespan only add to our suffering. In truth, there is no death, only the endless cycle of life and birth of the eternal soul that passes through both the physical and spiritual realms. By letting go of the fiction of death, we can focus on the present moment and find peace in living our lives as eternal immortal souls.

The Ego and ET/NHI

ET/NHIs understand the reality of life, death, and rebirth as part of the infinite Tao, and in their and our immortal and universal souls. They have learned to dissolve the ego into the Tao and have created ancient, long-lasting, and successful spiritual societies that are built around that reality. When we eliminate our egos, we show them that we have evolved enough spiritually so as to be ready for further development through our contact with them.

Conclusion

The pursuit of sensory pleasures and self-gratification through the ego is ultimately a fruitless endeavor that only leads to suffering and discontentment. By recognizing the true nature of the ego and letting go of desires and conflicts, we can attain enlightenment, a state of peace and inner contentment. This enlightenment and the means by which it can be found through the Tao and the Integral Way can and should be shared with others. It is how we refine and perfect ourselves. With ET/NHI quickly becoming the reality in a post-contact and post-disclosure, now is the time to dissolve our monkey-like ego, let go of sensory desires, conflicts, ideas, and the fiction of life and death, and live in a state of mindfulness and universal presence. Once we can begin to do this, then sustained peaceful positive contact with ET and NHIs and a better future for all beings will be our inevitable reality.

CHAPTER 11

Becoming One with the Tao

In this passage on becoming one with the Tao, Lao Tzu emphasizes the importance of transcending divisions and distinctions in order to experience Universal Consciousness, one's mindful unity and harmony with the subtle truth of the Tao. He suggests that attaching preferences and judgments to sensory experiences and mental constructs creates spiritual and cognitive separation. It is the dualistic way of thinking that prevents us from perceiving the true nature of things, the subtle truth, the Tao. By cultivating a quiet mind detached from judgment and duality, one can open themselves to a deeper understanding and alignment with the underlying unity of all things. With this deeper understanding of integral truth and the nature of all things and our mental, physical, and spiritual alignment with the Tao, we can prepare ourselves for meaningful contact with ET and NHIs who share with us the same understanding and alignment.

"Is your mind separated from itself? Do you find one scent or smell more appealing than another? Do you prefer one feeling or flavor over another? Is your work profane but your practice sacred? If you do any of these, then your mind is separated from both itself and the great Oneness of the Tao.

To be one with the Tao, your mind must be kept free of distinctions and divisions. Keep your mind detached and free of these things and it will become simple and quiet. When the mind is quiet and simple all things will then be able to exist harmoniously. When your mind begins to exist in harmony, then you will begin to perceive 'the subtle truth'. The subtle truth is that all,

**including yourself are one and infinitely connected in
and through the Tao."**

How to Become One with the Tao

We can all be victims of our own preferences and prejudices.
The Tao does not play favoritism. In this chapter we learn that
in order to become one with the Tao, our minds need to be
free of divisions and distinctions such as preferences for certain scents, flavors, and feelings. This is because having these
preferences separates us from oneness and the Tao, which is
the ultimate reality that pervades everything. By keeping our
minds free of these distinctions, we can begin to perceive the
subtle truth and exist in harmony with all things.

When life is simple and the mind is detached and quiet, it can
exist in a state of peace and oneness with the universe. This
detachment allows us to see beyond the surface-level distinctions, divisions, and fears that we often create in our minds.
These schisms are exemplified by Lao Tzu by the separation
between sacred and profane or work and spiritual practice,
to mention just two. There certainly are more. In reality, all
aspects of our lives can exist in harmony with each other as
long as we remain detached and present. Once we can do this,
every act, even the most mundane, can become a meditative
spiritual act, a sacred practice of mindfulness that connects us
to the Tao and with each other.

Conclusion

Making both the sacred and the profane one in the same can
be hard to wrap one's mind around. But understanding that
we can make even the most boring or arduous of tasks into
a meditative spiritual exercise is central to the practice of the
Integral Way. Nothing is too big or too small to deserve our
focus and attention when that attention is necessary.

To truly understand the Tao, the "subtle truth" of existence, therefore, we must first let go of our judgments, our preferences, and attachments and cultivate a quiet undistracted mind. Such a mind is one free from judgment, divisions, and dualistic distinctions like good and bad, young and old, ugly and beautiful and life and death. Their underlying unifying reality is the Tao. By doing as Lao Tzu instructs, we can experience the unity and indistinguishable oneness of all things and all beings and live in harmony with the world and with all beings. Among these beings are the ET and NHIs, the highest spiritual beings who inhabit both our world and the universe around us.

CHAPTER 12

The Highest Spiritual Beings

What Lao Tzu recognizes in this chapter is the need of all spiritual beings to inhabit sacred space, to seek the respect and companionship of other spiritual beings and be protected by powerful energy forces. These forces can be human. These forces can be Extraterrestrials and Non-human. They can be angelic and divine. All are part of the Tao and follow the Integral and Universal Way.

The passage suggests that by cherishing and practicing the Integral Way, as well as sharing its teachings with others, one can receive abundant blessings from the universe and its more advanced inhabitants. Here Lao Tzu introduces us to the idea of the "highest spiritual beings" and conveys the idea that living in alignment with spiritual principles can bring profound and infinite rewards. And so, for those who practice the Integral Way and teach it to others, it does.

> **"Is it sacred space that you wish to inhabit? Is it the companionship and respect of the highest of spiritual beings? Do you seek the protection of the guardians of the eight rays of energy? If you seek these, then it is the Integral Way that you must cherish. You should regard these teachings with reverence. Their truths practice. Illuminate others with them. Should you do these things, then from the universe, as many blessings will you receive as in the River of Timelessness are there grains of sand."**

The Highest Spiritual Beings

In this chapter, Lao Tzu mentions for the first time the "highest spiritual beings". He also tells us how to find their companionship and gain their respect. The identity of these sacred beings is not limited to human beings who have recognized their own divinity in the Tao but includes Universal beings who are not from this earth or even this dimension. Lao Tzu also alludes to otherwise supernatural powers that come to those who have found and entered the sacred space where the peace and tranquility of Tao is realized. The place where our minds begin to exist in harmony and perceive 'the subtle truth'.

Like elements attract. In such spiritual states, other spiritual beings will come to find us. These beings include ET/NHI.

In this quote Lao Tzu also teaches us that the blessings we can receive from practicing the Integral Way are vast and abundant, extending beyond what our minds can comprehend. It speaks to the idea that by living in alignment with the Tao and its spiritual principles, we can tap into the universal energy that surrounds us and bring about positive change in our lives and the lives of those around us.

Lao Tzu emphasizes the importance of following the Integral Way and cherishing its teachings with reverence. By doing so, we can inhabit sacred space, receive the respect and companionship of spiritual beings, (ET/NHIs) and be protected by the "guardians of the eight powerful energy rays". *

In order to completely follow the Integral Universal Way, we need to practice its truths and teach them and illuminate others. This means not only studying the teachings of Lao Tzu but also actively integrating them into our daily lives and sharing them with others. There is no greater gift than sharing these gifts. When we share the Tao with others, we become a vessel for the Tao and a conduit for the teachings of the Integral Way.

By doing so, we can receive innumerable and unimaginable blessings from the universe. These blessings include the presence of the highest spiritual beings in our lives.

Sacred Space

By following the Integral Way and cherishing its teachings with reverence, we can find and inhabit "sacred space" where we can tap into the Tao's spiritual realm and achieve a sense of meaning, purpose, and connection in our lives and with the rest of the highest spiritual inhabitants of the universe.

One's sacred space can but does not necessarily mean a physical space. Sacred space is a harmonious, calm, peaceful, mental and spiritual state where we can find peace of mind and inner peace. It is through this state that we can connect ourselves with the "highest spiritual beings" and "guardians", (ET and NHIs) about which Lao Tzu begins to introduce us here.

The Guardians of the Eight Powerful Energy Rays: Real Manifestations of Energy and Form Beyond Human Definition.

According to Taoist thought the "guardians of the eight powerful energy rays" are eight deities or spiritual entities that are associated with the eight energy bodies or energy centers, "shakras" in the human body. These guardians are said to be responsible for protecting and guiding individuals who are seeking to cultivate their spiritual development and achieve a full awakening of their being.

The eight guardians of the energy rays are also known as the "ba xian" in Chinese, which means "eight immortals". Each of the eight immortals is associated with a specific energy body or center* and is said to possess unique qualities and abilities that can help individuals overcome blockages in their energy flow and achieve greater balance and harmony.

The eight immortals are often depicted in Taoist art and mythology as wise sages or hermits who possess extraordinary spiritual abilities and profound insights into the nature of reality. They represent the ideal of spiritual perfection in Taoist philosophy and are revered as powerful allies in one's spiritual journey.

The Guardians of the Eight Powerful Energy Rays represent an aspect of the human journey towards enlightenment and spiritual growth. These guardians, wherever they may be from or however they are depicted or represented, are said to protect individuals on their spiritual paths, helping them overcome obstacles and reach higher levels of consciousness.

However, for those of us who have experienced ET/NHI (extraterrestrial/non-human intelligence) contact, we understand that the existence of these guardians and higher beings goes beyond art and mere allegory or human definition. We have seen them with our own eyes, felt their presence, and received their guidance, healing, and grace.

Whether these guardians take the form of angels, ET/NHI, or other manifestations, no matter what one calls them they are undoubtedly real manifestations of energies and often physical entities created and sent by the Tao, God, our divine source, to assist those who call upon them for aid, companionship and protection in times of need.

Those of us who have experienced ET/NHI contact know firsthand the profound impact these guardians and higher beings can have on our lives. Experiencing their presence is the experience of universal truth and the existential reassurance that we humans are neither alone and that the universe is a not a hostile place devoid of love or compassion. Contact with ET/NHIS brings us a deep sense of peace and protection, guiding us towards our highest spiritual path and helping us navigate the complexities of life.

To those who may be skeptical of the existence of these actual "guardians", approach the topic with an open mind. There are countless reports of individuals experiencing encounters with ET/NHI, guardian angels, and feeling in them the presence of peaceful, compassionate, and intelligent divine beings. These experiences are real and cannot be explained away as mere imagination or hallucination.

Instead, they represent a powerful connection to a force greater than us, a force that is here to help us on our journey towards spiritual growth and enlightenment. By calling upon ET/NHI, the "highest spiritual beings", the "Guardians of the Eight Powerful Energy Rays", we open ourselves up to this powerful benevolent force. When we open ourselves to it we can allow it to guide us towards contact and a greater understanding and wisdom about ourselves and the beings and universe that connects and surrounds us.

Connecting with ET/NHI

Lao Tzu's juxtaposition between his mention of the "companionship of the highest spiritual beings" and the existence of the "Guardians of the Eight Powerful Energy Rays" is no accident. It is a profound reminder of the interconnectedness of all beings and all things. While we may never fully describe them or know what they call themselves or yet understand the physical nature of these beings, we can rest assured that they are real and that they are here to help us on our journey and in our time of need. We should be open to this reality in order to explore the vastness of the universe, and to trust in the wisdom and guidance of those beings who exist beyond our own limited understanding and antiquated and limited descriptions. Contact with these divine and universal beings is an inevitable part of those who follow the Integral Universal Way and care to make friends and compassionate companions of them.

Finally, our connections with ET/NHI are made possible through our integral spiritual oneness with the divine, infinite and universal Tao. These connections are not limited to the spiritually elevated beings of this earthly world. In later chapters of this work, we will learn that the elevated state of our own spiritual nature extends out to all Integral universal beings throughout the cosmos. These beings, followers of the Tao and its integral way inevitably include ET and NHIs. Once we learn to calm our minds and find our inner peace, we can through meditation consciously invite and invoke their presence and enjoy the companionship and respect of our guardians, the highest of all spiritual beings. From them there are as many blessings for us to receive as there are in the River of Timelessness grains of sand.

*THE EIGHT ENERGY BODIES

The eight energy bodies in our being, each of which has its own unique function and contributes to our overall well-being.

The <u>first energy body</u> is the physical body, which is our tangible, material form that is sustained by the second energy body - the Qi, or chi body.

The <u>second energy body</u> is the chi or "ethereal" body. This body occupies and extends its aura out the physical body between 2" for those who are ill to 2' for those who are healthy and have great vitality. Chi energy body is responsible for fueling the physical body and maintaining its vitality.

The <u>third energy body</u>, the emotional body, is responsible for generating our emotions - both positive and negative. It is the source of our feelings of joy, anger, fear, love, and so on.

The <u>fourth energy body</u>, the mental body, is responsible for our thoughts and thinking patterns. It determines whether our thoughts are clear or confused and influences our ability to process information and make decisions.

The fifth energy body, the psychic body, allows us to access our hidden internal capacities and develop our intuition or psychic perceptions which may become more concrete over time.

The sixth energy body, the causal body, is linked to karma. It plays a role in causing the flow of karma in our lives - the consequences of our actions and the reactions we receive from them.

The seventh energy body, the body of individuality, enables the actual birth of our spiritual being, commonly referred to as our essence. It is responsible for bringing forth our unique qualities into the world.

The eighth energy body, the realization of the TAO or the entire universe. This universal or unity consciousness is something that is rare in that few people actualize it without the practice of spiritual education and self-cultivation. It is a state of complete oneness with the universe, where there is no separation between us and all that exists.

Understanding and working with these eight energy bodies can help us achieve greater balance, harmony, and self-awareness in our lives. By recognizing the interconnected nature of these bodies, we can begin to integrate them into our daily lives and improve our overall physical, mental and spiritual well-being.

CHAPTER 13

Boundlessness

The passage here highlights the limitations of our conceptual understanding when it comes to comprehending the vastness of the universe and the nature of the Tao. It suggests that our attempts to grasp and control the ineffable essence of the Tao through the mind's notions are futile. The Tao, being formless and beyond knowing, cannot be fully captured, managed through or truly understood by intellectual means. However, the passage offers solace by suggesting allegorically that by letting go of our knives and by surrendering to the Tao, we can experience a profound connection with it. In that state of surrender, the Tao becomes accessible and tangible to us making our consciousness a "direct link with life's origin" *. It is in this state that of surrender and letting go of our egos that we can best connect with the Tao and through it, connect ourselves with the highest spiritual beings and the guardians that the Tao provides for us, our spiritual enlightenment, protection and social evolution.

"The particles that form the universe are not tiny. Nor is the universe they form vast. Tiny and vast are relative notions of the mind that like a sharp knife constantly chips away at the Tao by trying to grasp and manage it. The Tao is beyond form. Hence it is ungraspable. The Tao is beyond knowing and so, it cannot be managed. However, there is one consolation. Once you let go of the knife, at your fingertips you will find the Tao."

The True Nature of the Universe

"Truly, we live with mysteries too marvelous to be understood."
- Mary Oliver

Just like American poet Mary Oliver's beautiful quote above, this passage of Lao Tzu above also speaks to that marvelous mystery and the inherent limitations of the human mind and its ability to perceive reality. We have to accept the fact that the universe is too complex to be able to fully grasp through reason alone. Besides our limited senses, our thoughts, ideas and conditioning often create boundaries that prevent us from fully experiencing and understanding the true nature of reality and appreciating the marvelous mystery of creation that is the Tao.

The idea that the tiny particles which form the universe are not truly "tiny" speaks to both relativism and the interconnectedness of all things. At the quantum level, particles are not separate entities, but rather they are part of a larger whole. Similarly, the universe itself is not truly "vast" in the sense that it is separate from us, but rather we are an integral part of something that is immeasurable and unlimited.

When we try to grasp and manage the Tao, especially with our five physical senses and three-dimensional minds, we are limiting ourselves and missing out on the magnificent infinite possibilities that exist beyond our understanding. It is only by letting go of our preconceived mental notions and ideas that we can truly access the Tao, and experience its boundlessness and the fullness and wonder of life.

So, let us all strive to surrender our mind's knives that want to dissect, parse and put names to things. In the physical relativistic world, although these actions have their place; in a world beyond material physical reality and constructs like time and space, by confining ourselves to these tools we limit our experience of the Tao and its universe. Instead, let us unravel the enigma by embracing the ungraspable, accepting and enigmatic unimaginable and unmanageable boundless nature of the Tao. In doing so, we may find that what we once sought

to understand and control and thought to beyond our reach
is waiting for us right at our fingertips.
                    *Gargi Mitra-Delmonte

CHAPTER 14

Integral Oneness

This chapter invites us to explore our own self cultivation and spiritual evolution through the dissolution of ego and the transcendence of dualistic thinking. Even though seeing ourselves in others and others in ourselves, Lao Tzu encourages us to let go of the concepts of self and other, as well as various dualities such as male and female, short and long, and life and death in order to see everything as the Tao. By releasing these dualistic notions and embracing the Tao without skepticism or panic, we can evolve spiritually and come closer to experiencing the original Integral Oneness that is the Tao.

The passage also advises us to avoid attaching exceptional or exalted qualities to Oneness. It emphasizes that Oneness is beyond such labels and descriptions—it is the direct experience of the Tao and its essential, and complete truth that is central to the core of our infinite, conscious spiritual existence. By approaching oneness with an open mind and without preconceived notions, we can deepen our understanding and connection with the fundamental infinite unity of all things. It is also upon this understanding that our fundamental connection with ET/NHIs lies.

"The Integral Way requires us to dissolve the ego. Can you do this? Can you abandon the notions of good and evil, short and long and of male and female? Can you relinquish these dualities and without panic or skepticism, accept the Tao and embrace it? If you can do these things, you will arrive at the heart of the Tao's integral oneness. On your path remember that the Tao is the complete, direct and essential truth. Because of its oneness, there is no need to think of it in terms of it

being transcendental, exalted, unusual or sublime. The Tao is beyond all that."

Dissolving the Ego

Dissolving the ego is central to the Universal Way and the experience of Integral Oneness. The concept of ego dissolution has been a topic of discussion in many philosophical and spiritual circles for centuries. It is the practice of abandoning the idea of self and embracing a state of unity with the universe. This process involves relinquishing all notions of duality, such as self and other, male and female, short and long, life and death, and accepting and embracing the Tao.

By dissolving our egos, we can reach the heart of the Integral Oneness, where and through which all beings including ETs and NHIs are consciously interconnected as integral parts of a greater whole. To achieve this state of being, we must let go of all skepticism and panic and simply accept the truth that is the great integral Oneness of the Tao.

However, this path, the path of dissolving ego is not necessarily an easy one. In today's modern world, where individualism and self-assertion are highly valued, it can be difficult to let go of the ego and the sense of self. It is easy to cling to one's identity and the idea of being separate from others. But by doing so, we are preventing ourselves from reaching Integral Oneness and experiencing the profound sense of compassion and connection that comes with it.

To dissolve the ego, we must first let go of all preconceived ideas of separateness and acknowledge that everything is interconnected. This means acknowledging and accepting that our actions and decisions affect not only us but those and the world around us. It requires us to accept the reality that we are all integral parts of a greater whole. It means embracing humility and truth and recognizing that as integral as we are, we are not the center of the universe.

Our dissolving of our egos is a necessary and critical step towards experiencing the Integral Oneness that is the Tao. By embracing the Tao and relinquishing the notions of self and other, we can reach a state of profound connection with the universe and all that it contains. This integral connection includes ETs and NHIs. While this path may not be easy, it is one that, for most, is worth taking, as it leads to a sense of fulfillment that cannot be found through individualistic endeavors. Ultimately, the pursuit of Integral Oneness requires us to let go of all notions that separate us from the unity of the universe and embrace the truth of our shared infinite and cosmic existence and that of the extraterrestrials and non-human intelligences that surround us. We are all integral parts of the same infinite, patient, loving and compassionate Tao.

CHAPTER 15

The Highly Evolved Being

This chapter again explores and develops the perspective what is a "highly evolved being", one who has transcended the notion of individuality and embraces a state of oneness with all so that there is no self or other. It suggests that for such a being, the concept of tolerance becomes irrelevant because in the oneness, there is no separation between self and others. Instead, this evolved being extends goodwill to all without prejudice. The state of such being is one of learning and existing in a continuous state of spiritual growth.

Secondly, this passage also highlights those attachments, such as love, hate, and expectations, hinder the growth of one's true being. The integral being, free from attachments, can relate to all beings with an open and unstructured attitude. By existing in this way, the highly evolved being benefits all things, as the boundaries between form and formlessness, and between action and rest, disappear and all are seen as equal in a constantly evolving continuum.

Finally, Lao Tzu emphasizes that this understanding that we call the Integral Way is not a religious invention but rather a subtle truth. Lao Tzu plainly states that only those who are highly evolved beings will grasp the depth of this perspective. And just like grasping the nature and existence of ET/NHIs, others simply, will not.

"For everyday human beings they ordinarily tolerate others. For highly evolved humans, tolerance does not exist because there is no 'other' to tolerate. The highly evolved give up the idea of individuality. Without prejudice they extend their magnanimity universally

with equanimity to all. Without hatred or rest, such beings never contest. They simply learn and be. Love, hate and expectation are all attachments. Attachments prevent the growth of one's own true being. The integral beings are ones who attach themselves to nothing. As a consequence, they are able to relate to everyone with an attitude that is unstructured. Because of their openness and non-attachment integral beings benefit everyone and everything. To them, that with form is equal to that with no form. That which is alive is equal to that which is no longer alive. The Integral Way is not a religious institution. Only the highly evolved understand this subtle truth."

"These are not aliens; they've been here forever. It's likely that the US government has had direct contact. There's a spiritual component to this". - Tucker Carlson

Transcending Tolerance

As human beings, we've grown accustomed to seeing ourselves as individuals, distinct and separate from others. We've learned to tolerate those who are different from us, to put up with their quirks and habits. But what if we could transcend tolerance altogether? What if we could become highly evolved beings, who see no "other", only an integral whole? The answer is that the key to true love, wisdom, and spiritual growth lies in dissolving ego and giving up the idea of individuality and embracing an unstructured attitude towards others and us.

The Integral Being

To understand this perspective fully, we must first understand the concept of integral being. As the quote from which the purpose of this analysis is derived describes, the integral being (IB) is someone who has given up all attachments, whether they be to ideas, people, or things. The Integral Being is universal. He or she does not resist or contest others, nor does the IB entertain expectations. In doing so, the IB liberates itself from the narrow confines of ego and enters the experience of the state of pure being. This state is characterized by unconditional love, acceptance, compassion and curiosity, qualities that enable the Integral Being to connect with others and the universe in a way that is rare, timeless and beautiful.

The question that naturally arises is: why as humans should we become highly evolved integral beings? After all, isn't tolerance enough? The answer is that, while tolerance is certainly commendable, it is limited by its very nature. When we tolerate others, we accept their existence grudgingly, ready to pounce at the first hint of a disagreement. We may be polite on the surface, but deep down, we are convinced of our superiority and their inferiority. This kind of attitude not only breeds resentment in others but also limits our own growth. We become stuck in our own biases and opinions, unable to see the world from another person's perspective.

In contrast, becoming an integral being opens up a universe of possibilities. When we give up the idea of individuality and enter into a state of pure being, we become like mirrors, reflecting the world and universe around us without distortion. We learn to be patient and to listen deeply. We begin to understand where others are coming from, appreciate their needs and to respond to them with compassion rather than ego and judgment. We also become more curious, more inventive, and more open to learning new things. We also become happier and more courageous, because we are no longer trapped in the endless cycle of desire and aversion. Instead, we find contentment in the present moment wherever we may be, in the simple act of being alive.

Conclusion

Of course, for some, becoming an integral being is not an easy task. It requires us to let go of our egos, our biases, and our fears. It requires us to be vulnerable, to acknowledge our mistakes, and to be willing to learn from others. But the rewards are worth it. When we become integral beings, we become agents of positive change not only in the world but in the universe, hence the term "Integral Universal Beings". Our very existence benefits all things, and as the quote says, we become more compassionate, wiser, and more loving.

The idea of a highly evolved human integral being may seem lofty and unattainable to some, but it is something that we can all work toward. It is something into which all spiritual beings can evolve if they so, by their free will, choose. By reassessing and releasing our attachment to ego and individuality and dissolving them into the Tao, we can enter into a state of being that is characterized throughout the universe in all integral beings by curiosity, love, and universal acceptance. We can be mirrors that reflect our world and the Tao in all its diversity and beauty. We can become the change we want to see in the world. We can have a magnanimous and equananimous effect on the universe. Finally, it is also through this quantum shift in being that we more easily avail ourselves to ET/NHI contact. ET/NHI contact is not just about seeing lights in the sky. It is about our own personal and societal evolution and spiritual refinement into the realm of higher spiritual beings. It is through this spiritual advancement that we make possible further meaningful ET/NHI contact and insure the inevitability of being counted amongst the highest spiritual beings that exist throughout the multiverse.

CHAPTER 16

Revealing the Entire Truth of the Universe

Religion and its dogma walls itself off from spiritual practice. Spiritual practice separates itself from the direct experience of the Tao. In this passage Lao Tzu expresses a perspective that many religions, even those at practice their own forms of spirituality can reinforce attachments to false concepts and prevent individuals from perceiving the Integral Oneness and experiencing it. He tells us that the highest virtue lies in taking personal responsibility for discovering and transmitting the whole truth. This is the seed from which our own self-cultivation springs.

Lao Tzu dismisses the idea of helping others solely or in part for personal gain, as well as cultivating oneself for the sake of pride. These approaches are tainted by ego. Because the ego is involved there is a quid pro quo for one's actions. These approaches, however admirable by others, can only provide us with a partial understanding of truth.

Instead of entangling ourselves in the false dualities promulgated by religious (and political) dogmas, the passage encourages us to seek the whole truth for its own sake. It emphasizes the necessity of practicing universal truth in our daily lives, and humbly sharing it with others. By improving ourselves for the betterment of the world, we can enter the realm of the divine and experience a deeper connection with the integral nature of the universe (and by way of implication), the "realm of the divine", the realm of the integral and highest spiritual beings of the universe and guardians that inhabit it. Finally, this chapter emphasizes the importance of compassionate self-less service and the pursuit of truth in order to transcend false concepts and achieve a greater understanding of oneself and the universe. It is both truth and compassion that create the "mystic gates" to our eternal conscious awareness and connection with the Tao.

"Most of the religions of the world only serve to strengthen attachments to concepts that, by their nature are untrue. These false concepts include those of life and death, self and other and heaven and earth, just to mention a few. By becoming entangled in these false ideas, our perception of the integral Oneness is prevented.

The highest virtue that can be exercised is for one to be responsible for the discovery and transmission of the whole truth. For the one who helps others in order for him to be admired or receive blessings, such actions are meaningless. For those who self-cultivate partly to serve others and partly to satisfy their pride, they, at best, will understand only half the truth.

However, for those who cultivate themselves for the world's sake, the entire truth of the universe will be revealed to them. Seek that which is the whole truth. In your own lives, practice it daily. With others, share it humbly. Should you do so, the path into the divine realm will be yours to enter."

Religion and the belief in a higher power have been a significant part of human history, with millions of people adhering to various religious views worldwide. Despite the rise and fall of numerous religions throughout the history of mankind, they have served to increase attachment to false concepts, preventing people from understanding the Integral Oneness.

Religions serve to grow and sustain themselves. To do so they manipulate and strengthen false concepts such as self and other, life and death, and heaven and earth, and reinforce social norms that separate us. * According to this viewpoint, those who become entangled personally or socially in these false ideas are prevented from perceiving the Integral Oneness - the concept of complete unity and interconnectedness of all things.

The highest virtue, according to the perspective of the Integral Way, is to accept the responsibility of both discovering and transmitting the whole truth. This means that the truth should not be selective, and any false concept should not influence it. For people who help others to receive blessings for the admiration they themselves desire, such acts are deemed meaningless as their motive is not pure. It is for either personal or secondary gain. Those who cultivate themselves partly to serve others and partly for their pride will only manage to understand half of the truth.

To obtain the whole truth of the universe, an individual should improve themselves, not only for the sake of self-improvement but for the sake of the world. This means that we can enter the realm of the divine by finding and accepting the whole truth and practicing it daily, by teaching it through our own living examples and sharing it humbly with others by both the spoken and written word. When we do so, we will realize and be granted access to the Tao, the whole truth of the universe. Thus, it is essential for each one of us to find the whole truth of the universe, our connection with the Tao and to practice it daily and share it with others. This is how we as human beings enter the realm of the divine. What we will find there and encounter is beyond our imagination but within the possibility of our own experience of ET/NHI and the divine immortals and universal beings who inhabit our world and the cosmos beyond.

*Gemeinschaft and Gesellschaft, the former meaning "community" bound by common norms and beliefs and the later meaning "society". associations in which the primary justification for membership is self-interest.

CHAPTER 17

The Source of the Subtle Truth

In this chapter, Lao Tzu advises against worshiping deities and religious institutions as the sole source of the subtle truth. It suggests that relying on intermediaries creates a separation between oneself and the divine, making one dependent on external sources for spiritual fulfillment. Instead, Lao Tzu encourages seeking the Tao within one's own heart as the true source of wisdom and connection with the divine.

By discovering the Tao within oneself, worship and reverence become personal and meaningful. This approach emphasizes the importance of internal exploration and self-realization to establish a genuine and profound connection with the divine. The passage invites individuals to look within and recognize their own inherent treasure present within themselves rather than seeking it externally.

"The source of the subtle truth cannot be found in religious institutions or in the worship of deities. Those who do so place these as intermediaries between themselves and the divine. They make themselves beggars who search outside for a treasure that lies hidden within their own breasts. If what you want is to worship the Tao, then discover it first within your own hearts. When you do, then its worship shall be meaningful."

"The kingdom of God is within you"
- Luke 17:21, KJV

Intercession and the Divine

Throughout human history, people have sought to understand the divine and their connection with it. They have created religions, worshipped deities, and erected religious institutions in order to come closer to the divine. However, according to many ancient texts, the real path to the divine is not through external worship but through an internal journey of self-discovery. As a consequence, in order to truly experience the divine, just as Jesus Christ instructed in Luke 17:21 that "The kingdom of God is within you.", we must first discover the divine, our ever-present connection with the Tao in our own hearts.

In addition to those mentioned above, many religious texts stress the importance of discovering the divine within oneself. For instance, Lao Tzu, the author of this passage in his book the Tao Te Ching, warns against looking outside for the divine. Rather, he implores us to seek the Tao, or the divine, within ourselves. The text, like those of the Christian theologians of the Protestant Reformation* warns that worshipping deities and religious institutions as the source of the subtle truth of the universe is to place intermediaries between ourselves and the divine.

Similarly, ancient Indian texts such as the Upanishads emphasize the importance of self-discovery. They describe the concept of Atman, or the true self, which is said to be identical to the divine. The texts state that by discovering this true self within us, we can come closer to the divine in ourselves and others.

In addition, modern science also lends credence to this idea. Many scientific studies have shown that practices such as meditation or mindfulness can have a profound impact on mental health and wellbeing. These practices encourage us to turn inward, focusing on our own thoughts and feelings. Parenthetically, it is through such states of mindfulness and meditation that we can reach out to ET/NHIs and initiate and successfully contact them. This HICE or Human Initiated Contact Experience is commonly referred to as "CE-5".

The true path to contact with ET/NHIs and the divine is through an internal journey of self-discovery. We cannot rely solely on external worship or religious, philosophical, or political institutions or their leaders to find the divine and experience the infinite. Rather, we must look within ourselves to discover the true nature of the divine and our connection with it. This internal journey can be challenging, but the rewards are great. By discovering the divine within us, we can experience a profound sense of peace, happiness, and fulfillment as well as our oneness with all the Tao's creations no matter where they are or whenever or however they appear.

*Generally, for the early seminal Protestant faiths, having a priest as an intercessor between man and God was unnecessary. Therefore, the idea of a "universal priesthood", one in which all baptized Christian believers where in the sight of God, "priests", became a foundational concept for them and their Protestant progeny in general. Today, in most Protestant faiths the idea of a priesthood as a group that is spiritually distinct from lay people is one that is rejected.

CHAPTER 18

How the Realize the Tao

The passage below highlights the idea that there is no single method for realizing the Tao. To rigidly adhere to a particular method can create a dualistic mindset and hinder one's understanding of the subtle truth that all things are inextricably interconnected with the Tao as their divine source. Instead, the passage suggests maintaining an unstructured attitude and being open to the pursuit of the Integral Way.

The passage emphasizes the importance of a flexible and open approach, as well as the qualities of sincerity and service, in fostering a profound connection with the Tao and experiencing spiritual growth. The "mature person" (a person of integral being), according to the passage, recognizes the limitations of external methodologies and seeks simply to dissolve the ego and its concepts of duality. They study the teachings of masters, serve others selflessly, and engage in inner cleansing without burdening their teacher unnecessarily. By eliminating obstacles to understanding, practicing unconditional truth, compassion and sincerity, and by embodying qualities such as humility, perseverance, and adaptability, they establish a deep spiritual connection and become filled with "divine light". This light, or "understanding" becomes a beacon to all, including the highest spiritual beings of the universe.

> "There is only one way to realize the Tao. To pursue any other path will create duality. Duality will delay your understanding of the subtle truth. One who is mature views the fruitlessness of methodologies that are inflexible and external. The mature person remembers this. He therefore keeps an unstructured attitude at all times. In this way he is free to follow the integral

Way. He will study the teachings of the masters. He terminates all dualism. He gives of himself freely in service to others. He cleanses himself internally. He preserves his subtle spiritual connection with the divine energy of his teacher by not disturbing himself with needless entanglements. Gently, he eliminates all impediments to his own understanding. He is constantly and unconditionally sincere. Through perseverance, adaptability and humility he evokes the universe to respond to him and he is filled with its divine light."

How to Evoke the Response of the Tao

The Tao and the study of it are beyond methodology. In order to experience the realization of the Tao, one must go beyond rigid external methodologies and cultivate a mature, unstructured, and integral attitude that embraces the subtle truth that all is inextricably connected, the teachings of the masters, the service to others, the inner cleansing, and the unconditional compassion, truth and sincerity, which evoke the response of the universe and fill one with divine light.

The Tao is often described as the Way, the Path, the Principle, or the Truth that underlies and transcends all phenomena and perspectives. The Tao is not a personal god, a fixed doctrine, or a magical formula, but a dynamic and indescribable reality that can be experienced but not explained, grasped or expressed by ordinary means. The Tao is the source of all creation, the balance of all opposites, and the goal of all spiritual quests. However, to attain realization of the Tao, one must overcome many obstacles and illusions, including the tendency to cling to external methodologies and dualistic concepts. Let such things go.

The Tao Te Ching, the classic text by Lao Tzu that holds within it the fundamental tenets of Taoism, warns against the danger of creating a duality by regarding any method as the method for attaining realization of the Tao. The Tao cannot be confined to any particular technique, system, or doctrine, for it transcends all forms and names. The mature person, therefore, perceives the fruitlessness of such rigid external methodologies and always keeps his attitude unstructured, remaining always free to pursue the Integral Way.

The Integral Way is not a fixed path, but a dynamic and flexible approach that integrates various dimensions of life and reality, such as the spiritual, the ethical, the aesthetic, the intellectual, and the practical. A mature person studies the teachings of the masters, not to imitate or follow them blindly, but to learn from their insights and experiences, and to apply them creatively and adaptively to his own context and situation.

Transcending Duality and Ego

The mature person, we are told, dissolves all concepts of duality, including the dichotomy of self and other, subject and object, mind, and body, and so on. He realizes that all dualities are mere projections of the ego. Our egos seek to control, manipulate, or possess reality. It obscures the unity and interdependence of all things. By transcending ego and duality, the mature person attains a balanced, holistic, and harmonious perspective that transcends all boundaries and limitations.

The mature person also pours himself out in service to others, not out of obligation or reward, but out of sincere compassion and true gratitude. They see others as extensions of themselves and consider themselves as servants of the universal Tao. By serving others, the mature person cultivates humility, empathy, generosity, and altruism, which refines, enhances, and perfects their spiritual growth and connection with the divine energy of the universe.

The mature person also performs his inner cleansing, which means that he purifies his thoughts, emotions, and desires from negative and divisive influences, such as attachment, aversion, ignorance, anger, greed, and delusion. He practices meditation, reflection, and contemplation, which enables him to observe his own mind and to transform his negative patterns into positive habits.

Finally, the mature person maintains his unconditional sincerity, which means that he is honest, authentic, and transparent in his dealings with himself, others, and the universe. He does not pretend to be what he is not, or to know what he does not, but expresses his true feelings, thoughts, and values those of others openly and respectfully. By being sincere, the mature person earns the trust, respect, and support of others, and creates a favorable environment for his spiritual growth and his attunement with the universe.

Ultimately, the realization of the Tao is not a matter of following a fixed methodology, but of cultivating a mature, unstructured, and integral attitude that embraces the subtle truth, the teachings of the masters, service to others, the inner cleansing, and unconditional truth, compassion and sincerity. Ultimately the Tao is not a means to an end, but an end in itself. This "end" transcends all means and ends. By going beyond methodology, we can become part and parcel of the Tao. It is through this personalized integration that we can fulfill our potential as human beings and our destiny as integral and universal beings and prepare ourselves individually and as a society for contact with the higher and spiritually more advanced beings and those "guardians" that inhabit the universe and the cosmos beyond.

CHAPTER 19

To the Everyday person

This passage by Lao Tzu invites us to challenge our ordinary perception and understanding of the world. It suggests that our concept of the vastness of humanity or the need to elevate others' awareness is a product of dualistic thinking. In truth, there is no inherent distinction between self and other. The divine creator and its creation are one in the same.

Furthermore, the passage highlights that perceiving certain places or things as sacred while disregarding others creates a false duality that goes against the truth. Highly evolved individuals, however, maintain a non-dualistic, undiscriminating perception. They see everything without labeling or categorizing, and they hold an awareness of the Great Oneness that permeates all.

By embracing this perspective, those who are highly evolved find support from the Great Oneness itself. The passage encourages us to transcend dualistic thinking and cultivate an all-encompassing perception that aligns with the underlying unity of existence and the Tao. It concludes with the fact for those beings that the Tao always provides for those who choose the path of truth, compassion and the Integral Universal Way.

"To the everyday person, the universe seems like a great and vast thing. In reality, the universe is neither great nor small by comparison to anything else. To the everyday person there are others whose awareness is in need of raising. The universal truth is that self and other do not exist.

To the everyday person, the temple is a sacred place, but the ordinary field is not. This, like self and other is a duality that runs contrary to the truth. For the highly evolved, their hallmark is the development of their ability and the maintenance of their undiscriminating perception. By observing all and not labeling anything, their awareness of the Great Oneness, the Tao is maintained. Thusly, the Tao supports those who are highly evolved."

"Through our eyes, the universe is perceiving itself. Through our ears, the universe is listening to its harmonies. We are the witnesses through which the universe becomes conscious of its glory, of its magnificence."- Alan Watts

How to Evolve

For everyday human beings they ordinarily tolerate others. For highly evolved humans, tolerance does not exist because there is no "other". The highly evolved give up the idea of individuality. Without prejudice they extend their goodwill universally with equanimity. Without hatred or rest, such beings never contest but simply learn and be. Love, hate, and expectation are all attachments. Attachments prevent the growth of our own true being. The integral beings of the universe are ones who attach themselves to nothing. They can relate to everyone paupers and princes alike with an attitude that is compassionate and unstructured.

Because of their openness and non-attachment integral beings benefit everyone and everything. To them, that with form is equal to that with no form. There is no distinction between being and non-being. That which is alive is equal to that which is no longer alive.

The Integral Way is not a religious institution. It is an enlightened approach to consciousness and to life. Only the highly evolved understand this subtle truth.

How to Raise Our Awareness

Increasing the awareness of the universal truth of the Great Oneness is central to our evolution from an everyday ordinary person who might have no spiritual awareness to one of elevated awareness of the Tao and the Integral Universal Way. Such an awareness goes beyond mere spirituality.

To the ordinary person, the world can be seen as a vast and divided place. As "individuals", we often feel separate and disconnected from each other, our environment, and even ourselves. We tend to label and judge everything based on our limited perceptions and conditioning, creating dualisms that distort reality and the integral truth of our existence. However, those who are highly evolved have a different perception. They see everything and label nothing, maintaining awareness of the Great Oneness that unites all things.

This Oneness is an indescribable universal consciousness. It is the infinite creative energy that flows through everything and connects us all. It is what gives us life, sustenance, and purpose. When we forget about our differences, our labels, and our egos, we can tap into this energy and experience the Tao, the true nature of our being. In this state we become one with the universe, the earth, and with each other.

Unfortunately, this awareness is often missing in our daily lives. We get caught up in our own problems, routines, and ambitions, forgetting about the interconnectedness of all things. We see certain places, things, and people as more important than others, ignoring the beauty and value of the Tao's diversity. We default and drift back into ego only to create unnecessary conflicts, divisions, and avoidable inequalities that only lead to suffering, chaos and loss.

However, we can change this. We can begin to cultivate ourselves by raising our awareness and connecting with the Great Oneness by embracing the following principles:

1.Non-dualism: We need to realize that everything is interconnected and interdependent. There is no self and no other, no good and no bad, no sacred and no profane. These dualisms are illusions that distort the truth. We are all part of the same whole.

2.Compassion: We need to cultivate a sense of kindness, empathy, and respect towards all living beings. We need to see ourselves in others and recognize their suffering and joys as our own. Compassion is the bridge that brings us together.

3.Mindfulness: We need to be present and aware of our thoughts, feelings, and actions. We need to observe without judging, labeling, or reacting. This way, we can train our minds to see beyond the surface and into the depth of reality.

4.Gratitude: We need to appreciate the abundance and beauty of life, recognizing the gifts we have received and the challenges that have made us stronger. Gratitude opens our hearts and expands our awareness.

By embracing these principles, we can become more evolved individuals and refined human beings and contribute to the evolution of humanity as a whole. We can see beyond our limitations and connect with the Great Oneness that unites us all. We can create a world of peace, harmony, and cooperation, where diversity is celebrated and differences are seen as opportunities for learning, enjoyment and growth.

Conclusion

The Great Oneness is not a mere concept, but a conscious reality that transcends our ordinary perception. To increase our awareness of it, we need to let go of our egos and our dualistic thinking. We must cultivate compassion, mindfulness, and gratitude within ourselves, and practice connecting with our true nature. Our connection with others will eventually become automatic. Only then can we contribute significantly to a better and more joyful and peaceful world, one in which even the ordinary everyday person becomes extraordinary by realizing the integral truth that lies within.

CHAPTER 20

<u>Clairvoyance, Telepathy and Telekinesis</u>

The passage by Lao Tzu highlights the limitations of certain extrasensory abilities and profound phenomena that lie within the relativistic realm of duality. While clairvoyance, telepathy, and telekinesis may have significance within a dualistic framework, they become meaningless when viewed from the perspective of the Great Oneness. In the Tao, the realm of non-being, the formless and the no-mind (universal being), these abilities lose their relevance as there is nothing so special about them.

The chapter also teaches us that within the Great Oneness, where all things are interconnected and in their proper places, there is no need for skills like clairvoyance to see things elsewhere, telepathy to communicate with others' minds, or telekinesis to move physical objects. All these are the ordinary manifestations of a higher physical and spiritual order that is available to even everyday people. They are only special for the dualistic mind.

The practical emphasis here is on transcending dualistic notions and recognizing the power of our all-encompassing understanding and interconnectedness within the Great Oneness that is the Tao. In this state of unity, all things are seen, understood, and harmoniously exist in an inherent order that avails itself to anyone who is open and ready for it.

"The clairvoyant see forms that are somewhere else. However, the formless they are unable to see. The telepath may directly communicate another's mind but they cannot do so with one who is of no-mind. Those who possess the power of telekinesis need not touch an object in order to move it, but they are unable to

move the intangible. These abilities have meaning only
in dualistic reality. As a consequence, they are really
without meaning. When all things are seen, things like
like telepathy, telekinesis and clairvoyance do not exist
within the great Oneness that is the Tao. Within the
great Oneness all things are forever seen and understood
and forever remain properly where they belong."

Looking for a Deeper Meaning

The realm of parapsychology has long been the subject of debate and fascination. Clairvoyance, telepathy, telekinesis, and
by modern implication, remote viewing, extra sensory perception (ESP) and human-initiated extraterrestrial/Non-Human
Intelligence (ET/NHI) contact (HICE) are abilities that are
thought to transcend the limitations of physical reality, allowing individuals to perceive, communicate, and manipulate the
world in ways that are beyond our concepts of physical reality
and time and space. As such these powers are understood not
to be ordinarily possible. They deserve a more in-depth look
for us to see whether there may be a deeper meaning and understanding of the universe behind them.

Lao Tzu tells us that these abilities are ultimately meaningless,
as they exist solely within the realm of duality. The argument
that these abilities are entirely "meaningless" though may be
a misconstruction as these phenomena offer valuable insights
into the nature of reality, consciousness and the quantum field
as well. Consequently, when these abilities are considered within the framework of Great Universal Oneness of the Tao, these
abilities take on new structure and meaning.

At the heart of the idea that these abilities are meaningless is
the idea that they exist only within the realm of duality. That
is, they depend on the existence of a separate subject and object,
a perceiver and the perceived. In this sense, they are seen as

limited and superficial, providing only a distorted and partial view of reality.

However, the reality that surrounds these abilities is much more complex and nuanced. The Great Oneness, the ultimate reality that underlies all existence, is not simply a void, an empty space devoid of attributes or qualities. Rather, it is a dynamic, alive, and conscious whole, in which all things, even though unseen, are connected and completely interdependent.

In this context, it is clear that clairvoyance, telepathy, telekinesis, ESP, remote viewing and human-initiated ET/NHI contact are not limited to the realm of relativism and duality. Rather, they are simply expressions of the underlying interconnectedness of reality, the ability of consciousness to perceive and interact with the world and the universe in a direct and immediate way, unmediated by the limitations of the physical body, the ego or by the constructs of time, space and physical reality as it is commonly understood.

The realm of clairvoyance, telepathy, telekinesis, ESP, remote viewing and human-initiated ET/NHI contact and other phenomena that may be classified generally to be in the fields of parapsychology are not something to be dismissed or disregarded because they may once have been within the province of the dualistic mind. Instead, when considered within the unified field of the Tao and the Great Oneness, the study of these abilities offers profound insights into the nature of consciousness and reality and challenge us to expand our understanding of the world and universe around us. By embracing these abilities and exploring their deeper implications, especially in light of non-locality and the sub-atomic world and the comparatively recent evolution of quantum physics, mechanics and quantum entanglement, we can unlock new levels of insight and awareness and tap into the infinite potential of the human mind.

Conclusion

Lao Tzu's insight into the integral nature of these types of phenomena gives these abilities a deeper meaning and significance than is often acknowledged. Rather than being mere curiosities or novelties, they offer a glimpse into the fundamental nature of reality, the infinite potential and creativity of consciousness, and the realization of our own innate divinity and connection with and ability to integrate and interact with them all.

By embracing these abilities and exploring their wider implications, we can deepen our understanding of ourselves, our world, and universe and our place within it and use these channels to contact other higher physical energies and advanced spiritual beings in whatever form or place in which they exist and employ their aid in our own spiritual and societal advancement.

CHAPTER 21

Spontaneity and the Essence of the Moment

In the passage below, Lao Tzu emphasizes the ephemeral nature of each moment. It suggests that past, present, and future moments cannot be grasped or held onto, despite their beauty, enjoyment, or desirability. The mind, however, tends to fixate on preserving and controlling the flow of time, becoming preoccupied with thoughts of the past or future. In doing so, it overlooks the inherent truth and clarity of the present moment.

The passage suggests that by dissolving the mind's attachments and expectations, one can suddenly discover the presence of the Tao at their feet. This implies a profound realization and connection with the underlying reality and essence of existence. By letting go of mental constructs and by being fully present in the moment, clarity and understanding can arise naturally. It encourages us to embrace the fragility and beauty of each passing moment and find the Tao within the present experience of simply being.

"Ephemeral and delicate are each moment. The present moment, no matter how beautiful, is fragile and fleeting. No matter how enjoyable, one can neither hold on to nor possess it. No matter how desirable, one cannot catch the future moment. Desperate is the mind to fix in place the river. By trying to hold on to images of the past and being preoccupied with ideas of the future, the moment's plain truth is overlooked. Dissolve your mind and clarity will be at hand. Then suddenly you will find that the Tao you search for will be at your feet."

N. MICHAEL MURBURG, JR.

Zeno and the Flight of a Butterfly

Zeno an ancient Greek philosopher famous for metaphysical trolling once devised a paradox that stated, "A moving arrow is at rest." The "Quantum Zeno Effect" now accepted in modern physics predicts that certain quantum events can be frozen through the act of observation. However, both the Princeton Engineering Anomalies Research Lab experiments that showed the observational presence of human consciousness can significantly affect the statistical outcomes of random number generations and Thomas Young's double slit experiment in 1801 and its progeny* that showed that observation and measurement collapses the probability function of a wave tell us that the observation of the wave function of the arrow travels tells us that by measuring the arrow we collapse its wave in fight. One can either have the arrow in flight or the arrow itself. One cannot have both. Or can we?

While the arrow is in superposition, it has the potential of being both until we decide how we want the arrow to be, static or in flight. At the very least both Zeno's paradox and research in the quantum field quantum confirm the fact that consciousness is an integral part of creating the world that we observe.

In the same regard, Lao Tzu tells us that each moment in life is a beautiful, fragile and fleeting thing. Like the arrow in fight, a moment of the past cannot be kept, even if it was beautiful. The moment of the present slips away from us even as we try desperately to hold onto it. But we cannot even try to hold on to it without destroying the beauty of either an arrow in flight or a butterfly for that matter. And just like the past and present, the moment of the future cannot be caught, however much we desire it.

Too often, our minds are possessed by ideas of the past or preoccupied with images of the future. This means we overlook the plain truth of the moment. We fail to be in and see the beauty of each passing moment or the fragility of life itself. But if we can dissolve our minds, we can suddenly discover the Tao at our feet. By dissolving the mind, clarity at hand.

Life is a journey, and each instance is a unique part of that journey. Each moment is an opportunity to experience something new, to learn something different, and to appreciate the world around us. But if we are too preoccupied with the past or the future, we will inevitably miss these opportunities.

Take, for example, a beautiful sunset. Many people would take a photograph of the sunset in order to remember it. But in doing so, they miss the beauty of the sunset itself. They miss out on the unique experience of watching the sun slowly dip below the horizon, changing the colors of the sky and casting beautiful shadows across the land. They become too focused on capturing the moment rather than experiencing and appreciating it fully. The same is true for our relationships, our work, and our hobbies.

Our minds are powerful things. They can bring us joy, but they can also bring us misery. Once we learn to dissolve our minds, we can see the world in a new way. We can see each moment for what it truly is – like a butterfly or an arrow in flight or water flowing in a clear mountain stream: fleeting, fragile, and beautiful. We can appreciate the present rather than being consumed by trying to hold on to the past or ruminating about the future. We can find clarity and peace by being in the moment and thereby freely experiencing the here and now.

Conclusion

Each moment is indeed fragile and fleeting. But rather than trying to hold onto it, we should learn to appreciate it while it lasts. It is only by embracing the present and dissolving our minds that we can truly discover the beauty of life and the clarity that comes with it. Here Lao Tzu encourages us all accept the present, to live in the moment, to appreciate what we have, and to find peace and clarity in the beauty of each passing moment.

In the end, it is that peace and clarity of being that we can project to each other and share with our fellow human beings and even our ET/NHI counterparts. Being in the moment with them as they appear is and can be a peak life experience when we let it happen.

* See also., John Bell's work in the later part of the twentieth century on quantum entanglement

CHAPTER 22

Cultivating Spiritual States of Awareness and Being

In this chapter Lao Tzu reflects on the nature of perceiving the divine Oneness. It suggests that the Tao, or the divine Oneness, is not limited to appearing in grand or extraordinary manifestations. Instead, it is always present and available in every moment and in every aspect of existence.

The passage highlights that to truly see the divine Oneness, we need to go beyond relying on external forms or seeking awe-inspiring experiences. It is when we transcend the limitations of speech and dissolve the restless mind that the divine Oneness reveals itself. By living simple and honest lives and by cultivating clarity, purity, and sincerity, we create the conditions for the divine Oneness to be unveiled. Meditation can assist in this process.

Moreover, the passage emphasizes that if we are willing to surrender and allow ourselves to be guided by the divine Oneness, we can perceive its presence everywhere, even in the most ordinary and mundane aspects of life. Lao Tzu invites us to cultivate a state of openness and receptivity to experience the divine in all aspects of existence. This is the path of all integral and universal beings. This is the path of the Integral Way.

"How can one see the divine Oneness? Is it in the forms of beauty, wonders that take one's breath away and miracles that inspire awe? The Tao is always present and available, yet it does not oblige herself to present itself in these ways. You will find it when you have exhausted your speech and have depleted your mind. In these times the Tao presents herself.

> Cultivate clarity and purity and she will also present herself to you. When unconditional is your sincerity, the Tao unveils herself. If you are willing to be loved by her, everywhere you will see her. She expresses herself even in the most ordinary."

(Discovering Divine Awareness)

The Tao is present everywhere and in all things. Its divine Oneness is a concept that has been contemplated and explored by many throughout history. It has been described in various ways, and its manifestation has been seen in different forms. Those who seek to understand the divine Oneness may wonder how it can be seen. Is the divine Oneness visible in beautiful forms, breathtaking wonders, or awe-inspiring miracles? The answer is that the divine Oneness is always present and always available, regardless of how it chooses to manifest itself.

One way to see the divine Oneness is through the cultivation of clarity and purity. By clearing the mind of clutter and allowing oneself to become still and focused, individuals can become aware of the divine Oneness within themselves and in the world around them. This can lead to a greater sense of connection and understanding of the interconnectedness of all things including ET and NHIs.

Another way to see the divine Oneness is through the practice of sincerity. To practice sincere means to be completely honest and without guile. When sincerity is unconditional, it opens the door for the divine Oneness to unveil itself. This means being honest and authentic in all aspects of life and allowing ourselves to be guided by the divine Oneness and to trust in it. This can lead to a deep sense of connection, purpose and fulfillment, as we feel a sense of alignment with the universe and our true selves.

Finally, the divine Oneness may reveal itself when our speech is exhausted, and the mind is finally dissolved. This suggests that the divine Oneness cannot be fully understood through intellectual pursuits alone, but rather must be experienced through a state of being. When we let go of our prejudices and preconceived notions and allow ourselves to be receptive to the divine Oneness, we can begin to see it and its divinity expressed in all beings and even the most ordinary of things.

Conclusion

The divine Oneness, though often elusive can be seen in a variety of ways. Whether through cultivating clarity and purity, practicing sincerity, or experiencing an unencumbered state of being, the divine Oneness is always present and available to those who need it. By opening ourselves up to the possibility of seeing the divine Oneness in all things, we can gain a wider and expanded consciousness and with it, the experience of true universality. In this lies for us, a greater sense of connection and a better understanding of our place in our own lives, our families, society, world and the universal reality in which we exist.

CHAPTER 23

Teaching Without Words

In this chapter Lao Tzu underscores the ineffable nature of the Tao expressed as the "highest truth". It suggests that attempting to express this truth in words is inherently limited and falls short of capturing its essence. Consequently, the greatest teacher, recognizing this limitation, transcends the need for verbal explanations.

Instead of relying on words, the passage highlights that the greatest teacher teaches by example. They offer themselves in selfless service. Through their actions and presence, they embody these teachings and transmit wisdom without the need for extensive verbal communication. This service is performed without worry or concern, as the master teacher is completely aligned with the flow of the Tao and trusts in its guidance.

The passage also emphasizes that the highest truth transcends linguistic expression, and that genuine teaching goes beyond mere words. It encourages the practice of selfless service and the cultivation of a state of non-worry, allowing the teachings to be lived and experienced rather than solely spoken or explained. When one trusts in the Tao, there is nothing about which to worry.

Living the Tao and exemplifying its teachings here and in the Tao Te Ching are what Integral Virtue and the Integral Way are all about. The highest spiritual beings in the universe and all of its guardians live by these teachings. By studying them and living by them mankind will be able to survive itself and become capable of acceptance into the realm of older and more highly advanced civilizations that inhabit this universe and the cosmos beyond.

"One cannot express the highest truth in words. Because of this, the greatest teacher is one who says nothing. He worries not and pours himself over into service to others."

The Ineffable Tao

The concept that the highest truth cannot be put into words is one that has been explored and analyzed by many philosophers and thinkers throughout history. Lao Tzu suggests that there are certain aspects of existence that are beyond the limits of language and cannot be fully expressed or understood through words alone.

The idea of the greatest teacher having nothing to say may seem paradoxical to some, but it is rooted in the belief that actions can speak louder than words. By giving ourselves in service and never worrying, we can embody the highest truth and lead by our example. This means being fully present in each moment, offering ourselves in service to others without expectation of reward or recognition, and trusting in the process of life that is being constantly orchestrated by the Tao.

The greatest teacher need not preach or lecture, but rather they can offer guidance through their actions and presence. This can inspire others to embody the highest truth themselves and become their own teachers. Through this process, individuals can cultivate their own connection to something greater than themselves and find meaning and purpose in their lives.

The notion that the highest truth cannot be put into words and that the greatest teacher has nothing to say may seem contradictory, but it highlights the importance of embodying the highest truth through action rather than relying solely on language and doctrine. By offering ourselves in service and trusting in the Tao, we can cultivate our own inner wisdom and connect to the eternal, something that is greater than what we think of as ourselves. When a society of individuals can accomplish this, then what are its limits?

CHAPTER 24

The Subtle Awareness

In this chapter, Lao Tzu emphasizes that the realization of the Tao, "the subtle awareness of the truth of the universe" should not be seen as an achievement to be obtained. He cautions against the mindset of viewing the Tao and its subtle truth as something external or separate from our own nature. Such dichotomous thinking is deemed erroneous and misleading.

According to the passage, our nature and the integral nature of the universe are inseparable and indescribable. They may appear eternally present, but they are internally and eternally interconnected. The invitation is to simply open ourselves to this inherent truth, recognizing that the Tao and our subtle awareness of it is already within us and part of our being.

Because of this, Lao Tzu encourages a shift in our perspective, away from the notion of achievement and separation, towards a revelation of the intrinsic connection between our own nature and the greater nature of the universe. By embracing this realization and understanding and opening ourselves up to it, we can experience a deeper awareness of the "subtle truth" and appreciate our otherwise unseen connectedness the great Integral Oneness of the Tao.

"One should not regard as an achievement their entry into the subtle awareness of universal truth. If you think in terms of achievement, you place the truth of the universe as something external to your own nature. To do so is as erroneous as it is deceptive and confusing. Your true nature is one in the same with the indescribable, eternal and integral nature of the

universe. To enter the subtle awareness of the universal truth, simply open yourself to it."

Becoming Aware of the Subtle Tao

The concept that the subtle awareness of the truth of the universe should not be regarded as an achievement is an important one. This suggestion highlights the idea that the understanding of the universe is not something that can be attained through external means or efforts, but rather is something that is already inherently present within us.

Because the Tao is unseen, it is called subtle. Because it is subtle, becoming aware of it and how it operates may require some work. To think of our becoming aware of the subtle Tao in terms of achievement is to impose limitations and boundaries that separate us from the inherent nature of the Tao. This creates a sense of duality and separation that is not reflective of the interconnectedness of all things. Instead, it is important to recognize that our true nature is one and the same as the integral Tao nature of the universe. This means that the subtle awareness of the Tao and truth of the universe is already present within us, constantly available for us to access and experience.

To simply open ourselves to this inherent truth is to recognize that the Tao is already art work within us and that we don't need to work to achieve it. This requires a deep sense of surrender and a willingness to let go of our preconceived notions and beliefs. By recognizing the subtle awareness of the universe as already present within us, we can reach within ourselves and begin to genuinely connect with the world around us in a more authentic and meaningful way.

The recognition of the subtle awareness of the truth of the universe should not be seen as an achievement, but rather as a manifesting of the most natural aspect of our inherent nature. By opening ourselves up to this truth, we can disengage from the false duality of separation and connect with the world and the rest of humanity and with the universe and ETs and NHIs in a more genuine, authentic and meaningful way.

CHAPTER 25

Avoiding Detours to the Integral Way

In this passage Lao Tzu highlights the notion that not all spiritual paths necessarily lead to the Harmonious Oneness. He suggests that many paths may serve as detours or distractions from the true essence. In contrast, the Integral Way is presented as a path of plainness and simplicity, offering a trustworthy and direct route.

Lao Tzu advocates for those who want to follow the Integral Way to live with unconditional sincerity and eliminating duality, emphasizing the celebration of the equality of all things. By embodying these principles and walking the Integral Way, one is said to align with truth in every moment.

The passage invites individuals to place their trust in the simplicity and authenticity of the Integral Way, recognizing it as a path that leads to the realization of the Harmonious Oneness that is the Tao. By cultivating unconditional sincerity and transcending dualistic thinking, we can establish a profound connection with the truth that pervades all aspects of existence.

"There are many spiritual paths. However, most constitute no more than distractions and are detours from the Harmonious Oneness.

Trust in the simplicity and plainness of the Tao's Integral Way. Make your sincerity unconditional. Eliminate all dualities. Celebrate the equality of all things. If you can do this, then in truth will you live each and every moment."

Eliminating Duality

The idea that not all spiritual paths lead to the Harmonious Oneness is one that has been explored by many spiritual traditions. It suggests that there are many ways to approach spirituality and our cultivation of it in our daily lives. However, despite being told somewhat enigmatically to celebrate the equality of all things that comprise the Tao, not all paths are equally effective at bringing us closer to its ultimate truth.

The suggestion to trust the plainness and simplicity of the Integral Way acknowledges that spiritual growth does not require grand gestures or elaborate techniques. Rather, spiritual self-cultivation is a process that dissolves the ego into the Tao. This dissolution begins with our eradicating the dualistic thinking and retaining the false beliefs that separate us from the truth of the universe. By living with unconditional truth and sincerity and by celebrating the equality of all things as manifestations of the Tao, we can begin to dissolve these barriers and connect ourselves more fully with the world and universe around us.

Living in Truth

The Integral Way emphasizes the importance of simplicity and a deep sense of experiencing presence in each moment. Lao Tzu tells us that we need not look outside of ourselves for answers or seek complex spiritual practices or ornate rituals in order to cultivate a deeper connection with the universe and with each other. Instead, we can live and trust in the inherent simplicity of our true nature and allow ourselves to be guided by the Tao as we experience it freely in each present moment.

Ultimately, living in truth requires a willingness to relinquish our preconceived notions and beliefs and embrace the inherent interconnectedness, the "equality" of all things. This letting go requires a deep sense of surrender and a genuine willingness to be guided by the Tao itself, rather than by our past conditioning and our egos and their own desires or attachments.

Conclusion

In the physical universe it seems that life is a battle between polar opposites. The energies of the ego seem to fight for dominance over the soul against that which is the Tao. Chaos and complexity seem pitted against simplicity and order. However, to think this way is to think dualistically. In order to cultivate and refine ourselves physically, mentally and spiritually, we must learn to stop thinking in dualistic terms.

By eradicating duality and cultivating a deep sense of presence and unconditional sincerity, we can reconnect with our spiritual core and move beyond a relativistic paradigm to connect more fully with the world and universe around us and experience the Harmonious Oneness of the Tao that underlies and ultimately governs all things.

Following the Integral way towards our own spiritual growth need not be complicated or elusive. However, it does require us to exercise our free will and make choices through our own discernment. There, in the absence of judgment as to what otherwise may appear to be a choice between polar opposites, we can receive spiritual guidance and understanding from the Tao. In this way we can heal ourselves of our toxic attachments and live through each present moment fully. In the end, all we each need to do is to follow the plainness and simplicity of the Integral Way and when in doubt of which path to take, trust in our subtle awareness and the underlying universal truth and reality that is the Tao.

CHAPTER 26

Worldly and Integral Blessings and Wisdom

The pursuit of wisdom and blessings has been a common aspiration for humanity throughout history. In this chapter Lao Tzu draws a distinction for us between two types of blessings and two types of wisdom. The first type relates to worldly blessings and wisdom, which are associated with good deeds and a conceptual understanding of experiences. These blessings and wisdom are relativistic and are confined within the realm of the mind, time, and space. While they have value, they are limited in their ultimate efficacy as they do not provide a direct understanding of the ultimate truth.

On the other hand, the passage introduces us to the concept of integral blessings and integral wisdom. Because they are integral, they arise from becoming aware of the Great Oneness that is the Tao. Integral wisdom and blessings transcend the limitations of the mind, time, and space. The receipt of integral blessings liberates us to experience boundless harmony and freedom within the consciousness that is the Tao. Integral wisdom involves our full and direct participation in each moment. There, the boundaries between the observer and the observed dissolve in pure awareness, free from mental concepts and attitudes.

The integral blessings and wisdom are those we obtain through practicing the Integral Way and guiding others towards it. Because of their selfless integral nature, these blessings and wisdom are immensely greater than all worldly blessings and wisdom combined. Lao Tzu does not neglect to highlight the transformative power these gifts from the Tao and the significance of aligning ourselves with the Great Oneness to experience our liberation from the physical realm and the relativistic mind to experience the integral and universal nature of existence and the infinite harmony that is the Tao.

"Blessings may be seen as being of two sorts. The first kind may be called 'worldly' blessings. These blessings are gained by one performing good deeds. Such blessings, however, involve the mind and thus, they are confined in space and time.

The second type of blessings are called 'integral' because they are bestowed upon those who enter the awareness of the great Oneness.

The awareness of the great Oneness liberates those who enter it from the mind's bondage, the bondage of time and space. The great Oneness allows those who enter it to fly freely throughout the infinite harmony that is the Tao.

Just as there are two kinds of blessings, so to is it that there are two kinds of wisdom.
The first of the two types of wisdom is called 'worldly' wisdom because it is conceptual by its nature and is based on the understanding of one's own participation in life. It follows in time and space subsequent to one's own experiences and the events that caused them. Because of its subjective nature, worldly wisdom inhibits one's direct understanding of the truth.

The second kind of wisdom is 'integral'. It is integral because it involves us participating directly in and being aware of each and every moment of that which constitutes the experience. In Integral Wisdom there is neither an observer nor an observed. Both are absorbed into the moment and the light of complete awareness that dissolves all mental attitudes and concepts. Without

attitudes and mental concepts present, the light is undimmed.

For those who practice the integral Way, they will certainly accrue integral wisdom and numerous blessings. But for those who practice the Integral Way and lead others toward it, their blessings will be a billion times greater than all the worldly wisdom and worldly blessings combined."

The Integral Way: A Path to Boundless Wisdom and Blessings

The concepts of worldly blessings and integral blessings, as well as worldly wisdom and integral wisdom, are widely explored by and discussed in various spiritual and philosophical traditions. Like Lao Tzu, these ideas suggest that there are two distinct types of rewards that individuals can receive, depending on their level of awareness and connection to the universe.

Worldly blessings refer to tangible rewards that are gained through good deeds and actions. These blessings are often related to physical and material wealth, success, and recognition. While they may bring temporary happiness and satisfaction, they are limited materially by time and space and are ultimately temporary and transitory.

Integral blessings, on the other hand, are eternal and stem from our becoming aware of and connection to the Great Oneness. These blessings do not resemble those that are worldly as integral blessings liberate us from the limitations of the mind, material, time, and space, and allow us to experience the boundless harmony and beauty of the universe. Integral blessings come in countless ways. They are not limited to any specific time or space. They can seem miraculous to the newly awakened as these blessings are boundless, and along with the wisdom that flows forth from the Tao, they continue to grow and evolve in this lifetime and the next as the individual consciousness that one many refer to as the "soul" achieves deeper levels of connection and experience with and understanding of the Tao.

Similarly, worldly wisdom refers to the conceptual understanding of life experiences, while integral wisdom involves a direct participation in each moment without the interference of mental concepts or attitudes. Integral wisdom allows us to experience truth directly, rather than through a filter of preconceived beliefs or ideas.

The idea that the blessings and wisdom that accrue to those who practice the Integral Way are a billion times greater than all worldly blessings and wisdom is a reflection of the profound significance that these concepts hold. It highlights the importance of cultivating ourselves through our direct awareness of the Great Oneness and our unbroken connection to the universe and embracing the boundless wisdom and harmony that is the Tao.

The ideas of worldly and integral blessings and wisdom suggest that there are two distinct paths that individuals can take in their spiritual journey. While worldly blessings and wisdom are ephemerally limited by time and space, integral blessings and wisdom allow individuals to experience the boundless beauty and harmony of the universe. The rewards that come from practicing the Integral Way and connecting with the Great Oneness are infinite and can transform every aspect of life. This transformation does not stop with our daily lives or spiritual practice but goes beyond them. It continues on eternally into our relationship with the universe and our communication and association with its higher spiritual beings.

The Gateway to Limitless Blessings

The Integral Way provides a profound opportunity for us to accrue integral wisdom and blessings. This path transcends the limitations of worldly knowledge and conventional blessings, promising a deeper understanding of life's interconnectedness and a more meaningful existence. Besides this, at the end of this passage about the Integral Way these teachings by Lao Tzu hold a profound promise. Not only does the Integral way offer us the opportunity to attain integral wisdom and blessings, but for those who choose to guide others to and along this path, they will experience blessings that far surpass any worldly wisdom or blessings combined.

While the pursuit of integral wisdom and blessings is undeniably rewarding, the true magnitude of these benefits becomes even more profound when one becomes a guide for others to the Integral Way. For those so inclined, there are invaluable and deeply transformative blessings to be found in the nature of revealing the Integral Way to others.

Teaching the Tao and its Integral Way can lead to boundless and an even more profound wisdom and blessings from the Tao. By guiding others towards this path, individuals not only amplify their own personal growth but also contribute to the elevation of collective consciousness. Guiding others to and through the Integral Way is an act of selflessness that allows us to perfect our spiritual development by sharing our acquired wisdom and blessings, empowering others to embark on their own timeless and transformative journey. This act of giving back creates a ripple effect of positive change, throughout the universe magnifying the blessings received exponentially.

The blessings attained by those who choose to become teachers and lead others along this path are immeasurable, dwarfing any worldly wisdom or blessings. Teaching others of the Integral Way not only enriches the lives of others but opens the door to boundless blessings that can bring about our own personal fulfillment and contribute to the betterment of humanity and the universe as a whole. Embracing the Integral Way and becoming its teacher is a true testament to the statement that "there is no greater blessing than to be able to practice and teach others about the Tao's Integral Way."

Conclusion

The Integral Way is a path to integral blessings and integral wisdom. It is a path that encompasses not only the cultivation of personal wisdom but also the act of sharing it with others. It encourages us to integrate every aspect of our lives into an interconnected whole, fostering harmony and balance within ourselves and the world and universe around us. By practicing the Integral Way, we embark on a journey of self-discovery and self-mastery, aligning our thoughts, actions, and emotions with the principles of the Tao.

Through the diligent practice of the Integral Way, we can accrue integral wisdom that is not limited to worldly knowledge or conventional understanding. Integral wisdom embraces a deeper comprehension of the interplay between the physical, mental, and spiritual realms. It cultivates an intuitive understanding of the interconnected nature of all things and grants us the ability to see beyond surface-level appearances. This wisdom enables us to navigate life's challenges with grace, make wise decisions, and live with a sense of purpose and fulfillment.

Finally, in addition to integral wisdom, the Integral Way promises limitless blessings for those who embark on this transformative path and leading others toward it. These blessings are not limited to material wealth or temporary pleasures but encompass a holistic sense of infinite love, compassion, abundance and well-being. By aligning ourselves with the Tao, we open ourselves up to the flow of universal energy, experiencing increased vitality, inner peace, and harmony with our surroundings and those within them. Moreover, the practice of the Integral Way cultivates virtues such as sincerity, compassion, empathy, and humility, enhancing our relationships with others and fostering a sense of peace and interconnectedness.

Finally, we should always remember and rejoice in the fact that there is no greater blessing than to be able to practice the Integral Way and to lead others to it.

CHAPTER 27

What is an Integral Being

In this chapter Lao Tzu extrapolates on what it means to teach the Integral way and emphasizes the perspective of an "integral being", one who has evolved spiritually to experience integral being. He tells us that such a being does not possess the ambition to enlighten or elevate others from worldly existence to a divine realm. This is because the integral being recognizes the absence of self and other, as well as the absence of dualistic distinctions like good and bad, life and death and heaven and hell. Therefore, there is no one to be raised or a destination to be attained. Teaching the Tao is not an ulterior goal-directed behavior towards others.

The passage also invites us to reflect on the importance of personal sincerity and inner alignment, rather than being consumed by efforts to change or elevate others. It highlights the self-focused nature of the integral being's journey and their commitment to living in accordance with their true nature. Teaching is not done by pedagogy but done by example. When approached and asked we can teach what we know to be true of the Tao. There is no need to convert or proselytize to the masses of everyday people. Those who seek enlightenment through the Tao will find us.

The passage further emphasizes that the primary concern of the integral being lies in their own sincerity. This suggests that the focus is on cultivating genuine authenticity and aligning with the integral truth within oneself. Rather than being preoccupied with external endeavors, the integral being prioritizes the virtue and integrity of their own inner state and the sincerity of their actions. These traits, importantly, are also those rudimentarily shared by the highest spiritual beings and guardians of the universe, hence the term "Integral Universal Being" less we forget that they too, just as we, are all Integral beings who share the same great Oneness and follow the same Tao and eternal Integral Way.

"One should not imagine that it is the ambition of an integral being to raise worldly people into the divine realm or to enlighten those who are unaware.

To the integral being, dualistic divisions like self and other do not exist. There is no heaven; nor is there any hell. Because of this, there is no one who needs to be saved or their enlightenment raised. Sincerity is the only concern of an Integral being."

Integral Being

The concept of an integral being is often associated with enlightenment and the elevation of humanity. However, according to some beliefs, this is not actually the case. Those who identify as integral beings view the world in a different way, and their primary concern is not with raising others up to a perceived higher plane of existence. Instead, as beings of truth and compassion, they prioritize sincerity as a daily concern above all else, recognizing that everyone and everything is interconnected by the Integral and Subtle Truth in a profound way.

Integral beings do not therefore view themselves and others as separate entities, but rather as interconnected components of a greater whole. In this view, there are no individuals to be uplifted or enlightened, as all beings are part of the same universal consciousness. When we raise our own consciousness, we raise that of the universe as well. Similarly, there is no concept of heaven or hell, as these are seen as false constructs, illusions of the mind that distract us from the deeper truth of existence.

Because of this worldview, integral beings are solely focused on the sincerity of their own integral being. By being honest, true and genuine in all aspects of their lives, they can help to promote a greater sense of interconnectedness and harmony in the world. This sincerity is not just a personal virtue, but rather a way of being that can have a positive effect on the wider world and beyond.

For those who are unfamiliar with this concept, the idea of an integral being may seem abstract or even nonsensical. However, it is a deeply held belief for many people across the world and beings throughout the universe. By understanding and respecting this perspective, we can gain greater insight into the experience of humans and non-human beings alike and the diverse ways in which we each seek to understand the universe, each other and our place in the cosmos

Conclusion

The idea of integral being is one that universally prioritizes sincerity and interconnectedness over enlightenment or spiritual elevation. By recognizing the fundamental unity of all beings and living lives of truth, compassion and personal sincerity, integral beings can help to create a more harmonious and compassionate world and universe. By integral beings living their lives universally upon the integral Way, things like enlightenment and spiritual elevation will come to them without striving. Upon their further path of return to the Tao, enlightenment, in the form of spiritual evolution and refinement and many other blessings will come naturally on their own. These blessings are those that are accorded to those who honor the Tao and practice the integral Way.

Making and fostering connections with ET/NHIs is also a true part of our spiritual advancement in this life and has ramifications in the next.

CHAPTER 28

Beyond Imagination

As awesome as a clear view of the heavens may be, in this chapter, Lao Tzu cautions against the temptation of associating the vast and luminous heavens with the body of the Tao. It suggests that viewing the Tao as something confined to a specific shape or form would be a mistake. Though it stretches our imagination to try and comprehend it, the Tao transcends such limitations.

By identifying the Tao with a particular shape or form, one would limit their understanding and perception of it. The passage implies that the true nature of the Tao cannot be fully grasped or comprehended by confining it to any specific visual or conceptual representation.

To truly perceive the Tao, we are encouraged to let go of preconceived notions and relinquish the desire to confine it within a particular shape or form. By doing so, there is a greater possibility for us to experience the boundless and formless essence of the Tao.

"As vast and luminous as the heavens might be, it is a tempting mistake to view them as the body of the Tao. The Tao cannot be identified with any particular form. You will never see the Tao if you try and identify it with any particular shape or thing."

The Essence of All Being and Existence Itself

The universe is an awe-inspiring realm that has captivated human fascination for centuries. It is easy to see why many view the heavens as the body of the Tao, the way that all things flow and interact. However, this simplistic view only limits our understanding of what Tao truly is. An entity as expansive and infinite as the Tao cannot be confined to any particular shape or form, for it is in constant motion and evolution.

The Tao is the essence of all being. It is the essence of non-being and worlds and universes yet to be formed. The Tao is the source of creation and evolution, and to view it as something finite is to miss the essence of its true nature. It is not limited to the heavens, nor is it contained within any physical boundaries. It is something that is ineffable and transcendent.

The essence of Tao is not something that can be captured or defined, for it exists beyond the constraints of language and the material world that our senses are able to perceive. It is not something that can be grasped or understood through mere words and concepts. Instead, it is something that is experienced at a very deep level, beyond the conscious mind.

It is a mistake to view the Tao as a particular shape or form, for it is something that is beyond form. It is a force, and an intelligent divine energy that permeates all things. It is the essence of existence itself. To experience and understand the Tao is to let go of preconceived notions, to let go of our attachment to labels and definitions, and to simply be in a state of openness and awareness. It is through experiencing this state of being that we can begin to truly grasp the infinite and complex nature of the universe and our place within it. Consequently, is in and through this state that we are best able to initiate and sustain contact with ET and NHIs and all the highest spiritual beings of the universe.

CHAPTER 29

The Great Secret

The great secret is no secret at all. Once enlightenment is entered, one must exercise discipline in order to maintain it. In this passage Lao Tzu emphasizes the importance of discipline and practice in entering into and maintaining our total awareness and whole enlightenment once we have awakened and have begun to experience it. He cautions against the egotistical belief that one can "achieve" these states or enter them without dedicated effort.

According to the passage, appropriate spiritual practice plays a significant role in channeling emotions and life energy towards the light. By proper practice, Lao Tzu does not mean some sort of religious practice. Almost anything can be spiritual, even making a bed, brushing one's teeth or cleaning the house if it is practiced with mindfulness and connection with the Tao can become a spiritual practice. In this way even simple daily rituals can provide us with a spiritual framework for focusing our intentions and aligning ourselves with higher consciousness. Without the discipline to engage in these rituals and practices, we may find ourselves constantly falling back into darkness.

The passage also reveals the great secret that high awareness of the subtle truth is not only gained through virtuous conduct and sustaining disciplines but also maintained through them. It rightfully suggests that the path to enlightenment requires ongoing commitment and adherence to these practices.

"Highly evolved beings", as described by Lao Tzu in the passage, understand and appreciate the truth of this principle. They recognize the importance of disciplined practice and virtuous conduct in nurturing and sustaining their awakened state of awareness.

Finally, Lao Tzu emphasizes the significance of continued discipline, practice, and virtuous conduct in the journey toward higher awareness and enlightenment. It highlights the transformative power of engaging in appropriate "proper practice" and maintaining ongoing dedication to these practices.

"Can one become totally and wholly aware without proper practice and discipline? To believe that one can do so is egomaniacal. In order to channel one's life energy and emotions toward the light, one needs the appropriate rituals and discipline. Without the discipline to practice appropriate rituals, one will constantly slip and fall, tumbling back into the darkness.

I will tell you a great secret. Just as your high awareness of the subtle truth is entered into through virtuous conduct and is sustained through proper discipline, it is through these things that both virtuous conduct and high awareness are maintained. Those beings who are highly evolved respect this truth and understand the necessity of sustaining their virtue and awareness through proper discipline."

Proper Practice and Discipline

This quote highlights the importance of discipline and practice in finding and entering the states of enlightenment and awareness. Without proper guidance and focus, it can be easy to become lost in the darkness and pitfalls of life.

The key to achieving total awareness and enlightenment is through regular practice and discipline. This often involves developing healthy habits, such as meditation or prayer, that help channel our emotions and heavy life energy towards the more refined or "light" ones. These practices can help us stay centered and focused, providing a solid foundation upon which we can build our spiritual growth.

It is important to remember, however, that becoming enlightened is a lifelong journey. It is not something that can be gained overnight, nor is it something that can be taken for granted. Maintaining this state of awareness requires constant attention and effort, and we must remain vigilant in guarding against the temptation to slip back into unhealthy old habits and patterns.

Finally, the key is to find a balance between discipline and flexibility. While discipline is necessary to find enlightenment, it is also important to remain open and flexible, allowing for the guidance and wisdom of others to guide us along our path. By cultivating these virtues in our lives, and by caring for our mental, physical and spiritual wellbeing, we can attain the high awareness of the subtle truth that is the hallmark of an evolved and enlightened beings.

Ultimately, these evolved and enlightened beings include not only human beings but include the highest spiritual beings of the universe and the ETs and NHIs among them. They too are aware of the great secret that maintenance of heightened spiritual states requires proper practice and discipline.

CHAPTER 30

The Importance of Direct Experience

In this chapter Lao Tzu beautifully expresses the limitations of language in conveying the true essence of things. He teaches that to truly understand and experience the beauty of a tree, the melody of a song, for example, or the Tao itself, direct personal experience with it is necessary.

According to the passage, the subtle truth of the universe is a profound spiritual experience beyond what can be expressed in words or comprehended through thought alone. Therefore, the highest teachings go beyond verbal explanations and concepts. While the words may serve as guidance or a prescription, they are not the ultimate medicine or destination themselves.

Instead of analyzing and intellectualizing the Tao, Lao Tzu advises embracing a silent and experiential approach. He encourages living in alignment with the Tao, with an undivided and harmonious being. The emphasis lies on direct experience and embodying the essence of the Tao rather than intellectualizing or dissecting it intellectually through words. As a consequence, Lao Tzu encourages us to use states of silence, mindfulness in order to achieve whole-hearted immersion in order to best experience and understand the harmonious essence of the living Tao.

"The beauty of a tree cannot be adequately conveyed by words. In order for the beauty of a tree to be understood, one must see it with one's own eyes (and touch it with his own hands). Similarly, a song's melody cannot be captured by language. One must hear it with one's own ears. It is the same with the Tao. One can only understand it by experiencing it directly. The subtle

truth of the universe is beyond thought and speech. It is unthinkable and unsayable.
The Tao can only be understood by directly experiencing it.

The highest teachings are without words. Even these words are not medicine but only a prescription. They do not form a destination but are merely a map to assist you in order to arrive there. When you reach your destination calm your mind and be silent.

The Tao cannot be analyzed, so do not attempt to. Instead, endeavor to silently live it undividedly with your entire harmonious being."

There is No Substitute for Direct Experience

We are reminded here again that the direct experience of something is the gold standard for which the lessons in life are best learned and conveyed. language and words can only go so far in conveying the beauty and essence of something as profound as the Tao. To truly understand the Tao, we must directly experience it and once we do, to live it.

The Tao is something that cannot be fully expressed through language or any other form of communication. It is something that must be directly experienced through transcendent moments of insight and awareness. As the quote suggests, the highest teachings are wordless, as they point towards something that goes beyond the limitations of language and concepts.

To truly live the Tao is to cultivate a peaceful state of mindfulness and inner harmony. To do this we must learn to quiet our minds, let go of our mental ruminations and analytical tendencies, and surrender ourselves to the flow of the universe. In doing so, we can tap into the subtle truths that underlie all things and experience a deep sense of peace and oneness with the world and beings around us.

We cannot fully understand or express the Integral Truth of the Tao through words alone. While language can be a helpful guide and like a map, pointing us in the general direction of the Tao and its Integral Way, it is ultimately up to us to directly experience the Tao through our own practices and insights. By doing what we can by living honest lives of simplicity, patience, and compassion, to best live the Tao, we can practice cultivating an inner state of harmony and awareness that is transformative and enlightening. This is the path of the Integral and universal being.

CHAPTER 31

Eternal and Omnipresent

In this chapter, Lao Tzu conveys the eternal and omnipresent nature of the Tao. He analogizes the Tao to the sky, emphasizing that seen or unseen, it is always and everywhere present, regardless of whether our minds are clouded and unable to perceive it.

According to the passage, all suffering and misery stem from the activity of the mind. It suggests that by letting go of the incessant chatter of words, ideas, attitudes, conditioning, and expectations, we can open themselves to the presence of the Tao. The invitation is to be still, turn inward, and observe. In doing so, just as the sky is there day or night or obscured by clouds or not, like the omnipresent sky, we can recognize that the Integral truth is always available and the Tao responsive.

The passage also encourages us to develop a state of mindfulness and inner reflection, where the noise of the mind is quieted, and the deeper truth can be experienced. It reminds us that the Tao is ever-present, waiting to be recognized and embraced. When we embrace the Tao, all things are possible.

Just like this passage, human initiated contact with ETs and NHIS is possible through realizing our connection with the Tao. Both CE-5 meditation and mindfulness highlight the importance of stillness, letting go of mental constructs, and turning inward to perceive the ever-present truth of the Tao and reaching out into the universe so that our needs are fulfilled and contact with the higher beings of the universe initiated. By meditating and transcending the limitations of the human mind, we can access a deeper awareness and connection with the eternal essence of existence and all higher spiritual beings to whom we are connected by it.

"The Tao is not something that leaves and returns. Always and everywhere like the sky, without coming or going, it is always present. When the mind is clouded one cannot see it. Because one cannot see it does not mean that it is not present.

It is the mind's activity that creates all misery. If you can let go of ideas, words, and attitudes as well as your own expectations, then into view the Tao will loom. If you can be still and look inside you will see that the truth is available, always, and forever responsive."

The Unified Field

This is truly a profound passage as it highlights the ever-present, all-encompassing nature of the Tao, which is always present but can be easily obscured by the activity of the mind. The Tao is a unified field of intelligent energy that runs through the entirety of its creation.

The Tao is like the sky, always present and unchanging. It is only our own mental clouds that prevent us from seeing it clearly. When we get lost in our own thoughts, ideas, and expectations, we become disconnected from the reality of the present moment and lose sight of the subtle truth that underlies all things.

To fully experience the Tao, we must be willing to let go of these mental constructs and expectations and look within ourselves with an open mind and compassionate heart. By meditating and stilling the mind and focusing our attention inward, we not only can get in touch with our inner Tao but we can begin to better perceive the world around us and see past our own physical, mental and spiritual limitations.

Physical pain in life is inevitable. It is an inseparable part of having a physical existence. However, suffering is optional. All misery is created by the activity of the mind, and it is only by quieting the mind and learning how to enter a state of inner stillness that we can begin to overcome our negative thoughts and unhealthy behavioral patterns. By letting go of thought, we can tap into the eternal truth of the Tao and gain a deeper understanding of ourselves and others and the universe around us.

Conclusion

No matter where one goes, there the Tao is. One of life's universal truths is that no matter who we are or what we are doing, the Tao is always present and available to us. However it is up to us to cultivate the stillness and the conscious awareness necessary to perceive it and ask what we need of it. By letting go of our past conditioning and mental constructs, by relaxing and being present in the moment and taking a breath and looking within, we can begin to experience pure integral being and gain a deeper appreciation for the subtle truths of the universe. When we consciously connect with the Tao and attain a state of profound inner peace and harmony all things are possible, even contact with ET and NHIs. This, ability along with our ability to sincerely project unconditional love and compassion is what we have to give and offer to share with ET and NHIs and the other integral universal beings the highest spiritual beings in the universe.

CHAPTER 32

Taxonomy and Comparison

"You can know the name of a bird in all the languages of the world, but when you're finished, you'll know absolutely nothing whatever about the bird...So let's look at the bird and see what it's doing — that's what counts. I learned very early the difference between knowing the name of something and knowing something." - Richard P. Feynman

In this chapter Lao Tzu sheds light on the illusory nature of the ego and its tendency to parse, categorize and conceptualize the world based on size, form, and purpose. He suggests, as it does that the ego creates distinctions and limitations that hinder our understanding of the underlying unity of existence.

According to the passage, the ego perceives the world as vast and the particles that compose it as tiny. The ego believes that the joining and dispersing of these various particles give rise to the appearance of a vast world. However, the subtle truth is that in an infinite universe the world and its particles are not inherently vast or tiny. The passage emphasizes the equality and interconnectedness of all things, where everything is equal to every other thing.

Names, concepts, and beliefs are seen as obstacles that cloud our perception of this Great Oneness. The passage encourages us to look beyond these mental constructs and delve into the deeper, silent, and complete truth of the Tao. By embracing this truth, we can transcend our bewilderment and realize the inherent unity that underlies all existence. In this realization, there is completeness.

In summary, the passage invites us to recognize the limitations of the ego's categorizations and to transcend conceptual thinking. By letting go of beliefs and attachments to labels, we can gain a deeper understanding of the profound truth of the Tao, where the distinctions of size, purpose, and perception dissolve into the unity of all things.

"Is the universe vast? Are particles that form it tiny? The ego tells us they are. It also tells us that when small particles coalesce, as worlds and universes they appear. When these things disperse, then their tiny particles reappear. These different ideas and names all entrance the ego. However, the subtle truth is that whether it be universes, worlds or even the most minuscule of particles, all are the same. Neither is vast nor tiny. Large or small, all things are equal in the great Oneness.

The ego creates names and concepts that distort our perception of the great Oneness and blur our understanding the unity of all things. Ignore these distinctions.

Internally, the ego continuously bewilders us. It makes us frantically struggle to compare and distinguish between things like large and small. It makes us search for purpose behind both the coalescence and dispersion of the great and small. The ego confuses us with questions about things like whether the universe is mechanical and blind or if it is the divine product of a conscious being.

If we learn to live outside of our egos, we begin to look beyond these beliefs and distinctions and we will see that having these beliefs or making comments on such things is needless. When we look beyond the ego's

confusion, we can then ascertain the silent, deep and complete truth of the Tao.

When the Tao is embraced, our bewilderment vanishes."

Abandoning Ego

The ego is a powerful force that can hold sway over every aspect of our lives. From our beliefs and values to our perceptions of the world around us, the ego shapes our understanding of reality. However, as Lao Tzu and the Tao teach us that the ego is only an illusion that prevents us from seeing the true nature of the universe.

Neither the world nor the universe is vast. Nor are the particles that form them tiny. Rather, all the worlds in the universe and all the particles are made of the same essence, neither large nor small. This great oneness is obscured by the ego, which is obsessed with divisions, names and concepts that only serve to block our perception of the truth of the great Oneness of the Tao.

Those who live inside their egos are continually bewildered by the complexities of the world. They struggle to understand the purpose of joining and dispersing, seeking out beliefs and making comments about things that have no grounds for such notions. But the Tao shows us that behind these illusions lies a deep, silent, complete, and infinite truth that we can only discern by abandoning our attachment to our egos and its constructs.

Therefore, it is wise for us to ignore the ego and its dichotomous obsession with names and concepts and look behind them instead to examine the phenomenon itself. There we will find the deep truth of the Tao. In this way, we can embrace this truth and experience it. In this way we can free ourselves from the ego and its illusions of separation that cause our bewilderment and confusion about the nature of the universe and the way things really are.

Conclusion

Inevitably, Lao Tzu reminds us that we are all interconnected to the Tao and every thing is equal to every other thing. It is all made up of the same indestructible energy and reconfiguring firmament. This is the true nature of the universe, beyond the illusions created to understand reality by the ego. When we let go of our egos and their limiting self-protective constructs, we free ourselves to dispel the illusion of separation, discover its truth and see the oneness and the interrelationship of all things and embrace the beauty, mystery and wonder of the Tao. This discovery and experience is the common ground that all integral beings that we share with ETs and NHIs share the highest spiritual beings and guardians of the universe.

CHAPTER 33

Allowing the Tao to Dwell Within

"There is providence in the fall of a sparrow."
- William S. Shakespeare*

This chapter by Lao Tzu certainly highlights the interconnect-edness between the Tao and the manifestations of the world, including human beings and ET/NHI and the synchronici-ties** that surround them. While the world and its particles, as well as cosmic bodies and individual bodies, may appear different, they are ultimately inseparable and interconnected expressions of the Tao.

The Tao, being beyond comprehension and analysis, cannot be fully grasped or categorized by the human mind. It transcends the limitations of human conceptual understanding. However, the passage tells us that the truth of the Tao is omnipresent and limited by our ability to understand it through traditional means, it can be realized through a simple but profound shift in our perspective.

To apprehend the Tao, Lao Tzu advises letting go of mental attachments and approaching it with an open heart. By cul-tivating a receptive and intuitive state, we can develop a deep connection with the Tao. In this way, the Tao becomes an internal presence, residing within the individual, and guiding their actions and understanding.

Ultimately, Lao Tzu invites us to recognize the inherent in-terconnectedness of all things and the transient nature of the manifestations of the Tao. While comprehending the totality of the Tao is beyond our intellectual grasp, it can be realized, embraced, appreciated and in some ways understood through a heartfelt connection and a surrendering of the mind's attempts to separate, categorize and analyze. By simply allowing the Tao to reside within us, we can experience its eternal truth and share that truth and ultimately its compassion with others.

> **"In the same way that the world can be revealed as particles, the Tao can reveal itself as human beings. Whether revealed as world or particle, neither is the same, nor are they different. Similarly, neither the cosmic body nor your body are the same, however; neither are they different. Whether it be world or particle, body or being, time or space: all of these expressions of the Tao are transient in nature. Invisible, ungraspable, the Tao cannot be captured, analyzed or categorized. Simultaneously, its truth is omnipresent. Let your mind let go of it. Envelop the Tao with your heart and it will live there inside of you forever."**

Synchronicity and the Subtle Expression of the Tao

The Tao speaks to us in subtle and oft times mysterious ways, often revealing itself through synchronicities and the world around us. Just as the world can reveal itself as particles, the Tao can reveal itself in nature and even through human beings as well as ET and NHIs. Although these many expressions of the Tao may seem different, they are in fact all one and the same.

The world and particles are not the same, but neither are they different. Similarly, the cosmic body and your physical, mental, and spiritual body are not the same, but neither are they different. All of the transient expressions of the Tao, including your own present life and existence are part of its infinite and eternal presence. Although the Tao may be unseeable and ungraspable in its ultimate form and intent, its truth is everywhere around us.

To truly understand the Tao, as this and the previous chapter suggest, we must let go of our attempts to analyze or categorize it. The Tao is beyond any such attempts, and to try to confine it in such a way is to miss the point of it entirely. Rather, we must surround the Tao with our hearts, allowing ourselves to fully embrace its truth and beauty and live with it consciously within us.

One of the key ways we can do this is by recognizing the Tao in human beings and the events that surround them. Each person represents a unique expression of the Tao, with their own experiences, perspectives, and ways of being in the world. When we see the Tao in others, we open ourselves up to a deeper understanding of ourselves and the unfolding of the universe around us.

Conclusion

The subtle truth of the Tao can be seen in everything, from the world around us to the people and beings with whom we interact. Although the Tao may seem unseeable and un-graspable, its truth is everywhere we turn. It reveals itself in synchronicity***. The highest spiritual beings of the universe understand and accept the Tao as their universal truth. By embracing the Tao with our hearts and recognizing it in others, we can unlock its infinite potential and live our lives in harmony with subtle truth and share its eternal presence and compassion with countless other human beings and the highest spiritual beings that inhabit the universe.

"In this quote, Hamlet rejects the notion that the will of the gods or fate can be divined and avoided and asserts that everything unfolds according to an immutable plan. If something is fated to happen, it will happen. If not now, then it will come later. If not later, then now. For the first time in the play, he finds a sense of acceptance and peace in the face of overwhelming circumstances. Even the smallest sacrifices (i.e. the fall of a sparrow) are part of a grander design that we cannot fathom with our limited human perception. Because you can't see the bigger picture, you can't outsmart it." - Evan Robertson

**Synchronicity: The term first coined and used by Carl G. Jung to describe the occurrence simultaneously of events that appear significantly related yet do not discernably have a causal connection, yet they arise in frequency or circumstance beyond the levels of mere chance.

***Synchronicity, in a more profound way is the revealing of the Tao, the underlying Source that orchestrates and connects all reality and experience. Much like Dorothy pulling back the curtain that reveals the Wizard orchestrating what we see as Oz, so is synchronicity. The Creator of the universe lets us pull back the ego's curtain of illusion we call "Maya" to reveal the Eternal One that is has always been there timelessly orchestrating reality. Once realised, one can never go back to seeing reality the same anymore. Recognizing the Tao, and parenthetically, the nature of synchronicity, is the transcendent awakening that is at the base of all spiritual enlightenment. The divine creator and its creation are one and the same. It is no wonder why Jung in his book Synchronicity cites the Tao Te Ching as authority for part of his prospective or that synchronicity plays so prevalent a role in explaining the UFO/UAP phenomenon in his subsequent work Flying Saucers: A Modern Myth of Things Seen in the Sky.

CHAPTER 34

Birth, Life, Death and Rebirth

This passage by Lao Tzu emphasizes the cyclical nature of existence and the importance of the energies to which we ourselves connect. Whether it is the form of a star or a person, all things in the universe go through a process of transitioning from the unseen "subtle" non-being to being, that which becomes manifest. By proceeding through the cycle of physical being it dies and returns to the subtle only to return again to the manifest. The cycle is eternal.

Subtle energy precedes the manifestation of life, and once life passes away, the subtle energy, or "soul" continues to exist. Once physical existence ends, subtle energy can either return to the subtle realm or attach itself to new manifestations. The quality of our existence is shaped by the energies to which we attach ourselves.

If we attach ourselves to gross energies, such as attachment, hatred, or indulgence, we will experience heavy and attached lives. This cycle can continue for a long time, leading to a tedious existence. On the other hand, the integral being chooses to connect with higher, more refined, and subtle energies.

By aligning with these higher and lighter energies, the integral being traverses refined, heavenly and subtle realms. Even when engaging with the world, they do so lightly and without attachment. This allows them to move freely and navigate any situation without losing their connection to the center of the universe.

In essence, the passage encourages us to be mindful of the energies we cultivate and with which we connect. By choosing to eschew dark base and gross energies and associating ourselves with higher refined and subtle energies, we can elevate our soul's existence and move harmoniously within and through the cycles of life, both manifest and subtle.

"In the universe all things move back and forth from the unseen and subtle into that which is the visible and manifest. Whether it is a star or a human being, the process remains the same. It starts with the existence of subtle energy that takes on life as it becomes physically manifest. Over time, its life eventually passes away. However, its subtle energy remains. At this stage, after the death of its physical host, the subtle energy either returns to remain in the subtle realm or once again it attaches itself to things that are either manifest or becoming manifest. This process can be tedious because it can go on throughout one's lifetime for a very long time.

Just as energies become defined by their host, the character of our own existence is characterized by the energies with which we connect ourselves during our lives. If we attach ourselves to gross energies by loving one person yet hating another, or habitually indulging in one experience while rejecting another, then we are destined to live a series of lives where the energies are heavy and very attached.

It is the way of the integral beings to unite with higher things and integrate themselves with those subtle energies which are light and refined. In that way the integral being can easily traverse the realms of the subtle and refined. When such a being enters a world he or she does so lightly and lacking of all attachments. This is how an integral being can travel anywhere throughout both the realms of the subtle and manifest without ever having to leave the center of the universe."

The Unruling Rulers and Uncreating Creators of the Tao's
Immortal Realm

Everything in the universe, from stars to people, goes through a
process of movement from subtle energies to manifested forms
and back again. This process works continually and affects our
lives and our future lives.

The process of energy movement in the universe works in a
specific way. First, subtle unseen energy exists in the universe.
Then, it becomes manifest into the material realm and takes
on life. After a time, life passes away, but the subtle energy goes
on and either returns to the subtle realm where it is unseen or
attaches itself again to manifest things. This process determines
the characteristics of our existence.

Our existence is determined by the energies to which we decide
to connect ourselves. If we connect to lower vibrational, darker
or "gross" energies, such as loving only a particular person or
hating a particular clan, then we are leading attached lives. This
can go on for a very long time and become monotonous. It can
also cause an endless succession of lives in the same mortal and
physical realm. This cycle of birth and rebirth into the lower
physical realms may be transcended, however.

The character of our existence can be transformed by connecting to higher, refined, and subtle energies of the Tao. The
way of an integral being is to join with these higher things and
traverse these refined and subtle realms lightly and without
attachment. This way, he or she can go anywhere without ever
leaving the center of the universe.

Finally, in this chapter Lao Tzu begins to introduce us to what
we will learn on chapter 60 to be the "unruling rulers and uncreating creators of the Tao's immortal realm". Not limited to
the realms of the manifest, they are integral beings who have
evolved themselves beyond the highest spiritual beings and

beyond the concepts of being and non-being and can travel without form anywhere throughout both the Tao's realms of the subtle and manifest.

Conclusion

Ultimately, the movement of energy in the universe affects everything from stars to people. Our existence is determined by the energies to which we connect ourselves while we are manifest. By joining with refined and subtle energies, we, just as all integral universal beings and the highest spiritual beings of the universe have, can ultimately transform our existence and traverse these realms "lightly and without attachment" as the progeny of the Tao, thus experiencing a complete integral existence and becoming the complete integral beings that we were brought by the Tao into the manifest to be.

CHAPTER 35

Knowledge and Insight

This passage by Lao Tzu highlights the distinction between intellectual knowledge and spiritual insight, emphasizing the enduring nature of the latter as compared to the transient nature of the former.

Intellectual knowledge is associated with the brain and the physical body. As the body is subject to mortality, any collection of facts and knowledge stored in the brain is also limited by the lifespan of the body. It is impermanent and will eventually expire.

In contrast, insight is linked to the spirit, or soul which persists through cycles of life, death, and rebirth. This innate immortality implies that the opportunity for cultivating insight transcends individual lifetimes. With each cycle, there is a chance to evolve spiritually and to refine and deepen one's insight, gradually reaching a state of purity, constancy, and unwavering clarity. This refinement can eventually result in human beings escaping the misery attendant to materiality and physical being and evolving into new and higher forms of in this lifetime beyond our human form and into higher physical and non-physical forms in the next.

By cultivating our personal spiritual insight over time, we can finally begin to touch upon a true form of conscious immortality. This immortality does not refer to physical existence but rather the enduring nature of wisdom, consciousness and spiritual understanding that accompanies us after we physically expire. It is the development of our spiritual insight that allows us to connect with something timeless and profound, persisting and exceeding the limitations of individual lives and beyond things like physical materiality, time, and space.

"What is the difference between intellectual knowledge and insight?
Intellectual knowledge is knowledge that lives in the brain and survives there because of it. Because the brain is part of a mortal body, despite its impressive size or prodigious collection of facts, inevitably, because the brain's nature is physical, it will one day expire.
Insight, on the other hand is not a function of the brain but of spirit. Because your spirit is eternal, it follows you through each of your cycles of life, death and rebirth. With each rebirth you will have the ongoing opportunity to cultivate your insight so that it becomes constant, refined, pure, reliable and unwavering.
Most importantly, it is through discovering and using your insight and not your intellect that your own immortality begins."

The Physical World vs. Spiritual Existence

When we think about intellectual knowledge, we typically think about facts, information, and memories that are stored in our brains. This knowledge is undoubtedly valuable as it helps us understand the world around us, make decisions, and communicate with others. However, there is a fundamental limitation to intellectual knowledge, one that is often overlooked; it is tied to our physical bodies.

Because our brains are part of our physical bodies, which will inevitably expire, so too will our intellectual knowledge with them. This extinction applies whether we are thinking about personal memories or the collective knowledge of humanity. Eventually, all of it will be forgotten and lost.

However, Lao Tzu teaches us that there is another kind of knowledge that is not tied to the body - insight. Insight is a spiritual function of the soul. It is a deeper understanding of the world, one that goes beyond facts and data. Unlike intellectual knowledge, insight is not limited by death. Because the spirit follows us through cycles of life, death, and rebirth, we have the opportunity to cultivate insight in an ongoing fashion through infinite time.

As we refine our insight over time in each life, it becomes pure, constant, and unwavering. Eventually, we no longer need to rely on our bodies to access it. This transition between physicality and spirituality is the beginning of immortality.

The Value of Immortality

The question then arises - what is the value of immortality? Is it simply a pleasant thought, or does it have deeper implications?

One possibility is that immortality allows us to continue our personal growth and development beyond the limitations of a single lifetime. We can continue to learn, explore, and deepen our understanding of the world without the pressure of finite time. This type of ongoing development could have profound and positive implications for humanity as a whole.

Another possibility is that insight is a form of knowledge that is inherently superior to intellectual knowledge. It allows us to access deeper truths about the world and our place in it. If this is true, then the pursuit of insight ultimately may be more valuable than the pursuit of intellectual knowledge.

Ultimately, while intellectual knowledge is undoubtedly valuable, it is limited by our physical bodies. Insight, on the other hand, is a form of knowledge that is not tied to the body. It allows us to cultivate a deeper understanding of the world that can continue beyond physical death and into future lifetimes.

Whether this is valuable or not is a matter of opinion, but there is no denying the potential implications for spiritual insight and personal growth and human understanding. There is also no denying that it is instrumental in our relating to and understanding the older and higher forms of physical and spiritual life that inhabit the cosmos around us.

Conclusion

Like this passage, we should encourage the cultivation of our own insight and that of others as a means to transcend the limitations of intellectual knowledge. In this way we can embark on a journey of spiritual wisdom and understanding towards an enlightened state of immortality. By accepting our own divine conscious nature as living beings and acknowledging the existence of our own immortality we can change and improve the world in which we and others after us will live. Finally, when we choose to evolve and refine ourselves spiritually, we can better understand and relate to the eternal Tao and its cosmos. It is the same eternal Tao and the same cosmos that surrounds us and all beings that inhabit it from the infinite reaches of the subtle realm to the material one as well.

CHAPTER 36

Undiscriminating Virtue and the Highest Spiritual Beings

In this passage Lao Tzu takes us to the next step by teaching us that besides achieving true immortality through spiritual practice, we can also experience freedom and absolute joy through the practice of undiscriminating virtue. But what is undiscriminating virtue? We practice undiscriminating virtue when we practice without exception kindness and selflessness. When we do this, we align our lives with the Tao's Integral Way, the path that transcends all boundaries and illusions.

As the illusions of separation between individuals and societies, darkness and light, and life and death are dissolved, Lao Tzu tells us that one gains the company of the "highest spiritual beings". This companionship offers us protection from negative energies and harmful influences. It ensures us that our life energy remains intact. Ultimately, this assists in leading us to the attainment of the immortality that Lao Tzu mentions and explains in the previous chapter.

It is important to note that the passage rightly acknowledges that those who cultivate wholeness and virtue may still encounter difficulties in life. As the saying goes, "Even after enlightenment, one still has to do the laundry," However, those who practice indiscriminating virtue can approach these challenges with calmness and openness, as they recognize that difficulties pave the very road to immortality. Overcoming them is how we get there. By facing obstacles with the help of the Tao and by joyfully developing ourselves in calm and poised response to these difficulties, we become as natural, complete, and eternal as the Tao itself.

"Immortality is entirely possible for one to have and so too is the experience of eternal absolute joy and freedom. The means to this end is the practice of undiscriminating virtue. By practicing kindness and selflessness, one naturally aligns one's life with the Integral Way.

When one aligns their life with the Integral Way, they begin to dissolve those imaginary boundaries between people and societies and things like light and dark and life and death. When these illusions are eliminated, one acquires the company of the highest of spiritual beings. It is in the company of these beings that one is protected from negative influences. In their company your one's energy will not be able to be dissolved.

In becoming immortal, remember that your cultivation of wholeness and virtue will not insulate you from encountering difficulties in life. It is in one encountering difficulties and overcoming them that one walks the very path to his or her immortality.

By meeting difficulties calmly and openly, they unfold and in response the Integral being's joyful development in response to them. As a consequence, facing difficulty becomes as complete, natural and eternal for the integral being as does the Tao itself."

Real Immortality

The human quest for immortality is one of the enduring pursuits of mankind throughout history. From ancient times to modern-day, the search for ways to prolong life and achieve everlasting existence has been a subject of both fascination and speculation. While science has made impressive strides in recent decades towards unlocking the secrets of longevity, the path to true immortality is not a mere physical one. Instead, it is by embracing the practice of undiscriminating virtue and aligning our lives with the Integral Way that we can attain real immortality.

The Integral Way is a spiritual path that encompasses the cultivation of virtues such as simplicity, patience, kindness, selflessness, and compassion. By practicing these virtues, we open ourselves up to a higher level of consciousness and become aligned with the flow of all life. In doing so, we begin to transcend the traditional boundaries that separate individuals and societies, and we develop a deep understanding of the interconnectedness of all things.

As we cultivate wholeness and undiscriminating virtue in ourselves, we become better able to handle the difficulties and challenges that life throws our way. Instead of seeing these challenges as obstacles, we begin to view them as opportunities for personal growth and spiritual development. By meeting problems and impediments directly, truthfully, calmly and openly, we learn spiritually. We evolve through experience to become more natural, more complete, and more forgiving, compassionate and eternal, like the Tao itself.

The practice of undiscriminating virtue is not a means to an end but a way of life. It influences our thinking, mediates our actions, and shapes our character. As we practice undiscriminating virtue, we become better equipped to handle the ups and downs of life by remaining centered amidst turmoil, and to remain poised, optimistic and hopeful in the face of adversity. In doing so, we become invincible as we begin to realize the nature of our own immortality and transcend the limitations of the physical body.

Attaining immortality is not just a spiritual quest but an achievable goal. By embracing the Integral Way and cultivating wholeness and virtue in ourselves, we align our lives with a higher purpose and become more than just material, physical beings. We become truly spiritual beings, free from the constraints of materiality, time and space.

Ultimately, this passage emphasizes the transformative power of undiscriminating virtue, the dissolution of dualistic illusions, especially those of life and death. It reassures us that it is the joyful embrace of life's challenges that is the means for us to align ourselves with the eternal nature of the Tao, to achieve immortality and integrate ourselves spiritually with the highest spiritual beings of the universe and all the Tao's creation itself.

Conclusion

The path to true immortality is not through any physical means through the spiritual practice of undiscriminating virtue and the alignment of our lives with the Tao's Integral Way. Though we may encounter difficulties in life, by cultivating undiscriminating virtue and wholeness and by responding to the challenges of life's trials and tribulations joyfully and with indiscriminate and unconditional patience, love and compassion, we become as natural, complete, and eternal as the Tao itself.

CHAPTER 37

The Superior Being

This chapter from the teachings of Lao Tzu highlights the perspective and actions of a "superior person". Unlike the concerns, goings and comings of an every day human being that are centered around caring for themselves, the superior person distinguishes themself by being one who cares for the well-being of all things. This caring is demonstrated by accepting responsibility for the energy manifested by them both actively and in the subtle realm.

When observing a tree, an everyday person might see it simply as a tree or something to provide shade or firewood. The superior person, on the other hand, sees beyond its isolated existence and recognizes the interconnectedness of its roots, leaves, trunk, water, soil, and sun. This interconnectedness extends to all aspects of existence, including oneself and others. Trees, animals, humans, insects, flowers, and birds are seen as active expressions of the subtle energies that permeate the universe. These energies flow from the stars, combining with earthly elements and each other to give rise to all living things. The superior person sees all this.

The superior person not only understands this connection and the interplay of energies but also recognizes their own role within it. They acknowledge and respect the earth as their mother, the heavens as their father, and all living things as their brothers and sisters. By caring for and giving to others, they understand the Oneness of the Tao and that they are caring for and giving to themselves. They maintain a state of peace with all beings, which in turn brings about their own inner peace.

The passage encourages us to become "superior" beings and engage ourselves in a holistic perspective in life, to understand our interconnectedness, and live with a sense of responsibility and undertake that leadership towards all living things. This undiscriminating responsibility as part of the Great Oneness to all life inevitably includes our responsibility to each other and to ETs and NHIs.

"Caring for the well-being of others is what distinguishes a superior being from others who are not so advanced. The superior being becomes so by being responsible for the energy he manifests both inside and outside of the subtle realm. When the superior being looks at a tree she sees not just a tree as an isolated occurrence but sees it as the relatedness of its trunk, boughs, leaves, roots, branches, earth, water, air, sun and sky. Looking at herself and others she sees the same relationship. Humans, trees, insects, flowers, and birds; all are animated images of the Tao's subtle energy, the energy that flows throughout the universe from the stars to and through us and all things.

By meeting and combining with each other and with the elements these subtle energies, the Tao gives rise to the formation and birth of all living things. The superior being understands both this relationship and the part that she and her own energies play in it. The superior being therefore respects the earth as if it were her mother. She honors the heavens as if they were her father and treats all living things as her brothers and sisters. She cares for them knowing that when she gives to and cares for them, she gives to and cares for herself. Because she is at peace with them, she is at peace with herself."

The Holistic Perspective and Responsibility to all Life

In today's world, people often forget the importance of caring not only for themselves but for for all living things. A superior person understands and practices this concept in their daily life. This person acknowledges the interconnectivity between all life forms and the energies that flow through them. They understand that their own actions—both physical and subtle—play a critical role in contributing to the well-being of all living things.

For a superior person, everything that they see conveys a deeper understanding of the world around them. For instance, when they look at a tree, they don't simply see it as an isolated object. Instead, they see the larger network of relationships that make up the tree. They observe how the roots, trunk, leaves, water, soil, and sun all interact with one another and contribute to the tree's overall growth. They recognize that a "tree" isn't just a single entity, but rather a complex system of events that are interrelated with one another. Even the light from the faintest star has some effect upon it.

This holistic perspective also extends to their interactions with other people and living things. A superior person understands that every person and creature is a unique manifestation of the subtle energies that flow through the universe. They treat all living things with care and respect, recognizing that other living beings are their brothers and sisters. They acknowledge that we are all connected to each other and to the spaces we inhabit.

Furthermore, a superior person sees themselves as a part of the larger ecosystem and takes responsibility for their actions. They recognize that their physical and subtle energies and what they say and do and how they behave affect others around them. They therefore strive to live in a way that benefits everyone.

They also understand that giving to others is also a form of giving to themselves.

Thus, a superior person leads a harmonious and peaceful life. By caring for the well-being of all things, they find balance and purpose. They see themselves as part of a larger cosmic whole, and work to make the world a better place for everyone. And why wouldn't they?

The concept of caring for all living things is a critical one that we all should do our best to understand, accept and incorporate into our lives. A truly integral being is superior person who embodies this idea of responsibility to and compassion for all in their daily practices, recognizing the interconnectedness of all life forms throughout the universe and their energies and undertake as much responsibility that can be reasonably handled toward that end. By living in harmony with the world and universe around them, superior beings find meaning, purpose, connection and fulfillment not in things but in their relations here on earth and with the ET and NHIs who are already here and those in the universe beyond.

CHAPTER 38

"Be still and know that I am God".
- Psalm 46:10

This chapter by Lao Tzu reminds us of the eternal truth, to be still and recognize the truth of the Tao, "God", Source that permeates everything around us. It advises against seeking truth through constant accumulation of knowledge, which can lead to doubt and an insatiable hunger for more knowledge. Instead, the wise person finds understanding in the subtle interplay between the named and the unnamed, between being and non-being.

The source of truth lies within oneself. By quieting the mind and observing the world with stillness and clarity, one can perceive the underlying harmony and interconnectedness of all things. The foolish, on the other hand, are driven by impulsive actions and are unaware of the subtle forces at play. They fail to see the perfect essence that exists before any action is taken.

Artificial actions and disturbances disrupt the inherent peace and harmony of the world. The passage encourages contentment, quietness, and the discovery of inner harmony. By embracing this harmony within oneself, one can gain everything and contribute to the restoration of a healthy world. Those who are unable to do so may remain lost in the shadows of confusion and unrest.

Overall, the passage emphasizes the importance of stillness, self-discovery, and understanding the subtle nature of existence in order to find contentment and contribute to the well-being of the world.

"To find the truth, look no further than the tip of your nose. One need not scamper about looking where to find it. In everything and every non-thing truth vibrates and abounds.

Can you quiet yourself and see the subtle truth of the universe in the deep ocean or in looking to the mountain aloft above you? Can you see it in the great oak or the tender shoot of new pine? Can you see the subtle truth in yourself?

Contrary to what many think, the truth is not found by accumulating more knowledge. The more one knows the more one doubts. Knowledge begets doubt and doubt begets the search for even more knowledge. One makes us more ravenous for the other. The cycle is unending. We dine on both, but we are never filled with enough to make the hunger stop.

The wise do not feast on knowledge. Instead. They dine on something far more subtle. Their banquet is found in understanding that all being comes from non-being and all that has a name was born from the nameless. They understand that all that can be described in the world emanates from a source that cannot be described. With the discovery of this subtle source inside of themselves they discover their complete contentment.

So who among you can be still and observe the great chess game that is the world? Observe that impulsive moves are always made by fools. The wise know better. They know that something more subtle governs both victory and defeat. They can see that a subtle perfection exists before any move is made. Knowing that artificial action deteriorates this subtle perfection, they stay quiet and content. They choose not to move so that the peace is not disturbed.

So, be silent. Remain still. If you can, you will discover
the harmony in your own being. By embracing it, you
will have everything there is to gain. Health as well will
return to the world once again. If you cannot do this,
then in the shadows both you and your world will be
lost forever."

The Importance of Stillness and Truth

This chapter speaks to the importance of stillness and seeking a deeper understanding of the world. The wise person
acknowledges that the truth is not something that can be found
by accumulating knowledge or external stimuli, but rather, is
something that is present within us and in the world around us.

By being still and quiet, we are able to better see the subtle
truths that exist in everything. We begin to see how life works,
that the named is born from the unnamed, and that all being
flows from non-being. The wise person realizes that the world
is not a chess game to be won or lost, but rather a complex
system where victory and defeat are decided by something far
more subtle.

The passage emphasizes that there is a subtle perfection that
exists before any action is taken, and that this perfection can be
lost when artificial actions are taken. The wise person, therefore, chooses to remain quiet and not disturb the peace. They
seek to discover the harmony in their own being and embrace
it fully. When they move, they avoid doing so on impulse. The
moves of the wise are well considered and are done in such a
way as to preserve the harmony and natural order of things.

By doing so, the wise person gains everything as their banquet
and helps to create a peaceful, healthy, and thriving world.
The passage warns of the dangers of being lost in the shadows

forever if one cannot step outside of ego to find their inner harmony.

Conclusion

Ultimately, the passage speaks to the importance of our finding stillness wherever we can find it. In that quietude lies the subtle realm within us. It cautions us to avoid false knowledge and disturbing the Tao's natural peace by taking impulsive and artificial actions. Lao Tzu encourages us to seek subtle truths, those found in the Tao and in finding our inner harmony through the Integral Way. By doing so, we are rewarded by living peaceful, wise and contented lives. So, embrace the perfect harmony that already exists within you and connect to the world and universe with which you are eternally surrounded.

CHAPTER 39

The Integral Truth of the Universe

At this point in the Hua Hu Ching, Lao Tzu begins to confide in us the deeper truths of the Tao and the Integral Way. In this chapter Lao Tzu introduces us to the Great Tai Chi. There will be much more about its permutations and how its energies may be harnessed in later chapters. But it all really begins here.

In introducing us to the Tao as expressed in the universally recognized symbol, Lao Tzu highlights the ineffable nature of the Tao as the Great Creator or the Source of the universe. Lao Tzu tells us that trying to search for this ultimate source will be futile, as it is ultimately unknowable. Instead, he presents the metaphor of a great invisible river flowing through a fertile valley, symbolizing the silent and uncreated nature of the source that gives rise to all things.

The passage also introduces us to the concept of yin and yang, the complementary and interdependent forces that are responsible for the creation and manifestation of all things. The dynamic and active nature of yang, represented by the pushing forward of the river. Yang combines with the still and receptive nature of yin, represented by the valley. Through the integration of both their male and female energies, the world of forms and appearances emerges.

This integration of yin and yang is referred to as the Great Tai Chi, which represents the integral truth of the universe. All things emanate from this energetic source. The passage emphasizes that everything in existence, including our bodies, the cosmic body, wisdom, energy, and the interactions of people, arises through the natural interplay of yin and yang. Because the Great Tai Chi is self-so, there is no need for the direction of any external creator or agitated effort. All one needs to do is to breathe, relax and find the flow of the Tao. The rest will take care of itself.

That is why this passage teaches us to meditate and to cultivate our awareness of the Tao, the Great Tai Chi, the subtle operation of the universe. By being attuned to this underlying harmony and its flow, we can align ourselves with the natural unfolding of creation, its transformation, growth and its inevitable physical decline. Lao Tzu encourages a state of mindfulness and recognition of the inherent wisdom and energy present in the universe.

As Integral and universal beings we should remember to take some time out each day and contemplate the mysterious and self-organizing nature of the universe, reminding ourselves that we are part of this vast unfolding and encouraging ourselves to be aware of the Great Tai Chi that permeates all things. When we realize this is ourselves, we can recognize it in others and especially in the ETs and NHIs whom we now have made some rudimentary and nascent forms of contact and with whom we will have the opportunity to meet, communicate and interact in the future. Both they and we are part of the Great Tai Chi and share its awareness.

"If one searches for the Great Creator, he will return empty handed. Ultimately unknowable is the source for the universe. Like the flowing of a great yet invisible river, it forever travels through a timeless valley that is both fertile and boundless. Though silent and unborn, the Tao gives birth and life to all things.

From the subtle realm all things are brought forth by the Tao through the Great Tai Chi that is formed by Yin and Yang. That which becomes manifest in the world comes from their mystical intercourse. Yang, like a powerful surging river, pushes forward into the receptive

and peaceful valley of Yin. It is through the mystical integration of both Yin and Yang that all things that come into being are born.

This Great Tai Chi is called 'the integral truth of the universe'. This truth is universal because everything can be broken down from it into its own tai chi. From the cosmic body to the human body, all is a tai chi. Whether it be energy or form, human or not, wisdom or appearance, the joining of male and female, the unions and dispersal of time and space, all are a tai chi at their core.

All that comes into being exists, maintains, and then disperses itself on its own accord. It does so without either prompting or direction by a creator. Every tai chi is self-directing. Even your own creation, self-transformation, accumulation of wisdom and energy, the rise, decline and cessation of your own physical existence: all of it is a tai chi. They are 'self-so' because they occur by themselves upon their own accord, within the subtle operation that which is the Tao.

Because of the integral truth of the world, the Great Tai Chi, learn to be patient. Understand that agitated or forceful effort is harmful and unnecessary. Right now, simply be aware of the Great Tai Chi and universal integral truth that springs forth from it. (There will be more to learn about it later)."

"Matter can neither be created nor destroyed. It merely may be arranged in space, or the entities associated with it may be changed in form. The quantity of mass is therefore conserved to remain constant as nothing can be added or removed."
- The Law of Conservation of Mass

The Great Hai Chi

We can learn so much about the universe, however, the ultimate source of the universe is ultimately unknowable. Here Lao Tzu recognizes this and resorts to explaining the concept he wishes to express by analogizing the Tao with the metaphor of an invisible river that flows through a vast and fertile valley. Just like the invisible river, the Great Creator is not something that can be found through searching, but rather something that simply exists and creates all things. There is no need to search for something that runs through you and exists right in front of us in plain sight.

Everything in existence is a Tai Chi. Everything in the universe - from the cosmic body to the union of people - is a Tai Chi. Essentially, everything is brought into existence through the integration of yin and yang, and maintains itself and disperses itself without the direction of any creator.

The idea conveyed here is that everything within the universe is connected in a harmonious way, and that everything flows from the Great Tai Chi. Agitated effort is not necessary; we simply need to be aware of the Great Tai Chi and work with it to make life easier and more peaceful and abundant.

Finally, this passage also speaks to the idea of our acceptance of the universe as it is and being content in simply being aware of its subtle operation. This is part of becoming integrally aware. When we can understand the Great Tai Chi and realize that everything is connected, we can live more harmonious, connected and fulfilling lives. Such a life is the life of an integral beings throughout the universe.

CHAPTER 40

The Natural Laws of the Universe

"Everything in moderation" - Cleobulus

At this point almost halfway through the Hua Hu Ching and three quarters of the way through both of Lao Tzu's works that constitute his teachings about the Tao and its Integral Way, we are getting to the esoteric teachings about the nature of the Tao's energies and those elemental universal laws that govern reality as we can come to know it as human integral beings. In this passage Lao Tzu emphasizes the presence of natural laws in the universe that are inviolable and govern various aspects of existence. He highlights the principle that energy condenses into substance. For example, food is consumed through the mouth, and neglecting to breathe has consequences. These simple examples illustrate the inherent order and functioning of the world.

Furthermore, in this passage Lao Tzu reminds us that our thoughts, words, and actions play a significant role in shaping our lives. While ordinary individuals may perceive this law as external to themselves, leading to a false sense of confinement and control, the superior person recognizes their intrinsic connection to this subtle law. By cultivating ourselves to align with this law, we bring moderation to our actions and clarity to our minds.

The superior person, ie., an integral being, understands that they are not separate from the divine and enlightened nature of the universe. They know it best to act and live in moderation. By harmonizing with the natural laws and principles, and avoiding extremes, we experience serenity, contentment, and a sense of oneness with all that is.

Lao Tzu emphasizes the profound and simple truth that we, as individual manifestations of the Tao are the sovereign masters of our own lives and destinies. What we do, the choices we make, and the actions we take shape our existence and that of the universe around us. By aligning with the natural order and living in accordance with it, we can find mastery, fulfillment, and a deeper connection to the divine essence within ourselves and the world. We can reach out to others and connect with them.

As manifest individuals and as integral beings and followers of the integral Way, we recognize the interconnectedness between ourselves and the laws of the universe. By living moderately and aligning our thoughts, words, and deeds with the Tao and her natural laws, we can experience harmony, peace, and a sense of empowerment in shaping our own lives to fulfill our own destinies and become examples of integral beings and followers of the Tao and its integral.

"Inviolable are the universe's natural laws. Energy condenses into matter. We eat food through our mouths, not our noses. If you stop breathing, you will turn blue and die. Simply, some things cannot be dismissed. The natural laws of the universe are part of the cosmic law that says that whatever we say and do in our lives determines what happens in us.

Everyday people believe that cosmic law is something external to them and that it confines and controls them. As a consequence, they let desire control their minds. In turn, desire troubles their spirit. Because their spirit is troubled, they live in constant turmoil with the world. They spend their whole lives struggling.

The superior being perceives that he and the subtle law are not two separate things. They are one inseparable being. The superior being therefore cultivates himself

to live in accord with the subtle law. He acts with
moderation. He keeps his mind clear. As a consequence
of these practices, he discovers that he and all are one
with everything that is enlightened and divine. In this
knowledge he passes his days serenely and
in contentment.

The simple yet profound truth of the cosmic law is that
we are all masters of our lives and deaths. We ultimately
are what we say and do."

Everything Matters: We Are What We Do

At some point on the path to the integral Way we become
enlightened to it by recognizing that we are the master of
our own lives and that what we say and do determines what
happens in our lives. Lao Tzu mentions that the natural laws
of the universe are inviolable and that it is also a part of the
cosmic law that our actions and words have an impact on our
lives and the web of universal life to which we are connected.
Everything that we do and say matters.

The ordinary every-day person often feels confined and controlled by this law and unnecessarily lives a life of constant
turmoil and struggle. By contrast, the superior person, one of
integral being, recognizes that they and the subtle law are one.
They cultivate themselves to accord with this law, bringing
moderation to their actions and clarity to their mind. They
rest when they are weary, eat when hungry, drink when thirsty
and go to the bathroom when they have to.

It may seem so simple but so many people ignore these laws.
By acting as integral beings living in moderation and aligning
ourselves with the cosmic law, we can find ourselves at one with
all that is divine and enlightened. This connectedness exists
and aligns us with all beings, terrestrial and otherwise. We can,
in this oneness, pass our days in serenity and contentment and

in the knowledge that we are not alone in the universe and that we are surrounded by friends both human and otherwise.

Conclusion

Despite the naysayers, those who abide in the contrary and those who may want or seek to own or control us, we are ultimately the masters of our own lives. That freedom and sovereignty is our divine birthright. It is not up to others to control us. It is up to us to exert self-control and self-discipline. This is what following the Integral Way requires of us.

Ultimately, what we do is who and what we are. By recognizing the power that we have over our own lives, we can cultivate the best version of ourselves and live in harmony with the universe, with ET, NHIs and all of universe's inhabitants. We are all one inseparable being. In that being, there is nothing that needs to be feared.

CHAPTER 41

The Undivided Mind

The chapter here by Lao Tzu here emphasizes the importance of the undivided mind and the futility of affirming or denying concepts such as good and bad, self and others, life and death. Engaging in judgment by making such mental exercises only perpetuates illusions, delusions, and shadows*. When the mind is preoccupied with holding onto specific ideas, conflicts and contradictions arise, leading to a fragmented and contradictory existence.

Instead, Lao Tzu teaches us that the path of the integral being is to keep the mind undivided. By letting go of fixed concepts and dissolving all ideas into the Tao, one can transcend the shadows and limitations of the mind and access a universal state of unity and harmony. The Tao, representing the underlying essence of existence, is beyond the realm of ego, judgment, dualistic thinking and conceptual divisions.

In order for individuals to free themselves from the mental and the shadows of egoic constructs that create divisions and conflicts, they can do so by embracing a state of undivided awareness (Universal Awareness, Universal Consciousness) and dissolving the ego and all its ideas into the boundless Tao. By doing this, one can experience a deeper level of unity, clarity, and transcendence that becomes an undifferentiated part of their daily lives and a basis for reaching out into the universe for ET/NHI contact.

"Why affirm or deny concepts like good and bad, life and death or self and other. Whether it is acceptance or denial, it is merely the mind that is being exercised. The integral being understands that the mind manipulates

through its shadows, dreams and delusions. When it holds onto one idea another comes to compete with it. Eventually, a third will enter the fray and further divide it. Eventually, all mental activity becomes contradiction and chatter. The integral being seeks instead to quiet his or her mind and keep it from being divided. They quiet their minds by letting all ideas dissolve themselves into the Tao."

<u>Eliminating the Shadow</u>

This passage speaks to the idea that concepts such as good and bad, self and others, life and death are constructs of the mind and ego which can lead to inner conflict and contradiction. The integral being recognizes that these "shadows" as manipulations of the mind and are merely dreams, delusions, and shadows.

Holding onto one idea leads to competition from another, which leads to endless conflict and contradiction. Instead, Lao Tzu tells us that the solution for those of us who choose to confront the shadow is to seek to keep our minds undivided and dissolve all ideas into the Tao.

The Tao can be thought of as the "way" or the ultimate reality, and seeking to dissolve our ideas into it means letting go of our preconceived notions and accepting the natural flow of the universe. By doing so, we can free ourselves from the constraints of the mind and ego and achieve a state of inner peace and harmony.

We therefore should not affirm or deny concepts, but rather seek to dissolve them into the natural flow of the universe. "Letting go", accepting impermanence and "going with the flow" are the keys to living a life of serenity and tranquility, free from the endless chatter and contradiction of the ego and the mind and the shadows they together create. This is the path that all integral beings throughout the universe follow.

*The idea and expanse of what shadows are, should be considered perhaps as more than just a metaphor for doubt and the darkness of ignorance. According to C.J Jung, <u>The Archetype and Collective Unconscious</u>, "The shadow personifies everything that the subject refuses to acknowledge about himself". It is is the emotional blind spot of the true self. This shadow aspect of the ego may appear as projections in various forms of thought including in dreams and visions. Its manifestations will largely depend on the individual's life experience. This is why the shadow develops in the individual's mind and is differs from individual to individual. The shadow need not be exclusively a personal one but one that dangerously can be projected as well as the shadow of society as well. It is a collective concept whose active body is fed by neglected and repressed collective values. See., Michael Fordham, Jungian Psychotherapy. Avon. p. 5. The collective shadow is one worth mentioning in light of its manifestations in the deaths of over 100 million human beings through wars and at the hands of the governments that ruled the major countries of the world in the twentieth century.

CHAPTER 42

The Golden Rule as Integral Truth

The passage here by Lao Tzu highlights something that becomes all too obvious as we age: the limitations of relying solely on the mind and the ever-changing nature of thoughts and ideologies. It tells us that finding true stability and unshakable understanding requires turning towards befriending the Tao, the underlying source of all existence.

By befriending the Tao, we begin by quieting the thinking process and letting go of analytical and divisive tendencies. By transcending the habit of making judgments and distinctions and recognizing the interconnectedness of all things, one can realize their intrinsic connection to the entire universe. This understanding or universal consciousness leads to a profound realization: that an action done to another is ultimately done to oneself.

In essence, as integral beings and followers of the Integral Way, we need to go beyond the fluctuating realm of thoughts and ideologies and embrace a deeper awareness of our unity with the Tao and all beings. By perceiving and embodying this great truth, we can cultivate a sense of harmony, compassion, and interconnectedness in all our actions and relationships with others.

"Within the two realms of both thought and ideology, nothing is absolute. Lean on either for too long and it will collapse. There is nothing more frustrating or futile than to rely on one's mind.

To become steadfast and unwavering, quiet your mind and stop thinking. When you do, you will become

friends with the Tao. Stop dividing things up. Stop distinguishing between one thing and another.

Stop the analysis.
Simply understand that you are at the center of the universe. Accept that all beings and things are part of your infinite integral body. As you do, you will begin to understand the great integral truth that that which you do unto others is that which you do unto yourself."

Nothing is Absolute: Befriending the Tao

Nothing in the realm of thoughts or ideologies is absolute. Lao Tzu points out that if we rely on the mind for too long, we will ultimately be disappointed because even though it tries to hold on to things in order to create a false sense of permanence, everything in the mind is subject to change, collapse, and contradiction.

Instead, in order to arrive at the unshakable, we must befriend the Tao. To do this, we must quiet our thinking and stop analyzing and dividing everything into separate parts. When we do this, we can begin to see ourselves as the center of the universe, with all things and beings as parts of our infinite body.

The key to this understanding is recognizing that any act done to another is done to us. When we can see ourselves in others and others in ourselves and all integral puzzle-pieces of one magnificent being we fully begin to understand this great truth of the great Oneness, and therein, we can find true peace and harmony.

Conclusion

This realization that all is inextricably connected to us is the key to unlocking the heart and its unshakable soul. This is how we avoid the futility and frustration of relying on the mind. By seeing ourselves as an integral part of the greater eternal and infinite whole, we can live in the now of a free and enlightened state of acceptance and understanding, free from the limitations of the mind and the constant struggle with the shadows of our own personal and collective egos.

CHAPTER 43

The Old Ways

This passage by Lao Tzu highlights the wisdom of ancient times when people lived holistic lives, integrating their mind, body, and spirit in all aspects. They valued knowledge but did not overemphasize it. They sought a balanced approach toward life and new inventions, considering both the benefits and potential challenges of these inventions. They respected proven effective practices from the past while being open to new ways if they proved effective.

To overcome confusion, Lao Tzu tells us that we should emulate these ancient folk by harmonizing body, mind, and spirit in our daily lives. This includes choosing natural and sustainable options for food, clothing, and shelter, relying on one's body for transportation, and integrating work and recreation. Engaging in exercises that nurture the whole being and listening to music that resonates with the three spheres of existence can also contribute beneficially to holistic living.

The passage further encourages the selection of leaders based on virtue rather than material wealth or power, and the simultaneous cultivation of oneself and one's service to others. True growth, it emphasizes, arises from meeting life's challenges in ways that harmonize with oneself and others.

By following these simple yet profound old ways, we can continually renew ourselves and live in alignment with the interconnectedness of mind, body, and spirit and create healthy environments in which to live.

"Long ago, people lived simple lives that were naturally holistic. There were no parts of their lives that were not interconnected to the whole. Intellect was not emphasized over the body or the spirit. In all things the ancient ones integrated their bodies, minds and spirits. This strategy allowed them to master knowledge rather than to be victimized by the mind and its concepts. When a new invention came along, they evaluated both the benefits it offered and the troubles it could potentially cause. People in times long past valued ways that had proven themselves to be effective.

If you want to stop your confusion, then emulate the ways of the old ones. In all that you do, combine the three spheres of your being. Select food, shelter and clothing that are in accord with nature. For transportation count on and use your own body. Let your work and recreation become one in the same. In exercise develop not only your body but the three spheres of your whole being. In music, select that which resonates with these spheres. For leaders, choose them not based on their wealth or power but upon their virtue and character.

Cultivate yourselves by being in service to others. Understand that true growth flows from you meeting life's problems and facing them and solving them in a manner that is in harmony with yourself and others. Do not ignore them as ultimately, you will find continual self-renewal by following the simple old ways."

Masters of Knowledge

Not everything new is good. Not everything good is new. In ancient times, people lived holistic lives and integrated their mind, body, and spirit in all things. By doing this, they were able to become masters of knowledge rather than victims of concepts. They sought balance between old and new ways, validating their overall effectiveness and impact on their lives before adopting them.

Today, there are a few ways that we can emulate these ancient folk in our modern lives. We can choose food, clothing, and shelter that accords with nature and its energies. We can rely on our own bodies for transportation. We can combine our work and recreation activities and participate in exercise that develops our whole being.

Additionally, we should listen to music that bridges the mind, the body and the spirit, the three spheres of our being. When it comes to governance, we can choose leaders for their virtue rather than their wealth or power. Finally, we should serve others and cultivate ourselves simultaneously, and understand that true growth comes from meeting and solving the problems of life harmoniously for ourselves and others.

If we follow these simple old ways, we will be continually renewed. This idea promotes a holistic, balanced approach to life that values the integration of the mind, body, and spirit. By doing so, we can achieve a sense of harmony and balance, and instead of knowledge mastering us, we can become like the ancients were, masters of knowledge itself.

CHAPTER 44

The Unenlightened Mind

Here, in this chapter Lao Tzu describes the nature of an unenlightened mind. He highlights its limitations and tendencies towards gathering only partial information, forming judgments based on previous judgments, and storing distorted concepts and ideas. This leads to confusion and vexation as mental energy flows through inappropriate channels.

To alleviate the vexation of the mind, Lao Tzu suggests a different approach. Instead of engaging in more mental activity, he encourages dissolving the mind and disengaging the mind. After letting go of thought one needs to consider entering a state of not-doing, or "non-doing". * This involves avoiding attachment to what is seen and thought, letting go of the notion of separation from the universal mind in order to recover one's original pure insight. By relinquishing attachment and embracing a state of not-knowing, one can approach situations with an open mind and thereby regain clarity and enlightenment, recognize the illusions of the mind and gain awareness of everything.

In this passage Lao Tzu emphasizes that clarity and enlightenment are inherent in one's own true nature and can be regained without any external movement or effort. He reminds us that by transcending the limitations of the mind and realizing our interconnectedness with the universe, we can rediscover our innate wisdom and insight.

"What is the nature of the unenlightened mind? The unenlightened mind relies on the sense organs. Because the sense organs are limited in their ability and scope they gather information randomly. This results in

partial information that arranges itself into judgments. Present judgments are based on previous judgments. And previous judgments incorporate the previous judgments of others and include them and other foolish ideas.

These judgments create ideas and false concepts that are stored in our highly selective memories. These distortions compound the next to cause our mental energy to flow into inappropriate and contorted channels. As a consequence, the more we use our minds the more confused we become.

One cannot successfully eliminate the mind's vexation by doing. The mechanics of the mind are only reinforced by doing. It is through dissolving the mind by non-doing that vexation is eliminated. To do this is simple. Merely avoid becoming attached to what you think and what you see. Let go of the notion of separation from the Tao and its all-knowing mind.

When you can do this, you will regain your original uncontaminated insight. You will be able to see through all illusion. By keeping the mind free, you will know nothing yet have awareness of everything. Remember that it was in your nature at birth to both be enlightened and to have complete clarity of vision. You can regain both again now without having to move even so much as an inch."

"If you hold on to it, you're stuck with it."
- Eckhart Tolle

The Enlightened Mind

The concept of enlightenment has been pondered for centuries by philosophers and thinkers alike. The unenlightened mind is described as one that gathers partial information through limited sense organs and arranges this information into judgments based on previously held often foolish notions and storing these ideas in a highly selective memory system. This process leads to distortion upon distortion, with the mental energy they create flowing through contorted and inappropriate channels. This energy eventually has an impact on what we do and affects the people, world and the entire universe of which we are a part.

To eliminate the vexation of the mind and become "enlightened", all we simply need to do is to avoid becoming attached to what we have seen or thought. That is the key. Relinquishing the notion of separation from the Tao, the all-knowing mind of the universe is also essential to the enlightened mind. This dissolution of the mind and not-doing is not achieved by doing something. Doing, striving to achieve a certain state merely reinforces the mechanics of the mind. However, by letting go of thoughts we empty the mind and by "knowing nothing" we keep the mind completely open. By doing so we remove the blockages to our ability to perceive and communicate. In this way we can become aware of everything. These steps also open the doors to ET/NHI contact.

Clarity and enlightenment are within our own nature, and though lost by years of the imposition of manufactured systems of "reality" and belief, the clarity of enlightenment can be regained without so much as moving an inch. The idea that one must do something to achieve clarity is a common misconception. Instead, by simply letting go, trusting in the Tao and in our own intuition, we can regain our original pure insight and see through all illusions. This is the path to regaining clarity. This is the way toward enlightenment.

Conclusion

The concept of enlightenment is a complex and elusive one. Ultimately, the unenlightened mind that gathers and processes information in a flawed manner is just as unreliable as incomplete or inherently flawed information is itself. Dissolving the mind is a matter of letting go of thought and the idea of having to do anything and by relinquishing the notion of separation from the all-knowing mind of the universe. Clarity and enlightenment are within the instinct and intuitive nature of all beings. Once lost, they can be regained through trusting in our own pure insight and seeing through all illusions. Unlearn what you know. Learn to trust your insight, instincts and intuition. Trust in the Tao. She will take you home.

The Taoist concept of wu wei can be translated as "non-action" or "non-doing". It is a principle in Taoism that involves intentionally letting things happen naturally and spontaneously, without forcing them or trying to control them. One cannot force crops to grow faster than they can. One cannot make the rain stop. Paint dries on its own accord. To everything there is a time for it under the heavens. Wu wei is often associated with the idea of effortless action, where one acts in accord with the natural flow of things without imposing one's own will on them. By practicing wu wei and relying on one's instinctual and intuitive connection with the Tao a person can live in harmony with the Tao, and follow its integral way, the natural way of the universe.

CHAPTER 45

Correcting the Mind

The chapter by Lao Tzu emphasizes the significance of the mind in shaping one's life. By correcting and aligning the mind with the natural flow of the Tao, the rest of life easily falls into place. Again, Lao Tzu uses the metaphor of a river as it flows through the proper channel in order to illustrate the harmonious functioning of life when the mind is clear and balanced.

The Integral Way, as described in the passage, involves a theme that is prominent throughout the Tao and other transcendental and Eastern religious thought. That theme is simplification and the process of decreasing rather than increasing. It advocates for not-doing, which means letting go of excessive thinking, attachments, and complications. By cultivating a detached and whole mind, we can eliminate mental confusion and achieve clarity. This includes quieting emotions and finding serenity within.

In this passage Lao Tzu also warns against getting caught up in distractions and false beliefs, comparing it to adding another head on top of the existing one. Lao Tzu encourages letting go of restless activities and embracing a state of stillness. By valuing being over unnecessary or nervous doing, Lao Tzu reassures us that we can reconnect with our integral nature, the Tao and allow our pure original insight to emerge.

"Every aspect of human life is governed by the mind. If your mind can be corrected, then your life will reveal itself and unfold for you. To correct the mind and let your life fall into its proper place rely on non-doing. Cease thinking and hanging on to complications. Keep your mind detached and whole.

When a river flows cleanly and clearly within its proper passage, all is well within its banks. Like the river, eliminate the muddy your waters to keep your mind crystal clear. Refrain from daydreaming. Eliminate the obscure and your pure original insight will emerge.

Lay your emotions to rest. Find the serene and abide in it. Avoid the insane worship of ideas, images and idols. To not do so is like putting one head on top of the one you have. The integral way depends not on increasing but decreasing. If you can decrease your activity and stop your restlessness, what will emerge is your own original pure and crystal-clear insight."

Simplification

> "Our life is frittered away by detail.
> Simplify, simplify, simplify."
> - Henry David Thoreau

There is great importance of cultivating a clear, uncluttered and focused mind in order to live an authentic and fulfilling life. The idea of the "Integral Way" suggests a holistic approach to living, where the mind, body, and spirit are all in alignment. The emphasis on decreasing, rather than increasing, tells us that simplicity and letting go of excess can lead to greater clarity and balance.

The practice of "not-doing" and by way of extrapolation, wu wei is a means of simplifying life to achieve serenity and access a deeper wisdom by letting go of distractions and attachments. The importance of a clear and tranquil mind in living an aligned and harmonious life is important to all integral beings. Consequently, it is important that we learn to simplify life and practice not doing and cultivate detachment. In this way we can enter an enlightened state of mind. Eventually these practices along with stillness, mindful meditation and cultivating a sense of inner peace and clarity is invaluable to the lives of all integral beings throughout the universe, followers of the integral Way.

CHAPTER 46

Walk, Do Not Run

"Wise men do not run. They walk,"
- Professor Phil Sutherland

Here in this chapter, Lao Tzu highlights the interconnectedness and unity of all things according to the principles of Tao. He introduces us to and explains the process of creation, starting with the Tao giving birth to the One, which then gives rise to yin and yang, the complementary forces that underlie all phenomena. However important they may be, consistent with the teachings of the last few chapters, this passage reemphasizes the importance of letting go of concepts, even these concepts and not clinging to them.

Lao Tzu also avises us again to forget about the ego, as pain and happiness are merely conditions of the ego. This passage also importantly extends what we have already learned in chapters 12, 30 and in chapter 36 about the "highest spiritual beings" of the universe. The fact that these beings are not necessarily human challenges our western notions of Anthropocentrism and of time and space as well. With the re-introduction to us of the reality of "supernatural beings" Lao Tzu underscores the existence and importance of these "guardians" in the limitless eternal cosmos in which they and we exist.

Lao Tzu notes that these "supernatural" beings are both with and without form, ie., they are seeable and the unseeable. These beings are not allegorical or archetypal but constitute a true and factual part of the universe created by the Tao. It is because these beings, like we, are part of that factual reality that they are important and purposefully described by Lao Tzu.

By considering these changing and illusory "supernatural be-ings" to include what we now know to be called ETs and NHIs, interdimensional and non-physical intelligences, we can understand that and why these beings should be seen as extensions of nature and the Tao. Because of their presence Lao Tzu emphasizes their inseparability from the natural world and our own ontological reality. But, as he instructs, forget this for now.

The subtle truth of the Tao lies in balancing the polarities and cultivating without neglect, our minds, bodies, and spirits. Importantly, Lao Tzu reminds us that if people understood and embodied this truth, world peace and universal harmony would naturally arise. However, consistent with Wu Wei, Lao Tzu discourages actively seeking understanding or trying to force harmony, as the universe already possesses inherent har-mony. It needs nothing to be added or subtracted. The universe knows when enough is enough.

Finally, in the pursuit of inner peace, just as he discouraged doing for the sake of doing, Lao Tzu advises against scurrying about to eliminate our anxiety find serenity and peaceful re-pose. Instead, he encourages realizing that inner peace already exists within us. By letting go of the striving we can embrace and experience the inherent harmony of the universe that un-derlies our existence. Ultimately, Lao Tzu again, in order to find our heartsease, urges us to let go of fixed concepts, em-brace the interconnectedness of all things, and find inner peace through the acceptance and realization of the one eternal Tao.

"To one does the Tao give birth. To yin and Yang does the one give birth. To all things do Yin and Yang give birth. Forget this now. The whole that is complete is the complete whole. So too are any of its parts. Forget this as well. Happiness and pain are merely circumstances of the ego. Forget the ego. Time and space are not real or fixed. They change and dissolve so that they can each be

> thought of as an accessory.
> You need not think of this either.
>
> There are supernatural beings who are without form.
> They extend themselves and their life force to support
> the formed and unformed beings of the universe. Like
> the natural, the supernatural, both are merely parts of
> nature. Disregard this as well.
>
> The entire truth lies in tai chi. In order to cultivate your
> mind, body and spirit merely balance the polarities of
> Yin and Yang. If only people would understand this,
> naturally world peace and harmony would arise. All
> things would then be one. Forget this as well.
>
> Simply realize that the universe already is a harmonious
> oneness. If you scurry about searching for inner peace
> then you will lose it."

<u>Forget This</u>

We as individuals and integral universal beings need to let go
of our egos and attachments, to embrace the natural balance
of the universe, and to cultivate a state of inner peace and
harmony by balancing the various polarities that exist within
ourselves and within the world around us. This passage reminds us to not scramble about in search of inner peace, as
this will only lead to losing it. Instead, we are urged to realize
that the universe is already a harmonious oneness, and we
need only surrender to the natural flow of existence in order
to find our inner peace as part of it. This is what all superior
beings do whoever they are and whatever forms they take. All
are children of the same eternal Tao.

Certainly, it is no great intellectual or spiritual stretch to in-
terpret the words and characters used to convey the idea of
'supernatural beings' to be the same as extraterrestrial beings

or non-human intelligences who visit Earth. This modern fact is no longer the fascinating perspective so often explored in science fiction and conspiracy theories. For centuries, if not eons, these 'supernatural' beings from advanced civilizations beyond our planet and dimension have had the ability to interact with Earth and its inhabitants. And they have and do.

In this more modern interpretation of 'supernatural beings' these extraterrestrial beings and non-human intelligences could well have been seen as 'supernatural' since they possessed advanced technologies and abilities far beyond our past and even our current understanding of what is natural and what is supernatural. Obviously, their advanced technologies and abilities are little understood even by modern science and might have and still do appear supernatural to us. The idea of them extending their life force and support to both formed and unformed beings on Earth should be perceived as their benevolent or guiding influence being offered to mankind as they too honor the Tao and are followers of the integral Way. The nature of their existence and purpose for their being here for us especially as practitioners of undiscriminating virtue and embodiments of the Tao will be further explored and explained infra.

CHAPTER 47

Embodying the Tao

In this passage Lao Tzu critiques and warns us about the various forms of dualism, religious practices, and materialism. He argues that dualistic thinking leads to sickness, and that religious practices often distort true spirituality. Materialism is described as cruel, while blind spirituality is seen as unreal. Chanting, prayer beads, and religious robes are all depicted as unnecessary and superficial.

Instead of getting caught up in these spiritual superficialities, the passage suggests living a quiet and simple life, free from the prison of ideas and concepts. Lao Tzu encourages us to prioritize inner virtue and selflessness over external trappings and spiritual practices that may distract us from living in accordance with the Tao. He emphasizes the importance of practicing undiscriminating virtue, by giving selflessly and anonymously to others and radiating light throughout the world. By doing so, one becomes a sanctuary for oneself and all beings and an embodiment of the Tao.

"Thinking dualistically is an illness, materialism cruel and religion a distortion. Blind spirituality is not real. Chanting is no more holy than the babbling of a brook. Prayer beads are as sacred as a simple breath. Religious garments are no more special than the clothes in which one works.

If you want to experience the oneness of the Tao, avoid the snare of spiritual superficialities. Live your life simply and quietly free of ideas and mental concepts. Be content in your practice of undiscriminating virtue. It is your one true power. Give to others anonymously and

selflessly. Let your light radiate throughout the world by eliminating your own darkness. Embody the Tao so that your virtue becomes a sanctuary for yourself and for all beings."

To Perceive the False is to Negate the False

This passage emphasizes the rejection of dualistic thinking and the transcendence of superficial aspects of spirituality. Consistent with his writings in the Tao Te Ching, Lao Tzu criticizes the distortion of religion, the cruelty of materialism, and the unreal nature of blind spirituality. All are products of the ego and manifestations of the mind's need for comfort and security, even if the manifestations that have been relied on for millennia are false.

In order to free ourselves from these entrapments, Lao Tzu tells how we can live quiet and simple lives, free from attachment to ideas and concepts through the practice of undiscriminating virtue. Lao Tzu highlighted it as the true source of power. Through undiscriminating compassion, selflessly giving to others we radiate true spiritual light and we become sanctuaries for ourselves and for all beings. These beings necessarily include ETs and NHIs. The Tao is the creator of all, and its subtle and universal laws apply not only to humans but to all advanced spiritual beings; those who practice undiscriminating virtue.

Finally, Lao Tzu tacitly recognizes that religion is nothing more than idolatry. Because they are ultimately manifestations of our own fears and egos that give us a false sense of comfort and separate us from each other, Lao Tzu encourages us to find contentment by embodying the Tao and its truth through our genuine acts of compassion and selflessness, rather than getting caught up in external forms worship or empty religious rituals. By doing these things and taking a holistic approach to spirituality and by focusing on our inner virtues and truth and the interconnectedness of all beings we can actualize ourselves as enlightened and integral beings of the eternal and universal Way.

CHAPTER 48

Two Paths to a Single Oneness

This passage by Lao Tzu presents the reader with two paths towards experiencing the natural unity of all things, the great oneness with the Tao. The first path, often called the shorter path, is the path of acceptance, which involves affirming everything and extending goodwill towards all things. By embracing all things as part of the Harmonious Oneness, the individual can begin to perceive it more clearly.

The second path, the longer one, is the path of denial, which involves recognizing that everything seen, or thought is a falsehood, an illusion that veils the truth. By peeling away these veils, the individual can arrive at the Oneness and achieve spontaneous awareness of the Great Oneness.

Ultimately, and very importantly, Lao Tzu emphasizes that both paths will deliver the individual to the same place: a state of unity with the Tao. Once this place is reached, the individual need not struggle to maintain their unity with it. Rather, they can simply participate in it and live in harmony with the natural flow of existence.

"If freeing yourself of emotional and mental knots is what you need, then become one with the Tao. To become one with the Tao, there are two paths that you may take. One is the path of acceptance. The other path is that of denial.

In the path of acceptance, everything and everyone is affirmed. One extends one's virtue and goodwill in all directions regardless of circumstance. When one is able

to embrace everything as part of the Tao's harmonious
oneness, then he or she will begin to see it.

In the second path, that of denial, one recognizes that
everything that one thinks or sees is nothing more than
an illusion, a veil of falsehood that covers the truth.
Unveil its layers and they who seek will arrive at the
Oneness. Even though these paths diverge and take
one in opposite directions, they deliver the traveler
to the exact same place, the place where one becomes
spontaneously aware of the great Oneness.

Once you have arrived there and entered the awareness
of the Great Oneness, you need not struggle in order to
maintain your unity within it. Importantly, all you must
do is to participate in it."

Acceptance and Denial

There are two paths to attain oneness with the Tao. The first
path is the simpler path, that of acceptance, where one affirms
and embraces everyone and everything, extending goodwill
and virtue in all directions. By perceiving all things as part of
the Harmonious Oneness, they begin to experience it.

The second path, the more complex one, is that of denial,
where one recognizes the illusory nature of everything seen and
thought. By peeling away the veils of falsehood and illusion,
one reaches the original Oneness. Despite being different paths,
both lead to the same destination: spontaneous awareness of
the Great Oneness. No matter which path is taken, one arrives
at this state and there is no need to struggle to maintain unity
with it. Instead, once aware, we simply need to participate in
it. We participate in it by being present in our own lives and by
being actively engaged in the flow of the Tao. By being aware
of the Tao, and of our place within it, we can use its energies

efficiently and accomplish what needs to be accomplished in the most effectively propitious of ways.

CHAPTER 49

How To Embody the Tao

Do you walk the walk, or do you just talk the talk? This passage by Lao Tzu emphasizes the importance of actually practicing the Integral Way rather than merely discussing or thinking about it. He compares talking about the Way to one talking about horsemanship without actually becoming a skilled rider. To embody the Tao, one is encouraged to still the mind, silence the chatter and engage in the active practice of walking the integral way.

The practice of the Way involves meditation, relaxing the body, quieting the senses, and returning the mind to its original clarity. It entails letting go of the illusion of separation from others and the Divine Source. Instead of thinking or being in awe of the Oneness, Lao Tzu suggests "merging" into truth and allowing it to envelop one's being. This means living a life of unvarnished truth and unwavering sincerity and compassion.

In essence, the passage highlights the transformative power of direct experience and practice. Lao Tzu urges individuals to transcend mere intellectual understanding and immerse themselves in the realization and embodiment of the Integral Way.

"Thinking and talking about something are not the same as one's actual participation in it. If you want to embody the Tao, then stop talking and begin to practice it. Whether it is riding a horse or writing a book, neither the rider nor the author ever became great without practice.

To practice embodying the Tao, let your body relax and your senses become quiet. Then let your mind return to

its original state of crystal-clear clarity. Do not worry about others or fret about separation from the Divine Source. Let go of these things and you will return to the experience of your innate Integral Oneness. If you think of it or become in awe of it, then you will lose it. Just allow it to surround you and let yourself merge with its simple truth."

Reaching Out to ET and NHI Through The Integral Way

The Integral Way is an essential practice for all of us who seek to integrate different aspects of the self to embody the Tao. While it is important for us to understand the principles and concepts underlying this practice, we must also emphasize the importance of putting it into the everyday practice and integrate the traits of absolute truth as well as those of simplicity, patience and compassion into a reflective and meditative yet active life.

As the passage suggests, thinking and talking about the Integral Way are not enough to embody the Tao. It is like being a good rider by merely talking about horses or being a good writer without ever writing. Instead, if we wish to merge into truth and become one with the Divine Source, we must stop chattering and start practicing. We have to stop talking the talk and begin walking the walk.

To begin this walk, we need to learn how to meditate and to relax our bodies and quiet our senses so we can return our minds to their original clarity. At the same time, we must not be separated from others or from the Divine Source. We must learn to "merge into truth", allowing it to surround us. We must move beyond thinking about Oneness or being in awe of it because this would only create a sense of separation and paralysis. We have to move beyond the awe.

Walking the walk is also true of our ET/NHI contact work. Through meditation and relaxing our minds and bodies and returning our minds to their original clarity we can merge into the truth of the reality of the integral Way and engage in ET/NHI contact. There, in a state of pure truth and clear intent, we can reach out to these beings and entities and invite them peacefully into our loving and compassionate presence. Without active engagement with the phenomenon, we are no more than chattering boxes and the writers who do not write and the horsemen who do not ride.

As integral universal beings it is our collective responsibility to focus on practicing the Integral Way in our everyday lives. This requires the integration of different aspects of the self and the cultivation of mindfulness regarding our intentions, thoughts, and actions. It also means that we should cultivate a sense of unity with others, including ET and NHIs through the Divine Source.

For those who want to become complete human beings or want to make contact with ET, NHIs and the highest spiritual beings in the multiverse, just learning about the Integral Way is necessary but it is insufficient. We must regularly and mindfully practice the Integral Way in our daily lives if we are to reach a sense of unity and merge into the truth of the universe and the great Oneness. Only then will we embody the Tao and become one with the Divine Source and properly be able to make open, profound and sustainable contact with ET/NHIs, Lao Tzu's 'supernatural beings' and the highest of all spiritual beings and "guardians" of the universe.

CHAPTER 50

The Integral Way

This passage presents us with questions about the value of accumulating material possessions and conforming to societal conventions, emphasizing that such pursuits are not in alignment with the Tao. In it Lao Tzu suggests that investing one's life in material accumulation goes against the natural flow of the Integral Way.

The passage also challenges the separation of spiritual and practical aspects of life. It tells us that an integral being sees no distinction between the two and lives in a simple and virtuous manner, true to their nature. It encourages individuals to let go of concepts of time and detach themselves from ideas and conventions. Instead, the focus is on embracing Oneness and aligning with the principles of the Integral Way.

In essence, Lao Tzu again advocates for a holistic and integrated approach to life, where material possessions and societal conventions hold less importance compared to living in harmony with one's true nature and the interconnectedness of all things.

"Spending one's life in pursuit of material things is not in keeping with the Tao. How does it benefit you to conform your behavior to the conventions of others. To do so is contrary to the inherent nature of your being. It will drain you of your energy.

It is pointless to separate your spiritual life from your practical one. An Integral Being does not distinguish one from the other. Live simply. Live virtuously. Live true to your own true nature. There is no need for distinguishing what constitutes what is spiritual and

what is not. Let go of concepts and ideas. Let go of time. Embrace Oneness. That is the Integral Way."

<u>Following the Integral Way</u>

This passage beautifully encapsulates the essence of Taoism and the Integral Way. It advises against spending our lives solely pursuing material possessions, as it goes against the natural flow of the Tao. Conforming to societal conventions can lead to a disconnect from our true nature, draining vital energy.

Following the Integral Way means the relentless pursuit of universal truth, living a simple, patient, compassionate and virtuous life, acknowledging that the spiritual and practical aspects of life are interconnected and should not be separated. It suggests embracing our true nature and not trying to be something or someone we naturally are not. Following the Way means thinking freely by letting go of conceptual distinctions, including those between the spiritual and the non-spiritual.

Embracing Oneness, finding inner peace and letting go of attachment to concepts and time aligns us with the core and following the timeless and eternal principles of the Tao. To follow its Integral Way means to live a balanced life, to emphasize harmony with the universe and live in that harmony and flow of existence in unity with all things.

CHAPTER 51

Virtue, the Mother of Abundance

It is said that virtue is the mother of all abundance. The passage by Lao Tzu highlights the importance of practicing four cardinal virtues for those seeking to understand the truth of the universe and walk the Integral Way. These virtues are:

1. Reverence for all life: This reverence involves cultivating unconditional love and respect for oneself and all beings, recognizing the inherent value and interconnectedness of life.

2. Natural sincerity: This type of sincerity entails being honest, sincere, and faithful in one's words and actions, embracing simplicity and authenticity.

3. Gentleness: This gentility encompasses kindness, compassion, and consideration for others, as well as maintaining sensitivity to spiritual truth.

4. Supportiveness: Being supportive involves selflessly serving others without expecting anything in return, offering assistance and support to those in need, no matter who they are.

These virtues are integral and are seen as intrinsic to one's original nature. When practiced, they lead to wisdom and the manifestation of five blessings: health, wealth, happiness, longevity, and peace. Lao Tzu's emphasis is on embodying these virtues in daily life rather than treating them as external rules or doctrines.

The four cardinal virtues are, therefore, essential components of the Integral Way. When we practice these virtues, we tap into our original nature and unlock the wisdom and blessings that come with living a virtuous life.

The Integral Way teaches us that there is no distinction between our spiritual life and our practical life. When we live a simple and virtuous life that is in tune with our true nature, we are able to naturally merge with and embody the principles of the Tao in all aspects of our lives. This means that we can ignore time, relinquish ideas and concepts, and embrace the Oneness that binds us all together.

Ultimately, the teachings of the Tao and the Integral Way remind us that our natural state is one of simplicity and spiritual unity. To embrace this state, we must let go of our attachment to material things and societal conventions and focus on living a simple, virtuous life that is true in itself and true to our own nature and the Oneness that unites all beings and things. By doing so, we can find greater meaning and purpose in life, and we can embody the principles of Tao. When we embody the Tao, we ready ourselves physically, mentally, spiritually, and ontologically so that both the seen and unseen universes and their inhabitants. As a consequence, the cosmos beyond will be ours to fearlessly explore.

"One practices the truth of the universe by practicing the 'four cardinal virtues'. The first of these virtues is reverence for all beings. This virtue manifests itself as unconditional love, self-respect and respect for all living things.

Natural sincerity is the second cardinal virtue. This virtue manifests itself as honesty, integrity, simplicity, and fidelity.

Gentleness is the third cardinal virtue. It manifests itself in universal compassion and kindness, being considerate of others and being sensitive to spiritual truth.

Supportiveness is the fourth cardinal virtue. Supportiveness manifests itself as being in service to others without expecting any reward in return.

These four virtues are within your original nature. They are not mere maxims or dogmatic beliefs. When these four virtues are practiced, they bring wisdom into the world and evoke 'the five blessings': health, longevity, happiness, wealth and peace."

The Four Cardinal Virtues and Their Five Blessings

This passage highlights the idea that living a life solely focused on material possessions is not aligned with the Tao, and that true fulfillment comes from embracing simplicity, virtue, and harmony with one's inherent nature.

In our modern society, it is all too easy to become caught up in the endless pursuit of status, wealth, and societal approval. We are bombarded with messages that suggest that having more material possessions and conforming to societal norms will lead to happiness and fulfillment. However, the teachings of the Tao and the Integral Way remind us that nothing could be further from the truth. That truth is that our true nature is one of simplicity and spiritual unity – and that living a life that is inconsistent with this nature can ultimately prove not only unsatisfying and unfulfilling but deadly to our own physical, mental and spiritual being.

The Accumulation of material possessions and things is not in keeping with the Tao. Hoarding is a fearful and unnatural state. Rather than accumulating more and more possessions, we should understand when enough is enough so we can focus on simplifying our lives and letting go of our attachment to consumer culture and unnecessary possessions. By doing so, we can simplify and find greater meaning and purpose in life, and we can develop a deeper sense of appreciation for the natural world and our interconnectedness with all the beings that inhabit our world and the universe beyond.

Similarly, we need to seriously question the value of conforming our behavior to societal conventions in general. Instead of blindly adhering to societal norms and expectations and caring what others think about us. Instead, we should look within ourselves and strive to live in a way that is true to our own nature and the Oneness. This means having the courage to take unconventional paths, to embrace our own creativity and unique identities, and to cultivate our own authentic spiritual practice.

The Integral Way teaches us that the pursuit of wisdom and truth and the beginning of our own spiritual practice begins with the practice of four cardinal virtues: reverence for all life, natural sincerity, gentleness, and supportiveness.

These virtues are not external dogmas imposed upon us from an external force, but rather they are intrinsic components of the Tao and our original nature. By tapping into these virtues, we can unlock our inner wisdom and bring the five blessings of health, wealth, happiness, longevity, and peace into our lives and those around us. These virtues are also infinitely important to engender and exemplify in our own lives if we want to make meaningful and extended ET and NHI contact.

The first cardinal virtue, reverence for all life, manifests as unconditional love and respect for ourselves and all other beings. When we practice this virtue, we honor the sacred essence and the interconnectedness of all life here on earth and otherwise. This, in turn, brings us into closer alignment with our true Tao nature and unveils to all intelligent beings and the highest spiritual beings of the universe the wisdom that flows from this understanding.

The second cardinal virtue, natural sincerity, manifests as honesty, simplicity, and faithfulness. This virtue encourages us to be true to ourselves and to be honest with and without guile in our dealings with others. When we practice natural sincerity, we remove the barriers to wisdom and unlock the flow of universal truth within ourselves. This truth then forms the basis for all our relationships.

The third cardinal virtue, gentleness, manifests as kindness, compassion, and consideration for all others. With this gentility comes sensitivity to spiritual truth. When we practice gentleness, we cultivate an attitude of compassion and empathy toward all beings, including our extraterrestrial brothers and sisters and other non-human intelligences. This leads us universally to greater wisdom, understanding, and connection with each other and all the more highly advanced spiritual beings in the universe.

The fourth cardinal virtue, supportiveness, manifests itself as altruism and indiscriminate service to others without expectation of reward. When we practice genuine supportiveness, we come into alignment with the true nature of the universe – one of giving and receiving. This virtue unlocks our inner wisdom and helps us to cultivate a deep sense of interconnectedness with each other and with other evolved and advanced non-human intelligences and extraterrestrial beings throughout the cosmos.

The four cardinal virtues are not some religious or philosophical concept or an external religious dogma but are integral parts of our original nature. When practiced, they not only give birth to wisdom and evoke the five blessings of health, wealth, happiness, longevity, and peace but prepare us to be citizens and societies worthy of being included in the higher levels of interstellar and inter-dimensional societies that populate the galaxy and the cosmos.

In a word, those who want to experience true peace, live in harmony, and know the truth of the universe and establish themselves as ET/NHI contactees should practice the four cardinal virtues as the cardinal tenets in their own lives. They need to let go of material attachments and concepts which are all the hallmarks of the ego that must be avoided for one to become a person of the Tao.

When we practice the fundamental principles of the Integral Way, we, like all advanced spiritual beings tap into our original Tao nature and unleash the wisdom and blessings that flow from a life lived in tune with the Tao. Finally, and because of its importance this cannot be overstated, by cultivating reverence, natural sincerity, gentleness, and supportiveness in our lives, we can not only bring greater meaning, purpose, peace and fulfilment into our own lives but into the world as well and ready it and its human inhabitants for their future inclusion and welcoming into the realm of the more technologically and spiritually advanced races and societies that follow the Integral Way and have already inhabited the cosmos for many billions of years.

CHAPTER 52

Integral Awareness

In this chapter Lao Tzu teaches us that, contrary to popular belief, constantly sitting in silent meditation alone may not lead to a clear mind. Instead, integral awareness, which is fluid and adaptable, should be cultivated. Integral awareness is described as present in all places and at all times, encompassing the ability to engage with the world. The Tao, which represents the natural order of things, is cited as an example of clarity and simplicity that doesn't avoid the world.

Lao Tzu then offers a practical approach to attaining clarity and simplicity. It encourages honoring family, showing love and support, maintaining strong relationships, fulfilling responsibilities, practicing virtue, and understanding profound truths while maintaining an ordinary manner. This integrated way of living is seen as a path to true mastery, clarity, and simplicity.

Finally, this passage emphasizes that true clarity and simplicity are not achieved by withdrawing from the world but by engaging with it in a harmonious and virtuous manner. Without compassionate engagement with the world and universe beyond we cannot perfect our complete integration with the Tao.

"Many believe that they can clear their minds by sitting in constant meditation. This kind of meditation narrows the mind and clouds it. Integral awareness is true meditation. Like the Tao, it is flowing and adaptable and is at all times and places present.

One also cannot attain simplicity and clarity by avoiding engagement with the world. True simplicity, true clarity

and true mastery are attained by honoring your parents, loving your children, helping your brothers and sisters.

To your friends be faithful. Care for and be a devoted mate. Joyfully and cooperatively complete your work. Accept and shoulder responsibility for problems that arise. Appreciate and truly understand the highest truths.

Be virtuous without first demanding it from others. Be unassuming. Keep an ordinary manner. Maintain the 'Common touch'. To do so is to practice the Integral Way. "

How to Practice the Integral Way

Lao Tzu and the Integral Way remind us that true meditation is a state of fluid and adaptable awareness that is present in all places and at all times. Rather than isolating ourselves in silent meditation, true clarity and simplicity come from fully engaging and embracing the world and practicing integral awareness of the connectedness of all things in all aspects of our lives.

In our fast-paced and often chaotic world, it is easy to become overwhelmed by the demands of modern life. Many people turn to silent meditation as a way to find peace and clarity amidst the chaos. Meditation is important, however; the Tao and the Integral Way teach us that true meditation is not about avoiding the world or narrowing our minds, but rather about embracing the world and cultivating a state of fluid and adaptable awareness and then going outside of ourselves and engage with others to perfect that awareness.

Sitting constantly in silent meditation can actually make our minds narrower, rather than clearer. Instead, Lao Tzu encourages us to practice integral awareness – a state of consciousness that is fluid and adaptable and present in all places and at all times. When we cultivate integral awareness, we can fully engage with the world and all its complexities, without becoming overwhelmed or losing our sense of inner clarity.

The Tao itself is a model of clear and simple awareness that is fully present in the world. Rather than isolating ourselves from the world, we should live to honor the Tao in our relationships with our parents, children, siblings, friends, and mates. We practice the Integral Way when we integrate our awareness with being the best parent, child, brother, sister, friend, and mate that we can be. We should complete our work cooperatively and joyfully, taking responsibility for problems and practicing virtue without first demanding it of others.

When we embody these principles in our lives, we achieve true clarity, simplicity, and mastery of the Integral Way. We understand the highest truths yet retain an ordinary manner, and common touch and we can fully engage with the world while maintaining a state of integral awareness.

Obviously, while silent meditation has its benefits, the Tao and the Integral Way remind us that true meditation is a state of fluid and adaptable awareness that we can cultivate in all aspects of our lives. By embracing the world and the universe beyond and by practicing integral awareness, we can achieve true clarity, simplicity, and mastery when we practice the Integral Way and fully engage with the world, humanity, and all integral and advanced spiritual beings in this universe and beyond.

CHAPTER 53

The Importance of Combining Awareness and Action

This passage from Lao Tzu again highlights the importance of combining awareness and action for those who practice the Integral Way. Enlightenment should not lead to indifference towards the suffering in the world but rather inspire individuals to increase their service and compassion. Those who genuinely embody the Tao are described as individuals who not only deepen their understanding of the Tao but also actively contribute to the well-being of others.

At its essence, the passage emphasizes the significance of aligning one's understanding with compassionate action. It suggests that true practitioners of the Tao and its Integral Way are those who integrate their awareness with a commitment to service and actively work towards alleviating suffering in the world.

> **"True understanding has two attributes in a person who practices the Integral Way. These attributes are awareness and action. Like the right and left hand of a person, they act together to naturally form a tai chi. To enjoy enlightenment yet still remaining indifferent to the world's suffering is not in keeping with the Integral Way. Only by increasing one's service (action) in combination with their understanding (awareness) can one be called a man or woman of the Tao."**

Cultivating True Understanding

Like the two hands of the potter that fashion a cup on his wheel, understanding and enlightenment requires both awareness and action – the yin and yang of a natural tai chi. Just like a car, one can start the engine, but without engaging the transmission, the vehicle goes nowhere. And so it is true with cultivating true understanding. Without action, our understanding remains theoretical, and without awareness, action risks becoming superficial. Therefore, to cultivate true understanding and be truly in harmony with the Tao, we must increase our service along with our understanding and respond to suffering in the world with compassion and action.

The Tao and the Integral Way remind us that true understanding and enlightenment require both awareness and action, the yin and yang of a natural tai chi. Too often, we become stuck in either the awareness or action aspects of this principle, failing to bring them together in harmony and balance.

To truly enjoy enlightenment in this world, we must combine awareness and action. It is not enough to simply understand the Tao conceptually; we must also act upon the insights we gain. Conversely, it is not enough to simply act in the world without first cultivating an awareness of the Tao and our place within it.

The core statement within this passage is that to simply call ourselves enlightened and remain indifferent to the suffering in the world is a falsehood. To be in harmony with the Tao, we must also be in harmony with the world around us and those who dwell within it. Therefore, we must learn to respond to suffering with compassion and action.

To be true men and women of the Tao, we must increase our service along with our understanding of the interrelationship of all things. This means we have to actively seek out ways to make a positive impact in the world, while, at the same time, also remain mindful of our place within the Tao and the interconnectedness of all things.

N. MICHAEL MURBURG, JR.

Conclusion

Ultimately, true understanding and enlightenment require both awareness and action, the yin and yang of a natural tai chi. By learning to combine these two principles harmoniously, we can cultivate a more profound and fulfilling relationship with the Tao and the world and people around us. Through service and compassion, we can respond to the suffering in the world and bring greater harmony, peace, and enlightenment into our lives and the lives of those around us and the universe beyond.

CHAPTER 54

Linking the Universal Mind with Individual Minds

At this point in the Hua Hu Ching, Lao Tzu begins to educate us about the arts and sciences of the ancients and about the various energies that underlie them. It is both useful and fascinating to consider the ancient holistic sciences and the idea of highly evolved spiritual beings developing them to aid in their own evolution and in that of others. The concept of linking individual minds with the universal mind plays itself out well in the following chapters.

There are indeed various traditional practices and spiritual disciplines that have been passed down through generations. As mentioned above, some of these will be discussed in the subsequent chapters of this book. These practices and disciplines are not mere window dressing. Engaging in such studies can have a positive impact on personal growth and contribute to the betterment of society. As part of their journey and path on the Integral Way it is important for individuals to explore and follow paths that resonate with their own spiritual journey.

"In times long past, highly evolved beings developed many of the holistic sciences in order to evolve and to help others to evolve as well. The subtle arts that they created linked the universal mind with individual minds.

Traditional teachers still teach these sciences to those who show virtue and an who exhibit a genuine desire to help others. When students seek out and study the wholistic arts they further mankind's evolution as well as their own spiritual blossoming and fruition.

To ignore these arts is to hinder the development of mankind and all beings."

The Need for Holistic Sciences

In Ancient times, "highly evolved beings" developed various holistic sciences that enabled their own evolution, as well as that of others. These subtle arts are said to have been created by linking individual minds with the universal mind. This concept is not an unusual one. The creation story of Ayahuasca and its medicinal and spiritual uses reads much the same way. *

Be that as it may, disparate cultures have developed their own holistic medicines based on trial and error for millennia to discover what in their natural world worked for them and what did not. Ancient masters of these arts believed that by developing a stronger connection to the universal mind, they could tap into a vast source of knowledge and wisdom that could assist in their own spiritual evolution. As they evolved, they shared their knowledge and imparted their teachings to their students for their own evolution and for the good of society itself.

Even today, traditional teachers are still passing on their teachings to those who display virtue and a desire to help others. For followers of the Integral Way, the same is true with the sciences that Lao Tzu mentions in this chapter. The students who seek out and study the teachings here and others elsewhere will have a significant impact on the evolution of mankind, as well as their own spiritual development. Conversely, the students who neglect these teachings are hindering not only their own development but the evolution of all beings.

The term "holistic sciences" used here refers to alternative healing modalities, such as acupuncture, Ayurveda, herbalism, chi gong, Feng Shui and yoga, to mention just a few, of which the reader may have knowledge or already encountered. These methods are holistic because they are not atomistic. They do not divide the human body and its experience of life and society into unconnected or antagonistic fragments. Instead, they treat the individual as a whole, a microcosm of the Tao and address not only physical symptoms but also emotional, mental, social and spiritual aspects of the person themself.

Traditional teachers who are still carrying on these teachings are responsible for upholding and preserving the ancient wisdom that has been passed down through generations. These teachers naturally, and consistent with the law of energy response, choose only the most dedicated and virtuous students to become apprentices and continue their work. The teachings, like those of Lao Tzu's in the Hua Hu Ching, are often passed down orally, preserving the purity and essence of the original message.

The benefits of studying these teachings are numerous. Students who immerse themselves in the holistic sciences are able to develop a deeper understanding of their own minds and bodies. They also learn to recognize and respect the interconnectedness of all beings. As they progress in their studies, they begin to access the universal mind and gain an even greater understanding of the universe, their place within it and how it works. As they continue to evolve, these students become invaluable contributors to the collective evolution of mankind and the social and collective evolution of all beings in the universe.

As Lao Tzu cautions, for those who neglect these teachings, they neglect their own holistic development and hinder the development of all beings. Ignoring the subtle arts means missing out on important knowledge about the human body, mind, and spirit and the energies that affect them. By neglecting this knowledge, one is not only limiting their own potential for spiritual evolution but also hindering the progress of others. Each person's evolution is interconnected, and by neglecting one's own development, they are limiting the influence they have on the rest of the world.

The subtle arts developed by ancient masters through linking individual minds with the universal mind hold immense power and potential for spiritual growth. Traditional teachers who still carry on these teachings guide aspirants to become valuable contributors to the collective evolution of mankind here on this planet. People who ignore these teachings cause a hindrance to their own and others' development. By studying these subtle arts, we can unlock our fullest potential and make significant contributions to the growth of all beings terrestrial and otherwise.

*Ayahuasca, "If you talk to the people they will say 'well the plants told us, but to western science this doesn't make a lot of sense you know, 'the plant the plants told you?'" - Dennis McKenna, PhD

CHAPTER 55

The Holistic Sciences

Learning about the Holistic Sciences is part of learning the Integral Way. Here Lao Tzu shares an extensive list of holistic practices from ancient times. It's impressive to see the wide range of disciplines that encompass science, art, and spiritual development. Each of these practices has its unique focus and purpose, contributing to the overall well-being and growth of an individual and the health of the world in which he or she lives. The study of the I Ching, in particular, is regarded as an important foundation for perceiving hidden influences and responding to them in a balanced and spiritually evolved manner. Each practice is not explained in depth here. Lao Tzu leaves further exploration to his students to find the ones that resonate best with them. Exploring these teachings can indeed be a means to serve universal unity, harmony, and wisdom and one's realization of the Tao.

"In order to create the ancient holistic practices, the masters of old integrated science and art with each person's spiritual development. The mind, the body and the spirit participated equally in this evolution.

These holistic practices include the healing science of Yi Yau. This healing art incorporates diagnosis and herbal medicine with therapeutic diet and acupuncture.

They also include Syang Ming. This healing art predicts the destiny of a person through the healer's observation of the patient's physical characteristics in the face, palms, skeleton and voice.

The third of these holistic arts and sciences is Feng Shui. In Feng Shui one studies the subtle energy rays that are present geographically to determine whether a location will support the construction or activities of a building or town in that location.

Next on the list is Fu Kua. This art, as in all Taoist practices, is founded in the study of The Book of Changes or I Ching. In Fu Kua the practitioner observes the subtle changes of yin and yang so that any decisions that are made are harmonious with both the hidden and apparent aspects of any given situation.

Wai Dan, Nei Dan and Fang Jung are the sciences whose purpose it is to refine a person's personal energy through chemistry, alchemy and the balancing and cultivation of sexual energy.

The holistic arts and sciences also include the practice of revitalization or Tai Syi that focuses on visualization and breathing techniques.

Chwun Shi, the modification and revision of one's spiritual nature by keeping one's thoughts in line with the Divine Source;

Shu Ser, the alignment of one's daily life with the cycle of universal energy;

Bi Gu, the practice of specific days of fasting to gather the life energy that comes from the harmonized positioning of specific stars.

Sau Yi, the science of joining and incorporating oneself with integral transcendental oneness in order to give birth to the 'mystical pearl';

Tai Chi Ch'uan; the engagement in certain physical exercises in order to master life and death. In this practice one initiates and directs the body's energy flows in in order to master the mind and physical body, including the internal organs through the breath.

Fu Chi, is the science of changing and reconstituting one's energies with herbs and foods that are unadulterated and pure.

Chuan Se, the visualization inward of both of one's inner and outer being.

Dzai Jing, the science performing certain ascetic practices for the purpose of purifying one's own energy.

Fu Jou, a holistic practice in which one writes and draws mystical pictures and recites mystical incantations to evoke a response from the Tao's subtle realm.

Tsan Syan, a process by which dissolves the ego and connects the practitioner with the Great Oneness. This is accomplished by the study of classical scriptures and through daily dialogues with an enlightened master.

Chi Men and Lyou Yen, the mystical sciences of linking one's energy in order to influence external affairs.

Finally, there is the study of I Ching, the most important subject for beginners. The I Ching enables one to see hidden influences present in every situation. This allows one a properly balanced and spiritually advanced response to those situations.

These holistic sciences deserve to be studied as they serve wisdom, harmony and lead to universal unity. They are all means for one to realize the Tao."

Realizing the Tao

Holistic practices of the ancient masters are a fascinating subject, as they integrate science, art, and personal spiritual development. These practices represent a deeply rooted cultural
heritage, and they aim to balance the mind, body, and spirit
equally. This essay will delve into the various holistic practices
of the ancient masters, including Yi Yau, Syang Ming, Feng
Shui, Fu Kua, Nei Dan, Wai Dan, Fang Jung, Tai Syi, Chwun
Shi, Shu-Ser, Bi Gu, Sau Yi, Tai Chi Ch'uan, and Fu Chi.
These are important subjects, so the following brief but useful
descriptions may help the reader decide which subjects resonate
with the reader and to investigate them further.

Yi Yau is a healing science that incorporates diagnosis, acupuncture, herbal medicine, therapeutic diet, and other techniques.
The practice is intended to balance yin and yang energies to
promote physical and emotional health, and it is based on the
principle that life energy, or Qi, (chi) flows through the body.

Syang Ming is a science that predicts a person's destiny by
observing the outward physical manifestations of his face,
skeleton, palms, and voice. Through the careful analysis of
these physical characteristics, Syang Ming seeks to identify an
individual's strengths and weaknesses, and to develop strategies
for achieving life goals.

Feng Shui, the science of discerning the subtle energy rays
present in a geographic location to determine whether they will
properly support the activities of a building or town construct-
ed there. Feng Shui principles guide the design and placement
of buildings, rooms, furniture, and other items to optimize the
flow of Qi energy, leading to greater balance and harmony.

Fu Kua is the observation of the subtle alterations of yin and
yang for the purpose of making decisions which are harmonious with the apparent and hidden aspects of a situation. This

practice is grounded in the study of the I Ching, or Book of Changes, and aims to help individuals make more informed decisions that align with universal principles.

Nei Dan, Wai Dan, and Fang Jung are the sciences of refining one's personal energy through alchemy, chemistry, and the cultivation of balanced sexual energy. These practices seek to maintain a balance of Qi energy within the body, leading to greater vitality, health, and spiritual development.

Tai Syi is the science of revitalization through breathing and visualization techniques. These practices aim to enrich the Qi flow in the body, leading to greater relaxation, clarity, and spiritual awareness.

Chwun Shi focuses on the transformation of one's spiritual essence through keeping their thoughts in accord with the Divine Source. By cultivating a closer relationship with the Divine, practitioners seek greater spiritual development and harmony.

Shu-Ser is the attunement of one's daily life to the cycle of universal energy rays. This practice involves making conscious choices about one's daily activities and aligning those activities with the natural flow of universal energy.

Bi Gu is the practice of fasting on specific days in order to gather life energy emanating from the harmonized positions of certain stars. This practice seeks to build up Qi energy within the body, leading to greater spiritual strength and awareness.

Sau Yi is the science of embracing integral transcendental oneness in order to accomplish conception of the 'mystical pearl'. By developing a closer relationship with universal principles, practitioners aim to attain greater spiritual awareness and harmony.

Tai Chi Ch'uan is the performance of physical exercises to induce and direct energy flows within the body to gain mastery of body, breath, mind, the internal organs, and life and death. This practice aims to promote physical health, mental clarity, and spiritual awareness.

Fu Chi is the science of reforming matter through the regulation of Qi energy flows. Practitioners seek to cultivate a deeper understanding of the fundamental principles of the universe and use this understanding to transform matter in a spiritually meaningful way.

Conclusion

The holistic practices of the ancient masters represent a deep and rich cultural heritage that continues to influence people throughout the world. Learning about them and the energies they involve is an important part of learning and understanding the Integral Way. By integrating science, art, and personal spiritual development, these practices seek to balance mind, body, and spirit equally, leading us to greater health, well-being, and spiritual awareness. This is why the holistic sciences deserve to be studied in more depth and integrated into our lives as they serve wisdom and harmony and lead to the natural integration of our mind, body and spiritual existences and serve universal unity and consciousness. They are all means by which we may realize the Tao and connect with it as our infinite, indestructible, intelligent and divine source.

CHAPTER 56

Becoming a Man or Woman of the Tao

These wise words by Lao Tzu below reflect the importance of dedication and wholeheartedness in the pursuit of the Integral Way and understanding and embodying the Tao. This path is one that requires a comprehensive approach and encompasses various aspects of life and wisdom. It emphasizes the interconnectedness of all things, where studying and practicing the Tao in its entirety can lead to a harmonious and reflective life. By immersing ourselves fully in the teachings and principles of the Tao, we may find alignment with the nature of life and offer that understanding to the world and beyond.

"If it is your desire to become a man or woman of the Tao, then pursue in your studies that which benefits the nature of all living things. Then offer it to the world. Be completely devoted to the Tao and its Integral Way. Do not be incomplete with either your practice or your discipline.

Just as one cannot understand the entire body by studying the finger, one cannot by studying one science understand the universe.

When one wholeheartedly studies the Tao, then everything in their life truly reflects it."

What being a Man or Woman of the Tao Means

Indeed, studying the Tao is a lifelong pursuit, and has infinite rewards, however; the integration of its teachings into our daily lives requires complete devotion and discipline. The Tao is not just one science or practice, but rather a holistic system that encompasses all aspects of life. To fully understand and embody the Tao, one must study and experience all of its teachings, from the healing sciences to the spiritual practices and beyond. Once learned, we can then engage ourselves with the world to offer what we have experienced and learned to others and the universe beyond. Being a man or woman of the Tao means that we are in service to the greater good beyond ourselves. By doing so, we can embody a higher level of spiritual awareness, harmony and understanding and live a life that is aligned with the timeless and universal principles of the Tao.

CHAPTER 57

The Radiant Energies of the Subtle Origin

To say that concept of the universe as a vast net of energy rays*
that emanate from the Tao's Subtle Origin and radiate like a
web throughout the entire universe is intriguing is a true un-
derstatement. In this passage, Lao Tzu begins to extend our
education about the Tao and its energies beyond the concepts
of Yin and Yang and Tai Chi by teaching us about their source.
It is from there that a primary positive and creative energy
emanates. This source, within the Tao, is referred to as the
Subtle Origin. The energies that radiate from this source create
a net of energy that exists throughout creation.

Lao Tzu teaches us here in this chapter that individuals can
convert subtle energy from this vast net into their own positive or negative "rays". Negative influences can affect one's
perception and hinder spiritual growth. To attain full human
evolution through the Integral Way and become an integral
universal being, it is important to be aware of these influences
and consciously integrate ourselves to align with positive energy
while avoiding or eliminating absorbing or projecting negative
ones. This process of self-awareness and discerning alignment
can enhance all aspects of life. By adopting the practices of the
Integral Way and reflecting and reconnecting with the Tao,
the Subtle Origin of the primary energy ray, we can merge all
the universe's rays and energies and dissolve them back into
the harmonious oneness that is the Tao.

**"The universe is composed of a vast web of energy rays.
These rays emanate from the primary ray that begins
in the Subtle Origin. The primary ray is completely
positive, entirely creative, and ultimately instructive.**

Every being converts the high energy of the primary ray into its own individual ray. Individual rays are of a lower energy than the primary one. They can be either positive or negative. They can be constructive. They may be destructive.

Individuals who are not yet spiritually evolved may be overwhelmed and be affected adversely by the net of negative energy that surrounds them. A common example for people who are not very evolved is when several negative energies and influences come together to affect him or her causing them to believe that they are not in control of their lives and that an oppressive invisible entity rules them.

Unfortunately, misconceptions like these can create significantly great difficulties and impediments to their enlightenment. In order to fully evolve and develop their status as an integral being, one must first become fully aware of this intricate matrix and its myriad of influences on them. One can enhance the aspects on one's life when they integrate the harmonious positive rays of energy with the positive components of their own being and eliminate the negative subtle influences. To do this, one simply ignores them.

In order to cultivate yourself, find and integrate the positive influences to which you may have access. Then consciously connect yourself to the Subtle Origin's primary ray and follow the Integral Way and adopt its practices. When you do, you will find that the web of subtle energy will combine and form a matrix around you that will merge and rejoin you with the Tao's harmonious oneness."

How to Eliminate Negative Energies and Refine the Higher Ones

If we want to fully evolve as humans and become integral beings, we must be aware of the intricate net of energy rays that make up the universe. This net is made up of the "primary ray" that emanates from the Tao, the "Subtle Origin". This radiating energy is entirely positive, creative, and constructive. However, each being converts the energy of this primary ray into its own ray, which can be positive or negative, constructive or destructive. An undeveloped person can be adversely affected by negative energy rays that radiate from the people, places and events that surround them. The frequency and vibration of these unhealthy energies lead to misconceptions and barriers to enlightenment.

To enhance all aspects of our lives, we need to integrate the Tao's positive, harmonious energy rays with the positive elements of our own being. We must eliminate both the overt and subtle negative influences that affect us. To achieve this, we must first be aware of the net of energies and its influences and those the negative inanimate and animated energies have on us. By adopting the practices of the Integral Way and reconnecting ourselves with the primary energy ray of the Subtle Origin, we can eliminate unhealthy negative influences and integrate the beneficial positive ones. This integration will merge all the rays in the net around us back into the Tao's subtle origin and its harmonious oneness. Dissolving ourselves, our egos and all the energies with which we are in contact into the Tao ultimately leads us not only to greater spiritual awareness and harmony, it is the quintessential means by which we refine and perfect our own spiritual being. All the advanced spiritual beings of the universe know and understand this and gauge their behaviors accordingly.

*Again, as we see here and in future chapters, it is not coincidental that the language and ideas Lao Tzu used over two

millennia ago is also completely consistent with the ideas and some of the terms used in modern science. For example, Radiant energy, "also known as electromagnetic radiation (EMR), is energy transmitted without the movement of mass. Practically speaking, this is the energy found in electromagnetic waves, also known as light. Light is made of individual particles called photons, each carrying a small 'packet' of energy." - https://energyeducation.ca

CHAPTER 58

Avoiding Extremist Approaches

In this passage Lao Tzu reiterates an important point about the necessity of holistic development and integration of mind, body, and spirit for sustained spiritual growth. Extremist approaches that prioritize one aspect of the body-mind-spirit complex over the others can lead to imbalances and adverse effects on one's well-being. The path of true self-cultivation involves harmonizing yin and yang, finding balance within oneself through practices aligned with the Integral Way. By achieving this unity, one can experience a state of complete equilibrium and grace, which manifests oneself in the world and in the universe around them. It is through this holistic integration that a person can cultivate their full potential and experience a longer life and more fulfilling spiritual journey.

"Without the equal development of the mind, the body and the spirit can either enlightenment or peak spiritual experiences take place. This is the reason why religions and ideologies that are extremist fail to bear fruit. Being forced into austerities that are unnatural or holding fast to external dogmas causes the body to grow sick and weak so that the body betrays its entire being. When one emphasizes the body to the extent that the mind and spirit are excluded, they both become like caged snakes, poisonously frenzied, unpredictably explosive and deleteriously toxic to one's person. These sorts of imbalances lead inevitably to exhaustion and the dissipation and death of one's life force.

True cultivation is all inclusive. It involves the complete integration of the body, the mind and the spirit. Through the practice of the Integral Way, one can

> balance his or her Yin and Yang energies and become both internally and externally complete. In the world, this unification expresses itself serenely to the universe as flawless equilibrium and perfect grace."

True Cultivation: The Art of Finding Balance, Flawless Equilibrium and Perfect Grace

Human beings are the embodiment of a mind, body, spiritual complex. If we want to enter the existence of our own spiritual peak; if we want sustain enlightenment, we must develop and fully integrate the mind, body, and spirit equally. This means that extremist religions and ideologies that force the mind and spirit into unnatural austerities or external dogmas ultimately fail. When the body is emphasized to the exclusion of the mind and spirit, it becomes like trapped snakes - frantic, explosive, and poisonous. Such imbalances inevitably lead to exhaustion and expiration of our life force.

True self-cultivation involves the holistic integration of mind, body, and spirit. By balancing yin and yang through the various practices of the Integral Way, we achieve complete unity within and without. This manifests in the world as perfect equilibrium and grace. Achieving this balance is critical to creating a balanced human Tai Chi, maintaining spiritual peak, and sustaining enlightenment.

A relaxed and well-balanced yin and yang human makes a beneficial and magnanimous Tai Chi. Becoming such a well-balanced human makes us better able to initiate and sustain meaningful contact with ETs and NHIs. This state of human physical and mental evolution and spiritual awareness is what all integral beings work toward throughout their lifetimes. It is what we share with other integral beings here on earth and with the highest spiritual beings of the universe. In the following chapters Lao Tzu begins to go into the truly esoteric depths of the Hua Hu Ching and tells us how we can cultivate and refine our energies as human beings and go beyond the confines of our human bodies and this planet. The journey toward Divine Realization, the mysteries of the universe and the nature of its inhabitants are about to be opened up to you. Enjoy

CHAPTER 59

It is the Angelic Teacher Who Finds the Student

The perspective Lao Tzu presents here is thought-provoking to say the least. It emphasizes the importance of virtue, service, and selflessness on the path to true attainment. It teaches us that the egoic desire for enlightenment and immortality driven by self-centeredness and dualism can hinder progress. Instead, by focusing on restoring our angelic qualities through virtuous actions and selfless service, we may draw the attention of "angelic teachers" who can guide in the methods of energy enhancement and integration necessary for spiritual growth.

The connection with the "divine realm" is said to come through high awareness and the practice of undiscriminating virtue, leading to enlightenment through the transmission of "ultimate subtle truths". This chapter highlights the difficulty of greed and the significance of selfless actions and our alignment with higher virtues on the journey towards divine realization and living as divine angelic beings of the immortal realm.

To become an angelic being of the divine immortal realm means never having to return to this one on earth in any lifetime after the lifetimes we complete here as humans. We can, by our own choices, evolve into higher and more spiritually enlightened and energetically pure beings in the next reincarnation should we choose to return after our departure to the world of form. That was clearly one of the messages contained in the download of 10/03/15. This is how we, as energies, are refined and evolve in a universe where the recycling of souls is its machinery and the Tao its creator.

"It matters not whether greed expresses itself as greed for enlightenment and immortality or for material wealth. Greed is still greed. Greed is a dualistic and

selfish expression of ego. It is an impediment to spiritual evolution and refinement and following the Integral Way.

States of enlightenment and immortality are rewards for the virtuous and cannot be entered whenever coveted. If your chosen path is to be a divine angelic immortal, an angel of the divine realm, then simply restore those divine and angelic qualities in yourself. This is done by developing your own virtue and being of service to others. Only in this way will you attract the immortals who can teach you the enhancement, integration and cultivation of energies necessary for you to enter the divine realm.

One cannot seek these teachers. They seek the student and appear only when the student is ready. Once one has evolved to a point of having high awareness and practices undiscriminating virtue and connects their divine energy with the divine realm, they will appear.

It is they who will transmit the ultimate subtle truths of the universe to you. All angels ultimately take this same path to the divine realm."

The Journey Toward Our Realization as a Divine Angelic Immortal, an Angel of the Divine Realm

If we choose the path toward enlightenment and divine angelic immortality, we must avoid the self-centered, greedy, egoic, materialist mindset that obstructs that path. This elimination is not selective but applies equally to all forms of greed. Whether it is for material wealth or spiritual advancement, greed is greed and greed is not good. States of enlightenment and immortality are not achieved by those who covet them; rather, they are the rewards of the virtuous who do not covet them but practice the Integral Way.

If our intent is to become highly developed spiritual beings, the divine immortal angels, either in this life or the highest spiritual beings of the universe in the next, we must restore the original innocent and angelic qualities of our being while incarnated here on earth through the practice of virtue and service. This is the only way for us to encounter and gain the attention of the immortals who teach the methods of energy enhancement and integration needed to enter the divine realm. These angelic teachers cannot be sought out; it is they who seek out the student. And they will appear when the student is ready. Unsurprisingly, these angelic teachers, the "immortals" as Lao Tzu calls them, may come in the form of other celestial beings. Call them whatever you will, "divine universal beings", "angels", "extraterrestrials", "energy beings" and "non-human intelligences", there are many different types in the multiverse. They are not imaginary. They are real and take on many forms. Just ask Sister Lucia and the 50,000 or more others present on the morning of Oct. 13, 1917, about the appearance of the Virgin Mary*. And query René Descartes about the angel who appeared to him in a dream on November 10, 1619, and gave him the key to the scientific method**. Or one might ask the historical Buddha himself about his own ET experience as recorded in Chapter 23 of the Lotus Sutra. There are so many examples of these beings appearing throughout recorded history and religion. They are described to the extent that the cultures within which they appear will allow. One might even ask the Hopi, the Sumerians or even Moses himself about their experiences with the divine. But I digress. The information is out there easily for the reader to discover and connect the dots.

Conclusion

Ultimately, what this passage tells us is that by connecting our energy with the divine realm through high awareness and the practice of undiscriminating virtue through service to others, we can succeed in following the path that all angels have taken to the divine realm. When we arrive, our teachers will naturally appear and the transmission of the ultimate subtle truths to us will follow. In this way, in this lifetime we can enter a state of enlightenment and immortality that transcends ego, self-centered greed and leaves us with an acute understanding that even we exist beyond our own physical deaths. This is the subtle truth of the universe. Let us live it as we understand it and integrate ourselves fully with the Tao and begin our encounter with all the highest spiritual beings in the universe.

*See., The sixth and final apparition in Fatima, Catholic News Herald: 02 August 2017
** "The conquest of nature is to be achieved through number and measure."

CHAPTER 60

The "Unruling Rulers and Uncreating Creators of the Universe's Divine Immortal Realm"

In a natural progression from the last chapter, in this one Lao Tzu's introduces us to a new description of the highest spiritual beings in the cosmos, the "unruling rulers and uncreating creators of the vast universe". In order to join the ranks of these beings, Lao Tzu again highlights the importance of transcending ego and the attachments and limitations of the worldly realm especially for those fond of learning about certain mystical techniques and understanding and experiencing immortality. To access these realms, just as it is "easier for a camel to go through the eye of a needle than for a rich man to enter the kingdom of God" *, one must dissolve the ego and its ties to duality, conflict, and dogma, and embrace a virtuous, integrated, and selfless life of simplicity, patience and compassion that goes beyond the materiality of the physical world.

Through the practices of the Integral Way, we can refine our physical, mental and spiritual energies from the gross and heavy to the subtle and transform our unenlightened everyday personality into a profound and divine presence. The journey along the Integral Way involves valuing the experience of the present moment and the truth of the unity of all things including the subtle realm over the world of material things and superficial worldly ambitions. By undergoing each stage of our spiritual cultivation and development, the "mystical gates" to immortality will begin open, allowing us to become among the highest spiritual beings of the universe and eventually, to join the ranks of unruling rulers and uncreating creators of the universe's divine immortal realm, who hold sway over its vastness. In order to arrive there, Lao Tzu emphasizes the importance of our inner transformation and aligning ourselves with the profound truths of the Tao and its subtle realm. In this way we become an integral being here on earth worthy of being counted among the highest spiritual beings of the universe and the cosmos of the Tao itself.

So after this rather weighty introduction, one might ask, "who exactly are these unruling rulers and uncreating creators"?

"The revelation of the transcendent spiritual or 'mystical' techniques for one's immortality happens after they detach from the duality, dogmas and conflicts formed by the gross energies of the worldly realm. If shallow worldly ambition exists in one's life, then the gates to immortality will not open.

In order to open the gates, we must live integrated, selfless and virtuous lives. Refine our heavy gross energies into energies that are light and subtle.

Follow and utilize the techniques and practices of the Integral Way. By doing this one can transform their worldly superficial personality into a presence that is both profound and divine.

By passing through each developmental stage along the Integral Way, one learns the value and the importance of being present today in the subtle realm and choosing it rather than that which is temporally desirable in the future from the worldly one.

Once one does this, the mystical gates to the divine immortal realm will open and unite those who pass through these gates with the 'unruling rulers and uncreating creators' of the universe's divine immortal realm."

The Unruling Rulers and Uncreating Creators of the Tao's Divine Immortal Realm

The takeaway of this passage is that the mystical techniques for achieving immortality are not given to just anybody, especially those who cling to the ego's gross worldly realm and its base energies. This worldly realm is that of materiality, duality, judgment, conflict, social, political, and religious confrontation and dogma. To access these mystical techniques about which Lao Tzu writes, we must begin by first dissolving the ego and all our ties to shallow worldly ambitions like fame and fortunes. Only when we have devoted ourselves to living a virtuous, integrated, and selfless life of truth and undiscriminating compassion will these the gates to the immortals open. Both truth and compassion form the mystical gates that enable us to make contact with the "highest spiritual beings", like those we now may call ET and NHIs, or as Lao Tzu calls them, the "unruling rulers and uncreating creators of the universe's divine immortal realm". These beings are of the highest spiritual order. Their presence is universal. They, as followers of the Integral Way themselves are our angelic teachers of old who have come to assist both the innocent and the spiritually evolved here in their own compassionate journey toward heightened spiritual being upon the Integral Way.

In the next twenty chapters, the reader will be exposed to new and deeper concepts and practices that constitute the Integral Way. For now, suffice it to say that through the practices of the Integral Way, pursuing truth and living virtuous simple lives of truth, patience and indiscriminate compassion, we can refine our energy from the dark, gross and heavy to the subtle and the light. By transforming our superficial worldly personality into a profound divine presence, we can pass through each stage of development along the Integral Way. In doing so, we can learn to value what is important in the unseen spiritual subtle realm today rather than what appears desirable in the worldly physical realm tomorrow. By practicing the Integral

Way, we can come to understand what is really important in a universe that, like us, is not only physically and mentally conscious but spiritually conscious as well.

Once we have sufficiently completed this journey, the mystical gates will inevitably begin to open for us, and we can begin to meet and join the unruling rulers and uncreating creators of the vast universe. This, however, is not always an easy path. There may be laughter and ridicule from those who are not spiritually well-enough advanced to understand or comprehend the true existence of the Tao. Not everyone is capable of this or following the Integral Way. Becoming highly evolved "superior beings" requires us to take the challenging path and surrender our egos and let go of what is ephemeral and shallow. It requires us to fully embrace the Tao and integrate into our daily lives the virtues and practices of the Integral Way.

Through selfless dedication to pursuing truth and living lives of simplicity, patience and compassion and the disciplines of the Integral Way, we can enter the highest levels of spiritual awareness and harmony in this lifetime. We can pass through the mystical gates to bring ourselves to be among the 'unruling rulers and uncreating creators' and into the universe's divine immortal realm. There we can experience a true state of immortality; one that transcends the limitations of our own temporal physical existence and extends our spiritual existence past the the limitations of time and space, life, and death and even birth and rebirth itself back into the material physical plane. We began as spiritual energy that came from the subtle realm into the physical one. It is from the physical one into the spiritual and subtle realm that we return. Welcome to the Tao's divine immortal realm. You have come a long way. There is still much to learn.

*See., The New Testament: Matthew 19:24, Luke 18:25 and the Qur'an 7:49

CHAPTER 61

Understanding the Universe

The concepts that Lao Tzu uses here to assist us in understanding the universe opening immortality's "Mystical Gates" draw from various philosophical and spiritual traditions, particularly from ancient Chinese philosophy. The concepts here mentioned, like those of the Tao, yin and yang, Tai Chi, the "Eight elements", "Harmonized Energy", the five elements, the six breaths, the I Ching and others, are part of ancient Chinese wisdom and provide a philosophical framework for Lao Tzu's understanding the world of 2500 years ago. They are often used metaphorically and symbolically to represent different aspects of nature, human life, and the interplay of forces. Despite their age, these ideas are nevertheless true.

Lao Tzu offers his insightful perspectives on understanding the universe and its dynamics through these concepts. While exploring these ideas can be fascinating, it's important to note that the understanding of the universe is a complex and ongoing field of study that involves multiple disciplines including but not limited to the study of mathematics, chemistry, physics, general relativity, special relativity, atomic energy, gravitational fields, and quantum physics as well as astrophysics, astronomy, ontology, cosmology, metaphysics and more.

It is crucial to approach these concepts with an open and critical mind, acknowledging that even as amazing as Lao Tzu's language and almost all-encompassing understanding of the universe might be our limited understanding of the universe today is continually evolving based on scientific research and empirical evidence that seem to either prove or buttress what Lao Tzu teaches us about the Tao and the nature of reality. Exploring both scientific knowledge and philosophical wisdom can not only help us to understand the writings of Lao Tzu but can contribute to a more holistic understanding of the universe and our place and relationship to all things and beings within it.

"In order for the universe to be understood, one must understand the following things. First, there is the Oneness of the Tao and its Great Tai chi. Second, there is the two forces of Yin and Yang. Third, one must understand the three main categories of heaven, earth and man that express themselves as spirit, mind, and body. Fourth, there are the four forces: weak, strong, heavy, and light. Fifth, there are the five elements that express themselves as earth, fire, wood, metal, and water. Sixth, there are the six breaths: wind, heat, cold, moisture and dryness which transform both the weather, the climate and one's internal organs as well. Seventh, there is change and its processes and how it recycles all things. Eighth, there are the 'Eight manifestations' as taught in the I Ching that express themselves as heaven, earth, fire, water, wind, lake and mountain and whose combinations reveal the subtle truth of all energies attendant to and present in all situations.

If one comes to understand these things, then one can utilize them internally to abandon and move on from what is aged and dead and accept and incorporate what is new and vital. By embracing these transformative internal alchemical processes, we open spiritual immortality's mystical gates up to ourselves."

<u>Comprehending the Mystical Nature of Existence and Achieving Spiritual Immortality</u>

The universe is an enormous entity that has since time immemorial captivated the minds of mankind. To comprehend the universe, it is essential to understand the foundational concepts that tie together its infinite complexity. As an introduction to them, and for the purpose of further study, Lao Tzu categorizes these foundational concepts into eight key elements that serve as the steppingstones towards achieving spiritual immortality. The eight core elements of the universe are the oneness, the Great Tai Chi, the forces of yin and yang, the Three Main Categories, the Four Forces, the Five Elements, the Six Breaths, Eternal rebirth and Change and the Eight Great Manifestations the I Ching. Understanding these elements gives an individual the tools to employ what is described as internal alchemy, allowing us to understand who and what we are and reconfigure ourselves around the truth that is the Tao and to leave behind of the old and dead and welcome that which is new and alive and eternal.

So, what do these categories expressed by Lao Tzu mean?

Oneness represents the universal source of all existence where there is no distinction between self and other. It is synonymous with the Great Tai Chi, which represents the state of perfect harmony of existence. This harmony is achieved through the interaction of the forces of yin and yang, which form the Great Tai Chi.

The Three Main Categories, which consist of Heaven, Earth, and Man, represent the three aspects of human nature: the physical body (earth), emotions and mental state (heaven), and the spirit (man). These three aspects work together cohesively, as a microcosm of the Tao and form a complete individual. The balance of these energies becomes part of our transformative alchemical process.

The Four Forces consist of strong, weak, light, and heavy. They represent the energies of what we now know to be fusion, electro-magnetic, chemical and fission. These are the fundamental forces that govern the universe.

The Five Elements, represented by water, fire, wood, metal, and earth, are the foundation of life. They represent the building blocks of all objects in existence.

The Six Breaths, represented by wind, cold, heat, moisture, dryness, and inflammation, transform the climate and the internal organs. They are the elements that keep everything in balance.

Lastly, the Eight Great Manifestations, including Heaven, Earth, Water, Fire, Thunder, Lake, Wind, and Mountain, represent the combinations of forces and elements that reveal the subtle energetic truth of all situations. This truth can be understood through the teachings of the I Ching.

To comprehend these forces and elements is to understand the foundation of the universe and to comprehend the mystical components of existence. Employing internal alchemy with this understanding can lead us consciously to spiritual immortality. By embracing what is alive and new, while simultaneously leaving behind the dead and old, we can reach a state of physical and mental health here on Earth and find spiritual completeness with the universe.

Conclusion

A basic understanding of the eight elements of the universe is essential for us to comprehend its infinite complexity and understand the Tao. Though simplified here in this chapter, each element forms a crucial foundation necessary for comprehending the mystical nature of existence and how it interplays alchemically with our physical, mental, and spiritual evolution toward spiritual immortality. By studying and embracing these concepts, we can begin to learn further how let go of the old and welcome the new and become the immortal universal beings we have always been meant to be. Ultimately, in this way, we can create in our lives a complete state of harmony within ourselves and with the Tao and the universe itself.

CHAPTER 62

The Three Main Energies

The pursuit of understanding and attaining the Tao is a profound journey that involves integrating various aspects of one's own being. Lao Tzu emphasizes three main energies: earth energy, heaven energy, and harmonized energy. Each of these energies corresponds to different aspects of human experience and development. Understanding them is an essential part of the Integral Way.

Earth energy, associated with the belly and sexuality, represents the physical aspect of our existence. Cultivating and mastering this energy as part of the Integral Way can lead to a partial purity.

Heaven energy, centered in the mind and associated with knowledge and wisdom, represents intellectual and cognitive development. Merging one's mind with the Universal Mind is considered within the Integral Way as another aspect of partial purity.

Harmonized energy, centered in the heart and associated with spiritual insight, represents the development of one's spiritual self. Nurturing this energy through the Integral Way can lead to another aspect of partial purity.

According to Lao Tzu, true purity of Tao is achieved when all three partially pure energies are harmoniously developed and combined to express themselves in an integral and virtuous life. This passage also tells us that integrating and balancing physical, intellectual, and spiritual aspects of one's being is essential in the quest for experiencing pure Tao.

"Do you seek to enter the realm and experience of pure Tao? If you do, then understand the universe's three principal energies and integrate them within yourself. The first of these energies is that of the earth. The second is that of heavenly energy. The third is harmonized energy.

Earth energy is centered in the abdomen. Its physical expression is that of sexuality. Cultivate and master it then partially pure you will be.

Heavenly energy finds its center in the mind. Knowledge and wisdom are its expressions. Merge your mind with the universal mind and you will be partially pure.

Harmonized energy finds its center in the heart. Spiritual insight is its expression. Develop spiritual insight and you will also be partially pure.

It is only when one masters all three of these energies and integrates and expresses them as one's own life of integral virtue does, he or she enter the realm and experience of pure Tao."

How to Experience Pure Tao

It's important to note that the concept of Tao and its interpretation can vary among different philosophical and spiritual traditions. This explanation is a simplified understanding based on the information that Lao Tzu provides here.

Integrating the three main energies of the universe is a key component to experiencing pure Tao. The earth energy, centered in the belly and expressed as sexuality, represents our physical nature. Mastering this energy allows us to reach a state of physical purity. On the other hand, the heaven energy, centered in the mind and expressed as knowledge and wisdom, represents only our mental state. Merging with the Universal Mind allows us to attain partial purity in the realm of the mind. Still, without more, the combination of these two states in incomplete and not "pure".

Finally, the harmonized energy, centered in the heart and expressed as spiritual insight, represents our spiritual nature. Developing spiritual insight leads to a greater understanding of the universe and fosters a state of virtuous integral life. To attain pure Tao, we must achieve mastery in all three areas and integrate them into our lives. Even though it may seem an incomplete work in progress, the message here is simple. Just as a stool requires three equal legs to stand and support its own weight, only by integrating the energies of earth, heaven and harmony, our holy energies of the body, the mind and the spirit can we achieve a state of complete harmony with the universe and experience pure Tao.

CHAPTER 63

The Three Layers of the Universe and the "Magnificent Magical Dance of the Divine Immortals"

In this passage Lao Tzu describes the universe as having three layers: Tai Ching, Shan Ching, and Yu Ching. These layers are associated with different states of existence and levels of harmony with the Tao.

In the lower layer, Tai Ching, and the middle layer, Shan Ching, the focus is on the hindrances and limitations of physical existence. Those who fail to live in accordance with the Tao reside in these layers, implying a state of disconnection from the underlying principles of harmony and unity.

In the upper layer, Yu Ching, only the Tao exists, and the constraints of form and physical existence are transcended. This layer is described as a realm where "immortal divine beings" engage in an exquisite energy dance.

To enter Yu Ching, one begins by following the Integral Way. This involves several practices: among these are simplifying one's life and deepening his or her personality, refining their sexual energy upward, integrating yin and yang in body, mind, and spirit, practicing patience and non-impulsiveness, and aligning one's conscience with "pure law". By following this path, we uncover truth after truth and enter the exquisite upper realm an Yu Ching. By following the Integral Way and making our consciences one with pure law, we enter the most exquisite upper realm of Yu Ching where all that exists is the "magnificent magical dance of the divine immortals".

So, what is pure law and what is Lao Tzu referring to when he describes the magnificent magical dance of the divine immortals? For now, it's important to approach these concepts with an open mind and recognize that they are part of a specific philosophical, ontological and spiritual framework that tries to best describe a reality that is both subjective and experiential. While they may provide insights and guidance for personal development and in our experience of what we call Interdimensionals, ETs and NHIs, it's essential to maintain an open-minded and balanced view and explore diverse perspectives in order to both cultivate a holistic understanding of life and the universe and understand who and what these "Immortals" are.

"The universe has three layers: the lower, the middle and the upper. The lower level is that of Tai Ching. Tai Ching requires the impediment of the physical body to exist. Shang Ching the middle level also requires the the physical body. Those who do not live consistently live in accord with the Tao live here.

In Yu Ching, the upper level, there is only the Tao. In this level, the servitude of form is dissolved. Those who seek to enter Yu Ching follow the Integral Way. To do this requires one to simplify their lives and uncomplicate their personalities. They should practice patience and non-impulsivity and cultivate to refine upwards their sexual energy. They make their consciences one with pure law. In this way they uncover truth after truth to enter the most exquisite upper realm of Yu Ching where all that exists is the magnificent magical dance of the divine immortals.

The path is simple to follow and quite clearly defined. However most lose their way in the ideological fogs they make for themselves."

Divine Energy, Li, Pure Law, Moral Law, and the Divine Immortals

There are three very different layers of the universe. The lower layer, Tai Ching, and the middle layer, Shan Ching, require the hindrance of a physical bodily existence. Those who fail to live in accordance with Tao reside in these lower layers. On the other hand, the upper layer, Yu Ching, is a realm where only the pure energy of the Tao exists, and the bondage of form is broken. Here, the lower energies have no hold on us. Here, there is only the exquisite energy dance of immortal divine beings. When we enter the state of Yu Ching we are capable of significant and meaningful contact with the Immortals, the Unruling Rulers and Uncreating Creators of the Tao's Divine Immortal Realm and to freely dance with them.

To enter Yu Ching, one follows the Integral Way. This involves simplifying one's life and personality, refining sexual energy and elevating it upwards, integrating yin and yang in body, mind, and spirit, practicing patience and non-impulsiveness, and making our consciences one with pure law.

Pure Law

So what is Pure Law? Simply, and very simply put Pure or "Natural Law" is in its essence, the Tao and its natural progression of intentional creation through cause and effect. It is the inexorable conclusion that both the Tao and all of reality including ourselves are self-determining or "self-so". It is the pure truth of being at heart, self-so and living complete truth with the Tao itself as one's own conscience. Pure Law is the pure nature of Natural Law. It is the Tao governing through us.

Pure Law*, is complete truth and honesty. It is the law of purity. When one lives the Integral Way, the complete truth and honesty of pure law entirely govern one's values and behavior. Pure law is commonly referred to as "Li". Li represents the highest level of our spiritual refinement. It known as the realm or state of absolute honesty in us. This pure honesty unites us with the pure honesty and truth of the Tao. In order to maintain this pure state, there must be no separation or deviation from Li, less one should fall from if. Even a small deviation puts the path at risk. That is why one doesn't lie about even the littlest of things. Li is the path of absolute truth. Absolute truth is the nature of the Tao all Integral Universal beings.

Li

In the final realm of Yu Ching, Li, commonly referred to as "pure law", comes to its paramount refinement. Li allows us to transcend the duality of Chi. Once one transcends Chi, they enter the realm of Li, the highest level of refinement. Li is above all. Within Li, one is no longer confined by duality or the distinctions of Chi energy found in Tai Ching and Shang Ching.

In Li, the rigidities of material force and form of the lower levels no longer apply. The dualistic distinctions of "free" and "not-free" are also of no relevance. Neither applies as all is governed not by matter or energy but by "Pure Law". In Li, complete honesty governs our values and behavior. There is no separation or deviation allowed from Li in order to maintain the state. Should one fail Li, then their spirit is lowered into the baser levels of Chi energy and Tai Ching's materiality and the flesh. There, one's bondage to matter and physicality is increased as they continue to fall lower and lower as they separate from Li. If one does deviate, one falls from this level back into the realm of duality between Chi and Li where they are again torn between two masters and the perplexities of duality once again become manifest. Here, one must again seek transcendence of Chi energy found in Tai Ching and Shang Ching

Life in Li is one of complete, unbent straightforwardness and unfailing rectitude with the universal truth and the natural universal law. In Li, one is always without guile and acts with complete directness. One must trust absolutely the freedom that lies within the ultimate truth that they find in Li.

In Li, high virtues are patiently perfected within Li's pure law. In Li, non-impulsiveness is the highest expression of the universal being. Within the realm of Yu Ching's Li, impatience and restlessness are unknown and a material, flesh-centered life becomes meaningless. The ego has become completely dissolved. Among the highly developed, one who has attained a life of complete truth and pure reason has his or her own conscience as pure law.

Moral Law

It should be mentioned that within Li, and pure law there also exists "moral law". Long ago before the development of modern complexities, the ancients saw how everything, and everyone were inseparably co-existent on their interdependence. A loss to one was a loss to all. The basis for "Moral law" was the common commitment among all people to each other to develop morally and spiritually as individuals. However, with civilization came materiality and a loss of the communality of interdependent spirits. Man lost his trust in the universe as things became more and more imbalanced. Man, lost trust in himself and his own nature. Man began to cling to things of material and of the flesh. Man became worldly and impulsive. Moral restraint disappeared as ego and duality crawled out of the darkness into ascendency.

The old moral law of an interdependent community gave way to Civilization and the laws of persons and property because the moral integrity of everyone had become so atrophied. Spiritual underdevelopment brought about the ascendency of self and egocentricity. With ego came restlessness and a loss of self-possession and control. Because man lacked self-control this shortcoming caused the evocation and passing of many laws.

This began the present downward spiral of mankind. All that was left eventually were the laws of human control and bondage on the material plane.

Conclusion

Following this path through the three layers of the universe allows us to uncover truth after truth and enter the exquisite upper realm of Yu Chung and experience Li. It is there where we find our consciences are once again in alignment with the moral law of the Tao our compassionate creator. It is important to note that despite the simplicity of this path, many individuals will still lose themselves in the ideological fogs of their own making. Therefore, it is important to stay mindful and focused on the path of absolute truth. By doing so we can continue to develop our understanding of the Tao and integrate the teachings of the Integral Way into our daily lives. When we do so, we too can evolve and refine our Chi energies into Li. As we do this, we can begin experiencing the company of the highest spiritual beings of the universe.

Within the pure law and of Li, we can truly begin to make profound and meaningful contact with the Immortals. Within our renewed common commitment among all people of the earth to each other to develop morally and spiritually as individuals and as a society and commit to ET and NHI in the same way, we will experience the profundity and benevolence of true contact. The nature of this contact is beyond time and space. It is through pure law and Li that once the servitude of form is dissolved, we will in the exclusive upper realm of Yu Ching not only see but get to dance the magnificent magical dance with the Unruling Rulers and Uncreating Creators of the Tao's Divine Immortal Realm.

CHAPTER 64

The Pinnacle of Spiritual Understanding

Here in this passage, Lao Tzu highlights a contrast between earlier times when people lived simply and serenely, attuned to the fluctuations of yin and yang. Even over two millennia ago, just as in our own in the present era, people lead hectic and impulsive lives, often ignoring these subtle changes. Whether in 500BCE or today, this lack of awareness leads to confusion, exhaustion, and frustration.

As a means to restore wholeness and clarity to the mind, Lao Tzu mentions the I Ching, an ancient Chinese divination text that deserves its own independent study. By studying the I Ching, one can begin to perceive the patterns and movements of yin and yang, which underlie all things. This understanding allows for a certain degree of predictability and a sense of peace and tranquility, akin to resting peacefully at night with the knowledge that inevitably daybreak will come.

The I Ching is a tool used to reveal the fluidity of things and to perceive the constancy and transformative power of the Tao—the underlying principle of creation and harmony. This understanding is considered the ultimate education and a source of solace.

While the study of the I Ching and the recognition of patterns can offer insights and guidance, it's important to recognize that finding solace and understanding can take different forms for different individuals. Exploring various philosophical and spiritual traditions can also provide our own personal context and a broader perspective on achieving peace of mind and a sense of wholeness in one's life within the greater context of the study of the Tao.

"In days long passed, because people lived serenely and simply, they were sensitive to the constant fluctuations that occurred about them. They could comfortably adjust to the energy that was present around them. Today, people live hysterically. They live impulsive lives. They are oblivious to yin and yang and their subtle alterations that influence all things. Their ignorance causes them confusion, frustration and exhaustion. However, despite the passage of time, one's clarity of mind and wholeness can be restored through the study of the Book of Change, the I Ching.

Similar to the cycle of night and day. The whole of existence is a Tai Chi that incorporates the movement of Yin and Yang. One who does not see the patterns in these movements is lost. However, if one consults the I Ching open-mindedly, then one begins to see the patterns that underlie all things.

At night, knowing that daybreak will come after the darkness allows us to peacefully rest. By our perceiving fluidity accurately in things, we begin to see the constancy of the boundless, immutable, creative, and transformative.
Tao that lies behind them.

Understanding this, is the ultimate solace and the apex of one's own education."

Perceiving Flow

People in earlier times lived simply and were more sensitive to the fluctuations that constantly occur. They saw things clearly and could adjust comfortably to the energy of the day. In contrast, today's society is perhaps even more impulsive and hysterical than the one in which Lao Tzu lived. People then and now often ignore the subtle alterations of yin and yang that influence all things. This lack of perception of the flow of the Tao can lead to our confusion, exhaustion, and frustration.

However daunting at times, it is still possible to restore wholeness and clarity to our minds. By studying the I Ching, as Lao Tzu suggests, individuals can become more attuned to the patterns underlying all things. The I Ching teaches that everything is a Tai Chi that incorporates movements between yin and yang in its predictions of energy flows and outcomes. The past, the present and the future are all related. Once the flow is perceived, the future is not such a mystery. It is no wonder that hindsight is 20/20. If we take time to pay attention to these movements between the energies of yin and yang over time, we can better understand the changes in the world around us and predict what the future might hold.

Accurately perceiving the fluidity of things also allows us to see not only the changes in life but the constancy behind them: the creative, transformative, boundless, immutable Tao. Seeing this, and that underlying and behind all change is the Tao is the pinnacle of our spiritual path. This realization is the ultimate education and our complete trust in the Tao is our ultimate reassuring solace. Our ultimate realization of the Tao allows us to rest peacefully at night, knowing that like the sun, seen or unseen, the Tao is always there. Whether we use the I Ching or not, by just paying close attention to the subtle fluctuations of yin and yang in the world around us, we can better understand the universe and cultivate a deeper sense of inner peace and harmony. With this sense, we can extend ourselves into our world and beyond and begin to understand who we are, what our place in the cosmos and how to relate to all its inhabitants.

CHAPTER 65

The Mysterious Mother

In this passage, Lao Tzu begins our further instruction in the interplay of the three levels of energy within the human being, Tai Ching, Sang Ching and Yu Ching, physical, mental and spiritual. In this chapter he begins to explore and teach us about our human sexual and reproductive energies and how to refine them upwards to create a heightened state of spiritual being. In the next few chapters Lao Tzu will illustrate this fully in more detail. This is an important area of study, not only bor us as evolving human beings but because by finding our sexual energies and sending them upwards, ET and NHIs begin to appear around us.

In this chapter, Lao Tzu begins his instruction by describing the mysterious interplay of yin and yang within the metaphorical context of the Mysterious Mother. This interplay creates the expansion and contraction of nature, and the entire universe is said to be formed through this reproductive dance. However, the universe itself is considered only a small part of the Mysterious Mother's being.

Similarly, the physical reproductive function is seen as a necessary part of human beings. However necessary though, the reproductive act is viewed as just a fraction of our complete existence. While many individuals focus on this biological impulse throughout their lives, it is suggested that there is more to our being than this aspect alone.

To unite with the heart and mind of the Mysterious Mother, it is proposed that one must integrate yin and yang within themselves and refine their fire upward. This suggests a process of inner cultivation and balance. By balancing the sexual energies of yin and yang, individuals gain the power to merge with the entirety of the Mysterious Mother's being, representing a state of true evolution often called "sexual sage hood".

It's important to note that the Mysterious Mother and the ideas presented are part of a specific seminal philosophical framework presented by Lao Tzu, and their interpretation over the millennia has metamorphosized into certain yogic and kundalini practices of the Hindu and Buddhists. They may also vary among both the same and very different traditions within which they are found. Exploring Lao Tzu's teachings along with these different perspectives and philosophies can contribute to a broader understanding of our existence and personal evolution and help us to make significant inroads in our abilities to make contact with ET and NHI.

"The Tao is the Mysterious Mother of all that comes into being. Within her womb, the interplay of Yin and Yang creates nature's expansion and contraction. Even though the entirety of the universe is created out of the Tao's reproductive dance, this is just a small portion of her being. Her heart and mind are the universal heart and mind.

The Tao's reproductive function is also a part of the reproductive function of human beings. In individuals, Yin and Yang are not complete. therefore, male and female pair up to integrate each other's Yin and Yang energies in order to create new life.

Most everyday people spend their entire lives enslaved to their biological and reproductive impulses. Yet, like the Tao, this is just a small percentage of our being. By being obsessed with the seed and egg, the physical or the lower Tai Ching energy we wed ourselves to the Mysterious Mother's reproductive womb. This marriage prevents us from knowing her.

Shan Ching and Yu Ching energies and her omniscient mind and unfathomable and inestimable heart.

In order to unite with her mind and heart you must cultivate your Yin and Yang and refine and direct their fiery energies through yourselves and upward. This upward refinement gives you the power to merge your being with the whole being of the Tao. This evolution is true evolution."

True Spiritual Evolution

Understanding the interplay of yin and yang within the womb of the Mysterious Mother is critical to our understanding of the Living Tao and how its Tai Chi operates. The expansion and contraction of nature, like the inhaling and exhaling of a billow, are created through the reproductive dance of yin and yang. While the Tao creates the universe and the "world of ten-thousand things" out of this dance, it is only a small portion of its being. The Universal Heart and Universal Mind are at the center of her universal being and gives it meaning.

The creative reproductive function is also a small but necessary part of being human. While individuals may spend their entire lives following this biological impulse, it is only a tiny portion of our beings. If one remains obsessed with only the seeds and eggs of physical reproduction, they are married only to the fertile reproductive valley of the Mysterious Mother but not to the sentient bosom of her immeasurable heart and the sapience of her all-knowing mind.

True spiritual evolution and self-cultivation involves integrating yin and yang within ourselves, and balancing them and refining their fiery sexual and reproductive energies upwards. But what does this mean and how is it done? In the next chapters to follow, we will find out. Once we have the power to merge with the whole being of the Mysterious Mother, we can then unite with her heart and mind. By learning how and doing so, we enrich not only our connection to the world around us, gaining a deeper understanding of the universe but strengthen our connection with and understanding of the Universal beings, the Divine Immortals, the highest spiritual beings of the universe, and the Unruling Rulers and Uncreating Creators of the Tao's Divine Immortal Realm

CHAPTER 66

The Three Integrations and Expressions
of Energy

In this passage Lao Tzu describes three integrations of yin and yang. Each integration is associated with different levels of existence and their outcomes. The first integration occurs within Tai Ching, the physical realm through the union of seed and egg within the womb. This represents the creation of new life. However wonderful, this integration is limited to the realm of flesh and blood. This realm is subject to eventual disintegration and mortality. The second integration is seen in the sexual union of mature males and females. This too is also within the physical realm. By its nature, this union is likewise concerned with the material and physical aspects of existence.

However, it is the third integration that is considered beyond mere physicality and to give birth to something immortal. The third integration involves a highly evolved individual who, through the practices of the Integral Way, joins the subtle inner energies of yin and yang under the light of spiritual understanding. This is called "self" or "Single Cultivation" *. By refining their energy from the gross and heavy energies of Tai Ching and Sang Ching to the ethereal and light energies of Yu Ching, they access a divine energy and the light of understanding. They become capable of penetrating the vast ocean of spiritual energy and complete wisdom that is the Tao. This life is pure consciousness beyond physical form. This is the essential nature of the Tao itself.

The new life resulting from this final integration of yin and yang within our own spiritual understanding is described as one that is self-aware yet without ego. It is capable of inhabiting a body but without attachment to it. It is a state of conscious being that is guided by wisdom rather than by emotion. Such a being is considered whole and virtuous, transcending the limitations of physical mortality. In human form, it properly may be called a "Divine" being. Such a being is capable of transcending the physical to become a "Universal" being once its lifecycle is over here on earth. As a universal being, there is no necessity to reincarnate.

However foreign or difficult these concepts may be to us, it is important to approach these concepts with an open mind, recognizing that they are part of a specific metaphysical, onto-logical, and spiritual framework. At their very least, they offer insights into the pursuit of spiritual evolution and our potential for transcending the limitations of the physical realm and the wheel of suffering and karma that keeps us returning after our deaths to repeat the lessons that we should have already learned. Ultimately, over the course of our many lifetimes, this transformation is what true spiritual evolution and refinement is all about. Without a clear roadmap for this journey, we would hardly know how and where to go, much less the point of the journey. Once we understand that we are immortal, neither we nor that understanding will ever pass away.

"The first integration of Yin and Yang is the union of seed and egg within the physical womb. Yin and Yang's second integration is the actual sexual union of a sexually mature male with a sexually mature female. These two integrations are bound to the physical realm by flesh and blood and are destined to live, grow old, deteriorate, and pass away.

Only in the third integration of yin and yang that something immortal can be born. In this third integration, an individual who is highly evolved takes his or her subtle internal yin and yang energies and joins them under the illumination of spiritual understanding. By following the practices of the Integral Way, one

refines their lower gross and heavy energies into energies that are divinely light and ethereal. This divine energy has the power to penetrate into the Tao's limitless ocean of complete wisdom and mighty spiritual energy.

In this third integration, a new form of intelligent life comes forth. This being is self-aware, yet it is without ego. Whole and virtuous, it is capable of inhabiting a physical body but it is not attached to it.
Rather than being guided by emotion, this being is guided by wisdom instead. Because the nature of this being is divine, it can never deteriorate or die. It is immortal as it can never pass away."

Understanding Our Own Immortality

Yin and yang are ancient concepts that ultimately became rooted in Chinese philosophy. They describe two complementary yet opposing principles and energies that make up the universe. Yin represents the feminine, soft, receptive, and yielding energy, while yang represents the masculine, active, and assertive energy. Both yin and yang have elements of the other embedded within them. They could not exist without both these conflicting and complementary energies to hold them together and to each other. In Taoist thought, the ultimate goal is to integrate these seemingly opposing energies in order to create balance and harmony in one's life and by way of extrapolation, in the universe.

According to Lao Tzu's teachings in the past chapters we have learned that there are three stages of integration relating to yin and yang. The first stage occurs during conception, when the seed and egg come together to energize to create new life within the mother's womb. The second stage relates to the sexual union of a mature male and female, which is also concerned with flesh and blood, and all that is conceived in this physical realm must one day die, disintegrate and pass away.

It is only the third integration which gives birth to something immortal. In this stage, an individual who is highly evolved will join the subtle inner energies of yin and yang under the love and light of spiritual understanding. Through the practices of the Integral Way, the "enlightened" self-cultivating individual will refine their gross, heavy energy into something ethereal and light. This divine "light" is an energy that has the capability of penetrating into the boundless mighty universe of spiritual energy and complete wisdom that is the Tao.

The new life created by this third and final integration is completely self-aware yet because its awareness of self, other and the Tao are one in the same. It is without ego. Although incapable of inhabiting a body, it is not attached to it. Because of this, this awareness is capable of inhabiting or sharing the body of another under the appropriate circumstances. Because this life is guided by wisdom rather than emotion its existence exists in an integrated state. Whole and virtuous, it consciously recognizes its own immortality and can never die.

Conclusion

Ultimately, the integration of yin and yang is something that not only can help individuals achieve balance and harmony in their lives but it can lead to our realization of the immortality of our own immortal consciousness and being. It is only when a person has reached a highly evolved state of self-cultivation that they are able to integrate their energies in a way that allows for the birth of something immortal. This self-cultivation is the path of all Integral beings, human and otherwise. Through the practices of the Integral Way, we can learn to refine our energies and create a life that, without ego, is guided by wisdom and compassion rather than by our emotions. In doing so, we can realize our own immortality.

As immortals, there is nothing that can kill us or harm us. This final stage of integration is beyond the realms of Tai Ching and Sang Ching through Yu Ching. It is the key to achieving true balance and harmony within us and with the universe and engaging constructively and on common ground, those ET/NHIs the children of the Mystical Mother who are the unruling rulers and uncreating creators of the vast universe that inhabit her creation.

*One of the ways that we can directly experience the integration of yin and yang into our own Tai Chi is through "Single Cultivation". The entry into higher states of consciousness and spheres of life and into higher spiritual realms require us initially to unite and refine our yin and yang energies into one balanced Tai Chi. When we do this by ourselves, it is called 'Single Cultivation'. The practice of Single Cultivation teaches us that one of high spiritual accomplishment and virtue can experience the transcendent nature of his or her own energy. The integration of balanced yin and yang energies can be channeled so that these energies may be used effectively for one's own further self-cultivation or be shared for the benefit of their mates and other of their fellow beings.

CHAPTER 67

Sexual Sage hood: The Dual Cultivation of Energies Through Human Sexual Intercourse

In this chapter, Lao Tzu takes us from Single Cultivation and introduces us to a new concept, that of Dual Cultivation and tells us who may undertake it properly. The topic of Dual Cultivation and its technique will be discussed in detail throughout the next few chapters. In introducing us to dual cultivation, Lao Tzu begins by emphasizing the continuous potential combination of new levels of yin and yang to achieve the highest levels of life's expression and experience and where to find these energies.

Single cultivation is a spiritually elevating experience with immeasurable benefits. We are surrounded by many forms of yin and yang energies. Lao Tzu tells us that the yang male energy can be found emanating from sources like the sun and mountains, while the female yin energy can be found reposed in the stillness of sources like the earth, moon, and lakes. By studying and understanding these dynamics, one can find the proper balance in yin and yang. By finding certain energies we can strengthen what needs to be strengthened and weaken that which needs to be weakened.

Unlike single cultivation, not everyone who embarks on a spiritual journey is ready for dual cultivation. However, in some cases, truly virtuous individuals who have cultivated themselves physically, mentally and spiritually may be chosen to learn and be instructed in the art of dual cultivation. In dual cultivation both yin and yang are directly integrated through sexual intercourse between a man and a woman. It is important to note that this practice requires genuine virtue and true mastery of self-cultivation in both participants. If these elements, along with others to be discussed later, are not present, then dual cultivation can have a destructive effect. However, when genuine virtue and true mastery of the Integral Way align in both participants, this practice can lead to profound balancing of one's gross and subtle energies and the miraculous transference and experience of the nature of being between the two partners themselves.

The result of this balancing and transfer can include improved health, harmonized emotions, the cessation of desires and impulses. At the highest level, dual cultivation, if properly practiced, results in the transcendent integration of the entire energy body formed by both partners. The circuitous exchange, leveling-out and the harmonizing of the yin and yang energies in the virtuous and masterful couple who can properly dually cultivate, results in a shared transcendent state of unity and profound harmony within them both.

"The highest levels of life are attainable, however; this requires one to continuously combine new and higher levels of Yin and Yang. In the natural world, the male energy Yang can be found in many sources. Most prominent among these powerful energy sources are the sun and the mountains.

The calming and receptive Yin energies can be found in sources like the moon, lakes and in the earth. But these bodies are only hinting as to where the energies of Yin and Yang may be found. Study these things and you will immeasurably benefit from it.

The conception of human life requires higher and more elevated Yin and Yang energies to accomplish its ends. Some genuinely virtuous students may be suited for instruction in the art of dual cultivation. In this practice both Yin and Yang are integrated directly through the

Tai chi formed by the male and female in
sexual intercourse.

In the practice of dual cultivation, the student must
be genuinely virtuous and the master who teaches the
discipline must be true otherwise, the practice will
end in calamity and have deleterious effects. However,
when done correctly, the experience and effects of dual
cultivation can be profound.

By balancing the student's gross and subtle Yin and Yang
energies, health can be improved, emotions harmonized,
impulses and desires caused to cease. At the highest
level of this discipline and practice, a transcendent
integration of the entire energy of the human
body occurs."

<u>Who Can Dually Cultivate</u>

Importantly, the passage above explores the concept of dual
cultivation. The instruction on how to combine new levels of
yin and yang through the sexual practice of dual cultivation
will follow in short order within the postscript for this chapter.

According to the teachings of Lao Tu, achieving the highest
levels of life requires a continual integration of higher and
higher levels of yin and yang. In nature, the male energy can
be found in sources such as the sun, the mountains and the
powerful rivers and waterfalls that flow beneath them. We can
absorb Yang energies by being close to these things. Female
energy can be found in sources such as the earth, the moon,
ponds, and lakes. When we are present near to these natural
phenomena, we absorb their calming yin qualities. By studying and understanding these energies, we can benefit greatly
from their integration. These profound energies resonate with
us because these same energies can also be found within male
and female human beings themselves.

For those who wish to integrate yin and yang in a more direct manner, through the yin and yang of the male and female human body, there is the practice of dual cultivation. This practice that appears to have begun with Lao Tzu involves the tai chi of sexual intercourse, where yin and yang energies are directly integrated. Because of its very powerful sexual nature, Lao Tzu teaches that because of the danger to the parties of doing it wrong, this practice must only be learned from a true master. Moreover, the participants must be genuinely virtuous and equally attracted to each other and the instruction must come from authentic sources. If dual cultivation is not taught by a true master or the student is not virtuous, dual cultivation can have a destructive and opposite effect from that which was intended.

When taught correctly and practiced virtuously, dual cultivation can bring about profound balancing of gross and subtle energies. It can result in improved health, harmonized emotions, the cessation of desires and impulses, and at the highest level, the transcendent integration of the entire energy body of yin and yang in the participating couple. By doing this, cou-les who are able can balance their spiritual energies and ready themselves for profound contact with ETs and NHIs. However evocative, dual cultivation is not necessary to invoke contact. Profound contact is most likely to be a result of Angelic Intercourse, a subject to be discussed infra.

POSTSCRIPT: THE PHYSICAL MECHANICS OF DUAL CULTIVATION

So, by now, you all must all be asking 'How is this all done and what are the mechanics involved in Dual Cultivation? Well, as taught to us by the Divine Immortals, in the practice of dual cultivation, the male's and female's energies are combined through the sexual act at what is also referred to as 'The Golden Pill'. The golden pill is the energetic epicenter that is created by the properly joined erect Yang penis and moist receptive vagina, yin. This accurate placement of male and female sexual organs is the union through which a complete sexual Tai Chi circuit is formed. In this dual cultivation of Tai Chi, each partner's intense Chi flows circuitously to and into the other partner and then back to the initiator again and again. When this physical energetic contact is maintained without orgasm, it creates a continuous spiritual circuit that builds energy and intensity. This intensity then is further magnified through and by the strength and amplitude of the sexual circuit as both partners continue to refrain from an involuntary orgasmic release as the pressure and compulsion to do so builds. The result can be quite a phenomenon, one that is a completely new experience for each half of the joined couple. Dual Cultivation goes well beyond orgasm. It is a sharing of both psyche and soul where one experiences the other's nature of being. It is the great gift of Universal Divine Energy that provides the remedy to complete, support and supplement the energy of those of truly great virtue.

The dual cultivation method is best taught by a proper master, but the proper and appropriate physical positioning for the "Golden Pill" is actually quite simple. When the truly virtuous couple is ready and the female physically able to be receptive, both may engage in the act of dual cultivation. First, and ideally, the male sits. Once the male is comfortably seated (on the floor or otherwise) and the male's penis is erect, the female straddles the male placing his penis inside of her vagina. Both the man and the woman remain seated with their torsos vertical and each facing the other. The heads of both remain above the torso so that the yin energies of each are at the top of the circuitous flow. Because both the man and woman are seated comfortably both are grounded in the earth allowing the yang polarity of the flow. The penis is placed into the vagina and the top of its head* is kept in contact with a special part the woman partner's vagina. **

This sensitive bean shaped area may feel a bit coarser than its surrounding area and is located about one to two inches or so on the anterior or upper side of the vaginal wall between the vagina and urethra. *** During arousal, this area becomes sexually sensitive to the female as it swells slightly and has a slightly corrugated or bumpy feel. This is the area where the top of the head and most sensitive portion of the male's penis needs to make and remain in contact throughout the coupling. Again, the purpose is not to orgasm, but it will sometimes happen, especially in younger and more sexually aroused. The greater the arousal, the greater the transfer of energy and control one can accomplish by not orgasming. The ability to not orgasm is what separates mankind's higher spiritual energy from that of other animals.

The great secret of dual cultivation, however, is that the actual physical position or form of intercourse is not really relevant at all. Because cultivation, whether singular or dual is a spiritual one, in order for one to achieve the immortality of being though it, what is important is for any Integral Universal being who wishes to cultivate, share and refine his or her energy, it is necessary for him or her to have sufficient yang energy to cultivate and refine. In order to do this, learning how to singularly cultivate oneself is of the utmost importance in approaching Dual Cultivation.

*The "glans" or head of the male penis is comparable to the female clitoris in that it has the most highly concentrated and most of the nerve endings in the male genitalia. Both the clitoris and glans, in fact, originate from the same material in utero and develop along x-y chromosomal lines throughout life and connect with the spinal cord through nerve roots in the spine beneath the lumbar area in the sacrum. Having about 4,000 nerve endings, compared to the 6,000-8,000 nerve endings in a woman's clitoris, the highest concentration of these nerves in men is around the outer ridge of the male glans making it the most physiologically and neurologically sensitive of all the external erogenous zones in the male body.

**Known today as the "Grafenberg spot" commonly referred to as the 'G-spot'.

***The G-spot is believed to be the female equivalent of the male prostate gland. The analysis of the G-spot or CUV complex is strictly connected with the experience of female sexual pleasure. The reflex arc responsible for orgasm starts from the receptors of the clitoral complex, which convey sensation through somatic afferents of the pudendal nerves including the dorsal nerve of the clitoris and the perineal branches up to the sacral spinal cord nerve roots S2–S4, from where visceral parasympathetic efferent fibers responsible for the vasodilation at genital level reach the erectile tissue [44]. https://link.springer.com/article/10.1007/s11930-021-00311-w#ref-CR44. Among other things, this female genital erection leads to sexual arousal and if continued it triggers orgasm through the sympathetic fibers from the T12 to L1 vertebrae. These nerves, in turn modify the orgasmic contraction of the muscles of the urethra, vagina and anal sphincters via autonomic innervation. They accompany sensitive, cognitive and emotional changes as well and provide at least part of a feedback loop for energy through the neurological system of one and both parties who engage in dual cultivation.

CHAPTER 68

Angelic Dual Cultivation

The concept Lao Tzu presents in this passage is that of Angelic Dual Cultivation, also known as Angelic Intercourse. Just as in Dual Cultivation, Lao Tzu also highlights the importance of sincerity and following the Tao in this form of dual cultivation. Angelic Intercourse is an important means of readying oneself for the initiating contact with ETs and NHIs through the consciousness driven CE-5* modality of contact.

The Tao, described as "elusive", reveals itself initially in form and image but ultimately dissolves into a subtle and indefinable essence. It is considered uncreated, yet it is the creator of all things. It has no substance and can enter spaces where there seems to be none. By returning to itself and remaining gentle and yielding, it achieves victories and overcomes the hardness of the world with its softness. It is with this yielding softness that we use our consciousnesses to enter Yu Ching, the Tao's Subtle Realm to invoke contact with the "divine immortals", the "highest spiritual beings" of the universe and watch as the "unruling rulers and uncreating creators of the universe's divine immortal realm" dance their "magnificent magical dance" for us.

Both Angelic Intercourse and CE-r imply the benefit of non-action and meditative silence. Non-action, also known as Wu Wei, does not refer to complete inactivity but rather aligning one's actions with the natural flow of the Tao. Angelic Dual Intercourse and CE-5 involves allowing things to unfold naturally without forcing or interfering, like water flowing effortlessly. Silence, both externally and internally, allows US to tune in to the subtle essence of the Tao and be receptive to its guidance BOTH WITH OUR angelic partners and ET/NHI.

Because non-action and silence provide an opportunity for deeper connection with the Tao, they also create space for inner stillness, observation, and attunement to the harmonious rhythms of existence. They allow for the dissolution of ego-driven desires and actions, enabling a more profound alignment with the natural order of the universe, with each other and the celestial beings that inhabit it.

By practicing non-action and silence in both CE-5 and in Angelic Dual Cultivation, we can cultivate a state of receptivity, clarity, and harmonious action, which can lead to a deeper understanding of each other, the Tao and its influence on our lives and our intimate connection to our partners and ET/NHI.

"From dual cultivation we move on to following the Tao and the Integral Way through the practice of angelic dual cultivation. Because angelic dual cultivation is illusive, this approach to the Tao requires one's complete and entire sincerity.

Angelic dual cultivation begins to first reveal itself in physical form and mental image. It then dissolves itself into the Tao's undefinable subtle essence.

Like the Tao, this unidentified subtle essence itself is uncreated yet all things are created by it. Because it is without substance, it can enter anywhere, even where there is no space at all. Gentle and yielding the subtle essence exercises itself by flowing outward and then returning to itself. Softer than all things, by being soft and yielding the Tao's subtle essence triumphs by overcoming anything hard. Its very existence is a demonstrative lesson about the benefit of silence and Wu Wei."

Angelic Dual Cultivation, Angelic Intercourse, ET/NHI CONTACT and World Peace

The concept of Angelic Dual Cultivation involves learning to follow the Tao, which can be elusive and difficult to comprehend, especially for those in the West whose history and beliefs have been steeped in the physical world of materialism. To approach the Tao, we must approach it with sincerity and dedication. The Tao is first revealed by what we see and sense in form and image, but it ultimately dissolves into subtle, indefinable essence. Despite being uncreated itself, the Tao creates all things. Because it has no substance, it can enter where there is no space and create substance wherever it chooses.

Exercising its power by returning to itself and winning victories by remaining gentle and yielding, the Tao, like water, is softer than anything and therefore can overcome everything hard. This teaches us about the benefit of non-action and silence. Silence is a very powerful thing. Whether we are alone or with others, through non-action and silence, we can cultivate our energy and reach a deeper understanding of the Tao and reach into her essence to invoke her blessings. ET/NHI contact is one of her blessings. This can be gained through Angelic Dual Cultivation, AKA, Angelic Intercourse.

In angelic dual cultivation, the focus is on cultivating energy through following the Tao and achieving a harmonious balance between yin and yang. The practice is not just about physical union, but rather about aligning oneself with the Tao and achieving a state of pure consciousness. This state can be attained through meditative silence and non-action, creating a profound understanding of the universe and one's place within it. This understanding is beyond time and space. It is also capable of being shared mentally, physically, and spiritually with each other and with ETs and NHIs.

The concept of angelic dual cultivation emphasizes following the Tao and achieving a harmonious balance in life. Through patient non-action and meditative silence, we can align ourselves with the Tao and achieve a state of pure consciousness. By doing so, we can gain a deeper understanding of the universe and our and the place of ET/NHIs and all other beings within it. By cultivating energy through the Tao and exercising patience and silence through Wu Wei we can also develop our abilities to make contact with ET/NHIs and the other highly advanced spiritual and divine beings throughout the universe, the "unruling rulers and uncreating creators of the vast universe" that inhabit the cosmos and both the Tao's mortal and her immortal realm.

CHAPTER 69

Sexuality and Spirituality: Dual Cultivation and Angelic Intercourse

Keeping in mind that Lao Tzu holds the immortals of the divine realm of the highest spiritual order, importantly, this passage discusses further the highest human spiritual practices of angelic and dual cultivation, the rudiments of which we were introduced in the preceding chapters. Here in chapter 69, Lao Tzu describes and highlights for us the different approaches to sexuality and their relationship to a person's level of spiritual evolution.

Lao Tzu rightly observes that unevolved individuals primarily focus on ordinary sexual intercourse, which places excessive emphasis on the sexual organs while neglecting the body's other organs and systems. In this rather base and animalistic approach, physical energy is accumulated and discharged for either reproduction or pleasure without consideration for the subtle energies they entail. This lack of concern leads to their dissipation and disorder. Regular or recreational sexual intercourse is therefore seen generally as a backward leap in terms of spiritual evolution, especially when these energies may be consciously amplified and internalized through the practices of single, dual and angelic cultivation.

For those aspiring to higher realms of living, in addition to the basics of single cultivation, self-cultivation also includes the practices of dual cultivation and angelic dual cultivation. In these practices, the emphasis shifts from the sexual organs (Tai Ching) to the integration of yin and yang energies throughout the body, mind, (Shang Ching) and spirit (Yu Ching). Dual Cultivation is based in human physicality and brings us beyond the sexual experience to a rather mystical energetic and spiritual one, the Li of Yu Ching. Angelic intercourse is described as being led by the spirit rather than solely relying on the sexual organs. It, like the other forms of self-cultivation, is characterized by relaxation, calmness, quietude, and a natural flow. These are all characteristics of the meditative state, and all are quintessential to both angelic intercourse and establishing ET/NHI contact.

Whereas ordinary intercourse focuses on the union of sex organs, and dual cultivation brings the focus away from the sexual organs, angelic cultivation does not require the use of the sexual organs in any special way. It aims to unite the spirits, minds, and every cell of one body with every cell of the other body. Instead of dissolution, it culminates in integration, offering an opportunity for mutual transformation and shared upliftment of both partners into a realm of conscious bliss and wholeness.

Finally, the sacred teachings of angelic intercourse are said to be imparted by individuals who have achieved total energy integration themselves and are only shared with devoted students who follow the Integral Way. As we know, this path involves seeking purification and pacification not only within oneself but also in the world at large. In modern times, bonafide teachers of angelic cultivation may be difficult to find. So, it is also important to note that Lao Tzu tells us that, in certain cases, individuals with radiant virtue may be able to receive these celestial teachings directly from the immortals in the subtle realm themselves. This is another confirmation from Lao Tzu that our teachers here on earth may not always be from here. Consequently, it is essential to approach one's teachers with discernment to respect diverse life forms and their different means of appearance and communication. This is true especially if one intends to incorporate the practices of dual and angelic cultivation in their own evolving Tao-centered life and into their contact and social intercourse with ETs and NHIs.

"One's approach to sexuality is an indicia of the level of one's own evolution. Those persons who are unevolved engage in ordinary sexual intercourse. This sort of coitus puts all its emphasis upon the sexual organs and ignores the body's other organs and systems. Such sexual practice is a great leap backwards because instead of heightening one's accumulated subtle energies, it summarily discharges, disorders and dissipates them. Angelic dual cultivation is a practice that is reserved for those who seek not the lower but the higher realms of life.

Because the body seeks balance and equilibrium, every part of the human body, mind, spirit complex desires and seeks the integration of Yin and Yang. The intercourse of higher beings is led not by the genitals but by the spirit. That is why this sort of intercourse is called 'Angelic Intercourse'.

Where regular intercourse takes effort, the angelic intercourse practiced in angelic dual cultivation is quiet, relaxed, calm and natural. In ordinary sexual intercourse the sexual organs are united. In angelic cultivation spirit unites with spirit, mind with mind and body unites with body even down to the cellular level.

The culmination of angelic dual cultivation results in the integration of the energies of body, mind and spirit, not their dissolution. Angelic dual cultivation is an opportunity for the mutual transformation and spiritual refinement of virtuous men and women and to elevate each other into the realm of wholeness and bliss.

A word of caution however, the ways of angelic intercourse are sacred and should be learned from a master who has achieved total energy integration. It should be taught only to virtuous students who have a

profound devotion to following the Integral way. Such
a student is one who seeks to purify and pacify not only
their own being but that of the entire world.

Finally, if one's virtue is exceptionally radiant it is
possible to open up a pathway into the subtle realm
of the Tao and receive instruction in these celestial
teachings from the immortals directly."

The Celestial Teachings of the Immortals

Do you have the most profound of devotions? Do you seek to
pacify your being and purify your own self-so? Do you thirst to
bring peace to the entire world along with your own suchnes?
If so, then you are ready for these teachings and move from the
physical and mental realms into the heightened spiritual ones.

Because of the requirement of self-control and placing the angelic world ahead of the animal one, one's approach to sexuality
is considered to be a sign of an individual's level of evolution.
Those who are unevolved practice ordinary sexual intercourse,
which emphasizes the sexual organs and physical orgasm yet
neglects other organs and energy systems of the body. This
leads to the accumulation and need to discharge physical energy, with one's subtle energies being disordered and dissipated.

For those who aspire to higher realms of living, there is the
concept of angelic dual cultivation, also known as "Angelic
Intercourse". This sacred practice is led by the spirit rather than
the sexual organs. Angelic intercourse involves the integration
of every portion of the body, mind, and spirit as all yearn for
the balancing and proper direction of yin and yang. Unlike
ordinary intercourse, angelic cultivation is calm, relaxed, quiet,
and natural. It unites spirit with spirit, mind with mind, and
every cell of one body with every cell of one body with another
body. The result is integration rather than dissolution, giving
individuals the opportunity to blend energies, and mutually

transform and uplift each other and their energies into a realm of bliss and wholeness.

Ultimately, the way in which we approach sexuality is considered an indication of our level of mental, physical and spiritual evolution. Because angelic intercourse is not based in human sexuality, ones who seek to enter and experience the joy and health attendant to higher physical, mental and spiritual realms of living can practice angelic dual cultivation to integrate, transform, and uplift their own and each partner's energies toward the Yu Ching state.

Finally, according to Lao Tzu the sacred ways of angelic intercourse are taught only by those who have achieved total energy integration. They are learned only by students who follow the Integral Way with profound devotion and nobly seek to purify and pacify the entire world along with their own being. However, even without a teacher, it is also possible for one's virtue to be especially radiant, thus opening a pathway to the subtle realm and allowing us to receive these celestial teachings directly from the "immortals", the ET/NHIs and divine beings of the angelic realm themselves. The forms of education and learning make themselves available to the virtuous as they share their virtue and compassion with others. If you build the temple within, your teachers will come to find you once you are ready.

POSTSCRIPT: THE MECHANICS OF ANGELIC DUAL CULTIVATION AND ANGELIC INTERCOURSE

The Mechanics of Angelic Dual Cultivation

The purpose of spiritual cultivation and immortal practice of Angelic Intercourse is to unite us with each other and bring the often-illusive sensation of oneness to realization and fruition by channeling our outward sexual energies and impulses inwardly to the mind and body. When this union of the essence of the mind and the essence of the body and spirit occurs, we can be said to be truly spiritually achieved in this very peculiarly special yet simple human way. This achievement can then be projected out in order to make contact with the Divine ones.

Lao Tzu does not go into detail about the mechanics of either dual or angelic cultivation, however; an understanding of the mechanics of both Dual Cultivation and Angelic Dual Cultivation are important in the pursuit of spiritual evolution as Integral beings. Whereas both Dual Cultivation and common sexual intercourse unite female and male sexual organs, like Angelic Cultivation, all forms of truly Angelic Dual Cultivation or "Angelic Intercourse" enigmatically, involve no sexual intercourse at all. Both Dual and Angelic Dual Cultivation involve the senses that unite the partners' mind with mind, spirit with spirit through the body's senses and organs of which touch and skin are very important ones. In this way, all the cells of one of the couple's bodies unite with the electromagnetic fields and all the bodily cells of the other. Instead of concluding in dissolution and energy disintegration, Angelic Intercourse is ultimately a heightened conscious meditative state that produces a unified energy current and electromagnetic field that culminates in the integration of mental, physical and spiritual energies. Without the element of sexual intercourse, Angelic dual cultivation provides an opportunity for both the man and the woman, especially those too old or infirm to engage in sexual intercourse to integrate, uplift and transform each other's physical body and consciousness into a realm of wholeness, compassion, and bliss without the necessity of sexual intercourse. Because Angelic intercourse is based on mutual love, care and compassion, Angelic Intercourse may even be engaged in without physical touching or contact whatsoever. It is mind meeting mind and soul meeting, surrendering and supplicating itself with another's in order to merge with divine energies of the Tao.

Our entire bodies, every portion, even our mind and spirit yearn for the integration of yin and yang into a balanced and harmonious Tai Chi. As in dual cultivation, Angelic dual cultivation involves a man and a woman. Unlike dual cultivation, however, angelic dual cultivation is not led by the sexual organs but only by the spirit of two virtuous, loving, sincere and compassionate people. Ordinary intercourse is full of effort. Even Dual Cultivation involves an intense sexual connection. Even though Angelic dual cultivation and Angelic intercourse may involve contact with all the parts of the physical bodies without neglect, the contact is directed entirely by the spirit itself, not the body. The body is merely the instrument through which the music of Angelic Intercourse is allowed to play.

Although some retired sexual energies may be involved, because Angelic Intercourse does not involve the "Golden Pill" formed by the sexual and energetic coupling of dual cultivation. It is technically neither a sexual refinement nor a physical practice. It is though, a mental and spiritual one. Angelic Intercourse is called "Angelic" because it not only exceeds the sexual realm but the physical realm altogether. According to Lao Tzu, it also can also place us in touch with the "Angels" of the divine realm. These are the ancient masters of the Integral Way, the unruling rulers and uncreating creators of the vast multi-universe, the Immortal Integral Universal Beings of the Divine Realm. These are the divine beings who taught the techniques of Single, Dual and Angelic cultivation to mankind long ago.

When done correctly, Angelic Intercourse is engaged in when a couple is in agreement. It can be properly performed when both participants are relaxed, calm, quiet and the inclination towards each other is natural. Angelic cultivation is done with little, if any exertion by the parties. It is done in a calm, meditative state, one that produces a crystal clear enlightened, elevated spiritual, mental and physical awareness. This awareness is one of the couples of themselves who are both acutely aware of each other and their surroundings. In this heightened state both are aware of what is happening to them and around them. Angelic Intercourse, at its essence, is a very special form of meditative Angelic communication. Ultimately. ET/NHI pick up on this and can be very easily attracted through the engaging the protocols of CE-5.

Self-Cultivation by the Divine Immortals and the Angelic Realm

But what if one is motivated to self-cultivation yet cannot find a teacher to further guide them through the various forms of spiritual cultivation? If this is the case, one should understands the immortal truth of life that all things are one and connected through the Tao, by extending their virtue selflessly and compassionately to the world, the immortal truth will become evident. Once it is evident, the Tao, the "Immortal Truth", will unite naturally with him or her. Those who have learned the immortal truth of life and extend their virtue to the world for the purpose of accomplishing world peace and purification will be prepared for the instruction and study the general principles of achieving energy integration in the ways that have been instructed in the past chapters and the present one.

When we follow the Integral Universal Way and extend our virtue and sincerity to the world, we naturally radiate our virtuous influence to the world. If we learn to cultivate ourselves correctly, we develop our subtle energy and reconnect ourselves with the Tao's subtle realm. Once we have learned to reconnect ourselves with the subtle realm. There we can make contact with the Angels of the Integral Wau and witjin the subtle realm initiate and engage in Angelic Intercourse with the Divine ones themselves.

Once one has learned to enter the Divine subtle realm, even without a human teacher or guide, Lao Tzu reassures us that the Divine immortals will come and appear themselves to guide and instruct us further. Sometimes their counsel, instruction and teaching will be beyond the sound of words. It is "gnosis at the level of understanding" *. To receive this guidance is the miraculous pinnacle of existence in our lifetime on this earth. Meeting the Divine ones through the interconnectedness of the Tao is the reason for all of our spiritual, mental and physical cultivations in this life and it forms the spiritual underpinnings for us in this life and all our other subsequent lives.

Conclusion

It is possible for us refine our sexual energies through Angelic Intercourse without Dual Cultivation so that we too may increase the probability of significant encounters the ancient immortals of whom Lao Tzu writes? In the Angelic realm of intercourse, physicality remains of little, if any relevance. The body and mind are merely tools for the eternal soul, the conscious spirit to exist in the physical material realm. Think of self-cultivation as the development of your soul through the recognition and development of your own spiritual energy. Mind unites with mind and spirit unites with spirit. Except for the purpose of maintaining life and doing the work of the Tao, it is not necessary for ones who have consciously entered the Angelic Realm of existence to be physical.

The Angelic realm is the highest elevation of the refined spiritual energy of the Tao. One need not go through Dual Cultivation in order to have profoundly refined spiritual elevation and to make contact with the Angelic Immortals. Practicing true and sincere virtue and having a true concern for the peace and wellbeing of your fellow human beings can be enough. If you have these things then the practice of Angelic intercourse can help accelerate and amplify your spiritual evolution and the probability of significant ET/NHI contact enormously.

Dedicated students of the Integral Way can self-cultivate and learn these teachings about Single, Dual and Angelic cultivation from their human teachers or even these celestial teachings directly from the "immortals", those angelic "unruling rulers and uncreating creators" who have entered the Tao's divine immortal realm. This realm incorporates those of both being and non-being. "Why or how can this happen?" one might ask. It can happen and will happen for those who pursue truth and follow the Tao.

Contact with ET/NHI is an inevitable outcome for those who practice virtue and share their compassion with others to put the world at peace and make it a better place. The law of energy response tells us that if this is the energy that we put out into the universe, the Tao will see to it that the universe will reflect that energy back to us. So, do not despair. Eventually, if you pursue truth and devote yourself to the practice of simplicity, patience and undiscriminating compassion and become a person of truth and lead by your example, your teachers will appear and the gifts they will bestow upon you, will be immeasurable. I write this from the humble sincerity born of my own experience and my own personal knowledge. - NMM

*Dr. Joseph Burkes

CHAPTER 70

The Benefits of Dual Cultivation and Angelic Intercourse

In this passage, Lao Tzu warns us of the difficulty ahead for the ones who choose the path of spiritual emancipation and freedom. He emphasizes the problematic entanglement of passion and desire, which creates a binding net around us so that we may be ensnared by them. Worldly confrontations further contribute to our petrification by stiffness and inflexibility, while the trap of duality holds us back from experiencing our singular liberation. Lao Tzu again emphasizes that through Duality Cultivation and Dual Angelic Cultivation that it is possible to unravel this net, soften rigidity, and dismantle the trap that duality presents to each and every one of us.

For those who need strength, by dissolving one's yin energy into the universal source of life and attracting yang energy from the same source, the individual transcends their individuality and merges with pure nature. For those who suffer from an overabundance of Yang energy, by dissolving their Yang energy into the Tao and attracting its divine yin energy of the one also transcends the individual ego and merges with pure nature. In this balanced state, free from ego, one lives in alignment with natural principles, works virtuously, and becomes infused with boundless vitality. This transformation leads not only to a better life but to his or her liberation from the cycle of death and rebirth.

Finally, this passage highlights the fact that our spiritual freedom and oneness with the Tao are not gifts randomly bestowed on us but are rewards that arise from each of our own conscious self-cultivation and our resultant self-transformation, evolution and spiritual refinement. It concludes that by consciously engaging in practices that dissolve ego, align with universal principles, and cultivate vitality, we can experience a permanent spiritual liberation and unity with the Tao.

"Oft times our own spiritual emancipation becomes a difficult task. Like the threads of a spider's web, passion and desire weave themselves around us. Unyielding and inflexible does our worldly confrontation make us. Duality's trap is tenacious. Trapped, bound and rigid, we are unable to experience true spiritual liberation.

However tight the cords and knots that bind us may be, the key to our own deliverance can be found in the practice of dual cultivation. Through dual cultivation, we can soften the bonds of our rigidity and free ourselves from duality's pernicious trap. When we dissolve our yin energy back into the Tao, the source of all life. From her, from that same source, we can attract new Yang energy. By dissolving our energy into the Tao and filling the void with the Tao's own subtle and most refined energy one abandons their own individuality and becomes pure nature, one with the Tao.

Free yourselves from the confines of ego and forever liberate yourselves from the constant cycle of life and death. We are free to live naturally and work virtuously.

If you understand anything, understand this. Our own spiritual freedom, our oneness with the Tao and eternal life are not gifts that are just randomly bestowed. They are the actual rewards of our own self cultivation and self-evolution and fruits of our spiritual refinement and self-transformation."

The Fruits of our own Self-cultivation, Spiritual Refinement and Self-transformation

The cords of passion and desire can be a binding net around us, causing us to become trapped in a cycle of duality and physical rebirth. Worldly confrontations can make us stiff and inflexible, unable to soften or to be flexible, we cannot experience liberation. However, through dual cultivation, it is possible to untie the knots, unravel this net, soften our rigidity, and dismantle the trap through our own Tao-like flexibility. Remember how Lao Tzu taught us to "Be like water".

We have, by now spent a dozen chapters learning about dual cultivation and the forms it takes. At its basic essence what is meant by "dual cultivation" is the practice of balancing the yin and yang energies within oneself and with another. It involves dissolving yin or yang energy through a partner into the source of universal life and attracting the appropriate yin or yang energy from that same source. It is because of these certain energies are naturally attracted to others. The goal of these transcendent practices of self-cultivation is to live naturally and leave behind individuality and become one with the natural energy of the Tao, free of ego.

Many may wonder why they should bother with these practices, especially ones that might involve sharing ourselves spiritually, mentally, or even physically with another. The answer is simple. The spiritual freedom and oneness with the Tao that we experience when we follow the Integral Way and by dual cultivation are not randomly bestowed gifts, but the rewards of conscious self-transformation and self-evolution. These are gifts that by their nature need to be shared whenever possible. When one become filled with inexhaustible vitality and are liberated forever from the cycle of death and rebirth through both deal and Angelic dual cultivation, they understand the true benefits and spiritual rewards of such practices.

So why does Lao Tzu bring up the subject of duality and the ego traps laid by passion and desire? It is because, in the realm of physical closeness, these things must be dissolved so that the spiritual realm may be entered. In order to engage in dual cultivation, one must jettison ego. Self-cultivation can be a long and arduous process, but it begins with recognizing the cords of passion and desire that are holding us back. We must learn to identify these cords and begin the process of unraveling them. This can be done through meditation, introspection, and a commitment to personal growth and transformation. The Integral Way may not be the only way, but it is a simple, patient and compassionate one

Whatever way one chooses to follow, they must open their hearts, work on softening their rigidity and dismantle the trap of duality. This can be achieved through practices such as yoga, tai chi, and other forms of movement meditation. By doing so, you will begin to attract the energy they need for example, to become one with nature and experience true freedom and vitality.

Ultimately, if we want to experience true spiritual freedom and oneness with the Tao, then we must commit ourselves to the practices of dual cultivation. It is not an easy path, but it is one that will bring about great rewards for those who are willing to put in the effort. So take the first step towards your connection with ET/NHIs and becoming one with someone you love and sharing the Tao with them and with the unruling rulers and uncreating creators of the vast universe. Begin the process of self-cultivation by freeing yourself from the cords of passion and desire. Experience freedom, true liberation and eternal life. This is the path of all true integral universal and divine beings throughout the universe. Once you have decided to enter and walk on this path you will be recognized as one of them by them all.

CHAPTER 71

Rome Was Not Built in a Day

In the passage below Lao Tzu emphasizes the gradual process of transformation towards divinity and eternal life. He teaches us that purification and upliftment of the heavy and gross energies of the body, mind, and spirit are necessary as a first step. Once the energy reaches a more refined and subtle level, self-mastery can realistically be pursued.

According to the passage, a wise instructor teaches the principles of self-integration only to those who virtuous students of self-cultivation who have already achieved a high level of self-purification and self-mastery. Furthermore, Lao Tzu reminds us that effective teaching follows the Law of Energy Response, meaning that the most suitable method is the one that harmoniously resonates with the student's natural energy. For some individuals who self-integrate, celibacy and self-cultivation may be appropriate, while for others, properly guided dual and Angelic dual cultivation may yield the greatest benefits. A discerning teacher will assess the right balance of practices for each individual.

It's important to note that all teachers and techniques are considered transitional in this context, serving as guides along the path of self-realization. The ultimate realization of the self comes from the direct merger of one's being with the divine energy of the Tao.

These teachings reflect a specific perspective and approach to spiritual development. Different philosophical and spiritual traditions may have varied views and practices. It's important for individuals to explore their own beliefs and values and find approaches that resonate with their own inner truth and experiences. However, for those who want to focus on their own self cultivation and the cultivation of their society towards a higher form of universal being there is the integral Way and the integration of one's being with the Tao. This is the path that the highest spiritual beings in the universe and their societies have followed for eons now. It is difficult to create another way when the present one works so efficiently and effectively. .

"The transformative road toward spiritual liberation and eternal life is a gradual one. First the heavy gross energies of the body, mind and spirit must be lightened, purified, and uplifted. When our awareness and energies ascend to the subtle level*, then one can truly seek self-mastery.

Wise instructors understand that the potent principles of self-cultivation and self-integration should only be reserved for those virtuous students who already have mastered high levels of self-mastery and self-purification. **

A wise instructor also knows that each student is different and will have certain natural proclivities and aptitudes. All proper instruction therefore should follow the Law of Energy Response. The most efficacious methods are those to which the natural energies of the student most harmoniously respond.

For some students, celibacy and self-cultivation will evoke the most productive response. For others, properly guided dual cultivation will appropriately provide the greatest benefit. A good teacher will determine the proper mix and balance of practices for each individual student.

However, if there is anything to remember about teaching, remember that all techniques and all teachers

are transitional. One's true and direct realization of the Tao comes only from the direct merger of the energies of the Tao with one's own being."

<u>The Path Towards Divine Being and Eternal Life</u>

Eternal life has been the dream of mankind since time immemorial, and many cultures and religions offer different paths towards achieving this goal. The path towards eternal life is not an easy one and requires the purification and upliftment of body, mind, and spirit. Moreover, one cannot achieve self-mastery until one has reached a high level of self-purification. A wise instructor teaches the principles of self-integration only to those who have already achieved a high level of self-mastery and the spiritual purification that they have found by following the Integral Way. The transformation towards eternal life is a gradual one. It is entered the doors of self-purification and then self-mastery.

The first step towards our conscious experience of eternal life is found in self-purification. The longer we live in the world of ten thousand things, the more the physical, mental and spiritual baggage that we accumulate. We need to purify the heavy, gross energies of body, mind, and spirit that we have accumulated over this lifetime and even from our earlier existences. This enlightenment requires discipline and dedication. One must first simplify one's life. Then follow a proper diet, exercise regularly, meditate and practice mindfulness. By doing this, one can cleanse negative energy and achieve inner peace. The next step is upliftment towards the subtle level. This can be achieved through meditation, yoga, qi gong, and other spiritual practices mentioned in earlier chapters that focus on the subtle energy of the body. In this way, one can connect with the divine energy of the Tao.

Once one has achieved a high level of self-purification, then self-mastery can be sought. Manifest the proper energy and the proper teacher will find you. This is one of the ways that the Law of Energy Response synchronistically operates.

All Teachers and Methods Are Transitory

Self-cultivation is a process. It happens in stages. A wise instructor teaches the powerful principles of self-integration only to those who have already achieved a high level of self-student's further mastery and purification. The teacher will also determine the proper balance of practices for each individual student, as the most effective method is always that to which the student's natural energy most harmoniously responds. For one, celibacy and self-cultivation will be appropriate, while for another, properly guided dual cultivation will derive the greatest benefit.

However, it is essential to note that all teachers and techniques are only transitional and transitory at best. True realization of one's own selfhood comes from the direct merger of one's being with the divine energy of the Tao. The ultimate aim of the self is to achieve oneness with the divine, and this can only be achieved through continued spiritual practice and dedication. This can and will happen with or without one ever actually finding a human teacher.

Ultimately, the path towards divinity and the conscious realization of eternal life requires self-discipline, self-dedication, and self-purification. Our own self-mastery can only be achieved once one has reached a sufficiently high level of self-purification. A wise instructor teaches the powerful principles of self-integration only to those who have already achieved a high level of self-mastery and purification. Without attaining such a level, the teachings of a master cannot be grasped.

However, despite the absence of any teacher, the Tao is there only to be discovered by each one of us. This is why all techniques and teachers are seen only as transitional. Our true realization of the Tao comes from the direct merger of our being with the divine energy of the Tao. This integration is a lifelong one. This merger is there for all who follow the Integral Way. With or without a teacher, it is therefore crucial for each of us to continue our spiritual practices and dedication towards having eternal life until we enter that realm whether it is here as divine beings in this lifetime or after as divine universal beings, the unruling rulers and uncreating creators of the vast universe.

*The level of Yu Ching where one's chi is realized and balanced
**A student's self-motivation to learn on his own and his or her levels of achievement without the benefit of the teachings of a true master shows the teacher how devoted and dedicated a student is.

CHAPTER 72

How to Unite with the Divine

In the last passage we learned that it is possible to realize our own divinity and oneness with the Tao, even if we never encounter a true teacher of the Integral Way in our daily lives. In this passage Lao Tzu begins to bring us all and his teachings full circle by teaching us exactly and simply how to become divine and enter eternal life. As he did in earlier chapters, Lao Tzu emphasizes the importance of us developing our true virtue and extending it to the world as a means to gain merit and to unite with the divine.

Lao Tzu reminds us to let go of elaborate theological concepts and imaginary ideas and instead engage in ordinary daily work, such as healing and in being of service to others. The focus for those who enter the Integral Way is on abandoning conflict and strife and practicing unwavering kindness and infinite patience. This is not only how we perfect ourselves as integral beings, but it is the behavior of all evolved intelligent life in the universe.

Lao Tzu also advises us against following destructive impulses and ambitious pursuits that disrupt the harmony of the mind and distance us from the Integral Way. He encourages maintaining awareness by being vigilant of circumstances without becoming excessively attached to them. Managing the mind involves recognizing the inherent emptiness of all things and releasing attachment to that emptiness.

These teachings also emphasize the value of virtuous actions and of simplicity, and mindfulness as a means to align with the divine and cultivate a harmonious existence. Lao Tzu finally reminds individuals to let go of negative tendencies, cultivate positive qualities, and maintain a balanced perspective.

> **"If you want to increase your merit and unify with the Tao then develop your virtue and then hold it forth and give it unconditionally to the world. If you have imaginary ideas or fancy thoughts, abandon them. Go out and do some ordinary daily work. Become a healer. Relinquish conflict. Let go of strife. Practice the wisdom of unwavering kindness and unceasing patience. Avoid being impulsive. Don't pursue ambitions that ruin your mind's wholeness or cause you separation from the Integral Way. Avoid obsession with circumstances, yet do not avoid your awareness of them. To guide your mind, understand that there is nothing (no thing). Then let go of all attachment to the nothingness. "**

How to Perfect One's Relationship with the Tao

To develop one's virtue is to gain merit and become one with the Tao. It is through acting in concert with the Tao that we bring our self-cultivation and integration with the Tao into fruition.

The pursuit of spiritual enlightenment has been a central theme in many cultures throughout history. If you wish to gain merit and become one with the divine, then it is crucial to develop your virtue and extend it to the world. In this passage Lao Tzu explores the importance of letting go of fancy theologies and imaginary ideas and doing some ordinary daily work. Because we all carry our wounds and do our best to either cope with them or conceal them, Lao Tzu advises us to become healers. We can all be healers by avoiding conflict and strife, practicing unconditional and indiscriminating kindness and patience, and managing our minds so as to relinquish all attachment and experience no-thing-ness; and finally, even to release ourselves from the experience of that nothingness itself.

Many people are drawn to theologies and ideas that promise extravagant rewards for spiritual practices. However, these ideas often come with rules, regulations, and strict adherence to certain rituals. By contrast, Lao Tzu points out that these complications are unnecessary for those who follow the Integral Way. Developing our innate virtue is a much simpler approach. Lao Tzu's method simply emphasizes self-improvement and through that, the betterment of the world. By cultivating virtues such as honesty, integrity, simplicity, patience, compassion, and humility, we can elevate our consciousness and through practicing mindfulness, we can all connect with the divine.

One practical way to improve our virtue is to be humble. Humility is found in doing ordinary daily work. It can be found in cleaning one's home or yard, by reconnecting with the earth and by growing things of sustenance and beauty. We can improve our virtue by first healing ourselves and then others by exercising compassion and forgiveness. We can improve our virtue by helping others. When we help others we demonstrate kindness, empathy, and selflessness, which are all important virtues. Whether one is a healthcare worker, a teacher, a volunteer, or somebody who is helpful around the office, the shop, the factory or the home. Every action we take to help others contributes to our spiritual growth and benefits the world and the universe beyond. There is no thought, word or deed that is not connected to everything else. Each has an effect on another. To understand this is to understand the nature of the Oneness.

Another crucial aspect of developing our virtue is by avoiding conflict and strife. Just as the body and the mind is connected so too is the individual and his or her environment. Conflict can be damaging to our mental and emotional health and can create a barrier to spiritual growth. By practicing unswerving kindness and unending patience, we can navigate difficult situations with grace and compassion and reduce the stress on ourselves and others thereby making the world and the universe beyond a more livable place.

Managing our own mind is also essential to gaining merit and becoming one with the divine. To manage the mind effectively, we need to know that there is nothing and then relinquish all attachment even to nothingness. This approach enables us to detach ourselves from negative thoughts and emotions, which can cloud our perception of reality. By focusing our minds on the present moment, we can enhance our awareness and connect with the divine.

In the end, developing our virtue is critical to gaining merit and becoming one with the divine. We can do this by avoiding dualistic and complicated theologies and eschewing the imaginary ideas of those whose philosophies would divide and conquer us. We can become manifestations of the Tao by doing ordinary daily work, by healing, and by avoiding conflict and strife, practicing kindness and patience, and managing our minds to relinquish all attachment to nothingness. We can elevate our consciousness and connect with the Tao and connect with all the highest spiritual beings and advanced non-human entities, the immortal angels who dwell within her and who follow the universal Integral Way.

CHAPTER 73

The Proper Student-Teacher Relationship

Some who seek to find their own conscious spiritual divinity and eternal life will have the good fortune to be found by a suitable mentor and teacher of the Integral Way. Because the relationship between the teacher and the student must be a pure one, spiritual contamination in the teacher-student relationship is an impediment that must be avoided. If it exists before the relationship begins then it must be cured before the relationship can begin and progress in earnest. Here, in this passage, Lao Tzu sets forth the spiritual underpinnings for the student teacher relationship.

According to Lao Tzu, spiritual purity is an elemental component of the teacher/student relationship. If the relationship is in danger of corruption in any way, the cleansing of spiritual contamination is the responsibility of the student, not the teacher. The student achieves this purification by selflessly offering his or her talents, resources, and life to the world. By offering one's pure energy, or even basic provisions like food, wine, or service to the teacher, a healthy student can contribute to the support of the teacher and the "immortal angels" by whom they are surrounded.

The student-teacher relationship is a reflection of the great Oneness, When the student gives without restraint, the barriers of individuality dissolve, and a profound unity is experienced. In this state, it becomes indistinguishable whether it is the student offering themselves to the teacher or vice versa. Only two immaculate beings are perceived, reflecting one another like mirrors.

"As long as a student is spiritually contaminated the teacher cannot aid him or her. It is not the teacher's responsibility to cleanse the student's spiritual contamination. It is the student's responsibility and the student's alone. The student's spiritual cleansing is done by the student offering up his or her talent, resources, and life up to the world.

To the teacher and the immortal angels who surround him (or her), a healthy student can offer up pure energy. A student whose energy is depleted can, at the very least, give food or wine or his or her service. Whenever and whatever one gives without restraint, the barriers created by individuality crumble. When individuality crumbles it is impossible to tell whether it is the student offering to the teacher or the teacher to the student. What only can be seen is two pure beings whose luminescence reflects each other like two brilliant mirrors."

Giving Whatever Can Be Given Without Restraint

This passage by Lao Tzu highlights the importance of selfless giving, the breakdown of individuality, and the potential for profound unity between the student and the teacher. It suggests that through generous acts and the dissolution of ego, just as it is with us and the Tao, a transformative connection can be established.

If one wishes to become a student of spiritual enlightenment, it is crucial for them to understand the importance of purity within the student-teacher relationship and that the cleaning of spiritual contamination is not the responsibility of the teacher, but the student's. To cleanse spiritual contamination, one must begin to dissolve their ego by offering their talent, resources, and life to the world. By doing so, devoid of ego-attachment, a healthy student can offer their pure energy to the teacher and the "immortal angels" that surround them. The student need not be wealthy and the offerings he or she brings to the teacher need not be large. Even a depleted student can offer something as simple as some food, a bit of wine, or helpful service.

When one gives whatever they can without restraint, the barriers of individuality break down. When this happens, one thinks of the other before thinking of themself. When the two give freely to the other, it no longer becomes possible to tell whether it is the student offering themselves to the teacher, or the teacher offering themselves to the student. Instead, one sees two immaculate beings reflecting each other like a pair of brilliant mirrors. It is within this form of relationship that true learning and spiritual evolution can take place.

It is important to recognize that spiritual cleansing is a personal responsibility and cannot be accomplished by someone else. A teacher can only aid a student whose spirit is pure and prepared for learning. By offering oneself to the world and embracing a selfless attitude, a ready can begin to cleanse their spirit and prepare themselves for the teachings of a spiritual teacher. These teachings inevitably include those that will result in contact with the "immortal angels", the highest spiritual beings in the universe by whom, seen or unseen, the teacher is surrounded.

Surrounding Ourselves with the Immortal Angles

Ultimately, whether one is a student or a teacher or involved in no such relationship, for those who follow the Integral Way, spiritual cleansing is an in delegable personal responsibility that must be accomplished through selfless service to others. By embracing a selfless attitude and offering ourselves to the world, we can begin to prepare ourselves for the teachings of Lao Tzu and those of those spiritual teachers who may live around us. Remember that no teacher can aid the student as long as the student's spirit is corrupted by ego. By cleansing our spirit and offering ourselves to the world, we can become immaculate beings who not only reflect the brilliance of the divine and eternal Tao but who are capable of becoming teachers and surrounding ourselves with "Immortal Angels", the highest forms of spiritual beings in the universe, the Unruling Rulers and Uncreating Creators of the Tao's Divine Immortal Realm.

CHAPTER 74

The Nature of True Worship

The passage by Lao Tzu below teaches us what is worthy of worship and why. Lao Tzu suggests various objects and places of worship for those who find energy and inspiration in such practices. These objects and places where certain energies may be found are all natural manifestations of the Tao. They include the sun and the moon as repositories of yang and yin energies respectively, the spiritual centers of men and women, the Eight Great Manifestations representing different aspects of nature, the sixty-four hexagrams of the I Ching symbolizing the underlying harmony of the universe, and the Great Tai Chi encompassing all things in a state of balance and repose.

Worship, in this context, can be seen as a way to connect with and honor these aspects of existence, tapping into their symbolic and energetic significance. It is important to note that the specific objects of worship may vary. The essence of worship lies in cultivating reverence, humility, gratitude, and a sense of connection to the divine or sacred principles represented by these entities.

Ultimately, the choice of worship and the way it is approached is a personal matter influenced by one's own individual spiritual path. Worship can serve as a means to deepen one's connection to the transcendent and foster a sense of harmony and reverence for the interconnectedness of all things and beings, the Oneness that is the Tao.

**"There are many who gain their energy from meditating on or worshipping deities or divine beings.
Those who feel so inclined to worship should direct the focus of their worship on the blazing sun, the repository**

THE TAO OF UFO

**of Yang energy or the aqueous moon, the repository
of Yin energy. Worship men's and women's spiritual
centers, for they too are angelic in every sense.
Worship the heavens, the earth, the water, the thunder,
the wind, the fire, the lakes, and mountains, or all of
these Eight Great Manifestations.**

**Worship the I Ching and its sixty-four hexagrams in
which the universe's underlying harmony is illuminated.
Finally, worship the Tao and the Great Tai Chi in which
all its forms are contained, balanced and find repose."**

What Is Worthy of Worship

The word worship has many facets and meanings. It includes
things like veneration, adoration, reverence, devotion, love, giving thanks and holding something or someone dear. However
multifaceted, not everyone is inclined to worship. Not every
entity is worthy of our feeling or expression of reverence or
adoration. However, for those who are inclined to worship,
there are many divine beings and guardians who inhabit the
cosmos and deities that one can meditate on and derive energy
from. Just as other integral parts of the great Oneness the Tao
certain expressions of it may still move us and be worthy of
the expression of reverence, adoration, and gratitude for their
existence.

The following are a few examples of entities that Lao Tzu suggests that one may worship and why:

Firstly, the fiery sun and watery moon are repositories of yang
and yin respectively and are worthy of worship. These celestial
bodies are ever-present and hold tremendous power and influence over the natural world and hold symbolic significance for
many cultures across the globe.

Secondly, the spiritual centers of men and women are angelic in every sense. The chakras or energy centers within our body represent a map of consciousness that can be used to deepen our spiritual journey and transcendence. Because of their importance, the spiritual cores of all sentient beings, that core is worthy of reverence and worship.

Thirdly, Lao Tzu teaches us the Eight Great Manifestations: Heaven, Earth, Water, Fire, Thunder, Lake, Wind, and Mountain. These are all embodiments of specific elemental energies that shape our world. Each is worthy of worship not only because of their beauty but because each plays a vital role in creating balance and harmony in the universe.

Fourthly, the sixty-four hexagrams of the I Ching illuminate the underlying harmony of the universe. The I Ching is a form of divination that can be used as a tool for spiritual insight and understanding. Because it is an outward manifestation of the Tao at work, it is worthy of worship.

Finally, Lao Tzu teaches that one may worship the Great Tai Chi, in which all things are contained, balanced, and reposed. Tai Chi symbolizes the interconnectivity of all things and can be used to cultivate balance between the physical, emotional, and spiritual aspects of our being. All these things make it worthy of our "worship".

Conclusion

Ultimately, there are many entities that we can worship if we feel inclined to do so. By meditating on these entities and our feelings toward them, we can derive spiritual energy and deepen our understanding of the underlying patterns and harmony of the universe. Whether we choose to "worship" the celestial bodies, spiritual centers, elemental manifestations, divination texts, ET/NHIs, immortal angels, the highest spiritual beings of the universe, the Great Tai Chi or the Tao itself, the energy that we "worship", I.e., adore, revere, love, hold dear, devote ourselves and give thanks to and invite into our lives ultimately guides us on our journey towards spiritual enlightenment, integral truth and our path home to the Tao.

CHAPTER 75

Our Own Self-Transformation, The Greatest Gift We Have to Give

The lower realms of existence are those visceral, dark and harmful physical and material energies that seek to destroy us. We can liberate ourselves from this realm of egoism and duality and the gross, heavy energy and the degradation and destruction that come with it.

This passage is a very important one because it tells us that there is a way out through self-liberation. Lao Tzu emphasizes the importance of personal transformation and self-awareness as a means to bring about positive change in ourselves and the world. It tells us that rather than getting caught up in shallow mass movements or external actions alone, we should focus on cultivating our own inner growth and awakening.

By diligently working on ourselves and eliminating those negative aspects within, we can then contribute to the elimination of suffering in the world. Lao Tzu encourages finding a teacher or guide if we can who embodies integral qualities and learning from their wisdom and virtue.

Through this process of self-transformation and reflection, individuals can become beacons of light and radiate their positive influence to others. The passage also tells us that the greatest gift we can offer to the world is our own journey of self-realization and by our example and accumulated wisdom share the positive impact of our transformation with the rest of the world.

Ultimately, Lao Tzu's message here conveys that personal growth and inner development are essential for creating a more peaceful and virtuous existence, both individually and collectively. Our lives and our examples are all that we really have to offer to the world. Let's make the best of it. People are in need of us.

"How do you liberate yourself from life's lower realms? Do you want to save the world from its destiny of degradation and destruction? Then distance yourself from shallow social movements. Step away from the crowd. Go to work silently and serenely on your own self-awareness.

If to waken humanity is what you want, then first you must entirely awaken yourself. If to eliminate the world's suffering is what you want, then get rid of what is negative and dark in yourself. Verily, the greatest gift that one has to give to the world is one's own self-transformation.

So find yourself a teacher. One who is an Integral being. One who is a beacon of light who extends his illumination and virtue equally and with ease to those who appreciate him and to those who do not. Fashion yourself by his example. Immerse yourself in his life-giving radiance and reflect it outward to the world. As you do, you will begin to understand one of the universe's eternal truths: that there is always a peaceful home for one who is a virtuous being."

How To Save Humanity and Chage the World

This passage is one of the most important chapters of the Hua Hu Ching. This is because it tells us how this world will eventually be changed by our actions.

If we wish to liberate ourselves from the lower realms of life and save the world from destruction, the first step is to step away from "shallow mass movements" like religion and politics and quietly work on our own self-awareness. The power to awaken and heal the world lies within each individual, and the key to unlocking this power is through self-transformation. We are the ones who are responsible for this. It is each of our own individual tasks and ours alone.

If you want to awaken all of humanity, the most effective way is to begin by awakening all of yourself. This may require facing uncomfortable truths, confronting negative patterns and beliefs, and striving towards a state of greater self-awareness and personal growth. By eliminating all that is dark and negative in yourself, you can become a beacon of light and positivity in the world.

To achieve such enlightenment, it is important to seek out a teacher who is an integral being, someone who embodies the qualities you aspire to have. This teacher should be someone who extends their light and virtue with equal ease to those who appreciate them and those who do not. Their presence should be nourishing and radiating, inspiring you to shape yourself in their mold and reflect their qualities to the rest of the world. This teacher may not even know that he or she is a teacher. But you will know it by their example. Learn from them.

You may also find the words and teachings of great teachers in books. Some are no longer living among us. Find the works of teachers whose words resonate with your own eternal truth. Read them and internalize their lessons.

Through this process of self-transformation and guidance from an integral teacher, you will come to understand an eternal truth: there is always a peaceful home for a virtuous being. By cultivating virtue within yourself and extending it to the world, you can create a peaceful and harmonious environment that benefits not only yourself but all those around you.

Lao Tzu, the great teacher himself does not understate the fact that the greatest gift we must give is that of our own self-transformation. By recognizing the power of personal growth and seeking guidance from an integral teacher, we can awaken all of ourselves, live virtuously and by our example, ultimately create a positive impact on the world.

CHAPTER 76

The Saviors of the World

Is the world worth saving? Implicit in this passage is the answer that it does. In this passage Lao Tzu addresses the world's need to be saved. He tells us that any individual who wholeheartedly embraces the teachings and principles he describes, and diligently applies them in their life, has the potential to contribute to the salvation and betterment of the world. This person who is capable of saving the world is described as someone who cultivates inner peace, remains focused, and develops a deep understanding of subtle truths.

By merging their own virtue with the universal virtue and selflessly extending it to the world, we become a source of positive influence and transformation. The emphasis by Lao Tzu is on acting without any expectation of personal reward and with a genuine desire to bring about positive change and uplift others.

The passage concludes that the salvation and improvement of the world, and by extrapolation, the universe, depends on the collective efforts of those virtuous individuals who embody the Tao and actively work towards creating a more harmonious and virtuous existence for all. This is the path of all true integral and universal beings who follow the Integral Way.

"Who is it who can save the world? Perhaps it is one who follows these teachings devoutly and calms his mind, who takes no notice of divergence and has become highly aware of the subtle truths. Such a savior will combine his virtue with the universal virtue that emanates from the Tao. Selflessly, without any expectation of reward at all, he or she will extend this

virtue to the world. Surely, whether a man or woman, such a person who does so indeed shall be the savior of the world."

How to Save the Universe

The world needs saving, and perhaps the ones who can do so are persons who wholeheartedly pursue the truth and follow the teachings of Lao Tzu. These people are ones who have learned to calm their minds, ignore all diversions, and develop a high awareness of the subtle truths that underlie our existence.

Most importantly, such people are ones who have learned to merge their own virtue with that of the universe and extend it to the world without any expectation of reward or recognition. This requires a deep and abiding commitment to selflessness and genuine care for the well-being of all living beings including ETs and NHIs.

A person who embodies the teachings of truth and virtue in everyday life, will indeed be the savior of the world. Through their example, they will inspire others to follow in their footsteps and work towards building a better world for all. Such beings do not go unnoticed by the Tao or its highest spiritual beings.

So, if you wish to save the world, the key is not to wait for someone else to do so, but to embrace these teachings and commit yourself to embodying them in your everyday life. By developing a calm mind, ignoring diversions, and merging your own virtue with that of the Tao, you can make a profound impact on the world around you and the universe beyond help pave the way towards a brighter future for all living beings.

CHAPTER 77

Intelligence vs. Wisdom

This passage by Lao Tzu highlights the distinction between intelligence and wisdom, pointing out that despite the growth of human intelligence, there is an apparent increase in trouble and a decrease in happiness. Lao Tzu attributes this to both the misuse of partial intelligence and the neglect of holistic wisdom. Consequently, humanity despite its so-called intelligence is not very wise.

When individuals and societies become consumed by physical desires, uncontrolled emotions, and ego, they lose touch with the benefits of a simple and natural life. They become slaves to materialistic pursuits and to things like power, imbalanced divisive religions and by extension, divisive political philosophies, and ideological beliefs. They eschew personal responsibility by creating psychological justifications for their harmful acts. This slavery leads to tyranny and confusion and to a reign of calamity wherever it exists.

However, all is not lost. Lao Tzu reassures us that during times of turmoil, superior individuals can and still do emerge as leaders who can guide others out of their suffering. The key to liberating the many lies in first liberating oneself. This liberation is not achieved by elevating oneself above others but by embracing the virtues of simplicity, modesty, and truth.

By integrating these qualities within us and embodying them fully, we discover our original pure nature, which is irrevocably interconnected with the Tao, the "pure nature of the universe". Through the release of divine energy and the transcendence of complicated situations through the grace that is the Tao, we bring about within ourselves and our surroundings a sense of balance, oneness and harmony.

Ultimately, the passage teaches us that by embracing wisdom and living as a living embodiment of divinity, our actions have a profound impact on the universe as a whole. The liberation of ourselves becomes a catalyst for the liberation and transformation of others and the world around them. This transformation not only has profound effects on us and the universe but the ramifications of this transformation extend throughout the cosmos and help further define its nature as our own.

"Humanity's intelligence grows daily. Clearly, however, there is more trouble and less happiness. Why is this? It is because intelligence and wisdom are not the same things. Moreover, society's intelligence is only partial intelligence. It is not a holistic one. By misusing partial intelligence and ignoring holistic wisdom, society causes its people to become amnesic of the benefits that flow from living lives that are simple and natural.

Desire, emotions and ego seduce everyday people. They become enslaved by luxury and the body's demands. They become addicted to power and the use of psychological excuses and the imbalance of religion. As they do, confusion begins and calamity reigns. Nevertheless, a superior being can awaken during these tumultuous times and lead others out of this hazardous quagmire.

How is it that one can lead the many? First, he or she must free themself and liberate his or her own being. Then such a being elevates his or her potential for leadership by lowering themself and integrating simplicity, modesty, and truth completely into his or her life. Ultimately such a being masters these things and completely emancipates themself from their

former false life by becoming one with the Tao through this integration.

Separated from his or her former false persona, one discovers his or her own original true pure nature. Without reservation he or she spontaneously releases his divine energy. Such a superior being is constantly able to transcend complicated situations. He or she attracts everything around them back to the original Oneness. When such a person acts, the universe acts in concert with him or her because this person is a living divine being, a divinity of the Tao."

Transcendent Leadership

Humanity's intelligence, knowledge and technology is growing geometrically, yet there seems to be less wisdom, less happiness and more trouble. This is because intelligence is not the same as wisdom.

Intelligence is the acquisition and application of knowledge. Wisdom is not only the quality of having good knowledge but having experience and good judgment that express themselves as soundness of one's actions and decisions. Ultimately, a society's wisdom is that which develops over time based on these same qualities their successful expressions. When a society has only partial knowledge or partial intelligence and acts on them and ignores holistic wisdom, the wisdom that comes from looking at something as a whole, rather than one or more of its parts, it forgets the benefits of a simple and natural life. Driven by desires, emotions, and egos, its people become slaves to their bodily desires, material luxuries, power, unbalanced religion, divisive philosophies, and psychological excuses. This leads to an abdication of personal responsibility and the calamity and confusion that go along with it.

However, during times of turmoil, superior people can and do awaken to lead others out of the mire. But how can one liberate the many? One can liberate the many first by liberating their own selves. In doing so, they remain humble. It is through that humility that they are elevated. They do not elevate themselves. The ones who lead the many out of chaos liberate by humbly lowering themselves to the service of others by integrating the simple, modest, and true into their lives, and becoming masters of simplicity, modesty, and truth. By doing so, these leaders are completely emancipated from their former false lives and discover the harmony of their original pure nature, which is the Tao, the pure nature of the universe.

The liberated individual then freely and spontaneously releases their divine energy, constantly transcending complicated situations and drawing everything around them back into an integral oneness. They are a living divinity, and when they act, the universe acts through them.

This process of self-liberation is not about increasing one's status or power but about returning to a state of original purity and interconnectedness. By doing so, the liberated individual becomes an instrument of harmony and balance in the world and beyond. He or she is recognized by all the highest spiritual beings of the universe as divine being a living embodiment of the Tao.

Conclusion

Sigmund Freud once said that "Most people do not really want freedom, because freedom involves responsibility, and most people are freighted of responsibility." The key to becoming a Superior Being and liberating the many is to first accept the responsibility of freeing oneself. The next step is actually liberating oneself. Liberating oneself involves living a modest life by integrating simplicity, patience, and truth into one's being and discovering their original pure and compassionate nature. By doing so, the liberated individual becomes self-so, a living divinity, who is part and parcel of the Tao. Such a divinity is constantly releasing their divine energy and drawing everything around them back into an integral oneness. They become an instrument of harmony and balance in the universe, and through their example, others may also be inspired to seek liberation and return to their natural state of purity and the interconnectedness of all things and all beings.

In the end though, any true follower of the Integral Way will tell you that the greatest wisdom of all is kindness and the greatest knowledge is of the self and the Tao, its creator. To know and understand this is to understand one's own divinity and become a divine superior being and a transcendent leader for all those who have fallen into chaos.

CHAPTER 78

The Integral Way

In Chapter 78 after so many chapters in the Tao Te Ching and the Hua Hu Ching about the Integral Way, Lao Tzu begins to bring us all home. In the passage below Lao Tzu expounds upon the danger posed by partial religions to which he introduced us to in the last chapter and contrasts them with the Integral Way. Partial religions are described as human inventions, reliant on manipulation and lacking in the transmission of the plain and natural truth. Conversely, He emphasizes the the Integral Way is no religion at all but a deep expression of the pure and universal mind.

The Integral Way is presented therefore, as a total reality, rejecting conceptual fanaticism and extravagant living. It encourages renouncing fashionable distractions and embracing honesty, plainness and virtue. By following the practices of the Integral Way, one is said to embody these qualities and undergo a complete transformation.

While partial pursuits result in partial transformation, the Integral Way offers the possibility of a profound metamorphosis, transcending emotional and biological limitations to reach a higher state of being. By following this path and staying true to its principles, one becomes extraordinary and unfathomable, embodying cosmic subtlety and transcending the constraints of time and space.

The passage emphasizes the importance of simplicity, honesty, and virtue in pursuing the Integral Way. It is through its practice, that we can realize the subtle truths of the universe and attain a profound level of spiritual development that reconnects us to our original source, the Tao.

"Of imperfect religions there are many. Yet there is only the one Integral Way. Biased and incomplete, these religions are clever yet desperate inventions of human origin. The Integral Way is a path, a profound expression of the whole, pure universal mind. Religions discriminate. They hypnotize and manipulate minds that are primitive and still undeveloped.

Contrary to discriminatory religions, the Integral Way is rooted in the free communication of the immutable plain and natural truth. Its reality is a total one. Its practice is neither a mysterious or esoteric one.

The Integral way shuns conceptional and abstract fanaticism. It eschews living extravagantly. It abstains from exotic foods and avoids harsh music and anything that spoils the mind's serenity and obstructs our spiritual development.

It renounces that which is transitory and fashionable. It embraces that which is honest, plain and virtuous. The Integral Way returns us to that which is life's subtle essence. By adopting the practices of the Integral Way, we become the Way itself, the subtle essence of the Tao, simple, honest, plain, virtuous, true, compassionate and complete.

Partial pursuits are only partially transformative. However, through Integral self-cultivation it is possible for us to completely metamorphize and transcend our biological and emotional limitations and by evolving into higher states of being and becoming a new form of being ourselves.

By remaining outside of the shadows and following the path and staying the simple course of the Integral Way we become one of the Tao's unfathomably extraordinary

and profound cosmic immortal subtle beings. By realizing the Tao, the universe's profound subtle truth we outlive time and space."

Partial Religions and The Integral Way

There are partial religions, and then there is the Integral Way. Partial religions are human inventions, whereas the Integral Way is a deep expression of the pure, whole, universal mind. Partial religions rely on the hypnotic manipulation of undeveloped minds, whereas the Integral Way is founded on the free transmission of the plain, natural, immutable truth. Unlike religion's focus on a partial reality, the focus of the Integral way is on the integration of the mind, the body and the spirit. It is not an occult practice but a total reality.

The Integral Way is a deep expression of the pure, whole, universal mind. The Integral Way is not about fanaticism or extravagance but rather embracing what is plain, honest, and virtuous. It is about renouncing what is fashionable and returning to the subtle essence of life. Its practices lead to honest and virtuous lives governed by simplicity, truth, patience, compassion and wholeness. By following the Integral Way, it is possible for us to achieve a complete metamorphosis, transcend emotional and biological limitations, and permanently evolve to an immortal higher state of being.

The path of integral self-cultivation is not about partial pursuits or transformation but rather achieving a complete metamorphosis. By staying out of the shadows and following a simple path, we can become an extraordinary, unfathomable being of profound cosmic subtlety. By realizing the subtle truth of the universe, we can outlive our present dimensional concepts of time and space and achieve an immortal conscious awareness.

CHAPTER 79

The Fruits of Practicing the Integral Way

In the passage below, Lao Tzu begins to bring us closure by this benediction emphasizing the timelessness of his teachings and the beneficence that flows from them. The Hua Hu Ching was not composed or written only for those of Lao Tzu's day but for humanity throughout the ages. Both it and the Tao Te Ching are comprised of deep universal truths. In this passage Lao Tzu emphasizes that future generations who study and practice the teachings of the Integral Way will be blessed with profound gifts.

Besides the blessings of contact with the highest spiritual beings of the universe outlined in prior chapters, those who learn and follow the Integral Way will acquire the subtle light of wisdom, which allows them to see clearly and penetrate obstacles. They will possess the mighty sword of clarity, enabling them to cut through any obstructions on their path. Additionally, they will attain the mystical pearl of understanding, which encompasses the entire universe and grants them deep insight into the integral truth of the Tao.

By following the truth with unwavering sincerity, those individuals who follow the integral Way and the Tao will not only understand it but become one with it. They will embody the qualities of wholeness, courage, indestructibility, and transcendence beyond conventional labels. This passage highlights the transformative power and profound benefits that await those who diligently study and practice these teachings in this and future generations.

Without following the integral Way, humans will never open the gates of their spiritual immortality and their societies will never evolve to a point where they will become an important part of the social organs that make up the advanced celestial civilizations of the cosmos whose entities freely traverse the barriers of time and space. Without the integral Way humankind will never come to be among the unruling rulers and uncreating creators of the vast universe.

"Blessed will be those who, in future generations, will study and practice the truth of these teachings. Theirs will be the subtle light of true vision to acquire. With it they will have clarity of vision, the mighty sword that cuts through all obstacles and the Mystical Pearl by which the entire universe is enveloped. Their insight will enable them to perceive the Tao's integral truth. With unwavering sincerity they will follow that truth and become one with it: whole, unnamable, courageous and indestructible."

The Highest Spiritual Beings in the Universe

Both here and in the Tao Te Ching, Lao Tzu speaks of the blessings that those in future generations who study and practice the truth of these teachings will receive. He talks about how they will acquire the subtle light of wisdom, the mighty sword of clarity that cuts through all obstruction, and the mystical pearl of understanding that envelops the entire universe. He explains that those who follow this truth with unabashed sincerity will become whole, courageous, indestructible, and unnamable. Therefore, it is crucial for everyone to make an effort to understand and practice the teachings of the Tao's Integral Way in order to attain the blessings about which Lao Tzu speaks.

Learning the teachings that constitute the Integral way is far more than making contact with ET/NHIs. The Tao constitutes a fundamental aspect of the universal reality that is often overlooked in modern human society. It is a way of being that emphasizes harmony, simplicity, and humility. This way of being is integral to all the highest spiritual beings of the universe. Those who practice the teachings of the Tao see the world in a new understanding and in a special light. Those who follow the Integral Way are able to see the interconnectedness of all things and can perceive the integral truth of the Tao. They can let go of their ego and desires, which allows them to attain the subtle light of wisdom about which Lao Tzu teaches.

Furthermore, the teachings of the Tao's Integral Way provide us with a powerful tool for navigating the challenges of life. The mighty sword of clarity that cuts through all obstructions is a reference to the ability to see through the illusions that impede and hamper us from seeing the truth. Those who practice the Integral Way can see through the distractions and noise of the world and capably focus on what is truly important. This skill is especially important in today's world, where people are bombarded with information and propaganda from social media, news outlets, and other sources.

Finally, the mystical pearl of understanding that envelops the entire universe is a reference to the deep sense of interconnectedness and understanding that those spiritual beings who practice the Tao's Integral Way experience. They can see the beauty and meaning in the world and understand their place in it. This broad perspective can lead to a sense of purpose and fulfillment that is difficult to find otherwise. This is the sense of spirit and fulfillment that all the highest beings of the universe share.

Ultimately, those in future generations who study and practice the truth of the Tao will be blessed with the subtle light of wisdom, the mighty sword of clarity, and the mystical pearl of understanding. These blessings are essential for all intelligent and highly spiritually advanced beings in the universe as they lead to a fulfilling and meaningful life. Therefore, it is important for everyone who seeks spiritual evolution and refinement to make an effort to understand and practice the teachings about the Tao and its Integral Wah by Lao Tzu. By doing so, they can become whole, courageous, indestructible, and unnamable – just like Lao Tsu describes and place themselves and their future societies among those from which their progeny are to be, the highest spiritual beings of the cosmos, the unruling rulers and uncreating creators of the vast universe.

CHAPTER 80

The Half-enlightened Masters

In this passage Lao Tzu warns us to recognize that the world is filled with half-enlightened masters who surround themselves with selfish pleasures and impart their confused teachings upon others. All one needs to do is to read about the many religious cults or turn their televisions and watch the jet-flying, million-dollar sports car driving preachers in their mega-churches who preach a gospel of abundance at the cost of their followers. They strive for spiritual climax and sacrifice the truth, deviating from the Tao. Their offerings of enlightenment to the world are rooted in their own confusion. The healing waters that they sell for a price is the water any person can receive from their own well.

True masters of the Integral Way understand that enlightenment is not an end in itself, but a means to the greater goal of virtue. They embrace the arduous journey of physical, mental, and spiritual cultivation, forsaking personal ambition and quietly assuming responsibilities. Without seeking recognition, they guide individuals who seek their own wisdom. They share their divine energy, supporting, challenging, and directing others toward the vast ocean of the Tao.

If we aspire to this mastery, we need not judge others in their ignorance but must root ourselves in the Tao, shedding negative habits and attitudes. Sincerity and truth become our strength as we engage with the real world and extend our virtue without discrimination. We strive to embody the truest versions of ourselves in every role—compassionate parents, loving siblings, loyal friends, and dedicated disciples. Humbly respecting and serving our teacher, we dedicate ourselves unwaveringly to self-cultivation. Through this transformative practice, we attain self-mastery and are able to guide others on their own paths of self-realization.

Why do we do this? It is because this is what true loving compassion does. This is our purpose in the world and in the eternal Tao.

"Be aware that the world is filled with half-enlightened masters. Unduly clever and overly sensitive, too delicate to live in an everyday world, they indulge themselves in egotistic pleasures and pander to the unwary with their glorious teachings. They precociously promote themselves as having reached some pinnacle of spiritual climax. They sacrifice the truth as they diverge from the Tao.

All they really have to offer the world is their confused minds. A true master understands that enlightenment is only the means and not the end. The master's goal is virtue. He accepts the long and often arduous path through the self-cultivation necessary to become virtuous.

The master does not scheme to become a leader. Quietly he or she humbly shoulders the mantle of responsibility for whatever task or responsibility befalls them. To accomplishments they are unattached. They take credit for nothing. By guiding those who come their way, they guide the whole world.

With those who are his students, the master shares his or her divine energy. The master encourages them and creates tests for them and trials to make them stronger. The master admonishes them to awaken their awareness and directs their energies and life streams toward the Infinite deep ocean that is the Tao.

If such mastery is that to which you aspire, then root yourself firmly in the Tao. Give up your negative attitudes and bad habits. Make your sincerity genuine and strong. Dissolve your ego. Live in the world of everyday people. Extend your virtue to them without discrimination in your usual daily activities.

If you are a father or mother, be the truest father or mother that you can be. If you are a brother or sister, friend, or disciple, be the truest one you can be. Serve your teacher with humble respect. With your entire self unwaveringly dedicate your whole being to self-cultivation. If you can do this then surely you will master your self and be able to help others to do the same."

The Path to True Mastery, Contact with ET and NHIs

The world is rife with half-enlightened masters who, rather than truly seeking wisdom and virtue, are obsessed with their own comfort, cleverness and spiritual achievements. They live in ivory towers, indulging in selfish pleasures while loudly proclaiming their grandiose teachings to anyone who will listen. However, their enlightenment, if it can even be called that, is ultimately empty and meaningless, for they remain disconnected from the truth and the Tao. They are lost souls.

Those who truly seek mastery understand that enlightenment is not the end, but the means to achieving a life of virtue and service to others. Such masters do not strive to become leaders or teachers in search of glory or power. Rather, they quietly take on whatever responsibilities fall to them, serving as true officials of the Tao.

To achieve true mastery, one must root oneself in the Tao and rid oneself of negative habits and attitudes. The Tao and its Integral Way teach us to live in the real world and to extend our virtue to it, treating all people with compassionate patience, respect and kindness without discrimination. We must strive to be the truest versions of ourselves, whether as fathers, mothers, brothers, sisters, friends, or disciples, exemplifying the virtues that we wish to cultivate in others.

To achieve self-mastery and guide others towards virtue, we must first follow the Integral Way and humbly respect and serve our teachers, dedicating our entire being to unwavering self-cultivation. We must be grateful for and willing to endure trials and tribulations to strengthen ourselves and awaken our true potential. And we must share our divine energy and knowledge with others, creating opportunities to guide and develop whoever comes to us with sincerity and good intentions.

True mastery is not about grandstanding or self-promotion. It is about living a life of sincere and humble service to others, guiding them towards the Tao and cultivating the virtues of wisdom, compassion, and integrity. By rooting ourselves in the Tao and committing ourselves to self-cultivation, we can become true officials and masters of the way, helping to teach and guide ourselves and others towards enlightenment and true fulfillment.

Therefore, I urge you to join us on this journey towards true mastery and meaningful personal and societal evolution and ET/NHI contact by rooting yourself in the Tao, relinquishing your negative habits and attitudes, living in the real world, and extending your virtue to it and the universe without discrimination. With dedication, sincerity, and hard work, we can all evolve to achieve self-mastery and help others do the same and ultimately make contact with the highest spiritual beings of the universe, the unruling rulers and uncreating creators of the vast universe and become one of and with them. Ultimately that is the path of those who embark on the Integral Way.

CHAPTER 81

The Final Chapter

"After a thousand millennia, why haven't we changed?
We are still barbarians."
- Jiddu Krishnamurti

We have now come full circle. In the midst of all these words, what has truly been conveyed that will elevate all who listen beyond the barbarianism that inhabits and stalks those who live on this planet? The answer is to become what the highest spiritual beings of the universe have become by being one with the Tao itself. We can do this and transform ourselves beyond our own barbarianism and brutal thinking by following the Integral Way.

Remember that what is spoken and heard are not the only reality. They are merely forms. The Tao's subtle truth cannot be fully encapsulated in language alone; it extends beyond the realm of words. Learn to breathe and just be. Take moments of silence and deep listening. Attune yourself to the unspoken wisdom, adhering to the law that surpasses written rules. Embrace the ineffable and worship the nameless.

Cherish your life and place your trust in the Tao. Do your best at what you do. Engage in the profound union with the invisible and subtle origin of the universe. If you do, you will find yourself without want and you will be abundantly fulfilled. Be thankful for your life and what you have been given. Your gratitude is the key to your continued abundance.

When you become one with the Tao, there is no need to seclude yourself permanently anywhere. Even amidst the bustling world, you can embody the qualities of a serene and contemplative sage, unaffected by external circumstances. Through your integral practices, you will find sustenance and rewards that surpass any material success and its measures.

Dissolve your ego into the Tao. Search out the truth of the universe. Live simply, patiently, and compassionately. Let your example lead others to their own enlightenment. As you inspire others, generously and without discrimination bestow your gifts upon all. Awaken and purify the world through your every movement and action. When you do, you will ascend to the divine realm even in the brightness of day.

The breath of the Tao whispers its wisdom. It speaks in its own way. Throughout the universe, those who are in harmony with it can discern its profound message clearly. It is they who become and are the highest forms of spiritual beings in the universe who will come to visit.

**"After all these words, what has really been said? One can point at the subtle truth with words, but words can neither contain nor adequately describe it.
Listen, take the time to understand that which is being said without words. Obey the laws that are too subtle to be written. Worship that which is unnamable. Embrace that which is unformed. Love the life you have. Trust the Tao. Become intimate and integrate yourself with its invisible subtle origin and the Tao will give you everything you need.**

You will have no need to forever ensconce yourself in spiritual retreats. With the Tao, the middle of everything, you can be a gentle contemplative hermit unaffected by the world; rewarded and sustained by your self-cultivation and integral practices.

Encourage others. Give freely to all. Awaken and purify the world. With each action and movement in broad

daylight you will ascend into the divine realm. The Tao speaks to each in its own way.

Those in harmony with it hear it quite clearly."

Becoming One with the Tao and All Its Celestial Inhabitants

The UFO/UAP phenomenon is beyond flying saucers. It is beyond the nuts and bolts of understanding how interstellar craft are built or propelled. Making contact with the extra-terrestrials and non-human intelligences who are the highest spiritual beings in the universe is not about them. It is not even about what is happening to us in this life and on this planet. It is not even about us. It is about taking responsibility for our own physical, mental, and spiritual health and evolution in this lifetime, making this planet a better place for all its inhabitants and where and how we might want to be exist in the next. This world needs to do its spiritual work if it wants to evolve and be accepted as equals among the more highly advanced societies of the cosmos. That was the message of October 3, 2015. This book has been a consequence of that meeting and event.

We, the Tao and all its beings are one in the same. To become one with the universe and all its celestial inhabitants, must pay attention and listen to the Breath of the Tao. To be among the highest spiritual beings of the universe, we must make its heartbeat and flow our own.

In a world dominated by words and empty rhetoric that cause divisions between even mankind itself, it is easy to lose sight of the subtle truth that lies beyond them. We each are capable of knowing the Tao and experiencing its pure, peaceful and subtle truth and beauty that cannot be contained by language. Our natural experience of the Tao, our creator and source is too deep and too mysterious to be captured by mere words.

As Lao Tzu reiterates here, it can only be pointed to, hinted at, and felt in the core of our own experience of being.

To truly hear the truth, we must learn to listen beyond words, to the silence that lies within and around us. We must obey the law that is too subtle to be written but easily understood. Trust in the Tao that speaks to us through the breath of life itself. For it is in this deep listening that we can begin to hear the voice of the subtle origin of the universe and embrace the unformed and unnamable essence that animates and governs all things. This essence is undoubtedly that of the ET/NHIs who are among the highest spiritual beings of the universe. Their presence here on this planet shows this awareness and attunement with the universal Integral Way.

When we learn to love our lives, to trust the Tao, and to make love with the invisible essence of the universe, we give ourselves everything we need. We no longer need to hide away behind the wall of religion or in spiritual retreats, for we can be gentle, contemplative, hermit-like masters of the Tao right in the midst of everything, sustained by the Tao and rewarded by our integral spiritual practices and by contact with ET/NHIs.

By encouraging others, giving freely to all, and awakening and purifying the world with each movement and action, we can ascend to the divine realm at any time. Through our conscious understanding and by following the Integral Way we become vessels of the divine energy that connects all things, and channels of the breath of the Tao that moves and animates the universe. We can become channelers of our love and compassion to ETs and NHIs.

So why not fall in love with our creator? Let us learn to listen deeply, to hear the subtle truth that lies beyond words, and to obey the law that is too subtle to be written. Let us trust the Tao that speaks to us through the breath of life and make love with the invisible essence of the universe. Let us be gentle, contemplative sages and masters of the Tao and its Integral Way.

In the midst of the world, we can become channels of the divine energy that connects all things. In doing so, we all can ascend to the divine and subtle realm. There we can make profound contact with the illustrious ET/NHI brothers and sisters who have become lovers and teachers of the Integral Way. This has been the purpose of this book. It is not about making contact with the highest forms of spiritual beings in the universe, the Unruling Rulers and Uncreating Creators of the Tao's Divine Immortal Realm the truest of the true masters the Immortal Angels of the integral Way but becoming one of and with them. Once that happens, they will inevitably find their way to us as Integral Beings and followers of the Integral Way.

END OF BOOK 2.

ABOUT THE AUTHOR

Norman Michael Murburg, Jr., "Mike", is a UFO "Experiencer" and "Contactee". Mike is a graduate of Princeton University, (B.A., History 1977) where he also took studies in the Departments of Religion and Classics. He is also an honors graduate of the Florida State University College of Law) and a former Florida Assistant State Attorney. He is a proud father of two children, a Gold Star dad. He has been practicing law since 1986. Since 2017 he has run a monthly CE-5, 5 (Close Encounters of the Fifth Kind, human initiated contact experiences*) 6 and 7 outreach and ET/NHI contact group at his ranch in Darby, Florida.

Mike has been a long-time practitioner of the Tao and a follower of its Integral way for many years. He is a lifetime UFO "Experiencer" and "Contactee". He is a student and practitioner of Tao and teaches and SINCE 2017 he conducted a monthly HICE (Human Initiated Close Encounter/Contact Experiences) - CE-5, CE-6 and CE-7 contact group at his ranch in Darby, Florida. Mike was a member of the Foundation for the

Research into Extraterrestrial and Extraordinary Experiencers (FREE) and a contributing author and editor of Chapter 12 of Volume 1 (Spirituality and the Contact Experience) of their book Beyond UFOs: The Science of Consciousness & Contact with Non-Human Intelligence**. This 820-page book published in 2018 is a detailed academic work. It is the world's first comprehensive multi-language quantitative and qualitative 5-year academic study of individuals who have had UFO/UAP related contact with Non-Human Intelligences (NHIS). Authored by Reinerio Hernandez, J.D. (Cornell), Rudy Schild, PH.D. (Harvard-Smithsonian Center for Astrophysics), Jon Klimo, PH.D. (Brown University, Arnold Fellowship, PH.D Argosy University), their study collected detailed responses to 3 extensive quantitative and qualitative surveys from over 4,200 individuals from over 100 countries. Their peer-reviewed study was the first of its kind to be undertaken. Chapter 12 documents Mike's contact history and appears as a case study and exemplary analysis of the positive and long-lasting effects of ET/NHI, (Extraterrestrial/Intelligent Non-human) contact within that book.

In 2014, after years of study, Mike began to unravel and better understand the Tao for himself. In 2015, while recuperating from a long physical illness, he finished his written notes and meditations on his study of the Tao Te Ching. He then began doing the same thing with Lao Tzu's other attributed work, the Hua Hu Ching. On October 3, 2015, at about 6 A.M. after having meditated upon and written throughout the night on chapters 11, 12, 14 and 14 Mike was visited by a "Golden Orb" that appeared at that time in the waning darkness outside of his apartment in downtown Tampa. During the hour before it left, Mike had a direct empathetic and telepathic communication with this celestial non-human intelligence. After receiving an extensive message in what has come to be known by fellow experiencers and contactees as the "download", Mike asked this entity, self-described as "universal being" and "a complex group combined intelligences" and was given its permission to photograph it as it began to depart that morning. The first of three photos appears as the cover of this book. The orb was photographed at 6:59 AM just before it left.

The entity's clarifications to Mike upon the Tao Te Ching and the Hua Hu Ching along with its unifying peace-giving message and lessons about unity-conscious and the nature of reality became immediately relevant to Mike's ongoing understanding of the relevance of the highly spiritual works of Lao Tzu in today's post-contact world. Because the nature of ET/NHI contact is a spiritual one and not just a physical one and has been since the beginning of man's time on this planet, Mike has intentionally incorporated the lessons received from the orb on October 3, 2014, into these two books. He has also incorporated them into his CE-5 teachings and practice as the basis for his group's ongoing successful direct and continuing contact with ET/NHIs.

So let Mike introduce you to the internal operating system of the universe of the Tao of UFO in Book 1. Then let him teach you about the Integral Way and explain the real and true existence and purpose of ET/NHI, these "angels" of the sky of ages gone by, these self-described "Universal", "Divine" or "Celestial" beings, the "unruling rulers and uncreating creators"*** of the universe's divine immortal realm that Lau Tzu describes in Book 2, the Hua Hu Ching.

* Dr. Joseph Burkes, MD
**https://www.amazon.com/Beyond-UFOs-Science-Consciousness-Intelligence/dp/1721088652
***Brian Browne Walker, The Unknown Teachings of Lao Tzu, Hua hu Ching, Harper San Francisco 1994